MW01244946

LOT VIEWING
Heritage Auction Galleries, 17th Floor
3500 Maple Avenue • Dallas, Texas 75219

Monday, February 2 – Wednesday, February 4, 2009
9:00 AM - 5:00 PM CT
By Appointment Only

Thursday, February 5 • 9:00 AM – 6:00 PM CT
Friday, February 6 • 9:00 AM – 6:00 PM CT

*View Lots and Video Lot Descriptions
Online at HA.com/Stamps*

LIVE FLOOR BIDDING
Bid in person during the floor sessions.

LIVE TELEPHONE BIDDING *(floor sessions only)*
Phone bidding must be arranged on or before
Wednesday, February 4, 2009, by 12:00 PM CT.
Client Service: 866-835-3243.

HERITAGE Live!™ BIDDING
Bid live from your location, anywhere in the world,
during the Auction using our HERITAGE Live!™ program
at HA.com/Live

INTERNET BIDDING
Internet absentee bidding ends at 10:00 PM CT
the evening before each session. HA.com/Stamps

FAX BIDDING
Fax bids must be received on or before Wednesday,
February 4, 2009, by 12:00 PM CT. Fax: 214-409-1425

MAIL BIDDING
Mail bids must be received on or before
Wednesday, February 4, 2009.

*Please see "Choose Your Bidding Method" in the back of this
catalog for specific details about each of these bidding methods.*

LIVE AUCTION
SIGNATURE® FLOOR SESSIONS 1-4
(Floor, Telephone, HERITAGE Live!,™ Internet, Fax, and Mail)

Heritage Auction Galleries, 1st Floor Auction Room
3500 Maple Avenue • Dallas, Texas 75219

SESSION 1
Thursday, February 5, 2009 • 12:00 PM CT • Lots 31001-31430

SESSION 2
Thursday, February 5, 2009 • 4:00 PM CT • Lots 31431-31838

SESSION 3
Friday, February 6, 2009 • 12:00 PM CT • Lots 31839–32290

SESSION 4
Friday, February 6, 2009 • 4:00 PM CT • Lots 32291–32666

NON FLOOR/NON PHONE BIDDING SESSION 5
(HERITAGE Live!,™ Internet, Fax, and Mail only)

SESSION 5
Saturday, February 7, 2009 • 12:00 PM CT • Lots 32667-33210

AUCTION RESULTS
Immediately available at HA.com/Stamps

LOT SETTLEMENT AND PICK-UP
Available immediately following each floor session or weekdays
9:00 AM – 5:00 PM CT by appointment only.

Extended Payment Terms available. See details in the back of this catalog.

*Lots are sold at an approximate rate of 125 lots per hour, but it
is not uncommon to sell 80 lots or 150 lots in any given hour.*

This auction is subject to a 19.5% Buyer's Premium.

THIS AUCTION IS PRESENTED AND CATALOGED BY HERITAGE AUCTIONS, INC.

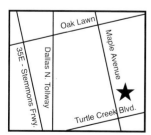

Heritage World Headquarters

HERITAGE HA.com
Auction Galleries

Home Office • 3500 Maple Avenue, 17th Floor • Dallas, Texas 75219
Design District Annex • 1518 Slocum Street • Dallas, Texas 75207
214.528.3500 | 800.872.6467 | 214.409.1425 (fax)
Direct Client Service Line: Toll Free 1.866.835.3243 • Email: Bid@HA.com

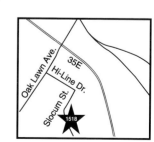

Heritage Design District Annex

TX Auctioneer licenses: Samuel Foose 11727; Robert Korver 13754; Scott Peterson 13256; Bob Merrill 13408; Mike Sadler 16129; Ed Griffith 16343; Andrea Voss 16406;
Jacob Walker 16413; Charlie Mead 16418; Eric Thomas 16421; Douglas Nyholm 16431; Patricia Gardner 16446. Associate 16142 Kathleen Guzman under sponsorship of
Andrea Voss 16406.

16261

Rare Stamp Specialists

Steve Ivy
CEO
Co-Chairman
of the Board

Leo Frese
Vice President

Steven Crippe
Director of
Philatelic Sales

Brian Degen
Director of
Philatelic Operations

Jim Halperin
Co-Chairman
of the Board

Greg Rohan
President

Paul Minshull
Chief Operating
Officer

3500 Maple Avenue, 17th Floor • Dallas, Texas 75219
Phone 214-528-3500 • 800-872-6467
HA.com/Stamps

DIRECTORY FOR DEPARTMENT SPECIALISTS AND SERVICES

COINS & CURRENCY

COINS – UNITED STATES

HA.com/Coins
U.S. Coins

Leo Frese, Ext. 1294
Leo@HA.com
Charles Clifford, Ext. 1477
CharlesC@HA.com
Sam Foose, Ext. 1227
SamF@HA.com
Jim Jelinski, Ext. 1257
JimJ@HA.com
Katherine Kurachek, Ext. 1389
KKurachek@HA.com
David Lisot, Ext. 1303
DavidL@HA.com
Bob Marino, Ext. 1374
BobMarino@HA.com
David Mayfield, Ext. 1277
DavidM@HA.com
Mike Sadler, Ext. 1332
MikeS@HA.com
Doug Nyholm, Ext. 1598
DNyholm@HA.com
Dave Lindvall, Ext. 1231
David@HA.com
Jason Friedman, Ext. 1582
JasonF@HA.com
Darrill Batté Ext. 1715
DarrillB@HA.com
Chris Dykstra Ext. 1380
ChrisD@HA.com
Shaunda Fry Ext. 1159
ShaundaF@HA.com
Dennis Nowicki Ext. 1121
DennisN@HA.com

COINS – WORLD

HA.com/WorldCoins
World Coins & Currencies

Warren Tucker, Ext. 1287
WTucker@HA.com
Scott Cordry, Ext. 1369
ScottC@HA.com
Cristiano Bierrenbach, Ext. 1661
CrisB@HA.com

CURRENCY

HA.com/Currency
Paper Money

Len Glazer, Ext. 1390
Len@HA.com
Allen Mincho, Ext. 1327
Allen@HA.com
Dustin Johnston, Ext. 1302
Dustin@HA.com
Jim Fitzgerald, Ext. 1348
JimF@HA.com
Michael Moczalla, Ext. 1481
MichaelM@HA.com

UNITED STATES COINS PRIVATE TREATY SALES

HA.com/Coins

Todd Imhof, Ext. 1313
Todd@HA.com

UNITED STATES COINS PURCHASED

HA.com/Coins

Jim Stoutjesdyk, Ext. 1310
JimS@HA.com

COMICS

HA.com/Comics
*Comics, Original Comic Art
and Related Memorabilia*

Ed Jaster, Ext. 1288
EdJ@HA.com
Lon Allen, Ext. 1261
LonA@HA.com
Barry Sandoval, Ext. 1377
BarryS@HA.com

FINE ART

ART OF THE AMERICAN WEST

HA.com/FineArt

Michael Duty, Ext. 1712
MichaelD@HA.com

DECORATIVE ARTS

HA.com/FineArt

Michael Wolf, Ext. 1541
MWolf@HA.com
Meredith Meuwly, Ext. 1631
MeredithM@HA.com

FINE ART

HA.com/FineArt

Edmund P. Pillsbury, Ph.D., Ext. 1533
EPP@HA.com
Kathleen Guzman, Ext. 1672
KathleenG@HA.com
Ed Jaster, Ext. 1288
EdJ@HA.com
Courtney Case, Ext. 1293
CourtneyC@HA.com

RUSSIAN ART

HA.com/FineArt

Douglass Brown, Ext. 1165
DouglassB@HA.com

ILLUSTRATION ART

HA.com/Illustration

Ed Jaster, Ext. 1288
EdJ@HA.com
Todd Hignite, Ext. 1790
ToddH@HA.com

PHOTOGRAPHY

HA.com/ArtPhotography

Lorraine Anne Davis, Ext. 1714
LorraineD@HA.com

SILVER & VERTU

HA.com/FineArt

Tim Rigdon, Ext. 1119
TimR@HA.com

20TH-CENTURY ART & DESIGN

HA.com/FineArt

Thom Pegg, Ext. 1742
ThomP@HA.com

TEXAS ART

HA.com/TexasArt

Atlee Phillips, Ext. 1786
AtleeP@HA.com

HISTORICAL

AMERICAN INDIAN ART

HA.com/AmericanIndian

Delia Sullivan, Ext. 1343
DeliaS@HA.com

AMERICANA & POLITICAL

HA.com/Historical
*Historical & Pop Culture Americana,
Vintage Toys, Presidential & Political
Memorabilia, Buttons & Medals,
Books & Manuscripts, First Editions
and Collectible Autographs*

Tom Slater, Ext. 1441
TomS@HA.com
Marsha Dixey, Ext. 1455
MarshaD@HA.com
John Hickey, Ext. 1264
JohnH@HA.com
Michael Riley, Ext. 1467
MichaelR@HA.com

CIVIL WAR ARTIFACTS

HA.com/CivilWar
*Artifacts, Documents and Memorabilia
Related to the American Civil War*

Dennis Lowe, Ext. 1182
DennisL@HA.com

RARE BOOKS

HA.com/Books

James Gannon, Ext. 1609
JamesG@HA.com

MANUSCRIPTS

HA.com/Manuscripts

Sandra Palomino, Ext. 1107
SandraP@HA.com

TEXANA

HA.com/Historical

Sandra Palomino, Ext. 1107
SandraP@HA.com

WESTERN AMERICANA

HA.com/Western

Russ Jorzig, Ext. 1633
RussJ@HA.com

JEWELRY & TIMEPIECES

JEWELRY

HA.com/Jewelry

Jill Burgum, Ext. 1697
JillB@HA.com

TIMEPIECES

HA.com/Timepieces

Jim Wolf, Ext. 1659
JWolf@HA.com

MOVIE POSTERS

HA.com/MoviePosters
*Posters, Lobby Cards, and
Hollywood Ephemera*

Grey Smith, Ext. 1367
GreySm@HA.com
Bruce Carteron, Ext. 1551
BruceC@HA.com
Isaiah Evans, Ext. 1201
IsaiahE@HA.com

MUSIC & ENTERTAINMENT MEMORABILIA

HA.com/Entertainment
*Autographs, Stage-worn Costumes, Film
and Television-used Props and Wardrobe,
Celebrity-played Instruments, Pop-Culture
Memorabilia, Rare Records and Acetates.*

Doug Norwine, Ext. 1452
DougN@HA.com

John Hickey, Ext. 1264
JohnH@HA.com
Garry Shrum, Ext. 1585
GarryS@HA.com
Jim Steele, Ext. 1328
JimSt@HA.com

NATURAL HISTORY

HA.com/NaturalHistory

David Herskowitz, Ext. 1610
DavidH@HA.com

SPORTS COLLECTIBLES

HA.com/Sports
*Sports Cards, Artifacts,
Game-Used Jerseys & Equipment*

Chris Ivy, Ext. 1319
CIvy@HA.com
Stephen Carlisle, Ext. 1292
StephenC@HA.com
Mike Gutierrez, Ext. 1183
MikeG@HA.com
Lee Iskowitz, Ext. 1601
LeeI@HA.com
Mark Jordan, Ext. 1187
MarkJ@HA.com
Jonathan Scheier, Ext. 1314
JonathanS@HA.com
Peter Calderon, Ext.1789
PeterC@HA.com

STAMPS

HA.com/Stamps

Steven Crippe, Ext.1777
StevenC@HA.com
Brian Degen, Ext.1767
BrianD@HA.com

CORPORATE & INSTITUTIONAL COLLECTIONS/VENTURES

Jared Green, Ext. 1279
Jared@HA.com

AUCTION OPERATIONS

Norma Gonzalez, Ext. 1242
V.P. Auction Operations
Norma@HA.com

CREDIT DEPARTMENT

Marti Korver, Ext 1248
Marti@HA.com
Eric Thomas, Ext. 1241
EricT@HA.com

MARKETING

Debbie Rexing, Ext. 1356
DebbieR@HA.com

MEDIA & PUBLIC RELATIONS

Kelley Norwine, Ext. 1583
KelleyN@HA.com

CORPORATE OFFICERS

R. Steven Ivy, Co-Chairman
James L. Halperin, Co-Chairman
Gregory J. Rohan, President
Paul Minshull, Chief Operating Officer
Todd Imhof, Executive Vice President
Leo Frese, Executive Vice President

WIRING INSTRUCTIONS

Bank Information:
JP Morgan Chase Bank, N.A.
270 Park Avenue, New York, NY 10017
Account Name:
Heritage Numismatic Auctions
Master Account
ABA Number: 021000021
Account Number: 1884827674
Swift Code: CHASUS33

Dear Fellow Collector,

After a 15-year hiatus, the time has finally arrived: Heritage Auction Galleries is re-entering the Rare Stamp market, Feb. 5-7, with an auction as important as it is anticipated. Steve Ivy, formerly of Steve Ivy Philatelic Auctions, then Ivy, Shreve, and Mader – not to mention being co-founder of Heritage, the world's largest collectibles auctioneer – is offering a special welcome to you, as one of our valued and discriminating clients, by being the first to receive a catalogue of our inaugural Signature Stamp Auction.

For longtime collectors and neophytes alike, a cornucopia of philately awaits: Pan-American Issue inverts, Trans –Mississippi Issues, Classic US Proofs and essays, Postal history, Back of the Book (including a strong US Revenue section), a very nice run of recently discovered Federal Duck Plate Proofs, British, Canadian, Rare foreign, PSE highest graded, Modern Errors and more are nestled within these pages. No level of buyer will be disappointed. Also, to instill absolute confidence, all single item lots are accompanied by current expert certificates from the most respected authorities specializing in that particular field.

"I hope to meet each and every person attending our auction," said Steven Crippe, a well-respected veteran of the Philatelic field, and Heritage's Director of Rare Stamps, "and I want to personally thank you all for helping to make Heritage Auction Galleries one of the most successful auction houses in the world. "

If you are not able to attend the auction in person at our uptown Dallas headquarters, remember that Heritage offers state-of-the-art technology, via our HERITAGE Live!™ Bidding platform, to view and bid, all in real time. Feel free to visit us at www.HA.com, where you can read detailed descriptions of each lot in the auction, as well as download detailed, enlargeable images.

There are a tremendous amount of great stamps in this auction; more than we could possibly list in this letter alone, but just to whet your appetite a bit, a few of the highlights from the auction include: the Scott # 1a PSE graded 98J, Mint original gum, previously hinged, the highest graded mint # 1, in any shade, known to date. It is a spectacular corner sheet margin example in dark brown, from Position 100. Or how about a beautifully centered $3 Columbian, PSE graded 98J, original gum, previously hinge. There's also the Great Britain 2p Blue (S.G. #5 / Scott #2), and several Pan- American inverts, which go perfectly with the largest known mint multiple of the non-denomination H "Yellow Hat" variety.

Oh yes, there's also a little stamp known as the Holy Grail of Philately; perhaps you've heard of it? It's one of the 100 stamps known, simply, as the "Inverted Jenny."

We encourage you to sit back, relax and enjoy this catalogue in anticipation of this great rare stamp auction on Feb. 5-7, and to hold on to it as the valuable library reference it will surely be for the future.

Sincerely,

Greg Rohan

Cataloguing and Grading Information

Condition and Grade are provided on all single item lots. Stamps that are third-party graded will include numerical and adjectival descriptive information, e.g., Superb 98, for example. On stamps that have been PSE Graded - PSE Population data and SMQ pricing information will be provided, courtesy of PSE. Stamps that have not been numerically graded will be assigned an adjectival "grade" only; e.g., "Very Fine." This description refers to stamp centering only.

TABLE OF GRADES

Numerical Grade	Description	Abbreviation
100	Gem	Gem
98	Superb	SUP
95	Extremely Fine – Superb	XF-Sup
90	Extremely Fine	XF
85	Very Fine - Extremely Fine	VF-XF
80	Very Fine	VF
75	Fine - Very Fine	F-VF
70	Fine	F
50	Very Good	VG
40	Good - Very Good	G-VG
30	Good	G
20	Fair - Good	FR-G
10	Fair	FR

A "J" when appended to the numerical grade refers to Jumbo margins (larger than is typically found on issue) For example; "XF-S 95J" refers to Extremely Fine- Superb 95 Jumbo

ABBREVIATIONS AND OTHER TERMS

Modifier	Description
OGnh	Original gum, never hinged
OGPh	Original gum, previously hinged
OG/OGh	Original gum, hinged
DOG	Disturbed original gum
POG	Partial original gum
NG	No original gum
RG	Regummed
NGAI	No gum (as originally issued)
J	Jumbo - unusually larger margins
Mint	Unused or new stamp - never cancelled.
Used	A used stamp - cancelled for postage or use.

CATALOGS USED

CATALOGS USED	ABBREVIATION
Stamp Market Quarterly	SMQ
Scott	Scott
Stanley Gibbons	Stanley Gibbons/(SG)
Unitrade	Unitrade
Dally	Dally

Catalog valuation is provided whenever possible and available. We use the current corresponding valuation in effect at the time of printing the catalog.

Table of Contents

SESSION ONE

Floor, Telephone, Heritage Live!™, Internet, Fax, and Mail Signature® Auction #1106
Thursday, February 5, 2009, 12:00 PM CT • Dallas, Texas • Lots 31001-31430

A 19.5% Buyer's Premium ($9 minimum) Will Be Added To All Lots
You can now view full-color images and bid via the Internet at the Heritage website: HA.com/Stamps

1847 REGULAR ISSUES

31001 **#1, 1847, 5c Red Brown XF 90 PSE.** (Used). Pretty copy, four margins, attractive light blue grid cancel. Extremely Fine PSE - Encapsulated. (SMQ $960; this being one of 60 attaining this grade as of 10/08, with 41 graded higher).

Estimate: $900+

Minimum Bid: $450

31002 **#1, 1847, 5c Red Brn XF 90 PSE.** (Used). Red grid cancel, nice four-margin example. Extremely Fine PSE - Encapsulated. (SMQ $960; this being one of 60 attaining this grade as of 10/08, with 41 graded higher).

Estimate: $800+

Minimum Bid: $400

31003 **#1, 1847, 5c Red Brown, VF-XF 85 PSE.** (Used). Position 80R - Double Transfer "A" variety. Red grid cancel, four full margins. Very Fine to Extremely Fine; 2006 PSE - Graded Certificate. (SMQ $710; this being one of 38 attaining this grade as of 10/08, with 102 graded higher)

Estimate: $750+

Minimum Bid: $375

31004 **#1, 1847, 5c Red Brown, VF-XF 85 PSE.** (Used). Gorgeous four margin example with a red grid cancel and an extraneous inking line at the bottom right. Very Fine to Extremely Fine; 2005 PSE - Graded Certificate. (SMQ $710; this being one of 38 attaining this grade as of 10/08, with 102 graded higher).

Estimate: $700+

Minimum Bid: $350

31005 **#1, 1847, 5c Red Brown.** (Used). A gorgeous four margin single, margins vary from generous at the bottom to monstrous at the left. Attractive red cancel. Cert notes "darkening of the color" at the top, very difficult to detect, if at all. Very Fine; 2008 PSE Certificate. (Scott $600).

Estimate: $500+

Minimum Bid: $250

31006 **#1, 1847, 5c Brown.** (Used). Wonderful used example tied to an original piece by a red circular grid cancel and a matching red Boston circular date stamp (c.d.s.) cancel, four full margins. Very Fine; 2008 PSE Certificate. (Scott $600).

Estimate: $600+

Minimum Bid: $300

31007 #1a, 1847, 5c Dark Brown, SUP 98J PSE. (Original Gum - Previously Hinged). Bottom right sheet corner margin single, Position 100R, believed to be the *unique* mint example that unquestionably proves its plate position. Outstanding in stature, this important stamp is *ex-Newbury* (1962, Lot 521 where this stamp sold for $800), and boasts an overall freshness and quality that makes it a prime focus for the crème-de-la-crème of collections. Aside from the simply monstrous margins right and bottom as a result of the sheet margins, this beauty sports large to huge margins top and left. Sumptuous color that has hardly, if at all, been affected by its 160+ years, on what is clearly bluish paper, with original gum that has been but extremely lightly kissed at the top by previous hinging, and shows what appears to be a small spot of short gumming at the bottom center well below the stamp. Of particular interest is that considering how delicate and porous the paper used for this issue is by nature, this exquisite masterpiece is sound, say for only trivial tiny specks of gum penetration are evident. a far cry less than could, or even should be expected. A truly Superb showpiece that will likely not be seen in the marketplace again for many a year to come. 2007 PSE - Graded Certificate. While this is but one of the two highest graded examples (as of 10/08), its uniqueness places it in a class of its own.

Estimate: $100,000+
Minimum Bid: $50,000

31008 **#1a, 1847, 5c Dark Brown, VF-XF 85 PSE.** (Used). Rich shade, largely face-free black grid cancel. Very Fine to Extremely Fine PSE - Encapsulated. (SMQ $860; this being one of 8 attaining this grade as of 10/08, with 26 graded higher).

Estimate: $800+

Minimum Bid: $400

31009 **#2, 1847, 10c Black, VF-XF 85 PSE.** (No Gum). Rare and underappreciated in this lofty grade, a true world class condition rarity. Jet black color with four ample to huge margins, unbelievable preservation of this 161 year old stamp, light expertising mark on the back (hard to tell, but appears to be "Calves"), a gem of this quality might not appear on the market again for quite some time. Very Fine to Extremely Fine PSE - Encapsulated.
(SMQ $17,500; this being one of 2 attaining this grade as of 10/08, with *none* graded higher).

Estimate: $17,000+

Minimum Bid: $8,500

31010 **#2, 1847, July 1, 10c Black SUP 98 PSE.** (Used). One of the finest examples of this highly sought after issue, stunning with a light red cancel, absolutely enormous margins, belongs in the finest collection. Superb; 2008 PSE - Graded Certificate, Also, 1999 PF Certificate, (SMQ $8,650; this being one of 7 attaining this grade as of 10/08, with only 2 graded higher).

Estimate: $9,000+

Minimum Bid: $4,500

31011 **#2, 1847, 10c Black, VF-XF 85 PSE.** (Used). Jet Black color, sharp detailed impression, attractive light blue grid cancel. Four margin copy. Very Fine to Extremely Fine PSE - Encapsulated. (SMQ $1,650; this being one of 23 attaining this grade as of 10/08, with 83 graded higher).

Estimate: $1,500+

Minimum Bid: $750

31012 **#2, 1847, 10c Black, VF-XF 85 PSE.** (Used). A visually striking used single, well centered within generous margins, intense color and detailed impression on fresh bluish paper, with light, unobtrusive blue grid cancel. Very Fine to Extremely Fine; 2008 PSE - Graded Certificate.
(SMQ without premium for color cancel $1,650; this being one of 23 attaining this grade as of 10/08, with 83 graded higher).

Estimate: $1,500+

Minimum Bid: $750

31013 **#2, 1847, 10c Black, VF 80 PSE.** (Used). Four margins, very attractive and unobtrusive red cancel. Very Fine PSE - Encapsulated. (SMQ $1,350; this being one of 25 attaining this grade as of 10/08, with 106 graded higher).

Estimate: $1,000+

Minimum Bid: $500

31014 **#2, 1847, 10c Black, VF 80 PSE.** (Used). Alluring example, large balanced margins, extremely attractive light red cancel, pencil notation on back. Very Fine PSE - Encapsulated. (SMQ $1,350; this being one of 25 attaining this grade as of 10/08, with 106 graded higher).

Estimate: $1,000+

Minimum Bid: $500

31015 **#2, 1847, 10c Black, VF 80 PSE.** (Used). Four margins, bottom margin large, very light red cancel. Very Fine PSE - Encapsulated. (SMQ $1,350; this being one of 25 attaining this grade as of 10/08, with 106 graded higher).

Estimate: $1,000+

Minimum Bid: $500

31016 **#2, 1847, 10c Black, VF 80 PSE.** (Used). A handsome used sheet margin single, well centered within very large margins, with red grid cancel, and an inconsequential small corner crease at the lower left, visible only under magnification and even then only barely. Very Fine; 2007 PSE - Graded Certificate. (SMQ $1,350; this being one of 25 attaining this grade as of 10/08, with 106 graded higher).

Estimate: $900+

Minimum Bid: $450

31017 **#2, 1847, 10c Black, F 70 PSE.** (Used). Very light cancel, three very nice margins, a little close at bottom, but still clear of design. Fine PSE - Encapsulated. (SMQ $750; this being one of 19 attaining this grade as of 10/08, with 144 graded higher).

Estimate: $650+

Minimum Bid: $325

31018 **#2 (A), 1847, 10c Black, F 70 PSE.** (Used). Double Transfer in 'X' at lower right. Well-defined and clearly visible. (Pencil mark on back) Minute traces of Blue cancel. Pretty stamp. Fine PSE - Encapsulated. (This Double Transfer unlisted in SMQ or in the PSE Population Records)

Estimate: $1,500+

Minimum Bid: $750

1875 REPRODUCTIONS
OF 1847 ISSUE

31019 **#3, 1875 Reproduction, 5c Red Brown, VF 80 PSE.** (No Gum As Issued). Appealing example with a lovely warm appearance, clean back. Very Fine PSE - Encapsulated. (SMQ $750; this being one of 12 attaining this grade as of 10/08, with 38 graded higher).

Estimate: $700+

Minimum Bid: $350

31020 **#3, 1875 Reproduction, 5c Red Brown.** (No Gum As Issued). Clean crisp mint example, quality stamp in all respects, Very Fine; 2008 PSE Certificate. (Scott $800).
Estimate: $750+
Minimum Bid: $375

31021 **#4, 1875 Reproduction, 10c Black, VF-XF 85 PSE.** (No Gum As Issued). Sharp Impression. Light pencil '3' on back. Very Fine to Extremely Fine PSE - Encapsulated. (SMQ $1,200; this being one of 15 attaining this grade as of 10/08, with 23 graded higher).
Estimate: $1,000+
Minimum Bid: $500

31022 **#4, 1875 Reproduction, 10c Black, VF 80J PSE.** (No Gum As Issued). An attention-grabbing sheet margin single, generous to huge margins and a proof-like impression. Very Fine; 2008 PSE - Graded Certificate. (this being one of 1 attaining this grade as of 10/08, with 41 graded higher).
Estimate: $1,000+
Minimum Bid: $500

31023 **#4, 1875 Reproduction, 10c Black, F-VF 75 PSE.** (No Gum As Issued). Handsome unused single. Intense impression, VF appearance. Fine to Very Fine; 2008 PSE - Graded Certificate. (SMQ unvalued grade 75 ; this being one of 5 attaining this grade as of 10/08, with 49 graded higher).
Estimate: $800+
Minimum Bid: $400

1851-57 FIRST ISSUES - IMPERF

31024 **#5A, 1851, 1c Blue.** (Used). Very fine appearing 5A, rare stamp in any condition, used Position 6RIE, red and black cancels with tiny thins above the head and a light vertical crease. Very Fine; 2006 PF Certificate, 1986 PF Certificate. (Scott $8,500).
Estimate: $3,500+
Minimum Bid: $1,750

31025 #6, 1851, 1c Blue, VF-XF 85 PF. (Used). TY Ia. Choice example. Position 95R4 clearly showing curl in "C" of Cents, with town cancel. This very pretty stamp worth well over standard CV. Very Fine to Extremely Fine; 2007 PF Graded Certificate. (Scott $14,000).

Estimate: $27,500+

Minimum Bid: $13,750

31026 #6, 1851, 1c Blue. (Used). Gorgeous example of this hard to find stamp, neat black cancel, tiny facial scuff in the upper right edge. Gem; 2008 PSE Certificate, 1974 PF Certificate. (Scott $12,500) .

Estimate: $6,500+

Minimum Bid: $3,250

31027 #6, 1851, 1c Blue. (Used). Extremely rare used example, Position 97L4,with a black New York circular date stamp (c.d.s.). Horizontal crease from the center to the right edge, large margins on three sides, crisp blue color, pencil notation on back. Very Good to Fine PSE Certificate. (Scott $12,500).

Estimate: $6,500+

Minimum Bid: $3,250

31028 #6b, 1851, 1c Blue. (Used). Position 96R4 with town cancel, several thins, two creases and overall soiling, very pretty appearing example, rare. F-VF; 2007 PSE Certificate. (Scott $2,750).

Estimate: $2,000+

Minimum Bid: $1,000

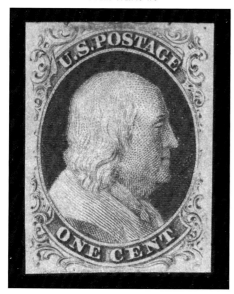

31029 **#7, 1851, 1c Blue XF-S 95 PSE.** (Original Gum - Previously Hinged). Among the very finest examples in existence. Huge margins bordering on a Jumbo designation, all design elements clearly visible. Beautiful blue color, incredible stamp. Extremely Fine to Superb PSE - Encapsulated. (SMQ $5,000; this being one of 2 attaining this grade as of 10/08, with only 3 graded higher).

Estimate: $5,500+

Minimum Bid: $2,750

WIDE MARGIN MINT #7

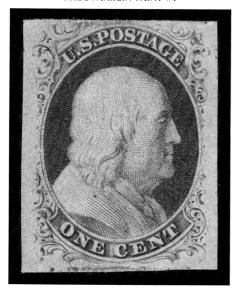

31030 **#7, 1851, 1c Blue, XF-S 95 PSE.** (Original Gum - Hinged). An extraordinary mint single, especially well-centered within generous to large margins, with part of the adjoining stamp showing at the bottom, and minute traces of the adjoining stamps showing left and right, rich and vibrant with finely etched detail. Fresh original gum showing only light traces of previous hinging, an Extremely Fine to Superb gem infrequently offered in premium grade such as this; PSE - Graded Certificate. (SMQ $5,000; this being one of 2 attaining this grade as of 10/08, with only 3 graded higher).

Estimate: $6,000+

Minimum Bid: $3,000

31031 **#7, 1851, 1c Blue, XF-S 95J PSE.** (Used). A captivating used single, well centered within generous to huge margins, with portions of the adjacent stamps clearly showing top, bottom, and left, light non-obtrusive town cancel. Extremely Fine to Superb; 2008 PSE - Graded Certificate. (this being one of 9 attaining this grade as of 10/08, with 10 graded higher).

Estimate: $1,500+

Minimum Bid: $750

31032 **#7, 1851, 1c Blue, XF 90J PSE.** (Used). Super size Jumbo margins. Attractive. Extremely Fine; 2008 PSE - Graded Certificate. (SMQ $405; this being one of 5 attaining this grade as of 10/08, with 32 graded higher).

Estimate: $600+

Minimum Bid: $300

31033 **#8, 1851, 1c Blue, VF-XF 85 PSE.** (Used). Lovely example. Four margins, deep color and strong impression. Very Fine to Extremely Fine PSE - Encapsulated. (SMQ $4,900; this being one of 5 attaining this grade as of 10/08, with 11 graded higher).

Estimate: $4,500+

Minimum Bid: $2,250

31034 **#8A, 1851, 1c Blue VF-XF 85 PSE.** (Used). Ty IIIa. 2mm+ break in top outer line. Very pretty copy, intense shade and strong impression. Black grid cancel. Very Fine to Extremely Fine PSE - Encapsulated. (SMQ $1,600; this being one of 7 attaining this grade as of 10/08, with 20 graded higher).

Estimate: $1,500+

Minimum Bid: $750

31035 **#8A, 1851, 1c Blue, XF 90J PSE.** (Used). Type IIIa. Wonderfully bright color and paper. Jumbo margins, unobtrusive cancel. Extremely Fine; 2008 PSE - Graded Certificate. (this being one of 2 attaining this grade as of 10/08, with only 8 graded higher).

Estimate: $3,500+

Minimum Bid: $1,750

31036 **#8A, 1851, 1c Blue, F 70 PSE.** (Used). Ty IIIa, attractive example, Plate 4, E relief, fresh with decent margins, bold blue color. Fine PSE - Encapsulated. (SMQ $570; this being one of 2 attaining this grade as of 10/08, with 34 graded higher).

Estimate: $700+

Minimum Bid: $350

31037 **#9, 1851, 1c Blue, SUP 98J PF.** (Used). Position 9R1L, Horizontal manuscript cancel. Huge side margins, with large portion of adjoining stamps at right and left. Superb; 2007 PF Graded Certificate.

Estimate: $1,500+

Minimum Bid: $750

31038 **#9, 1851, 1c Blue, SUP 98 PSE.** (Used). Mouthwatering used example, truly jumbo margins although not certified as such, breakout candidate, post office fresh with outstanding color, black New York circular cancel. Superb PSE - Encapsulated. (SMQ $1,850; this being one of 5 attaining this grade as of 10/08, with 16 graded higher).

Estimate: $2,000+

Minimum Bid: $1,000

31039 **#9, 1851, 1c Blue, XF-S 95 PSE.** (Used). Alluring used example with black town cancel, recut at the top and twice at the bottom. Extremely Fine to Superb; 2005 PSE -Graded Certificate, 2002 PF Certificate. (SMQ $860; this being one of 27 attaining this grade as of 10/08, with 35 graded higher).

Estimate: $800+

Minimum Bid: $400

31040 **#9, 1851, 1c Blue, XF-S 95; PSE.** (Used). Wonderfully attractive, face free cancel. Extremely Fine to Superb PSE - Encapsulated. (SMQ $860; this being one of 27 attaining this grade as of 10/08, with 35 graded higher).

Estimate: $800+

Minimum Bid: $400

31041 **#9, 1851, 1c Blue, XF-S 95 PSE.** (Used). Well centered within generous to large margins, with portions of the adjoining stamps clearly showing top and bottom, bright fresh color, multiple black circular date stamp (c.d.s.) cancels. Extremely Fine to Superb; 2008 PSE - Graded Certificate. (SMQ $860; this being one of 27 attaining this grade as of 10/08, with 35 graded higher).

Estimate: $800+

Minimum Bid: $400

31042 **#10, 1851, 3c Orange Brown, XF 90 PSE.** (Used). Rich shade, fabulous color, very sharp appearance for this issue. Black circular grid cancel, plate position pencil notation on back. Extremely Fine PSE - Encapsulated. (SMQ $385; this being one of 7 attaining this grade as of 10/08, with only 7 graded higher).

Estimate: $425+

Minimum Bid: $212

31043 **#11, 1851, 3c Brownish Carmine, SUP 98J PSE.** (Used). An astonishing used single of this shade variety, boasting huge balanced margins top and bottom, and a large part of the adjoining stamps left and right, blue circular date stamp (c.d.s.) cancel. Superb; 2007 PSE - Graded Certificate. (this being one of 12 attaining this grade as of 10/08, with only 6 graded higher).

Estimate: $1,200+

Minimum Bid: $600

HIGHEST GRADED ORIGINAL GUM #11A

31044 **#11A, 1851, 3c Dull Red, VF-XF 85J PSE.** (Original Gum - Previously Hinged). An attention grabbing, jumbo margined mint example with parts of the adjoining stamps right and left. Light hinge marks on the back. Very Fine to Extremely Fine PSE - Encapsulated. (this being the first stamp to attain this grade as of 10/08, none have been graded higher).

Estimate: $1,000+

Minimum Bid: $500

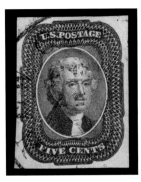

31045 **#12, 1856, 5c Red Brown, XF-S 95 PSE.** (Used). Few and far between example, deep rich red brown color, large balanced margins, black circular date stamp cancel, light pencil notation on back. Extremely Fine to Superb PSE - Encapsulated. (SMQ $2,850; this being one of 14 attaining this grade as of 10/08, with only 8 graded higher).

Estimate: $2,400+

Minimum Bid: $1,200

31046 **#12, 1856, 5c Red Brown, XF-S 95 PSE.** (Used). Exquisite four margin example with very light attractive black town cancel, perfect back, one of the best. Extremely Fine to Superb; 2007 PSE - Graded Certificate.
(SMQ $2,850; this being one of 14 attaining this grade as of 10/08, with only 8 graded higher).

Estimate: $2,500+

Minimum Bid: $1,250

31047 **#12, 1856, 5c Red Brown, XF 90 PSE.** (Used). Deep Shade; face-free cancel. Extremely Fine PSE - Encapsulated. (SMQ $1,350; this being one of 17 attaining this grade as of 10/08, with 26 graded higher).

Estimate: $1,100+

Minimum Bid: $550

31048 **#12, 1856, 5c Red Brown, VF-XF 85 PSE.** (Used). Very pleasing used example with circular date stamp (c.d.s.) cancel, Very Fine to Extremely Fine PSE - Encapsulated. (SMQ $1,000; this being one of 11 attaining this grade as of 10/08, with 44 graded higher).

Estimate: $900+

Minimum Bid: $450

31049 **#13, 1855, 10c Green, XF-S 95 PSE.** (Used). Exceptionally choice example, eye-catching green color, large well balanced margins on all sides, black circular date stamp (c.d.s.), and attractive traces or red cancel as well. Extremely Fine to Superb PSE - Encapsulated. (SMQ $3,400; this being one of 11 attaining this grade as of 10/08, with only 4 graded higher).

Estimate: $3,100+

Minimum Bid: $1,550

31050 **#13, 1855, 10c Green, XF-S 95 PSE.** (Used). Erased pencil marks on back. Large margins. Extremely Fine to Superb PSE - Encapsulated. (SMQ $3,400; this being one of 11 attaining this grade as of 10/08, with only 4 graded higher).

Estimate: $2,700+

Minimum Bid: $1,350

31051 **#13, 1855, 10c Green, XF 90 PSE.** (Used). Very attractive used example with several black grid cancels, terrific eye-appeal. Extremely Fine; 2005 PSE - Graded Certificate, 1998 PF Certificate. (SMQ $1,800; this being one of 10 attaining this grade as of 10/08, with 18 graded higher).

Estimate: $1,500+

Minimum Bid: $750

31052 **#14, 1855, 10c Green, XF-S 95J PSE.** (Used). Deep color, Jumbo margins. Extremely Fine to Superb; 2008 PSE - Graded Certificate. (this being one of 2 attaining this grade as of 10/08, with 10 graded higher).

Estimate: $900+

Minimum Bid: $450

31053 **#14, 1855, 10c Green, XF-S 95 PSE.** (Used). Absolutely wonderful used example with a black circular date stamp (c.d.s.), Extremely Fine to Superb; 2006 PSE - Graded Certificate. (SMQ $780; this being one of 40 attaining this grade as of 10/08, with 12 graded higher).

Estimate: $700+

Minimum Bid: $350

31054 **#14, 1855, 10c Green, XF-S 95 PSE.** (Used). Unobtrusive and very light cancel. Extremely Fine to Superb PSE - Encapsulated. (SMQ $780; this being one of 40 attaining this grade as of 10/08, with 12 graded higher).

Estimate: $650+

Minimum Bid: $325

31055 **#14, 1855, 10c Green, XF-S 95 PSE.** (Used). Beautiful copy with a nice New Orleans town cancel, large four margin example, pencil notation on back. Extremely Fine to Superb PSE - Encapsulated. (SMQ $780; this being one of 40 attaining this grade as of 10/08, with 12 graded higher).

Estimate: $700+

Minimum Bid: $350

31056 **#15, 1855, 10c Green, XF-S 95 PSE.** (Used). Nice used copy with blue circular date stamp (c.d.s.) cancel, four full large margins, pencil notation on back. Extremely Fine to Superb PSE - Encapsulated. (SMQ $780; this being one of 34 attaining this grade as of 10/08, with 16 graded higher).

Estimate: $700+

Minimum Bid: $350

31057 **#16, 1855, 10c Green, VF 80 PSE.** (Used). Very attractive stamp. Unobtrusive black grid cancel, four full margins. Position 65L1. Very Fine PSE - Encapsulated. (SMQ $1,700; this being one of 7 attaining this grade as of 10/08, with 22 graded higher).

Estimate: $1,500+

Minimum Bid: $750

31058 **#16, 1855, 10c Green, VG 50 PSE.** (Used). Recut at top, Pos 65L1, CV is Scott, SMQ does not value pos 65L1. Very Good PSE - Encapsulated. (SCV $1700; this being one of 6 attaining this grade as of 10/08, with 35 graded higher).

Estimate: $750+

Minimum Bid: $375

MINT UNUSED - UNCOMMON
WITH **4** MARGINS

31059 **#17, 1851, 12c Black VF-XF 85 PSE.** (No Gum). An exceptional unused single, precisely centered within generous margins, gloriously rich on fresh clean paper. Very Fine to Extremely Fine; 2007 PSE - Graded Certificate. (SMQ $2,400; this being one of 1 attaining this grade as of 10/08, with only 1 graded higher).

Estimate: $2,500+

Minimum Bid: $1,250

31060 **#17, 1851, 12c Black, SUP 98J PSE.** (Used). Portions of adjoining stamps at both sides, black grid cancel. Superb; 2006 PSE - Graded Certificate. (this being one of 6 attaining this grade as of 10/08, with only 2 graded higher).

Estimate: $5,000+

Minimum Bid: $2,500

VERY PRETTY - 4 MARGINS
FACE FREE CANCELS

31061 **#17, 1851, 12c Black, XF-S 95; PSE.** (Used). Awesome example with black and red cancels, spacious margins showing a portion of adjoining stamp. Extremely Fine to Superb PSE - Encapsulated. (SMQ $1,900; this being one of 20 attaining this grade as of 10/08, with 21 graded higher).

Estimate: $1,900+

Minimum Bid: $950

GORGEOUS USED PAIR

31062 **#17, 1851, 12c Black.** (Used). A gorgeous used horizontal pair, precisely centered within ample to large margins, intense color and detailed impression on crisp white paper, with black canceling date stamp (c.d.s.) cancels, and part of a red numeral foreign credit marking. Very Fine to Extremely Fine; 2008 PSE Certificate. (Scott $770).

Estimate: $800+

Minimum Bid: $400

1857-61 FIRST ISSUES - PERFS

TOP OF THE POP

31063 **#18, 1857, 1c Blue, XF 90 PSE.** (Original Gum - Previously Hinged). A prime mint example of this first perforated issue, concisely centered. Small portion of prior remnant. Extremely Fine and choice; PSE - Encapsulated. (SMQ $6,000; this being one of 6 attaining this grade as of 10/08, with *none* graded higher).

Estimate: $6,000+

Minimum Bid: $3,000

31064 **#18, 1857, 1c Blue, F 70 PSE.** (Original Gum - Hinged). Pretty example with bold blue color, light hinge marks and some pencil marks on gum. Fine PSE - Encapsulated. (SMQ $1,300; this being one of 1 attaining this grade as of 10/08, with only 9 graded higher).

Estimate: $900+

Minimum Bid: $450

31065 **#18, 1857, 1c Blue, VF-XF 85 PSE.** (Used). Difficult issue to find well centered, lovely example with attractive black town cancel. Very Fine to Extremely Fine; 2008 PSE - Graded Certificate. (SMQ $1,050; this being one of 5 attaining this grade as of 10/08, with only 8 graded higher).

Estimate: $900+

Minimum Bid: $450

31066 **#19, 1857, 1c Blue XF 90 PSE.** (Used). Type 1a perforated - Bottom Row, position 92R4. Beautifully centered with neat black and red unobtrusive cancels. Because of the extra height of this stamp, it is likely that this stamp is one of the *wide spacing* examples from a small segment of the bottom row which was sometimes perforated at a slight angle. Only a handful of perforated Type 1a stamps exist in VF or better grade. Extremely Fine; 2008 PSE - Graded Certificate. Also, 2008 PF Certificate. (SMQ $42,000; this being one of 1 attaining this grade as of 10/08, with only 2 graded higher).

Estimate: $50,000+
Minimum Bid: $25,000

31067 **#19, 1857, 1c Blue.** (Used). Tied on the corner of an original envelope by blue Cincinnati, O. canceling date stamp (c.d.s.) cancel, with a trivial unpunched perf at the bottom and scissor clipped perfs at the top, Very Good to Fine; 2008 PSE Certificate. (Scott $11,000).

Estimate: $3,000+

Minimum Bid: $1,500

CHOICE QUALITY - ONE OF THE NICEST #21'S IN EXISTENCE

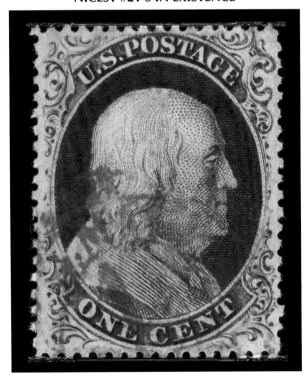

31068 **#21, 1857, 1c Blue, XF-S 95 PSE.** (Used). A magnificent example for the collector desiring to acquire the finest. Impeccable example in every respect, stunning blue color amidst symmetrical fabulous margins, enhancing light red carrier cancel. Full, intact perforations with a crisp detailed impression. Seldom encountered in this premium grade. Extremely Fine to Superb PSE - Encapsulated. (SMQ $16,500.00; this being one of 8 attaining this grade as of 10/08, with *none* graded higher).

Estimate: $20,000+

Minimum Bid: $10,000

31069 **#21, 1857, 1c Blue, XF 90 PSE.** (Used). Sharply detailed impression with deep blue color, unobtrusive black cancel, perfect back. Extremely Fine; 2005 PSE - Graded Certificate, 2004 PF Certification.
(SMQ $6950; this being one of 13 attaining this grade as of 10/08, with only 8 graded higher).

Estimate: $6,000+

Minimum Bid: $3,000

31070 **#22, 1857, 1c Blue.** (Partial Original Gum). A handsome mint example from Plate 11, with intense color and detailed impression, part original gum with a hinge remnant not mentioned on the certificate. Fine to Very Fine; 2005 PSE Certificate. (Scott $2,750).

Estimate: $1,500+

Minimum Bid: $750

31071 **#22, 1857, 1c Blue, XF 90 PSE.** (Used). Intense blue color, black grid cancel with very light plating notes in pencil on the back. Extremely Fine; 2005 PSE - Graded Certificate,1996 PF Certificate.
(SMQ $1,600; this being one of 11 attaining this grade as of 10/08, with only 8 graded higher).

Estimate: $1,350+

Minimum Bid: $675

31072 #24, 1857, 1c Blue, XF-S 95 PSE.
(Original Gum - Previously Hinged). Fabulous example, bold color throughout, marvelously well centered. Prior hinge mark only, no remnant. Extremely Fine to Superb PSE - Encapsulated.
(SMQ $740; this being one of 3 attaining this grade as of 10/08, with *none* graded higher).
Estimate: $740+
Minimum Bid: $370

31073 #25, 1857, 3c Rose, XF 90 PSE.
(Used). Highly desirable example, appealing, blue circular date stamp (c.d.s.), pencil notations on back. Extremely Fine PSE - Encapsulated (SMQ $690; this being one of 14 attaining this grade as of 10/08, with only 2 graded higher).
Estimate: $550+
Minimum Bid: $275

STUNNING HIGH GRADE FIRST ISSUE

31074 #26, 1857, 3c Dull Red, SUP 98 PSE.
(Original Gum - Never Hinged). A monstrous, attention-grabbing mint top sheet margin single, flawlessly centered, with large parts of all adjoining stamps and selvage included all around, essentially providing a picture frame for this gem. Vividly fresh, with immaculate full and fresh original gum Superb; 2007 PSE - Graded Certificate.
(SMQ $3,500; this being one of 2 attaining this grade as of 10/08, with *none* graded higher).
Estimate: $5,000+
Minimum Bid: $2,500

31075 #26, 1857, 3c Dull Red, XF-S 95 PSE.
(Original Gum - Never Hinged). Extremely fresh example, very hard to find this nice. Extremely Fine to Superb PSE - Encapsulated.
(SMQ $1,150; this being one of 6 attaining this grade as of 10/08, with only 2 graded higher).
Estimate: $1,450+
Minimum Bid: $725

31076 #26, 1857, 3c Brownish Carmine, XF-S 95 PSE.
(Original Gum - Never Hinged). Tough stamp Never Hinged. Fresh gum for issue. The Brownish Carmine shade, worth a premium. PSE POP does not distinguish shades on this issue, still low POP regardless. Extremely Fine to Superb; 2007 PSE - Graded Certificate.
(this being one of 6 attaining this grade as of 10/08, with only 2 graded higher).
Estimate: $1,500+
Minimum Bid: $750

SCARCE GREEN CANCEL ON BETTER SHADE

31077 #26, 1857, 3c Brownish Carmine XF-S 95 PSE.
(Used). Generously margined and well centered copy with lovely green town cancel. (SMQ value does not include premium for the green cancel). Extremely Fine to Superb; 2008 PSE - Graded Certificate. (SMQ $375; this being one of 17 attaining this grade as of 10/08, with 10 graded higher).
Estimate: $500+
Minimum Bid: $250

31078 #27, 1857, 5c Brick Red, VF-XF 85 PSE. (Used). Rich brick red color with large even margins for this issue, used example with a black New Orleans Feb 1859 circular date stamp (c.d.s.) cancel. Very Fine to Extremely Fine; 2005 PSE - Graded Certificate, 1985 PF Certificate,
(SMQ $2,800; this being one of 3 attaining this grade as of 10/08, with 10 graded higher).

Estimate: $2,400+

Minimum Bid: $1,200

31079 #27, 1857, 5c Brick Red. (Used). Tough issue in any grade, true brick color for this used example with black New Orleans, La. circular date stamp (c.d.s.) cancel, Fine; 2008 PSE Certificate.
(Scott $1,800).

Estimate: $900+

Minimum Bid: $450

31080 #29, 1857, 5c Brown XF 90 PF. (Used). An intriguingly high quality used single, exceptionally well centered within the usually tight margins, with a trace of red cancel at the top left Extremely Fine; 2007 PF Graded Certificate.

Estimate: $1,200+

Minimum Bid: $600

31081 #29, 1857, 5c Brown, VF-XF 85 PSE. (Used). Appealing used example with a black grid cancel, Very Fine to Extremely Fine; 2005 PSE - Graded Certificate, 1986 PF Certificate. (SMQ $700; this being one of 5 attaining this grade as of 10/08, with 14 graded higher).

Estimate: $600+

Minimum Bid: $300

31082 #30A, 1857, 5c Brown, XF 90; PSE. (Original Gum - Previously Hinged). A superlative mint example of this classic era Jefferson issue. Marvelously well centered with full even perforations all around. Fresh warm color and detailed impression on crisp paper, full original gum showing only insignificant traces of previous hinging. Extremely Fine PSE - Encapsulated.
(SMQ $5,500; this being one of 3 attaining this grade as of 10/08, with only 1 graded higher).

Estimate: $6,500+

Minimum Bid: $3,250

31083 #30A, 1857, 5c Brown. (Partial Original Gum). An attractive mint single, post office fresh color and detailed impression, well centered, previously hinged with traces of original gum, small hinge remnant. Very Fine; 2004 PF Certificate.
(Scott $2,400).

Estimate: $1,200+

Minimum Bid: $600

31084 **#30A, 1857, 5c Brown, XF 90 PSE.** (Used). Black Grid Cancel. Extremely Fine PSE - Graded Certificate. (SMQ $890; this being one of 9 attaining this grade as of 10/08, with only 8 graded higher).

Estimate: $800+

Minimum Bid: $400

31085 **#31, 1857, 10c Green.** (Used). Handsome example with a black 'PAID' in circle cancel, one nibbed perf at the bottom that is not visually distracting, nice stamp Very Fine; 2008 PSE Certificate. (Scott $1,300).

Estimate: $650+

Minimum Bid: $325

31086 **#31, 1857, 10c Green.** (Used). Extremely attractive example, ample to large margins with a light black circular date stamp (c.d.s.) cancel Very Fine; 2008 PSE Certificate. (Scott $1,300).

Estimate: $950+

Minimum Bid: $475

31087 **#32, 1857, 10c Green, XF-S 95 PSE.** (Used). Magnificent used example, very light black circular date stamp (c.d.s.) cancel, extremely well centered, perfect perforations. Extremely Fine to Superb PSE - Encapsulated. (SMQ $2,800; this being one of 13 attaining this grade as of 10/08, with only 1 graded higher).

Estimate: $2,600+

Minimum Bid: $1,300

31088 **#32, 1857, 10c Green, XF-S 95 PSE.** (Used). An outstanding used gem, flawlessly centered amidst generous margins that very nearly boarder on being jumbo for the issue. Full intact perforations all around, luxuriously rich color and finely etched detail on crisp clean paper. Non-obtrusive black New Orleans, LA c.d.s. cancel. Extremely Fine to Superbjewel typically impossible to find in such extraordinary quality. 2008 PSE - Graded Certificate. (SMQ $2,800; this being one of 13 attaining this grade as of 10/08, with only 1 graded higher).

Estimate: $3,500+

Minimum Bid: $1,750

31089 **#32, 1857, 10c Green, XF 90 PSE.** (Used). An impressive used single, precisely centered amidst generous margins, detailed impression with color that almost glows, light cancel, with an inconsequential unpunched perf at the top right. Extremely Fine; 2008 PSE - Graded Certificate. (SMQ $830; this being one of 11 attaining this grade as of 10/08, with 14 graded higher).

Estimate: $1,000+

Minimum Bid: $500

CONDITION RARITY + 'YANKEE JIMS' CANCEL

31090 **#33, 1857, 10c Green, XF-S 95 PSE.** (Used). An incomparable used single, flawlessly centered amidst enormous well balanced margins for the issue, bright and vibrant, vividly detailed, with a non-obtrusive black Yankee Jims c.d.s. cancel. Extremely Fine to Superb,condition rarity whose equal would be extremely difficult if not outright impossible to find; 2008 PSE - Graded Certificate. (SMQ $2,800; this being one of 9 attaining this grade as of 10/08, with only 1 graded higher).

Estimate: $3,000+

Minimum Bid: $1,500

31091 **#34, 1857, 10c Green.** (Used). Black cds and red crayon cancels and two unpunched perfs. Very Fine to Extremely Fine; 2008 PSE Certificate.

Estimate: $2,000+
Minimum Bid: $1,000

31092 **#35, 1857, 10c Green, XF-S 95 PSE.** (Used). Wonderful used example with huge side margins, black circular date stamp (c.d.s.) cancel. Extremely Fine to Superb; 2008 PSE - Graded Certificate, 1984 PF Certification. (SMQ $590; this being one of 19 attaining this grade as of 10/08, with only 2 graded higher).

Estimate: $500+
Minimum Bid: $250

31093 **#36, 1857, 12c Black, XF-S 95 PSE.** (Used). A truly magnificent used example of this tough to find issue, huge margins for this issue, fresh with black town cancel. Extremely Fine to Superb PSE - Encapsulated. (SMQ $3,700; this being one of 6 attaining this grade as of 10/08, with only 1 graded higher).

Estimate: $3,200+
Minimum Bid: $1,600

31094 **#36, 1857, 12c Black, XF 90 PSE.** (Used). Very fresh example with unobtrusive black grid and trace red cancels. Very attractive example. Extremely Fine; 2005 PSE - Graded Certificate, 1991 PF Certificate.
(SMQ $1,000; this being one of 11 attaining this grade as of 10/08, with only 7 graded higher).

Estimate: $900+
Minimum Bid: $450

31095 **#35, 1857, 10c Green, XF-S 95 PSE.** (Used). Beautiful lightly canceled stamp (red cancel) with huge evenly centered side margins, Extremely Fine to Superb PSE - Encapsulated. (SMQ $590; this being one of 19, attaining this grade as of 10/08, with only 2 graded higher) .

Estimate: $550+
Minimum Bid: $275

31096 **#36, 1857, 12c Black, XF 90 PSE.** (Used). A stunning used single, perfectly centered, with vivid color and deeply etched impression on white paper, with complimentary black c.d.s. and red transit cancels. Extremely Fine; 2007 PSE - Graded Certificate. (SMQ $1,000; this being one of 11 attaining this grade as of 10/08, with only 7 graded higher).

Estimate: $900+
Minimum Bid: $450

31097 **#36, 1857, 12c Black, XF 90 PSE.** (Used). An exceptional used single, very well-centered, rich and vibrant, with a black circular date stamp (c.d.s.) cancel. Extremely Fine example for the connoisseur of quality used stamps; 2008 PSE - Graded Certificate and 2004 PF Certificate.
(SMQ $1,000; this being one of 11 attaining this grade as of 10/08, with only 7 graded higher).

Estimate: $800+
Minimum Bid: $400

31098 **#37, 1860, 24c Gray Lilac XF-S 95 PSE.** (Used). Exceptional example, unbelievable freshness on this used stamp, a red grid cancel that frames the portrait. Extremely Fine to Superb; 2008 PSE - Graded Certificate,
(SMQ $4,000; this being one of 8 attaining this grade as of 10/08, with only 3 graded higher).

Estimate: $5,500+

Minimum Bid: $2,750

RARE AS USED

31099 **#39, 1860, 90c Blue.** (Used). Extremely rare issue in used condition, deepest of blue color with complimenting red cancel, some light toning in the lower right margin, pencil notation on back. Fine; 2007 PSE Certificate. (Scott $9,500).

Estimate: $5,000+

Minimum Bid: $2,500

1875 REPRINT OF
1857-61 ISSUE

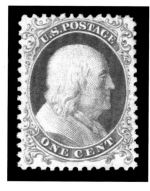

31100 **#40, 1875 Reprint, 1c Bright Blue, XF 90 PF.** (No Gum As Issued). Bright, fresh and beautiful, clean back. Extremely Fine; 2008 PF Graded Certificate, 1984 PF Certificate. (Scott $625).

Estimate: $625+

Minimum Bid: $312

RARE REPRINT - ONLY 516 SOLD IN 1875

31101 **#43, 1875 Reprint, 10c Blue Green, F-VF 75 PSE.** (No Gum As Issued). Impressive blue green color on fresh white paper, sharp impression, first rate example of this difficult stamp. Fine to Very Fine; 2008 PSE - Graded Certificate.
(this being one of 2 attaining this grade as of 10/08, with only 8 graded higher).

Estimate: $3,000+

Minimum Bid: $1,500

31102 **#46, 1875 Reprint, 30c Yellow Orange, XF 90 PSE.** (No Gum As Issued). One of the finest examples of this very rare issue, the yellow orange color looks like it is embossed on the white background, virtually perfect centering for this issue. Extremely Fine; 2004 PSE - Graded Certificate, 1965 PF Certificate.
(SMQ $9,500; this being one of 6 attaining this grade as of 10/08, with only 2 graded higher).

Estimate: $8,500+

Minimum Bid: $4,250

RARE REPRINT - ONLY 454 SOLD IN 1875

31103 **#47, 1875 Reprint, 90c Deep Blue VF 80 PSE.** (No Gum As Issued). Intensely deep rich color. Only 454 sold. Very Fine PSE - Graded Certificate.
(SMQ $4750; this being one of 2 attaining this grade as of 10/08, with only 7 graded higher).

Estimate: $5,000+

Minimum Bid: $2,500

31104 **#47, 1875 Reprint, 90c Deep Blue, VF 80 PF.** (No Gum As Issued). Very scarce and undervalued. Only 454 stamps were issued. Intense deep blue color and prooflike impression, great stamp. Very Fine; 2008 PF Graded Certificate. (Scott $4,750).

Estimate: $5,000+

Minimum Bid: $2,500

1861-66 SECOND ISSUES

31105 **#56, 1861, 3c Brown Rose.** (Original Gum - Previously Hinged). Simply gorgeous example with some gum disturbances from hinge removal and some gum toning, (August Issue 65-E15h). Fine to Very Fine; 2008 PF Certificate. (Scott very fine appearance $550).

Estimate: $500+

Minimum Bid: $250

31106 **#65, 1861, 3c Rose.** (Original Gum - Never Hinged). As bright and fresh as the day it was minted, terrific eye-appeal. Fine to Very Fine; 2008 PSE Certificate. (Scott $150.00).

Estimate: $125+

Minimum Bid: $1

31107 **#67, 1861, 5c Buff, VG 50 PSE.** (No Gum). Very rare mint stamp in any condition, fresh with rich buff color, overall nice example. Very Good PSE - Encapsulated. (SMQ $2,600; this being one of 1 attaining this grade as of 10/08, with only 1 graded higher).

Estimate: $1,900+

Minimum Bid: $950

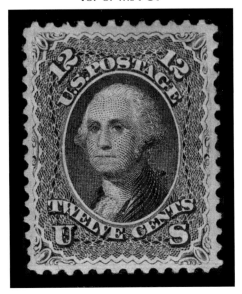

31108 **#69, 1861, 12c Black, XF 90; PSE.** (Original Gum - Previously Hinged). Magnificent. A stunning mint single, incomparably well centered, rich and vibrant color. Razor sharp impression on crisp clean paper, and original gum that has only a light prior hinge mark. Extremely Fine PSE - Encapsulated. (SMQ $5,050; this being one of 4 attaining this grade as of 10/08, with *none* graded higher).

Estimate: $7,500+

Minimum Bid: $3,750

31109 **#69, 1861, 12c Black, XF-S 95 PSE.** (Used). Neat black wedge cork cancel, well centered with fresh color. Extremely Fine to Superb PSE - Encapsulated. (SMQ $1,050; this being one of 23 attaining this grade as of 10/08, with only 8 graded higher).

Estimate: $1,000+

Minimum Bid: $500

31110 **#70, 1861, 24c Red Lilac XF 90 PSE.** (Used). Beautifully centered example with dynamic red violet color, neat black circle cancel. Extremely Fine; 2005 PSE - Graded Certificate. (SMQ $1,000; this being one of 10 attaining this grade as of 10/08, with only 5 graded higher).
Estimate: $850+
Minimum Bid: $425

31111 **#70c, 1861, 24c Violet, VF 80 PSE.** (Used). Terrific used example, bright fresh violet color, ample well centered margins, black grid cancels, very attractive overall. Very Fine; 2007 PSE - Graded Certificate, 2006 PSE Certificate. (SMQ $2,050; this being one of 2 attaining this grade as of 10/08, with only 5 graded higher).
Estimate: $1,800+
Minimum Bid: $900

31112 **#72, 1861, 90c Blue, XF 90 PSE.** (Used). Exceptional color and strong impression, black grid cancel. Extremely Fine; 2005 PSE - Graded Certificate,1985 and 1989 PF Certificate. (SMQ $1450; this being one of 7 attaining this grade as of 10/08, 12 graded higher).
Estimate: $1,200+
Minimum Bid: $600

31113 **#73, 1861, 2c Black, XF-S 95 PSE.** (Used). Black New Orleans town and target cancels. Extremely Fine to Superb; 2005 PSE - Graded Certificate. Also, 2003 PF Certificate. (SMQ $1,000; this being one of 12 attaining this grade as of 10/08, with only 2 graded higher).
Estimate: $900+
Minimum Bid: $450

31114 **#78a, 1863, 24c Grayish Lilac, XF 90 PSE.** (Used). Black target cancel and trace red cancels. Pencil note on back; "70(b)" Extremely Fine PSE - Encapsulated. (SMQ $680; this being one of 4 attaining this grade as of 10/08, with only 3 graded higher).
Estimate: $500+
Minimum Bid: $250

31115 **#83, 1867, 3c Rose.** (Original Gum - Previously Hinged). A scarce mint example of this "C" grilled issue, fresh and clean, with a strong well defined grill, light hinge mark only with no remnant. Fine; 2004 PF Certificate and 1999 PSE Certificate.
(Scott $6,500) .
Estimate: $4,000+
Minimum Bid: $2,000

31116 **#85, 1867, 3c Rose, XF 90 PSE.** (Used). Circle of V's cancel, well-centered and choice. Extremely Fine PSE - Encapsulated.
(SMQ $3,000; this being one of 5 attaining this grade as of 10/08, with only 4 graded higher).
Estimate: $3,000+
Minimum Bid: $1,500

31117 #85, 1867, 3c Rose. (Used). Three large margins, black quartered cork cancel. Very Fine; 2008 PSE Certificate.
(Scott $1,200).
Estimate: $800+
Minimum Bid: $400

31118 #85, 1867, 3c Rose. (Used). Circle of V's cancel. Trivial corner creases at the top right and bottom right, two diagonal creases at the upper right and a nibbed perf at the lower right. Pencil notation on back. Fine; 2008 PSE Certificate. (Scott $1,200).
Estimate: $900+
Minimum Bid: $450

31119 #85B, 1867, 2c Black. (Partial Original Gum). Rare in Mint condition. Part original gum, gum soaks in the grill and perforation tips. This issue plagued by rough perfs, this copy with reasonably nice perfs, only a single pulled perforation at top left. Very Good to Fine; 2007 PF Certificate.
(Scott $15,000).
Estimate: $3,800+
Minimum Bid: $1,900

HIGH GRADE "Z" GRILL

31120 #85B, 1867, 2c Black, XF-S 95 PSE. (Used). A breathtaking example of this rarity. Impeccably well-centered amidst beautifully balanced margins, captivatingly bright and fresh, with a black circle of "V"s cancel. An Extremely Fine to Superb example which is very difficult to find in such premier quality; 2008 PSE - Graded Certificate. (SMQ $12,400; this being one of 3 attaining this grade as of 10/08, with only 2 graded higher).
Estimate: $15,000+
Minimum Bid: $7,500

31121 **#85C, 1867, 3c Rose.** (Used). A well centered and sound used example of this difficult "Z" grill, the grill being very strong and showing well, even from the face, with a rosette cancel. Very Fine and choice example of this difficult stamp; 1976 and 2008 PF Certificates. (Scott $3,750).

Estimate: $3,500+
Minimum Bid: $1,750

31122 **#85E, 1867, 12c Black, VF-XF 85 PSE.** (Used). A stunning used example of this "Z" grill issue, precisely centered amidst generous margins. Vibrant color with complimentary black cork cancel. Insignificant short perf at the lower right. Very Fine to Extremely Fine; 2008 PSE - Graded Certificate.
(SMQ $4,050; this being one of 2 attaining this grade as of 10/08, with only 3 graded higher).

Estimate: $4,000+
Minimum Bid: $2,000

31123 **#87, 1867, 2c Black, XF-S 95 PSE.** (Used). Precisely centered within generous well balanced margins, black fancy cork cancel. Extremely Fine to Superb PSE - Encapsulated. (SMQ $2,100; this being one of 6 attaining this grade as of 10/08, with only 3 graded higher).

Estimate: $2,000+
Minimum Bid: $1,000

31124 **#88, 1867, 3c Rose.** (Original Gum - Previously Hinged). A mint example of the 3c "E" grill, fresh with a full strong grill clearly visible from the face. Light hinge mark only. Very Fine; 1994 and 2005 PF Certificates. (Scott $1,200) .

Estimate: $1,200+
Minimum Bid: $600

31125 **#90, 1867, 12c Black, XF-S 95 PSE.** (Used). Well centered with larger than usual margins, jet black color on white paper, black cancel, tiny pencil notation on back, beautiful. Extremely Fine to Superb PSE - Encapsulated. (SMQ $3,700; this being one of 7 attaining this grade as of 10/08, with only 1 graded higher).

Estimate: $3,200+
Minimum Bid: $1,600

31126 **#90, 1867, 12c Black, XF 90 PSE.** (Used). Choice large margin example, unobtrusive cancel. Extremely Fine; 2005 PSE - Graded Certificate, 2000 PF Certificate. (SMQ $1,000; this being one of 7 attaining this grade as of 10/08, with only 9 graded higher).

Estimate: $900+
Minimum Bid: $450

31127 **#91, 1867, 15c Black.** (Original Gum - Previously Hinged). Gorgeous example of this rare issue, extremely fresh with vivid black color and sharp impression, lightly hinged on the back. Fine to Very Fine; 2008 PSE Certificate. 1988 and 2002 PF Certificate. (Scott $13,500).

Estimate: $8,500+
Minimum Bid: $4,250

31128 **#96, 1867, 10c Green.** (Original Gum - Previously Hinged). Outstanding mint example with rich dark color, minor hinging marks and some pencil notations on the back. Fine; 2006 PF Certificate. (Scott $3,500).
Estimate: $1,750+
Minimum Bid: $875

31129 **#97, 1867, 12c Black XF-S 95 PSE.** (Used). Absolutely perfect example, wonderfully balanced margins with a prooflike impression, black circle of wedges cancel. Extremely Fine to Superb PSE - Encapsulated. (SMQ $2700; this being one of 10 attaining this grade as of 10/08, with only 2 graded higher).
Estimate: $2,500+
Minimum Bid: $1,250

31130 **#100, 1867, 30c Orange, VF 80 PSE.** (Used). An attractive used single, precisely centered amidst typically tight margins, fresh color and detailed impression on white paper, strong clear grill, with a quartered cork cancel, and trivial light pencil notations on the back, not detracting from the overall desirability. Very Fine; 2006 PSE - Graded Certificate.
(SMQ $900; this being one of 3 attaining this grade as of 10/08, with only 8 graded higher).
Estimate: $1,000+
Minimum Bid: $500

1875 RE-ISSUE OF 1861-66 ISSUES

STUNNING QUALITY - EX-HETHERINGTON

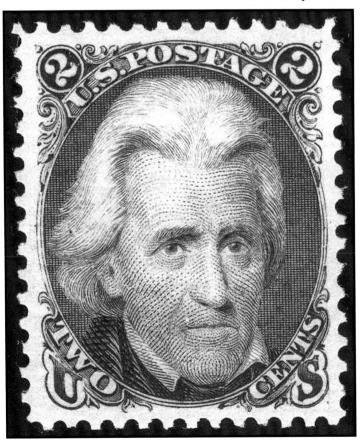

31131 **#103, 1875 Re-Issue, 2c Black XF-S 95 PSE.** (Original Gum - Previously Hinged). Wonderfully detailed and sharp impression. Only 979 sold. Tremendously well-centered. PSE Certificate: "Never Hinged," however, we detect a trivial mark that looks like a prior hinge mark to us, so we are offering as "Previously Hinged." Ex-Hetherington, 1957. Extremely Fine to Superb; 2007 PSE - Graded Certificate.
Estimate: $25,000+
Minimum Bid: $12,500

RARE 1875 RE-ISSUE

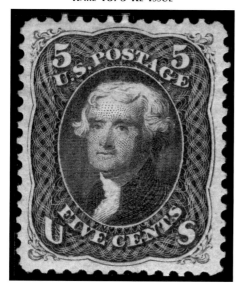

RARITY - ONLY 389 SOLD IN 1875

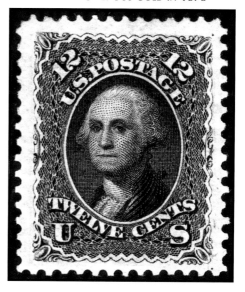

31132 **#105, 1875 Re-Issue, 5c Brown, XF-S 95 PSE.** (Original Gum - Previously Hinged). A magnificent example of this scarce Re-Issue, exceptionally well centered, detailed impression, original gum that shows evidence of previous hinging in the top third of the stamp. Extremely Fine to Superb, rarely seen this choice; *one of only 672 issued*; PSE - Encapsulated.

(SMQ $14,400; this being one of 7 attaining this grade as of 10/08, with only 1 graded higher).

Estimate: $15,000+

Minimum Bid: $7,500

31134 **#107, 1875 Re-Issue, 12c Black, XF 90J PSE.** (Original Gum - Previously Hinged). Intense Color and Sharp detailed impression. large margins. light hinge marks and slight gum discolorations. Extremely Fine; 2005 PSE - Graded Certificate. Also, 1999 PF Certificate. (this being one of 2 attaining this grade as of 10/08, with only 4 graded higher).

Estimate: $15,000+

Minimum Bid: $7,500

RARE 1875 RE-ISSUE

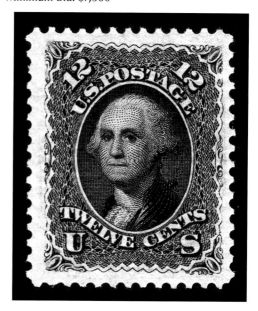

31133 **#106, 1875 Re-Issue, 10c Green, XF-S 95 PSE.** (Original Gum - Previously Hinged). Decisively wonderful, radiantly bright on white paper, finely detailed impression, original gum showing only very light evidence of previous hinging towards the top. Extremely Fine to Superb and scarce; *one of only 451 issued*; PSE - Encapsulated. (SMQ $15,500; this being one of 2 attaining this grade as of 10/08, with only 2 graded higher).

Estimate: $15,000+

Minimum Bid: $7,500

31135 **#107, 1875 Re-Issue, 12c Black, VF-XF 85J PSE.** (Original Gum - Hinged). Eye-pleasing large margins. Small hinge remnant and small pencil mark on gum. Very Fine to Extremely Fine; 2006 PSE - Graded Certificate. (this being one of 2 attaining this grade as of 10/08, with only 7 graded higher).

Estimate: $11,000+

Minimum Bid: $5,500

31136 **#112, 1869, 1c Buff, XF 90 PF.** (Original Gum - Previously Hinged). Wonderful Stamp. Obviously undergraded by PF, just look at the centering! Rich color and sharp impression. Fresh gum, portion of prior remnant. Extremely Fine; 2006 PF Graded Certificate.

Estimate: $3,500+

Minimum Bid: $1,750

31137 **#112, 1869, 1c Buff, VF-XF 85 PSE.** (Original Gum - Previously Hinged). Gorgeous example with wide even margins, small hinge remnant and pencil mark on the back. Very Fine to Extremely Fine PSE - Graded Certificate. (Scott $850).

Estimate: $750+

Minimum Bid: $375

31138 **#113, 1869, 2c Brown, XF 90 PSE.** (Original Gum - Previously Hinged). Post Horse and Rider. Excellent example, very appealing, lightly hinged. Extremely Fine; 2005 PSE - Graded Certificate, 1997 PF Certificate. (SMQ $1,850; this being one of 9 attaining this grade as of 10/08, with only 7 graded higher).

Estimate: $1,600+

Minimum Bid: $800

31139 **#113, 1869, 2c Brown, XF 90 PSE.** (Original Gum - Hinged). Post Horse and Rider. Bright, fresh, and fabulous example, vivid impression. Extremely Fine; 2008 PSE - Graded Certificate. (SMQ $1,850; this being one of 9 attaining this grade as of 10/08, with only 7 graded higher).

Estimate: $1,600+

Minimum Bid: $800

RARE - NO GRILL

31140 **#113b, 1869, 2c Without Grill F-VF 75 PSE.** (Original Gum - Previously Hinged). Post Horse and Rider. Attractive example of this rare no grill, rich brown color with sharp impression, hinge remnant, small gum void at lower right and pencil notation on back. Fine to Very Fine PSE - Encapsulated. (SMQ -unlisted and unpriced)

Estimate: $4,000+

Minimum Bid: $2,000

SCARCE DOUBLE VARIETY

31141 **#113, 1869, 2c Dark Brown.** (No Gum). Post Horse and Rider. Pretty variety, unused with no gum. Double grill (one split) variety. A short perforation at the right and a natural straight edge at the left. Very Good to Fine; 2008 PSE Certificate.

Estimate: $500+

Minimum Bid: $250

31142 **#113, 1869, 2c Brown, VF 80J PSE.** (Used). Post Horse and Rider. Large margins for issue. Very Fine; 2007 PSE - Graded Certificate. (this being one of attaining this grade as of 10/08, with none graded higher).

Estimate: $600+

Minimum Bid: $300

CONDITION RARITY
SPLIT GRILL VARIETY !

31143 **#114, 1869, 3c Ultramarine, SUP 98 PSE.** (Original Gum - Never Hinged). Stand-out Pictorial issue. Split Grill variety, tremendously well-centered. Few exist nicer. Superb; 2008 PSE - Graded Certificate. (SMQ $6,250; this being one of 2 attaining this grade as of 10/08, with None graded higher).

Estimate: $9,500+

Minimum Bid: $4,750

31144 **#114, 1869, 3c Ultramarine, XF-S 95 PSE.** (Original Gum - Never Hinged). Locomotive. Among the finest examples to date, bright white paper surrounds a wonderfully centered image, unbelievable quality for the grade. Extremely Fine to Superb PSE - Encapsulated. (SMQ $3,500; this being one of 5 attaining this grade as of 10/08, with only 2 graded higher).

Estimate: $4,500+

Minimum Bid: $2,250

31145 **#114, 1869, 3c Ultramarine, XF-S 95 PSE.** (Original Gum - Never Hinged). Locomotive. Rare and beautiful Pictorial. Almost perfect centering combined with a rich ultramarine color (visually brightened by the crisp white paper), exceptional impression. Extremely Fine to Superb; 2008 PSE - Graded Certificate. (SMQ $3,500; this being one of 5 attaining this grade as of 10/08, with only 2 graded higher).

Estimate: $4,500+

Minimum Bid: $2,250

31146 **#114, 1869, 3c Ultramarine VF-XF 85J PSE.** (Original Gum - Never Hinged). Locomotive. Magnificent example, fresh as the day it was minted, very bright color, super fresh. Very Fine to Extremely Fine; 2007 PSE - Graded Certificate. (this being one of 1 attaining this grade as of 10/08, with 16 graded higher).

Estimate: $800+

Minimum Bid: $400

31147 #114, 1869, 3c Ultramarine, XF-S 95J PSE. (Used). A huge monster of a used stamp, fabulously centered within tremendous well balanced margins, fancy cancel a tad heavy. Extremely Fine to Superb; 2007 PSE - Graded Certificate. (this being one of 5 attaining this grade as of 10/08, with only 1 graded higher).

Estimate: $600+

Minimum Bid: $300

31148 #115, 1869, 6c Ultramarine, XF 90 PF. (No Gum). Bright color on fresh white paper. Tough stamp with nice margins like these. Extremely Fine; 2007 PF Graded Certificate..

Estimate: $2,500+

Minimum Bid: $1,250

31149 #115, 1869, 6c Ultramarine, XF 90J PSE. (Used). Truly oversized margins for this issue, black grid cancel. Very tough stamp with good sized margins, much less with decent centering. Extremely Fine; 2007 PSE - Graded Certificate. (this being one of 4 attaining this grade as of 10/08, with only 2 graded higher).

Estimate: $950+

Minimum Bid: $475

31150 #116, 1869, 10c Yellow, XF-S 95 PSE. (No Gum). Eagle and Shield. Bold and Rich color on fresh white paper. (tiny dirt speck just to the right of eagle) Extremely Fine to Superb PSE - Encapsulated. (SMQ $2,150; this being one of 2 attaining this grade as of 10/08, with *none* graded higher).

Estimate: $1,350+

Minimum Bid: $675

STEAMSHIP CANCEL

31151 #116, 1869, 10c Yellow, XF-S 95 PSE. (Used). Eagle and Shield. Outstanding example. Rich shade and exceptional margins. STEAMSHIP cancel. Extremely Fine to Superb PSE - Encapsulated.
(SMQ for common cancel; $1,200, this being one of 12 attaining this grade as of 10/08, with only 3 graded higher, which refers to all PSE Graded 116's, not necessarily those copies with a desirable and scarce cancel such as this copy).

Estimate: $2,000+

Minimum Bid: $1,000

31152 #116, 1869, 10c Yellow, XF 90J PSE. (Used). Eagle and Shield. Gorgeous and Rich color with design-free, light and attractive cancel. Oversize margins for issue. Extremely Fine; 2006PSE - Graded Certificate. (this being one of 2 attaining this grade as of 10/08, with 16 graded higher).

Estimate: $900+

Minimum Bid: $450

31153 **#116, 1869, 10c Yellowish Orange, XF 90 PSE.** (Used). Eagle and Shield. Black Target Cancel, Bold color. Extremely Fine PSE - Encapsulated. (SMQ $395; this being one of 30 attaining this grade as of 10/08, with 17 graded higher).

Estimate: $400+

Minimum Bid: $200

31154 **#117, 1869, 12c Green, VF-XF 85 PSE.** (No Gum). S.S. Adriatic. Bright color, fresh white paper. Very Fine to Extremely Fine PSE - Encapsulated. (SMQ $1,150; this being one of 3 attaining this grade as of 10/08, with only 6 graded higher).

Estimate: $800+

Minimum Bid: $400

Gorgeous Color on Fresh White Paper

31155 **#117, 1869, 12c Green, VF 80 PSE.** (Original Gum - Previously Hinged). S.S. Adriatic. Very pleasing example, bright green color, original gum, portion of prior hinge remnant. Very Fine PSE - Encapsulated. (SMQ $3,000; this being one of 4 attaining this grade as of 10/08, with 11 graded higher).

Estimate: $3,000+

Minimum Bid: $1,500

31156 **#117, 1869, 12c Green, XF-S 95J; PSE.** (Used). S.S. Adriatic. A Gorgeous example of the twelve cent Pictorial issue, fresh vibrant appearance, and well centered within generously large margins. Unobtrusive circle of wedges cancel. Extremely Fine to Superb PSE - Encapsulated.
(this being one of 5 attaining this grade as of 10/08, with only 7 graded higher).

Estimate: $1,000+

Minimum Bid: $500

31157 **#117, 1869, 12c Green, XF-S 95 PSE.** (Used). S.S. Adriatic. A stunning used example, nearly perfectly framed within generous well balanced margins, fresh and rich. Extremely Fine to Superb; 2006 PSE - Graded Certificate. (SMQ $1,250; this being one of 7 attaining this grade as of 10/08, with 12 graded higher).

Estimate: $1,250+

Minimum Bid: $625

31158 **#117, 1869, 12c Green, XF 90 PSE.** (Used). S.S. Adriatic. Very light cancel, attractive copy. Extremely Fine; 2005 PSE - Graded Certificate. (SMQ $425; this being one of 33 attaining this grade as of 10/08, with 23 graded higher).

Estimate: $500+

Minimum Bid: $250

DELICIOUS RED 'PAINT' CANCEL

31159 #117, 1869, 12c Green, VF-XF 85 PSE. (Used). S.S. Adriatic. Very strong '85', with scarce Red "paint" cancel. (SMQ value does not include an allowance for the red cancel) Very Fine to Extremely Fine; 2008 PSE - Graded Certificate. (SMQ $260; this being one of 13 attaining this grade as of 10/08, with 59 graded higher).

Estimate: $700+

Minimum Bid: $350

#118 USED JUMBO - GREAT CENTERING

31160 #118, 1869, 15c Brown & Blue, XF-S 95J PSE. (Used). Landing of Coulmbus. Lavishly large jumbo margins, very light and unobtrusive circular date stamp (c.d.s.) cancel, Beautiful brown and blue color, stunning overall. Extremely Fine to Superb; 2008 PSE - Graded Certificate. (this being one of 1 attaining this grade as of 10/08, with only 2 graded higher).

Estimate: $6,500+

Minimum Bid: $3,250

31161 #118, 1869, 15c Brown And Blue XF-S 95 PSE. (Used). Landing of Coulmbus. Brilliant Color and sharp impression. Appears to have missed a Jumbo grade by a whisker. Extremely Fine to Superb; 2005 PSE - Graded Certificate. (SMQ $4,850; this being one of 7 attaining this grade as of 10/08, with only 3 graded higher).

Estimate: $5,000+

Minimum Bid: $2,500

31162 #118, 1869, 15c Brown & Blue, XF 90 PSE. (Used). Landing of Coulmbus. Extremely light cork cancel on a beautifully centered pictorial, outstanding color with crisp impression. Extremely Fine PSE - Encapsulated. (SMQ $1,850; this being one of 8 attaining this grade as of 10/08, with 16 graded higher).

Estimate: $1,800+

Minimum Bid: $900

31163 #118 Var, 1869, 15c Brown And Blue. (Used). Landing of Coulmbus. Double Grill Variety, black segmented cork cancel. Fine to Very Fine; 2008 PSE Certificate. Also, 2000 PF Certificate. (Scott $950).

Estimate: $750+

Minimum Bid: $375

31164 **#119, 1869, 15c Brown & Blue, XF 90 PSE.** (Used). Landing of Coulmbus. Handsome used example with neat black cork cancel, very pretty example. Extremely Fine; 2008 PSE - Graded Certificate.
(SMQ $680; this being one of 15 attaining this grade as of 10/08, with only 6 graded higher).

Estimate: $550+

Minimum Bid: $275

31165 **#119, 1869, 15c Brown & Blue, XF 90 PSE.** (Used). Landing of Coulmbus. Deep and rich color, unobtrusive cancel. Extremely Fine PSE - Encapsulated. (SMQ $680; this being one of 15 attaining this grade as of 10/08, with only 6 graded higher).

Estimate: $650+

Minimum Bid: $325

31166 **#119, 1869, 15c Brown And Blue, VF-XF 85 PSE.** (Used). Landing of Coulmbus. Very Fine to Extremely Fine; 2006 PSE - Graded Certificate. Also, 2006 PF Certificate Graded VF-XF 85. (SMQ $430; this being one of 12 attaining this grade as of 10/08, with 21 graded higher) .

Estimate: $400+

Minimum Bid: $200

31167 **#120, 1869, 24c Green And Violet, VF 80 PSE.** (Original Gum - Previously Hinged). The Declaration of Independence. Quite rare, with only 6 PSE graded total original gum copies. Handsome example, bright and fresh, small hinge remnant, light pencil and neat owners mark on back. Very Fine PSE - Encapsulated.
(SMQ $11,000; this being one of 1 attaining this grade as of 10/08, with only 2 graded higher).

Estimate: $10,000+

Minimum Bid: $5,000

31168 **#120, 1869, 24c Green & Violet, XF 90 PSE.** (Used). Declaration of Independence. Extremely fine used example with attractive black cork cancel, bright color and wide margins. Extremely Fine; 2005 PSE - Graded Certificate, 2003 PSE Certificate, 1982 PF Certificate. (SMQ $1,850; this being one of 12 attaining this grade as of 10/08, with only 9 graded higher).

Estimate: $1,250+

Minimum Bid: $625

31169 **#120, 1869, 24c Green & Violet, XF 90 PSE.** (Used). Declaration of Independence. A phenomenal used example of the 24c 1869 Pictorial issue, perfectly centered with full perforations all around, gloriously bright in color and detail, and sporting a strong grill. Extremely Fine and typically difficult to find in this high quality Extremely Fine; 2008 PSE - Graded Certificate. (SMQ $1,850; this being one of 12 attaining this grade as of 10/08, with only 9 graded higher).

Estimate: $1,600+

Minimum Bid: $800

31170 **#120, 1869, 24c Green And Violet, VF 80 PSE.** (Used). Declaration of Independence. Circle of Wedges cancel. Very Fine; 2008 PSE - Graded Certificate. (SMQ $760; this being one of 8 attaining this grade as of 10/08, with 32 graded higher).

Estimate: $800+

Minimum Bid: $400

RARE INVERTED CENTER

31171 **#120b, 1869, 24c Green & Violet, Center Inverted, FR-G 20 PSE.** (Used). Declaration of Independence. A used example of this highly sought after and rare invert of the 24c 1869 Pictorial issue. The engraving of the entire stamp shifted to the left, including the inverted vignette, most known examples having faults of one kind or another. This example has a 1mm tear at the right not affecting the design, even with the grade of Fair to Good this is a rare stamp missing from most collections. PSE - Encapsulated. (this being the sole example attaining this grade as of 10/08, with only 2 graded higher).

Estimate: $15,000+

Minimum Bid: $7,500

31172 **#121, 1869, 30c Ultramarine & Carmine, VF-XF 85 PSE.** (No Gum). Eagle, Shield and Flags. A gorgeous unused single, bright and fresh, well centered for this, clear grill shifted just down from center, Very Fine to Extremely Fine and choice; PSE - Encapsulated. (SMQ $3,350; this being the only example attaining this grade as of 10/08, with only 3 graded higher).

Estimate: $2,500+

Minimum Bid: $1,250

INVERTED CENTER

31173 **#121b, 1869, 30c Ultramarine & Carmine, Flags Inverted, VG 50 PSE.** (Used). Eagle, Shield and Flags. A handsome example of this very rare Pictorial Issue invert, well centered, with a distinct inversion of the flags, with a circle of "V"'s cancel, owner's marks on the reverse, and a repair at the lower right visible from the face only under very close examination, more obvious from the reverse. Very Good example of this notably rare invert, with an overall very fine to extremely fine appearance; PSE - Encapsulated. (SMQ $66,000; this being the sole example attaining this grade as of 10/08, with only 1 graded higher).

Estimate: $60,000+

Minimum Bid: $30,000

31174 **#122, 1869, 90c Carmine And Black.** (Partial Original Gum). Abraham Lincoln. Fresh mint example, strong carmine color with complimenting black vignette. Margin is close on the right but with ample white showing between the perforations and the design, other margins are very good to huge, overall a wonderful example with partial original gum, tiny perf repair at lower right. Fine; 2008 PSE Certificate. (Scott $13,000).

Estimate: $7,500+

Minimum Bid: $3,750

31175 **#122, 1869, 90c Carmine And Black.** (Disturbed Original Gum). Abraham Lincoln. Outstanding example, fresh mint color and sharp impression with large to very large margins, gum disturbance is largely natural offset and some small amount of missing gum. Very Fine to Extremely Fine; 2008 PF Certificate,1990 PF Certificate. (Scott $13,000).

Estimate: $11,500+

Minimum Bid: $5,750

31176 **#122, 1869, 90c Carmine And Black, VF 80J PSE.** (No Gum). Abraham Lincoln. Rich colors and strong, detailed engraving. Very Fine PSE - Encapsulated. (this being one of 1 attaining this grade as of 10/08, with only 4 graded higher).

Estimate: $5,000+

Minimum Bid: $2,500

31177 **#122, 1869, 90c Carmine & Black, XF 90 PSE.** (Used). Abraham Lincoln. Light crease. (the 'light crease' is *extremely* hard to detect). Extremely Fine PSE - Encapsulated. (SMQ $4,850; this being one of 13 attaining this grade as of 10/08, with 11 graded higher).

Estimate: $3,000+

Minimum Bid: $1,500

31178 **#122, 1869, 90c Carmine & Black, XF 90 PSE.** (Used). Abraham Lincoln. A gorgeous used single, marvelously centered, stunningly bright and vibrant with an over-all proof-like quality, black (quartered) cork cancel, Extremely Fine and choice for the most refined collections; 2008 PSE - Graded Certificate. (SMQ $4,850; this being one of 13 attaining this grade as of 10/08, with 11 graded higher).

Estimate: $4,000+

Minimum Bid: $2,000

31179 **#122, 1869, 90c Carmine And Black, VF-XF 85 PSE.** (Used). Abraham Lincoln. Strong color and impression. Mild cancel. Very Fine to Extremely Fine PSE - Encapsulated. (SMQ $3,400; this being one of 7 attaining this grade as of 10/08, with 24 graded higher).

Estimate: $3,000+

Minimum Bid: $1,500

31180 **#122, 1869, 90c Carmine & Black, VF-XF 85 PF.** (Used). Abraham Lincoln. Bold Color and very neat fancy cancel. Very Fine to Extremely Fine; 2006 PF Graded Certificate.

Estimate: $4,000+

Minimum Bid: $2,000

31181 **#122, 1869, 90c Carmine & Black.** (Used). Abraham Lincoln. Beautifully centered, bright colors on white paper, light black cancel. Very Fine to Extremely Fine; 2008 PSE Certificate. (Scott $2,500).

Estimate: $1,800+

Minimum Bid: $900

1875-81 RE-ISSUES OF 1869 PICTORIALS

31182 **#124, 1875 Re-Issue, 2c Brown.** (Original Gum - Previously Hinged). Post Horse and Rider. An attractive mint example of this 1869 Pictorial re-issue, bright and vibrant with finely detailed impression on bright white paper, original gum, tiny hinge remnant with slightly toned gum. Only 4,755 issued Very Fine; 2004 PSE Certificate. (Scott $800).

Estimate: $750+

Minimum Bid: $375

31183 **#125, 1875 Re-Issue, 3c Blue, XF 90 PSE.** (Original Gum - Previously Hinged). Locomotive. Finest mint example for the perfectionist, bright blue color with large well balanced margins, very fresh overall appearance, small hinge remnant and pencil notation on back. Extremely Fine PSE - Encapsulated. (SMQ $12,900; this being one of 2 attaining this grade as of 10/08, with none graded higher).

Estimate: $12,500+

Minimum Bid: $6,250

31184 **#125, 1875 Re-Issue, 3c Blue.** (No Gum). Locomotive. Pretty unused example with light soiling at the upper left, a short perforation at the top, a thin at the top center and a light red staining on the back, still a desirable example of this rare issue. Very Fine to Extremely Fine; 2008 PSE Certificate. (Scott $3,250).

Estimate: $1,600+

Minimum Bid: $800

Only 1,947 Issued in 1875

31185 **#127, 1875 Re-Issue, 10c Yellow, XF-S 95 PSE.** (No Gum). Shield and Eagle. Wonderfully well-centered. Brilliant color on fresh white paper. Beautiful Re-Issue. Extremely Fine to Superb; 2008 PSE - Graded Certificate. (SMQ $2,350; this being one of 2 attaining this grade as of 10/08, with none graded higher).

Estimate: $2,750+

Minimum Bid: $1,375

Only 1,947 Issued in 1875

31186 **#127, 1875 Re-Issue, 10c Yellow.** (No Gum). Shield and Eagle. A sensational unused example of this difficult re-issue of the 10c 1869 Pictorial issue, gloriously bright and vibrant, and precisely centered. Very Fine to Extremely Fine and undercatalogued, this being one of only 1,947 issued; 2004 APS Certificate. (Scott $1,150).

Estimate: $1,500+

Minimum Bid: $750

31187 **#128, 1875 Re-Issue, 12c Green.** (Original Gum - Previously Hinged). S.S. Adriatic. Luscious green color, nicely etched impression, crisp clean overall look, lightly hinged with a couple of short perforations. No remnant. Fine; 2008 PSE Certificate.
(Scott $3,000).

Estimate: $1,400+

Minimum Bid: $700

31188 **#129, 1875 Re-Issue, 15c Brown & Blue, XF 90 PSE.** (Original Gum - Hinged). Landing of Coulmbus. A spectacular mint example of this 15c Pictorial type III (Re-Issue), splendidly centered within large balanced margins, vivid and bright with a proof-like impression. Some small hinge remnants and pencil notations on the back. Extremely Fine; *Only 1,981 issued.* PSE - Encapsulated. (SMQ $3,800; this being one of 4 attaining this grade as of 10/08, with only 4 graded higher).

Estimate: $3,500+

Minimum Bid: $1,750

31189 **#129, 1875 Re-Issue, 15c Brown And Blue.** (Original Gum - Previously Hinged). Landing of Coulmbus. Post office fresh example, blindingly bright color, extraordinary impression, proof-like beauty. Lightly hinged with no remnant. Very Fine to Extremely Fine; 2008 PSE Certificate.
(Scott $1,900).

Estimate: $1,800+

Minimum Bid: $900

31190 **#129, 1875 Re-Issue, 15c Brown And Blue, XF 90 PSE.** (Used). Declaration of Independence. Outstanding copy of this scarce Re-Issue. Around 70 copies exist in total. Extremely Fine; 2005 PSE - Graded Certificate.
(SMQ $2,750; this being one of 4 attaining this grade as of 10/08, with *none* graded higher).

Estimate: $3,000+

Minimum Bid: $1,500

31191 **#130, 1875 Re-Issue, 24c Green & Violet, VF-XF 85 PSE.** (Original Gum - Previously Hinged). Declaration of Independence. A beautiful mint single, well centered, bright and vibrant with a proof-like appearance. Somewhat obvious previous hinging. Very Fine to Extremely Fine and choice; *one of only 2,091 issued*; PSE - Encapsulated. (SMQ $3,900; this being one of 4 attaining this grade as of 10/08, with 10 graded higher).

Estimate: $3,500+

Minimum Bid: $1,750

31192 **#130, 1875 Re-Issue, 24c Green & Violet, VF-XF 85 PSE.** (Original Gum - Hinged). Declaration of Independence. Shorter perfs noted, bright color and strong impression, full original gum, obvious prior hinging with some remnant present. Very Fine to Extremely Fine PSE - Encapsulated. (SMQ $3,900; this being one of 4 attaining this grade as of 10/08, with 10 graded higher).

Estimate: $2,000+

Minimum Bid: $1,000

31195 **#130, 1875 Re-Issue, 24c Green & Violet, F 70 PSE.** (Used). Rare used. Cancel a tad heavy, but vignette still visible. Fine PSE - Encapsulated.
(SMQ $830; this being one of 1 attaining this grade as of 10/08, with only 6 graded higher).

Estimate: $600+

Minimum Bid: $300

31193 **#130, 1875 Re-Issue, 24c Green & Violet, VF-XF 85 PSE.** (Original Gum - Previously Hinged). Declaration of Independence. A sensational mint example of this highly sought after issue sporting an overall glowing presence with such sharp detail as to appear virtually three dimensional. Light traces of hinge markings at the top. 2008 PSE - Graded Certificate and 2004 PF Certificate. Very Fine to Extremely Fine. (SMQ $3,900; this being one of 4 attaining this grade as of 10/08, with 10 graded higher)

Estimate: $3,500+

Minimum Bid: $1,750

31196 **#131, 1875 Re-Issue, 30c Ultramarine & Carmine, XF 90 PSE.** (No Gum). Eagle, Shield and Flags. Absolutely stunning example, large fairly balanced margins, superb color on white paper, clean back, no gum. Gorgeous. Extremely Fine; 2007 PSE - Graded Certificate. (SMQ $2,100; this being one of 3 attaining this grade as of 10/08, with only 1 graded higher).

Estimate: $1,900+

Minimum Bid: $950

31194 **#130, 1875 Re-Issue, 24c Green & Violet, F-VF 75 PSE.** (Partial Original Gum). Declaration of Independence. Handsome example of this scarce re-issue, pretty mint example, part original gum. Fine to Very Fine; 2007 PSE - Graded Certificate.
(this being one of 2 attaining this grade as of 10/08, with 16 graded higher).

Estimate: $700+

Minimum Bid: $350

31197 **#132, 1875 Re-Issue, 90c Carmine & Black, XF 90 PSE.** (Original Gum). Abraham Lincoln. A charming example of this Pictorial high value Re-Issue, intensely bright and fresh color, proof-like impression, original gum that has been largely disturbed by previous hinging, Extremely Fine and select; *one of only 1,356 issued.* PSE - Encapsulated. (SMQ $9,450; this being one of 8 attaining this grade as of 10/08, with 12 graded higher).

Estimate: $8,500+

Minimum Bid: $4,250

31198 **#132, 1875 Re-Issue, 90c Carmine And Black.** (Original Gum - Previously Hinged). Incredible example, the color and impression are so intense that it looks like a proof, fabulous stamp. Lightly hinged with no remnant. Very Fine; 2008 PSE Certificate. (Scott $4,750).

Estimate: $4,000+

Minimum Bid: $2,000

1870-71 NATIONAL BANK NOTE CO. ISSUES - GRILLED

HIGHEST GRADED NO GUM COPY

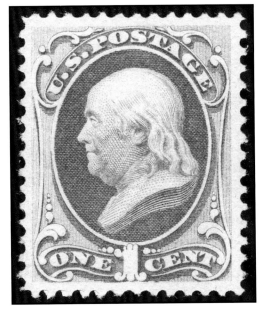

31199 **#134, 1870, 1c Ultramarine XF 90 PSE.** (No Gum). An awesome unused example of this grilled Bank Note issue, perfectly centered with full perforations all around, with a luscious almost pastel coloring and vivid impression on bright white paper, an Extremely Fine gem destined for the finest collection; 2007 PSE - Graded Certificate and 1983 PF Certificate.
(SMQ $1,700; this being the highest graded as of 10/08).

Estimate: $2,500+

Minimum Bid: $1,250

31200 **#135, 1870, 2c Red Brown, XF 90 PSE.** (Used). "I" Grill, very light cancel. Extremely Fine; 2006 PSE - Graded Certificate. (SMQ $210; this being one of 7 attaining this grade as of 10/08, with 13 graded higher).
Estimate: $350+
Minimum Bid: $175

31202 **#141, 1870, 15c Orange, VF 80 PSE.** (Used). Cork cancel. Prior owner marks in very light pencil on back Very Fine PSE - Encapsulated. (SMQ $1,250; this being one of 1 attaining this grade as of 10/08, with only 6 graded higher).
Estimate: $800+
Minimum Bid: $400

31203 **#143, 1870, 30c Black, VG-F 60 PSE.** (Used). Light cancel, shorter perfs at right. Very Good to Fine PSE - Encapsulated. (this being one of 1 attaining this grade as of 10/08, with only 3 graded higher).
Estimate: $1,500+
Minimum Bid: $750

31201 **#138, 1870, 7c Vermilion, XF-S 95 PSE.** (Used). Unlike any we've seen before, very bright and fresh example, an orange color that looks like it was printed yesterday, sharp impression, black circular date stamp (c.d.s.) coupled with a rare premium orange-red cancel. Very fresh back with extremely light pencil mark outlining the grill. Extremely Fine to Superb PSE - Encapsulated. (SMQ $3,550; this being one of 2 attaining this grade as of 10/08, with only 2 graded higher).
Estimate: $4,000+
Minimum Bid: $2,000

31204 **#144, 1870, 90c Carmine, VF 80 PSE.** (Used). Attractive used example, very nice black cork cancel, scarce in used, Very Fine; 2006 PSE - Graded Certificate. (SMQ $2,500; this being one of 2 attaining this grade as of 10/08, with only 2 graded higher).
Estimate: $2,000+
Minimum Bid: $1,000

1870-71 NATIONAL BANK NOTE CO. ISSUES - W/O GRILL

31205 **#149, 1871, 7c Vermilion, F-VF 75 PSE.** (Original Gum - Previously Hinged). Bright and Fresh color, strong impression. Small hinge remnant only. Fine to Very Fine PSE - Encapsulated. (this being one of 1 attaining this grade as of 10/08, with only 3 graded higher).
Estimate: $950+
Minimum Bid: $475

31206 **#153, 1870, 24c Purple, XF 90 PSE.** (Original Gum - Previously Hinged). Soft pastel purple, large margins for this series, very well-centered. Light hinge remnant, wonderful stamp. Extremely Fine PSE - Encapsulated. (SMQ $6,000; this being one of 4 attaining this grade as of 10/08, with only 4 graded higher).
Estimate: $6,500+
Minimum Bid: $3,250

31207 **#153, 1870, 24c Purple, XF 90 PSE.** (Original Gum - Previously Hinged). Rich color and very sharp impression on crisp white paper. Wonderfully fresh gum with only a slight hinge mark. One of the brightest mint 153's in existence. Extremely Fine; 2005 PSE - Graded Certificate. (SMQ $6,000; this being one of 4 attaining this grade as of 10/08, with only 4 graded higher).
Estimate: $6,500+
Minimum Bid: $3,250

31208 **#153, 1870, 24c Purple, VF 80 PSE.** (Original Gum - Hinged). Very pretty example with terrific purple color. Very Fine; 2008 PSE - Graded Certificate. (SMQ $2,400; this being one of 1 attaining this grade as of 10/08, with only 8 graded higher).

Estimate: $2,100+

Minimum Bid: $1,050

31209 **#153, 1870, 24c Purple.** (Disturbed Original Gum). Handsome example with darkly toned gum. Fine; 2006 PF Certificate.
(Scott $2,300)

Estimate: $900+

Minimum Bid: $450

31210 **#153, 1870, 24c Purple, XF-S 95 PSE.** (Used). Visually striking example with complimenting red New York foreign mail cancel, lovely pastel color, large even margins. Extremely Fine to Superb PSE - Encapsulated. (SMQ $1,400; this being one of 12 attaining this grade as of 10/08, with only 1 graded higher).

Estimate: $1,500+

Minimum Bid: $750

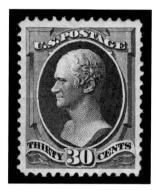

31211 **#154, 1870, 30c Black, XF 90; PSE.** (Original Gum - Previously Hinged). A sensational example of a rare stamp. A mint example of the thirty cent 1870 National Bank Note Co. issue without grill, precisely centered, with a warm yet rich color and finely etched detail on fresh paper. Full original gum, only a prior hinge mark, no remnant. Extremely Fine PSE - Encapsulated.
(SMQ $18,500; this being one of 2 attaining this grade as of 10/08, with only 1 graded higher).

Estimate: $20,000+

Minimum Bid: $10,000

31212 **#154, 1870, 30c Black, XF 90 PSE.** (No Gum). Intense color and impression, fresh white paper. Full, even perforations. Highest graded NG example, according to PSE POP. Extremely Fine PSE - Encapsulated.
(SMQ $4,050; this being one of 1 attaining this grade as of 10/08, with *none* graded higher).

Estimate: $3,250+

Minimum Bid: $1,625

31213 **#154, 1870, 30c Black, XF-S 95 PSE.** (Used). Mild cork cancel. Choice quality. Extremely Fine to Superb PSE - Encapsulated
(SMQ $2,100; this being one of 8 attaining this grade as of 10/08, with only 4 graded higher).

Estimate: $2,100+

Minimum Bid: $1,050

31214 **#155, 1870, 90c Carmine, XF 90 PSE.** (Used). Exceptional example, beautiful color framed inside well balance margins, very light "Circle of V's " cancel. Extremely Fine PSE - Encapsulated. (SMQ $900; this being one of 13 attaining this grade as of 10/08, with only 4 graded higher).

Estimate: $800+

Minimum Bid: $400

1873 CONTINENTAL BANK NOTE CO. ISSUES

31215 **#157, 1873, 2c Brown, XF-S 95 PSE.** (Original Gum - Hinged). A magnificent mint single, remarkably well centered, deep rich color and finely etched detail on crisp paper, original gum showing evidence of previous hinging over most of the top half, Extremely Fine to Superb; PSE - Encapsulated.
(SMQ $2,200; this being one of 2 attaining this grade as of 10/08, with only 1 graded higher).

Estimate: $2,000+

Minimum Bid: $1,000

31216 **#158, 1873, 3c Green, VF-XF 85 PSE.** (Original Gum - Never Hinged). A magnificently stunning mint example of this 3c Bank Note issue, precisely centered within substantial margins, gorgeously rich and vibrant giving it an almost proof-like quality, immaculate original gum. Very Fine to Extremely Fine; 2007 PSE - Graded Certificate. (SMQ unvalued as Never Hinged ; this being one of 2 attaining this grade as of 10/08, with only 4 graded higher).

Estimate: $1,500+

Minimum Bid: $750

31217 **#159b, 1873, 6c Carmine.** (Original Gum - Previously Hinged). Handsome example of this classic with grill, lovely color and impression, small hinge remnant and pencil notation on the back. Very Good to Fine; 2007 PF Certificate.
(Scott $1,800).

Estimate: $1,400+

Minimum Bid: $700

31218 **#160, 1873, 7c Vermilion, XF 90 PSE.** (No Gum). Rich color and strongly detailed impression. Full, even perforations, white paper. Extremely Fine PSE - Encapsulated. (SMQ $830; this being one of 1 attaining this grade as of 10/08, with none graded higher).

Estimate: $700+

Minimum Bid: $350

31219 **#161, 1873, 10c Brown, XF-S 95 PSE.** (Original Gum - Previously Hinged). Bold and rich color, detailed impression. Owners handstamp in lower right corner. Extremely Fine to Superb PSE - Encapsulated. (SMQ $6,750; this being one of 4 attaining this grade as of 10/08, with only 3 graded higher).

Estimate: $6,500+

Minimum Bid: $3,250

31220 **#165, 1873, 30c Greenish Black.** (Original Gum - Previously Hinged). An outstanding mint example of this slightly less common shade, concisely centered and sporting remarkably warm color and finely etched impression, original gum, previously hinged showing only minimal traces of prior hinging. Very Fine; 2007 PF Certificate. (Scott $3,500).

Estimate: $3,500+
Minimum Bid: $1,750

31222 **#174, 1875 Special Print, 15c Bright Orange, VG 50 PSE.** (No Gum As Issued). Typical for this rare stamp (38 known), is the scissor-cut perfs, but this copy, while also scissor-cut, was cut skillfully, as the perfs appear mostly intact. Very Good PSE - Graded Certificate. (SMQ $14,700; this being one of 1 attaining this grade as of 10/08, with only 1 graded higher).

Estimate: $17,500+
Minimum Bid: $8,750

1875 SPECIAL PRINTING OF 1873 CBN ISSUE

SPECIAL PRINTING - 70 COPIES KNOWN

1879 AMERICAN BANK NOTE CO. ISSUES

31223 **#183, 1879, 2c Vermilion XF 90 PSE.** (Original Gum - Never Hinged). Marvelously fresh example of this 129 year old stamp, impression, color, and balance are all first rate. Extremely Fine; 2007 PSE - Graded Certificate. (SMQ $1,250; this being one of 7 attaining this grade as of 10/08, with only 5 graded higher).

Estimate: $1,100+
Minimum Bid: $550

31221 **#173, 1875 Special Print, 12c Dark Violet.** (No Gum). Strong color and impression. 70 copies known. Fine; 2008 PF Certificate. (Scott $8,000).

Estimate: $5,500+
Minimum Bid: $2,750

31224 **#183, 1879, 2c Vermilion, XF 90 PSE.** (Original Gum - Never Hinged). An impressive mint single, bright pastel-like color and detailed impression on fresh clean paper, precisely centered. Choice. Extremely Fine; 2008 PSE - Graded Certificate. (SMQ $1,250; this being one of 7 attaining this grade as of 10/08, with only 5 graded higher).

Estimate: $1,100+

Minimum Bid: $550

31225 #183, 1879, 2c Vermillion, VF 80 PSE. (Original Gum - Never Hinged). Deep shade and strong color, with detailed impression, super fresh front and back. Very Fine; 2008 PSE - Graded Certificate. (SMQ $435; this being one of 4 attaining this grade as of 10/08, with 13 graded higher).

Estimate: $350+

Minimum Bid: $175

31226 #182, 1879, 1c Dark Ultramarine, XF 90 PF. (Original Gum - Never Hinged). Extremely scarce never hinged, very well centered example with large margins, some gum toning not mentioned on the certificate. Extremely Fine; 2007 PF Graded Certificate, 2002 PF Certificate. (Scott $1,100 for Very Fine).

Estimate: $2,000+

Minimum Bid: $1,000

31227 #184, 1879, 3c Green, XF-S 95 PSE. (Original Gum - Previously Hinged). Rich detailed impression. Very attractive stamp, fresh white paper, nice even perforations. Prior hinge mark, no remnant. Extremely Fine to Superb PSE - Encapsulated. (SMQ $480; this being one of 2 attaining this grade as of 10/08, with *none* graded higher).

Estimate: $500+

Minimum Bid: $250

ENORMOUS MARGINS

31228 #184, 1879, 3c Green, XF-S 95J PSE. (Used). Face-free cancel, Huge margins. Extremely Fine to Superb; 2007 PSE - Graded Certificate. (this being one of 14 attaining this grade as of 10/08, with only 2 graded higher).

Estimate: $700+

Minimum Bid: $350

31229 #185, 1879, 5c Blue, XF-S 95 PSE. (Original Gum - Previously Hinged). Eye Pleasing example. Detailed impression. Pencil mark on gum, and portion of hinge remnant. Extremely Fine to Superb PSE - Encapsulated. (SMQ $2,050; this being one of 3 attaining this grade as of 10/08, with only 1 graded higher).

Estimate: $2,000+

Minimum Bid: $1,000

31230 #189, 1879, 15c Red Orange, SUP 98 PSE. (Original Gum - Never Hinged). A tremendous showpiece for the most discriminating collector, extremely rare in high grade never hinged, visually perfect margins on all sides, fresh mint red orange color, spectacular example. Superb PSE - Encapsulated. (SMQ $15,800; this being one of 3 attaining this grade as of 10/08, with none graded higher).

Estimate: $15,000+

Minimum Bid: $7,500

TREMENDOUS QUALITY

31231 **#189, 1879, 15c Red Orange, XF-S 95 PSE.** (Original Gum - Never Hinged). Hard to believe this stamp was minted in 1879, "fresh" does not do it justice. The red orange color is difficult to preserve over time and this looks Post Office Fresh. Extremely Fine to Superb PSE - Encapsulated. (SMQ $7,350; this being one of 5 attaining this grade as of 10/08, with only 3 graded higher).

Estimate: $8,000+

Minimum Bid: $4,000

31232 **#189, 1879, 15c Red Orange, XF 90J PSE.** (Original Gum - Hinged). Huge even margins for this tight margined issue, scarce with Jumbo margins. Portion of prior remnant. Extremely Fine; 2004 PSE - Graded Certificate. (this being one of 2 attaining this grade as of 10/08, with only 5 graded higher).

Estimate: $800+

Minimum Bid: $400

31233 **#189, 1879, 15c Red Orange, XF 90 PSE.** (Original Gum - Never Hinged). Sharp detailed, proof-like impression on fresh white paper Extremely Fine PSE - Encapsulated. (SMQ $2,850; this being one of 8 attaining this grade as of 10/08, with only 9 graded higher).

Estimate: $2,200+

Minimum Bid: $1,100

31234 **#189, 1879, 15c Red Orange, VF-XF 85 PSE.** (Original Gum - Never Hinged). Nicely centered example with extra wide margins, attractive stamp. Very Fine to Extremely Fine; 2007 PSE - Graded Certificate.
(SMQ $1,800; this being one of 3 attaining this grade as of 10/08, with 18 graded higher).

Estimate: $1,600+

Minimum Bid: $800

31235 **#190, 1879, 30c Full Black, VF 80 PSE.** (Original Gum - Previously Hinged). Fantastic color with razor sharp impression, very fresh and barely hinged Very Fine PSE - Encapsulated. (SMQ $1,100; this being one of 5 attaining this grade as of 10/08, with 14 graded higher).

Estimate: $900+

Minimum Bid: $450

31236 **#191, 1879, 90c Carmine, VF-XF 85J PSE.** (No Gum). An outstanding unused example of this high value Bank Note issue, well centered within monstrous picture frame margins, with an overall soft pastel coloring with sharp detail on unblemished white paper, and remarkably sound for this typically faulty issue. a Very Fine to Extremely Fine; 2008 PSE - Graded Certificate.
(SMQ as non-Jumbo $950; this being one of attaining this grade as of 10/08, with *none* graded higher).

Estimate: $1,500+

Minimum Bid: $750

1880 SPECIAL PRINTING OF 1879 ABN ISSUES

RARITY - ONLY 47 KNOWN TO EXIST

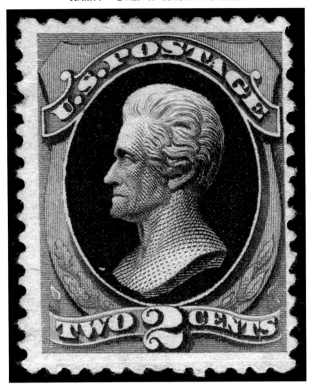

31237 **#193, 1880 Special Print, 2c Black Brown.** (No Gum).
Rich color. 47 known, many are faulty, this copy sound.
Fine; 2008 PF Certificate. Also, 1974 PF Certificate. (Scott
$27,500).

Estimate: $18,000+

Minimum Bid: $9,000

RARE SPECIAL PRINTING - 80 COPIES EXIST

31238 **#196, 1880 Special Print, 7c Scarlet Vermilion, VF-XF
85 PSE.** (No Gum As Issued). Tantalizing sharp detailed
impression, rich color. Loads of eye-appeal here, one
of the best centered copies in existence. Approximately
80 total copies exist. Very Fine to Extremely Fine PSE -
Encapsulated. (SMQ $16,900; this being one of 2 attaining
this grade as of 10/08, with only 1 graded higher).

Estimate: $17,500+

Minimum Bid: $8,750

31239 **#196, 1880 Special Print, 7c Scar Vermilion.** (No Gum
As Issued). Bold Color. Around 80 copies exist only. Fine;
2008 PF Certificate. (Scott $9,000).

Estimate: $8,000+

Minimum Bid: $4,000

31240 **#196, 1880 Special Print, 7c Scarlet Vermilion.** (No Gum).
Bright color, very sharp and detailed impression. Less than
80 known. Fine to Very Fine; 2006 PF Certificate. (Scott
$9,000).

Estimate: $7,500+

Minimum Bid: $3,750

ONLY 60 KNOWN TO EXIST
MOST WITH FAULTS - THIS COPY SOUND

31241 **#198, 1880 Special Print, 12c Black Purple.** (No Gum).
Intense Shade and Impression. Fine; 2008 PF Certificate.
(Scott $15,000).

Estimate: $9,500+

Minimum Bid: $4,750

1881-82 DESIGNS OF 1873 RE-ENGRAVED

31242 #200, 1880 Special Print, 24c Dark Violet. (No Gum). Without gum as issued, rich color and sharp impression. PF Cert: "tiny repaired tear" in a perf hole at right. There is a small hairline printing void in portrait oval, not mentioned on the certificate. 66 copies reported to exist. Fine to Very Fine; 2008 PF Certificate.(Scott $14,000).

Estimate: $10,000+

Minimum Bid: $5,000

31244 #207, 1881, 3c Blue Green, XF 90 PSE. (Original Gum - Never Hinged). Undervalued in never hinged condition, bright, fresh and very well centered. Extremely Fine; 2005 PSE - Graded Certificate. (SMQ $880; this being one of 4 attaining this grade as of 10/08, with only 3 graded higher).

Estimate: $900+

Minimum Bid: $450

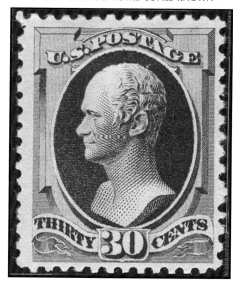

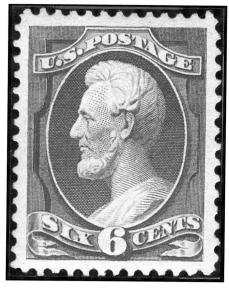

31243 #201, 1880 Special Print, 30c Greenish Black, F-VF 75 PSE. (No Gum As Issued). Razor sharp detailed impression. Intact and full perforations. Fewer than 50 examples of this rarity exist. Fine to Very Fine PSE - Encapsulated. (this being one of 3 attaining this grade as of 10/08, with only 2 graded higher).

Estimate: $35,000+

Minimum Bid: $17,500

31245 #208a, 1881, 6c Deep Brown Red, SUP 98 PSE. (Original Gum - Previously Hinged). An engraved masterpiece that commands awe and reverence, boasting flawless centering within large well balanced margins, color that is both intense and radiant at the same time, masterfully engraved giving an almost three-dimensional sculpted appearance to the bust of Lincoln, and full original gum that requires very close examination to identify any evidence of previous hinging. A Superb world class condition rarity destined for the finest collection; PSE - Encapsulated. (SMQ $3,850; this being *sole example attaining this grade* as of 10/08, with *none graded higher*).

Estimate: $5,000+

Minimum Bid: $2,500

31246 **#208a, 1881, 6c Deep Brown Red, XF-S 95 PSE.** (Original Gum - Previously Hinged). Intense and warm shade, well-defined impression on white paper. Prior hinge mark only. Extremely Fine to Superb; 2007 PSE - Graded Certificate. (SMQ $2,300; this being one of 5 attaining this grade as of 10/08, with only 1 graded higher).

Estimate: $2,500+
Minimum Bid: $1,250

31247 **#208, 1881, 6c Rose, XF-S 95 PSE.** (Original Gum - Previously Hinged). Exceptional copy. Very detailed impression and engraving. Only the very slightest evidence of a prior hinge, a tiny mark only. Extremely Fine to Superb PSE - Encapsulated. (SMQ $2,950; this being one of 5 attaining this grade as of 10/08, with none graded higher).

Estimate: $3,000+
Minimum Bid: $1,500

31248 **#209, 1881, 10c Brown, XF-S 95 PSE.** (Original Gum - Previously Hinged). Gorgeous color and detailed impression. Only trace evidence of prior hinging, no remnant at all. Extremely Fine to Superb PSE - Encapsulated.
(SMQ $750; this being one of 7 attaining this grade as of 10/08, with only 1 graded higher).

Estimate: $750+
Minimum Bid: $375

1883 AMERICAN BANK NOTE CO. ISSUES

TOP OF THE POP

31249 **#210, 1883, 2c Red Brown, SUP 98 PSE.** (Used). A true condition rarity, flawlessly centered, with full intact perforations all around, fresh and bright, with an extremely light cancel that does not detract from the appearance in any way, a Superb and matchless gem. 2008 PSE - Graded Certificate. (SMQ $450; this being the *unique example attaining this grade* as of 10/08, with *none graded higher*).

Estimate: $750+
Minimum Bid: $375

31250 **#210, 1883, 2c Red Brown, XF-S 95 PSE.** (Original Gum - Never Hinged). Dazzling color and impression, very large well balanced margins. Extremely Fine to Superb; 2008 PSE - Graded Certificate. (SMQ $1,250; this being one of 2 attaining this grade as of 10/08, with only 1 graded higher).

Estimate: $1,200+
Minimum Bid: $600

31251 **#211, 1883, 4c Blue Green, VF-XF 85 PSE.** (Original Gum - Never Hinged). Excellent example with vivid color, very pretty stamp, Very Fine to Extremely Fine; 2005 PSE - Graded Certificate, Also, 1996 PF Certificate. (SMQ $1,850; this being one of 5 attaining this grade as of 10/08, with only 6 graded higher).

Estimate: $1,700+
Minimum Bid: $850

1883-85 SPECIAL PRINTING OF 1883 ABN ISSUES

31252 #211B, 1883 Special Print, 2c Pale Red Brown, VF-XF 85 PSE. (Original Gum - Hinged). A marvelous example of this special trial printing by the new steam-powered American Bank Note Company press, finely detailed, bright and fresh, original gum, with an inconsequential small hinged remnant, and an expertising mark on the reverse. Very Fine to Extremely Fine and undercatalogued with only 1,000 having been issued; PSE - Encapsulated. (SMQ $560; this being the only example attaining this grade as of 10/08, with only 2 graded higher).

Estimate: $750+

Minimum Bid: $375

1887-88 AMERICAN BANK NOTE CO. ISSUES

31253 #213, 1887, 2c Green, XF 90 PSE. (Original Gum - Never Hinged). Nearly perfect example, Strong 90, original gum, Never Hinged, Extremely Fine; 2007 PSE - Graded Certificate. (SMQ $460; this being one of 12 attaining this grade as of 10/08, with only 6 graded higher).

Estimate: $450+

Minimum Bid: $225

31254 #214, 1887, 3c Vermilion, SUP 98J PSE. (Original Gum - Previously Hinged). Enormous margins, rich color, enticing copy. Very light hinge mark only. Superb PSE - Encapsulated. (this being one of 1 attaining this grade as of 10/08, with none graded higher).

Estimate: $1,000+

Minimum Bid: $500

31255 #215, 1888, 4c Carmine SUP 98 PSE. (Original Gum - Previously Hinged). A simply marvelous mint single, splendidly centered, bright and fresh, full original gum that shows only very light evidence of previous hinging, a Superb stamp for the collector who requires nothing but the best. PSE - Encapsulated. (SMQ $1,900; this being the *only example attaining this grade* as of 10/08, with *none graded higher*).

Estimate: $1,500+

Minimum Bid: $750

31256 #216, 1888, 5c Indigo, XF 90 PSE. (Original Gum - Never Hinged). An exceptional mint Never Hinged example of this late Bank Note issue, concisely centered with full even perforations all around, rich vibrant color and nearly proof-like impression on bright white paper, pristine full original gum. Extremely Fine. 2008 PSE - Graded Certificate. (SMQ $2,600; this being one of 3 attaining this grade as of 10/08, with only 5 graded higher).

Estimate: $4,000+

Minimum Bid: $2,000

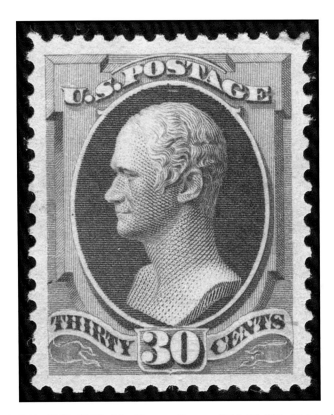

31257 #217, 1888, 30c Orange Brown, XF-S 95 PSE. (Original Gum - Never Hinged). A marvelously captivating mint single, well-centered within attractive margins stunningly rich color and finely detailed impression on bright paper, immaculate full original gum, simply said, "Fabulous", Extremely Fine to Superb and perfect for the gem collector. 2007 PSE - Graded Certificate and also with 1985 and 1998 PF Certificates. (SMQ $8,600; this being one of 4 attaining this grade as of 10/08, with only 1 graded higher).

Estimate: $10,000+

Minimum Bid: $5,000

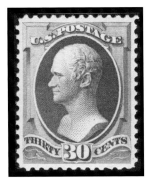

31258 #217, 1888, 30c Orange Brown, XF 90 PSE. (Original Gum - Previously Hinged). Very small hinge mark, tiny piece of prior hinge remnant only. Extremely Fine PSE - Encapsulated. (SMQ $940; this being one of 7 attaining this grade as of 10/08, with only 5 graded higher).

Estimate: $900+

Minimum Bid: $450

31259 #218, 1888, 90c Purple, XF-S 95 PSE. (Disturbed Original Gum). Gorgeous mint example, bright and fresh with great color, PSE indicates "slightly disturbed original gum", PF "previously hinged." Gum is missing at the very top of the stamp. Extremely light pencil notation on the back. Extremely Fine to Superb; 2008 PSE - Graded Certificate, 1987 PF Certificate. (SMQ $3,950; this being one of 2 attaining this grade as of 10/08, with none graded higher).

Estimate: $2,500+

Minimum Bid: $1,250

31260 #218, 1888, 90c Purple, XF 90 PSE. (Used). A striking used single, perfectly centered amidst rather large margins, with luminous pastel color and detailed impression on bright white paper, and a tad heavy black New York double oval Registry cancels. Extremely Fine; 2005 PSE - Graded Certificate. Also, 2003 and 1990 PF Certificates. (SMQ $680; this being one of 10 attaining this grade as of 10/08, with only 9 graded higher).

Estimate: $600+

Minimum Bid: $300

31261 #218, 1888, 90c Purple, XF 90 PSE. (Used). Attractive used example with a light black New York Registry cancel, excellent color. Extremely Fine; 2008 PSE - Graded Certificate. (SMQ $680; this being one of 10 attaining this grade as of 10/08, with only 9 graded higher).

Estimate: $550+

Minimum Bid: $275

1890-93 SMALL BANK NOTES

31262   #219D, 1890, 2c Lake, XF-S 95 PSE. (Original Gum - Never Hinged). Unmistakable Lake color, showpiece for the finest collection, visually perfect centering, upper end for the grade, crisp clear impression, spellbinding. Extremely Fine to Superb PSE - Encapsulated. (SMQ $1,200; this being one of 6 attaining this grade as of 10/08, with only 2 graded higher).

Estimate: $8,500+

Minimum Bid: $4,250

31263   #219D, 1890, 2c Lake, XF 90 PSE. (Original Gum - Previously Hinged). Fantastic color. Sharp impression on crisp white paper. Two small hinge marks only. Extremely Fine; 2007 PSE - Graded Certificate. (SMQ $540; this being one of 6 attaining this grade as of 10/08, with only 6 graded higher).

Estimate: $700+

Minimum Bid: $350

31264   #219D, 1890, 2c Lake. (Original Gum - Previously Hinged). Bottom margin imprint pair, fabulous lake color, barely hinged. Very Fine to Extremely Fine; 2008 PSE Certificate. (Scott as singles $500).

Estimate: $400+

Minimum Bid: $200

HUGE USED JUMBO

31265   #219D, 1890, 2c Lake, XF-S 95J PSE. (Used). Bold Lake shade, attractive light cancel with **enormous** margins. Extremely Fine to Superb Jumbo. 2004 PSE - Graded Certificate. (this being one of 2 attaining this grade as of 10/08, with only 3 graded higher).

Estimate: $400+

Minimum Bid: $200

TOUGH LITTLE USED STAMP - TOP POP

31266   #220c, 1890, 2c Carmine, SUP 98 PSE. (Used). Perfection. Choice used example, highest grade to date. Superb; 2008 PSE - Graded Certificate. (SMQ $1,550; this being one of 1 attaining this grade as of 10/08, with *none* graded higher).

Estimate: $1,500+

Minimum Bid: $750

31267   #224, 1890, 6c Brown Red, XF-S 95 PSE. (Original Gum - Never Hinged). A visually striking mint top sheet margin single that simply screams quality, sporting perfect centering, rich yet warm pastel coloring and vivid impression on clean paper, pristine original gum. Extremely Fine to Superb; 2008 PSE - Graded Certificate. (SMQ $2,900; this being one of 13 attaining this grade as of 10/08, with only 6 graded higher).

Estimate: $3,500+

Minimum Bid: $1,750

31268   #224, 1890, 6c Brown Red, XF-S 95; PSE. (Original Gum - Never Hinged). A superior mint top sheet margin single, with lovely color, nearly perfect centering, and immaculate full original gum, the top selvage having been removed since its original certification. Extremely Fine to Superb; 2005 PSE - Graded Certificate. (SMQ $2,900; this being one of 13 attaining this grade as of 10/08, with only 6 graded higher).

Estimate: $2,500+

Minimum Bid: $1,250

31269 **#227, 1890, 15c Indigo, XF-S 95 PSE.** (Original Gum - Never Hinged). A gem for the connoisseur, extremely rare in this lofty grade, true indigo color with well balance large margins, showpiece. Extremely Fine to Superb PSE - Encapsulated. (SMQ $9,500; this being one of 8 attaining this grade as of 10/08, with only 1 graded higher).

Estimate: $9,500+

Minimum Bid: $4,750

31270 **#227, 1890, 15c Indigo, VF 80J PSE.** (Original Gum - Never Hinged). Bold color on fresh white paper. Jumbo margins. Very Fine PSE - Encapsulated.

(this being one of 1 attaining this grade as of 10/08, with 21 graded higher).

Estimate: $700+

Minimum Bid: $350

31271 **#228, 1890, 30c Black, XF 90 PSE.** (Original Gum - Previously Hinged). Fabulous jet black color, hinge remnant and slightly darkened gum. Extremely Fine. 2006 PSE - Graded Certificate. (SMQ $900; this being one of 6 attaining this grade as of 10/08, with only 4 graded higher).

Estimate: $800+

Minimum Bid: $400

31272 **#228, 1890, 30c Black, VF 80J PSE.** (Original Gum - Never Hinged). A captivating mint Never hinged single, especially well centered for the issue, bright and vibrant, with immaculate original gum. Very Fine; 2008 PSE - Graded Certificate.

(this being one of 1 attaining this grade as of 10/08, with 16 graded higher).

Estimate: $1,750+

Minimum Bid: $875

31273 **#229, 1890, 90c Orange, XF 90 PSE.** (Original Gum - Never Hinged). Fiery rich shade and ultra strong impression. Gorgeous stamp. Extremely Fine PSE - Encapsulated. (SMQ $5,450; this being one of 5 attaining this grade as of 10/08, with only 4 graded higher).

Estimate: $5,000+

Minimum Bid: $2,500

31274 **#229, 1890, 90c Orange, VF-XF 85J PSE.** (Original Gum - Hinged). Hinge remnant, bold color and proof-like impression, amid large margins. Very Fine to Extremely Fine PSE - Encapsulated. (this being one of 2 attaining this grade as of 10/08, with 13 graded higher).

Estimate: $800+

Minimum Bid: $400

31275 **#229, 1890, 90c Orange, XF 90J PSE.** (Used). Double Oval Registry cancel, oversize margins for issue. Extremely Fine; 2008 PSE - Graded Certificate. (this being one of 5 attaining this grade as of 10/08, with 4 graded higher).

Estimate: $500+

Minimum Bid: $250

1893 COLUMBIAN EXPOSITION ISSUE

31276 **#230, 1893, 1c Deep Blue, XF-S 95J PSE.** (Original Gum - Never Hinged). Columbus In Sight Of Land. Massive jumbo with deep blue color, incredible impression, Extremely Fine to Superb; 2004 PSE - Graded Certificate, 1988 PF Certificate. (this being one of 10 attaining this grade as of 10/08, with 16 graded higher).

Estimate: $800+

Minimum Bid: $400

31277 **#230, 1893, 1c Deep Blue, XF-S 95; PSE.** (Original Gum - Never Hinged). Columbus in Sight of Land. Extremely Fine to Superb PSE - Encapsulated.
(SMQ $600; this being one of 58 attaining this grade as of 10/08, with 26 graded higher).

Estimate: $500+

Minimum Bid: $250

31278 **#230, 1893, 1c Deep Blue, XF-S 95 PSE.** (Original Gum - Never Hinged). Columbus in Sight of Land. Spectacular example. Intense deep blue color with large even margins all around. Fresh. Extremely Fine to Superb; 2006 PSE - Graded Certificate.
(SMQ $600; this being one of 58 attaining this grade as of 10/08, with 26 graded higher).

Estimate: $550+

Minimum Bid: $275

31279 **#230, 1893, 1c Deep Blue XF-S 95 PF.** (Original Gum - Never Hinged). Columbus in Sight of Land. A bright and vibrant mint single, precisely centered, with full perforations all around, unblemished full original gum. Extremely Fine to Superbgem that will realize multiples of its catalog value; 2007 PF Graded Certificate.
(Scott for the typical Very Fine $60.00).

Estimate: $500+

Minimum Bid: $250

31280 **#230, 1893, 1c Deep Blue, XF-S 95 PSE.** (Original Gum - Never Hinged). Columbus in Sight of Land. Amazing color and spectacular impression. Extremely Fine to Superb PSE - Encapsulated. (SMQ $600; this being one of 58 attaining this grade as of 10/08, with 26 graded higher).

Estimate: $500+

Minimum Bid: $250

31281 #230, 1893, 1c Deep Blue, XF-S 95 PSE. (Original Gum - Never Hinged). Columbus in Sight of Land. Irresistible example, large well-balanced margins, choice. Extremely Fine to Superb PSE - Encapsulated. (SMQ $600; this being one of 58 attaining this grade as of 10/08, with 26 graded higher).

Estimate: $500+

Minimum Bid: $250

31282 #230, 1893, 1c Deep Blue, XF-S 95 PSE. (Original Gum - Never Hinged). Columbus in Sight of Land. Bright deep blue color with a stunning impression. Fresh. Extremely Fine to Superb. 2005 PSE - Graded Certificate. (SMQ $600; this being one of 58 attaining this grade as of 10/08, with 26 graded higher).

Estimate: $500+

Minimum Bid: $250

31283 #231, 1893, 2c Brown Violet, SUP 98 PSE. (Original Gum - Never Hinged). Landing of Columbus. A must have for the serious Columbian collector, post office fresh, large superb margins, terrific impression and color. Superb PSE - Encapsulated. (SMQ $2,800; this being one of 8 attaining this grade as of 10/08, with only 9 graded higher).

Estimate: $2,500+

Minimum Bid: $1,250

31284 #231 Var, 1893, 2c Brown, XF-S 95 PSE. (Original Gum - Never Hinged). Landing of Columbus. Beautifully well-centered "**Broken Hat**" variety. Rare in high grade. Extremely Fine to Superb PSE - Encapsulated. (SMQ Broken Hat $2,000; PSE Population not listed or tracked for this scarce variety).

Estimate: $2,000+

Minimum Bid: $1,000

31285 #231, 1893, 2c Brown Violet, XF-S 95 PSE. (Original Gum - Never Hinged). Landing of Columbus. A magnificent mint example, precisely centered amidst margins bordering on huge, gorgeously rich and vibrant. Extremely Fine to Superb; 2008 PSE - Graded Certificate. (SMQ $640; this being one of 38 attaining this grade as of 10/08, with 30 graded higher).

Estimate: $700+

Minimum Bid: $350

31286 **#231 Var, 1893, 2c Brown Violet, VF-XF 85 PSE.** (Original Gum - Never Hinged). Landing of Columbus. **"Broken Hat"** variety. Very Fine to Extremely Fine; 2006 PSE - Graded Certificate. (SMQ Broken Hat $270; PSE Population not listed or tracked for this scarce variety).

Estimate: $350+

Minimum Bid: $175

31287 **#232, 1893, 3c Green, XF-S 95 PSE.** (Original Gum - Never Hinged). Flag Ship of Columbus. Very desirable example, huge margins with nice centering, deep color. Post Office Fresh. Extremely Fine to Superb PSE - Encapsulated. (SMQ $1,350; this being one of 53 attaining this grade as of 10/08, with 31 graded higher).

Estimate: $1,250+

Minimum Bid: $625

31288 **#232, 1893, 3c Green, XF-S 95 PSE.** (Original Gum - Never Hinged). Flag Ship of Columbus. Huge bottom plate# 56 single, breathe away from a Jumbo. Extremely Fine to Superb. 2004 PSE - Graded Certificate. (SMQ $1,350; this being one of 53 attaining this grade as of 10/08, with 31 graded higher).

Estimate: $1,200+

Minimum Bid: $600

31289 **#232, 1893, 3c Green XF-S 95 PSE.** (Original Gum - Never Hinged). Flag Ship Of Columbus. Fabulous centering with wide margins, very attractive. Extremely Fine to Superb PSE - Graded Certificate. (SMQ $1,350; this being one of 53 attaining this grade as of 10/08, with 31 graded higher).

Estimate: $1,100+

Minimum Bid: $550

31290 **#232, 1893, 3c Green, XF-S 95 PSE.** (Original Gum - Never Hinged). Flag Ship of Columbus. Exceptional example, sharply detailed impression. Fresh. Extremely Fine to Superb; 2004 PSE - Graded Certificate. (SMQ $1,350; this being one of 53 attaining this grade as of 10/08, with 31 graded higher).

Estimate: $1,200+

Minimum Bid: $600

31291 **#232, 1893, 3c Green, XF-S 95 PSE.** (Original Gum - Never Hinged). Flag Ship Of Columbus, wonderful example, attractive eye-appeal. Extremely Fine to Superb; 2007 PSE - Graded Certificate. (SMQ $1,350; this being one of 53 attaining this grade as of 10/08, with 31 graded higher).

Estimate: $1,200+

Minimum Bid: $600

31292 #233, 1893, 4c Ultramarine, XF-S 95 PSE. (Original Gum - Never Hinged). Fleet of Columbus. Wonderfully bright and fresh, strong detailed impression on fresh white paper. Extremely Fine to Superb PSE - Encapsulated. (SMQ $2,200; this being one of 35 attaining this grade as of 10/08, with 28 graded higher).

Estimate: $2,000+

Minimum Bid: $1,000

31293 #233, 1893, 4c Ultramarine, XF-S 95J PSE. (Original Gum - Never Hinged). Fleet Of Columbus. Enormous margins. Soft pastel ultramarine color with a striking impression. Extremely Fine to Superb; 2004 PSE - Graded Certificate. (this being one of 12 attaining this grade as of 10/08, with 16 graded higher).

Estimate: $3,000+

Minimum Bid: $1,500

31294 #233, 1893, 4c Ultramarine, XF-S 95 PSE. (Original Gum - Never Hinged). Fleet of Columbus. Terrific example bright fresh color, wide even margins, crisp impression, stamp has great eye-appeal. Extremely Fine to Superb; 2006 PSE - Graded Certificate. (SMQ $2,200; this being one of 35 attaining this grade as of 10/08, with 28 graded higher).

Estimate: $2,200+

Minimum Bid: $1,100

31295 #233, 1893, 4c Ultramarine, XF-S 95 PSE. (Original Gum - Never Hinged). Fleet of Columbus. Wonderfully centered example with balanced even margins on all four sides, soft muted ultramarine color, very pretty. Extremely Fine to Superb; 2006 PSE - Graded Certificate. (SMQ $2,200; this being one of 35 attaining this grade as of 10/08, with 28 graded higher).

Estimate: $2,000+

Minimum Bid: $1,000

31296 #233, 1893, 4c Ultramarine, XF-S 95 PSE. (Original Gum - Never Hinged). Fleet of Columbus. Mint fresh example with a dark, appropriately saturated ultramarine color, fantastic eye-appeal. Extremely Fine to Superb; 2005 PSE - Graded Certificate. (SMQ $2,200; this being one of 35 attaining this grade as of 10/08, with 28 graded higher).

Estimate: $2,000+

Minimum Bid: $1,000

31297 #233 Var, 1893, 4c Ultramarine, XF-S 95 PSE. (Original Gum - Never Hinged). Fleet of Columbus. Three-Leaf Variety. Extremely Fine to Superb; 2005 PSE - Graded Certificate.(Unlisted in SMQ or PSE Population Reports).

Estimate: $2,500+

Minimum Bid: $1,250

31298 **#233, 1893, 4c Ultramarine, XF-S 95 PSE.** (Original Gum - Never Hinged). Fleet of Columbus. Post Office Fresh. Extremely Fine to Superb PSE - Encapsulated. (SMQ $2,200; this being one of 35 attaining this grade as of 10/08, with 28 graded higher).
Estimate: $1,800+
Minimum Bid: $900

31299 **#233 Var, 1893, 4c Ultramarine, XF-S 95 PSE.** (Original Gum - Never Hinged). Fleet of Columbus. An intensely rich and vibrant mint example of the three leaf in right 4 variety. Extremely Fine to Superb; 2008 PSE - Graded Certificate. (SMQ $2,200; this being one of 35 attaining this grade as of 10/08, with 28 graded higher).
Estimate: $2,200+
Minimum Bid: $1,100

31300 **#233, 1893, 4c Ultramarine, XF 90 PSE.** (Original Gum - Never Hinged). Fleet of Coulmbus. Fresh. Extremely Fine PSE - Encapsulated. (SMQ $660; this being one of 45 attaining this grade as of 10/08, with 69 graded higher).
Estimate: $500+
Minimum Bid: $250

31301 **#233, 1893, 4c Ultramarine, XF 90 PSE.** (Original Gum - Never Hinged). Fleet of Columbus. Fresh. Extremely Fine PSE - Encapsulated. (SMQ $660; this being one of 45 attaining this grade as of 10/08, with 69 graded higher).
Estimate: $500+
Minimum Bid: $250

31302 **#233, 1893, 4c Ultramarine, VF-XF 85 PSE.** (Original Gum - Never Hinged). Fleet of Columbus. Bright and Fresh. Very Fine to Extremely Fine PSE - Graded Certificate. (SMQ $365; this being one of 26 attaining this grade as of 10/08, with 117 graded higher).
Estimate: $350+
Minimum Bid: $175

31303 **#234, 1893, 5c Chocolate, XF-S 95J PSE.** (Original Gum - Never Hinged). Columbus Soliciting Aid Of Isabella. Absolutely stunning jumbo example. Delicious chocolate color. Extremely Fine to Superb. 2008 PSE - Graded Certificate.
(this being one of 4 attaining this grade as of 10/08, with 20 graded higher).
Estimate: $3,000+
Minimum Bid: $1,500

31304 **#234, 1893, 5c Chocolate, XF-S 95 PSE.** (Original Gum - Never Hinged). Columbus Soliciting the Aid of Isabella. Intense impression, large, eye-pleasing margins with vivid chocolate color. Extremely Fine to Superb PSE - Encapsulated. (SMQ $2,450; this being one of 34 attaining this grade as of 10/08, with 24 graded higher).
Estimate: $2,450+
Minimum Bid: $1,225

31305 **#234, 1893, 5c Chocolate, XF-S 95 PSE.** (Original Gum - Never Hinged). Columbus Soliciting the Aid of Isabella. Rich chocolate color and detailed impression, spectacular. Extremely Fine to Superb PSE - Encapsulated. (SMQ $2,450; this being one of 34 attaining this grade as of 10/08, with 24 graded higher).
Estimate: $2,200+
Minimum Bid: $1,100

31306 **#234, 1893, 5c Chocolate, XF-S 95 PSE.** (Original Gum - Never Hinged). Columbus Soliciting Aid Of Isabella, One of the nicest example we have seen at this grade, huge margins, rich chocolate color, incredible impression. Extremely Fine to Superb; 2007 PSE - Graded Certificate. (SMQ $2,450; this being one of 34 attaining this grade as of 10/08, with 24 graded higher).

Estimate: $2,100+

Minimum Bid: $1,050

31307 **#234, 1893, 5c Chocolate, XF 90 PSE.** (Original Gum - Never Hinged). Columbus Soliciting Aid of Isabella. Rich Shade. Fresh. Extremely Fine; 2005 PSE - Graded Certificate. (SMQ $740; this being one of 37 attaining this grade as of 10/08, with 70 graded higher).

Estimate: $650+

Minimum Bid: $325

31308 **#234, 1893, 5c Chocolate, XF 90 PSE.** (Original Gum - Never Hinged). Columbus Soliciting Aid of Isabella. Extremely Fine PSE - Encapsulated.
(SMQ $740; this being one of 37 attaining this grade as of 10/08, with 70 graded higher).

Estimate: $700+

Minimum Bid: $350

31309 **#235, 1893, 6c Purple, XF-S 95 PSE.** (Original Gum - Never Hinged). Columbus Welcomed at Barcelona. Intense and exquisite deep color with exceptionally well-balanced margins. Strong 95. Extremely Fine to Superb PSE - Encapsulated. (SMQ 2,200; this being one of 24 attaining this grade as of 10/08, with only 9 graded higher).

Estimate: $2,000+

Minimum Bid: $1,000

31310 **#235, 1893, 6c Purple, XF 90; PSE.** (Original Gum - Never Hinged). Columbus Welcomed at Barcelona. A charming and fresh mint single with bright vibrant pastel color and detailed impression on crisp clean paper, pristine original gum. Extremely Fine PSE - Encapsulated. (SMQ $660; this being one of 32 attaining this grade as of 10/08, with 34 graded higher).

Estimate: $600+

Minimum Bid: $300

31311 **#235, 1893, 6c Purple, XF-S 95 PSE.** (Original Gum - Never Hinged). Columbus Welcomed at Barcelona. Detailed impression, deep, rich shade. Post Office fresh. Extremely Fine to Superb; 2005 PSE - Graded Certificate. (SMQ $2200; this being one of 24 attaining this grade as of 10/08, with only 9 graded higher).

Estimate: $1,800+

Minimum Bid: $900

31312 #235, 1893, 6c Purple, XF-S 95 PSE. (Original Gum - Never Hinged). Columbus Welcomed at Barcelona. Finely detailed impression and fresh vibrant color, gorgeous eye appeal. Extremely Fine to Superb; 2008 PSE - Graded Certificate. (SMQ $2200; this being one of 24 attaining this grade as of 10/08, with only 9 graded higher).

Estimate: $2,000+

Minimum Bid: $1,000

31313 #235, 1893, 6c Purple, XF-S 95 PSE. (Original Gum - Never Hinged). Columbus Welcomed At Barcelona. Eye-catching bright purple color. Fabulous overall look. Extremely Fine to Superb; 2003 PSE - Graded Certificate. (SMQ $2,200; this being one of 24 attaining this grade as of 10/08, with only 9 graded higher).

Estimate: $2,000+

Minimum Bid: $1,000

31314 #235, 1893, 6c Purple, VF-XF 85J PSE. (Original Gum - Never Hinged). Columbus Welcomed at Barcelona. Bright and Fresh. Large Margins, well-balanced. Very Fine to Extremely Fine; 2005 PSE - Graded Certificate. (this being one of 5 attaining this grade as of 10/08, with 73 graded higher).

Estimate: $500+

Minimum Bid: $250

31315 #236, 1893, 8c Magenta, XF-S 95 PSE. (Original Gum - Never Hinged). Columbus Restored to Favor. Extremely Fine to Superb; 2007 PSE - Graded Certificate. (SMQ $2,150; this being one of 23 attaining this grade as of 10/08, with 15 graded higher).

Estimate: $2,000+

Minimum Bid: $1,000

31316 #236, 1893, 8c Magenta, XF-S 95 PSE. (Original Gum - Never Hinged). Columbus Restored to Favor. Radiant magenta color, sharp impression on fresh white paper. Extremely Fine to Superb PSE - Encapsulated. (SMQ $2,150; this being one of 23 attaining this grade as of 10/08, with 15 graded higher).

Estimate: $1,900+

Minimum Bid: $950

31317 #236, 1893, 8c Magenta, XF 90 PSE. (Original Gum - Never Hinged). Columbus Restored To Favor. Razor sharp impression and fresh. Extremely Fine; 2005 PSE - Graded Certificate. (SMQ $620, this being one of 45 attaining this grade as of 10/08, with 47 graded higher).

Estimate: $550+

Minimum Bid: $275

31318 **#236, 1893, 8c Magenta, XF 90 PSE.** (Original Gum - Never Hinged). Columbus Returned to Favor. Fresh color and gum. Extremely Fine; 2005 PSE - Graded Certificate. (SMQ $620; this being one of 45 attaining this grade as of 10/08, with 47 graded higher).

Estimate: $500+
Minimum Bid: $250

31319 **#237, 1893, 10c Black Brown, XF-S 95; PSE.** (Original Gum - Never Hinged). Columbus Presenting Natives. A visibly striking mint single, impeccably centered with full intact perforations all around, stunning color and a deeply etched impression on bright fresh paper Extremely Fine to Superb; 2006 PSE - Graded Certificate. (SMQ $3,650; this being one of 17 attaining this grade as of 10/08, with only 9 graded higher).

Estimate: $3,500+
Minimum Bid: $1,750

31320 **#237, 1893, 10c Black Brown, XF-S 95 PSE.** (Original Gum - Never Hinged). Columbus Presenting Natives. A bright and vividly detailed mint single. Extremely Fine to Superb; 2008 PSE - Graded Certificate. (SMQ $3,650; this being one of 17 attaining this grade as of 10/08, with only 9 graded higher).

Estimate: $3,500+
Minimum Bid: $1,750

31321 **#237, 1893, 10c Black Brown, XF-S 95 PSE.** (Original Gum - Never Hinged). Columbus Presenting Natives. An absolutely delightful example, near perfect margins surround a captivating scene enveloped in a rich color and impression. Extremely Fine to Superb; 2007 PSE - Graded Certificate. (SMQ $3,650; this being one of 17 attaining this grade as of 10/08, with only 9 graded higher).

Estimate: $3,500+
Minimum Bid: $1,750

31322 **#237, 1893, 10c Black Brown, XF 90 PSE.** (Original Gum - Never Hinged). Columbus Presenting Natives. Attractive example with true brown black color and a precise, strongly detailed impression. Extremely Fine; 2004 PSE - Graded Certificate. (SMQ $1,150; this being one of 26 attaining this grade as of 10/08, with 30 graded higher).

Estimate: $900+
Minimum Bid: $450

31323 **#237, 1893, 10c Black Brown, XF 90 PSE.** (Original Gum - Never Hinged). Columbus Presenting Natives, extremely fresh. Extremely Fine; 2006 PSE - Graded Certificate. (SMQ $1,150; this being one of 26 attaining this grade as of 10/08, with 30 graded higher).

Estimate: $900+
Minimum Bid: $450

31324 **#237, 1893, 10c Black Brown, XF 90 PSE.** (Original Gum - Never Hinged). Columbus Presenting Natives. Extremely Fine PSE - Encapsulated.
(SMQ $1,150; this being one of 26 attaining this grade as of 10/08, with 30 graded higher).
Estimate: $900+
Minimum Bid: $450

31325 **#237, 1893, 10c Black Brown, VF-XF 85 PSE.** (Original Gum - Never Hinged). Columbus Presenting Natives. Very Fine to Extremely Fine; 2004 PSE - Graded Certificate. (SMQ $640; this being one of 14 attaining this grade as of 10/08, with 59 graded higher).
Estimate: $550+
Minimum Bid: $275

31326 **#238, 1893, 15c Dark Green, VF-XF 85 PSE.** (Original Gum - Never Hinged). Columbus Announcing His Discovery. almost 3-D impression, very fresh. Very Fine to Extremely Fine; 2006 PSE - Graded Certificate. (SMQ $1,200; this being one of 9 attaining this grade as of 10/08, with 32 graded higher).
Estimate: $1,000+
Minimum Bid: $500

31327 **#238, 1893, 15c Dark Green, VF-XF 85 PSE.** (Original Gum - Never Hinged). Columbus Announcing his Discovery. Very Fine to Extremely Fine; 2005 PSE - Graded Certificate. (SMQ $1,200; this being one of 9 attaining this grade as of 10/08, with 32 graded higher).
Estimate: $1,000+
Minimum Bid: $500

31328 **#238, 1893, 15c Dark Green, VF 80 PSE.** (Original Gum - Never Hinged). Columbus Announcing his Discovery. Huge corner margin single, very well centered with sharp clear impression, extremely high end for the grade. Very Fine PSE - Graded Certificate. (SMQ $740; this being one of 11 attaining this grade as of 10/08, with 41 graded higher).
Estimate: $750+
Minimum Bid: $375

31329 **#238, 1893, 15c Dark Green, XF 90J PSE.** (Used). Columbus Announcing his Discovery. Moderate New York double oval REGISTRY cancel. Jumbo Margins. Extremely Fine; 2008 PSE - Graded Certificate.
(this being one of 2 attaining this grade as of 10/08, with only 5 graded higher).
Estimate: $650+
Minimum Bid: $325

FANTASTIC QUALITY 30C COLUMBIAN

31330 **#239, 1893, 30c Orange Brown, SUP 98 PSE.** (Original Gum - Never Hinged). Columbus at La Rabida. An exquisite, fresh, vibrant, and flawless Superb condition rarity for the serious Columbian collector. 2008 PSE - Graded Certificate. (SMQ $24,500; this being one of 8 attaining this grade as of 10/08, with only 2 graded higher).

Estimate: $25,000+

Minimum Bid: $12,500

31331 **#239, 1893, 30c Orange Brown, XF-S 95J PSE.** (Original Gum - Never Hinged). Columbus at La Rabida. A spectacular huge margined example. Finely etched impression, immaculate full original gum. Extremely Fine to Superb PSE - Graded Certificate. (this being one of 4 attaining this grade as of 10/08, with 10 graded higher).

Estimate: $10,000+

Minimum Bid: $5,000

31332 **#239, 1893, 30c Orange Brown, XF-S 95J PSE.** (Original Gum - Never Hinged). Columbus at La Rabida. Prooflike impression. Nice large Jumbo margins. Extremely Fine to Superb PSE - Encapsulated. (This being one of 4 attaining this grade as of 10/08, with 10 graded higher).

Estimate: $9,000+

Minimum Bid: $4,500

31333 **#239, 1893, 30c Orange Brown, XF-S 95 PSE.** (Original Gum - Never Hinged). Columbus At La Rabida . Rich orange brown color with an intense impression. Beautiful. Extremely Fine to Superb; 2006 PSE - Graded Certificate. (SMQ $6,850; this being one of 28 attaining this grade as of 10/08, with 14 graded higher).

Estimate: $6,000+

Minimum Bid: $3,000

31334 **#239, 1893, 30c Orange Brown, XF-S 95 PSE.** (Original Gum - Previously Hinged). Columbus at La Rabida. Very small hinge remnant at top right. Extremely Fine to Superb; 2006 PSE - Graded Certificate. (SMQ $880; this being one of 9 attaining this grade as of 10/08, with only 6 graded higher).

Estimate: $700+

Minimum Bid: $350

31335 **#239, 1893, 30c Orange Brown, XF 90 PSE.** (Original Gum - Previously Hinged). Columbus At La Rabida. Exceptional color and impression. Very lightly hinged with no remnant. Extremely Fine; 2007 PSE - Graded Certificate. (SMQ $510; this being one of 16 attaining this grade as of 10/08, with only 17 graded higher).

Estimate: $500+

Minimum Bid: $250

31336 **#239, 1893, 30c Orange Brown, XF 90 PSE.** (Original Gum - Never Hinged). Columbus at La Rabida. Exceptionally nice 90, balanced margins.. Extremely Fine; 2007 PSE - Graded Certificate. (SMQ $2,350; this being one of 17 attaining this grade as of 10/08, with 43 graded higher).

Estimate: $2,100+

Minimum Bid: $1,050

31337 **#239, 1893, 30c Orange Brown, XF 90 PSE.** (Original Gum - Never Hinged). Columbus at La Rabida. Extremely Fine; 2007 PSE - Graded Certificate. (SMQ $2,350; this being one of 17 attaining this grade as of 10/08, with 43 graded higher).

Estimate: $2,000+

Minimum Bid: $1,000

31338 **#239, 1893, 30c Orange Brown, VF 80J PSE.** (Original Gum - Never Hinged). Columbus at La Rabida. Delightful jumbo example, lovely orange brown hue with good saturation, vivid impression. Very Fine; 2005 PSE - Graded Certificate. (this being one of 1 attaining this grade as of 10/08, with 43 graded higher).

Estimate: $900+

Minimum Bid: $450

31339 **#240, 1893, 50c Slate Blue, XF-S 95 PSE.** (Original Gum - Hinged). Recall of Columbus. Darkest slate blue imaginable, life-like appearance to the figures surrounding Columbus, moderately hinged with no remnant. Extremely Fine to Superb PSE - Encapsulated. (SMQ $1,850; this being one of 8 attaining this grade as of 10/08, with only 2 graded higher).

Estimate: $1,700+

Minimum Bid: $850

31340 **#240, 1893, 50c Slate Blue, XF 90 PSE.** (Original Gum - Previously Hinged). Recall Of Columbus, beautiful example with large even margins, pretty. Hinge remnant at the top left. Extremely Fine; 2006 PSE - Graded Certificate. (SMQ $1,050; this being one of 30 attaining this grade as of 10/08, with 10 graded higher).

> Estimate: $900+
> Minimum Bid: $450

CONDITION RARITY - NEVER HINGED

31341 **#240, 1893, 50c Slate Blue, VF-XF 85 PSE.** (Original Gum - Never Hinged). Recall of Columbus. Very Fine to Extremely Fine; 2007 PSE - Graded Certificate. Also, 2006 PF Certificate Graded VF-XF 85. (SMQ $2,950; this being one of 5 attaining this grade as of 10/08, with 17 graded higher) .

> Estimate: $2,500+
> Minimum Bid: $1,250

CONDITION RARITY - NEVER HINGED

31342 **#240, 1893, 50c Slate Blue, VF-XF 85 PSE.** (Original Gum - Never Hinged). Recall Of Columbus. Handsome example with large margins. Very Fine to Extremely Fine; 2005 PSE - Graded Certificate. (SMQ $2,950; this being one of 5 attaining this grade as of 10/08, with 17 graded higher).

> Estimate: $2,400+
> Minimum Bid: $1,200

31343 **#240, 1893, 50c Slate Blue, VF-XF 85 PSE.** (Original Gum - Previously Hinged). Recall of Columbus. Perfect slate blue color, impressive example for the grade. Very light touch of a hinge mark with no remnant. Very Fine to Extremely Fine PSE - Graded Certificate. (SMQ $780; this being one of 16 attaining this grade as of 10/08, with 42 graded higher).

> Estimate: $700+
> Minimum Bid: $350

31344 **#240, 1893, 50c Slate Blue, XF 90 PSE.** (Used). Recall of Columbus. Moderate Cancel. Extremely Fine; 2007 PSE - Graded Certificate. (SMQ $455; this being one of 7 attaining this grade as of 10/08, with 12 graded higher).

> Estimate: $400+
> Minimum Bid: $200

31345 **#240, 1893, 50c Slate Blue, XF 90 PSE.** (Used). Recall of Columbus. Black cork cancel. Extremely Fine; 2005 PSE - Graded Certificate. (SMQ $455; this being one of 7 attaining this grade as of 10/08, with 12 graded higher).

> Estimate: $400+
> Minimum Bid: $200

31346 **#241, 1893, $1 Salmon, XF-S 95J PSE.** (No Gum). Isabella Pledging her Jewels. Incredible example, Rare with margins this large. Very well centered with vivid color. Extremely Fine to Superb; 2008 PSE - Graded Certificate, 1992 PF Certificate. (this being one of 1 attaining this grade as of 10/08, with *none* graded higher).

> Estimate: $1,500+
> Minimum Bid: $750

31347 **#241, 1893, $1 Salmon, XF 90 PSE.** (Original Gum - Never Hinged). Isabella Pledging her Jewels. Deep, rich color and proof-like impression. A masterpiece of the printers art on a tiny canvas. One of the most strikingly deep colored 241's we've ever seen. Extremely Fine PSE - Encapsulated. (SMQ $13,500; this being one of 4 attaining this grade as of 10/08, with only 3 graded higher).

Estimate: $20,000+

Minimum Bid: $10,000

31348 **#241, 1893, $1 Salmon, XF 90 PSE.** (Original Gum - Previously Hinged). Isabella Pledging her Jewels. Choice mint example with very attractive appearance. Very lightly hinged with no hinge remnant. Extremely Fine; 2006 PSE - Graded Certificate. (SMQ $2,000; this being one of 14 attaining this grade as of 10/08, with 10 graded higher).

Estimate: $1,800+

Minimum Bid: $900

31349 **#241, 1893, $1 Salmon, XF 90 PSE.** (Original Gum - Never Hinged). Isabella Pledging Her Jewels, Rare stamp never hinged. Fresh. Extremely Fine; 2004 PSE - Graded Certificate. (SMQ $13,500; this being one of 4 attaining this grade as of 10/08, with only 3 graded higher).
Estimate: $15,000+
Minimum Bid: $7,500

CONDITION RARITY - NEVER HINGED

31350 **#241, 1893, $1 Salmon, XF 90 PSE.** (No Gum). Isabella pledging her jewels. A beautiful unused stamp, precisely centered, gorgeous fresh color and detailed impression on white paper. Extremely Fine; PSE - Encapsulated.(SMQ $860; this being one of 7 attaining this grade as of 10/08, with only 1 graded higher).
Estimate: $750+
Minimum Bid: $375

31351 **#241, 1893, $1 Salmon, VF 80 PSE.** (Original Gum - Previously Hinged). Isabella Pledging her Jewels. Lovely example with ample margins. Very Fine; 2007 PSE - Graded Certificate. (SMQ $1,250; this being one of 11 attaining this grade as of 10/08, with 31 graded higher).
Estimate: $1,100+
Minimum Bid: $550

31352 **#241, 1893, $1 Salmon, VF 80 PSE.** (Original Gum - Never Hinged). Isabella Pledging her Jewels. Very difficult stamp in Never Hinged Condition. This copy with deep and rich color, strong impression on fresh white paper. Very Fine; 2005 PSE - Graded Certificate. (SMQ $3,850; this being one of 3 attaining this grade as of 10/08, with only 7 graded higher).
Estimate: $3,750+
Minimum Bid: $1,875

31353 **#241, 1893, $1 Salmon, XF 90 PSE.** (Used). Isabella Pledging her Jewels. Large margin example. Double oval REGISTRY cancel. Extremely Fine; 2005 PSE - Graded Certificate. (SMQ $1,350; this being one of 14 attaining this grade as of 10/08, with only 5 graded higher).

Estimate: $1,100+

Minimum Bid: $550

31354 **#241, 1893, $1 Salmon, XF 90 PSE.** (Used). Isabella Pledging Her Jewels. Choice example with a black New York duplex cancel, fiery color and a clean back. Extremely Fine; 2005 PSE - Graded Certificate. Also, 1986 PF Certificate. (SMQ $1,350; this being one of 14 attaining this grade as of 10/08, with only 5 graded higher).

Estimate: $1,100+

Minimum Bid: $550

31355 **#241, 1893, $1 Salmon, VF 80 PSE.** (Used). Isabella Pledging her Jewels. Town cancel. Very Fine; 2008 PSE - Graded Certificate. (SMQ $670; this being one of 8 attaining this grade as of 10/08, with 24 graded higher).

Estimate: $600+

Minimum Bid: $300

31356 **#241, 1893, $1 Salmon, VF 80 PSE.** (Used). Isabella Pledging her Jewels. Wonderfully centered used example with a black duplex cancel, lovely salmon color. Very Fine; 2005 PSE - Graded Certificate. (SMQ $670; this being one of 8 attaining this grade as of 10/08, with 24 graded higher).

Estimate: $550+

Minimum Bid: $275

Condition Rarity - Never Hinged

31357 **#242, 1893, $2 Brown Red, XF 90 PSE.** (Original Gum - Never Hinged). Columbus in Chains. Spectacular, crisp color, balanced margins, clean white paper, very strong 90. Extremely Fine PSE - Encapsulated. (SMQ $18,900; this being one of 3 attaining this grade as of 10/08, with only 2 graded higher).

Estimate: $20,000+

Minimum Bid: $10,000

31358 **#242, 1893, $2 Brown Red, VF-XF 85 PF.** (Original Gum - Previously Hinged). Columbus in Chains. Rich color and strong impression. Nearly perfect gum with only trace evidence of a prior hinge. Very Fine to Extremely Fine; 2008 PF Graded Certificate..

Estimate: $3,000+

Minimum Bid: $1,500

Condition Rarity - Never Hinged

31359 **#242, 1893, $2 Brown Red, VF 80 PF.** (Original Gum - Never Hinged). Columbus in Chains. Intense shade and detailed impression on fresh white paper. Super fresh gum; 2007 PF Graded Certificate. (Scott $4,250).

Estimate: $4,250+

Minimum Bid: $2,125

31360 **#242, 1893, $2 Brown Red, XF 90 PSE.** (Used). Columbus in Chains. Very well-centered, better than the assigned 90, with a likely 5 point reduction for the cancel. Extremely Fine; 2006 PSE - Graded Certificate.
(SMQ $1,400; this being one of 11 attaining this grade as of 10/08, with only 6 graded higher).

Estimate: $1,200+

Minimum Bid: $600

31361 **#242, 1893, $2 Brown Red, XF 90 PSE.** (Used). Columbus In Chains. Superbly centered example with large margins with a black Springfield, Mass. boxed town cancel. Extremely Fine; 2006 PSE - Graded Certificate, 2000 PSE Certificate. (SMQ $1,400; this being one of 11 attaining this grade as of 10/08, with only 6 graded higher).

Estimate: $1,100+

Minimum Bid: $550

31362 **#242, 1893, $2 Brown Red, VF 80 PSE.** (Used). Columbus in Chains. Excellent example with a black stars and stripe (flag) machine cancel. Handsome. Very Fine; 2005 PSE - Graded Certificate. (SMQ $700; this being one of 4 attaining this grade as of 10/08, with 23 graded higher).

Estimate: $600+

Minimum Bid: $300

 A 19.5% Buyer's Premium ($9 min.) Applies To All Lots

ONE OF THE BEST MINT $3
COLUMBIANS IN EXISTENCE

31363 #243, 1893, $3 Yellow Green, SUP 98 PSE. (Original Gum - Previously Hinged). Columbus Describing Third Voyage. One of the finest examples we have ever seen. Deep dark yellow green color with a perfect impression, wide balanced margins that frame the design. Light outline mark of prior hinge only, no remnant. World class piece for the finest collection. Superb; 2006 PSE - Graded Certificate. (SMQ $11,700; this being one of 3 attaining this grade as of 10/08, with **none** graded higher).

Estimate: $20,000+

Minimum Bid: $10,000

CONDITION RARITY - NEVER HINGED

31364 #243, 1893, $3 Yellow Green XF 90 PSE. (Original Gum - Never Hinged). Columbus Describing Third Voyage. Extraordinary example with outstanding centering, richly detailed and colorful impression. Extremely Fine PSE - Encapsulated. (SMQ $17,400; this being one of 2 attaining this grade as of 10/08, with only 2 graded higher).

Estimate: $20,000+

Minimum Bid: $10,000

31365 **#243a, 1893, $3 Olive Green, VF-XF 85 PSE.** (No Gum). Columbus describing Third Voyage. Bright and fresh unused single, well centered within generous to large margins, Very Fine to Extremely; Fine PSE - Encapsulated. (SMQ $1,100; this being one of 2 attaining this grade as of 10/08, with only 2 graded higher).

Estimate: $1,000+

Minimum Bid: $500

31367 **#243a, 1893, $3 Olive Green VF 80 PSE.** (Original Gum - Hinged). Columbus Describing Third Voyage. Tremendous deep olive green color and much better than usual impression, moderate hinging. Very Fine; 2007 PSE - Graded Certificate. (SMQ $1950; this being one of 3 attaining this grade as of 10/08, with 15 graded higher).

Estimate: $1,800+

Minimum Bid: $900

31369 **#243, 1893, $3 Olive Green, XF 90 PSE.** (Used). Columbus Describing Third Voyage. Moderate double oval REGISTRY cancel. Rich color, white paper. Extremely Fine; 2006 PSE - Graded Certificate. (SMQ $2,100; this being one of 10 attaining this grade as of 10/08, with only 4 graded higher).

Estimate: $1,800+

Minimum Bid: $900

31366 **#243, 1893, $3 Yellow Green, VF 80 PSE.** (Original Gum - Never Hinged). Columbus Describing Third Voyage. Very Fine PSE - Graded Certificate. (SMQ $6100; this being one of 2 attaining this grade as of 10/08, with only 6 graded higher).

Estimate: $5,500+

Minimum Bid: $2,750

31368 **#243, 1893, $3 Yellow Green, XF 90 PSE.** (Used). Columbus Describing Third Voyage. Exquisite color and impression with light black cancel, light pencil notation on the back. Extremely Fine; 2005 PSE - Graded Certificate,1990 PF Certification.(SMQ $2100; this being one of 10 attaining this grade as of 10/08, with only 4 graded higher).

Estimate: $1,700+

Minimum Bid: $850

31370 **#244, 1893, $4 Crimson Lake, XF-S 95 PSE.** (Original Gum - Previously Hinged). Columbus and Isabella. Absolutely superb example, terrific crimson lake color with an excellent impression, very fresh overall. Barest trace of hinging. Extremely Fine to Superb; 2007 PSE - Graded Certificate. (SMQ $4,350; this being one of 5 attaining this grade as of 10/08, with only 3 graded higher).

Estimate: $4,000+

Minimum Bid: $2,000

Please visit HA.com to view other collectibles auctions. *A 19.5% Buyer's Premium ($9 min.) Applies To All Lots*

31371 #244, 1893, $4 Crimson Lake, XF 90 PSE. (Original Gum - Never Hinged). Columbus and Isabella. A simply gorgeous copy. As fresh as the day printed, exceptional eye appeal. Sharp impression, detailed impression on fresh white paper, full perforations and gorgeous gum. Extremely Fine; 2004 PSE - Graded Certificate. Also, 1996 PF Certificate. (SMQ $24,000; this being one of 5 attaining this grade as of 10/08, with only 3 graded higher).

Estimate: $30,000+

Minimum Bid: $15,000

31372 #244, 1893, $4 Crimson Lake, XF 90 PSE. (Original Gum - Hinged). Columbus and Isabella. An absolutely stunning example with bright fresh crimson lake color, large margins are emphasized by the etched impression, very light hinge mark. Extremely Fine; 2004 PSE - Graded Certificate. (SMQ $4,350; this being one of 12 attaining this grade as of 10/08, with only 9 graded higher).

Estimate: $4,000+

Minimum Bid: $2,000

31373 #244a, 1893, $4 Rose Carmine, VF 80 PSE. (Original Gum - Previously Hinged). Columbus and Isabella. Soft pastel rose carmine color on fresh white paper, ample to large margins, lightly hinged. Very Fine; 2007 PSE - Graded Certificate. (SMQ $2,700; this being one of 1 attaining this grade as of 10/08, with only 4 graded higher).

Estimate: $2,500+

Minimum Bid: $1,250

31374 #244, 1893, $4 Crimson Lake VF 80 PSE. (Original Gum - Previously Hinged). Columbus and Isabella. Handsome example, very fresh, lightly hinged. Very Fine; 2007 PSE - Graded Certificate. (SMQ $2,700; this being one of 5 attaining this grade as of 10/08, with 29 graded higher).

Estimate: $2,400+

Minimum Bid: $1,200

31375 **#244, 1893, $4 Crimson Lake, XF 90 PSE.** (Used). Isabella and Columbus. Gorgeous used example. Light bulls-eye cancel, Fantastic Rich color. Extremely Fine; 2005 PSE - Graded Certificate. (SMQ $2,700; this being one of 10 attaining this grade as of 10/08, with only 3 graded higher).

Estimate: $3,000+

Minimum Bid: $1,500

31376 **#244, 1893, $4 Crimson Lake, XF 90 PSE.** (Used). Columbus and Isabella. Huge used margined example with black double oval Registry cancel. Extremely Fine; 2005 PSE - Graded Certificate. (SMQ $2700; this being one of 10 attaining this grade as of 10/08, with only 3 graded higher).

Estimate: $2,300+

Minimum Bid: $1,150

31377 **#244, 1893, $4 Crimson Lake, VF 80 PSE.** (Used). Columbus and Isabella. New York registry cancel. Very Fine PSE - Encapsulated. (SMQ $1350; this being one of 3 attaining this grade as of 10/08, with 19 graded higher).

Estimate: $900+

Minimum Bid: $450

31378 **#245, 1893, $5 Black, XF-S 95 PSE.** (Original Gum - Previously Hinged). Columbus. Extremely fresh and sharp example. Distinctive deep black color with strongly etched impression. Very lightly touched by a hinge. Extremely Fine to Superb; 2007 PSE - Graded Certificate,1988 and 1998 PF Certificate. (SMQ $9,550; this being one of 14 attaining this grade as of 10/08, with only 8 graded higher).

Estimate: $9,000+

Minimum Bid: $4,500

31379 **#245, 1893, $5 Black, XF-S 95 PSE.** (Original Gum - Previously Hinged). Columbus. Very light hinge mark only. Extremely Fine to Superb; 2004 PSE - Graded Certificate. (SMQ $9,550; this being one of 14 attaining this grade as of 10/08, with only 8 graded higher).
Estimate: $9,500+
Minimum Bid: $4,750

31380 **#245, 1893, $5 Black, XF-S 95 PSE.** (Original Gum - Hinged). Columbus. Splendid and fresh mint single, concisely centered, vividly intense, original gum, a few hinges marks but overall pretty nice. Extremely Fine to Superb; PSE - Encapsulated. (SMQ $9,550; this being one of 14 attaining this grade as of 10/08, with only 8 graded higher).
Estimate: $8,500+
Minimum Bid: $4,250

31381 **#245, 1893, $5 Black, XF 90; PSE.** (Original Gum - Previously Hinged). Columbus. A visually striking mint single sporting rich color and vivid impression, choice centering, and original gum showing just minor impression of previous hinging. Extremely Fine PSE - Encapsulated. (SMQ $4,800; this being one of 14 attaining this grade as of 10/08, with 27 graded higher).
Estimate: $4,500+
Minimum Bid: $2,250

31382 **#245, 1893, $5 Black, VF-XF 85 PSE.** (Original Gum - Previously Hinged). Columbus. Dynamic jet black color accentuated by a razor sharp impression, ample to large margins, just a touch of hinge mark, wonderful example. Very Fine to Extremely Fine; 2005 PSE - Graded Certificate. (SMQ $3,750; this being one of 7 attaining this grade as of 10/08, with 41 graded higher).
Estimate: $3,400+
Minimum Bid: $1,700

31383 **#245, 1893, $5 Black VF 80 PSE.** (Original Gum - Never Hinged). Columbus. Sharp engraving and impression. Strong eye appeal, super fresh paper and gum. Strong 80. Very Fine; 2007 PSE - Graded Certificate. (SMQ $10,500; this being one of 3 attaining this grade as of 10/08, with only 3 graded higher).

Estimate: $10,000+

Minimum Bid: $5,000

31384 **#245, 1893, $5 Black, VF 80 PSE.** (Original Gum - Hinged). Columbus. Very fine mint example, beautiful black color with ample margins, great eye-appeal for the grade, minor gum disturbances from hinge removal with small hinge remnant. Very Fine PSE - Graded Certificate. (SMQ $3,000; this being one of 5 attaining this grade as of 10/08, with 48 graded higher).

Estimate: $2,600+

Minimum Bid: $1,300

31385 **#245, 1893, $5 Black, F 70 PSE.** (Original Gum - Never Hinged). Columbus. Bright and fresh example with a very attractive appearance for the grade. Fine; 2007 PSE - Graded Certificate. (SMQ $4,100; this being one of 2 attaining this grade as of 10/08, with only 7 graded higher).

Estimate: $3,500+

Minimum Bid: $1,750

31386 **#245, 1893, $5 Black.** (Original Gum - Previously Hinged). Columbus. Sharp detailed impression, strong color, fresh white paper amid large well-proportioned margins. Two small hinge remnants. Extremely Fine; 2006 PF Certificate. (Scott $3000).

Estimate: $4,500+

Minimum Bid: $2,250

31387 **#245, 1893, $5 Black.** (Original Gum - Previously Hinged). Columbus. Excellent example with rich black color, key to the series, bold impression, two large hinge impressions on the back. VF-XF; 2008 PF Certificate. (Scott $3,000).

Estimate: $3,500+

Minimum Bid: $1,750

31388 **#245, 1893, $5 Black, XF 90 PSE.** (Used). Columbus. Fantastic used example. Jet black color with very large margins, face free black circular date stamp cancel (c.d.s.), Extremely Fine; 2006 PSE - Graded Certificate, Also, 1995 PF Certificate. (SMQ $3,100; this being one of 7 attaining this grade as of 10/08, with only 6 graded higher).

Estimate: $3,000+

Minimum Bid: $1,500

31389 **#245, 1893, $5 Black, XF 90 PSE.** (Used). Columbus. Eye-pleasing example. Very light cancel Extremely Fine; 2008 PSE - Graded Certificate. (SMQ $3,100; this being one of 7 attaining this grade as of 10/08, with only 6 graded higher).

Estimate: $3,000+

Minimum Bid: $1,500

1894 BUREAU ISSUES - UNWATERMARKED

31390 **#246, 1894, 1c Ultramarine, XF-S 95 PSE.** (Original Gum - Never Hinged). Impressive example, rare deeply saturated color, lovely. Extremely Fine to Superb PSE - Encapsulated. (SMQ $1,250; this being one of 3 attaining this grade as of 10/08, with only 6 graded higher).

Estimate: $1,250+

Minimum Bid: $625

31391 **#249, 1894, 2c Carmine Lake, XF-S 95 PSE.** (Original Gum - Never Hinged). Rare and beautiful carmine lake example, perfectly centered within large margins, radiant color, magnificent overall impression. Extremely Fine to Superb PSE - Encapsulated. (SMQ $5,350; this being one of 4 attaining this grade as of 10/08, with only 2 graded higher).

Estimate: $5,350+

Minimum Bid: $2,675

31392 **#250, 1894, 2c Carmine, XF-S 95 PSE.** (Original Gum - Never Hinged). Immaculate mint state example, near jumbo well centered margins, brilliant color. Extremely Fine to Superb PSE - Encapsulated. (SMQ $ 1,150; this being one of 7 attaining this grade as of 10/08, with only 3 graded higher).

Estimate: $1,150+

Minimum Bid: $575

31393 **#252, 1894, 2c Carmine, VF-XF 85 PF.** (Original Gum - Never Hinged). Type III. Bright color. Very Fine to Extremely Fine; 2007 PF Graded Certificate.
(Scott CV for Very Fine $400.00).

Estimate: $650+

Minimum Bid: $325

31394 **#254, 1894, 4c Dark Brown, XF-S 95 PSE.** (Original Gum - Never Hinged). Pristine mint example, rich dark brown color, sharply etched impression, overall tremendous eye-appeal. Extremely Fine to Superb PSE - Encapsulated.
(SMQ $5,300; this being one of 5 attaining this grade as of 10/08, with only 5 graded higher).

Estimate: $5,300+

Minimum Bid: $2,650

31395 **#260, 1894, 50c Orange, VF-XF 85 PSE.** (Original Gum - Never Hinged). Scarce stamp in this condition. Bright and fresh. Very Fine to Extremely Fine PSE - Encapsulated. (SMQ $3,200; this being one of 6 attaining this grade as of 10/08, with only 7 graded higher).

Estimate: $3,000+

Minimum Bid: $1,500

31396 **#260, 1894, 50c Orange, F-VF 75J PSE.** (Original Gum - Hinged). Sharp looking example, ample to large margins, deep orange color, hinge remnant. Fine to Very Fine; 2007 PSE - Graded Certificate. (PSE POP does not list 75J Grade, there are 15 graded higher).

Estimate: $450+

Minimum Bid: $225

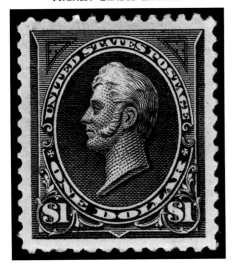

31397 #261, 1894, $1 Black, SUP 98J PSE. (Original Gum - Hinged). A superlative mint single, flawlessly centered within large balanced margins. Boldly intense with a deeply etched impression that produces an almost three-dimensional effect. Original gum showing clear evidence of previous hinging throughout the top half, a Superb example. PSE - Encapsulated. (this being the *only example attaining this grade* as of 10/08, with *none graded higher*).

Estimate: $10,000+

Minimum Bid: $5,000

31398 #261, 1894, $1 Black, XF-S 95J PSE. (Original Gum - Previously Hinged). A spectacular mint single, remarkably centered within giant margins, deeply intense color and impression on fresh white paper, full original gum, with only the absolute barest trace of having been previously hinged, appearing never hinged at a glance. This stamp is an Extremely Fine to Superb gem whose equal would be difficult to find; 2008 PSE - Graded Certificate. (this being one of 4 attaining this grade as of 10/08, with only 1 graded higher).

Estimate: $6,000+

Minimum Bid: $3,000

31399 #261, 1894, $1 Black, XF 90 PSE. (Original Gum - Previously Hinged). Intense Black, detailed and sharp impression. Hinge remnant, light pencil mark on back; "261." Extremely Fine PSE - Encapsulated. (SMQ $2,500; this being one of 8 attaining this grade as of 10/08, with only 8 graded higher).

Estimate: $2,000+

Minimum Bid: $1,000

31400 #261A, 1894, $1 Black, F 70 PSE. (Original Gum - Never Hinged). Handsome and fresh mint single. Fine; PSE - Encapsulated. (SMQ $2,700; this being one of 2 attaining this grade as of 10/08, with 12 graded higher).

Estimate: $2,000+

Minimum Bid: $1,000

31401 #262, 1894, $2 Bright Blue. (Original Gum - Previously Hinged). A handsome mint example of this $2 Bureau issue, both intense and radiant at the same time, with a deeply etched impression that gives the portrait a nearly life-like quality. Beautiful original gum with only mild evidence of previous hinging. Very Fine and choice; 2008 PSE Certificate and 1982 PF Certificate. (Scott $3,250).

Estimate: $2,500+

Minimum Bid: $1,250

31402 #263, 1894, $5 Dark Green. (Original Gum - Hinged). A gorgeous mint single, deep rich color and nearly proof-like impression. Some tiny hinge remnants are attached. Very Fine to Extremely Fine and choice; 1998 & 2008 PSE Certificates and 2000 PF Certificate. (Scott $5,000).

Estimate: $4,000+

Minimum Bid: $2,000

1895 BUREAU ISSUES - WATERMARKED

31403 **#264, 1895, 1c Blue, SUP 98 PSE.** (Original Gum - Never Hinged). Wonderfully well-centered, absolutely flawless. Brilliant color and sharp detailed impression. Superb PSE - Encapsulated. (SMQ $1,250; this being one of 9 attaining this grade as of 10/08, with only 2 graded higher).

Estimate: $1,250+

Minimum Bid: $625

31404 **#264, 1895, 1c Blue, XF-S 95J PSE.** (Original Gum - Never Hinged). Plate# 299, Right side single with Jumbo margins, Super fresh. Extremely Fine to Superb; 2008 PSE - Graded Certificate. (this being one of 5 attaining this grade as of 10/08, with 11 graded higher).

Estimate: $500+

Minimum Bid: $250

31405 **#264, 1895, 1c Blue, SUP 98 PSE.** (Used). Lovely little used single with mathematically balanced margins. Superb; 2008 PSE - Graded Certificate. (SMQ $660; this being one of 2 attaining this grade as of 10/08, with only 1 graded higher).

Estimate: $700+

Minimum Bid: $350

31406 **#265, 1895, 2c Carmine, XF-S 95 PSE.** (Original Gum - Never Hinged). Incredibly fresh with radiant color, highest graded to date, wonderful example, original gum, Never Hinged, Extremely Fine to Superb PSE - Encapsulated. (SMQ $1,150; this being one of 8 attaining this grade as of 10/08, with *none* graded higher).

Estimate: $1,150+

Minimum Bid: $575

31407 **#267, 1895, 2c Carmine SUP 98 PSE.** (Original Gum - Never Hinged). Hard to imagine a nicer #267, terrific margins, brilliant color, great impression, super fresh. Superb PSE - Encapsulated. (SMQ $1,100; this being one of 2 attaining this grade as of 10/08, with only 2 graded higher).

Estimate: $1,100+

Minimum Bid: $550

1897-1903 BUREAU ISSUES

31408 **#279, 1898, 1c Deep Green, XF-S 95 PSE.** (Original Gum - Never Hinged). Bold, bright and Fresh. Very strong 95, in our book. Extremely Fine to Superb PSE - Encapsulated. (SMQ $475; this being one of 18 attaining this grade as of 10/08, with 10 graded higher).

Estimate: $500+

Minimum Bid: $250

1895 BUREAU ISSUES - WATERMARKED

31409 **#270, 1895, 5c Chocolate, XF-S 95 PSE.** (Original Gum - Never Hinged). Amazing example, vivid fresh color with sharp, detailed impression. Extremely Fine to Superb PSE - Encapsulated. (SMQ $1,300; this being one of 9 attaining this grade as of 10/08, with only 7 graded higher).

Estimate: $1,300+

Minimum Bid: $650

31410 **#270, 1895, 5c Chocolate, XF 90 PSE.** (Original Gum - Never Hinged). Plate# 189, Deep and Rich shade. Pretty strong 90. Extremely Fine; 2006 PSE - Graded Certificate. (SMQ $420; this being one of 15 attaining this grade as of 10/08, with 17 graded higher).

Estimate: $400+

Minimum Bid: $200

31411 **#271, 1895, 6c Dull Brown, VF-XF 85 PF.** (Original Gum - Never Hinged). A premium mint single, marvelously precise centering with full even perforations all around. Soft, yet lovely color with a finely detailed impression. Very Fine to Extremely Fine; 2008 PF Graded Certificateand 1998 PF Certificate.

Estimate: $1,200+

Minimum Bid: $600

31412 **#272, 1895, 8c Violet Brown XF-S 95 PSE.** (Original Gum - Never Hinged). Fantastic eye-appeal, the brightest white paper imaginable, almost jumbo margins evenly balanced, finest violet brown color, spectacular impression. Very fresh. Extremely Fine to Superb PSE - Encapsulated. (SMQ $2,450; this being one of 8 attaining this grade as of 10/08, with only 3 graded higher).

Estimate: $2,450+

Minimum Bid: $1,225

31413 **#272, 1895, 8c Violet Brown, XF-S 95; PSE.** (Original Gum - Never Hinged). An outstanding mint single, fresh as the day printed, exceptionally well centered with generous and balanced margins. Extremely Fine to Superb; 2006 PSE - Graded Certificate. (SMQ $2,450; this being one of 8 attaining this grade as of 10/08, with only 3 graded higher).

Estimate: $2,500+

Minimum Bid: $1,250

31414 **#276, 1895, $1 Black, VF-XF 85 PSE.** (Original Gum - Never Hinged). Incredible impression gives the portrait a cameo appearance. Bold, jet black color on fresh white paper. Plate #76. Very Fine to Extremely Fine; 2007 PSE - Graded Certificate. (SMQ $3,550; this being one of 4 attaining this grade as of 10/08, with only 2 graded higher).

Estimate: $3,500+

Minimum Bid: $1,750

31415 **#277a, 1895, $2 Dark Blue, SUP 98 PSE.** (Original Gum - Previously Hinged). Perfectly centered, intense and radiant, with a deeply etched impression giving the portrait of Madison an almost life-like appearance, fresh original gum showing only light evidence of previous hinging. Superb and virtually unrivalled in quality. 2008 PSE - Graded Certificate. (SMQ $7,300; this being one of 3 attaining this grade as of 10/08, with *none* graded higher).

Estimate: $7,000+

Minimum Bid: $3,500

31416 **#277a, 1895, $2 Dark Blue, XF 90 PSE.** (Original Gum - Hinged). Fantastic example, rich dark blue color on fresh paper, ample to large margins. Richly detailed impression, simply stunning for a 90. Heavy hinge markings at top, small hinge remnant and pencil notation on the back. Extremely Fine; 2007 PSE - Graded Certificate,1985 PF Certificate. (SMQ $2,350; this being one of 5 attaining this grade as of 10/08, with only 5 graded higher).

Estimate: $2,500+

Minimum Bid: $1,250

31417 **#277a, 1895, $2 Dark Blue, VF-XF 85 PSE.** (Original Gum - Previously Hinged). Choice example of the Dark Blue shade. Rich color, strong impression on fresh white paper. A very strong '85' in our opinion. Light hinge mark only. Very Fine to Extremely Fine; 2008 PSE - Graded Certificate. (SMQ $1650; this being one of 5 attaining this grade as of 10/08, with 10 graded higher).

Estimate: $1,600+

Minimum Bid: $800

31418 **#277, 1895, $2 Bright Blue, XF-S 95 PSE.** (Used). Moderate cancel, very well-centered. Extremely Fine to Superb PSE - Encapsulated. (SMQ $3300; this being one of 3 attaining this grade as of 10/08, with only 1 graded higher).

Estimate: $2,750+

Minimum Bid: $1,375

31419 **#278, 1895, $5 Dark Green, XF-S 95 PSE.** (Original Gum - Previously Hinged). A sensational mint example of this difficult high value, especially fresh and vibrant, splendidly centered within generous well balanced margins. Original gum showing only the barest traces of hinging, and even then only under close examination, Extremely Fine to Superb gem, nearly unrivalled in quality. PSE - Encapsulated. (SMQ $7,450; this being one of 5 attaining this grade as of 10/08, with only 3 graded higher).

Estimate: $7,000+

Minimum Bid: $3,500

31420 **#278, 1895, $5 Dark Green XF-S 95 PSE.** (Original Gum - Previously Hinged). A dazzling mint single sporting precision centering, intense rich color and finely etched impression of white paper, original gum showing a very slight light discoloration from previous hinging, (not visible from front). Extremely Fine to Superb; PSE - Encapsulated. (SMQ $7,450; this being one of 5 attaining this grade as of 10/08, with only 3 graded higher).

Estimate: $7,000+

Minimum Bid: $3,500

31421 **#278, 1895, $5 Dark Green, XF 90 PSE.** (Original Gum - Hinged). Deep dark green color, razor sharp impression, very strong 90. Small hinge remnant. Extremely Fine; 2008 PSE - Graded Certificate, 2007 PF Certificate. (SMQ $4,800; this being one of 10 attaining this grade as of 10/08, with only 8 graded higher).

Estimate: $5,000+

Minimum Bid: $2,500

31422 **#278, 1895, $5 Dark Green, VF 80 PSE.** (Original Gum - Previously Hinged). Well centered mint single, deep rich color, original gum, with only light traces of previous hinging, Very Fine; PSE - Encapsulated. (SMQ $2,400; this being one of 5 attaining this grade as of 10/08, with 22 graded higher).

Estimate: $2,000+

Minimum Bid: $1,000

31423 **#278, 1895, $5 Dark Green, VF 80 PSE.** (Original Gum - Hinged). Hinge mark at top, very small hinge remnant at right side center. Very Fine PSE - Encapsulated. (SMQ $2,400; this being one of 5 attaining this grade as of 10/08, with 22 graded higher).

Estimate: $1,500+

Minimum Bid: $750

31424 **#278, 1895, $5 Dark Green, XF 90 PSE.** (Used). Elegant example, rich and deep color, large margins for this issue, black double oval New York registry cancel, pencil notion on back. Extremely Fine PSE - Encapsulated. (SMQ $1,300; this being one of 15 attaining this grade as of 10/08, with only 3 graded higher).

Estimate: $1,200+

Minimum Bid: $600

31425 **#278, 1895, $5 Dark Green, VF-XF 85 PSE.** (Used). Intense color and impression, used with black New York registry cancel. Very Fine to Extremely Fine; 2005 PSE - Graded Certificate. (SMQ $900; this being one of 6 attaining this grade as of 10/08, with 18 graded higher).

Estimate: $750+

Minimum Bid: $375

1897-1903 BUREAU ISSUES

31426 **#279, 1898, 1c Deep Green, SUP 98 PSE.** (Original Gum - Never Hinged). The whitest of white paper embossed with deep emerald green design, among the finest of this issue hands down, spectacular example for someone, previously hinged in the selvage only. (Stamp is NH). Superb; 2006 PSE - Graded Certificate.
(SMQ $1,750; this being one of 8 attaining this grade as of 10/08, with none graded higher).

Estimate: $2,000+

Minimum Bid: $1,000

31427 **#279, 1898, 1c Deep Green, SUP 98 PSE.** (Original Gum - Never Hinged). Marvelous example, fresh in every respect. Superb PSE - Encapsulated. (SMQ $1,750; this being one of 8 attaining this grade as of 10/08, with none graded higher).
Estimate: $1,750+
Minimum Bid: $875

31429 **#281, 1898, 5c Dark Blue, SUP 98 PSE.** (Used). Choice condition. Bold color, unobtrusive cancel. Superb; 2007 PSE - Graded Certificate. (SMQ $900; this being one of 2 attaining this grade as of 10/08, with none graded higher).
Estimate: $2,000+
Minimum Bid: $1,000

31428 **#280, 1898, 4c Rose Brown, XF-S 95 PSE.** (Original Gum - Never Hinged). Post office fresh beauty, extremely well centered with accurate rose brown color. Extremely Fine to Superb PSE - Encapsulated. (SMQ $1150; this being one of 4 attaining this grade as of 10/08, with none graded higher).
Estimate: $1,150+
Minimum Bid: $575

31430 **#284, 1898, 15c Olive Green, XF-S 95 PSE.** (Used). Phenomenal. precisely centered, with a warm pastel-like glow, and an especially light non-obtrusive cancel. Extremely Fine to Superb, 2008 PSE - Graded Certificate. (SMQ $400; this being one of 2 attaining this grade as of 10/08, with *none* graded higher).
Estimate: $500+
Minimum Bid: $250

End of Session One

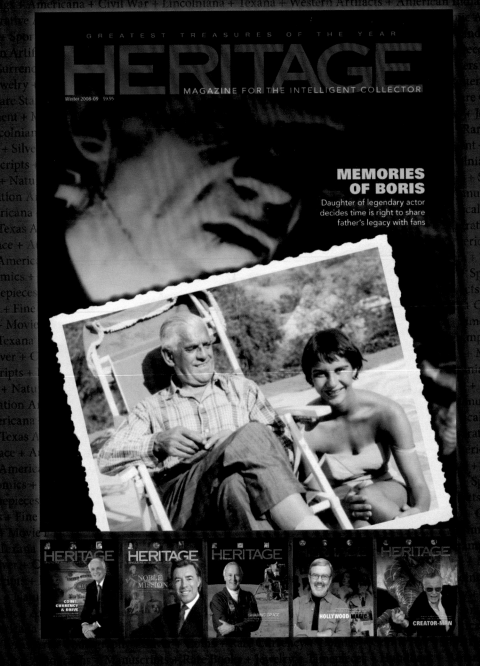

SESSION TWO

Floor, Telephone, Heritage Live!™, Internet, Fax, and Mail Signature® Auction #1106
Thursday, February 5, 2009, 4:00 PM CT • Dallas, Texas • Lots 31431-31838

A 19.5% Buyer's Premium ($9 minimum) Will Be Added To All Lots
You can now view full-color images and bid via the Internet at the Heritage website: HA.com/Stamps

1898 TRANS-MISSISSIPPI EXPOSITION ISSUE

31431 **#285, 1898, 1c Dark Yellow Green, SUP 98 PSE.** (Original Gum - Never Hinged). Marquette on the Mississippi. An astounding mint single, rich and fresh, impeccably centered within generous well balanced margins. Super fresh. Especially scarce this choice. 2008 PSE - Graded Certificate. (SMQ $3,450; this being one of 9 attaining this grade as of 10/08, with none graded higher).
Estimate: $3,500+
Minimum Bid: $1,750

31432 **#285, 1898, 1c Dark Yellow Green, XF-S 95 PSE.** (Original Gum - Never Hinged). Marquette on the Mississippi. Deep Rich color. Extremely Fine to Superb PSE - Encapsulated. (SMQ $1,050; this being one of 29 attaining this grade as of 10/08, with 14 graded higher).
Estimate: $1,000+
Minimum Bid: $500

31433 **#285, 1898, 1c Dark Yellow Green, XF-S 95 PSE.** (Original Gum - Never Hinged). Marquette on the Mississippi. Absolutely beautiful example, wonderful impression and rich color. Extremely Fine to Superb PSE - Encapsulated. (SMQ $1,050; this being one of 29 attaining this grade as of 10/08, with 14 graded higher).
Estimate: $1,050+
Minimum Bid: $525

31434 **#285, 1898, 1c Dark Yellow Green, XF-S 95 PSE.** (Used). Marquette on the Mississippi. Attractive copy, good color and face-free cancel. Extremely Fine to Superb; 2008 PSE - Graded Certificate. (SMQ $245; this being one of 6 attaining this grade as of 10/08, with only 4 graded higher).
Estimate: $450+
Minimum Bid: $225

31435 **#286, 1898, 2c Copper Red, XF-S 95 PSE.** (Original Gum - Never Hinged). Farming in the West. Magnificent color and impression, rich looking example. Post Office Fresh. Extremely Fine to Superb PSE - Encapsulated. (SMQ $1,050; this being one of 29 attaining this grade as of 10/08, with only 8 graded higher).

Estimate: $900+

Minimum Bid: $450

31436 **#286, 1898, 2c Copper Red, XF-S 95 PSE.** (Original Gum - Never Hinged). Farming in the West. Exciting example of this copper red beauty. Extremely Fine to Superb; 2007 PSE - Graded Certificate. (SMQ $1,050; this being one of 29 attaining this grade as of 10/08, with only 8 graded higher).

Estimate: $900+

Minimum Bid: $450

31437 **#287, 1898, 4c Orange, XF-S 95; PSE.** (Original Gum - Never Hinged). Indian Hunting Buffalo. Remarkably striking in every detail, a spectacular mint single that is precisely centered within generous well balanced margins, with full even perforations all around, strikingly bright and vibrant color and vivid impression on fresh white paper. Immaculate gum. Extremely Fine to Superb; 2006 PSE - Graded Certificate.
(SMQ $4,450; this being one of 24 attaining this grade as of 10/08, with only 6 graded higher).

Estimate: $4,000+

Minimum Bid: $2,000

31438 **#287, 1898, 4c Orange, XF-S 95 PSE.** (Original Gum - Never Hinged). Indian Hunting Buffalo. An eye-appealing beauty for the connoisseur. Brilliant orange color, very large margins, crisp impression. Extremely Fine to Superb PSE - Encapsulated. (SMQ $4,450; this being one of 24 attaining this grade as of 10/08, with only 6 graded higher).

Estimate: $4,000+

Minimum Bid: $2,000

31439 **#287, 1898, 4c Orange, VF-XF 85 PSE.** (Original Gum - Never Hinged). Indian Hunting Buffalo Bold and Rich color, sparkling fresh gum. Very Fine to Extremely Fine; 2005 PSE - Graded Certificate. (SMQ $700; this being one of 13 attaining this grade as of 10/08, with 61 graded higher).

Estimate: $700+

Minimum Bid: $350

31440 **#287, 1898, 4c Orange, XF 90J PSE.** (Used). Indian Hunting Buffalo. Bold and bright color on nice white paper. Mild cancel. A reasonably strong 90 in our opinion, very large margins for issue. Extremely Fine; 2005 PSE - Graded Certificate. (this being one of 1 attaining this grade as of 10/08, with only 2 graded higher).

Estimate: $400+

Minimum Bid: $200

31441 #288, 1898, 5c Dull Blue, XF-S 95; PSE. (Original Gum - Never Hinged). Fremont on the Rocky Mountains. A phenomenal mint single, gloriously deep rich color and proof-like impression on bright white paper. Precisely centered within generous well balanced margins, pristine gum. Extremely Fine to Superb; 2006 PSE - Graded Certificate. (SMQ $4,450; this being one of 20 attaining this grade as of 10/08, with only 4 graded higher).

Estimate: $4,000+

Minimum Bid: $2,000

31442 #288, 1898, 5c Dull Blue, XF-S 95 PSE. (Original Gum - Never Hinged). Fremont on the Rocky Mountains. Essentially perfect, rich color with a razor sharp impression, beautifully centered. Extremely Fine to Superb PSE - Encapsulated. (SMQ $4,450; this being one of 20 attaining this grade as of 10/08, with only 4 graded higher).

Estimate: $4,000+

Minimum Bid: $2,000

31443 #288, 1898, 5c Dull Blue, XF 90; PSE. (Original Gum - Never Hinged). Fremont on the Rocky Mountains. An exceptional example of this popular issue, with rich vibrant color and proof-like impression on bright paper. Immaculate gum. Extremely Fine PSE - Encapsulated. (SMQ $1,250; this being one of 23 attaining this grade as of 10/08, with 29 graded higher).

Estimate: $1,000+

Minimum Bid: $500

31444 #288, 1898, 5c Dull Blue, XF 90 PSE. (Original Gum - Never Hinged). Fremont on the Rocky Mountains. Dark bright blue example of dull blue issue, white crisp paper. Fresh gum. Extremely Fine; 2006 PSE - Graded Certificate. (SMQ $1,250; this being one of 23 attaining this grade as of 10/08, with 29 graded higher).

Estimate: $1,000+

Minimum Bid: $500

31445 #288, 1898, 5c Dull Blue, VF-XF 85 PSE. (Original Gum - Never Hinged). Fremont on the Rocky Mountains. Blazing rich color and impression. Very strong eye appeal and freshness. Very Fine to Extremely Fine; 2005 PSE - Graded Certificate. Also, 2008 PF Certificate Graded VF-XF 85. (SMQ $700; this being one of 16 attaining this grade as of 10/08, with 53 graded higher)..

Estimate: $700+

Minimum Bid: $350

31446 #289, 1898, 8c Violet Brown, VF-XF 85 PSE. (Original Gum - Never Hinged). Troops Guarding Train. Sharply detailed impression with Rich Color on fresh white paper. Very Fine to Extremely Fine; 2005 PSE - Graded Certificate. (SMQ $1,100; this being one of 16 attaining this grade as of 10/08, with 16 graded higher).

Estimate: $1,000+

Minimum Bid: $500

31447 **#289, 1898, 8c Violet Brown, VF-XF 85 PSE.** (Original Gum - Never Hinged). Troops Guarding Train. Rich violet brown color with sharp impression. Very Fine to Extremely Fine; 2008 PSE - Graded Certificate. (SMQ $1,100; this being one of 16 attaining this grade as of 10/08, with 16 graded higher).

Estimate: $900+

Minimum Bid: $450

31448 **#289, 1898, 8c Violet Brown, VF 80 PSE.** (Original Gum - Never Hinged). Troops Guarding Train. Choice left bottom corner margin example with vivid color. Post Office Fresh. Very Fine; 2008 PSE - Graded Certificate. (SMQ $600; this being one of 9 attaining this grade as of 10/08, with 32 graded higher).

Estimate: $500+

Minimum Bid: $250

31449 **#289, 1898, 8c Violet Brown, XF-S 95 PSE.** (Used). Troops Guarding Train. Tough stamp. Not an easy stamp in this grade used. Extremely Fine to Superb; 2008 PSE - Graded Certificate. (SMQ $600; this being one of 3 attaining this grade as of 10/08, with only 2 graded higher).

Estimate: $600+

Minimum Bid: $300

31450 **#290, 1898, 10c Gray Violet, VF-XF 85 PSE.** (Original Gum - Never Hinged). Hardships of Emigration. Wonderfully fresh, front and back. Rich color and impression. Very Fine to Extremely Fine; 2008 PSE - Graded Certificate. Also, 2007 PF VFXF85 Certificate. (SMQ $980; this being one of 11 attaining this grade as of 10/08, with 46 graded higher).

Estimate: $1,000+

Minimum Bid: $500

31451 **#291, 1898, 50c Sage Green, XF-S 95 PSE.** (Original Gum - Previously Hinged). Western Mining Prospector. A captivatingly bright and fresh mint single, concisely centered, original gum with light traces of previous hinging at the top center only. Extremely Fine to Superb; PSE - Encapsulated. (SMQ $2,350; this being one of 10 attaining this grade as of 10/08, with only 1 graded higher).

Estimate: $2,000+

Minimum Bid: $1,000

31452 **#291, 1898, 50c Sage Green, VF 80 PSE.** (Original Gum - Never Hinged). Western Mining Prospectors. Very pretty color and impression. Super Fresh Gum. Very Fine; 2005 PSE - Graded Certificate. Also, 2004 PF Ungraded Certificate.
(SMQ $2,200; this being one of 5 attaining this grade as of 10/08, with 10 graded higher).

Estimate: $2,000+

Minimum Bid: $1,000

31453 **#291, 1898, 50c Sage Green, VF-XF 85 PSE.** (Used). Western Mining Prospectors. Black New York double oval REGISTRY and blue crayon cancels. Very Fine to Extremely Fine; 2005 PSE - Graded Certificate. Also, 2006 PF Certificate graded VF-XF 85. (SMQ $300; this being one of 5 attaining this grade as of 10/08, with 22 graded higher).

Estimate: $400+

Minimum Bid: $200

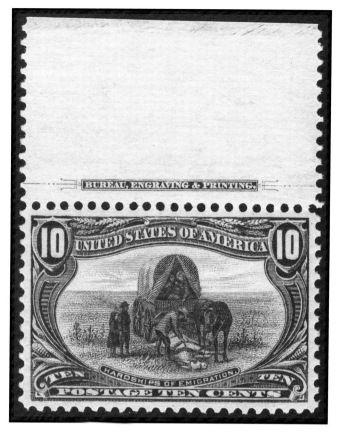

31454 **#290, 1898, 10c Gray Violet, XF-S 95 PSE.** (Original Gum - Never Hinged). Hardships of Emigration. Richly detailed and strong impression, very fresh example. Extremely Fine to Superb PSE - Encapsulated. (SMQ $6,150; this being one of 15 attaining this grade as of 10/08, with only 5 graded higher).

Estimate: $5,500+

Minimum Bid: $2,750

31455 **#290, 1898, 10c Gray Violet, XF-S 95; PSE.** (Original Gum - Never Hinged). Hardships of Emigration. An awe inspiring mint top sheet margin single with full imprint, flawlessly centered with full even perforations all around, post office fresh in every detail. Extremely Fine to Superb; 2007 PSE - Graded Certificate.
(SMQ $6,150; this being one of 15 attaining this grade as of 10/08, with only 5 graded higher).

Estimate: $6,000+

Minimum Bid: $3,000

31456 **#290, 1898, 10c Gray Violet, VF 80 PSE.** (Original Gum - Never Hinged). Hardships of Emigration. Bright color and fresh, neat overall appearance. Very Fine; 2005 PSE - Graded Certificate. (SMQ $540; this being one of 8 attaining this grade as of 10/08, with 57 graded higher).

Estimate: $500+

Minimum Bid: $250

31457 **#292, 1898, $1 Black, XF-S 95 PSE.** (Original Gum - Previously Hinged). Cattle in the Storm. Darkest black color imaginable, breathtaking example, at first glance appears never hinged, so very lightly hinged only. Extremely Fine to Superb; 2004 PSE - Graded Certificate. (SMQ $4,150; this being one of 18 attaining this grade as of 10/08, with only 2 graded higher).

Estimate: $3,800+

Minimum Bid: $1,900

CONDITION RARITY - NEVER HINGED

31458 **#292, 1898, $1 Black. XF 90 PSE.** (Original Gum - Never Hinged). Cattle in the Storm. Distinctive mint example. Razor sharp impression, Jet Black color. Post Office Fresh. One of the most popular USA Commemoratives of all time. Extremely Fine PSE - Encapsulated. (SMQ $11,400; this being one of 8 attaining this grade as of 10/08, with only 6 graded higher).

Estimate: $15,000+

Minimum Bid: $7,500

31459 #292, 1898, $1 Black, XF 90 PF. (Original Gum - Never Hinged). Cattle in the Storm. A magnificently fresh stamp, uncharacteristically large and precisely centered, both gloriously rich and intense, with an overall strong proof-like quality, sheet guide line across top perfs. Flawless full original gum. Extremely Fine; 2007 PF Graded Certificate.

Estimate: $11,000+

Minimum Bid: $5,500

31460 #292, 1898, $1 Black, VF-XF 85 PSE. (Original Gum - Never Hinged). Cattle in the Storm. Extremely fresh example with vibrant black color, the most sought after design of the Trans-Mississippi Exposition Issue. Guideline along top perfs. Very Fine to Extremely Fine; 2007 PSE - Graded Certificate. (SMQ $6,450; this being one of 5 attaining this grade as of 10/08, with 14 graded higher).

Estimate: $6,500+

Minimum Bid: $3,250

31461 **#292, 1898, $1 Black, VF-XF 85 PSE.** (Original Gum - Never Hinged). Cattle in the Storm. Jet Black Color, vivid impression. Fresh. Very Fine to Extremely Fine; 2007 PSE - Graded Certificate. Also, 2007 PF Certificate Graded VF 85 (SMQ $6,450; this being one of 5 attaining this grade as of 10/08, with 14 graded higher).

Estimate: $6,000+

Minimum Bid: $3,000

31462 **#292, 1898, $1 Black, VF-XF 85 PSE.** (Original Gum - Previously Hinged). Cattle in the Storm. Wonderfully centered fresh example with marvelous eye-appeal, very well-centered for an 85, obvious 5 point reduction for guide line. Light traces of a hinge mark. Very Fine to Extremely Fine; 2005 PSE - Graded Certificate. (SMQ $1,600; this being one of 25 attaining this grade as of 10/08, with only 39 graded higher).

Estimate: $1,500+

Minimum Bid: $750

31463 **#292, 1898, $1 Black, F-VF 75 PSE.** (Original Gum - Previously Hinged). Cattle in the Storm. Fabulous black color on white paper, attractive and fresh. Lightly hinged with no remnant. Fine to Very Fine PSE - Graded Certificate. (this being one of 12 attaining this grade as of 10/08, with 78 graded higher).

Estimate: $700+

Minimum Bid: $350

31464 **#292, 1898, $1 Black.** (Original Gum - Never Hinged). Cattle in the Storm. An attractive mint single, rich vibrant color and detailed impression, fresh original gum. Fine. 2008 PF Certificate. (Scott $3,750).

Estimate: $1,700+

Minimum Bid: $1,000

31465 **#292, 1898, $1 Black, XF 90 PSE.** (Used). Cattle in the Storm. Extremely Fine; 2008 PSE - Graded Certificate. (SMQ $1,500; this being one of 8 attaining this grade as of 10/08, with only 6 graded higher).

Estimate: $1,200+

Minimum Bid: $600

31466 **#292, 1898, $1 Black, VF-XF 85 PSE.** (Used). Cattle in the Storm. Black New York double oval REGISTRY cancel. Very Fine to Extremely Fine; 2006 PSE - Graded Certificate. (SMQ $950; this being one of 10 attaining this grade as of 10/08, with 14 graded higher).

Estimate: $700+

Minimum Bid: $350

31467 **#292, 1898, $1 Black, VF 80 PSE.** (Used). Cattle in the Storm. Extremely light black cancel on black stamp, attractive, clean back. Very Fine PSE - Graded Certificate. (SMQ $650; this being one of 8 attaining this grade as of 10/08, with 24 graded higher).

Estimate: $550+

Minimum Bid: $275

 A 19.5% Buyer's Premium ($9 min.) Applies To All Lots

31468 **#293, 1898, $2 Orange Brown, XF-S 95 PSE.** (Original Gum - Previously Hinged). Mississippi River Bridge. Exceptional Trans-Mississippi Exposition Issue, key to the series. Warm orange brown. Elegant example. Light outline of hinge mark with no remnant. Extremely Fine to Superb PSE - Graded Certificate. (SMQ $7,050; this being one of 10 attaining this grade as of 10/08, with none graded higher).

Estimate: $6,500+

Minimum Bid: $3,250

31469 **#293, 1898, $2 Orange Brown, XF-S 95 PSE.** (Original Gum - Hinged). Mississippi River Bridge. A lovely copy. Wide paper (old style) hinge remnant. Brilliant color and strong impression. Extremely Fine to Superb PSE - Encapsulated. (SMQ $7,050; this being one of 10 attaining this grade as of 10/08, with *none* graded higher).

Estimate: $6,000+

Minimum Bid: $3,000

31470 **#293, 1898, $2 Orange Brown, XF 90 PSE.** (Original Gum - Previously Hinged). Mississippi River Bridge. Extremely fresh example with a rich orange brown color. Well-centered beauty. Light hinge marks at the top. Extremely Fine; 2008 PSE - Graded Certificate, 2007 PF Certificate. (SMQ $3,550; this being one of 13 attaining this grade as of 10/08, with 11 graded higher).

Estimate: $4,400+

Minimum Bid: $2,200

31471 **#293, 1898, $2 Orange Brown, XF 90 PSE.** (No Gum). Mississippi River Bridge. Large margins for issue, quite well-centered for a 90. Extremely Fine; 2008 PSE - Graded Certificate. (SMQ $1,450; this being one of 1 attaining this grade as of 10/08, with only 2 graded higher).

Estimate: $1,500+

Minimum Bid: $750

31472 **#293, 1898, $2 Orange Brown, VF-XF 85 PF.** (Original Gum - Previously Hinged). Mississippi River Bridge. Choice copy. Sweet color and sharp impression. Large margins for issue, Extremely light hinge mark on very fresh appearing gum. Very Fine to Extremely Fine; 2007 PF Graded Certificate..

Estimate: $3,700+

Minimum Bid: $1,850

31473 **#293, 1898, $2 Orange Brown VF 80 PSE.** (Original Gum - Never Hinged). Mississippi River Bridge. Fresh. Very Fine; 2007 PSE - Graded Certificate.
(SMQ $6,600; this being one of 3 attaining this grade as of 10/08, with only 7 graded higher) Also, PF Certificate Graded VF 80.
Estimate: $6,000+
Minimum Bid: $3,000

31476 **#293, 1898, $2 Orange Brown, VF 80 PSE.** (Used). Mississippi River Bridge. Extremely light cancel. Rich color. Very Fine PSE - Graded Certificate. Also, 2002 PF Certificate. (SMQ $1,100; this being one of 2 attaining this grade as of 10/08, with 11 graded higher).
Estimate: $1,000+
Minimum Bid: $500

31478 **#294, 1901, 1c Green And Black, XF-S 95 PSE.** (Original Gum - Never Hinged). Fast Lake Navigation. Top margin plate number single; Plate#1179. Extremely Fine to Superb; 2008 PSE - Graded Certificate. (SMQ $445; this being one of 26 attaining this grade as of 10/08, with 15 graded higher).
Estimate: $400+
Minimum Bid: $200

31474 **#293, 1898, $2 Orange Brown, VF 80 PSE.** (Original Gum - Previously Hinged). Mississippi River Bridge. Strong color, detailed impression. Fresh gum with small portion of prior hinge remnant only. Very Fine PSE - Graded Certificate.
(SMQ $2,200; this being one of 6 attaining this grade as of 10/08, with 34 graded higher).
Estimate: $2,200+
Minimum Bid: $1,100

31477 **#293, 1898, $2 Orange Brown, F-VF 75 PSE.** (Used). Mississippi River Bridge. Strong color, mild cancel. Fine to Very Fine PSE - Encapsulated. (this being one of 3 attaining this grade as of 10/08, with 13 graded higher).
Estimate: $700+
Minimum Bid: $350

31479 **#294, 1901, 1c Green XF-S 95 PSE.** (Original Gum - Never Hinged). Fast Lake Navigation. Bright, fresh, and well centered. Extremely Fine to Superb; 2007 PSE - Graded Certificate. (SMQ $445; this being one of 26 attaining this grade as of 10/08, with 15 graded higher).
Estimate: $400+
Minimum Bid: $200

31475 **#293, 1898, $2 Orange Brown.** (Original Gum - Never Hinged). Mississippi River Bridge. Lovely mint example with crisp impression, pristine gum, scarce never hinged. Fine; 2007 PSE Certificate. (Scott $6,500).
Estimate: $3,500+
Minimum Bid: $1,750

31480 #295, 1901, 2c Carmine And Black, SUP 98 PSE. (Original Gum - Never Hinged). Empire State Express. Absolutely perfect, giant even margins, fresh color and sharply detailed impression. Superb; 2008 PSE - Graded Certificate. (SMQ $1,300; this being one of 18 attaining this grade as of 10/08, with only 5 graded higher).

Estimate: $1,200+
Minimum Bid: $600

TOP OF THE POP FOR USED

31481 #295, 1901, 2c Carmine And Black, SUP 98 PSE. (Used). Empire State Express. Undervalued in high grade used, highest graded to date, sensational with a black straight line machine cancel. Superb; 2008 PSE - Graded Certificate. (SMQ $660; this being one of 1 attaining this grade as of 10/08, with *none* graded higher).

Estimate: $750+
Minimum Bid: $375

RARE AND SOUGHT AFTER INVERT
THIS EXAMPLE WITH EXCELLENT GUM

31482 #295a, 1901, 2c Carmine and Black, Inverted Center, F 70 PSE. (Original Gum - Previously Hinged). Fast Express. Inverted Center. Approximately 155 unused copies exist. The vast majority have disturbed gum, this example with very fresh and shiny gum, and only a trivial light line at the top from prior hinging. Fine PSE - Encapsulated. (SMQ $44,700; this being one of 1 attaining this grade as of 10/08, with only 4 graded higher).

Estimate: $70,000+

Minimum Bid: $35,000

31484 #296, 1901, 4c Deep Red Brown and Black, XF-S 95 PSE. (Original Gum - Never Hinged). Electric Automobile in Washington. Perfect balanced margins, rich warm color, unblemished front and back. Extremely Fine to Superb PSE - Encapsulated.

(SMQ $1,550; this being one of 39 attaining this grade as of 10/08, with only 4 graded higher).

Estimate: $1,500+

Minimum Bid: $750

31483 #296, 1901, 4c Deep Red Brown And Black, XF-S 95J PSE. (Original Gum - Never Hinged). Electric Automobile in Washington. Extraordinarily rare example in high grade, jumbo margins on all sides, bottom imprint example with etched impression and bright color, one of the finest in existence. Extremely Fine to Superb PSE - Graded Certificate. (this being one of 2 attaining this grade as of 10/08, with only 3 graded higher).

Estimate: $2,500+

Minimum Bid: $1,250

31485 #296, 1901, 4c Deep Red Brown And Black, XF-S 95 PSE. (Original Gum - Never Hinged). Electric Automobile in Washington. Pristine example of this wonderful issue, large margins for this issue with lovely color. Fresh. Extremely Fine to Superb PSE - Encapsulated. SMQ $1,550; this being one of 39 attaining this grade as of 10/08, with only 4 graded higher).

Estimate: $1,500+

Minimum Bid: $750

ONE OF THE RAREST INVERTS

31486 #296a, 1901, 4c, Deep Red Brown and Black, Center Inverted. (Original Gum - Previously Hinged). Electric Automobile in Washington. The 4c Pan-American Invert is a special printing. Almost all have partial or disturbed gum. This copy, freshly certified by PSE has full original undisturbed gum, with only a light hinge mark. Centered FINE, with rich and bold deep red brown color on reasonably fresh white paper, with one nibbed perforation at top center left. Further evidence of the scarcity and demand for this stamp, is the 100% increase in value (from $35,000 2008) in the 2009 Scott Specialized Catalog. Fine; 2008 PSE Certificate. (Scott $70000).

Estimate: $45,000+
Minimum Bid: $22,500

Please visit HA.com to view other collectibles auctions. *A 19.5% Buyer's Premium ($9 min.) Applies To All Lots*

31487 **#296Sa, 1901, 4c Deep Red Brown And Black.** (Disturbed Original Gum). Electric Automobile in Washington. Exceedingly rare Pan-American, center inverted, specimen overprint. Rich deep red color with a dark black inverted center, perforations touch into the design at the bottom only, some disturbed original gum typical for the issue. Light diagonal crease at the center, light purple specimen overprint, a must for the invert collector. Very Good; 2008 PSE Certificate. (Scott $10,000).

Estimate: $6,500+

Minimum Bid: $3,250

"Knock-out" Quality

31488 **#297, 1901, 5c Ultramarine, SUP 98 PSE.** (Original Gum - Never Hinged). Bridge at Niagara Falls. Knock out gorgeous example, highest graded with none higher. Typically very tightly margined, this is probably the toughest of the series to find well-centered, and with large margins. Superb; 2007 PSE - Graded Certificate. (SMQ $5,000; this being one of 6 attaining this grade as of 10/08, with none graded higher).

Estimate: $5,000+

Minimum Bid: $2,500

31489 **#297, 1901, 5c Ultramarine, XF-S 95 PSE.** (Original Gum - Never Hinged). Bridge at Niagara Falls. Bright and Fresh. Nearly perfect margins on all sides. Extremely Fine to Superb PSE - Graded Certificate. (SMQ $1,600; this being one of 19 attaining this grade as of 10/08, with only 7 graded higher).

Estimate: $1,400+

Minimum Bid: $700

31490 **#297, 1901, 5c Ultramarine XF 90 PSE.** (Original Gum - Never Hinged). Bridge at Niagara Falls. Top plate number single (and printer marks) in a rich ultramarine color. Extremely Fine; 2007 PSE - Graded Certificate. (SMQ $530; this being one of 21 attaining this grade as of 10/08, with 27 graded higher).

Estimate: $600+

Minimum Bid: $300

31491 **#297, 1901, 5c Ultramarine And Black, XF 90 PSE.** (Original Gum - Never Hinged). Bridge at Niagara Falls. Bold and Bright Color. Extremely Fine PSE - Encapsulated. (SMQ $530; this being one of 21 attaining this grade as of 10/08, with 27 graded higher).

Estimate: $500+

Minimum Bid: $250

31492 **#297, 1901, 5c Ultramarine & Black, XF 90 PF.** (Original Gum - Never Hinged). Bridge at Niagara falls. Rich shade and detailed impression. Post Office Fresh. Not an easy stamp this nice. Extremely Fine; 2007 PF Graded Certificate.

Estimate: $500+

Minimum Bid: $250

31493 **#298, 1901, 8c Brown Violet, & Black, XF-S 95 PSE.** (Original Gum - Never Hinged). Canal Locks at Sault Ste. Marie. Absolutely gorgeous example with choice centering, desirable quality. Extremely Fine to Superb; 2004 PSE - Graded Certificate. (SMQ $1,850; this being one of 28 attaining this grade as of 10/08, with only 6 graded higher).

Estimate: $1,500+

Minimum Bid: $750

31494 **#298, 1901, 8c Brown Violet And Black, XF-S 95 PSE.** (Original Gum - Never Hinged). Canal Locks at Sault Ste. Marie. Deeply engraved impression with picture perfect color, Post Office Fresh. Extremely Fine to Superb; 2005 PSE - Graded Certificate. (SMQ $1,850; this being one of 28 attaining this grade as of 10/08, with only 6 graded higher).

Estimate: $1,500+

Minimum Bid: $750

31495 **#299, 1901, 10c Yellow Brown And Black, SUP 98 PSE.** (Original Gum - Previously Hinged). Fast Ocean Navigation. Pleasant color, single hinge remnant. Superb PSE - Encapsulated. (SMQ $710; this being one of 2 attaining this grade as of 10/08, with none graded higher).

Estimate: $700+

Minimum Bid: $350

31496 **#299, 1901, 10c Yellow Brown And Black XF-S 95 PSE.** (Original Gum - Never Hinged). Fast Ocean Navigation. Premium mint quality throughout. Sharp detailed impression, Post Office Fresh. Extremely Fine to Superb; 2003 PSE - Graded Certificate. (SMQ $2,500; this being one of 18 attaining this grade as of 10/08, with only 1 graded higher).

Estimate: $2,400+

Minimum Bid: $1,200

1902-08 REGULAR ISSUES

31497 **#300, 1903, 1c Blue Green, XF-S 95J; PSE.** (Original Gum - Never Hinged). A visually striking mint single, impeccably centered amidst uncommonly large margins. Post Office fresh and vibrant. Extremely Fine to Superb PSE - Encapsulated. (this being one of 7 attaining this grade as of 10/08, with only 5 graded higher).

Estimate: $700+

Minimum Bid: $350

31498 **#300, 1903, 1c Deep Green, XF-S 95J PSE.** (Original Gum - Never Hinged). Deep Color and strong impression, plus large margins for issue. The Deep Green shade not encountered all that often on this issue. Extremely Fine to Superb Jumbo; 2008 PSE - Graded Certificate. (this being one of 7 attaining this grade as of 10/08, with only 5 graded higher).

Estimate: $950+

Minimum Bid: $475

CHOICE QUALITY

31499 **#302, 1903, 3c Bright Violet, SUP 98 PSE.** (Original Gum - Never Hinged). Perfection on paper, very close to a 100 grade, centering is unimprovable from any angle, the sharp impression brings out all the design elements, perfect hue for a bright violet, unblemished front and back. Superb PSE - Encapsulated. (SMQ $4,750; this being one of 4 attaining this grade as of 10/08, with only 3 graded higher).

Estimate: $5,500+

Minimum Bid: $2,750

31500 **#302, 1903, 3c Bright Violet, XF-S 95 PSE.** (Original Gum - Never Hinged). Wonderfully centered and fresh, very strong eye appeal for the grade. Extremely Fine to Superb PSE - Encapsulated. (SMQ $1,500; this being one of 15 attaining this grade as of 10/08, with 11 graded higher).

Estimate: $1,400+

Minimum Bid: $700

31501 **#302, 1903, 3c Bright Violet, XF-S 95; PSE.** (Original Gum - Never Hinged). An impressive mint single, fresh and vibrant, sensationally centered, with flawless original gum. Extremely Fine to Superb; 2007 PSE - Graded Certificate. (SMQ $1,500; this being one of 15 attaining this grade as of 10/08, with 11 graded higher).

Estimate: $1,400+

Minimum Bid: $700

31502 **#304, 1903, 5c Blue, XF-S 95J PSE.** (Original Gum - Never Hinged). Enormous jumbo with richly saturated color and exceptional impression, masterpiece in all aspects. Extremely Fine to Superb PSE - Encapsulated.
(SMQ $1,650 ; this being one of 3 attaining this grade as of 10/08, with only 3 graded higher).

Estimate: $2,000+

Minimum Bid: $1,000

31503 **#304, 1903, 5c Blue, XF-S 95; PSE.** (Original Gum - Never Hinged). A magnificent mint single whose color is considerably deeper than typical, precisely centered on bright fresh paper, with immaculate gum. Looks like "Jumbo" upgrade candidate to us. Extremely Fine to Superb PSE - Encapsulated.
(SMQ $1,650; this being one of 18 attaining this grade as of 10/08, with only 6 graded higher).

Estimate: $1,500+

Minimum Bid: $750

31504 **#305, 1903, 6c Claret, XF-S 95 PSE.** (Original Gum - Never Hinged). Attractive scarce example, nicely centered with ample margins, rich claret color. Extremely Fine to Superb PSE - Encapsulated. (SMQ $1,850; this being one of 7 attaining this grade as of 10/08, with only 2 graded higher).

Estimate: $1,700+

Minimum Bid: $850

31505 **#306, 1902, 8c Violet Black, XF-S 95; PSE.** (Original Gum - Never Hinged). A visually captivating example, phenomenal in all aspects, from its intensely rich color and deeply etched impression, to its exceptional centering. Extremely Fine to Superb PSE - Encapsulated. (SMQ $1,250; this being one of 12 attaining this grade as of 10/08, with only 6 graded higher).

Estimate: $1,200+

Minimum Bid: $600

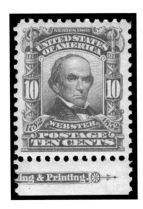

31506 **#307, 1903, 10c Pale Red Brown, XF-S 95 PSE.** (Original Gum - Never Hinged). Bottom margin imprint single with intense color and impression. Post office fresh, balanced centering, ample margins. Extremely Fine to Superb PSE - Encapsulated. (SMQ $1,850; this being one of 18 attaining this grade as of 10/08, with only 1 graded higher).

Estimate: $1,850+

Minimum Bid: $925

31507 **#307, 1903, 10c Pale Red Brown, XF-S 95 PSE.** (Original Gum - Never Hinged). Splendid well centered example, soft pastel color is very fresh, appealing. Extremely Fine to Superb PSE - Encapsulated. (SMQ $1,850; this being one of 18 attaining this grade as of 10/08, with only 1 graded higher).

Estimate: $1,600+

Minimum Bid: $800

31508 **#307, 1903, 10c Pale Red Brown, SUP 98J PSE.** (Used). Highest graded used example, virtually perfect with Jumbo margins. Light black cancel. Superb; 2008 PSE - Graded Certificate.
(this being one of 1 attaining this grade as of 10/08, with none graded higher).

Estimate: $500+

Minimum Bid: $250

31509 **#308, 1902, 13c Purple Black, SUP 98 PSE.** (Original Gum - Never Hinged). Outstanding example rarely seen in this unbelievable quality, luscious purple black color with an impression that dazzles. Superb PSE - Encapsulated. (SMQ $4,050; this being one of 5 attaining this grade as of 10/08, with only 4 graded higher).

Estimate: $4,000+

Minimum Bid: $2,000

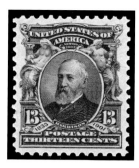

31510 **#308, 1902, 13c Purple Black, SUP 98 PF.** (Original Gum - Never Hinged). A sensational mint single boasting perfect centering within beautifully balanced margins. Full even perforations all around, strikingly warm color, a deeply etched impression, and immaculate stamp the likes of which are seldom seen. 2006 PF Graded Certificate and 2001 PF Certificate.

Estimate: $3,500+

Minimum Bid: $1,750

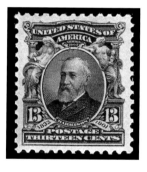

31511 **#308, 1902, 13c Purple Black, XF-S 95; PSE.** (Original Gum - Never Hinged). An outstanding mint single, fresh as the day it was printed, flawlessly centered Extremely Fine to Superb PSE - Encapsulated. (SMQ $1,200; this being one of 29 attaining this grade as of 10/08, with 15 graded higher).

Estimate: $1,000+

Minimum Bid: $500

31512 **#308, 1902, 13c Purple Black, XF-S 95 PSE.** (Original Gum - Never Hinged). Vivid prooflike impression brings out the rich color. Extremely Fine to Superb PSE - Encapsulated. (SMQ $1,200; this being one of 29 attaining this grade as of 10/08, with 15 graded higher).

Estimate: $1,000+

Minimum Bid: $500

31513 **#308, 1902, 13c Purple Black, XF-S 95; PSE.** (Original Gum - Never Hinged). An outstanding mint example, fresh as the day printed, near perfect centering. Extremely Fine to Superb PSE - Encapsulated. (SMQ $1,200; this being one of 29 attaining this grade as of 10/08, with 15 graded higher).

Estimate: $1,000+

Minimum Bid: $500

31514 **#309, 1903, 15c Olive Green, XF-S 95 PSE.** (Original Gum - Never Hinged). An absolutely gorgeous example, deep olive green color framed with precise margins, unblemished gum. Extremely Fine to Superb PSE - Encapsulated. (SMQ $5,300, this being one of 3 attaining this grade as of 10/08, with only 2 graded higher).

Estimate: $5,000+

Minimum Bid: $2,500

STUPENDOUS QUALITY

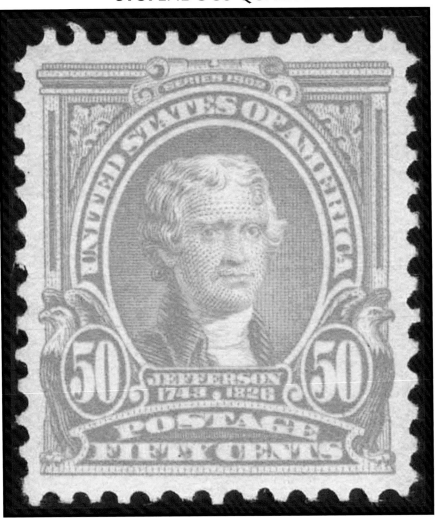

31515 **#310, 1903, 50c Orange, XF-S 95 PSE.** (Original Gum - Never Hinged). An unbelievable example of this scarce stamp. Intense shade and color, large margins for this issue. Gleaming fresh gum. Extremely Fine to Superb PSE - Encapsulated. (SMQ $11,500; this being one of 3 attaining this grade as of 10/08, with only 2 graded higher).

Estimate: $11,500+

Minimum Bid: $5,750

31516 **#310, 1903, 50c Orange, XF 90 PSE.** (Original Gum - Never Hinged). Exciting fresh example, very well centered, deep bright orange color, extremely light "310" pencil marking on gum, not mentioned by PSE. Extremely Fine PSE - Encapsulated. (SMQ $4,000; this being one of 19 attaining this grade as of 10/08, with only 6 graded higher).

Estimate: $3,500+

Minimum Bid: $1,750

STUNNING EYE APPEAL

31517 **#311, 1903, $1 Black XF-S 95 PSE.** (Original Gum - Never Hinged). One of the finest mint examples in existence. Rich dark color enhanced by the razor sharp impression. Unblemished gum. Extremely Fine to Superb PSE - Encapsulated. (SMQ $12,700; this being one of 9 attaining this grade as of 10/08, with only 2 graded higher).

Estimate: $12,700+

Minimum Bid: $6,350

31518 **#311, 1903, $1 Black, VF-XF 85 PSE.** (Original Gum - Hinged). Attractive example with great color and impression. Hinge remnant at the top. Very Fine to Extremely Fine; 2008 PSE - Graded Certificate, 1992 PF Certificate. (SMQ $870; this being one of 11 attaining this grade as of 10/08, with 31 graded higher).

Estimate: $700+

Minimum Bid: $350

31519 #311, 1903, $1 Black VF-XF 85J PSE. (Used). Very large margins, looks like the cancel may have cost the stamp 5 points, as it sure looks better centered than 85. Very Fine to Extremely Fine; 2006 PSE - Graded Certificate. (this being one of 2 attaining this grade as of 10/08, with 29 graded higher).

Estimate: $400+

Minimum Bid: $200

HIGHEST GRADED ORIGINAL GUM COPY

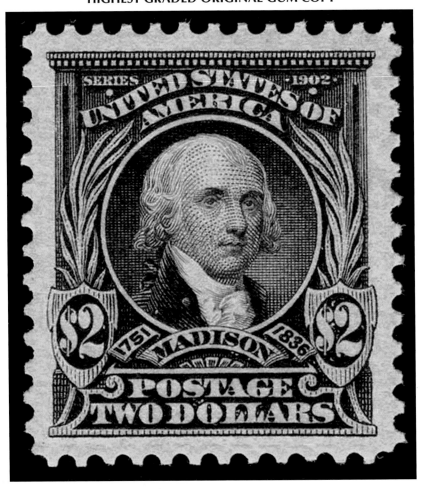

31520 #312, 1903, $2 Dark Blue, GEM 100 PSE. (Original Gum - Previously Hinged). A world class condition rarity. A phenomenal mint single of unrivalled quality, perfectly centered within enormous and flawlessly balanced margins. Full intact and even perforations all around, gloriously rich yet radiant color and razor sharp impression on fresh white paper, fresh original gum that has been previously hinged twice, once at the top, and again toward the bottom with a tiny inconsequential hinge remnant not noted on the certificate, a ravishing **Gem** that will probably not come on the market again for quite some time; 2007 PSE - Graded Certificate. Also, 1999 PF Certificate. (SMQ unvalued; this being the *unique example attaining this grade* as of 10/08, with *none graded higher*).

Estimate: $10,000+

Minimum Bid: $5,000

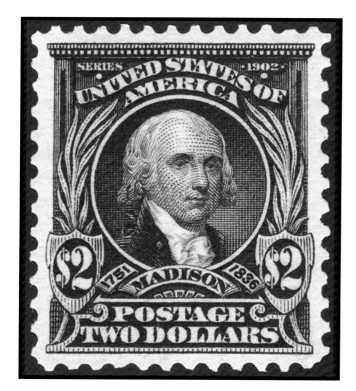

31521 #312, 1903, $2 Dark Blue, XF-S 95; PF. (Original Gum
- Never Hinged). Pure splendor. A mint example that exem-
plifies the definition of quality, flawlessly centered within completely symmetric margins, with full perforations
all around, luxuriously deep rich color and razor sharp
impression on crisp clean paper, unblemished full original
gum, an Extremely Fine to Superb condition rarity, perfect
for the gem collector; 2006 PF Graded Certificate, as well
as 1992 and 1999 PF Certificates.

Estimate: $15,000+

Minimum Bid: $7,500

31522 #312, 1903, $2 Dark Blue, XF-S 95 PSE. (Original Gum
- Previously Hinged). Intense and vivid, choice centering within evenly generous margins, original gum, light
hinge mark with no remnant, an Extremely Fine to Superb
example whose equal would be difficult to find; PSE -
Encapsulated. (SMQ $2,500; this being one of 7 attaining
this grade as of 10/08, with only 4 graded higher).

Estimate: $3,000+

Minimum Bid: $1,500

31523 #313, 1903, $5 Dark Green, XF-S 95 PSE. (Original Gum
- Previously Hinged). Gorgeously rich and vibrant, with
a deeply etched proof-like impression, full original gum
with only a very small disturbance from previous hinging. Extremely Fine to Superb; PSE - Encapsulated. (SMQ
$6,000; this being one of 13 attaining this grade as of
10/08, with only 4 graded higher).

Estimate: $5,500+

Minimum Bid: $2,750

31524 #313, 1903, $5 Dark Green, XF-S 95 PSE. (Original Gum -
Previously Hinged). Bright color and sharp impression, single hinge remnant at top center. Extremely Fine to Superb
PSE - Encapsulated. (SMQ $6,000; this being one of 13
attaining this grade as of 10/08, with only 4 graded higher).

Estimate: $5,500+

Minimum Bid: $2,750

31525 #313, 1903, $5 Dark Green, VF 80 PSE. (Original Gum - Previously Hinged). Outstanding color and impression. Very lightly hinged with no remnant. Very Fine; 2008 PSE - Graded Certificate, Also 1990 PSE Certificate. (SMQ $2,700; this being one of 14 attaining this grade as of 10/08, with 41 graded higher).

Estimate: $2,200+

Minimum Bid: $1,100

31526 #313, 1903, $5 Dark Green. (Original Gum - Previously Hinged). Exceptional dark green color and impression. Light hinge mark with no remnant. Very Fine; 2006 PSE Certificate. (Scott $3,000).

Estimate: $2,500+

Minimum Bid: $1,250

31527 #313, 1903, $5 Dark Green. (Original Gum - Previously Hinged). Intense and vibrant, well centered, previous hinge mark only, in the upper right corner. Fine to Very Fine; 2008 PSE Certificate. (Scott $3,000).

Estimate: $2,000+

Minimum Bid: $1,000

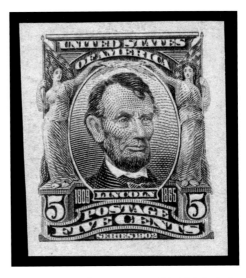

31528 #315, 1906, 5c Blue, SUP 98 PSE. (Original Gum - Never Hinged). Perfect example. Bright color and crisp white paper. Super fresh gum. Very large margins. Superb; 2008 PSE - Graded Certificate. (SMQ $820; this being one of 9 attaining this grade as of 10/08, with only 2 graded higher).

Estimate: $1,100+

Minimum Bid: $550

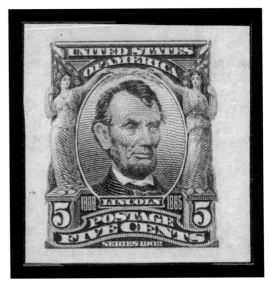

31529 #315, 1906, 5c Blue, XF-S 95J PSE. (Original Gum - Never Hinged). Fantastic jumbo margins, cool blue color, terrific eye-appeal. Extremely Fine to Superb PSE - Encapsulated. (this being one of 3 attaining this grade as of 10/08, with 11 graded higher).

Estimate: $750+

Minimum Bid: $375

31530 #317, 1908, 5c Blue. (Original Gum - Previously Hinged). Rich Shade and strong impression on this RARE coil pair. Guideline along top perforations. Missing from most collections. Pencil mark on gum, lightly hinged across the middle. Very Fine; 2005 PF Certificate. (Scott $17,500).

Estimate: $16,500+

Minimum Bid: $8,250

RARE PAIR - HIGHEST GRADED

31531 #318, 1908, 1c Blue Green, VF-XF 85 PSE. (Original Gum - Previously Hinged). Coil Pair. Sharp detailed impression, rich color. Prior hinge evidence. Very Fine to Extremely Fine PSE - Encapsulated. (SMQ $15,500; this being one of 3 attaining this grade as of 10/08, with none graded higher).

Estimate: $15,000+

Minimum Bid: $7,500

1904 LOUISIANA PURCHASE EXPOSITION ISSUE

31532 **#324, 1904, 2c Carmine, XF-S 95 PSE.** (Original Gum - Never Hinged). Thomas Jefferson. Rich and deep color, exceptional eye-appeal. Extremely Fine to Superb PSE - Graded Certificate. (SMQ $880; this being one of 20 attaining this grade as of 10/08, with only 2 graded higher).

Estimate: $800+

Minimum Bid: $400

31533 **#325, 1904, 3c Violet, XF-S 95 PSE.** (Original Gum - Never Hinged). James Monroe. Dazzling impression. Vivid violet color. Extremely Fine to Superb; 2008 PSE - Graded Certificate. (SMQ $2,000; this being one of 34 attaining this grade as of 10/08, with 14 graded higher).

Estimate: $1,800+

Minimum Bid: $900

31534 **#325, 1904, 3c Violet XF-S 95 PSE.** (Original Gum - Never Hinged). James Monroe. Nearly perfect centering and margins, very high end. Extremely Fine to Superb; 2006 PSE - Graded Certificate. (SMQ $2,000; this being one of 34 attaining this grade as of 10/08, with 14 graded higher).

Estimate: $1,900+

Minimum Bid: $950

31535 **#325, 1904, 3c Violet, XF-S 95 PSE.** (Original Gum - Never Hinged). James Monroe. Spectacular example Extremely Fine to Superb; 2008 PSE - Graded Certificate. (SMQ $2,000; this being one of 34 attaining this grade as of 10/08, with 14 graded higher).

Estimate: $1,900+

Minimum Bid: $950

31536 **#325, 1904, 3c Violet, XF-S 95 PSE.** (Original Gum - Never Hinged). James Monroe. Bright and Fresh. Extremely Fine to Superb PSE - Encapsulated. (SMQ $2,000; this being one of 34 attaining this grade as of 10/08, with 14 graded higher).

Estimate: $1,900+

Minimum Bid: $950

31537 **#325, 1904, 3c Violet, XF 90 PSE.** (Original Gum - Never Hinged). James Monroe. Very choice example of this typically tight margined issue. Extremely Fine; 2004 PSE - Graded Certificate. (SMQ $580; this being one of 36 attaining this grade as of 10/08, with 49 graded higher).

Estimate: $500+

Minimum Bid: $250

31538 **#326, 1904, 5c Dark Blue, XF-S 95J PSE.** (Original Gum - Never Hinged). William McKinley. Spectacular example with very eye-pleasing Jumbo margins. Deep rich dark blue color, sharply etched impression. Extremely Fine to Superb PSE - Encapsulated. (this being one of 3 attaining this grade as of 10/08, with only 3 graded higher).

Estimate: $3,500+

Minimum Bid: $1,750

31539 #326, 1904, 5c Dark Blue, XF-S 95J PSE. (Original Gum - Never Hinged). William McKinley, Rich and Deep Color, Super fresh gum with large margins. Extremely Fine to Superb Jumbo; 2008 PSE - Graded Certificate. (this being one of 3 attaining this grade as of 10/08, with only 3 graded higher).

Estimate: $3,500+
Minimum Bid: $1,750

31540 #326, 1904, 5c Dark Blue, XF-S 95 PSE. (Original Gum - Never Hinged). William McKinley. Gorgeous deep color, and sharp detailed impression. Tough stamp in this condition and grade. Extremely Fine to Superb; 2005 PSE - Graded Certificate. (SMQ $2,650; this being one of 12 attaining this grade as of 10/08, with only 6 graded higher).

Estimate: $2,000+
Minimum Bid: $1,000

31541 #327, 1904, 10c Red Brown, XF-S 95 PSE. (Original Gum - Never Hinged). Map of Louisiana Purchase. Virtually perfect centering. Key to the set. Extremely Fine to Superb; 2005 PSE - Graded Certificate. (SMQ $3,550; this being one of 20 attaining this grade as of 10/08, with only 6 graded higher).

Estimate: $3,100+
Minimum Bid: $1,550

31542 #327, 1904, 10c Red Brown, VF-XF 85 PSE. (Original Gum - Never Hinged). Map of Louisiana Purchase. Key to the set. Huge top margin plate number single, eye-catching example. Very Fine to Extremely Fine; 2007 PSE - Graded Certificate.
(SMQ $670; this being one of 23 attaining this grade as of 10/08, with 45 graded higher).

Estimate: $550+
Minimum Bid: $275

31543 #327, 1904, 10c Red Brown, VF-XF 85 PSE. (Original Gum - Never Hinged). Map of Louisiana Purchase. Key to the set..Fresh example with ample to huge margins. Very Fine to Extremely Fine; 2005 PSE - Graded Certificate.
(SMQ $670; this being one of 23 attaining this grade as of 10/08, with 45 graded higher).

Estimate: $550+
Minimum Bid: $275

31544 #327, 1904, 10c Red Brown. (Original Gum - Never Hinged). Map of Louisiana Purchase. Key to the set. XF margins for this typically tightly margined series, sharp impression. fresh. Extremely Fine; 2008 PSE Certificate.

Estimate: $750+
Minimum Bid: $375

1907 JAMESTOWN EXPOSITION ISSUE

31545 **#328, 1907, 1c Green, XF-S 95 PSE.** (Original Gum - Never Hinged). Captain John Smith. Extremely fine centering and margins for this issue, vivid color. Guideline at left. Extremely Fine to Superb; 2003 PSE - Graded Certificate.
(SMQ $880; this being one of 18 attaining this grade as of 10/08, with only 5 graded higher).

Estimate: $750+

Minimum Bid: $375

31546 **#329, 1907, 2c Carmine XF-S 95 PSE.** (Original Gum - Never Hinged). Founding of Jamestown. Terrific example in every aspect -super fresh. Extremely Fine to Superb; 2008 PSE - Graded Certificate. (SMQ $1,000; this being one of 14 attaining this grade as of 10/08, with only 5 graded higher).

Estimate: $900+

Minimum Bid: $450

31547 **#330, 1907, 5c Blue, XF-S 95 PSE.** (Original Gum - Never Hinged). Pocahontas. Exceptional example, large margins for this very tight margined issue. Extremely Fine to Superb PSE - Encapsulated. (SMQ $3,500; this being one of 14 attaining this grade as of 10/08, with only 2 graded higher).

Estimate: $3,000+

Minimum Bid: $1,500

31548 **#330, 1907, 5c Blue, XF 90 PSE.** (Original Gum - Never Hinged). Pocahontas. Vibrant deep blue color with very large margins for this issue. Choice. Extremely Fine; 2007 PSE - Graded Certificate. (SMQ $1,050; this being one of 27 attaining this grade as of 10/08, with 18 graded higher).

Estimate: $900+

Minimum Bid: $450

1908-09 WASHINGTON FRANKLIN ISSUE - DBL. LINE WMK.

31549 **#331, 1908, 1c Green, SUP 98J PSE.** (Used). A world class used condition rarity, perfectly centered within tremendous well balanced margins, fresh and rich, finely detailed impression, with a non-obtrusive wavy line machine cancel, a Superb stamp whose equal would be extremely difficult to find; PSE - Encapsulated. (this being one of 11 attaining this grade as of 10/08, with only 2 graded higher).

Estimate: $500+

Minimum Bid: $250

31550 **#334, 1908, 4c Orange Brown, XF-S 95 PSE.** (Original Gum - Never Hinged). Luscious example bordering on jumbo designation, great color, sharp detailed impression. Extremely Fine to Superb PSE - Encapsulated. (SMQ $1,200; this being one of 15 attaining this grade as of 10/08, with only 7 graded higher).

Estimate: $1,200+

Minimum Bid: $600

31551 **#334, 1908, 4c Orange Brown, XF-S 95 PSE.** (Original Gum - Never Hinged). Post Office Fresh. Extremely Fine to Superb; 2005 PSE - Graded Certificate. Also, 2003 PF Certificate. (SMQ $1,200; this being one of 15 attaining this grade as of 10/08, with only 7 graded higher).

Estimate: $1,000+

Minimum Bid: $500

31552 **#336, 1908, 6c Red Orange, SUP 98 PSE.** (Original Gum - Previously Hinged). A spectacular example, radiantly bright and vibrant, flawlessly centered, with full intact perforations all around, only a trace of a hinge mark. 2008 PSE - Graded Certificate. (SMQ $530; this being one of 1 attaining this grade as of 10/08, with only 1 graded higher).

Estimate: $500+

Minimum Bid: $250

31553 **#336, 1909, 6c Red Orange, XF-S 95 PSE.** (Original Gum - Never Hinged). Spectacular red orange beauty, bright and fresh. Extremely Fine to Superb PSE - Encapsulated. (SMQ $1,750; this being one of 5 attaining this grade as of 10/08, with only 2 graded higher).

Estimate: $1,500+

Minimum Bid: $750

31554 **#337, 1908, 8c Olive Green, XF-S 95 PSE.** (Original Gum - Never Hinged). Handsome example with visually attractive centering, dreamy appearance. Extremely Fine to Superb PSE - Encapsulated. (SMQ $1,300; this being one of 8 attaining this grade as of 10/08, with only 2 graded higher).

Estimate: $1,200+

Minimum Bid: $600

31555 **#338, 1909, 10c Yellow XF 90J PSE.** (Original Gum - Never Hinged). Sweet position piece, fresh as could be. Extremely Fine; 2006 PSE - Graded Certificate. (this being one of 9 attaining this grade as of 10/08, with only 5 graded higher).

Estimate: $1,000+

Minimum Bid: $500

31556 **#339, 1909, 13c Blue Green, XF-S 95 PSE.** (Original Gum - Never Hinged). Brilliant blue green color with very fresh appearance, lovely example. Extremely Fine to Superb PSE - Encapsulated. (SMQ $1,200; this being one of 16 attaining this grade as of 10/08, with only 4 graded higher).

Estimate: $1,200+

Minimum Bid: $600

31557 **#340, 1909, 15c Pale Ultramarine, XF-S 95 PSE.** (Original Gum - Never Hinged). Delicate pastel color with large margins, intriguing example. Extremely Fine to Superb PSE - Encapsulated. (SMQ $1,750; this being one of 12 attaining this grade as of 10/08, with only 3 graded higher).

Estimate: $1,500+

Minimum Bid: $750

31558 **#340, 1909, 15c Pale Ultramarine, XF-S 95 PSE.** (Original Gum - Never Hinged). Beautiful example with rich color and wide margins, Extremely Fine - Superb2008 PSE - Graded Certificate. Also, 2000 PF Certificate. Extremely Fine to Superb; 2008 PSE - Graded Certificate. (SMQ $1,750; this being one of 12 attaining this grade as of 10/08, with only 3 graded higher).

Estimate: $1,500+

Minimum Bid: $750

31559 **#342, 1909, $1 Violet Brown, XF 90 PSE.** (Original Gum - Previously Hinged). Rich color. Very minimal evidence of prior hinge. Extremely Fine; 2008 PSE - Graded Certificate. (SMQ $870; this being one of 19 attaining this grade as of 10/08, with only 6 graded higher).

Estimate: $700+

Minimum Bid: $350

TOP OF THE POP

31560 **#348, 1908, 1c Green, XF-S 95 PSE.** (Used). Coil guide line pair. A spectacular used Line Pair. Precision centering, unobtrusive cancel. Extremely Fine to Superb; 2008 PSE - Graded Certificate and 2008 APS Certificate. (SMQ $2,800; this being the *unique example attaining this grade* as of 10/08, with *none graded higher*).

Estimate: $3,000+

Minimum Bid: $1,500

31561 **#349, 1908, 2c Carmine, XF-S 95 PSE.** (Original Gum - Never Hinged). Coil Pair. Fantastic quality, very low population. Bold color, appealing example Extremely Fine to Superb PSE - Encapsulated. (SMQ $2,550; this being one of 4 attaining this grade as of 10/08, with none graded higher).

Estimate: $2,500+

Minimum Bid: $1,250

TOP OF THE POP

31562 **#349, 1908, 2c Carmine, XF-S 95 PSE.** (Original Gum - Never Hinged). Coil Single. One of the rarest coils in high grade. Beautiful example. Extremely Fine to Superb PSE - Encapsulated. (SMQ $1200; this being one of 4 attaining this grade as of 10/08, with *none* graded higher).

Estimate: $1,500+

Minimum Bid: $750

31563 **#350, 1908, 4c Orange Brown, XF-S 95 PSE.** (Original Gum - Never Hinged). Coil Single. Extremely rare coil, wonderful rich color. Fresh. Extremely Fine to Superb PSE - Encapsulated. (SMQ $2,050; this being one of 2 attaining this grade as of 10/08, with only 2 graded higher).

Estimate: $1,900+

Minimum Bid: $950

31564 **#351, 1908, 5c Blue, XF-S 95 PSE.** (Original Gum - Never Hinged). Coil Guide Line Pair. Spectacular example of this rare coil, near perfectly balanced margins surround this choice example. Extremely Fine to Superb PSE - Encapsulated. (SMQ $11,400; this being one of 5 attaining this grade as of 10/08, with only 1 graded higher).

Estimate: $12,000+

Minimum Bid: $6,000

31565 **#351, 1908, 5c Blue, VF 80 PSE.** (Original Gum - Never Hinged). Coil Guide Line Pair. Rich color and overall fresh. Very Fine; 2008 PSE - Graded Certificate. (SMQ $2,450; this being one of 3 attaining this grade as of 10/08, with only 12 graded higher).

Estimate: $2,200+

Minimum Bid: $1,100

31566 **#351, 1908, 5c Blue.** (Disturbed Original Gum). Coil Guide Line Pair. Rich color. Cert notes gum disturbance, which is nothing more than a result of the hinge removal in the top stamp. Fine to Very Fineand choice; 2003PF Certificate. (Scott $1,150).

Estimate: $500+

Minimum Bid: $250

31567 **#351, 1908, 5c Blue, XF-S 95 PSE.** (Original Gum - Never Hinged). Coil Single. Rich and warm color. Very well-centered. fresh. Extremely Fine to Superb PSE - Encapsulated. (SMQ $2,150; this being one of 5 attaining this grade as of 10/08, with only 3 graded higher).

Estimate: $2,150+

Minimum Bid: $1,075

31568 **#352, 1909, 1c Green.** (Original Gum - Previously Hinged). Coil Guide Line Pair. Nicely centered, with fresh vibrant color. Lightly hinged. Very Fine to Extremely Fineand choice; 2001 PF Certificate. (Scott $825).

Estimate: $750+

Minimum Bid: $375

RARE NEVER HINGED COIL LINE PAIR

31569 #356, 1909, 10c Yellow F-VF 75 PSE. (Original Gum - Never Hinged). Only Two Never Hinged Coil Joint Line Pairs have been graded by PSE. This line pair in absolutely Choice condition with vibrant and bold color on fresh white paper. Flawless, fresh gum. Condition rarity. Fine to Very Fine PSE - Encapsulated. (This being one of 1 attaining this grade as of 10/08, with only 1 graded higher).

Estimate: $50,000+

Minimum Bid: $25,000

31570 #356, 1909, 10c Yellow XF-S 95 PSE. (Original Gum - Previously Hinged). Coil Pair. The highest graded OG example to date with none higher, magnificent mint coil pair, bright yellow color with a sharp detailed impression. Wonderful centering with large to huge margins, very lightly hinged, otherwise with fresh gleaming gum. Extremely Fine to Superb; 2008 PSE - Graded Certificate,1989 PF Certificate. (SMQ $14,500; this being one of 1 attaining this grade as of 10/08, with none graded higher).
Estimate: $20,000+
Minimum Bid: $10,000

31571 #356, 1909, 10c Yellow, F-VF 75 PSE. (Original Gum - Hinged). Coil Pair. Bright color and strong impression. Noticeable hinge removal, but no remnant. Fine to Very Fine PSE - Encapsulated. (this being one of 2 attaining this grade as of 10/08, with only 3 graded higher).
Estimate: $5,000+
Minimum Bid: $2,500

31572 #353, 1909, 2c Carmine. (Original Gum - Previously Hinged). Coil Guide Line Pair. Luscious carmine color. Short corner perf at the right top of the left stamp. Barely hinged at the top. Fine to Very Fine; 2008 PSE Certificate. (Scott $750).
Estimate: $400+
Minimum Bid: $200

1909 BLUISH PAPERS

31573 #357, 1909, 1c Green, SUP 98 PSE. (Original Gum - Never Hinged). Spectacular showpiece. This Bluish paper does not typically run 'nice', in fact the majority are poorly centered. This copy is a condition rarity. Completely Fresh. Superb PSE - Encapsulated. (SMQ $6,600; this being one of 3 attaining this grade as of 10/08, with only 1 graded higher).

Estimate: $6,500+

Minimum Bid: $3,250

31574 #358, 1909, 2c Carmine, XF-S 95 PSE. (Original Gum - Never Hinged). Choice example of this tough Bluish paper. Post Office Fresh. Extremely Fine to Superb PSE - Encapsulated. (SMQ $2,100; this being one of 6 attaining this grade as of 10/08, with only 4 graded higher).

Estimate: $2,000+

Minimum Bid: $1,000

31575 #361, 1909, 5c Blue. (Original Gum - Previously Hinged). Very attractive left side margin part imprint single, ample to large margins all around, previously hinged with a hinge remnant on the side margin. Fine to Very Fine; 2008 PSE Certificate. (Scott $6,000).

Estimate: $4,500+

Minimum Bid: $2,250

31576 #361, 1909, 5c Blue. (Original Gum - Previously Hinged). Strong Impression and deep color. Very light prior hinging mark and a small owners handstamp. Better margins and centering than usually encountered on this rare stamp. Very Fine; 2006 PF Certificate. (Scott $6,000).

Estimate: $8,500+

Minimum Bid: $4,250

CONDITION AND GRADE RARITY

31577 #365, 1909, 13c Blue Green, XF-S 95 PSE. (Original Gum - Previously Hinged). A magnificent mint example of this 13c Bluish paper issue, concisely centered, bold rich color and finely etched impression on fresh bluish paper, full original gum that appears never hinged, requiring extremely close examination to find any traces of previous hinging. Extremely Fine to Superb; PSE - Encapsulated. (SMQ $6,950; this being one of 4 attaining this grade as of 10/08, with *none graded higher*).

Estimate: $7,000+

Minimum Bid: $3,500

 A 19.5% Buyer's Premium ($9 min.) Applies To All Lots

31578 **#365, 1909, 13c Blue Green.** (Original Gum - Never Hinged). Attractive with a pastel-like color and sharp impression that seems to almost radiate, very pristine original gum. Very Fine and choice; 2008 PF Certificate. (Scott $6,500).

Estimate: $6,500+

Minimum Bid: $3,250

RARE BLUISH PAPER - NEVER HINGED
TOP OF THE POP

31579 **#366, 1909, 15c Pale Ultramarine XF 90 PSE.** (Original Gum - Never Hinged). Very tough stamp in this condition. Post Office Fresh front and back. Rare Bluish paper. Extremely Fine PSE - Encapsulated. (SMQ $8,850; this being one of 3 attaining this grade as of 10/08, with *none* graded higher).

Estimate: $10,000+

Minimum Bid: $5,000

31580 **#366, 1909, 15c Pale Ultramarine.** (Original Gum - Never Hinged). A stunning example of this 15c Bluish Paper Washington issue, warm pastel color, well centered for the issue. Very Fine to Extremely Fine; 2008 PSE Certificate and 2001 PF Certificate. (Scott $3,500).

Estimate: $2,500+

Minimum Bid: $1,250

1909 COMMEMORATIVES

31581 **#367, 1909, 2c Carmine, SUP 98 PSE.** (Original Gum - Never Hinged). Amazing example, bright and fresh. Superb PSE - Encapsulated. (SMQ $460; this being one of 9 attaining this grade as of 10/08, with only 2 graded higher).

Estimate: $500+

Minimum Bid: $250

31582 **#369, 1909, 2c Carmine, XF-S 95 PSE.** (Original Gum - Never Hinged). Absolutely phenomenal example, beautifully balance margins, Fresh. Extremely Fine to Superb PSE - Encapsulated. (SMQ $1,650; this being one of 19 attaining this grade as of 10/08, with only 7 graded higher).

Estimate: $1,500+

Minimum Bid: $750

31583 **#370, 1909, 2c Carmine, SUP 98 PSE.** (Original Gum - Never Hinged). A visually striking mint single, fresh and vibrant. Superb PSE - Encapsulated. (SMQ $410; this being one of 34 attaining this grade as of 10/08, with only 2 graded higher).

Estimate: $500+

Minimum Bid: $250

TOP MARGIN IMPRINT SINGLE - USED

31584 **#371, 1909, 2c Carmine. SUP 98J PSE.** (Used). Attractive top margin Imprint copy. Nice light black 1909 Duplex cancel. Not at all an easy item in this condition. Superb; 2005 PSE - Graded Certificate. (this being one of 2 attaining this grade as of 10/08, with only 2 graded higher).

Estimate: $450+

Minimum Bid: $225

31585 **#372, 1909, 2c Carmine, SUP 98 PSE.** (Original Gum - Never Hinged). Bold color, fresh. Superb PSE - Encapsulated. (SMQ $600; this being one of 13 attaining this grade as of 10/08, with only 3 graded higher).

Estimate: $500+

Minimum Bid: $250

31586 **#372, 1909, 2c Carmine, SUP 98 PSE.** (Original Gum - Never Hinged). Bright, fresh, and perfect. Superb; 2006 PSE - Graded Certificate. (SMQ $600; this being one of 13 attaining this grade as of 10/08, with only 3 graded higher).

Estimate: $500+

Minimum Bid: $250

31587 **#372, 1909, 2c Carmine, SUP 98 PSE.** (Original Gum - Never Hinged). Very large wide margins with precise centering, detailed impression. Fresh Superb; 2005 PSE - Graded Certificate. (SMQ $600; this being one of 13 attaining this grade as of 10/08, with only 3 graded higher).

Estimate: $500+

Minimum Bid: $250

1910-11 WASHINGTON-FRANKLIN ISSUE - SGL. LINE WMK.

31588 #375, 1910, 2c Carmine, SUP 98 PSE. (Original Gum - Never Hinged). Deep dark rich color surrounded by huge margins, exceptional for the grade. Superb PSE - Encapsulated. (SMQ $960; this being one of 5 attaining this grade as of 10/08, with only 5 graded higher).

Estimate: $800+

Minimum Bid: $400

31589 #376, 1910, 3c Deep Violet, SUP 98 PSE. (Original Gum - Never Hinged). Fantastic deep violet color with an exceptional impression, wide margins on very white paper. Superb PSE - Encapsulated. (SMQ $2,100; this being one of 5 attaining this grade as of 10/08, with only 1 graded higher).

Estimate: $2,000+

Minimum Bid: $1,000

31590 #376, 1910, 3c Deep Violet. XF-S 95 PSE. (Original Gum - Never Hinged). Rich color. Plate# 6052, top margin single. Extremely Fine to Superb; 2003 PSE - Graded Certificate. (SMQ $580; this being one of 15 attaining this grade as of 10/08, with 20 graded higher).

Estimate: $500+

Minimum Bid: $250

31591 #377, 1911, 4c Brown, XF-S 95J PSE. (Original Gum - Never Hinged). Jumbo with tremendous eye-appeal. Extremely Fine to Superb PSE - Encapsulated. (this being one of 16 attaining this grade as of 10/08, with only 4 graded higher).

Estimate: $1,000+

Minimum Bid: $500

31592 #377, 1911, 4c Brown, XF-S 95J PSE. (Original Gum - Never Hinged). An attention-grabbing monster of a stamp, fabulously centered with massive margins bordering on boardwalk in size, intense color and deeply etched impression on crisp clean paper. Unblemished full original gum, Extremely Fine to Superb; 2005 PSE - Graded Certificate and 1999 PF Certificate. (this being one of 16 attaining this grade as of 10/08, with only 4 graded higher).

Estimate: $1,600+

Minimum Bid: $800

31593 #378, 1911, 5c Blue SUP 98 PSE. (Original Gum - Never Hinged). Extremely fresh and attractive gem, deep intense blue color enhanced by bright white paper, well balanced margins, rarely seen this nice, original gum, Never Hinged. Superb PSE - Encapsulated. (SMQ $3,200; this being one of 5 attaining this grade as of 10/08, with only 2 graded higher).

Estimate: $3,200+

Minimum Bid: $1,600

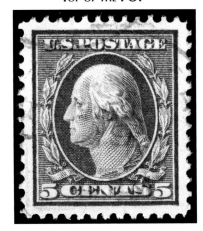

31594 **#378, 1911, 5c Blue XF-S, 95J PSE.** (Original Gum - Never Hinged). Eye-catching, bright blue color with jumbo margins. Extremely Fine to Superb; 2003 PSE - Graded Certificate and 1991 PSE Certificate. (this being one of 5 attaining this grade as of 10/08, with only 7 graded higher).
Estimate: $1,000+
Minimum Bid: $500

31596 **#378, 1911, 5c Blue, GEM 100J PSE.** (Used). The ultimate grade for the serious collector, used with very light black cancel. Gem; 2008 PSE - Graded Certificate. (this being the *only example attaining this grade* as of 10/08, with *none graded higher*).
Estimate: $1,000+
Minimum Bid: $500

31598 **#379, 1911, 6c Red Orange, XF-S 95 PSE.** (Original Gum - Never Hinged). Absolutely gorgeous example, bright, vibrant, and fresh. Extremely Fine to Superb. 2008 PSE - Graded Certificate. (SMQ $1,150; this being one of 23 attaining this grade as of 10/08, with only 7 graded higher).
Estimate: $1,000+
Minimum Bid: $500

31595 **#378, 1911, 5c Blue XF-S, 95 PSE.** (Original Gum - Never Hinged). Vibrant top margin mint single. Extremely Fine to Superb; 2007 PSE - Graded Certificate. (SMQ $1,000; this being one of 13 attaining this grade as of 10/08, with 12 graded higher).
Estimate: $800+
Minimum Bid: $400

31597 **#379, 1911, 6c Red Orange, SUP 98 PSE.** (Original Gum - Never Hinged). Sensational example in every aspect, luscious red orange color, symmetrically balanced margins, pinpoint impression, scarce in high grade. Superb PSE - Encapsulated. (SMQ $3,500; this being one of 4 attaining this grade as of 10/08, with only 2 graded higher).
Estimate: $4,000+
Minimum Bid: $2,000

31599 **#380, 1911, 8c Olive Green, XF-S 95 PSE.** (Original Gum - Never Hinged). Especially handsome example, large balanced margins, gorgeous color, original gum, Never hinged, Extremely Fine to Superb PSE - Encapsulated. (SMQ $2,500; this being one of 8 attaining this grade as of 10/08, with only 4 graded higher).
Estimate: $2,500+
Minimum Bid: $1,250

31600 **#381, 1911, 10c Yellow, VF-XF 85 PSE.** (Original Gum - Never Hinged). A couple of mount fibers on gum, not mentioned on the certificate. Fine to Extremely Fine. PSE - Encapsulated. (SMQ $450; this being one of 9 attaining this grade as of 10/08, with 24 graded higher).

Estimate: $300+

Minimum Bid: $150

31601 **#382, 1911, 15c Pale Ultramarine, XF-S 95 PSE.** (Original Gum - Never Hinged). Spectacular color, rich, and vibrant, well centered with generous margins, rare in this quality. Extremely Fine to Superb PSE - Encapsulated. (SMQ $5,300; this being one of 9 attaining this grade as of 10/08, with only 1 graded higher).

Estimate: $5,300+

Minimum Bid: $2,650

SPECTACULAR GUIDE LINE PAIR

31602 **#388, 1910, 2c Carmine, VF-XF 85 PSE.** (Original Gum - Previously Hinged). A superlative mint coil guide line pair, especially well centered, vibrant and finely detailed, original gum with only minimal evidence of previous hinging at top center of the pair. Very Fine to Extremely Fine and destined for the finest collection. PSE - Encapsulated. (SMQ $11,000; this being the only example attaining this grade as of 10/08, with only 1 graded higher).

Estimate: $10,000+

Minimum Bid: $5,000

31603 **#388, 1910, 2c Carmine.** (Original Gum - Hinged). Extremely rare coil guide line pair. Clean crisp impression with deep rich carmine color, hinge remnant across the top of both stamps. Fine. 2008 PSE Certificate and 1970 PF Certificate. (Scott $8,750).

   Estimate: $5,000+
   Minimum Bid: $2,500

HIGHEST GRADED

31604 **#388, 1910, 2c Carmine, SUP 98 PSE.** (Original Gum - Previously Hinged). A true condition rarity, deep rich carmine color set between perfect margins, barely hinged with small pencil notation on the back. Superb. 2007 PSE - Graded Certificate. (SMQ $7,400; this being the *sole example attaining this grade* as of 10/08, with *none graded higher*).

   Estimate: $9,000+
   Minimum Bid: $4,500

31605 #389, 1911, 3c Deep Violet. (Used). Very deep and rich color. This rarity is seldom encountered in Sound condition. Wavy line Orangeburg, NY machine cancel. Fine. 2006 PF Certificate. (Scott $11,000).

Estimate: $9,000+

Minimum Bid: $4,500

31607 #391, 1910, 2c Carmine, XF 90 PSE. (Original Gum - Never Hinged). Coil Pair. Gorgeous color. Post Office Fresh. Extremely Fine; 2008 PSE - Graded Certificate and 2000 PF Certificate. (SMQ $540; this being one of 3 attaining this grade as of 10/08, with only 4 graded higher).

Estimate: $500+

Minimum Bid: $250

31606 #390, 1910, 1c Green, SUP 98 PSE. (Original Gum - Never Hinged). Coil Guide Line Pair. Superb. 2007 PSE - Graded Certificate. (SMQ $640; this being one of 11 attaining this grade as of 10/08, with only 9 graded higher).

Estimate: $500+

Minimum Bid: $250

31608 #391, 1910, 2c Carmine, XF-S 95J PSE. (Original Gum - Never Hinged). Coil Single. Spectacularly fresh and luminous color, precisely centered, with flawless gum. Oversize margins. Extremely Fine to Superb example whose equal would be impossible to find. 2008 PSE - Graded Certificate. (this being the *unique example attaining this grade* as of 10/08, with *none graded higher*).

Estimate: $750+

Minimum Bid: $375

31609 #392, 1910, 1c Green, VF 80 PSE. (Original Gum - Never Hinged). Coil Guide Line Pair. Bright and fresh color, post office fresh gum. Very Fine. PSE - Encapsulated. (SMQ $425; this being one of 3 attaining this grade as of 10/08, with 15 graded higher).

Estimate: $350+

Minimum Bid: $175

1913-15 PANAMA-PACIFIC EXPOSITION ISSUE

31610 **#393, 1910, 2c Carmine, XF 90J PSE.** (Original Gum - Never Hinged). Coil Pair. Stunning example, with fantastic color. Extremely Fine. 2008 PSE - Graded Certificate. (this being one of 8 attaining this grade as of 10/08, with 10 graded higher).

Estimate: $600+

Minimum Bid: $300

31611 **#395, 1912, 4c Brown, XF 90 PSE.** (Original Gum - Previously Hinged). Coil Guide Line Pair. Beautifully centered, fresh and vibrant, original gum, with light trace of previous hinging at the top center of the pair. Extremely Fine. 2007 PSE - Graded Certificate. (SMQ $620; this being one of 3 attaining this grade as of 10/08, with only 7 graded higher).

Estimate: $550+

Minimum Bid: $275

31612 **#396, 1913, 5c Blue, SUP 98 PSE.** (Original Gum - Never Hinged). Coil Single. Huge margins surround this deep blue colored example (perfect perforations). Superb. PSE - Encapsulated. (SMQ $1,500; this being one of 6, attaining this grade as of 10/08, with only 2 graded higher).

Estimate: $1,300+

Minimum Bid: $650

31613 **#397, 1913, 1c Green, SUP 98 PSE.** (Original Gum - Never Hinged). Balboa. Fresh and vibrant, flawlessly centered, pristine full original gum. A Superb example for the serious collector. PSE - Encapsulated. (SMQ $1,200; this being one of 26 attaining this grade as of 10/08, with only 6 graded higher).

Estimate: $1,500+

Minimum Bid: $750

31614 **#397, 1913, 1c Green, SUP 98 PSE.** (Original Gum - Never Hinged). Balboa. An exquisite mint single, impeccably centered, deeply intense color and etched impression on fresh white paper. Immaculate gum. 2007 PSE - Graded Certificate. (SMQ $1,200; this being one of 26 attaining this grade as of 10/08, with only 6 graded higher).

Estimate: $1,500+

Minimum Bid: $750

31615 **#397, 1913, 1c Green, XF-S 95J PSE.** (Original Gum - Never Hinged). Balboa. Bright and Fresh, small fingerprint on gum. Extremely Fine to Superb. 2005 PSE - Graded Certificate. (this being one of 14 attaining this grade as of 10/08, with 32 graded higher).

Estimate: $500+

Minimum Bid: $250

31616 **#398, 1913, 2c Carmine, SUP 98 PSE.** (Original Gum - Never Hinged). Panama Canal. A picture window perfect view, intense in detail and vibrant in color, all framed within generous perfectly balanced margins. Fresh, unblemished full original gum. Superb; PSE - Encapsulated. (SMQ $1,250; this being one of 17 attaining this grade as of 10/08, with only 4 graded higher).

Estimate: $1,500+

Minimum Bid: $750

31617 **#399, 1913, 5c Blue, SUP 98 PSE.** (Original Gum - Never Hinged). Golden Gate. Rich and radiant, deeply etched impression, perfectly centered, with full even perforations all around. PSE - Encapsulated. (SMQ $4,000; this being one of 12 attaining this grade as of 10/08, with only 3 graded higher).

Estimate: $4,000+

Minimum Bid: $2,000

31618 **#399, 1913, 5c Blue, XF-S 95 PSE.** (Original Gum - Never Hinged). Golden Gate. Rich dark blue color and wide even margins. A lovely example. Extremely Fine to Superb. PSE - Encapsulated. (SMQ $1,300; this being one of 24 attaining this grade as of 10/08, with 21 graded higher).

Estimate: $1,000+

Minimum Bid: $500

31619 **#399, 1913, 5c Blue, XF-S 95 PSE.** (Original Gum - Never Hinged). Golden Gate. Intensely rich color on this example, large margins very well balanced. Extremely Fine to Superb. PSE - Encapsulated. (SMQ $1,300; this being one of 24 attaining this grade as of 10/08, with 21 graded higher).

Estimate: $1,000+

Minimum Bid: $500

31620 **#400, 1913, 10c Orange Yellow, SUP 98 PSE.** (Original Gum - Never Hinged). Discovery of San Francisco Bay. An eye-popping premium mint example of this popular commemorative, perfectly centered with full even perforations all around, intensely bright and vibrant, with an overall crisp freshness, a wonderful example suited for the most discriminating collector. 2006 PSE - Graded Certificateand 1978 PF Certificate. Superb; 2006 PSE - Graded Certificate. (SMQ $6,100; this being one of 9 attaining this grade as of 10/08, with only 3 graded higher).

Estimate: $6,500+

Minimum Bid: $3,250

31621 **#400, 1913, 10c Orange Yellow, XF-S 95 PSE.** (Original Gum - Never Hinged). Discovery of San Francisco Bay. Marvelous overall freshness, sharp impression, great eye appeal. Extremely Fine to Superb. PSE - Encapsulated. (SMQ $2,100; this being one of 27 attaining this grade as of 10/08, with 16 graded higher).

Estimate: $2,000+

Minimum Bid: $1,000

31622 **#400, 1913, 10c Orange Yellow, XF-S 95 PSE.** (Original Gum - Never Hinged). Discovery of San Francisco Bay. Bright and Fresh. Gorgeous Gum. Extremely Fine to Superb. 2005 PSE - Graded Certificate. (SMQ $2,100; this being one of 27 attaining this grade as of 10/08, with 16 graded higher).

Estimate: $1,900+

Minimum Bid: $950

31623 **#400, 1913, 10c Orange Yellow XF-S 95 PSE.** (Original Gum - Previously Hinged). Discovery of San Francisco Bay. A magnificent mint single, deep rich color and impression, precisely centered, with full even perforations all around, original gum that has been just barely kissed by hinging, appears never hinged at first glance. Extremely Fine to Superb. 2008 PSE - Graded Certificate. (SMQ $405; this being one of 12 attaining this grade as of 10/08, with only 6 graded higher).

Estimate: $400+

Minimum Bid: $200

31624 **#400, 1913, 10c Orange Yellow, XF-S 95 PSE.** (Used). Discovery of San Francisco Bay. Pretty stamp, nicely centered with double oval town cancel. Extremely Fine to Superb PSE - Encapsulated. (SMQ $310; this being one of 4 attaining this grade as of 10/08, with only 1 graded higher).

Estimate: $300+

Minimum Bid: $150

31625 **#400A, 1913, 10c Orange, SUP 98 PSE.** (Original Gum - Never Hinged). Discovery of San Francisco Bay. Sumptuously rich and vibrant, impeccably centered. A Superb stamp for the finest collection. PSE - Encapsulated. (SMQ $8,600; this being one of 13 attaining this grade as of 10/08, with only 3 graded higher).

Estimate: $10,000+

Minimum Bid: $5,000

31626 **#400A, 1913, 10c Orange, SUP 98 PSE.** (Original Gum - Previously Hinged). Discovery of San Francisco Bay. An especially well centered beauty, super light hinge mark, no remnant. Superb. 2007 PSE - Graded Certificate. (SMQ $1,250; this being one of 3 attaining this grade as of 10/08, with only 1 graded higher).

Estimate: $1,000+

Minimum Bid: $500

31627 #400A, 1913, 10c Orange, XF-S 95 PSE. (Original Gum - Never Hinged). Discovery of San Francisco Bay. Post Office Fresh. Extremely Fine to Superb. PSE-Encapsulated.(SMQ$3,250;this being one of 24 attaining this grade as of 10/08, with 22 graded higher).

Estimate: $2,500+

Minimum Bid: $1,250

31628 #400A, 1913, 10c Orange, XF-S 95 PSE. (Original Gum - Never Hinged). Discovery of San Francisco Bay. Bright and rich true orange color on white crisp paper, well balanced on all sides. Alluring example. Extremely Fine to Superb. PSE - Encapsulated. (SMQ $3,250; this being one of 24 attaining this grade as of 10/08, with 22 graded higher).

Estimate: $2,500+

Minimum Bid: $1,250

31629 #400A, 1913, 10c Orange, XF 90 PSE. (Original Gum - Never Hinged). Discovery of San Francisco Bay. Choice example with deep orange color and massive margins all around. Extremely Fine. 2007 PSE - Graded Certificate. (SMQ $1,200; this being one of 27 attaining this grade as of 10/08, with 50 graded higher).

Estimate: $1,000+

Minimum Bid: $500

31630 #400A, 1913, 10c Orange, XF-S 95J PSE. (Used). Discovery of San Francisco Bay. Gorgeous used example, jumbo well centered margins, unobtrusive black cancel, clean back. Extremely Fine to Superb. 2008 PSE - Graded Certificate. (this being one of 4 attaining this grade as of 10/08, with only 3 graded higher).

Estimate: $350+

Minimum Bid: $175

31631 #401, 1914, 1c Green, SUP 98 PSE. (Original Gum - Never Hinged). Balboa. Warm and vibrant, finely detailed, and precisely centered within generous margins. A Superb stamp of the highest quality. PSE - Encapsulated. (SMQ $2,000; this being one ot 8 attaining this grade as of 10/08, with none graded higher).

Estimate: $2,500+

Minimum Bid: $1,250

31632 #401, 1914, 1c Green, XF-S 95J PSE. (Original Gum - Never Hinged). Balboa. Magnificent jumbo with fabulously rich dark green color. Extremely Fine to Superb. 2006 PSE - Graded Certificate. (this being one of 3 attaining this grade as of 10/08, with only 8 graded higher).

Estimate: $600+

Minimum Bid: $300

31633 #401, 1914, 1c Green, XF-S 95 PSE. (Original Gum - Never Hinged). Balboa. Fresh and gorgeous, wide margined example. Extremely Fine to Superb. PSE - Encapsulated. (SMQ $600; this being one of 23 attaining this grade as of 10/08, with 11 graded higher).

Estimate: $500+

Minimum Bid: $250

31634 #401, 1914, 1c Green, XF-S 95 PSE. (Original Gum - Never Hinged). Balboa. A very high end example with superb color and impression. Extremely Fine to Superb. 2005 PSE - Graded Certificate and 2003 PF Certificate. (SMQ $600; this being one of 23 attaining this grade as of 10/08, with 11 graded higher).

Estimate: $500+

Minimum Bid: $250

31635 #402, 1914, 2c Carmine, SUP 98 PSE. (Original Gum - Never Hinged). Panama Canal. Post Office fresh with a warm pastel color, unblemished full original gum. A Superb stamp whose equal would be very difficult to find; PSE - Encapsulated. (SMQ $5,000; this being one of 6 attaining this grade as of 10/08, with none graded higher).

Estimate: $7,500+
Minimum Bid: $3,750

31636 #402, 1914, 2c Carmine, XF-S 95 PSE. (Original Gum - Never Hinged). Panama Canal. A gorgeous mint single, exceptionally centered within large balanced margins, bright yet warm pastel color and detailed impression. Extremely Fine to Superb. PSE - Encapsulated. (SMQ $1,550; this being one of 7 attaining this grade as of 10/08, with only 9 graded higher).

Estimate: $1,300+
Minimum Bid: $650

31637 #403, 1914, 5c Blue, SUP 98 PSE. (Original Gum - Previously Hinged). Golden Gate. Impressive color and impression. Crisp white paper with only a very light prior hinge mark. Superb. 2008 PSE - Graded Certificate. (SMQ $1,100; this being one of 2 attaining this grade as of 10/08, with only 1 graded higher).

Estimate: $1,000+
Minimum Bid: $500

31638 #403, 1914, 5c Blue XF-S 95J PSE. (Original Gum - Never Hinged). Golden Gate. A flashy example with monster margins, draped in a magnificent blue color. Extremely Fine to Superb. 2006 PSE - Graded Certificate. (this being one of 2 attaining this grade as of 10/08, with only 6 graded higher).

Estimate: $4,500+
Minimum Bid: $2,250

31639 #403, 1914, 5c Blue, VF-XF 85 PSE. (Original Gum - Never Hinged). Golden Gate. A beautiful example with deep blue color and large balanced margins. Very Fine to Extremely Fine. 2008 PSE - Graded Certificate. (SMQ $680; this being one of 22 attaining this grade as of 10/08, with 42 graded higher).
Estimate: $550+
Minimum Bid: $275

31640 #403, 1914, 5c Blue, VF-XF 85 PSE. (Original Gum - Never Hinged). Golden Gate. Attractive example with large even margins and fresh blue color. Extremely Fine. 2005 PSE - Graded Certificate. (SMQ $680; this being one of 22 attaining this grade as of 10/08, with 42 graded higher).
Estimate: $550+
Minimum Bid: $275

31641 #404, 1914, 10c Orange, XF-S 95 PSE. (Original Gum - Never Hinged). Discovery of San Francisco Bay. Rare and beautiful to behold, sporting an orange color so fresh it looks like it was printed yesterday. White crisp borders, portrait-like impression, unblemished original gum. Extremely Fine to Superb.2007 PSE - Graded Certificate. (SMQ $9,450; this being one of 9 attaining this grade as of 10/08, with only 7 graded higher).
Estimate: $8,500+
Minimum Bid: $4,250

1912-14 WASHINGTON-FRANKLIN ISSUE

31642   #404, 1914, 10c Orange, XF-S 95 PSE. (Original Gum - Never Hinged). Discovery of San Francisco Bay. Gleaming fresh color combined with a razor sharp impression on white paper, with exaggerated margins all around. Extremely Fine to Superb. PSE - Graded Certificate. (SMQ $9,450; this being one of 9 attaining this grade as of 10/08, with only 7 graded higher).

Estimate: $8,500+

Minimum Bid: $4,250

31644   #406, 1912, 2c Carmine SUP 98J PSE. (Original Gum - Never Hinged). Unbelievable deep carmine color, enormous jumbo margins, the finest example to date. Superb. 2008 PSE - Graded Certificate. (this being the *only example attaining this grade* as of 10/08, with *none graded higher*).

Estimate: $1,000+

Minimum Bid: $500

31643   #404, 1914, 10c Orange, XF 90J PSE. (Used). Discovery of San Francisco Bay. Enormous well centered jumbo with a black Boston Mass. double oval cancel. Extremely Fine. 2008 PSE - Graded Certificate. (this being one of 6 attaining this grade as of 10/08, with only 8 graded higher).

Estimate: $400+

Minimum Bid: $200

31645   #406, 1912, 2c Carmine, SUP 98J PSE. (Used). Oversize margins, wavy line cancel. Superb. 2005 PSE - Graded Certificate. (this being one of 2 attaining this grade as of 10/08, with only 3 graded higher).

Estimate: $500+

Minimum Bid: $250

31646   #407, 1912, 7c Black, XF-S 95 PSE. (Original Gum - Never Hinged). One of the nicest examples of this tough to find stamp. Extremely Fine to Superb. 2007 PSE - Graded Certificate. (SMQ $1,800; this being one of 13 attaining this grade as of 10/08, with only 3 graded higher).

Estimate: $1,500+

Minimum Bid: $750

31649 **#412, 1912, 1c Green, XF-S 95 PSE.** (Original Gum - Never Hinged). Coil Guide Line Pair. Fabulously fresh. Extremely Fine to Superb. 2005 PSE - Graded Certificate. (SMQ $1,150; this being one of 8 attaining this grade as of 10/08, with 11 graded higher).

Estimate: $900+

Minimum Bid: $450

31652 **#415, 1912, 9c Salmon Red, XF-S 95 PSE.** (Original Gum - Never Hinged). Choice stamp, pleasing overall appearance. Extremely Fine to Superb. PSE - Encapsulated. (SMQ $1,400; this being one of 12 attaining this grade as of 10/08, with only 1 graded higher).

Estimate: $1,200+

Minimum Bid: $600

31647 **#411, 1912, 2c Carmine XF-S 95 PSE.** (Original Gum - Never Hinged). Coil guide line pair. Intense shade and rich color, fresh. Extremely Fine to Superb. 2008 PSE - Graded Certificate. (SMQ $510; this being one of 6 attaining this grade as of 10/08, with only 3 graded higher).

Estimate: $500+

Minimum Bid: $250

31650 **#414, 1912, 8c Pale Olive Green, XF-S 95J PSE.** (Original Gum - Never Hinged). Magnificently enormous margins. Extremely Fine to Superb. 2007 PSE - Graded Certificate and 2001 PF Certification. (this being one of 4 attaining this grade as of 10/08, with only 5 graded higher).

Estimate: $1,200+

Minimum Bid: $600

31653 **#416, 1912, 10c Orange Yellow SUP 98 PSE.** (Original Gum - Previously Hinged). Rich shade, portion of hinge remnant. Superb. PSE - Encapsulated. (SMQ $385; this being one of 4 attaining this grade as of 10/08, with only 3 graded higher).

Estimate: $450+

Minimum Bid: $225

31648 **#411, 1912, 2c Carmine, SUP 98J PSE.** (Original Gum - Never Hinged). Coil Single. Simply gorgeous color and strike. Superb. PSE - Encapsulated. (this being one of 2 attaining this grade as of 10/08, with only 1 graded higher).

Estimate: $450+

Minimum Bid: $225

31651 **#415, 1912, 9c Salmon Red, XF-S 95 PSE.** (Original Gum - Never Hinged). Bright and gorgeous. Extremely Fine to Superb. PSE - Encapsulated. (SMQ $1,400; this being one of 12 attaining this grade as of 10/08, with only 1 graded higher).

Estimate: $1,200+

Minimum Bid: $600

31654 **#416, 1912, 10c Orange Yellow, XF-S 95 PSE.** (Original Gum - Never Hinged). Radiant and intense in color and impression. Extremely Fine to Superb. PSE - Encapsulated. (SMQ $1,200; this being one of 18 attaining this grade as of 10/08, with only 5 graded higher).

Estimate: $1,100+

Minimum Bid: $550

31655 **#416, 1912, 10c Orange Yellow, XF-S 95 PSE.** (Original Gum - Never Hinged). Glowing orange yellow beauty, highly desirable example. Extremely Fine to Superb. PSE - Encapsulated. (SMQ $1,200; this being one of 18 attaining this grade as of 10/08, with only 5 graded higher).

Estimate: $1,000+

Minimum Bid: $500

31656 **#416, 1912, 10c Orange Yellow, XF-S 95 PSE.** (Original Gum - Never Hinged). A spectacular, nearly blinding example. Extremely Fine to Superb and choice selection for the serious collector. 2008 PSE - Graded Certificate. (SMQ $1,200; this being one of 18 attaining this grade as of 10/08, with only 5 graded higher).

Estimate: $1,000+

Minimum Bid: $500

31657 **#417, 1912, 12c Claret Brown, SUP 98 PSE.** (Original Gum - Previously Hinged). Light hinge mark only, no remnant. Superb. 2006 PSE - Graded Certificate. (SMQ $400; this being one of 4 attaining this grade as of 10/08, with none graded higher).

Estimate: $400+

Minimum Bid: $200

31658 **#417, 1912, 12c Claret Brown, XF-S 95 PSE.** (Original Gum - Never Hinged). Rich and deep color. Fresh white paper. Choice. Extremely Fine to Superb PSE - Encapsulated. (SMQ $1,300; this being one of 12 attaining this grade as of 10/08, with only 7 graded higher).

Estimate: $1,300+

Minimum Bid: $650

31659 **#418, 1912, 15c Gray, XF-S 95 PSE.** (Original Gum - Never Hinged). A splendid fresh example. Deep color and excellent centering. Extremely Fine to Superb. PSE - Encapsulated. (SMQ $1,850; this being one of 10 attaining this grade as of 10/08, with only 9 graded higher).

Estimate: $1,500+

Minimum Bid: $750

31660 **#419, 1912, 20c Ultramarine, XF-S 95 PSE.** (Original Gum - Never Hinged). Exceptionally choice. Extremely well-centered with deep rich ultramarine color. Extremely Fine to Superb. PSE - Encapsulated. (SMQ $3,600; this being one of 9 attaining this grade as of 10/08, with only 4 graded higher).

Estimate: $3,250+

Minimum Bid: $1,625

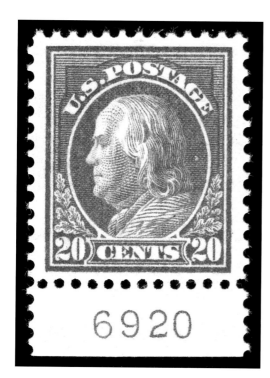

31661 #419, 1912, 20c Ultramarine, XF 90 PSE. (Original Gum - Never Hinged). Bottom Plate No. 6920 single. Fantastic dark ultramarine color and lavish margins. Extremely Fine. 2004 PSE - Graded Certificate. (this being one of 9 attaining this grade as of 10/08, with 13 graded higher).

Estimate: $1,100+

Minimum Bid: $550

TOP OF THE POP

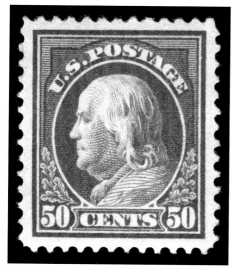

31662 #421, 1912, 50c Violet GEM 100 PSE. (Original Gum - Previously Hinged). Radiant shade and color, and a strong impression on fresh white paper, light hinge mark only. Gem. 2007 PSE - Graded Certificate and 2001 PF Certificate. (this being the *only example attaining this grade* as of 10/08, with *none graded higher*).

Estimate: $6,500+

Minimum Bid: $3,250

31663 #421, 1912, 50c Violet, SUP 98 PSE. (Original Gum - Previously Hinged). A beautiful mint single, perfectly centered, with full even perforations all around, vibrant pastel color and detailed impression, the gum showing only very light traces of previous hinging. A Superb example for the discriminating collector. 2007 PSE - Graded Certificate and 1992 PF Certificate for block of four from which this is the bottom right stamp. (SMQ $2,500; this being one of 5 attaining this grade as of 10/08, with only 1 graded higher).

Estimate: $2,500+

Minimum Bid: $1,250

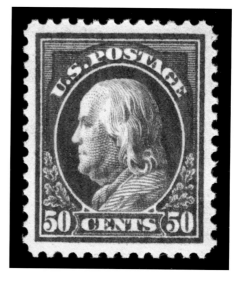

31664 #421, 1912, 50c Violet, XF-S 95 PSE. (Original Gum - Never Hinged). Deeply penetrating violet color printed on bright white paper. Visually perfect centering within symmetrical margins. Overall stunning eye-appeal. Extremely Fine to Superb. PSE - Encapsulated. (SMQ $7,350; this being one of 8 attaining this grade as of 10/08, with only 4 graded higher).

Estimate: $7,400+

Minimum Bid: $3,700

31665 **#422, 1912, 50c Violet, XF-S 95 PSE.** (Original Gum - Never Hinged). Warm and rich color. Post Office fresh. Extremely Fine to Superb. PSE - Encapsulated. (SMQ $4,600; this being one of 7 attaining this grade as of 10/08, with only 1 graded higher).

Estimate: $5,000+

Minimum Bid: $2,500

31666 **#423, 1912, $1 Violet Brown, XF-S 95J PSE.** (Original Gum - Previously Hinged). A remarkable mint single boasting prime centering within large margins. Intensely rich color and deeply etched impression, full original gum that requires extremely close examination to identify any previous hinging. Extremely Fine to Superb and choice. 2007 PSE - Graded Certificate, as well as 2007 PSE and 1983 PF Certificates. (this being one of 4 attaining this grade as of 10/08, with only 2 graded higher).

Estimate: $2,000+

Minimum Bid: $1,000

31667 **#423, 1912, $1 Violet Brown, XF-S 95 PSE.** (Original Gum - Never Hinged). An exquisite example with gigantic margins. Extremely Fine to Superb. 2007 PSE - Graded Certificate. (SMQ $1,550; this being one of 9 attaining this grade as of 10/08, with only 6 graded higher).

Estimate: $1,400+

Minimum Bid: $700

31668 **#423, 1912, $1 Violet Brown, XF 90J PSE.** (Used). Huge and gorgeous used single. Extremely Fine. PSE - Encapsulated. (this being one of 3 attaining this grade as of 10/08, with only 2 graded higher).

Estimate: $450+

Minimum Bid: $225

1913-15 WASHINGTON-FRANKLIN ISSUE - SGL. LINE WMK.

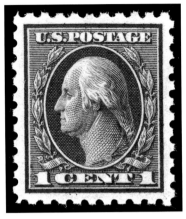

31669 **#424, 1914, 1c Green, GEM 100 PSE.** (Original Gum - Never Hinged). Dead-on centering. Rich color and strong impression. Gem. 2008 PSE - Graded Certificate. (this being one of 2 attaining this grade as of 10/08, with none graded higher).

Estimate: $1,000+

Minimum Bid: $500

TOP OF THE POP

31670 **#425, 1914, 2c Rose Red GEM 100 PSE.** (Original Gum - Never Hinged). Exciting quality single that can best be described as flawless perfection. Perfectly centered within balanced margins, an overall radiant example. 2008 PSE - Graded Certificate. (SMQ unvalued; this being one of 2 attaining this grade as of 10/08, with *none graded higher*).

Estimate: $1,000+

Minimum Bid: $500

Please visit HA.com to view other collectibles auctions.

31671 **#425, 1914, 2c Rose Red, SUP 98 PSE.** (Original Gum - Never Hinged). An extraordinary show-piece. Superb PSE - Encapsulated. (SMQ $465; this being one of 6 attaining this grade as of 10/08, with only 4 graded higher).
Estimate: $500+
Minimum Bid: $250

31672 **#426, 1914, 3c Deep Violet, SUP 98 PSE.** (Original Gum - Never Hinged). Deep color that is both intense and radiant at the same time. Superb. PSE - Encapsulated. (SMQ $1,550; this being one of 8 attaining this grade as of 10/08, with only 1 graded higher).
Estimate: $1,600+
Minimum Bid: $800

31673 **#426, 1914, 3c Deep Violet, XF-S 95 PSE.** (Original Gum - Never Hinged). Rich and fresh. Extremely Fine to Superb PSE - Encapsulated. (SMQ $490; this being one of 14 attaining this grade as of 10/08, with 12 graded higher).
Estimate: $500+
Minimum Bid: $250

31674 **#427, 1914, 4c Brown, XF-S 95 PSE.** (Original Gum - Never Hinged). Remarkably fresh and strong for grade. Extremely Fine to Superb. PSE - Encapsulated. (SMQ $1,050; this being one of 15 attaining this grade as of 10/08, with only 6 graded higher).
Estimate: $1,000+
Minimum Bid: $500

31675 **#428, 1914, 5c Blue, XF-S 95 PSE.** (Original Gum - Never Hinged). Rich penetrating blue color and perfect margins. Extremely Fine to Superb. 2008 PSE - Graded Certificate. (SMQ $1,050; this being one of 25 attaining this grade as of 10/08, with only 3 graded higher).
Estimate: $900+
Minimum Bid: $450

31676 **#428, 1914, 5c Blue, XF-S 95 PSE.** (Original Gum - Never Hinged). Fresh and delightful. Extremely Fine to Superb PSE - Encapsulated. (SMQ $1,050; this being one of 25 attaining this grade as of 10/08, with only 3 graded higher).
Estimate: $900+
Minimum Bid: $450

31677 **#428, 1914, 5c Blue, XF-S 95 PSE.** (Original Gum - Never Hinged). Refreshing deep blue color, very large margins. Extremely Fine to Superb. PSE - Encapsulated. (SMQ $1,050; this being one of 25 attaining this grade as of 10/08, with only 3 graded higher).
Estimate: $900+
Minimum Bid: $450

31678 **#429, 1914, 6c Red Orange, XF-S 95 PSE.** (Original Gum - Never Hinged). Warm pastel color amid large even margins. Extremely Fine to Superb PSE - Encapsulated. (SMQ $1,300; this being one of 13 attaining this grade as of 10/08, with only 4 graded higher).
Estimate: $1,300+
Minimum Bid: $650

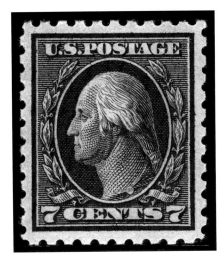

31679 #430, 1914, 7c Black, XF-S 95 PSE. (Original Gum - Never Hinged). Vibrant color and sharp impression. Fresh. Extremely Fine to Superb. PSE - Encapsulated. (SMQ $2,150; this being one of 11 attaining this grade as of 10/08, with only 2 graded higher).

Estimate: $2,100+

Minimum Bid: $1,050

31680 #431, 1914, 8c Pale Olive Green, SUP 98 PSE. (Original Gum - Never Hinged). Fresh and Bright. Superb. PSE - Encapsulated. (SMQ $3,300; this being one of 6 attaining this grade as of 10/08, with only 2 graded higher).

Estimate: $3,300+

Minimum Bid: $1,650

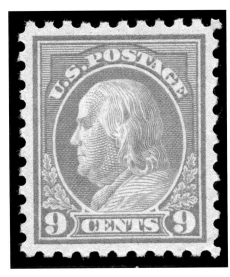

31681 #432, 1914, 9c Salmon Red SUP 98 PSE. (Original Gum - Never Hinged). Fresh and lively with wonderfully balanced margins. Superb. 2008 PSE - Graded Certificate and 1992 PF Certificate. (SMQ $3,450; this being one of 2 attaining this grade as of 10/08, with none graded higher).

Estimate: $4,250+

Minimum Bid: $2,125

31682 #432, 1914, 9c Salmon Red, XF-S 95 PSE. (Original Gum - Never Hinged). Stunning shade and color. Must have missed a J designator by only a whisker. Extremely Fine to Superb. PSE - Encapsulated. (SMQ $1,300; this being one of 11 attaining this grade as of 10/08, with only 4 graded higher).

Estimate: $1,300+

Minimum Bid: $650

31683 #433, 1914, 10c Orange Yellow, XF-S 95J PSE. (Original Gum - Never Hinged). Spectacular jumbo. Unbelievably fresh. Extremely Fine to Superb. 2007 PSE - Graded Certificate and 2004 PF Certificate. (this being one of 3 attaining this grade as of 10/08, with only 3 graded higher).

Estimate: $1,200+

Minimum Bid: $600

31684 #433, 1914, 10c Orange Yellow, XF-S 95 PSE. (Original Gum - Never Hinged). Pristine example with wide even margins. Extremely Fine to Superb. PSE - Encapsulated. (SMQ $1,250; this being one of 14 attaining this grade as of 10/08, with only 6 graded higher).

Estimate: $1,000+

Minimum Bid: $500

31685 #433, 1914, 10c Orange Yellow, XF-S 95 PSE. (Original Gum - Never Hinged). Blindingly radiant, fresh and pristine, a glaring jewel of exquisite quality. Extremely Fine to Superb. 2008 PSE - Graded Certificate. (SMQ $1,250; this being one of 14 attaining this grade as of 10/08, with only 6 graded higher).

Estimate: $1,000+

Minimum Bid: $500

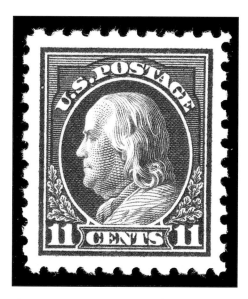

31686 **#434, 1914, 11c Dark Green, XF-S 95J PSE.** (Original Gum - Never Hinged). A superior mint single, flawlessly centered within giant well balanced margins, intense and vibrant. Immaculate full original gum. Extremely Fine to Superb for the serious collector. 2005 PSE - Graded Certificate and 2004 PF Certificate for block of four from which this is the bottom left stamp. (this being one of 3 attaining this grade as of 10/08, with only 5 graded higher).

Estimate: $1,250+

Minimum Bid: $625

31687 **#434, 1914, 11c Dark Green, XF-S 95 PSE.** (Original Gum - Never Hinged). Intense color and vivid impression. Extremely Fine to Superb. PSE - Encapsulated. (SMQ $810; this being one of 13 attaining this grade as of 10/08, with only 8 graded higher).

Estimate: $800+

Minimum Bid: $400

31688 **#434, 1914, 11c Dark Green, XF-S 95 PSE.** (Original Gum - Never Hinged). A magnificently fresh mint single. Extremely Fine to Superb. 2007 PSE - Graded Certificate. (SMQ $810; this being one of 13 attaining this grade as of 10/08, with only 8 graded higher).

Estimate: $800+

Minimum Bid: $400

31689 **#435, 1914, 12c Claret Brown, XF-S 95 PSE.** (Original Gum - Never Hinged). Stunning color and strong, detailed impression on fresh white paper. Extremely Fine to Superb. PSE - Encapsulated. (SMQ $880; this being one of 13 attaining this grade as of 10/08, with only 4 graded higher).

Estimate: $800+

Minimum Bid: $400

31690 **#437, 1914, 15c Gray, SUP 98 PSE.** (Original Gum - Previously Hinged). A gorgeous mint right sheet margin single, precisely centered, with a warm pastel color and finely detailed impression on fresh white paper, original gum, the gum showing only a very light traces from having been previously hinged. A Superb example. 2006 PSE - Graded Certificate. (SMQ $950; this being one of 3, attaining this grade as of 10/08, with only 1 graded higher).

Estimate: $1,100+

Minimum Bid: $550

31691 **#437, 1914, 15c Gray, XF-S 95 PSE.** (Original Gum - Never Hinged). Vivid color and detailed impression. Extremely Fine to Superb and elusive in high grade. PSE - Encapsulated. (SMQ $2,750; this being one of 8 attaining this grade as of 10/08, with only 2 graded higher).

Estimate: $2,500+

Minimum Bid: $1,250

31692 **#439, 1914, 30c Orange Red XF-S 95 PSE.** (Original Gum - Never Hinged). Dazzling bright color and razor sharp impression. Extremely Fine to Superb. PSE - Encapsulated. (SMQ $4,700; this being one of 5 attaining this grade as of 10/08, with only 3 graded higher).

Estimate: $4,000+

Minimum Bid: $2,000

31693 **#439, 1914, 30c Orange Red, XF-S 95 PSE.** (Original Gum - Never Hinged). Bright and vivid color, detailed impression. Fresh. Extremely Fine to Superb PSE - Encapsulated. (SMQ $4,700; this being one of 5 attaining this grade as of 10/08, with only 3 graded higher).

Estimate: $4,000+

Minimum Bid: $2,000

31694 **#440, 1915, 50c Violet SUP 98 PSE.** (Original Gum - Never Hinged). Absolutely stunning, the margins are wide and balanced on all sides, the paper crisp and clean both front and back, the gum is pristine. A Superb example for the record books. 2007 PSE - Graded Certificate. (SMQ $20,500; this being one of 4 attaining this grade as of 10/08, with none graded higher).

Estimate: $25,000+

Minimum Bid: $12,500

31695 **#440, 1915, 50c Violet, XF-S 95 PSE.** (Original Gum - Never Hinged). A luxuriously warm and vibrant mint single, impeccably centered and fresh as the day printed, with pristine full original gum. An Extremely Fine to Superb example for the connoisseur of true quality. 2007 PSE - Graded Certificate and 1994 PF Certificate. (SMQ $8,800; this being one of 6 attaining this grade as of 10/08, with only 5 graded higher).

Estimate: $9,000+

Minimum Bid: $4,500

31696 **#441, 1914, 1c Green, SUP 98J PSE.** (Original Gum - Never Hinged). The best color and impression combination possible, plus magnificent jumbo margins. Superb. 2008 PSE - Graded Certificate. (this being one of 5 attaining this grade as of 10/08, with only 4 graded higher).

Estimate: $400+

Minimum Bid: $200

31697 **#445, 1914, 3c Violet, XF-S 95 PSE.** (Original Gum - Previously Hinged). Coil Guide Line Pair. Prior hinge mark, no remnant, and eye-pleasing centering. Extremely Fine to Superb. 2003 PSE - Graded Certificate. (SMQ $2,700; this being one of 4 attaining this grade as of 10/08, with only 1 graded higher).

Estimate: $2,500+

Minimum Bid: $1,250

31698 **#445, 1914, 3c Violet.** (Original Gum - Never Hinged). Coil Guide Line Pair. Deep dark color, ample to large margins. Very Fine. 2008 PSE Certificate. (Scott $2,800).

Estimate: $2,000+

Minimum Bid: $1,000

31699 **#445, 1914, 3c Violet, XF-S 95 PSE.** (Original Gum - Previously Hinged). Coil Pair. A spectacular example with wide, even margins and great color, original gum showing light disturbance from previous hinging at approximately mid-height across the pair. Extremely Fine - Superb and rare in high grade. 2006 PSE - Graded Certificate, as well as 2001 PSE and 1976 PF Certificates. (SMQ $1,250; this being one of 4 attaining this grade as of 10/08, with only 1 graded higher).

Estimate: $1,000+

Minimum Bid: $500

31700 **#445, 1914, 3c Violet, VF-XF 85 PSE.** (Original Gum - Hinged). Coil Pair. Hinge remnant at top center. Very Fine to Extremely Fine. PSE - Encapsulated. (SMQ $690; this being one of 7 attaining this grade as of 10/08, with 12 graded higher).

Estimate: $500+

Minimum Bid: $250

31701 **#445, 1914, 3c Violet, XF-S 95 PSE.** (Used). Coil Pair. Very light non-obtrusive black cancel. Extremely Fine to Superb. 2008 PSE - Graded Certificate. (SMQ $3,350; this being one of 2 attaining this grade as of 10/08, with *none graded higher*).

Estimate: $3,100+

Minimum Bid: $1,550

31702 **#446, 1914, 4c Brown, SUP 98 PSE.** (Original Gum - Previously Hinged). Coil Guide Line Pair. Rich and thick color, sharp and detailed, with extra large to huge margins. Very light hinge mark with no remnant. 2008 PSE - Graded Certificate and 1980 PF Certificate. (SMQ $2,500; this being one of 2 attaining this grade as of 10/08, with none graded higher).

Estimate: $3,500+

Minimum Bid: $1,750

31703 **#446, 1914, 4c Brown, VF-XF 85 PSE.** (Original Gum - Previously Hinged). Coil Guide Line Pair. Fresh Color. Very light prior hinge mark only. Very Fine to Extremely Fine. PSE - Encapsulated. (SMQ $920; this being the only example attaining this grade as of 10/08, with only 9 graded higher).

Estimate: $700+

Minimum Bid: $350

31704 **#446, 1914, 4c Brown.** (Original Gum - Never Hinged). Coil Guide Line Pair. Intense color and sharp impression. Fine to Very Fine. 2008 PSE Certificate. (Scott $1,650).

Estimate: $1,200+

Minimum Bid: $600

31705 **#446, 1914, 4c Brown, XF-S 95 PSE.** (Original Gum - Never Hinged). Coil Pair. Very fresh with monster margins. Extremely Fine to Superb PSE - Encapsulated. (SMQ $2,750; this being one of 3 attaining this grade as of 10/08, with only 3 graded higher).

Estimate: $2,400+

Minimum Bid: $1,200

31706 **#446, 1914, 4c Brown GEM 100 PSE.** (Original Gum - Never Hinged). Coil Single. Unmatched perfection, enormous perfectly matched margins, an impression that looks carved into the bright paper, with a lovely rich almost chocolate brown color, and unblemished gleaming gum. A true world record candidate Gem. 2008 PSE - Graded Certificate. (this being the *unique example attaining this grade* as of 10/08, with *none graded higher*).

Estimate: $10,000+

Minimum Bid: $5,000

31707 **#447, 1914, 5c Blue, XF-S 95 PSE.** (Original Gum - Never Hinged). Coil Guide Line Pair. Marvelously bright and fresh with ample margins. Extremely Fine to Superb. PSE - Encapsulated. (SMQ $2,150; this being one of 7 attaining this grade as of 10/08, with only 8 graded higher).

Estimate: $2,000+

Minimum Bid: $1,000

31708 **#448, 1915, 1c Green, SUP 98 PSE.** (Original Gum - Never Hinged). Coil Pair. Stunning and Superb. 2008 PSE - Graded Certificate. (SMQ $710; this being one of 2 attaining this grade as of 10/08, with only 4 graded higher).

Estimate: $600+

Minimum Bid: $300

HIGHEST GRADED NEVER HINGED GUIDE LINE PAIR

31709 **#449, 1915, 2c Red, VF 80 PSE.** (Original Gum - Never Hinged). One of the rarest Coil Guide Line Pairs. Gorgeous red color with ample margins. Very Fine and nearly impossible to acquire in any condition. PSE - Encapsulated. (SMQ $29,000; this being the *sole example attaining this grade* as of 10/08, with *none graded higher*).

Estimate: $29,000+

Minimum Bid: $14,500

31710 **#452, 1914, 1c Green, XF-S 95 PSE.** (Original Gum - Never Hinged). Coil Guide Line Pair. Nicely balanced, with soft warm color. Extremely Fine to Superb. PSE - Encapsulated. (SMQ $600; this being one of 4, attaining this grade as of 10/08, with only 3 graded higher).

Estimate: $450+

Minimum Bid: $225

31711 **#452, 1914, 1c Green, XF-S 95 PSE.** (Original Gum - Never Hinged). Coil Joint Line Pair. Fresh and vibrant. Extremely Fine to Superb. 2008 PSE - Graded Certificate. (SMQ $600; this being one of 12 attaining this grade as of 10/08, with only 3 graded higher).

Estimate: $450+

Minimum Bid: $225

31712 **#453, 1914, 2c Carmine Rose, VF 80 PSE.** (Original Gum - Never Hinged). Coil Joint Line Pair. Attractive and fresh. Very Fine. 2008 PSE - Graded Certificate. (SMQ $1,650; this being one of 2 attaining this grade as of 10/08, with 15 graded higher).

Estimate: $1,400+

Minimum Bid: $700

31713 **#453, 1914, 2c Carmine Rose, XF 90 PSE.** (Original Gum - Previously Hinged). Coil Pair. Magnificently centered, fresh and vibrant, with only light traces of previous hinging. Extremely Fine. 2005 PSE - Graded Certificate. (SMQ $510; this being one of 3 attaining this grade as of 10/08, with only 2 graded higher).

Estimate: $450+

Minimum Bid: $225

31714 **#453, 1914, 2c Carmine Rose, XF-S 95 PSE.** (Original Gum - Never Hinged). Coil Single. Virtual perfection, nice color with well-balanced margins. Extremely Fine to Superb. PSE - Encapsulated. (SMQ $1,500; this being one of 8 attaining this grade as of 10/08, with only 1 graded higher).

Estimate: $1,500+

Minimum Bid: $750

HIGHEST GRADED PAIR

31715 **#454, 1915, 2c Red, SUP 98 PSE.** (Original Gum - Never Hinged). Coil Pair. Fresh and vibrant. Superb PSE - Encapsulated. (SMQ $1,250; this being the *sole example attaining this grade as of 10/08, with none graded higher*).

Estimate: $1,250+

Minimum Bid: $625

31716 **#454, 1915, 2c Red, XF 90 PSE.** (Original Gum - Never Hinged). Coil Pair. Fresh color and gum. Extremely Fine PSE - Encapsulated. (SMQ $630; this being one of 6 attaining this grade as of 10/08, with only 5 graded higher).

Estimate: $500+

Minimum Bid: $250

31717 **#455, 1915, 2c Carmine SUP 98 PSE.** (Original Gum - Never Hinged). Coil Joint Line Pair. Delightfully fresh and scarce. Superb. 2008 PSE - Graded Certificate. (SMQ $770; one of 6 attaining this grade as of 10/08, with only 2 graded higher).

Estimate: $700+

Minimum Bid: $350

31718 **#456, 1916, 3c Violet.** (Original Gum - Previously Hinged). Coil Joint Line Pair. Exceptionally well-centered, fresh pastel color and detailed impression, light hinge mark on both stamps. Very Fine to Extremely Fine; 2004 and 1981 PF Certificates. (Scott $1,250).

Estimate: $1,000+

Minimum Bid: $500

SWEET QUALITY

31719 **#456, 1916, 3c Violet, XF-S 95 PSE.** (Original Gum - Never Hinged). Coil Pair. Nearly perfect centering and luxuriously fresh. Extremely Fine to Superb. PSE - Encapsulated. (SMQ $4,550; this being the only example attaining this grade as of 10/08, with only 2 graded higher).

Estimate: $4,550+

Minimum Bid: $2,275

31720 **#456, 1916, 3c Red Violet, SUP 98 PSE.** (Used). Coil Single. Dead-on centering, with a wonderful pastel color, light wavy line machine cancel. Superb. 2008 PSE - Graded Certificate. (SMQ $2500; this being the *only example attaining this grade* as of 10/08, with *none graded higher*).

Estimate: $3,000+

Minimum Bid: $1,500

31721 **#458, 1916, 5c Blue, XF-S 95 PSE.** (Original Gum - Never Hinged). Coil Joint Line Pair. Well-centered within ample margins, deep fresh color, and pristine original gum. Extremely Fine to Superb. PSE - Encapsulated. (SMQ $1,400; this being one of 2 attaining this grade as of 10/08, with only 3 graded higher).

Estimate: $1,400+

Minimum Bid: $700

31722 **#458, 1916, 5c Blue, XF 90 PSE.** (Original Gum - Never Hinged). Coil Joint Line Pair. Each stamp precisely centered, rich and vibrant. Extremely Fine for the quality conscious collector. 2007 PSE - Graded Certificate. (SMQ $720; this being one of 3 attaining this grade as of 10/08, with 11 graded higher).

Estimate: $750+

Minimum Bid: $375

31723 **#458, 1916, 5c Blue, SUP 98 PSE.** (Original Gum - Never Hinged). Coil Pair. Perfectly balanced margins and deep rich color. Superb. PSE - Encapsulated. (SMQ $1,050; this being one of 3 attaining this grade as of 10/08, with none graded higher).

Estimate: $1,050+

Minimum Bid: $525

31724 **#458, 1916, 5c Blue, XF-S 95 PSE.** (Original Gum - Never Hinged). Coil Pair. Bright and Fresh. Extremely Fine to Superb. PSE - Encapsulated. (SMQ $600; this being one of 6 attaining this grade as of 10/08, with only 5 graded higher).

Estimate: $450+

Minimum Bid: $225

31725 **#458, 1916, 5c Blue, SUP 98 PSE.** (Original Gum - Never Hinged). Coil Single. Gorgeous and fresh. Superb. 2008 PSE - Graded Certificate. (SMQ $550; this being one of 3 attaining this grade as of 10/08, with none graded higher).

Estimate: $500+

Minimum Bid: $250

31726 **#459, 1914, 2c Carmine, SUP 98 PSE.** (Original Gum - Never Hinged). Imperforate Coil Pair. Bright color on crisp white paper. Superb. PSE - Encapsulated. (SMQ $900; this being one of 5 attaining this grade as of 10/08, with none graded higher).

Estimate: $800+

Minimum Bid: $400

31727 **#459, 1914, 2c Carmine, SUP 98 PSE.** (Original Gum - Never Hinged). Imperforate Coil Pair. Fresh and vibrant. Superb. 2005 PSE - Graded Certificate. (SMQ $900; this being one of 5 attaining this grade as of 10/08, with none graded higher).

Estimate: $800+

Minimum Bid: $400

31728 **#459, 1914, 2c Carmine, XF-S 95; PSE.** (Original Gum - Never Hinged). Imperforate Coil Pair. Dazzlingly bright color and razor sharp impression. Extremely Fine to Superb. PSE - Encapsulated. (SMQ $760; this being one of 19 attaining this grade as of 10/08, with only 5 graded higher).

Estimate: $700+

Minimum Bid: $350

31729 **#460, 1915, $1 Violet Black, SUP 98 PSE.** (Original Gum - Previously Hinged). Spectacular Centering. Light prior hinge mark only. Superb PSE - Encapsulated. (SMQ $3,850; this being one of 4 attaining this grade as of 10/08, with none graded higher).

Estimate: $2,750+

Minimum Bid: $1,375

TOP OF THE POP - GEM 100

31730 **#461, 1915, 2c Pale Carmine Red, GEM 100 PSE.** (No Gum). Absolutely perfect in every aspect, showpiece of perfection, fabulous pale carmine red color, mint no gum. Gem. 2008 PSE - Graded Certificate. (this being the *only example attaining this grade* as of 10/08, with *none graded higher*).

Estimate: $1,500+

Minimum Bid: $750

31731 **#461, 1915, 2c Pale Carmine Red, XF-S 95 PSE.** (Original Gum - Never Hinged). Post Office fresh. Extremely Fine to Superb. 2008 PSE - Graded Certificate. (SMQ $2,850; this being one of 9 attaining this grade as of 10/08, with only 1 graded higher).

Estimate: $3,000+

Minimum Bid: $1,500

31732 **#461, 1915, 2c Pale Carmine Red, XF-S 95 PSE.** (Original Gum - Previously Hinged). Stellar condition with light trace of previous hinging. Extremely Fine to Superb. 2007 PSE - Graded Certificate. (SMQ $435; this being one of 4 attaining this grade as of 10/08, with only 2 graded higher).

Estimate: $450+

Minimum Bid: $225

31733 **#461, 1915, 2c Pale Carmine Red, XF 90 PF.** (Original Gum - Never Hinged). An attention-grabbing example, post office fresh and exceptionally well-centered for the issue. Extremely Fine. 2006 PF Graded Certificate.

Estimate: $1,000+

Minimum Bid: $500

Please visit <u>HA.com</u> to view other collectibles auctions. *A 19.5% Buyer's Premium ($9 min.) Applies To All Lots*

1916-22 WASHINGTON-FRANKLIN ISSUE - UNWATERMARKED

31734 **#463, 1916, 2c Carmine, SUP 98J PSE.** (Original Gum - Never Hinged). Terrific jumbo left Plate No.7942 single, fresh and vibrant. Superb. 2008 PSE - Graded Certificate. (this being one of 2 attaining this grade as of 10/08, with only 1 graded higher).

Estimate: $500+

Minimum Bid: $250

31735 **#464, 1916, 3c Violet, XF-S 95 PSE.** (Original Gum   Never Hinged). Soft pastel tones, ample balanced margins, alluring overall appeal. Extremely Fine to Superb. PSE - Encapsulated. (SMQ $1,700; this being one of 9 attaining this grade as of 10/08, with only 1 graded higher).

Estimate: $1,500+

Minimum Bid: $750

31736 **#464, 1916, 3c Violet XF-S 95 PSE.** (Original Gum - Never Hinged). Very strong for grade. Deep shade and strong impression. Extremely Fine to Superb. 2008 PSE - Graded Certificate. (SMQ $1,700; this being one of 9 attaining this grade as of 10/08, with only 1 graded higher).

Estimate: $1,500+

Minimum Bid: $750

31737 **#465, 1916, 4c Orange Brown, XF-S 95 PSE.** (Original Gum - Never Hinged). Choice example, super bright and fresh. Extremely Fine to Superb. PSE - Encapsulated. (SMQ $1,200; this being one of 11 attaining this grade as of 10/08, with only 7 graded higher).

Estimate: $1,200+

Minimum Bid: $600

31738 **#466, 1916, 5c Blue, XF-S 95J PSE.** (Original Gum - Never Hinged). Extraordinarily warm and fresh, brilliantly centered within Jumbo balanced margins. Extremely Fine to Superb and destined for the finest collection. 2008 PSE - Graded Certificate and 2002 PF Certificate. (this being one of 4 attaining this grade as of 10/08, with only 2 graded higher).

Estimate: $2,000+

Minimum Bid: $1,000

31739 **#466, 1916, 5c Blue, XF-S 95 PSE.** (Original Gum - Never Hinged). Well-centered with deep rich color. Extremely Fine to Superb. PSE - Encapsulated. (SMQ $1,700; this being one of 3 attaining this grade as of 10/08, with only 6 graded higher).

Estimate: $1,700+

Minimum Bid: $850

ERROR OF COLOR - GRAND SHOWPIECE

31740 **#467, 1916, 5c Carmine, SUP 98 PSE.** (Original Gum - Never Hinged). A magnificent large margined showpiece showing portions of all the eight adjoining stamps. The finest graded to date. Superb. PSE - Encapsulated. (SMQ $17,400; this being one of 2 attaining this grade as of 10/08, with none graded higher).

Estimate: $14,000+

Minimum Bid: $7,000

31741 **#467, 1916, 5c Carmine, XF-S 95 PSE.** (Original Gum - Never Hinged). A Post Office fresh masterpiece. Extremely Fine to Superb and rare in high grade. 2008 PSE - Graded Certificate and 2003 PF Certificate. (SMQ $7,950; this being one of 9 attaining this grade as of 10/08, with only 2 graded higher).

Estimate: $6,500+

Minimum Bid: $3,250

31742 **#467, 1916, 5c Carmine, XF 90 PSE.** (Original Gum - Never Hinged). An outstanding mint example with small portions of the adjoining stamps attached left and right. Fresh and vibrant. Extremely Fine. 2005 PSE - Graded Certificate and 1996 PF Certificate. (SMQ $2,900; this being one of 6 attaining this grade as of 10/08, with 12 graded higher).

Estimate: $2,400+

Minimum Bid: $1,200

31743 **#468, 1916, 6c Red Orange, XF-S 95 PSE.** (Original Gum - Never Hinged). Splendidly centered with bright, nearly blinding color and deeply etched impression. Extremely Fine to Superb. PSE - Encapsulated. (SMQ $2,150; this being one of 9 attaining this grade as of 10/08, with only 4 graded higher).

Estimate: $2,000+

Minimum Bid: $1,000

31744 **#470, 1916, 8c Olive Green, XF-S 95 PSE.** (Original Gum - Never Hinged). Spectacular and fresh, well-centered with a luxuriously rich color and detailed impression. Extremely Fine to Superb. PSE - Encapsulated. (SMQ $1,550; this being one of 8 attaining this grade as of 10/08, with only 9 graded higher).

Estimate: $1,400+

Minimum Bid: $700

31746 **#471, 1916, 9c Salmon Red, XF-S 95 PSE.** (Original Gum - Never Hinged). Post Office fresh. Extremely Fine to Superb. 2005 PSE - Graded Certificate and 2001 PF Certificate. (SMQ $1,550; this being one of 12 attaining this grade as of 10/08, with only 4 graded higher).

Estimate: $1,200+

Minimum Bid: $600

31748 **#472, 1916, 10c Orange Yellow, XF-S 95 PSE.** (Original Gum - Never Hinged). Impressively well-centered with a sharp impression and glowing color. Extremely Fine to Superb. PSE - Encapsulated. (SMQ $2,400; this being one of 11 attaining this grade as of 10/08, with only 3 graded higher).

Estimate: $2,000+

Minimum Bid: $1,000

31745 **#471, 1916, 9c Salmon Red, XF-S 95 PSE.** (Original Gum - Never Hinged). Bright and fresh. A strong 95. Extremely Fine to Superb. PSE - Encapsulated. (SMQ $1,550; this being one of 12 attaining this grade as of 10/08, with only 4 graded higher).

Estimate: $1,200+

Minimum Bid: $600

31747 **#472, 1916, 10c Orange Yellow, XF-S 95 PSE.** (Original Gum - Never Hinged). Spectacular eye-appeal, perfect centering with large balanced margins, lavish rich color. Extremely Fine to Superb. PSE - Encapsulated. (SMQ $2,400; this being one of 11 attaining this grade as of 10/08, with only 3 graded higher).

Estimate: $2,000+

Minimum Bid: $1,000

31749 **#473, 1916, 11c Dark Green, XF-S 95 PSE.** (Original Gum - Never Hinged). Splendidly centered with a sharp impression and intensely rich color. Extremely Fine to Superb. PSE - Encapsulated. (SMQ $1,150; this being one of 11 attaining this grade as of 10/08, with 10 graded higher).

Estimate: $900+

Minimum Bid: $450

31750 **#473, 1916, 11c Dark Green, XF-S 95 PSE.** (Original Gum - Never Hinged). Precisely centered with blazing color and detailed impression. Extremely Fine to Superb. PSE - Encapsulated. (SMQ $1,150; this being one of 11 attaining this grade as of 10/08, with only 10 graded higher).

Estimate: $900+

Minimum Bid: $450

31751 **#474, 1916, 12c Claret Brown, XF-S 95 PSE.** (Original Gum - Never Hinged). Rich shade and sharp detailed impression. Strong for 95. Extremely Fine to Superb. PSE - Encapsulated. (SMQ $1,500; this being one of 8 attaining this grade as of 10/08, with only 2 graded higher).

Estimate: $1,500+

Minimum Bid: $750

31752 **#475, 1916, 15c Gray, XF-S 95 PSE.** (Original Gum - Never Hinged). Exciting and attractive. Precisely centered and fresh. Extremely Fine to Superb. PSE - Encapsulated. (SMQ $3,750; this being one of 13 attaining this grade as of 10/08, with only 5 graded higher).

Estimate: $3,500+

Minimum Bid: $1,750

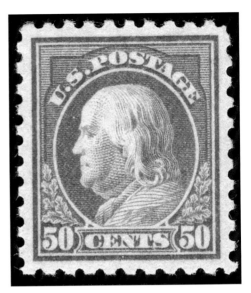

31753 **#477, 1916, 50c Light Violet, SUP 98 PSE.** (Original Gum - Previously Hinged). A superlative mint single, perfectly centered, with full even perforations all around, finely detailed with warm pastel color, original gum with a light hinge mark only. A Superb stamp. 2007 PSE - Graded Certificate. (SMQ $4,800; this being one of 2 attaining this grade as of 10/08, with none graded higher).

Estimate: $5,000+

Minimum Bid: $2,500

31754 **#477, 1916, 50c Light Violet, XF-S 95 PSE.** (Original Gum - Never Hinged). A gorgeous stamp of uncommon premium grade. Precisely centered, with a soft pastel color on crisp white paper. Extremely Fine to Superb. PSE - Encapsulated. (SMQ $13,600; this being one of 6 attaining this grade as of 10/08, with only 2 graded higher).

Estimate: $14,000+

Minimum Bid: $7,000

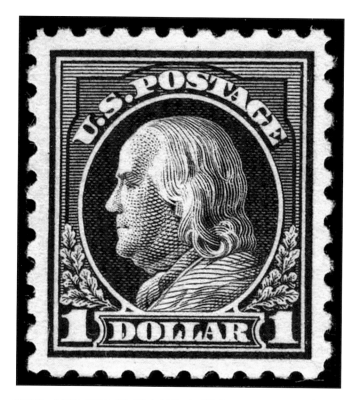

31755 #478, 1916, $1 Violet Black, XF-S 95 PSE. (Original Gum - Never Hinged). A handsome mint single, strong 95. Well-centered with large symmetrically balanced margins, a true violet black color unaffected by the passage of time. Post Office fresh in all respects. Extremely Fine to Superb PSE - Encapsulated. (SMQ $10,800; this being one of 10 attaining this grade as of 10/08, with only 1 graded higher).
Estimate: $11,000+
Minimum Bid: $5,500

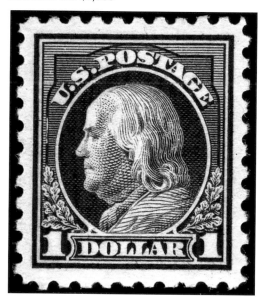

31756 #478, 1916, $1 Violet Black, XF 90 PSE. (Original Gum - Never Hinged). Vivacious color on clean white paper, with large even margins. Extremely Fine. PSE - Encapsulated. (SMQ $4,200; this being one of 11 attaining this grade as of 10/08, with 11 graded higher).
Estimate: $4,000+
Minimum Bid: $2,000

31757 #478, 1916, $1 Violet Black, XF 90 PSE. (Original Gum - Hinged). Gorgeous and fresh, with obvious hinge mark resulting from slightly untidy hinge removal. Extremely Fine. PSE - Encapsulated. (SMQ $1,100; this being one of 8 attaining this grade as of 10/08, with 16 graded higher).
Estimate: $900+
Minimum Bid: $450

31758 #478, 1916, $1 Violet Black, XF 90 PSE. (Original Gum - Hinged). A charming mint single, well centered, deep rich color and finely etched detail on white paper, original gum, previously hinged including a small hinge remnant. Extremely Fine. 2008 PSE - Graded Certificate. (SMQ $1,100; this being one of 8 attaining this grade as of 10/08, with 16 graded higher).
Estimate: $950+
Minimum Bid: $475

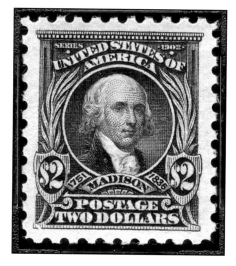

31759 #479, 1917, $2 Dark Blue, SUP 98 PSE. (Original Gum - Never Hinged). Perfectly centered, nearly jumbo, with intense color on crisp white paper. Superb. PSE - Encapsulated. (SMQ $4,250; this being one of 7 attaining this grade as of 10/08, with only 1 graded higher).
Estimate: $3,750+
Minimum Bid: $1,875

31760 **#479, 1917, $2 Dark Blue, XF-S 95 PSE.** (Original Gum - Never Hinged). Precisely centered, with striking color and a razor sharp impression. Extremely Fine to Superb. PSE - Encapsulated. (SMQ $2,300; this being one of 20 attaining this grade as of 10/08, with only 8 graded higher).

Estimate: $2,000+

Minimum Bid: $1,000

31761 **#479, 1917, $2 Dark Blue, XF-S 95 PSE.** (Original Gum - Never Hinged). Gloriously rich and vibrant, perfectly centered within generous margins. Extremely Fine to Superb; 2008 PSE - Graded Certificate. (SMQ $2,300; this being one of 20 attaining this grade as of 10/08, with only 8 graded higher).

Estimate: $2,000+

Minimum Bid: $1,000

31762 **#479, 1917, $2 Dark Blue, XF-S 95 PSE.** (Original Gum - Never Hinged). A visually striking mint single, beautifully centered amongst lavish margins, with full even perforations all around. Luxuriously rich color and a razor sharp impression, flawless full original gum. Extremely Fine to Superb and desirable. 2005 PSE - Graded Certificate. (SMQ $2,300; this being one of 20, attaining this grade as of 10/08, with only 8 graded higher).

Estimate: $2,000+

Minimum Bid: $1,000

31763 **#480, 1917, $5 Light Green, SUP 98 PSE.** (Original Gum - Never Hinged). Intense color with detailed impression on fresh white paper. Superb. 2007 PSE - Graded Certificate. (SMQ $3,450; this being one of 6 attaining this grade as of 10/08, with none graded higher).

Estimate: $4,000+

Minimum Bid: $2,000

31764 **#480, 1917, $5 Light Green, XF-S 95 PSE.** (Original Gum - Never Hinged). Very fresh color and impression. Extremely Fine to Superb. PSE - Encapsulated. (SMQ $1,950; this being one of 29 attaining this grade as of 10/08, with 11 graded higher).

Estimate: $1,600+

Minimum Bid: $800

31765 **#480, 1917, $5 Light Green, XF-S 95 PSE.** (Original Gum - Never Hinged). Tremendous example with bright color and sharp impression. Extremely Fine to Superb. 2006 PSE - Graded Certificate. (SMQ $1,950; this being one of 29 attaining this grade as of 10/08, with 11 graded higher).

Estimate: $1,600+

Minimum Bid: $800

RARE TYPE IA

31766 **#482A, 1916, 2c Deep Rose, Type Ia.** (Used). Type Ia with Type III Schermack private vending machine perforations. Insignificant tiny nick at upper right opposite the "E" in "Postage". 2005 PF Certificate. (Scott $65,000).
Estimate: $55,000+
Minimum Bid: $27,500

31767 **#485, 1917, 5c Carmine, SUP 98J PSE.** (Original Gum - Never Hinged). Imperforate Error of Denomination. Fresh and vibrant with Jumbo margins. Superb. 2006 PSE - Graded Certificate. (this being the only example attaining this grade as of 10/08, with only 1 graded higher). (SMQ does not value this stamp).

Estimate: $35,000+
Minimum Bid: $17,500

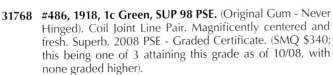

31768 **#486, 1918, 1c Green, SUP 98 PSE.** (Original Gum - Never Hinged). Coil Joint Line Pair. Magnificently centered and fresh. Superb. 2008 PSE - Graded Certificate. (SMQ $340; this being one of 3 attaining this grade as of 10/08, with none graded higher).

Estimate: $350+
Minimum Bid: $175

31769 **#487, 1916, 2c Carmine, SUP 98 PSE.** (Original Gum - Never Hinged). Coil Pair. Luxuriously fresh and precisely centered. Superb PSE - Encapsulated. (SMQ $560; this being one of 2 attaining this grade as of 10/08, with none graded higher).

Estimate: $600+
Minimum Bid: $300

31770 #491, 1916, 2c Carmine. (Original Gum - Previously Hinged). Coil Joint Line Pair. Fresh and bright with only the barest trace of a hinge mark on each stamp. Fine to Very Fine. 2008 PSE Certificate. (Scott $14,000).
Estimate: $10,000+
Minimum Bid: $5,000

31771 #491, 1916, 2c Carmine, F 70 PSE. (Used). Coil Pair. Type II with double oval cancel. Fine PSE - Encapsulated. (SMQ $1950; this being one of 2 attaining this grade as of 10/08, with only 3 graded higher).
Estimate: $1,200+
Minimum Bid: $600

31772 #492, 1916, 2c Carmine, SUP 98 PSE. (Original Gum - Never Hinged). Coil Pair. Perfectly centered and fresh. Superb PSE - Encapsulated. (SMQ $480; this being one of 3 attaining this grade as of 10/08, with none graded higher).
Estimate: $500+
Minimum Bid: $250

31773 #495, 1917, 4c Orange Brown, SUP 98 PSE. (Original Gum - Never Hinged). Coil Line Pair. Superb PSE - Encapsulated. (SMQ $1700; this being one of 9 attaining this grade as of 10/08, with none graded higher).
Estimate: $2,000+
Minimum Bid: $1,000

31774 #500, 1917, 2c Deep Rose, XF-S 95 PSE. (Original Gum - Never Hinged). Type Ia. A pristine example with outstanding eye appeal. Extremely Fine to Superb. PSE - Encapsulated. (SMQ $4,200; this being one of 3 attaining this grade as of 10/08, with only 5 graded higher).

Estimate: $4,000+

Minimum Bid: $2,000

1917-19 WASHINGTON-FRANKLIN ISSUE - PERF 11

31775 #503, 1917, 4c Brown, SUP 98 PSE. (Original Gum - Never Hinged). Choice and fresh with rich color and a crisp impression. Superb PSE - Encapsulated. (SMQ $870; this being one of 8 attaining this grade as of 10/08, with only 7 graded higher).

Estimate: $800+

Minimum Bid: $400

TOP OF THE POP ERROR OF DENOMINATION

31776 #505, 1917, 5c Rose SUP 98 PSE. (Original Gum - Hinged). Almost perfect mint example, sporting wide margins all around and gleaming color, original gum, light hinge marks with tiny remnant. Superb. 2008 PSE - Graded Certificate. (SMQ $1,500; this being the *sole example attaining this grade* as of 10/08, with *none graded higher*).

Estimate: $1,500+

Minimum Bid: $750

31777 #505, 1917, 5c Rose, XF-S 95 PSE. (Original Gum - Never Hinged). Rich and fresh with huge well-balanced margins. Extremely Fine to Superb. PSE - Encapsulated. (SMQ $4,300; this being one of 15, attaining this grade as of 10/08, with only 7 graded higher).

Estimate: $4,000+

Minimum Bid: $2,000

31778 #505, 1917, 5c Rose, XF 90 PSE. (Original Gum - Never Hinged). Precisely centered, fresh and rich. Extremely Fine. 2008 PSE - Graded Certificate. (SMQ $1,800; this being one of 10 attaining this grade as of 10/08, with 22 graded higher).

Estimate: $1,500+

Minimum Bid: $750

31779 #507, 1917, 7c Black, XF-S 95 PSE. (Original Gum - Never Hinged). Fresh and rich. Extremely Fine to Superb. PSE - Encapsulated. (SMQ $670; this being one of 32 attaining this grade as of 10/08, with 10 graded higher).

Estimate: $600+

Minimum Bid: $300

31780 #507, 1917, 7c Black XF-S 95 PSE. (Original Gum - Never Hinged). Ample well-balanced margins, rich and fresh. Extremely Fine to Superb. PSE - Encapsulated. (SMQ $670; this being one of 32, attaining this grade as of 10/08, with 10 graded higher).

Estimate: $600+

Minimum Bid: $300

31781 #507, 1917, 7c Black, XF-S 95 PSE. (Original Gum - Never Hinged). Post Office fresh. Extremely Fine to Superb. PSE - Encapsulated. (SMQ $670; this being one of 32 attaining this grade as of 10/08, with 10 graded higher).

Estimate: $600+

Minimum Bid: $300

31782 #509, 1917, 9c Salmon Red, SUP 98 PSE. (Original Gum - Never Hinged). Lovely pastel shade and finely detailed. Superb PSE - Encapsulated. (SMQ $1,100; this being one of 8 attaining this grade as of 10/08, with only 1 graded higher).

Estimate: $1,000+
Minimum Bid: $500

31783 #510, 1917, 10c Orange Yellow, SUP 98 PSE. (Original Gum - Never Hinged). Lustrous and lovely. Superb PSE - Encapsulated. (SMQ $1,350; this being one of 5 attaining this grade as of 10/08, with only 1 graded higher).

Estimate: $1,200+
Minimum Bid: $600

31784 #510a, 1917, 10c Brown Yellow. (Original Gum - Previously Hinged). Typically poorly centered, this copy better at F-VF. Small hinge remnant. Significantly undervalued in Scott. Fine to Very Fine. 2006 PF Certificate. (Scott $1,500).

Estimate: $3,000+
Minimum Bid: $1,500

31785 #512, 1917, 12c Claret Brown, SUP 98 PSE. (Original Gum - Never Hinged). Sharp and pristine. Superb. 2008 PSE - Graded Certificate. (SMQ $800; this being the only example attaining this grade as of 10/08, with only 2 graded higher).

Estimate: $700+
Minimum Bid: $350

31786 #512a, 1917, 12c Brown Carmine, SUP 98 PSE. (Original Gum - Never Hinged). Gorgeous and Fresh. Superb. 2008 PSE - Graded Certificate. (SMQ $870; this being one of 2 attaining this grade as of 10/08, with only 2 graded higher).

Estimate: $950+
Minimum Bid: $475

31787 #513, 1919, 13c Pale Apple Green, XF-S 95J PSE. (Original Gum - Never Hinged). Gorgeous Post Office fresh example with oversize margins. Extremely Fine to Superb and huge. 2007 PSE - Graded Certificate. (this being one of 9 attaining this grade as of 10/08, with 13 graded higher).

Estimate: $450+
Minimum Bid: $225

31788 #514, 1917, 15c Gray, SUP 98 PSE. (Original Gum - Never Hinged). Deliciously attractive, deep robust color with wide parallel margins, fresh. Superb. PSE - Encapsulated. (SMQ $2,550; this being one of 12 attaining this grade as of 10/08, with only 1 graded higher).

Estimate: $2,000+
Minimum Bid: $1,000

31789 **#514, 1917, 15c Gray, SUP 98 PSE.** (Original Gum - Never Hinged). Fresh and vibrant. Superb. PSE - Encapsulated. (SMQ $2,550; this being one of 12 attaining this grade as of 10/08, with only 1 graded higher).

Estimate: $2,000+

Minimum Bid: $1,000

31790 **#514, 1917, 15c Gray, SUP 98 PSE.** (Original Gum - Never Hinged). Bright and fresh with warm pastel color surrounded by large even margins. Superb. PSE - Encapsulated. (SMQ $2,550; this being one of 12 attaining this grade as of 10/08, with only 1 graded higher).

Estimate: $2,000+

Minimum Bid: $1,000

31791 **#515, 1917, 20c Light Ultramarine SUP 98J PSE.** (Original Gum - Never Hinged). A phenomenally monstrous mint bottom sheet margin single boasting unparalleled centering within boardwalk margins, stunningly warm pastel color and precisely etched detail, with pristine full original gum. A Superb gem typically impossible to find in such premium quality. 2007 PSE - Graded Certificate and 2001 PSE Certificate. (this being one of 5 attaining this grade as of 10/08, with none graded higher).

Estimate: $5,000+

Minimum Bid: $2,500

31792 **#515, 1917, 20c Light Ultramarine, XF-S 95 PSE.** (Original Gum - Never Hinged). Fresh and vibrant. Extremely Fine to Superb. 2007 PSE - Graded Certificate. (SMQ $1,000; this being one of 25 attaining this grade as of 10/08, with 14 graded higher).

Estimate: $800+

Minimum Bid: $400

31793 **#515, 1917, 20c Light Ultramarine, XF-S 95 PSE.** (Original Gum - Never Hinged). Rich and fresh. Extremely Fine to Superb. 2005 PSE - Graded Certificate. (SMQ $1,000; this being one of 25 attaining this grade as of 10/08, with 14 graded higher).

Estimate: $800+

Minimum Bid: $400

31794 **#516, 1917, 30c Orange Red, SUP 98 PSE.** (Original Gum - Never Hinged). Beautifully centered with broad margins, rich vibrant color. Superb PSE - Encapsulated. (SMQ $2,550; this being one of 10 attaining this grade as of 10/08, with only 3 graded higher).

Estimate: $2,000+

Minimum Bid: $1,000

31795 **#516, 1917, 30c Orange Red, SUP 98 PSE.** (Original Gum - Never Hinged). Exquisite example with gorgeously rich color on fresh white paper. Superb. PSE - Encapsulated. (SMQ $2,550; this being one of 10 attaining this grade as of 10/08, with only 3 graded higher).

Estimate: $2,000+

Minimum Bid: $1,000

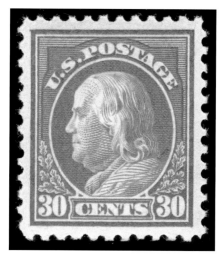

31796 **#516, 1917, 30c Orange Red, SUP 98 PSE.** (Original Gum - Never Hinged). Deeply etched impression and luscious color. Superb. PSE - Encapsulated. (SMQ $2,550; this being one of 10 attaining this grade as of 10/08, with only 3 graded higher).
Estimate: $2,000+
Minimum Bid: $1,000

MONSTER MARGINED PERFECTION

31797 **#517, 1917, 50c Red Violet, GEM 100J PSE.** (Original Gum - Never Hinged). World Class conditionally Unique. The epitome of perfection, with zero space for improvement of any kind. A tremendous mint Never Hinged GEM that is pristine, with an almost proof-like quality. An unrivalled Gem destined for the finest collection. 2007 PSE - Graded Certificate as well as 1987 and 2003 PF Certificates. (this being the *unique example attaining this grade* as of 10/08, with *none graded higher*).
Estimate: $10,000+
Minimum Bid: $5,000

31798 **#517, 1917, 50c Red Violet, SUP 98 PSE.** (Original Gum - Never Hinged). Sensational fresh example. Incredible centered within lavish margins. Superb. PSE - Encapsulated. (SMQ $2,800; this being one of 15 attaining this grade as of 10/08, with only 7 graded higher).

Estimate: $2,400+

Minimum Bid: $1,200

31799 **#517, 1917, 50c Red Violet, SUP 98 PSE.** (Original Gum - Never Hinged). Fresh and pristine. Superb. PSE - Encapsulated. (SMQ $2,800; this being one of 15 attaining this grade as of 10/08, with only 7 graded higher).

Estimate: $2,400+

Minimum Bid: $1,200

31800 **#517, 1917, 50c Red Violet, XF-S 95 PSE.** (Original Gum - Never Hinged). Awesome and fresh. Extremely Fine to Superb. 2007 PSE - Graded Certificate. (SMQ $1,100; this being one of 39 attaining this grade as of 10/08, with 28 graded higher).

Estimate: $900+

Minimum Bid: $450

31801 **#518, 1917, $1 Violet Brown SUP 98 PSE.** (Original Gum - Never Hinged). Perfectly centered with a finely detailed impression complimented by vivid color. Superb. 2006 PSE - Graded Certificate. (SMQ $2,550; this being one of 17 attaining this grade as of 10/08, with only 6 graded higher).

Estimate: $2,400+

Minimum Bid: $1,200

31802 **#518, 1917, $1 Violet Brown, SUP 98 PSE.** (Original Gum - Never Hinged). Perfectly centered, with a razor sharp impression and vibrant color. Superb. PSE - Encapsulated. (SMQ $2,550; this being one of 17 attaining this grade as of 10/08, with only 6 graded higher).

Estimate: $2,400+

Minimum Bid: $1,200

31803 **#518, 1917, $1 Violet Brown, SUP 98 PSE.** (Original Gum - Never Hinged). Marvelously fresh and very close to perfection. Superb. PSE - Encapsulated. (SMQ $2,550; this being one of 17 attaining this grade as of 10/08, with only 6 graded higher).

Estimate: $2,400+

Minimum Bid: $1,200

31804 **#518, 1917, $1 Violet Brown, XF-S 95 PSE.** (Original Gum - Never Hinged). Stunning and fresh. Extremely Fine to Superb. 2007 PSE - Graded Certificate. (SMQ $950; this being one of 48 attaining this grade as of 10/08, with 31 graded higher).

Estimate: $800+

Minimum Bid: $400

31805 **#518, 1917, $1 Violet Brown, XF-S 95 PSE.** (Original Gum - Never Hinged). Rich and fresh. Extremely Fine to Superb. 2004 PSE - Graded Certificate. (SMQ $950; this being one of 48 attaining this grade as of 10/08, with 31 graded higher).

Estimate: $800+

Minimum Bid: $400

31806 **#518b, 1917, $1 Deep Brown.** (Used). A Fine used example of this seldom found, yet rare color variety, with a trivial faint corner crease that can barely be seen under magnification; 2008 PF Certificate. (Scott $1,250).

Estimate: $500+

Minimum Bid: $250

31807 **#523, 1918, $2 Orange Red & Black, SUP 98 PSE.** (Original Gum - Never Hinged). Virtual perfection for the connoisseur, perfectly centered amidst enormous even margins, radiantly bright and fresh. Superb PSE - Encapsulated. (SMQ $10,000; this being one of 3 attaining this grade as of 10/08, with only 1 graded higher).

Estimate: $9,000+

Minimum Bid: $4,500

31808 **#523, 1918, $2 Orange Red & Black, XF 90 PSE.** (Original Gum - Never Hinged). Fresh and attractive. Extremely Fine. 2008 PSE - Graded Certificate. (SMQ $2,350; this being one of 11 attaining this grade as of 10/08, with 18 graded higher).

Estimate: $2,000+

Minimum Bid: $1,000

31809 **#523, 1918, $2 Orange Red & Black, XF 90 PSE.** (Original Gum - Previously Hinged). Light portion of prior hinge remnant. Extremely Fine. 2007 PSE - Graded Certificate. (SMQ $870; this being one of 18 attaining this grade as of 10/08, with 17 graded higher).

Estimate: $750+

Minimum Bid: $375

31810 **#523, 1918, $2 Orange Red & Black, F-VF 75 PSE.** (Original Gum - Never Hinged). Post Office fresh. Fine to Very Fine. PSE - Encapsulated. (this being one of 8 attaining this grade as of 10/08, with 49 graded higher).

Estimate: $800+

Minimum Bid: $400

31811 **#523, 1918, $2 Orange Red & Black, XF 90 PSE.** (Used). Los Angeles double oval cancel. Extremely Fine. 2005 PSE - Graded Certificate. (SMQ $490; this being one of 4 attaining this grade as of 10/08, with 11 graded higher).

Estimate: $450+

Minimum Bid: $225

31812 **#524, 1918, $5 Deep Green & Black, SUP 98 PSE.** (Original Gum - Never Hinged). Precisely centered, rich and bright. Superb. PSE - Encapsulated. (SMQ $4,300; this being one of 8 attaining this grade as of 10/08, with only 1 graded higher).

Estimate: $4,000+

Minimum Bid: $2,000

31813 **#524, 1918, $5 Deep Green & Black, XF-S 95 PSE.** (Original Gum - Never Hinged). Especially lovely and vibrant. Extremely Fine to Superb. PSE - Encapsulated. (SMQ $1,600; this being one of 25 attaining this grade as of 10/08, with 10 graded higher).

Estimate: $1,300+

Minimum Bid: $650

1918-20 WASHINGTON-FRANKLIN ISSUE - OFFSET ISSUES

31814 **#526, 1918, 2c Carmine, SUP 98 PSE.** (Original Gum - Never Hinged). A visually striking left sheet margin single, perfectly centered within margins approaching huge. Bright and vibrant with a deeply etched impression, and unblemished full original gum, fresh as the day printed. Absolutely Superb and virtually unrivalled. 2008 PSE - Graded Certificate. (SMQ $2,100; this being one of 4 attaining this grade as of 10/08, with only 2 graded higher).

Estimate: $2,400+

Minimum Bid: $1,200

31815 **#528, 1918, 2c Carmine, SUP 98 PSE.** (Original Gum - Never Hinged). A stunning condition rarity deserving of this lofty grade. Superb. PSE - Encapsulated. (SMQ $830; this being one of 3 attaining this grade as of 10/08, with only 4 graded higher).

Estimate: $800+

Minimum Bid: $400

31816 **#530, 1918, 3c Violet, SUP 98 PSE.** (Original Gum - Never Hinged). Exceptionally fresh and scarce in such high grade. Superb. PSE - Encapsulated. (SMQ $385; this being one of 2 attaining this grade as of 10/08, with only 3 graded higher).

Estimate: $400+

Minimum Bid: $200

31817 #531, 1919, 1c Green, GEM 100 PSE. (Used). Monster margined used example. Soft pastel color with very light double oval cancel. A Gem by definition. 2008 PSE - Graded Certificate. (this being the *only example attaining this grade* as of 10/08, with *none graded higher*).

Estimate: $450+

Minimum Bid: $225

31818 #532, 1918, 2c Carmine Rose, GEM 100J PSE. (Original Gum - Never Hinged). A world class condition rarity. a mint left sheet margin Plate No. 10918 single showing portions of the adjoining stamps, deeply rich and vibrant on fresh unblemished paper, with pristine full original gum. A true Gem in every sense of the word. 2008 PSE - Graded Certificate. (SMQ unvalued in such distinct grade; this being one of 13, attaining this grade as of 10/08, with none graded higher).

Estimate: $500+

Minimum Bid: $250

31819 #533, 1918, 2c Carmine, SUP 98 PSE. (Original Gum - Never Hinged). A magnificent bottom right, sheet corner margin single, luxuriously vibrant and detailed on immaculate white paper, with pristine full original gum. Superb. 2007 PSE - Graded Certificate. (SMQ $475; this being one of 5 attaining this grade as of 10/08, with only 5 graded higher).

Estimate: $500+

Minimum Bid: $250

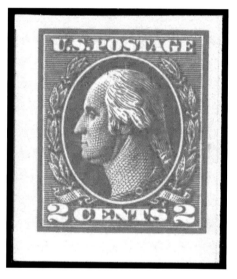

31820 #534B, 1918, 2c Carmine, XF 90J PSE. (Original Gum - Never Hinged). Fresh and bright, surprisingly detailed for an offset printing especially considering the slab label notation of a weak impression, which we really don't see any evidence of. Extremely Fine. PSE - Encapsulated. (this being the only example attaining this grade as of 10/08, with only 9 graded higher).

Estimate: $4,500+

Minimum Bid: $2,250

RARE USED PAIR - HUGE MARGINS

31821 **#534B, 1918, 2c Carmine.** (Used). A monstrous used pair tied on piece by black New Hampshire duplex cancel. A Gem destined for the finest collection. 2005 PSE Certificate. (Scott $4,500).

Estimate: $6,000+
Minimum Bid: $3,000

31822 **#536, 1919, 1c Gray Green, XF-S 95J PSE.** (Original Gum - Never Hinged). A tremendous mint jewel for the serious collector, perfectly centered within monstrous margins, full intact perforations all around, gloriously rich and vibrant. Extremely Fine to Superb. 2008 PSE - Graded Certificate. (this being one of 9 attaining this grade as of 10/08, with 10 graded higher).

Estimate: $1,000+
Minimum Bid: $500

1919-20 ISSUES

ELUSIVE SHADE AND CONDITION RARITY

31823 **#537a, 1919, 3c Deep Red Violet, XF 90 PSE.** (Original Gum - Previously Hinged). Only four original gum copies graded by PSE so far, this being one of the top two. Gum is super fresh, except for a narrow and short line of a prior hinge mark at top. Well-centered 537a's are nearly impossible to locate. Undervalued in SMQ. Extremely Fine. 2004 PSE - Graded Certificate. (SMQ $2,000; this being the only example attaining this grade as of 10/08, with only 1 graded higher).

Estimate: $2,500+
Minimum Bid: $1,250

31824 **#538, 1919, 1c Green SUP 98 PSE.** (Original Gum - Never Hinged). An extraordinary example, perfectly centered. Superb; 2004 PSE - Graded Certificate. (SMQ $950; this being one of 7 attaining this grade as of 10/08, with only 2 graded higher).

Estimate: $1,250+
Minimum Bid: $625

CONDITION RARITY

31825 **#539, 1919, 2c Carmine Rose.** (Original Gum - Never Hinged). Rotary Perf 11 x 10. One of the rarest 20th Century US Stamps. Stunning rich color and Choice centering. Shiny fresh gum. The vast majority of 539's are very poorly centered. Extremely Fine; 2005 PF Certificate,1994 PF Certificate. (Scott in grade of FINE = $4,250).

Estimate: $20,000+

Minimum Bid: $10,000

RARE UNUSED ROTARY PRESS SHEET WASTE

31826 **#544, 1923, 1c Green F 70 PSE.** (No Gum). Rich, vibrant, and reasonably well-centered for this Rotary Press Sheet Waste issue. Fine, 2007 PSE - Graded Certificate. (SMQ unvalued as No Gum, $35,000 as OGph; this being the *unique graded unused example* of this nearly impossible issue).

Estimate: $15,000+

Minimum Bid: $7,500

31827 **#544, 1923, 1c Green VF 80 PSE.** (Used). Well-centered example with a black wavy line machine cancel. Very Fine. 2007 PSE - Graded Certificate. (SMQ $7,500; this being one of 2 attaining this grade as of 10/08, with only 1 graded higher).

Estimate: $6,500+

Minimum Bid: $3,250

31828 **#544PR, 1923, 1c Green.** (Used). Horizontal pair centered above average for the issue, with a black slogan machine cancel and a tiny thin spot at the center of the right stamp. Fine. 2008 PSE Certificate, as well as 1941 American Board of Experts and 1966 PF Certificates. (Scott $7,500).

Estimate: $6,000+

Minimum Bid: $3,000

31829 **#546, 1921, 2c Carmine Rose XF-S 95 PSE.** (Original Gum - Never Hinged). As fresh as the day it was printed, with radiant color and perfect margins. Extremely Fine to Superb. 2007 PSE - Graded Certificate. (SMQ $2,300; this being one of 7 attaining this grade as of 10/08, with only 2 graded higher).

Estimate: $2,500+

Minimum Bid: $1,250

31830 **#546, 1921, 2c Carmine Rose, XF 90J PSE.** (Original Gum - Never Hinged). A magnificent example of this difficult issue sporting rarely found with Jumbo margins. Deep rich color. Extremely Fine. 2008 PSE - Graded Certificate and 1989 PF Certificate. (this being one of 3 attaining this grade as of 10/08, with 10 graded higher).

Estimate: $1,000+

Minimum Bid: $500

31831 **#546, 1921, 2c Carmine Rose XF 90J PSE.** (Original Gum - Never Hinged). A magnificent example of this "coil waste" issue, precisely centered within large well balanced margins, warm nearly pastel-like color and fresh impression, with unblemished full original gum. Extremely Fine. 2005 PSE - Graded Certificate. (this being one of 3 attaining this grade as of 10/08, with 10 graded higher).

Estimate: $1,000+

Minimum Bid: $500

31832 **#547, 1920, $2 Carmine & Black, XF-S 95J PSE.** (Original Gum - Never Hinged). Magnificently centered within huge well-balanced margins. Fresh with exceptional eye appeal. Extremely Fine to Superb. PSE - Encapsulated. (this being one of 2 attaining this grade as of 10/08, with only 3 graded higher).

Estimate: $1,500+

Minimum Bid: $750

31833 **#547, 1920, $2 Carmine & Black, XF-S 95 PSE.** (Original Gum - Never Hinged). Beautifully centered, rich and vibrant. A magnificent example. Extremely Fine to Superb. PSE - Graded Certificate. (SMQ $1,350; this being one of 34 attaining this grade as of 10/08, with only 5 graded higher).

Estimate: $1,200+

Minimum Bid: $600

31834 **#547, 1920, $2 Carmine & Black, XF-S 95 PSE.** (Original Gum - Never Hinged). A beautiful example, well-centered and with bright color. Extremely Fine to Superb. 2007 PSE - Graded Certificate. (SMQ $1,350; this being one of 34 attaining this grade as of 10/08, with only 5 graded higher).

Estimate: $1,200+

Minimum Bid: $600

31835 **#547, 1920, $2 Carmine & Black XF-S 95 PSE.** (Original Gum - Never Hinged). Bright and fresh. Gorgeously centered. Extremely Fine to Superb. 2008 PSE - Graded Certificate. (SMQ $1,350; this being one of 34 attaining this grade as of 10/08, with only 5 graded higher).

Estimate: $1,200+

Minimum Bid: $600

31836 **#547, 1920, $2 Carmine & Black, XF-S 95 PSE.** (Used). A magnificent used single, precisely centered within large well balanced margins, both intense and bold at the same time, with a light unobtrusive double oval Chicago cancel. Extremely Fine to Superb. 2008 PSE - Graded Certificate. (SMQ $230; this being one of 2 attaining this grade as of 10/08, with none graded higher).

Estimate: $500+

Minimum Bid: $250

1920 PILGRIM TERCENTENARY ISSUE

31837 **#550, 1920, 5c Deep Blue, XF-S 95J PSE.** (Original Gum - Never Hinged). Signing of the Compact. Magnificent and enormous with bright vibrant color. Extremely Fine to Superb. 2007 PSE - Graded Certificate. (this being one of 11 attaining this grade as of 10/08, with only 6 graded higher).

Estimate: $850+

Minimum Bid: $425

31838 **#550, 1920, 5c Deep Blue, XF-S 95 PSE.** (Original Gum - Never Hinged). Signing of the Compact. Rich and fresh. Extremely Fine to Superb. 2005 PSE - Graded Certificate. (SMQ $840; this being one of 27 attaining this grade as of 10/08, with 17 graded higher).

Estimate: $700+

Minimum Bid: $350

End of Session Two

Want to see your stamps in our next catalog?

Don't leave money on the table. Talk to Heritage before selling.

Q: How can you choose the right firm to auction your stamp collection?

A: Simple. Choose the company that will not only market your stamps to the hardcore collector, but also to 500,000 collectors outside the field, many of whom eagerly buy across multiple categories.

That's what Heritage Auction Galleries – formerly Ivy, Shreve & Mader – gives you that no one else can. There's a reason that Heritage is the World's Largest Collectibles Auctioneer. Come and see for yourself at www.HA.com.

Please contact Steve Crippe for a no-obligation proposal for your collection with a minimum pre-auction estimate of $5,000.

Receive a free copy of the next stamp catalog, or one from another Heritage category. Register on-line at HA.com/CATB16261 or call 866-835-3243 and mention reference #CATB16261. The entire catalog will go online approximately July 13th at HA.com/Stamps.

Steven Crippe, Director,
800-872-6467, ext. 1777
or StevenC@HA.com

SESSION THREE

Floor, Telephone, Heritage Live!™, Internet, Fax, and Mail Signature® Auction #1106
Friday, February 6, 2009, 12:00 PM CT • Dallas, Texas • Lots 31839-32290

A 19.5% Buyer's Premium ($9 minimum) Will Be Added To All Lots
You can now view full-color images and bid via the Internet at the Heritage website: HA.com/Stamps

1922-25 DEFINITIVES

31839 **#553, 1925, 1½c Yellow Brown, SUP 98J PSE.** (Original Gum - Never Hinged). Spectacular example with huge margins and radiant color. Superb. PSE - Encapsulated. (this being one of 8 attaining this grade as of 10/08, with only 2 graded higher).

Estimate: $400+

Minimum Bid: $200

31840 **#554, 1923, 2c Carmine, GEM 100 PSE.** (Original Gum - Never Hinged). A gem for the perfectionist. Perfectly centered within precisely balanced margins, luxuriously vibrant. Gem PSE - Encapsulated. (this being one of 6 attaining this grade as of 10/08, with none graded higher).

Estimate: $750+

Minimum Bid: $375

31841 **#555, 1923, 3c Violet, SUP 98 PSE.** (Original Gum - Never Hinged). Rich luminescent color and precision centering. Superb. PSE - Encapsulated. (SMQ $1,200; this being one of 13 attaining this grade as of 10/08, with only 1 graded higher).

Estimate: $1,000+

Minimum Bid: $600

31842 **#555, 1923, 3c Violet, SUP 98 PSE.** (Original Gum - Never Hinged). A fabulously centered example, bright and fresh. Superb. 2007 PSE - Graded Certificate. (SMQ $1,200; this being one of 13 attaining this grade as of 10/08, with only 1 graded higher).

Estimate: $1,000+

Minimum Bid: $600

31843 **#555, 1923, 3c Violet, XF-S 95 PSE.** (Original Gum - Never Hinged). Fresh and vibrant. Extremely Fine to Superb. PSE - Encapsulated. (SMQ $325; this being one of 45 attaining this grade as of 10/08, with 21 graded higher).

Estimate: $325+

Minimum Bid: $162

31844 **#556, 1923, 4c Yellow Brown, XF-S 95 PSE.** (Original Gum - Never Hinged). Post Office fresh. Extremely Fine to Superb. 2006 PSE - Graded Certificate. (SMQ $410; this being one of 31 attaining this grade as of 10/08, with 11 graded higher).

Estimate: $400+

Minimum Bid: $200

31845 **#557, 1922, 5c Dark Blue XF-S 95 PSE.** (Original Gum - Never Hinged). Extremely Fine to Superb. PSE - Encapsulated. (SMQ $410; this being one of 24 attaining this grade as of 10/08, with only 9 graded higher).

Estimate: $500+

Minimum Bid: $250

31846 **#558, 1922, 6c Red Orange XF-S 95 PSE.** (Original Gum - Never Hinged). Bright and vibrant. Extremely Fine to Superb. PSE - Encapsulated. (SMQ $540; this being one of 38 attaining this grade as of 10/08, with only 6 graded higher).

Estimate: $450+

Minimum Bid: $300

31847 **#558, 1922, 6c Red Orange XF-S 95 PSE.** (Original Gum - Never Hinged). Gorgeously rich and bold, with an almost proof-like quality. Extremely Fine to Superb. 2006 PSE - Graded Certificate. (SMQ $540; this being one of 38 attaining this grade as of 10/08, with only 6 graded higher).

Estimate: $450+

Minimum Bid: $225

31848 **#559, 1923, 7c Black, SUP 98 PSE.** (Original Gum - Never Hinged). Splendidly centered and fresh. Superb. PSE - Encapsulated. (SMQ $540; this being one of 21 attaining this grade as of 10/08, with only 6 graded higher).

Estimate: $500+

Minimum Bid: $250

31849 **#559, 1923, 7c Black, SUP 98 PSE.** (Original Gum - Never Hinged). A visually striking mint single. Precisely centered within beautifully balanced margins, fresh and vibrant, with pristine original gum. A Superb stamp for the serious collector. PSE - Encapsulated. (SMQ $540; this being one of 21 attaining this grade as of 10/08, with only 6 graded higher).

Estimate: $500+

Minimum Bid: $250

31850 **#560, 1923, 8c Olive Green XF-S 95 PSE.** (Original Gum - Never Hinged). Gloriously rich pastel color. Extremely Fine to Superb. PSE - Encapsulated. (SMQ $650; this being one of 21 attaining this grade as of 10/08, with only 6 graded higher).

Estimate: $550+

Minimum Bid: $300

31851 **#560, 1923, 8c Olive Green, XF-S 95 PSE.** (Original Gum - Never Hinged). Fresh and rich. Extremely Fine to Superb. PSE - Graded Certificate. (SMQ $650; this being one of 21 attaining this grade as of 10/08, with only 6 graded higher).

Estimate: $550+

Minimum Bid: $275

NONE GRADED HIGHER

31852 **#561, 1923, 9c Rose, SUP 98J PSE.** (Original Gum - Never Hinged). Meticulously centered within enormous, perfectly balanced margins, with fresh color. Superb. 2006 PSE - Graded Certificate. (this being one of 2 attaining this grade as of 10/08, with none graded higher).

Estimate: $750+

Minimum Bid: $375

31853 **#561, 1923, 9c Rose, SUP 98 PSE.** (Original Gum - Never Hinged). Marvelous fresh and vibrant. Superb PSE - Encapsulated. (SMQ $890; this being one of 16 attaining this grade as of 10/08, with only 2 graded higher).

Estimate: $800+

Minimum Bid: $400

31854 **#561, 1923, 9c Rose, SUP 98 PSE.** (Original Gum - Never Hinged). Precisely centered within wide even margins, with deep rich color and detailed impression. Superb. PSE - Graded Certificate. (SMQ $890; this being one of 16 attaining this grade as of 10/08, with only 2 graded higher).

Estimate: $800+

Minimum Bid: $400

31855 **#561, 1923, 9c Rose, XF-S 95J PSE.** (Original Gum - Never Hinged). A magnificent bottom sheet margin single boasting huge well-balanced margins and a luxuriously rich pastel color. Extremely Fine to Superb. 2006 PSE - Graded Certificate. (this being one of 5 attaining this grade as of 10/08, with 18 graded higher).

Estimate: $500+

Minimum Bid: $250

31856 **#563, 1922, 11c Greenish Blue, SUP 98 PSE.** (Original Gum - Never Hinged). Delightfully fresh and vibrant. Superb. PSE - Graded Certificate. (SMQ $520; this being one of 11 attaining this grade as of 10/08, with only 8 graded higher).

Estimate: $450+

Minimum Bid: $225

31857 **#564, 1923, 12c Brown Violet SUP 98J PSE.** (Original Gum - Never Hinged). A gorgeous stamp. Perfectly centered within huge margins. Luxuriously fresh. Superb PSE - Encapsulated. (this being one of 6 attaining this grade as of 10/08, with only 2 graded higher).

Estimate: $500+

Minimum Bid: $250

31858 **#565, 1923, 14c Blue, GEM 100 PSE.** (Original Gum - Never Hinged). The epitome of perfection, flawless in all respects. A virtually matchless Gem. 2008 PSE - Graded Certificate. (this being one of 5 attaining this grade as of 10/08, with none graded higher).

Estimate: $750+

Minimum Bid: $375

31859 **#566, 1922, 15c Gray, SUP 98 PSE.** (Original Gum - Never Hinged). A perfectly centered jewel with a warm pastel hue and detailed impression. Superb. PSE - Encapsulated. (SMQ $1,300; this being one of 23 attaining this grade as of 10/08, with only 5 graded higher).

Estimate: $1,000+

Minimum Bid: $500

31860 **#566, 1922, 15c Gray, SUP 98 PSE.** (Original Gum - Never Hinged). Incredibly well-centered within visually perfect margins. Superb. PSE - Encapsulated. (SMQ $1,300; this being one of 23 attaining this grade as of 10/08, with only 5 graded higher).

Estimate: $1,000+

Minimum Bid: $500

31861 **#566, 1922, 15c Gray, SUP 98 PSE.** (Original Gum - Never Hinged). Delicate proof-like detail on fresh "bleach white" paper, full original gum. A Superb stamp for the elite collector. PSE - Encapsulated. (SMQ $1,300; this being one of 23 attaining this grade as of 10/08, with only 5 graded higher).

Estimate: $1,000+

Minimum Bid: $500

31862 **#567, 1923, 20c Carmine Rose SUP 98 PSE.** (Original Gum - Never Hinged). Precisely centered example with brilliant color on bright white paper. Superb. PSE - Encapsulated. (SMQ $1,300; this being one of 16 attaining this grade as of 10/08, with only 7 graded higher).

Estimate: $1,000+

Minimum Bid: $500

31863 **#567, 1923, 20c Carmine Rose, XF-S 95J PSE.** (Original Gum - Never Hinged). A tremendous showpiece. Finely centered within huge portrait-like margins, fresh and vibrant. Extremely Fine to Superb. PSE - Encapsulated. (this being one of 7 attaining this grade as of 10/08, with 23 graded higher).

Estimate: $400+

Minimum Bid: $200

31864 **#568, 1922, 25c Yellow Green, GEM 100 PSE.** (Original Gum - Never Hinged). A perfect stamp, centered dead-on. Gem. 2008 PSE - Graded Certificate. (this being the *sole example attaining this grade* as of 10/08, with *none graded higher*).

Estimate: $1,500+

Minimum Bid: $750

31865 **#568, 1922, 25c Yellow Green, SUP 98 PSE.** (Original Gum - Never Hinged). Gorgeous example with vivid color. Superb. 2008 PSE - Graded Certificate. (SMQ $1,300; this being one of 16 attaining this grade as of 10/08, with only 2 graded higher).

Estimate: $1,000+

Minimum Bid: $500

31866 **#568, 1922, 25c Yellow Green, SUP 98J PSE.** (Used). An incomparable giant, fresh and bright, vivid in detail, with a double line in rectangle Franklin, Texas cancel. Superb. 2008 PSE - Graded Certificate. (this being the *unique example attaining this grade* as of 10/08, with *none graded higher*).

Estimate: $750+

Minimum Bid: $375

31867 **#569, 1923, 30c Olive Brown, SUP 98 PSE.** (Original Gum - Never Hinged). Fresh and beautiful. Superb PSE - Encapsulated. (SMQ $1,850; this being one of 11 attaining this grade as of 10/08, with only 6 graded higher).

Estimate: $1,500+

Minimum Bid: $750

31868 **#569, 1923, 30c Olive Brown, XF-S 95 PSE.** (Original Gum - Never Hinged). A portrait-like beauty. Extremely Fine to Superb. PSE - Encapsulated. (SMQ $470; this being one of 25 attaining this grade as of 10/08, with 31 graded higher).

Estimate: $450+

Minimum Bid: $225

31869 **#570, 1922, 50c Lilac, SUP 98 PSE.** (Original Gum - Never Hinged). Lovely deep rich shade enhanced by balanced margins. Superb. PSE - Encapsulated. (SMQ $2,200; this being one of 8 attaining this grade as of 10/08, with only 5 graded higher).

Estimate: $2,000+

Minimum Bid: $1,000

31870 **#570, 1922, 50c Lilac XF-S 95 PSE.** (Original Gum - Never Hinged). Fresh and bright. Extremely Fine to Superb. PSE - Graded Certificate. (SMQ $620; this being one of 33 attaining this grade as of 10/08, with 22 graded higher).

Estimate: $600+

Minimum Bid: $300

31871 **#570, 1922, 50c Lilac, XF-S 95 PSE.** (Original Gum - Never Hinged). Post Office fresh. Extremely Fine to Superb. PSE - Encapsulated. (SMQ $620; this being one of 33 attaining this grade as of 10/08, with 22 graded higher).

Estimate: $600+

Minimum Bid: $300

31872 **#571, 1922, $1 Violet Black, SUP 98 PSE.** (Original Gum - Never Hinged). A superlative example. Precisely centered within wonderfully balanced margins, with rich dark color and well defined impression. Superb. PSE - Encapsulated. (SMQ $2,100; this being one of 17 attaining this grade as of 10/08, with only 2 graded higher).

Estimate: $2,000+

Minimum Bid: $1,000

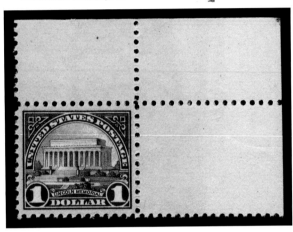

31873 **#571, 1923, $1 Violet Black, XF-S 95 PSE.** (Original Gum - Never Hinged). Top right sheet corner margin single. Luxuriously fresh and vibrant. Extremely Fine to Superb. 2003 PSE - Graded Certificate. (SMQ $600; this being one of 56 attaining this grade as of 10/08, with 21 graded higher).

Estimate: $550+

Minimum Bid: $275

31874 **#571, 1923, $1 Violet Black, XF-S 95 PSE.** (Original Gum - Never Hinged). Spectacular color and impression. Fresh. Extremely Fine to Superb. 2007 PSE - Graded Certificate. (SMQ $600; this being one of 56 attaining this grade as of 10/08, with only 21 graded higher).

Estimate: $500+

Minimum Bid: $250

31875 **#572, 1923, $2 Deep Blue, SUP 98J; PSE.** (Original Gum - Never Hinged). A flawless mint example of this highly popular issue. Perfectly centered amidst uncharacteristically large well balanced margins, remarkably rich and vibrant in color and detail, with pristine full original gum. A Superb Jumbo stamp that would enhance the finest of collections. PSE - Encapsulated. (this being one of 3 attaining this grade as of 10/08, with only 3 graded higher).

Estimate: $2,500+

Minimum Bid: $1,250

31876 **#572, 1923, $2 Deep Blue SUP 98 PSE.** (Original Gum - Never Hinged). U.S. Capitol. Deep blue jewel, 'dead-on' centered. Superb. PSE - Encapsulated. (SMQ $2,150; this being one of 26 attaining this grade as of 10/08, with only 6 graded higher).

Estimate: $1,900+

Minimum Bid: $950

31877 **#572, 1923, $2 Deep Blue, SUP 98 PSE.** (Original Gum - Never Hinged). Fresh with deep color. Superb PSE - Graded Certificate. (SMQ $2,150; this being one of 26 attaining this grade as of 10/08, with only 6 graded higher).
Estimate: $1,900+
Minimum Bid: $950

31878 **#572, 1923, $2 Deep Blue, SUP 98 PSE.** (Original Gum - Never Hinged). Fabulously fresh with a detailed impression. Superb PSE - Encapsulated. (SMQ $2,150; this being one of 26 attaining this grade as of 10/08, with only 6 graded higher).
Estimate: $1,900+
Minimum Bid: $950

31879 **#572, 1923, $2 Deep Blue XF-S 95 PSE.** (Original Gum - Never Hinged). Bright and fresh. Extremely Fine to Superb. 2007 PSE - Graded Certificate. (SMQ $660; this being one of 57 attaining this grade as of 10/08, with 36 graded higher).
Estimate: $550+
Minimum Bid: $275

31880 **#572, 1923, $2 Deep Blue XF-S 95 PSE.** (Original Gum - Never Hinged). U.S. Capitol. Post Office fresh. Extremely Fine to Superb. 2007 PSE - Graded Certificate. (SMQ $660; this being one of 57 attaining this grade as of 10/08, with 36 graded higher).
Estimate: $550+
Minimum Bid: $275

31881 **#572, 1923, $2 Deep Blue, XF-S 95 PSE.** (Original Gum - Never Hinged). Rich and fresh. Extremely Fine to Superb. 2006 PSE - Graded Certificate. (SMQ $660; this being one of 57 attaining this grade as of 10/08, with 36 graded higher).
Estimate: $550+
Minimum Bid: $275

31882 **#572, 1923, $2 Deep Blue, XF-S 95 PSE.** (Original Gum - Never Hinged). A huge margined stamp with extraordinary color and impression. Extremely Fine to Superb. 2007 PSE - Graded Certificate and 1982 PF Certificate. (SMQ $660; this being one of 57 attaining this grade as of 10/08, with 36 graded higher).
Estimate: $550+
Minimum Bid: $275

31883 **#573, 1923, $5 Carmine And Blue SUP 98 PSE.** (Original Gum - Never Hinged). Rich and radiant on bright white paper. Superb. PSE - Encapsulated. (SMQ $2,350; this being one of 27 attaining this grade as of 10/08, with none graded higher).

Estimate: $2,500+

Minimum Bid: $1,350

31884 **#573, 1923, $5 Carmine & Blue, SUP 98 PSE.** (Original Gum - Never Hinged). Fresh and finely detailed. Superb. 2006 PSE - Graded Certificate. (SMQ $2,350; this being one of 27 attaining this grade as of 10/08, with none graded higher).

Estimate: $2,500+

Minimum Bid: $1,350

31885 **#573, 1923, $5 Carmine And Blue XF-S 95 PSE.** (Original Gum - Never Hinged). Visually striking and fresh. Extremely Fine to Superb. PSE - Encapsulated. (SMQ $770; this being one of 74 attaining this grade as of 10/08, with 31 graded higher).

Estimate: $700+

Minimum Bid: $350

31886 **#573, 1923, $5 Carmine & Blue, XF-S 95 PSE.** (Original Gum - Never Hinged). Exceptionally fresh. Extremely Fine to Superb. 2007 PSE - Graded Certificate. (SMQ $770; this being one of 74 attaining this grade as of 10/08, with 31 graded higher).

Estimate: $650+

Minimum Bid: $325

31887 **#573, 1923, $5 Carmine & Blue, XF-S 95 PSE.** (Original Gum - Never Hinged). Outstanding example with vivid color and impression. Extremely Fine to Superb. 2007 PSE - Graded Certificate. (SMQ $770; this being one of 74, attaining this grade as of 10/08, with 31 graded higher).

Estimate: $650+

Minimum Bid: $325

31888 **#573a, 1923, $5 Carmine Lake & Dark Blue, XF 90 PSE.** (Original Gum - Never Hinged). Strong for grade. Extremely Fine. PSE - Encapsulated. (SMQ $500; this being one of 15 attaining this grade as of 10/08, with 18 graded higher).
Estimate: $400+
Minimum Bid: $200

31889 **#578, 1923, 1c Green XF-S 95 PSE.** (Original Gum - Never Hinged). Fabulously centered example of this often off-centered stamp. Rich and fresh. Extremely Fine to Superb. 2005 PSE - Graded Certificate. (SMQ $1,300; this being one of 8 attaining this grade as of 10/08, with only 1 graded higher).
Estimate: $1,000+
Minimum Bid: $500

NONE GRADED HIGHER

31890 **#581, 1923, 1c Green, SUP 98 PSE.** (Original Gum - Never Hinged). Highest graded to date, virtually perfect, superb mint example, super fresh and perfectly centered. Perf 10 issues are very difficult in this high grade. Superb. 2008 PSE - Graded Certificate. (SMQ $1,350; this being one of 5 attaining this grade as of 10/08, with none graded higher).
Estimate: $1,500+
Minimum Bid: $750

31891 **#582, 1925, 1½c Brown, SUP 98 PSE.** (Original Gum - Never Hinged). Pristine with a sharp impression. Superb PSE - Encapsulated. (SMQ $770; this being one of 12 attaining this grade as of 10/08, with none graded higher).
Estimate: $700+
Minimum Bid: $350

31892 **#583, 1924, 2c Carmine, SUP 98 PSE.** (Original Gum - Never Hinged). Highly desirable. Well centered within sizeable margins for this. Lovely color and detailed impression. Superb PSE - Encapsulated. (SMQ $495; this being one of 5 attaining this grade as of 10/08, with only 4 graded higher).
Estimate: $450+
Minimum Bid: $225

31893 **#584, 1925, 3c Violet, XF-S 95 PSE.** (Original Gum - Never Hinged). Brilliant color and sharp impression. Extremely Fine to Superb. 2005 PSE - Graded Certificate. (SMQ $670; this being one of 13 attaining this grade as of 10/08, with 12 graded higher).
Estimate: $500+
Minimum Bid: $250

31894 **#585, 1925, 4c Yellow Brown, SUP 98 PSE.** (Original Gum - Never Hinged). Choice example with nice big margins, very fresh and sharp. Superb. PSE - Encapsulated. (SMQ $1,700; this being one of 9 attaining this grade as of 10/08, with only 3 graded higher).

Estimate: $1,500+

Minimum Bid: $750

31895 **#585, 1925, 4c Yellow Brown SUP 98 PSE.** (Original Gum - Never Hinged). Magnificent color and impression. Well-centered within large even margins. Superb. 2008 PSE - Graded Certificate. (SMQ $1,700; this being one of 9 attaining this grade as of 10/08, with only 3 graded higher).

Estimate: $1,500+

Minimum Bid: $750

31896 **#585, 1925, 4c Deep Yellow Brown, SUP 98 PSE.** (Original Gum -Never Hinged). Remarkably rich and fresh. Superb. 2008 PSE - Graded Certificate. (SMQ $1,700; this being one of 9 attaining this grade as of 10/08, with only 3 graded higher).

Estimate: $1,500+

Minimum Bid: $750

31897 **#585, 1925, 4c Yellow Brown, XF-S 95 PSE.** (Original Gum - Never Hinged). Pretty and fresh. nearly a jumbo for this. Extremely Fine to Superb. 2008 PSE - Graded Certificate. (SMQ $500; this being one of 18 attaining this grade as of 10/08, with 13 graded higher).

Estimate: $450+

Minimum Bid: $225

31898 **#585, 1925, 4c Yellow Brown, XF-S 95 PSE.** (Original Gum - Never Hinged). Post Office fresh and vibrant. Extremely Fine to Superb. 2005 PSE - Graded Certificate. (SMQ $500; this being one of 18 attaining this grade as of 10/08, with 13 graded higher).

Estimate: $450+

Minimum Bid: $225

31899 **#586, 1924, 5c Blue, XF-S 95 PSE.** (Original Gum - Never Hinged). Vivid color and detailed impression. Extremely Fine to Superb. 2008 PSE - Graded Certificate. (SMQ $500; this being one of 6 attaining this grade as of 10/08, with none graded higher).

Estimate: $450+

Minimum Bid: $225

31900 **#587, 1925, 6c Red Orange SUP 98 PSE.** (Original Gum - Never Hinged). Fabulously centered amidst generous well-balanced margins, with luxuriously fresh color and detail impression. Superb PSE - Encapsulated. (SMQ $1,200; this being one of 9 attaining this grade as of 10/08, with none graded higher).

Estimate: $1,200+

Minimum Bid: $600

31901 **#588, 1926, 7c Black, SUP 98 PSE.** (Original Gum - Never Hinged). Spectacularly centered within ample margins. Rich and fresh. Superb. PSE - Encapsulated. (SMQ $1,400; this being one of 7 attaining this grade as of 10/08, with only 1 graded higher).
Estimate: $1,200+
Minimum Bid: $600

31902 **#588, 1926, 7c Black, SUP 98 PSE.** (Original Gum - Never Hinged). Gorgeous. Perfectly centered. Radiantly fresh. Superb. 2007 PSE - Graded Certificate. (SMQ $1,400; this being one of 7 attaining this grade as of 10/08, with only 1 graded higher).
Estimate: $1,200+
Minimum Bid: $600

31903 **#590, 1926, 9c Rose, SUP 98 PSE.** (Original Gum - Never Hinged). Perfectly centered with a brilliant rich color. Superb. 2007 PSE - Graded Certificate. (SMQ $790; this being one of 13 attaining this grade as of 10/08, with only 2 graded higher).
Estimate: $700+
Minimum Bid: $350

RARE USED ROTARY PRESS
COIL WASTE - 594

31904 **#594, 1923, 1c Green VG 50 PSE.** (Used). Fewer than 100 used copies exist, Rare stamp. Centering about typical. Reasonably light and attractive cancel. Very Good. PSE - Encapsulated. (SMQ $11,000; this being the only example attaining this grade as of 10/08, with only 3 graded higher).
Estimate: $8,500+
Minimum Bid: $4,250

HIGHEST GRADED TYPE II COIL PAIR

31905 **#599A, 1929, 2c Carmine, SUP 98 PSE.** (Original Gum - Never Hinged). Coil Pair. Rich lavish color, superb centering and evenly balanced margins, a coil collectors dream. Superb. PSE - Encapsulated. (SMQ $4,250; this being one of 6 attaining this grade as of 10/08, with none graded higher).

   Estimate: $4,000+

   Minimum Bid: $2,000

31906 **#599A, 1929, 2c Carmine, XF-S 95 PSE.** (Original Gum - Never Hinged). Coil Pair, Type II, Bright and Fresh. Extremely Fine to Superb. PSE - Encapsulated. (SMQ $1850; this being one of 5 attaining this grade as of 10/08, with only 6 graded higher).

   Estimate: $1,300+

   Minimum Bid: $650

RARE SHADE - CARMINE LAKE

31907 **#606a, 1923, 2c Carmine Lake, XF 90 PSE.** (Original Gum - Never Hinged). Coil Pair. Rare Shade. Extremely Fine. 2006 PSE - Graded Certificate. (this being one of 8 attaining this grade as of 10/08, with only 3 graded higher).

   Estimate: $3,500+

   Minimum Bid: $1,750

31908 **#606a, 1923, 2c Carmine Lake, XF 90 PSE.** (Original Gum - Never Hinged). Coil Single. Scarce color variety. Extremely Fine. PSE - Encapsulated. (this being one of 8 attaining this grade as of 10/08, with only 3 graded higher).

Estimate: $1,000+

Minimum Bid: $500

31909 **#610, 1923, 2c Black, SUP 98J; PSE.** (Original Gum - Never Hinged). A captivating mint bottom sheet margin single sporting uncharacteristically large, beautifully balanced margins with full even perforations all around. Overall fresh, including pristine full original gum, that epitomizes the grade of Superb. 2006 PSE - Graded Certificate. (this being one of 3, attaining this grade as of 10/08, with only 4 graded higher).

Estimate: $900+

Minimum Bid: $450

31910 **#612, 1923, 2c Black SUP 98; PSE.** (Original Gum - Never Hinged). An exceptional mint example flawlessly centered amidst beautifully balanced margins, lovely and fresh, with unblemished full original gum. A Superb stamp destined for the finest of collections. 2005 PSE - Graded Certificate. (SMQ $1,200; this being one of 7 attaining this grade as of 10/08, with only 3 graded higher).

Estimate: $1,200+

Minimum Bid: $600

1924-29 COMMEMORATIVE ISSUES

31911 **#614, 1924, 1c Dark Green, SUP 98 PSE.** (Original Gum - Never Hinged). Huguenot-Walloon Tercentenary. Perfectly centered and lush. Superb. PSE - Encapsulated. (SMQ $510; this being one of 9 attaining this grade as of 10/08, with none graded higher).

Estimate: $500+

Minimum Bid: $250

31912 **#614, 1924, 1c Dark Green SUP 98 PSE.** (Original Gum - Never Hinged). Huguenot-Walloon Tercentenary. Absolutely fabulous example. The color and impression bring the ship to life. Superb. 2007 PSE - Graded Certificate. (SMQ $510; this being one of 9 attaining this grade as of 10/08, with none graded higher).

Estimate: $500+

Minimum Bid: $250

31913 **#616, 1924, 5c Dark Blue SUP 98J; PSE.** (Original Gum - Never Hinged). Huguenot-Walloon Tercentenary. A superlative mint example of virtually unrivalled quality, exquisitely centered amidst huge beautifully balanced margins, with gloriously rich color and deeply etched impression on bright paper. Full fresh original gum. 2005 PSE - Graded Certificate. (this being one of 3 attaining this grade as of 10/08, with only 1 graded higher).

Estimate: $2,500+

Minimum Bid: $1,250

31914 **#616, 1924, 5c Dark Blue SUP 98 PSE.** (Original Gum - Never Hinged). Huguenot-Walloon Tercentenary. Bold and bright color, choice centering. A truly remarkable example. Superb. PSE - Encapsulated. (SMQ $1,400; this being one of 12 attaining this grade as of 10/08, with only 4 graded higher).

Estimate: $1,400+

Minimum Bid: $700

31915 **#616, 1924, 5c Dark Blue SUP 98 PSE.** (Original Gum - Never Hinged). Huguenot-Walloon Tercentenary. Unimprovable color and impression, plus visually perfect centering. Superb. 2006 PSE - Graded Certificate. (SMQ $1,400; this being one of 12 attaining this grade as of 10/08, with only 4 graded higher).

Estimate: $1,400+

Minimum Bid: $700

31916 **#619, 1925, 5c Dark Blue, SUP 98 PSE.** (Original Gum - Never Hinged). The Minute Man. Superb bordering on a jumbo. Superb. PSE - Encapsulated. (SMQ $660; this being one of 32 attaining this grade as of 10/08, with only 3 graded higher).

Estimate: $600+

Minimum Bid: $300

31917 **#619, 1925, 5c Dark Blue, SUP 98 PSE.** (Original Gum - Never Hinged). The Minute Man. Fabulously centered within large margins. Superb. 2008 PSE - Graded Certificate. (SMQ $660; this being one of 32 attaining this grade as of 10/08, with only 3 graded higher).

Estimate: $550+

Minimum Bid: $275

31918 **#619, 1925, 5c Dark Blue, SUP 98 PSE.** (Original Gum - Never Hinged). The Minute Man. Post Office fresh beauty with large even margins. Superb. 2005 PSE - Graded Certificate. (SMQ $660; this being one of 32 attaining this grade as of 10/08, with only 3 graded higher).

Estimate: $600+

Minimum Bid: $300

TOP OF THE POP

31919 **#620, 1925, 2c Carmine & Black GEM 100 PSE.** (Original Gum - Never Hinged). Norse-American Centennial. Absolutely perfect in every respect, huge mathematically equal margins, rich vibrant color and detailed impressions on fresh white paper. A Gem for the finest collection. PSE - Graded Certificate. (this being one of 5 attaining this grade as of 10/08, with *none* graded higher).

Estimate: $1,500+

Minimum Bid: $750

31920 **#622, 1926, 13c Green, SUP 98J PSE.** (Original Gum - Never Hinged). Sensationally beautiful in all respects, luxuriously fresh color and masterfully detailed impression on crisp paper, perfectly centered, pristine full original gum. PSE - Encapsulated. (this being one of 6 attaining this grade as of 10/08, with only 3 graded higher).

Estimate: $600+

Minimum Bid: $300

31921 **#622, 1926, 13c Green, SUP 98 PSE.** (Original Gum - Never Hinged). Substantial well-balanced margins and deep crisp color. Superb. PSE - Encapsulated. (SMQ $520; this being one of 24 attaining this grade as of 10/08, with only 9 graded higher).

Estimate: $500+

Minimum Bid: $250

31922 **#622, 1926, 13c Green, SUP 98; PSE.** (Original Gum - Never Hinged). A stunning mint single, precisely centered and fresh as the day it was printed, unblemished full original gum. Superb for the serious collector. PSE - Encapsulated. (SMQ $520; this being one of 24 attaining this grade as of 10/08, with only 9 graded higher).

Estimate: $500+

Minimum Bid: $250

31923 **#622, 1926, 13c Green, SUP 98 PSE.** (Original Gum - Never Hinged). Radiant color and vibrant impression. Superb. 2005 PSE - Graded Certificate. (SMQ $520; this being one of 24 attaining this grade as of 10/08, with only 9 graded higher).

Estimate: $500+

Minimum Bid: $250

31924 **#623, 1925, 17c Gray Black GEM 100 PSE.** (Original Gum - Never Hinged). Spectacularly centered within substantial well-balanced margins, with fresh vibrant color and razor sharp impression. Gem. 2008 PSE - Graded Certificate. (this being one of 4 attaining this grade as of 10/08, with none graded higher).

Estimate: $1,500+

Minimum Bid: $750

31925 **#623, 1925, 17c Black, SUP 98J; PSE.** (Original Gum - Never Hinged). A stunning mint single, flawlessly centered amidst mammoth balanced margins, with intense color and a proof-like impression on crisp fresh paper, and pristine full original gum. A Superb stamp that would enhance the finest of collections. 2007 PSE - Graded Certificate. (this being one of 3 attaining this grade as of 10/08, with only 4 graded higher).

Estimate: $750+

Minimum Bid: $375

31926 **#623, 1925, 17c Black, SUP 98 PSE.** (Original Gum - Never Hinged). Lovely example. Precisely centered with deep rich color. Superb. PSE - Encapsulated. (SMQ $530; this being one of 23 attaining this grade as of 10/08, with only 7 graded higher).

Estimate: $500+

Minimum Bid: $250

31927 **#623, 1925, 17c Black, SUP 98 PSE.** (Original Gum - Never Hinged). Marvelously fresh with a razor sharp impression. Superb. 2008 PSE - Graded Certificate. (SMQ $530; this being one of 23 attaining this grade as of 10/08, with only 7 graded higher).

Estimate: $500+

Minimum Bid: $250

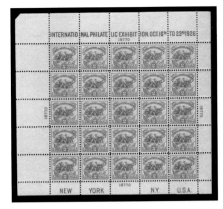

31928 **#630, 1926, 2c Carmine Rose.** (Original Gum - Never Hinged). White Plains Souvenir Sheet. Only 150,000 issued. This example, from the upper let position, with exceptional centering throughout. Natural gum wrinkle noted in position 3 and 8. (A sheet centered this well, typically sells above the Very Fine Catalog value of $600). Extremely Fine to Superb. 2008 PSE Certificate. (Scott $600).

Estimate: $800+

Minimum Bid: $400

31929 **#634A, 1928, 2c Carmine XF-S 95 PSE.** (Original Gum - Never Hinged). Type II. Very fresh left margin example, fantastic color. Extremely Fine to Superb. 2008 PSE - Graded Certificate. (SMQ $3,350; this being one of 7 attaining this grade as of 10/08, with only 6 graded higher).

Estimate: $3,000+

Minimum Bid: $1,500

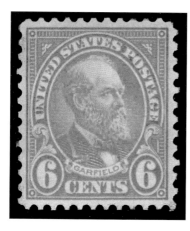

31930 **#638, 1927, 6c Red Orange, SUP 98 PSE.** (Original Gum - Never Hinged). Spectacularly well-centered. Rich and vibrant. Superb. PSE - Encapsulated. (SMQ $440; this being one of 7 attaining this grade as of 10/08, with none graded higher).

Estimate: $400+

Minimum Bid: $200

31931 **#639, 1927, 7c Black, GEM 100 PSE.** (Original Gum - Never Hinged). A GEM for the perfectionist. Smack-on centering. Perfect. Gem 100. PSE - Encapsulated. (this being one of 9 attaining this grade as of 10/08, with none graded higher).

Estimate: $1,500+

Minimum Bid: $750

TOP OF THE POP

31932 **#646, 1928, 2c Carmine GEM 100 PSE.** (Original Gum - Never Hinged). Molly Pitcher. Flawless gem, perfect in all aspects. Post Office Fresh. Gem. PSE - Encapsulated. (this being one of 6 attaining this grade as of 10/08, with only 1 graded higher).

Estimate: $800+

Minimum Bid: $400

31933 **#648, 1928, 5c Dark Blue, SUP 98 PSE.** (Original Gum - Never Hinged). Hawaii Sesquicentennial. A nearly perfect example of this stamp, typically difficult to find in high grade. Superb. 2007 PSE - Graded Certificate. (SMQ $690; this being one of 11 attaining this grade as of 10/08, with only 1 graded higher).

Estimate: $600+

Minimum Bid: $300

31934 **#650, 1928, 5c Blue, GEM 100 PSE.** (Original Gum - Never Hinged). Globe and Airplane. Perfectly centered within tremendous well-balanced margins. Post Office fresh. Gem. 2008 PSE - Graded Certificate. (this being one of 6 attaining this grade as of 10/08, with *none* graded higher).

Estimate: $1,300+

Minimum Bid: $650

31935 **#650, 1928, 5c Blue, SUP 98J PSE.** (Original Gum - Never Hinged). Globe and Airplane. Fabulously centered. Both rich and bold at the same time. Superb. 2008 PSE - Graded Certificate. (this being one of 8 attaining this grade as of 10/08, with only 6 graded higher).

Estimate: $500+

Minimum Bid: $250

TOP POP

31936 **#656, 1929, 2c Carmine Rose, SUP 98 PSE.** (Used). Coil Single. Very rare and undervalued in high grade used. Nice black wavy line cancel. Superb. 2008 PSE - Graded Certificate. (SMQ $210; this being the *only example attaining this grade* as of 10/08, with *none graded higher*).

Estimate: $500+

Minimum Bid: $250

1929 KANSAS / NEBRASKA OVERPRINTS

31937 **#658, 1929, 1c Green, SUP 98 PSE.** (Original Gum - Never Hinged). Fresh and captivating, with an uncommon warm glow. Superb; 2008 PSE - Graded Certificate. (SMQ $470; this being one of 5 attaining this grade as of 10/08, with only 3 graded higher).

Estimate: $450+

Minimum Bid: $225

31938 **#660, 1929, 2c Carmine, SUP 98 PSE.** (Original Gum - Never Hinged). Kansas Overprint. Exceptionally well-centered. Rich and bold. Superb. 2008 PSE - Graded Certificate. (SMQ $540; this being one of 10 attaining this grade as of 10/08, with none graded higher).

Estimate: $500+

Minimum Bid: $250

31939 **#661, 1929, 3c Violet, SUP 98 PSE.** (Original Gum - Never Hinged). Kansas Overprint. Splendidly centered, brilliant and fresh color. Superb PSE - Encapsulated. (SMQ $1,450; this being one of 5 attaining this grade as of 10/08, with only 2 graded higher).

Estimate: $1,500+

Minimum Bid: $800

31940 **#661, 1929, 3c Violet, XF-S 95J PSE.** (Original Gum - Never Hinged). Kansas Overprint. Amazingly centered within Jumbo margins for this typically tightly margined issue. Extremely Fine to Superb. 2004 PSE - Graded Certificate. (this being one of 2 attaining this grade as of 10/08, with only 7 graded higher).

Estimate: $650+

Minimum Bid: $325

31941 **#662, 1929, 4c Yellow Brown, SUP 98 PSE.** (Original Gum - Never Hinged). Kansas Overprint. Extremely attractive with gorgeous color and sharp impression. Superb PSE - Encapsulated. (SMQ $1,450; this being one of 8 attaining this grade as of 10/08, with only 3 graded higher).

Estimate: $1,500+

Minimum Bid: $800

31942 **#662, 1929, 4c Yellow Brown, SUP 98 PSE.** (Original Gum - Never Hinged). Kansas Overprint. Fantastically centered and bright. Superb. 2008 PSE - Graded Certificate. (SMQ $1,450; this being one of 8 attaining this grade as of 10/08, with only 3 graded higher).

Estimate: $1,500+

Minimum Bid: $800

31943 **#664, 1929, 6c Red Orange, SUP 98 PSE.** (Original Gum - Never Hinged). Kansas Overprint. Wonderful in all respects. Superb. PSE - Encapsulated. (SMQ $2,100; this being one of 10 attaining this grade as of 10/08, with only 1 graded higher).

Estimate: $2,000+

Minimum Bid: $1,150

31944 **#664, 1929, 6c Red Orange, XF-S 95 PSE.** (Original Gum - Never Hinged). Kansas Overprint. Left sheet margin single. Brilliant and fresh. Extremely Fine to Superb. 2005 PSE - Graded Certificate. (SMQ $670; this being one of 24 attaining this grade as of 10/08, with 14 graded higher).

Estimate: $600+

Minimum Bid: $300

31945 **#664, 1929, 6c Red Orange, XF-S 95 PSE.** (Original Gum - Never Hinged). Kansas Overprint. Handsome example. Extremely Fine to Superb. 2005 PSE - Graded Certificate. (SMQ $670; this being one of 24 attaining this grade as of 10/08, with 14 graded higher).

Estimate: $550+

Minimum Bid: $275

31946 **#665, 1929, 7c Black, SUP 98 PSE.** (Original Gum - Never Hinged). Kansas Overprint. Choice quality. Tough issue in this grade. Superb PSE - Encapsulated. (SMQ $1,800; this being one of 8 attaining this grade as of 10/08, with only 1 graded higher).

Estimate: $1,700+

Minimum Bid: $1,000

31947 **#666, 1929, 8c Olive Green, SUP 98 PSE.** (Original Gum - Never Hinged). Kansas Overprint. Sensational example. Precisely centered amidst generous well-balanced margins with intense yet warm pastel color. Post Office fresh. Superb. PSE - Encapsulated. (SMQ $3,100; this being one of 6 attaining this grade as of 10/08, with only 1 graded higher).

Estimate: $3,000+

Minimum Bid: $1,625

31948 **#666, 1929, 8c Olive Green, XF-S 95 PSE.** (Original Gum - Never Hinged). Kansas Overprint. Fresh and bright. Extremely Fine to Superb. 2005 PSE - Graded Certificate. (SMQ $1,050; this being one of 22 attaining this grade as of 10/08, with only 9 graded higher).

Estimate: $900+

Minimum Bid: $450

31949 **#666, 1929, 8c Olive Green XF-S 95 PSE.** (Original Gum - Never Hinged). Kansas Overprint. Post Office fresh. Extremely Fine to Superb. 2008 PSE - Graded Certificate. (SMQ $1,050; this being one of 22 attaining this grade as of 10/08, with only 9 graded higher).

Estimate: $900+

Minimum Bid: $450

31950 **#667, 1929, 9c Light Rose, SUP 98 PSE.** (Original Gum - Never Hinged). Kansas Overprint. A virtually unrivalled beauty, fresh pastel color, flawlessly centered with full even perforations all around, crisp fresh overprint, unblemished full original gum. A Superb stamp destined for the finest collection. PSE - Encapsulated. (SMQ $1,200; this being one of 9 attaining this grade as of 10/08, with none graded higher).

Estimate: $1,100+

Minimum Bid: $750

31951 **#671, 1929, 2c Carmine, SUP 98J PSE.** (Original Gum - Never Hinged). Nebraska Overprint. A spectacular and fresh mint single, bright and vibrant, uncharacteristically well centered amidst balanced margins, unblemished full original gum. Superb for the serious collector. 2006 PSE - Graded Certificate. (this being one of 2 attaining this grade as of 10/08, with only 1 graded higher).

Estimate: $750+

Minimum Bid: $375

31952 **#671, 1929, 2c Carmine, SUP 98 PSE.** (Original Gum - Never Hinged). Nebraska Overprint. Deep color with sharp impression. Fresh. Superb. PSE - Encapsulated. (SMQ $480; this being one of 6 attaining this grade as of 10/08, with only 3 graded higher).

Estimate: $450+

Minimum Bid: $225

31953 **#672, 1929, 3c Violet, SUP 98 PSE.** (Original Gum - Never Hinged). Nebraska Overprint. Perfect centering, rich vibrant color, and crisp impression. Superb. PSE - Encapsulated. (SMQ $1,150; this being one of 15 attaining this grade as of 10/08, with only 3 graded higher).

Estimate: $950+

Minimum Bid: $600

31954 **#673, 1929, 4c Yellow Brown, SUP 98 PSE.** (Original Gum - Never Hinged). Nebraska Overprint. Extraordinary quality for this often difficult stamp. Superb. PSE - Encapsulated. (SMQ $1,500; this being one of 7 attaining this grade as of 10/08, with only 1 graded higher).

Estimate: $1,300+

Minimum Bid: $1,000

31955 **#675, 1929, 6c Red Orange, SUP 98 PSE.** (Original Gum - Never Hinged). Nebraska Overprint. Virtual perfection with large even margins. Superb PSE - Encapsulated. (SMQ $2,200; this being one of 8 attaining this grade as of 10/08, with only 5 graded higher).

Estimate: $1,900+

Minimum Bid: $1,050

31956 **#675, 1929, 6c Red Orange, XF-S 95 PSE.** (Original Gum - Never Hinged). Nebraska Overprint. Excellent example. Extremely Fine to Superb. 2006 PSE - Graded Certificate. (SMQ $780; this being one of 17 attaining this grade as of 10/08, with 16 graded higher).

Estimate: $650+

Minimum Bid: $325

31957 **#676, 1929, 7c Black, XF-S 95 PSE.** (Original Gum - Never Hinged). Nebraska Overprint. Precisely centered with deep rich color and finely etched impression. Extremely Fine to Superb. PSE - Encapsulated. (SMQ $500; this being one of 18 attaining this grade as of 10/08, with only 5 graded higher).

Estimate: $500+

Minimum Bid: $250

31958 **#677, 1929, 8c Olive Green, XF-S 95 PSE.** (Original Gum - Never Hinged). Nebraska Overprint. Post Office Fresh. Extremely Fine to Superb. 2005 PSE - Graded Certificate. (SMQ $700; this being one of 11 attaining this grade as of 10/08, with only 3 graded higher).

Estimate: $600+

Minimum Bid: $300

31959 **#677, 1929, 8c Olive Green, XF-S 95 PSE.** (Original Gum - Never Hinged). Nebraska Overprint. Extremely Fine to Superb. 2008 PSE - Graded Certificate. (SMQ $700; this being one of 11 attaining this grade as of 10/08, with 3 graded higher).

Estimate: $600+

Minimum Bid: $300

31960 **#678, 1929, 9c Light Rose, XF-S 95 PSE.** (Original Gum - Never Hinged). Nebraska Overprint. Splendidly centered example, finely detailed with a warm pastel color. Extremely Fine to Superb. 2008 PSE - Graded Certificate. (SMQ $730; this being one of 9 attaining this grade as of 10/08, with only 9 graded higher).

Estimate: $600+

Minimum Bid: $300

31961 **#679, 1929, 10c Orange Yellow, SUP 98 PSE.** (Original Gum - Never Hinged). Nebraska Overprint. Rich and bold portrait perfectly centered within large balanced margins. Superb. PSE - Encapsulated. (SMQ $2,600; this being one of 8 attaining this grade as of 10/08, with only 1 graded higher).

Estimate: $2,500+

Minimum Bid: $1,350

1930 TO DATE

UNLISTED COLOR VARIETY - CARMINE LAKE

31962 **#680, 1929, 2c Carmine Lake, SUP 98J PSE.** (Original Gum - Never Hinged). Unlisted Color variety; Carmine Lake. An impressive mint bottom sheet margin single, post office fresh and vibrant. Superb. 2008 PSE - Graded Certificate. (this being one of 4 #680's attaining this grade as of 10/08, with only 3 graded higher).

Estimate: $1,000+

Minimum Bid: $500

TOP OF THE POP

31963 **#690, 1931, 2c Carmine Rose GEM 100J PSE.** (Original Gum - Never Hinged). General Pulaski. Perfection to an extreme. Top sheet margin Plate No. 20427 single. A monstrous and unrivalled Gem. 2008 PSE - Graded Certificate. (this being the *sole example attaining this grade* as of 10/08, with *none graded higher*).

Estimate: $1,500+

Minimum Bid: $750

31964 **#693, 1931, 12c Brown Violet, GEM 100 PSE.** (Original Gum - Never Hinged). Bottom right sheet corner margin Plate No. 20614 single. Perfect in all respects. Gem. PSE - Graded Certificate. (this being the *only example attaining this grade* as of 10/08, with *none graded higher*).

Estimate: $1,000+

Minimum Bid: $500

31965 **#701, 1931, 50c Red Lilac, SUP 98 PSE.** (Original Gum - Never Hinged). Precisely centered within evenly balanced margins, with a bright pastel color. Superb. PSE - Graded Certificate. (SMQ $880; this being one of 18 attaining this grade as of 10/08, with only 5 graded higher).

Estimate: $750+

Minimum Bid: $375

31966 **#705, 1932, 1c Green SUP 98J PSE.** (Original Gum - Never Hinged). Nearly impossible to find this issue in Jumbo. Superb PSE - Encapsulated. (SMQ $500; this being one of 2 attaining this grade as of 10/08, with none graded higher).

Estimate: $450+

Minimum Bid: $225

31967 #738, 1934, 3c Deep Violet, GEM 100J PSE. (Original Gum - Never Hinged). Mothers of America. Huge and perfect. Gem. PSE - Encapsulated. (this being the *sole example attaining this grade* as of 10/08, with *none graded higher*).

Estimate: $500+

Minimum Bid: $250

HIGHEST GRADED

31968 #740, 1934, 1c Green, GEM 100J PSE. (Original Gum - Never Hinged). El Capitan, Yosemite. Perfect and huge. Gem PSE - Encapsulated. (this being the *only example attaining this lofty grade* as of 10/08, with *none graded higher*).

Estimate: $1,000+

Minimum Bid: $500

31969 #805, 1938, 1½c Bister Brown, GEM 100 PSE. (Original Gum - Never Hinged). A gem for the connoisseur, well centered with large margins, crisp impression, and robust color. Gem. PSE - Encapsulated. (SMQ $620; this being one of 8 attaining this grade as of 10/08, with none grading higher).

Estimate: $500+

Minimum Bid: $250

31970 #808, 1938, 4c Red Violet, GEM 100 PSE. (Original Gum - Never Hinged). Perfect margins, fresh appearance, and stunning color, well deserving of the 100. Gem. PSE - Encapsulated. (SMQ $620; this being one of 9 attaining this grade as of 10/08, with none graded higher).

Estimate: $600+

Minimum Bid: $300

31971 #810, 1938, 5c Bright Blue GEM 100 PSE. (Original Gum - Never Hinged). Perfect with large margins for this issue. Gem. PSE - Encapsulated. (SMQ $560; this being one of 15 attaining this grade as of 10/08, with none graded higher).

Estimate: $450+

Minimum Bid: $225

31972 #810, 1938, 5c Bright Blue GEM 100; PSE. (Original Gum - Never Hinged). Bright and fresh. Gem. PSE - Encapsulated. (SMQ $560; this being one of 15 attaining this grade as of 10/08, with none graded higher).

Estimate: $500+

Minimum Bid: $250

31973 #814, 1938, 9c Rose Pink, GEM 100; PSE. (Original Gum - Never Hinged). Perfect with warm pastel color. Gem PSE - Encapsulated. (SMQ $620; this being one of 8 attaining this grade as of 10/08, with none graded higher).

Estimate: $600+

Minimum Bid: $300

31974 #816, 1938, 11c Ultra GEM 100; PSE. (Original Gum - Never Hinged). Gloriously fresh. Gem. PSE - Encapsulated. (SMQ $640; this being one of 7 attaining this grade as of 10/08, with none graded higher).

Estimate: $600+

Minimum Bid: $300

31975 #818, 1938, 13c Blue Green GEM 100; PSE. (Original Gum - Never Hinged). Rich and vibrant. Gem. PSE - Encapsulated. (SMQ $710; this being one of 4 attaining this grade as of 10/08, with none graded higher).

Estimate: $700+

Minimum Bid: $350

31976 #820, 1938, 15c Blue Gray, GEM 100; PSE. (Original Gum - Never Hinged). Post Office fresh. Gem. PSE - Encapsulated. (SMQ $650; this being one of 6 attaining this grade as of 10/08, with none graded higher).

Estimate: $600+

Minimum Bid: $300

31977 #821, 1938, 16c Black, GEM 100; PSE. (Original Gum - Never Hinged). Perfect with an almost sculpted-like image. Gem. PSE - Encapsulated. (SMQ $620; this being one of 10 attaining this grade as of 10/08, with none graded higher).

Estimate: $600+

Minimum Bid: $300

31978 #1054A, 1960, 1¼c Turquoise, GEM 100 PSE. (Original Gum - Never Hinged). Palace of the Governors. Coil Pair. Bright, vibrant, and fresh. Gem. 2006 PSE - Graded Certificate. (this being one of 2 attaining this grade as of 10/08, with *none* graded higher).

Estimate: $750+

Minimum Bid: $375

AIRMAIL ISSUES

31979 #C1, 1918, 6c Orange, SUP 98 PSE. (Original Gum - Never Hinged). Magnificently centered within large, nearly jumbo margins. Bright fresh color and finely detailed impression. Superb. PSE - Encapsulated. (SMQ $1,550; this being one of 12 attaining this grade as of 10/08, with none graded higher).

Estimate: $1,500+

Minimum Bid: $750

31980 **#C1, 1918, 6c Orange, XF-S 95 PSE.** (Original Gum - Never Hinged). Strong for grade. Wonderfully centered within substantial margins, with bold rich color. Extremely Fine to Superb. PSE - Encapsulated. (SMQ $640; this being one of 40 attaining this grade as of 10/08, with 12 graded higher).

Estimate: $600+

Minimum Bid: $300

31981 **#C2, 1918, 16c Green, XF-S 95 PSE.** (Original Gum - Never Hinged). Exceptionally choice. Well centered with large margins. Extremely Fine to Superb. PSE - Encapsulated. (SMQ $640; this being one of 46 attaining this grade as of 10/08, with 17 graded higher).

Estimate: $500+

Minimum Bid: $250

31982 **#C2, 1918, 16c Green, XF-S 95 PSE.** (Original Gum - Never Hinged). Post Office Fresh. Extremely Fine to Superb. PSE - Encapsulated. (SMQ $640; this being one of 46 attaining this grade as of 10/08, with 17 graded higher).

Estimate: $500+

Minimum Bid: $250

31983 **#C3, 1918, 24c Carmine Rose & Blue, XF-S 95J PSE.** (Original Gum - Never Hinged). Top sheet margin Plate No. 8493 single. Precisely centered amidst enormous margins. Extremely Fine to Superb. PSE - Encapsulated. (this being one of 13 attaining this grade as of 10/08, with 25 graded higher).

Estimate: $700+

Minimum Bid: $350

31984 **#C3, 1918, 24c Carmine & Black, XF-S 95J PSE.** (Original Gum - Never Hinged). Top sheet margin Plate No. 8493 single. Exceptionally well-centered within enormous margins. The vignette shifted slightly to the left giving the appearance of an 'fast flyer.' Extremely Fine to Superb. PSE - Encapsulated. (this being one of 13 attaining this grade as of 10/08, with 25 graded higher).

Estimate: $700+

Minimum Bid: $350

31985 **#C3, 1918, 24c Carmine Rose & Blue, XF-S 95 PSE.** (Original Gum - Never Hinged). Bright and fresh. The vignette shifted slightly downward giving the appearance of a 'landing' plane. Extremely Fine to Superb. PSE - Encapsulated. (SMQ $640; this being one of 42 attaining this grade as of 10/08, with 38 graded higher).

Estimate: $550+

Minimum Bid: $275

31986 **#C3, 1918, 24c Carmine Rose & Blue, XF-S 95 PSE.** (Original Gum - Never Hinged). Fresh and bright. Extremely Fine to Superb. 2008 PSE - Graded Certificate. (SMQ $640; this being one of 42 attaining this grade as of 10/08, with 38 graded higher).

Estimate: $500+

Minimum Bid: $250

31987 #C3a, 1918, 24c Carmine Rose & Blue F 70 PSE. (Original Gum - Previously Hinged). The Holy Grail of United States stamps; *"The Inverted Jenny"*. A single full pane of 100 was originally discovered and purchased by William T. Robey at the New York Avenue post office in Washington D.C. on May 14, 1918. Each stamp was subsequently numbered lightly in pencil on the reverse in the lower right corner shortly after discovery..This copy, now encapsulated and graded Fine 70 by the PSE, is Position 22 from that pane.

The overall design framework is shifted slightly downward, the vignette appearing to be meticulously centered within that framework, albeit upside-down. The gum side showing light traces of previous hinging dead-center of the stamp, overall inconsequential to the prominence of this highly celebrated rarity. Fine. PSE - Encapsulated. *ex-Colonel Edward H. R. Green and ex-Eugene Klein.*

(SMQ $380,000; this being one of 2 attaining this grade as of 10/08, with only 3 graded higher).

Estimate: $400,000+

Minimum Bid: $200,000

"GROUNDED" PLANE VARIETY

31988 **#C3 Var, 1918, 24c Carmine Rose And Blue F 70 PF.** (Original Gum - Never Hinged). True Grounded Plane; wheels 'well into' Cents. Post Office Fresh, Fine; 2008 PF Graded Certificate.

Estimate: $7,500+

Minimum Bid: $3,750

31989 **#C5, 1923, 16c Dark Blue, XF-S 95 PSE.** (Original Gum - Never Hinged). Rich, bold and fresh. Extremely Fine to Superb. PSE - Encapsulated. (SMQ $640; this being one of 61 attaining this grade as of 10/08, with 25 graded higher).

Estimate: $600+

Minimum Bid: $300

31990 **#C5, 1923, 16c Dark Blue, XF-S 95 PSE.** (Original Gum - Never Hinged). Bright and fresh. Strong for the grade. Extremely Fine to Superb. PSE - Encapsulated. (SMQ $640; this being one of 61 attaining this grade as of 10/08, with 25 graded higher).

Estimate: $600+

Minimum Bid: $300

31991 **#C6, 1923, 24c Carmine, XF-S 95 PSE.** (Original Gum - Never Hinged). Bright and fresh. Extremely Fine to Superb. PSE - Encapsulated. (SMQ $660; this being one of 52 attaining this grade as of 10/08, with 30 graded higher).

Estimate: $600+

Minimum Bid: $300

31992 #C6, 1923, 24c Carmine XF-S 95 PSE. (Original Gum - Never Hinged). Well-centered and bright. Extremely Fine to Superb. PSE - Encapsulated. (SMQ $660; this being one of 52 attaining this grade as of 10/08, with 30 graded higher).

Estimate: $600+

Minimum Bid: $300

31993 #C6, 1923, 24c Carmine, XF-S 95 PSE. (Original Gum - Never Hinged). Rich bold color and proof-like impression, centered within large even margins. Extremely Fine to Superb. PSE - Graded Certificate. (SMQ $660; this being one of 52 attaining this grade as of 10/08, with only 30 graded higher).

Estimate: $600+

Minimum Bid: $300

31994 #C6, 1923, 24c Carmine, XF-S 95 PSE. (Original Gum - Never Hinged). Fabulous color and impression. Extremely Fine to Superb. 2005 PSE - Graded Certificate. (SMQ $660; this being one of 52 attaining this grade as of 10/08, with 30 graded higher).

Estimate: $550+

Minimum Bid: $275

Unrivaled Perfection!

31995 #C6, 1923, 24c Carmine GEM 100 PSE. (Used). Unique Perfection. An incredible stamp in extraordinary condition with huge margins, deep rich color, and unimprovable centering. This is the only gem 100 used airmail for any C1-C6 as of 10/08. A true world class example that could be a once in a lifetime addition. Gem PSE - Encapsulated. (this being the *unique example attaining this grade* as of 10/08, with *none graded higher*).

Estimate: $1,500+

Minimum Bid: $750

Highest Graded

31996 #C7, 1926, 10c Dark Blue, GEM 100 PSE. (Original Gum - Never Hinged). Shear perfection. A true Gem for the collector who can settle for nothing less than the absolute best. Boasting the perfect intensity of color and detail on immaculate white paper, perfect centering, and pristine full original gum free from the natural gum bends that usually plague the issue. PSE - Encapsulated. (this being one of 3 attaining this grade as of 10/08, with *none graded higher*).

Estimate: $2,500+

Minimum Bid: $1,250

31997 #C8, 1926, 15c Olive Brown, SUP 98J PSE. (Original Gum - Never Hinged). Absolutely perfect, stamp has it all - jumbo margins, great color, dead-on centering, and pristine gum. Superb. PSE - Encapsulated. (this being one of 3 attaining this grade as of 10/08, with only 3 graded higher).

Estimate: $500+

Minimum Bid: $250

31998 **#C12, 1930, 5c Violet, SUP 98J; PSE.** (Original Gum - Never Hinged). A flawless mint example, perfectly centered amidst mammoth well balanced margins with full even perforations all around. With radiant color that virtually glows, a vivid proof-like impression, and pristine full original gum. A Superb stamp the likes of which are nearly never seen. 2005 PSE - Graded Certificate. (this being one of 7 attaining this grade as of 10/08, with only 2 graded higher).

Estimate: $750+
Minimum Bid: $375

31999 **#C13, 1930, 65c Green, XF-S 95 PSE.** (Original Gum - Never Hinged). Extremely Fine to Superb PSE - Encapsulated. (SMQ $880; this being one of 89 attaining this grade as of 10/08, with 33 graded higher).

Estimate: $750+
Minimum Bid: $375

32000 **#C13, 1930, 65c Green XF 90J PSE.** (Original Gum - Never Hinged). Enormous. Extremely Fine. PSE - Graded Certificate. (this being one of 3 attaining this grade as of 10/08, with 30 graded higher).

Estimate: $600+
Minimum Bid: $300

32001 **#C13, 1930, 65c Green, XF 90 PSE.** (Original Gum - Never Hinged). Fresh. Extremely Fine. PSE - Encapsulated. (SMQ $610; this being one of 133 attaining this grade as of 10/08, with 133 graded higher).

Estimate: $550+
Minimum Bid: $275

32002 **#C13, 1930, 65c Green XF 90 PSE.** (Original Gum - Never Hinged). Post Office fresh. Extremely Fine PSE - Encapsulated. (SMQ $610; this being one of 133 attaining this grade as of 10/08, with 133 graded higher).

Estimate: $450+
Minimum Bid: $225

32003 **#C13, 1930, 65c Green XF 90 PSE.** (Original Gum - Never Hinged). Post Office fresh. Extremely Fine. PSE - Encapsulated. (SMQ $610; this being one of 133 attaining this grade as of 10/08, with 133 graded higher).

Estimate: $450+
Minimum Bid: $225

32004 **#C13, 1930, 65c Green, VF-XF 85 PSE.** (Original Gum - Never Hinged). Post Office fresh and without the typical natural gum bends. Very Fine to Extremely Fine. PSE - Encapsulated. (SMQ $470; this being one of 145 attaining this grade as of 10/08, with 279 graded higher).

Estimate: $400+
Minimum Bid: $200

32005 **#C14, 1930, $1.30 Brown, XF-S 95 PSE.** (Original Gum - Never Hinged). Post Office Fresh. Extremely Fine to Superb. PSE - Encapsulated. (SMQ $1,700; this being one of 79 attaining this grade as of 10/08, with 32 graded higher).

Estimate: $1,450+

Minimum Bid: $725

32006 **#C14, 1930, $1.30 Brown, VF-XF 85 PSE.** (Original Gum - Never Hinged). Handsome example. Very Fine to Extremely Fine. PSE - Graded Certificate. (SMQ $910; this being one of 119 attaining this grade as of 10/08, with 254 graded higher).

Estimate: $750+

Minimum Bid: $375

32007 **#C14, 1930, $1.30 Brown, VF 80 PSE.** (Original Gum - Never Hinged). Post Office Fresh. Very Fine. PSE - Encapsulated. (SMQ $790; this being one of 160 attaining this grade as of 10/08, with 373 graded higher).

Estimate: $600+

Minimum Bid: $300

32008 **#C14, 1930, $1.30 Brown, VF 80 PSE.** (Original Gum - Never Hinged). Very Fine. PSE - Graded Certificate. (SMQ $790; this being one of 160 attaining this grade as of 10/08, with 373 graded higher).

Estimate: $650+

Minimum Bid: $325

32009 **#C14, 1930, $1.30 Brown.** (Original Gum - Never Hinged). A magnificent plate block of six was broken up resulting in this example becoming available as a single, perfect balanced margins all around, bright crisp brown color, detailed impression. Extra Fine-Superb; 2006 PF Certificate.

Estimate: $1,500+

Minimum Bid: $750

32010 **#C14, 1930, $1.30 Brown, XF-S 95 PSE.** (Used). Very fresh with Warrick Street Station cancel. Extremely Fine to Superb. PSE - Encapsulated. (SMQ $850; this being one of 18 attaining this grade as of 10/08, with only 5 graded higher).

Estimate: $850+

Minimum Bid: $425

32011 **#C15, 1930, $2.60 Blue, XF-S 95J PSE.** (Original Gum - Never Hinged). A premium mint example of this highly popular issue sporting an overall freshness, and flawless gum *without the usual natural gum bends*. Extremely Fine to Superb. PSE - Encapsulated. (this being one of 5 attaining this grade as of 10/08, with 24 graded higher).

Estimate: $2,500+

Minimum Bid: $1,250

32012 **#C15, 1930, $2.60 Blue, XF-S 95J PSE.** (Original Gum - Previously Hinged). Luscious color with a razor sharp impression, with light previous hinging. Extremely Fine to Superb. PSE - Graded Certificate. (this being one of 2 attaining this grade as of 10/08, with 10 graded higher).

Estimate: $1,000+

Minimum Bid: $500

32013 **#C15, 1930, $2.60 Blue XF-S 95 PSE.** (Original Gum - Never Hinged). Bright and Fresh. Extremely Fine to Superb PSE - Encapsulated. (SMQ $2,650; this being one of 84 attaining this grade as of 10/08, with 29 graded higher).

Estimate: $2,000+

Minimum Bid: $1,000

32014 **#C15, 1930, $2.60 Blue, XF-S 95 PSE.** (Original Gum - Never Hinged). Vivid and fresh. Extremely Fine to Superb. 2007 PSE - Graded Certificate. (SMQ $2,650; this being one of 84 attaining this grade as of 10/08, with 29 graded higher).

Estimate: $2,500+

Minimum Bid: $1,250

32015 **#C15, 1930, $2.60 Blue, XF 90 PSE.** (Original Gum - Never Hinged). Post Office fresh, slightly over-inked giving a warm feel, immaculate full original gum, with a few natural gum bends visible from the reverse only. Extremely Fine. PSE - Encapsulated. (SMQ $1,850; this being one of 119 attaining this grade as of 10/08, with 117 graded higher).

Estimate: $1,500+

Minimum Bid: $750

32016 **#C15, 1930, $2.60 Blue, XF 90 PSE.** (Original Gum - Never Hinged). Attractive and fresh. Extremely Fine. 2008 PSE - Graded Certificate. (SMQ $1,850; this being one of 119 attaining this grade as of 10/08, with 117 graded higher).

Estimate: $1,500+

Minimum Bid: $750

32017 #C15, 1930, $2.60 Blue, XF 90 PSE. (Original Gum - Hinged). Small hinge remnant. Extremely Fine. 2008 PSE - Graded Certificate. (SMQ $830; this being one of 27 attaining this grade as of 10/08, with 29 graded higher).
Estimate: $750+
Minimum Bid: $375

32018 #C15, 1930, $2.60 Blue VF-XF 85 PSE. (Original Gum - Never Hinged). Tiny inclusion above 'T' of United. Very Fine to Extremely Fine. PSE - Encapsulated. (SMQ $1,450; this being one of 150 attaining this grade as of 10/08, with 239 graded higher).
Estimate: $800+
Minimum Bid: $400

32019 #C15, 1930, $2.60 Blue, VF 80 PSE. (Original Gum - Never Hinged). Right sheet margin Plate No. 20091 single. Very Fine. PSE - Graded Certificate. (SMQ $1,200; this being one of 144 attaining this grade as of 10/08, with 389 graded higher).
Estimate: $850+
Minimum Bid: $425

32020 #C15, 1930, $2.60 Blue XF-S 95 PSE. (Used). Black Varny St. Station cancel. Extremely Fine to Superb. 2008 PSE - Graded Certificate. (SMQ $1,400; this being one of 7 attaining this grade as of 10/08, with only 2 graded higher).
Estimate: $1,200+
Minimum Bid: $600

32021 #C15, 1930, $2.60 Blue XF 90 PSE. (Used). Very well-centered for a 90, five points deducted for guide line on perf tips at left. Moderate cancel. Extremely Fine PSE - Encapsulated. (SMQ $940; this being one of 14 attaining this grade as of 10/08, with only 9 graded higher).
Estimate: $750+
Minimum Bid: $375

ONE OF THE HIGHEST GRADED ZEP SETS IN EXISTENCE

32022 #C13-15, 1930, 65c - $2.60 Zeppelins, SUP 98J PSE. (Original Gum - Never Hinged). THE most sought after Airmail stamps in the World - United States Graf Zeppelins. This widely popular set of three stamps was placed on sale by the United States Post Office Department at the height of the Great Depression in 1930. After thirty-seven days, 61,296 sets had been sold, they were then removed from sale and all unsold copies were destroyed. At the time, the Face Value of $4.55 was out of reach for the vast majority of collectors. This set has appreciated handsomely above original cost the last over the 78 years and is the key set to completion of a USA Airmail stamp collection.

The hand-picked set offered here is one of the Top three GRADED sets in existence. Only two sets with slightly higher grades exist. The highest graded Zeppelin set, formerly known as the "Westchester PSE Registry Set", was sold by Private Treaty in early 2008 for over $100,000.

Professional Stamp Experts (PSE) has graded 646 C13's. Only three stamps grade higher than the copy offered here. 593 C14's have been graded by PSE, only two stamps grade higher than the copy offered in this set and the C15 of which 581 copies have been graded by PSE, only a single stamp is graded higher (and it's currently sequestered in the ex-Westchester set referenced above, as are the other top-grade copies of C13 and C14).

Each stamp is Post Office Fresh. The C13 is PSE Capsule Graded Superb 98J, The C14 is PSE Paper Certificate, Graded Superb 98J (and Ex Killien), The C15 is PSE Capsule Graded Superb 98..

Estimate: $30,000+

Minimum Bid: $15,000

32023 **#C13-15, 1930, 65c - $2.60 Zeppelins, XF90 PSE.** (Original Gum - Never Hinged). Complete "XF 90" graded set of three. Extremely Fine. Each stamp with 2008 PSE - Graded Certificate. (SMQ $3,660; this being one of 122 possible sets attaining this grade as of 10/08).

Estimate: $2,800+

Minimum Bid: $1,400

32024 **#C13-15, 1930, 65c - $2.60 Zeppelins, XF-S 95 PSE.** (Original Gum - Never Hinged). Complete matched set for the airmail collector. Extremely Fine to Superb. PSE - Graded Certificate. (SMQ $5,230; this being one of 83 possible sets attaining this grade as of 10/08, with 21 graded higher).

Estimate: $4,500+

Minimum Bid: $2,250

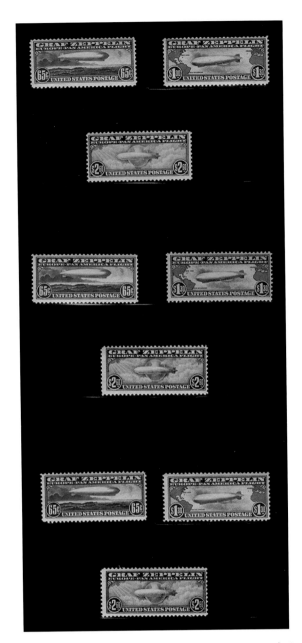

32026 **#C13-15, 1930, 65¢ - $2.60 Zeppelin, XF90 PSE.** (Original Gum - Never Hinged). Complete set of three Graf Zeppelins. Bright fresh, well centered, original gum, Never Hinged, Extremely Fine PSE - Graded Certificate. (SMQ $3660).

Estimate: $2,700+

Minimum Bid: $1,050

32025 **#C13-15, 1930, 65c - $2.60 COLOR.** (Original Gum - Never Hinged). Three (3) complete mint Never Hinged sets. Post office fresh, with full original gum, Fine to Very Fine; each stamp with either 2008 or 2007 PSE Certificate (9) Certificates total.
(Scott $7,800).

Estimate: $4,500+

Minimum Bid: $2,250

Please visit HA.com to view other collectibles auctions.   *A 19.5% Buyer's Premium ($9 min.) Applies To All Lots*

32027 **#C13-15, 1930, 65c - $2.60 COLOR.** (Original Gum - Never Hinged). A complete set of mint sheet margin singles, the 65c and $1.30 being top sheet margin singles, and the $2.60 being from the right sheet margin, original gum, Never hinged, Fine to Very Fine; each stamp with 2007 PSE Certificate. (Scott $2600).

Estimate: $1,500+
Minimum Bid: $750

32028 **#C13-15, 1930, 65c - $2.60 Zeppelins.** (Original Gum - Never Hinged). Complete set. Fine to Very Fine. The 65c with 2007 and the others with 2008 PSE Certificates. (Scott $2600).

Estimate: $1,500+
Minimum Bid: $750

32029 **#C16, 1931, 5c Violet, XF-S 95J PSE.** (Original Gum - Never Hinged). A magnificent mint example of this Winged Globe issue with uncharacteristically large and well balanced margins all around, lovely pastel color, razor sharp impression, and immaculate original gum. Extremely Fine to Superb PSE - Encapsulated. (this being one of 5, attaining this grade as of 10/08, with 10 graded higher).

Estimate: $500+
Minimum Bid: $250

SPECIAL DELIVERY ISSUES

32030 **#E1, 1885, 10c Blue XF 90 PF.** (Original Gum - Previously Hinged). Messenger Running. PF Certificate says "XQ" [Exceptional Quality] and we agree. Deserves a "J" designator also, as margins are very large for issue. Deep and strong color on fresh white paper. Light hinge mark only. Impressive stamp. Extremely Fine. 2008 PF Graded Certificate. (Scott $500).

Estimate: $1,000+

Minimum Bid: $500

32031 **#E3, 1893, 10c Orange, XF-S 95 PSE.** (Original Gum - Previously Hinged). Messenger on Foot. Bright color, very faint hinge mark only. Extremely Fine to Superb. 2008 PSE - Graded Certificate. (SMQ $790; this being one of 4 attaining this grade as of 10/08, with only 2 graded higher).

Estimate: $700+

Minimum Bid: $350

32032 **#E3, 1893, 10c Orange, XF 90 PSE.** (Original Gum - Never Hinged). Eye-catching example with wonderfully bright color. Extremely Fine. 2006 PSE - Graded Certificate. (SMQ $1,700; this being one of 7 attaining this grade as of 10/08, with only 4 graded higher).

Estimate: $1,500+

Minimum Bid: $750

32033 **#E4, 1894, 10c Blue, XF-S 95 PSE.** (Original Gum - Previously Hinged). A pristine example with excellent eye-appeal. The barest trace of hinging. Extremely Fine to Superb. 2006 PSE - Graded Certificate and 2000 PF Certificate. (SMQ $3,200; this being the only example attaining this grade as of 10/08, with only 5 graded higher).

Estimate: $2,800+

Minimum Bid: $1,400

HIGHEST GRADED USED

32034 **#E4, 1894, 10c Blue, SUP 98J PSE.** (Used). Messenger Running. Huge jumbo with a black town cancel, pencil notation on back. E4 does not come this big ordinarily, this copy rather unbelievable. Superb. 2008 PSE - Graded Certificate. (this being the *only example attaining this grade* as of 10/08, with *none graded higher*).

Estimate: $1,500+

Minimum Bid: $750

32035 **#E5, 1895, 10c Blue, SUP 98 PSE.** (Original Gum - Hinged). Messenger Running. Huge perfect margins, deep rich color and finely etched impression, with a small prior hinge remnant only. Superb. 2008 PSE - Graded Certificate. (SMQ $7,750; this being one of 3 attaining this grade as of 10/08, with none graded higher).

Estimate: $1,100+

Minimum Bid: $550

32036 **#E5, 1895, 10c Blue, SUP 98 PSE.** (Disturbed Original Gum). Messenger Running. Top sheet margin single with imprint. Phenomenally centered, with blazing rich color and detailed impression. PSE has however judged this stamp to have "disturbed original gum" a harsh call in our estimation, merely a slightly careless hinge removal. Gum is actually very close to what one would expect on a previously hinged stamp, at the worst. Superb. 2007 PSE - Graded Certificate and 1995 PF Certificate for a strip of three from which this is the middle stamp. (SMQ $1,150; this being the *only example attaining this grade* as of 10/08, with *none graded higher*).

Estimate: $1,500+

Minimum Bid: $750

TOP GRADE VARIETY

32037 **#E5var, 1895, 10c Blue, XF-S 95 PSE.** (Original Gum - Never Hinged). Messenger Running. Gorgeous rare variety *(now listed as #E5a)*, the Scott listed dots in curve frame variety only occurs on plate number 882, This particular example is very well centered with wide margins and excellent color. Extremely Fine to Superb. 2005 PSE - Graded Certificate and 2000 PF Certificate. (SMQ $3,600; this being one of 11 attaining this grade as of 10/08, with none graded higher, which includes all E5's, not necessarily the dot's variety).

Estimate: $5,000+

Minimum Bid: $2,500

32038 **#E5, 1895, 10c Blue, XF-S 95 PSE.** Messenger Running. (Original Gum - Never Hinged). Extremely large margins for this issue, with perfect gum. Extremely Fine to Superb PSE - Encapsulated. (SMQ $3,600; this being one of 11 attaining this grade as of 10/08, with none graded higher).

Estimate: $3,500+

Minimum Bid: $1,750

32039 **#E5, 1895, 10c Blue, XF-S 95 PSE.** Messenger Running. (Original Gum - Never Hinged). Uncharacteristically large margins. Extremely Fine to Superb PSE - Encapsulated. (SMQ $3,600; this being one of 11 attaining this grade as of 10/08, with none graded higher).

Estimate: $3,500+

Minimum Bid: $1,750

32040 **#E6, 1902, 10c Ultramarine, XF 90J PSE.** (Original Gum - Never Hinged). Messenger on Bicycle. Wonderful fresh jumbo with razor sharp impression. Extremely Fine. 2007 PSE - Graded Certificate. (this being one of 3 attaining this grade as of 10/08, with 4 graded higher).

Estimate: $2,500+

Minimum Bid: $1,250

32041 **#E7, 1908, 10c Green XF-S 95 PSE.** (Original Gum - Never Hinged). Lovely fresh stamp. Nicely balanced, bright and finely detailed. Extremely Fine to Superb. PSE - Encapsulated. (SMQ $840; this being one of 22 attaining this grade as of 10/08, with only 6 graded higher).

Estimate: $750+

Minimum Bid: $375

32042 **#E7, 1908, 10c Green XF-S 95 PSE.** (Original Gum - Never Hinged). Tremendous. Extremely Fine to Superb. 2004 PSE - Graded Certificate. (SMQ $840; this being one of 22 attaining this grade as of 10/08, with only 6 graded higher).

Estimate: $750+

Minimum Bid: $375

32043 **#E8, 1911, 10c Ultramarine, XF-S 95 PSE.** (Original Gum - Never Hinged). Messenger on Bicycle. Truly exceptional quality, dark rich ultramarine color, large margins, and crisp white paper. A very strong 95. Extremely Fine to Superb. PSE - Encapsulated. (SMQ $1,450; this being one of 4 attaining this grade as of 10/08, with only 7 graded higher).

Estimate: $1,500+

Minimum Bid: $750

32044 **#E8, 1911, 10c Ultramarine, XF 90J PSE.** (Original Gum - Never Hinged). Messenger on Bicycle. Bottom Plate No. 5513 single. Bright and fresh with a strong impression. Extremely Fine Jumbo. 2007 PSE - Graded Certificate. (this being one of 5 attaining this grade as of 10/08, with 13 graded higher).

Estimate: $950+

Minimum Bid: $475

32045 **#E9, 1914, 10c Ultramarine, XF-S 95 PSE.** (Original Gum - Never Hinged). Messenger on Bicycle. Remarkably well centered with a soft pastel color. Extremely Fine to Superb PSE - Encapsulated. (SMQ $1,500; this being one of 13 attaining this grade as of 10/08, with only 6 graded higher).

Estimate: $1,500+

Minimum Bid: $750

32046 **#E9, 1914, 10c Ultramarine, XF-S 95 PSE.** (Original Gum - Never Hinged). Messenger on Bicycle. Huge top Plate No. 5854 single. Deep dark color and detailed impression. Extremely Fine to Superb. 2004 PSE - Graded Certificate and 1994 PF Certificate. (SMQ $1,500; this being one of 13 attaining this grade as of 10/08, with only 6 graded higher).

Estimate: $2,000+

Minimum Bid: $1,000

32047 **#E9var, 1914, 10c Dark Ultramarine, VF-XF 85 PF.** (Original Gum - Never Hinged). Messenger on Bicycle. Unlisted Shade; Dark Ultramarine. Post Office fresh. Very Fine to Extremely Fine. 2006 PF Graded Certificate.

Estimate: $800+

Minimum Bid: $400

32048 **#E9a, 1914, 10c Blue, XF-S 95 PSE.** (Original Gum - Never Hinged). Messenger on Bicycle. Extremely rare and undervalued. Post Office fresh. Extremely Fine to Superb PSE - Encapsulated. (SMQ $1,900; this being one of 3 attaining this grade as of 10/08, with only 1 graded higher).

Estimate: $2,000+

Minimum Bid: $1,000

32049 **#E10, 1916, 10c Pale Ultramarine, XF-S 95 PSE.** (Original Gum - Never Hinged). Messenger on Bicycle. Difficult stamp to find in high grade. Fresh with a warm pastel color. Extremely Fine to Superb PSE - Encapsulated. (SMQ $2,350; this being one of 9 attaining this grade as of 10/08, with only 4 graded higher)

Estimate: $2,000+

Minimum Bid: $1,100

32050 **#E10, 1916, 10c Pale Ultramarine, XF-S 95 PSE.** Messenger on Bicycle. (Original Gum - Never Hinged). Especially handsome example with very large margins and a post office fresh appearance. Extremely Fine to Superb PSE to Encapsulated. (SMQ $2,350; this being one of 9 attaining this grade as of 10/08, with only 4 graded higher).

Estimate: $2,000+

Minimum Bid: $1,100

32051 **#E10, 1916, 10c Pale Ultramarine, XF-S 95 PSE.** Messenger on Bicycle. (Original Gum - Never Hinged). Deep rich color and spacious margins all around. Extremely Fine to Superb. 2008 PSE - Graded Certificate, as well as 1993 PF Certificate and 1991 PF Certificate for block of four from which this is the upper right stamp. (SMQ $2,350; this being one of 9 attaining this grade as of 10/08, with only 4 graded higher).

Estimate: $2,100+

Minimum Bid: $1,200

32053 **#E11, 1917, 10c Ultramarine, XF-S 95J PSE.** (Original Gum - Never Hinged). Messenger on Bicycle. Stunningly huge. Eye-pleasing color and shade. Post Office Fresh. Extremely Fine to Superb. 2008 PSE - Graded Certificate. (this being one of 15 attaining this grade as of 10/08, with only 7 graded higher).

Estimate: $1,500+

Minimum Bid: $750

32052 **#E11, 1917, 10c Ultramarine, SUP 98J PSE.** Messenger on Bicycle. (Original Gum - Never Hinged). Monstrous. Superb Jumbo for the finest collection. 2008 PSE - Graded Certificate and 1991 PF Certificate. (this being one of 2 attaining this grade as of 10/08, with only 1 graded higher).

Estimate: $700+

Minimum Bid: $350

32054 **#E12, 1922, 10c Gray Violet, XF-S 95J PSE.** Messenger on Motorcycle. (Original Gum - Never Hinged). Scarce jumbo with terrific color and impression. Extremely Fine to Superb. 2006 PSE - Graded Certificate. (this being one of 2 attaining this grade as of 10/08, with only 4 graded higher).

Estimate: $550+

Minimum Bid: $275

32055 **#E12, 1922, 10c Gray Violet, XF-S 95 PSE.** Messenger on Motorcycle. (Original Gum - Never Hinged). Rich and fresh. Extremely Fine to Superb. PSE - Encapsulated. (SMQ $550; this being one of 9 attaining this grade as of 10/08, with only 6 graded higher).

Estimate: $500+

Minimum Bid: $250

32056 **#E12, 1922, 10c Gray Violet, XF-S 95 PSE.** Messenger on Motorcycle. (Original Gum - Never Hinged). Impressive. Extremely Fine to Superb. 2006 PSE - Graded Certificate. (SMQ $550; this being one of 9 attaining this grade as of 10/08, with only 6 graded higher).

Estimate: $500+

Minimum Bid: $250

32057 **#E12, 1922, 10c Gray Violet XF-S 95 PF.** Messenger on Motorcycle. (Original Gum - Never Hinged). Almost a jumbo. Very bright and fresh. Extremely Fine to Superb. 2007 PF Graded Certificate.

Estimate: $500+

Minimum Bid: $250

32058 **#E12a, 1922, 10c Deep Ultramarine, SUP 98 PSE.** Messenger on Motorcycle. (Original Gum - Never Hinged). Fantastic color and razor sharp impression. Rare quality. Superb. PSE - Encapsulated. (SMQ $1,450; this being one of 5 attaining this grade as of 10/08, with only 2 graded higher).

Estimate: $1,400+

Minimum Bid: $700

32059 **#F1, 1911, 10c Ultramarine, XF-S 95 PSE.** (Original Gum - Never Hinged). Outstanding. Extremely Fine to Superb. PSE - Encapsulated. (SMQ $560; this being one of 16 attaining this grade as of 10/08, with only 7 graded higher).

Estimate: $500+

Minimum Bid: $250

32060 **#F1, 1911, 10c Ultramarine, XF-S 95 PSE.** (Original Gum - Never Hinged). Fresh and bright. Extremely Fine to Superb. 2005 PSE - Graded Certificate and 2001 PF Certificate. (SMQ $560; this being one of 16 attaining this grade as of 10/08, with only 7 graded higher).

Estimate: $500+

Minimum Bid: $250

POSTAGE DUE ISSUES

32061 **#J1, 1879, 1c Brown XF-S 95 PSE.** (Used). Warm pastel color and vivid detail, precisely centered. Extremely Fine to Superb. 2008 PSE - Graded Certificate. (this being the only example attaining this grade as of 10/08, with only 1 graded higher).

Estimate: $400+

Minimum Bid: $200

32062 **#J4, 1879, 5c Brown.** (Original Gum - Previously Hinged). A handsome mint example, warm color and finely etched, with original gum that shows light traces of previous hinging. Very Fine. 2008 PSE Certificate. (Scott $825.00).

Estimate: $600+

Minimum Bid: $300

HIGHEST GRADED USED

32063 **#J16, 1884, 2c Red Brown, SUP 98J PSE.** (Used). A stunning stamp with enormous margins. Superb. 2008 PSE - Graded Certificate. (this being the *only example attaining this grade* as of 10/08, with *none graded higher*).

Estimate: $900+

Minimum Bid: $450

32064 **#J17, 1884, 3c Red Brown.** (Original Gum - Previously Hinged). Handsome and fresh. Lightly hinged with no remnant. Fine to Very Fine. 2008 PSE Certificate. (Scott $1,150).

Estimate: $800+

Minimum Bid: $400

32065 **#J18, 1884, 5c Red Brown.** (Original Gum - Previously Hinged). A stunningly beautiful premium mint example. Flawlessly centered with an almost proof-like appearance and original gum that shows only the barest of kisses from a hinge. Very Fine to Extremely Fine. 2002 PSE Certificate. (Scott $625).

Estimate: $600+

Minimum Bid: $300

32066 **#J20, 1884, 30c Red Brown, VF 80J PSE.** (Original Gum - Never Hinged). Jumbo top margin single with partial imprint. Very Fine. 2008 PSE - Graded Certificate. (this being the only example attaining this grade as of 10/08, with only 9 graded higher).

Estimate: $600+

Minimum Bid: $300

32067 **#J33, 1894, 3c Deep Claret, VF-XF 85 PSE.** (Original Gum - Never Hinged). Intensely rich and vibrant. Very Fine to Extremely Fine. PSE - Encapsulated. (SMQ $760; this being one of 1 attaining this grade as of 10/08, with only 5 graded higher).

Estimate: $500+

Minimum Bid: $250

32068 **#J36b, 1894, 30c Pale Rose.** (Original Gum - Never Hinged). A bright and vibrant mint single, with finely detailed impression, beautifully centered. Very Fine to Extremely Fine. 2008 PSE Certificate and 2003 PF Certificate. (Scott $1,250).

Estimate: $1,000+

Minimum Bid: $500

SWEET DUE - TOP POP

32069 **#J41, 1895, 5c Deep Claret SUP 98 PSE.** (Original Gum - Never Hinged). Brilliant color, sparkling fresh gum. Superb. 2005 PSE - Graded Certificate. (SMQ $2,400; this being one of 6 attaining this grade as of 10/08, with none graded higher).

Estimate: $2,400+
Minimum Bid: $1,200

32070 **#J47, 1910, 3c Deep Claret, VF-XF 85 PF.** (Original Gum - Previously Hinged). Brilliant color and sharp impression, with only slight trace of prior hinge. Undervalued in Scott. Very Fine to Extremely Fine. 2008 PF Graded Certificate.

Estimate: $1,000+
Minimum Bid: $500

32071 **#J47, 1910, 3c Deep Claret.** (Original Gum - Never Hinged). Luxuriously deep rich color on bright white paper. Very Fine and select. 2008 PSE Certificate and 2002 PF Certificate. (Scott $1,750).

Estimate: $1,200+
Minimum Bid: $600

ONE OF THE BEST CENTERED J58'S IN EXISTENCE

32072 **#J58, 1914, 50c Carmine Lake.** (Original Gum - Previously Hinged). The Rarest Postage Due. Wonderfully centered with rich color and impression, and fresh gum with only a very light hinge mark. Inconsequential natural perforation disc impression on gum. Very Fine. 2007 PF Certificate. (Scott $17,500).

Estimate: $13,000+
Minimum Bid: $6,500

1913 PARCEL POST ISSUES

32073 **#J66, 1917, 30c Deep Claret, XF-S 95 PSE.** (Original Gum - Never Hinged). Beautifully centered, bright and fresh. Extremely Fine to Superb. 2007 PSE - Graded Certificate. (SMQ $750; this being the *only one attaining this grade* as of 10/08, with *none graded higher*).

Estimate: $750+

Minimum Bid: $375

32075 **#JQ1, 1913, 1c Dark Green, SUP 98 PSE.** (Original Gum - Never Hinged). Gorgeous and fresh. Superb for the finest collection. PSE - Encapsulated. (SMQ $590; this being one of 3 attaining this grade as of 10/08, with none graded higher).

Estimate: $600+

Minimum Bid: $300

32077 **#JQ4, 1913, 10c Dark Green XF-S 95 PSE.** (Original Gum - Never Hinged). Wonderful showpiece with impressive margins and glowing color. Extremely Fine to Superb. PSE - Encapsulated. (SMQ $2,150; this being one of 10 attaining this grade as of 10/08, with none graded higher).

Estimate: $2,200+

Minimum Bid: $1,100

32074 **#J73, 1930, 5c Carmine SUP 98 PSE.** (Original Gum - Never Hinged). Fresh and vibrant, unparalleled centering, with immaculate full original gum, Never Hinged, a Superb gem for the serious collector; 2008 PSE - Graded Certificate.
(SMQ $560; this being one of 1 attaining this grade as of 10/08, with none graded higher).

Estimate: $500+

Minimum Bid: $250

32076 **#JQ2, 1913, 2c Dark Green, XF-S 95 PSE.** (Original Gum - Never Hinged). Fresh mint example with large balanced margins. Pristine. Extremely Fine to Superb. PSE - Encapsulated. (SMQ $1,200; this being one of 4 attaining this grade as of 10/08, with only 1 graded higher).

Estimate: $1,200+

Minimum Bid: $600

32078 **#JQ4, 1913, 10c Dark Green, XF-S 95 PSE.** (Original Gum - Never Hinged). Top ten beauty. Extremely Fine to Superb. PSE - Encapsulated. (SMQ $2,150; this being one of 10 attaining this grade as of 10/08, with none graded higher).

Estimate: $2,150+

Minimum Bid: $1,075

32079 #JQ5, 1913, 25c Dark Green, XF-S 95 PSE. (Original Gum - Never Hinged). Tremendous Stamp. Brilliant color on fresh white paper, with glistening gum. Undervalued in SMQ. Extremely Fine to Superb. 2007 PSE - Graded Certificate. (SMQ $1,350; this being one of 3 attaining this grade as of 10/08, with only 3 graded higher).

Estimate: $3,500+

Minimum Bid: $1,750

1919-22 SHANGHAI OVERPRINTS

GORGEOUS HIGH GRADE SHANGHAI

32080 #K1, 1919, 2c on 1c Green, SUP 98 PSE. (Original Gum - Never Hinged). 'Gemmy' Shanghai overprint, perfect balanced margins, and great color. Superb. 2007 PSE - Graded Certificate. (SMQ $1,450; this being one of 7 attaining this grade as of 10/08, with only 1 graded higher).

Estimate: $2,000+

Minimum Bid: $1,000

32081 #K3, 1919, 6c on 3c Violet, XF-S 95 PSE. (Original Gum - Never Hinged). Stunning eye-appeal. Gorgeously rich and vibrant. Extremely Fine to Superb PSE - Encapsulated. (SMQ $1,150; this being one of 5 attaining this grade as of 10/08, with none graded higher).

Estimate: $1,100+

Minimum Bid: $550

32082 #K5, 1919, 10c on 5c Blue, XF-S 95 PSE. (Original Gum - Never Hinged). Fabulously centered within well-balanced margins. Pristine. Extremely Fine to Superb PSE - Encapsulated. (SMQ $1,200; this being one of 9 attaining this grade as of 10/08, with only 6 graded higher).

Estimate: $1,200+

Minimum Bid: $600

32083 #K6, 1919, 12c on 6c, Red Orange XF-S 95 PSE. (Original Gum - Never Hinged). Spectacular bright color. Unbelievably fresh. Extremely Fine to Superb PSE - Encapsulated. (SMQ $1,450; this being one of 9 attaining this grade as of 10/08, with only 2 graded higher).

Estimate: $1,400+

Minimum Bid: $700

32084 #K8, 1919, 16c on 8c, Olive Bister XF-S 95 PSE. (Original Gum - Never Hinged). Virtually flawless. Extremely Fine to Superb for the discriminating collector. PSE - Encapsulated. (SMQ $1,250; this being one of 8 attaining this grade as of 10/08, with only 4 graded higher).

Estimate: $1,200+

Minimum Bid: $600

32085 #K9, 1919, 18c on 9c Salmon Red, XF-S 95 PSE. (Original Gum - Never Hinged). Captivating. Exceptionally fresh and vibrant. Extremely Fine to Superb PSE - Encapsulated. (SMQ $1,200; this being one of 5 attaining this grade as of 10/08, with only 2 graded higher).

Estimate: $1,200+

Minimum Bid: $600

32086 #K9, 1919, 18c on 9c Salmon Red, XF 90 PSE. (Original Gum - Never Hinged). Bright and fresh. Extremely Fine. 2007 PSE - Graded Certificate. (SMQ $410; this being one of 10 attaining this grade as of 10/08, with only 7 graded higher).

Estimate: $375+

Minimum Bid: $188

32087 #K10, 1919, 20c on 10c Orange Yellow, XF-S 95 PSE. (Original Gum - Never Hinged). Hard to imagine a nicer 95. Perfect in every aspect. Extremely Fine to Superb PSE - Encapsulated. (SMQ $1,200; this being one of 6 attaining this grade as of 10/08, with only 1 graded higher).

Estimate: $1,200+

Minimum Bid: $600

32088 #K13, 1919, 40c on 20c Deep Ultramarine, XF-S 95 PSE. (Original Gum - Never Hinged). Rare and exquisite. Exceptionally well-centered, with deep rich color. Extremely Fine to Superb PSE - Encapsulated. (SMQ $1,950; this being one of 3 attaining this grade as of 10/08, with only 2 graded higher).

Estimate: $2,000+

Minimum Bid: $1,000

32089 #K15, 1919, $1 on 50c Light Violet, VF 80 PSE. (Original Gum - Previously Hinged). Wonderfully bold pastel color, with generously wide margins. Very light hinge mark. Very Fine. 2007 PSE - Graded Certificate. (SMQ $550; this being one of 4 attaining this grade as of 10/08, with 19 graded higher).

Estimate: $450+

Minimum Bid: $225

TOP OF THE POP

32090 #K17, 1922, 2c on 1c Green, SUP 98 PSE. (Original Gum - Never Hinged). Spectacular. Especially well-centered for the issue, rich and bold. Superb. PSE - Encapsulated. (SMQ $3,750; this being one of 7 attaining this grade as of 10/08, with none graded higher).

Estimate: $3,750+

Minimum Bid: $1,875

OFFICIAL ISSUES

RARE OVERPRINT ERROR

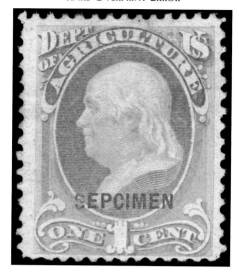

32091 #O1Sa, 1875, 1c Yellow F 70 PF. (No Gum). Rarely seen "Sepcimen" overprint error. Both handsome and captivating. Fine. 2008 PF Graded Certificate. (Scott $2,500).

Estimate: $2,000+

Minimum Bid: $1,000

32092 #O6, 1873, 12c Yellow. (Original Gum - Previously Hinged). A choice mint single, beautifully centered within picture frame margins, bright and vibrant, prior hinge very lightly brushed. Very Fineand a desirable example. 2004 PF Certificate. (Scott $450.00).

Estimate: $400+

Minimum Bid: $200

32093 #O69, 1873, $5 Green And Black F 70 PSE. (Original Gum - Previously Hinged). Slight gum disturbances. (gum disturbance mostly at top from less than careful hinge removal). This copy the only O69 OG stamp PSE has graded to date. Fine PSE - Encapsulated.
(SMQ $4,500; this being one of 1 attaining this grade as of 10/08, with none graded higher).

Estimate: $3,000+

Minimum Bid: $1,500

32094 #O69, 1873, $5 Green And Black F 70 PSE. (Partial Original Gum). Elusive in mint grade, fresh color, pencil notation on back, Fine; 2002 PSE - Graded Certificate.
(SMQ $4,500; this being one of 1 attaining this grade as of 10/08, with only 0 graded higher).

Estimate: $2,900+

Minimum Bid: $1,450

32095 #O69, 1873, $5 Green And Black. (Original Gum - Hinged). Handsome example, striking black vignette with great depth and contrast, ample to large margins, three short perforations at the bottom, small hinge remnant and pencil notation on the back, scarce stamp. Very Fine; 2008 PSE Certificate. (Scott $7,500).

Estimate: $3,000+

Minimum Bid: $1,500

32096 **#O70, 1873, $10 Green & Black.** (Original Gum - Previously Hinged). A bright and vibrant mint top sheet margin example of this high value State Department issue, with partial imprint, original gum, lightly hinged in the selvage, the stamp appearing never hinged. Fine to Very Fineand choice; color photocopy of 2008 PSE Certificatefor a vertical pair of which this is the top stamp.
(Scott $5,000).
Estimate: $5,000+
Minimum Bid: $2,500

32097 **#O70, 1873, $10 Green & Black.** (Original Gum - Hinged). A gorgeous mint example of this difficult State Department issue, fresh and vibrant, with light traces of multiple prior hinging's affecting most of the gum. Very Fine to Extremely Fine; 2008 PSE Certificate.
(Scott $5,000).
Estimate: $4,500+
Minimum Bid: $2,250

32098 **#O71, 1873, $20 Green & Black VG-F 60 PSE.** (Disturbed Original Gum). Intensely brilliant color, short perf. Hinge remnant and gum that is somewhat disturbed, but mostly present. Very Good to Fine PSE - Encapsulated.
(this being one of 1 attaining this grade as of 10/08, with only 2 graded higher).
Estimate: $2,000+
Minimum Bid: $1,000

32099 **#O71, 1873, $20 Green And Black.** (Original Gum - Hinged). One of the rarest of the officials in original gum, PSE has only graded two to date, fine centering with fresh green and black color, small hinged remnant. Fine; 2008 PSE Certificate.
Estimate: $1,800+
Minimum Bid: $900

32100 **#O71, 1873, $20 Green & Black.** (Used). A distinctively bright and vibrant used example of this often difficult high value State Department issue, cleaned, with horizontal pen cancel removed (from across the bust), with large part original gum still intact, a Fine to Very Fine example; 2006 APS Certificate.
(Scott $5,000).
Estimate: $2,000+
Minimum Bid: $1,000

NEWSPAPER ISSUES

32101 **#O94, 1879, 1c Yellow.** (No Gum As Issued). Exceedingly rare agriculture official issue, well centered example with much better than average color, two tiny thin spots at the top center, Fine to Very Fine; 2008 PSE Certificate. (Scott $6,000).

Estimate: $2,500+
Minimum Bid: $1,250

LOVELY NEVER HINGED OFFICIAL

32102 **#O100, 1879, 10c Vermillion XF 90 PSE.** (Original Gum - Never Hinged). Brilliant color, fresh and very well centered. Scarce as Never Hinged. Extremely Fine; 2008 PSE - Graded Certificate. (SMQ as previously hinged $270; this being one of 3 attaining this grade as of 10/08, with only 2 graded higher).

Estimate: $700+
Minimum Bid: $350

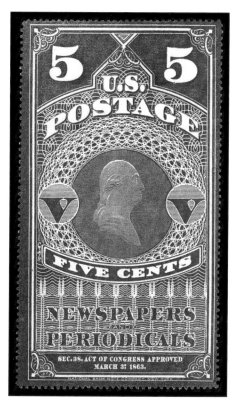

32103 **#PR1, 1865, 5c Dark Blue.** (No Gum As Issued). An outstanding mint example free of the faults that typically plague the issue. Both intense and radiant at the same time. Very Fine and rare thus; 2005 **PSE Certificate.** (Scott $750.00).

Estimate: $1,250+
Minimum Bid: $625

32104 **#PR27, 1875, $9 Yellow Orange.** (Original Gum - Previously Hinged). Bright and vibrant, precisely centered, inconsequential small thin spot at the right of the head. Lightly hinged with no remnant. Very Fine to Extremely Fine appearance for this difficult issue; 2006 PF Certificate. (Scott $4,000).

Estimate: $2,000+
Minimum Bid: $1,000

32105 **#PR29, 1875, $24 Dark Gray Violet.** (No Gum). Bright and fresh with no gum, pencil notations on the back. Very Fine; 2008 PSE Certificate.

Estimate: $850+
Minimum Bid: $425

SPECIAL PRINTING OF 1875 ISSUE

32106 **#PR36, 1875, 6c Gray Black.** (No Gum As Issued). An exhilarating mint example, free of the faults that typically plague this Continental Bank Note Co. Special Printing, no gum as issued. Very Fine to Extremely Fine. *Only 2,348 issued*; 2004 PF Certificate. (Scott $850.00).

Estimate: $700+
Minimum Bid: $350

32107 **#PR37, 1875, 8c Gray Black.** (No Gum As Issued). Brilliantly fresh gray black example, attractive, Fine to Very Fine; 2008 PSE Certificate. (Scott $950).

Estimate: $800+

Minimum Bid: $400

32108 **#PR38, 1875, 9c Gray Black.** (No Gum As Issued). Perforations barely cut into the design on the left side only, the color and impression are outstanding, overall a pretty stamp, Fine; 2008 PSE Certificate. (Scott $1,050).

Estimate: $600+

Minimum Bid: $300

32109 **#PR40, 1875, 12c Rose.** (No Gum As Issued). A striking shade variety of this scarce Special Printing, well-centered, with a luxurious pastel color and smooth yet detailed impression on white paper. Very Fine to Extremely Fineand under-valued in Scott. 2004PF Certificate. (Scott $1,500).

Estimate: $2,000+

Minimum Bid: $1,000

32110 **#PR71, 1879, $1.92 Pale Brown.** (Original Gum - Hinged). Extremely under-priced issue in original gum, PSE has only graded four with original gum to date, warm pale brown color accentuated with a sharp impression, great stamp, small hinge remnant. Very Fine; 2008 PSE Certificate. (Scott $550).

Estimate: $500+

Minimum Bid: $250

32111 **#PR73, 1879, $6 Blue.** (Original Gum - Hinged). Very rare, only five original gum previously hinged stamps graded by PSE to date, perforations barely cut into the design on the left side at a few points, color and strike are very good, small hinge remnant. Fine; 2008 PSE Certificate. (Scott $1,050).

Estimate: $350+

Minimum Bid: $175

32112 **#PR77, 1879, $36 Indian Red.** (Original Gum - Never Hinged). Rich and warm, fresh with pristine full original gum. Very Fine; 2008 PSE Certificate. (Scott as hinged $850).

Estimate: $1,000+

Minimum Bid: $500

32113 **#PR90, 1894, 1c Intense Black.**
(Original Gum - Never Hinged).
Well centered and fresh as the
day issued. Very Fine; 2008 PSE
Certificate.
(Scott $1,000).

Estimate: $700+

Minimum Bid: $350

32114 **#PR90, 1894, 1c Intense Black.**
(Original Gum - Never Hinged).
Intensely rich and detailed, bright
and fresh, pristine gum, with a trivial short corner perf at the top left
that does not really detract from
the overall appeal, Very Fine and
select; 2005 PSE Certificate.
(Scott $1,000).

Estimate: $500+

Minimum Bid: $250

32115 **#PR93, 1894, 6c Intense Black.**
(Original Gum - Never Hinged).
A visually stunning mint Never
Hinged single featuring a proof-like
appearance and full original gum,
with a trivial paper tear at the top
right that is difficult to find even
under magnification. Masterfully
repaired, a natural inclusion at the
bottom, Very Fine and select; 2004
PF Certificate.
(Scott as hinged $3750).

Estimate: $2,500+

Minimum Bid: $1,250

32116 **#PR104, 1895, 5c Black.** (Original
Gum - Never Hinged). A spec-
tacular mint Never Hinged bottom sheet margin single with part
imprint, fresh as the day printed,
with an intense proof-like impression, Extremely Fine and choice;
2004 PF Certificate.
(Scott $650).

Estimate: $400+

Minimum Bid: $200

1913 PARCEL POST ISSUES

32117 **#Q1, 1913, 1c Carmine Rose, SUP 98J PSE.** (Original Gum - Never Hinged). Post Office Clerk. Fantastic color and impression. Superb. 2006 PSE - Graded Certificate. (this being one of 5 attaining this grade as of 10/08, with only 2 graded higher).

Estimate: $650+

Minimum Bid: $325

32118 **#Q3, 1913, 3c Carmine XF-S 95J PSE.** (Original Gum - Never Hinged). Railway Postal Clerk. A magnificent mint single, both intense and radiant at the same time, precisely centered within huge well balanced margins. Full intact perforations all around. Extremely Fine to Superb. 2006 PSE - Graded Certificate. (this being one of 16 attaining this grade as of 10/08, with 10 graded higher).

Estimate: $750+

Minimum Bid: $375

32119 **#Q3, 1913, 3c Carmine XF-S 95J PSE.** (Original Gum - Never Hinged). Railway Postal Clerk. Jumbo with a dark rich color and razor sharp impression. Extremely Fine to Superb. 2006 PSE - Graded Certificate. (this being one of 16 attaining this grade as of 10/08, with 10 graded higher).

Estimate: $700+

Minimum Bid: $350

32120 **#Q3, 1913, 3c Carmine, XF-S 95 PSE.** (Original Gum - Never Hinged). Railway Postal Clerk. Choice example. Extremely Fine to Superb PSE - Encapsulated. (SMQ $440; this being one of 27 attaining this grade as of 10/08, with 26 graded higher).

Estimate: $400+

Minimum Bid: $200

32121 **#Q4, 1913, 4c Carmine Rose XF-S 95 PSE.** (Original Gum - Never Hinged). Rural Carrier. Gorgeous. Deep rich color and huge side margins. Extremely Fine to Superb. 2003 PSE - Graded Certificate. (SMQ $850; this being one of 9 attaining this grade as of 10/08, with only 6 graded higher).

Estimate: $750+

Minimum Bid: $375

32122 **#Q5, 1913, 5c Carmine Rose, XF-S 95 PSE.** (Original Gum - Never Hinged). Mail Train. Lovely Post Office fresh example. Bright and vibrant. Extremely Fine to Superb. PSE - Encapsulated. (SMQ $730; this being one of 13 attaining this grade as of 10/08, with only 9 graded higher).

Estimate: $700+

Minimum Bid: $350

32123 **#Q6, 1913, 10c Carmine Rose, SUP 98 PSE.** (Original Gum - Never Hinged). Steamship and Mail Tender. Tantalizing bright and bold color. Superb. PSE - Encapsulated. (SMQ $2,450; this being one of 7 attaining this grade as of 10/08, with none graded higher).

Estimate: $3,000+
Minimum Bid: $1,500

32124 **#Q6, 1913, 10c Carmine Rose XF-S 95 PSE.** (Original Gum - Never Hinged). Steamship and Mail Tender. Rich color. Fantastic eye-appeal. Extremely Fine to Superb. 2005 PSE - Graded Certificate. (SMQ $930; this being one of 12 attaining this grade as of 10/08, with 13 graded higher).

Estimate: $800+
Minimum Bid: $400

32125 **#Q7, 1913, 15c Carmine, Rose XF-S 95 PSE.** (Original Gum - Never Hinged). Dark rich color. Extremely Fine to Superb. PSE - Encapsulated. (SMQ $1,250; this being one of 7 attaining this grade as of 10/08, with only 4 graded higher).

Estimate: $1,200+
Minimum Bid: $600

32126 #Q9, 1913, 25c Carmine Rose, XF-S 95 PSE. (Original Gum - Never Hinged). Manufacturing. Nice large margins; very close to jumbo designation. Extremely Fine to Superb. PSE - Encapsulated. (SMQ $1,250; this being one of 4 attaining this grade as of 10/08, with only 8 graded higher).

Estimate: $1,200+

Minimum Bid: $600

32127 #Q10, 1913, 50c Carmine Rose, XF-S 95 PSE. (Original Gum - Never Hinged). Dairying. Dazzling bright color, large white balanced margins. Strong for grade. Extremely Fine to Superb. PSE - Encapsulated. (SMQ $3,750; this being one of 13 attaining this grade as of 10/08, with only 6 graded higher).

Estimate: $4,000+

Minimum Bid: $2,000

32128 #Q10, 1913, 50c Carmine Rose, XF 90 PSE. (Original Gum - Never Hinged). Dairying. Pretty example with well balanced margins. Extremely Fine. 2004 PSE - Graded Certificate. (SMQ $1,700; this being one of 19 attaining this grade as of 10/08, with 19 graded higher).

Estimate: $1,500+

Minimum Bid: $750

UNIQUELY GLORIOUS PERFECTION

32129 #Q11, 1913, 75c Carmine Rose, GEM 100J PSE. (Original Gum - Previously Hinged). Harvesting. For the collector that must have the absolute best of the best. This example is a phenomenal stamp, flawlessly centered within tremendous well balanced margins. Full even perforations all around, bright and fresh, original gum, only light traces of previous hinging near the top center. A true world class Gem in every respect. 2007 PSE - Graded Certificate. (this being *unique example attaining this grade* as of 10/08, with *none graded higher*).

Estimate: $3,000+

Minimum Bid: $1,500

32130 **#Q11, 1913, 75c Carmine Rose SUP 98 PSE.** (Original Gum - Never Hinged). Harvesting. Absolute beauty. A showpiece. NEARLY impossible to improve upon, stunning color, impression, and WONDERFUL centering. Superb PSE - Encapsulated. (SMQ $3,800; this being one of 8 attaining this grade as of 10/08, with none graded higher).

Estimate: $4,000+
Minimum Bid: $2,000

32131 **#Q12, 1913, $1 Carmine Rose, XF-S 95 PSE.** (Original Gum - Never Hinged). Fruit Growing. A real beauty. Bright and fresh within large even margins. Extremely Fine to Superb. PSE - Encapsulated. (SMQ $4,500; this being one of 14 attaining this grade as of 10/08, with only 8 graded higher).

Estimate: $4,000+
Minimum Bid: $2,000

32132 **#Q12, 1913, $1 Carmine Rose, XF-S 95 PSE.** (Original Gum - Never Hinged). Fruit Growing. Crisp, clean and fresh. Extremely Fine to Superb PSE - Encapsulated. (SMQ $4,500; this being one of 14 attaining this grade as of 10/08, with only 8 graded higher).

Estimate: $4,000+
Minimum Bid: $2,000

SPECIAL HANDLING ISSUES

32133 **#QE4, 1925, 25c Yellow Green, SUP 98 PSE.** (Original Gum - Never Hinged). Top sheet margin Plate No.17097 single. Superb. 2004 PSE - Graded Certificate. (SMQ $440; this being one of 26 attaining this grade as of 10/08, with only 2 graded higher).

Estimate: $400+
Minimum Bid: $200

LOCALS & CARRIERS

32134 **#10LB1, 1854 Bishop's City Post, Blue on Wove Paper.** (Original Gum - Hinged). A scarce mint single, intense color, original gum with paper adherance. Very Fine. 2007 APS Certificate. (Scott $5,000).

Estimate: $4,000+

Minimum Bid: $2,000

32135 **#40L1, 1842, 3c Black On Grayish Paper.** (No Gum). Gorgeous example with an attention-grabbing pressed out pre-print paper fold; with an additional small pre-print paper fold at lower left. Extremely Fine to Superb. 2008 PF Certificate. (Scott for normal $375).

Estimate: $500+

Minimum Bid: $250

32136 **#52L2, 1856, 1c Red.** (Used). Nice used example tied on piece by a black oval "Cornwall's Madison Square Post Office" cancel. Fine. 2002 PSE Certificate. (Scott $600).

Estimate: $500+

Minimum Bid: $250

REVENUE ISSUES

32137 **#R2a, 1862, 1c Red.** (Used). Nice used four margin example with a manuscript cancel and two light horizontal creases. Fine to Very Fine. 2008 PSE Certificate. 1992 PSE Certificate. (Scott $1,800).

Estimate: $1,300+

Minimum Bid: $650

DOUBLE TRANSFER VARIETY

32138 **#R7a var, 1862, 2c Blue.** (Used). An exceptional example of the double transfer T7 variety, with a distinct black 1863 handstamp cancel. Very Fine. 2008 PSE Certificate. (Scott $400).

Estimate: $850+

Minimum Bid: $425

32139 **#R9a, 1862, 2c Blue.** (Used). An attention-grabbing vertical block of 12 with manuscript cancels. Extremely Fine. 2008 PSE Certificate (Scott as blocks of four $480).

Estimate: $1,000+

Minimum Bid: $500

RARE REVENUE - POSSIBLY UNIQUE AS MINT

32140 #R17a, 1862, 3c Green. (No Gum). Playing Cards. One of the rarest US Revenue stamps. Very fresh, four margins, possibly left side sheet margin copy. Beautiful deep rich color, strongly detailed engraving. Catalog value for used ($25,000) - is irrelevant. This copy apparently unique as Mint. Very Fine to Extremely Fine; 2008 PF Certificate. Scott Catalog Value does not list value for unused revenues. Scott editors note that unused revenues exist and that they sell for prices above the stated used values.

Estimate: $90,000+
Minimum Bid: $45,000

32141 **#R31c, 1871, 6c Orange.** (Used). Rare stamp. A.M.F.G. (Gianelli, Genoa Italy) handstamp cancel. Small thins at the top, a thin and short corner perf at the upper left and a tiny margin tear at the bottom. Bright color and very nice appearing for this rare stamp. Fine; 2008 PSE Certificate. (Scott with faults $2000).

Estimate: $1,500+

Minimum Bid: $875

32142 **#R33b, 1862, 10c Blue.** (Used). Deep color, cert says 'used', we cannot find any evidence of a cancel. Light horizontal crease in the top margin at right. Very Fine; 2008 PSE Certificate. (Scott $750).

Estimate: $700+

Minimum Bid: $350

32143 **#R43a, 1862, 25c Red.** (Used). Horizontal pair, manuscript cancel. Attractive. Very Fine; 2008 PSE Certificate. (Scott $675).

Estimate: $650+

Minimum Bid: $325

32144 **#R65a, 1862, 70c Green.** (Used). Wonderful Quality. Deep and Rich color, large margins and a sweet Blue "Socked on the Nose" handstamp cancel. CV irrelevant on this beauty. Extremely Fine; 2008 PSE Certificate. (Scott $600).

Estimate: $2,500+

Minimum Bid: $1,250

32145 **#R74a, 1862, $1 Red.** (Used). Top sheet margin pair, manuscript cancel. Very Fine; 2008 PSE Certificate. (Scott $650).

Estimate: $900+

Minimum Bid: $450

32146 **#R77c, 1862, $1.30 Orange.** (Used). Choice pair, with delectable blue Robinson Cox handstamp cancel on each stamp. Very Fine; 2008 PSE Certificate. (Scott Manuscript cancel $190).

Estimate: $500+

Minimum Bid: $250

32147 **#R81a, 1862, $2 Red.** (Used). Top sheet margin, and with extra large margins all around. Manuscript cancel. (traces of light toning at the top). Very Fine; 2008 PSE Certificate. (Scott $160).

Estimate: $375+

Minimum Bid: $188

CHOICE CANCEL

32148 **#R83a, 1863, $2 Red.** (Used). Choice example. Lovely 1863 handstamp cancel. Fine to Very Fine; 2008 PSE Certificate. (Scott $5500).

Estimate: $4,500+

Minimum Bid: $2,250

32149 **#R83a, 1863, $2 Red.** (Used). Bright and scarce used example, excellent red color with a manuscript cancel. Light horizontal crease at the bottom. Very Fine to Extremely Fine; 2008 PSE Certificate. (Scott $5,500).

Estimate: $2,200+

Minimum Bid: $1,100

CONDITION RARITY - SCARCE REVENUE

32150 **#R84a, 1863, $2.50 Purple.** (Used). Rich and enthralling deep color. This stamp is not commonly found in sound condition. This copy very nice. Very Fine; 2008 PSE Certificate. (Scott $7000).

Estimate: $6,500+

Minimum Bid: $3,250

32151 **#R87a, 1863, $3.50 Blue.** (Used). Stunning used example. Deep blue color with a sharp impression and light manuscript cancel. Sealed 4 mm tear at the bottom. Very Fine; 2008 PSE Certificate. (Scott $7,000).

Estimate: $4,000+

Minimum Bid: $2,000

32152 **#R89a, 1862, $5 Red.** (Used). Terrific used horizontal pair, right sheet margin and vertical gutter-line. Canceled by a black hand stamp cancel and a manuscript cancel. Scarce. Very Fine; 2008 PSE Certificate.

Estimate: $500+

Minimum Bid: $250

32153 #R93a, 1862, $10 Green. (Used). Incredible color and impression, black manuscript cancel. Extremely Fine; 2008 PSE Certificate. (Scott $750).

Estimate: $750+
Minimum Bid: $375

32154 #R95a, 1862, $10 Green. (Used). Excellent used example, dark green color with extra-wide margins. Black manuscript cancel. Extremely Fine to Superb; 2008 PSE Certificate. (Scott $650).

Estimate: $700+
Minimum Bid: $350

32155 #R96a, 1862, $10 Probate of Will, Green. (Used). A used single with generous to large margins all around. Manuscript cancel, with light diagonal crease only visible from the back. Small toned spot at the bottom right, neither of which detracts from the overall appearance. Very Fine; 2008 PF Certificate.

Estimate: $1,000+
Minimum Bid: $500

32156 #R97a, 1862, $15 Blue. (Used). Rare used revenue with deep blue color and very fresh appearance, manuscript cancel, Fine to Very Fine; 2008 PSE Certificate. (Scott $2,700).

Estimate: $2,500+
Minimum Bid: $1,250

32157 #R99a, 1862, $20 Orange. (Used). Attractive example with a manuscript cancel, a small corner crease at the lower left and very slightly sulphurated color. Very Fine to Extremely Fine; 2008 PSE Certificate. (Scott $2,000).

Estimate: $1,750+
Minimum Bid: $875

32158 #R99c, 1862, $20 Orange. (Used). Extraordinary used example, two attractive black hand stamp cancels. Fine; 2008 PSE Certificate. (Scott $2,000).

Estimate: $1,500+
Minimum Bid: $750

32159 #R100a, 1863, $25 Red. (Used). Fantastic used example with wide well centered margins, light black manuscript cancel. Very Fine to Extremely Fine; 2008 PSE Certificate. (Scott $1,500).

Estimate: $1,350+

Minimum Bid: $675

32160 #R100a, 1863, $25 Red. (Used). Fine used example with a manuscript cancel. Fine; 2008 PSE Certificate. (Scott $1,500).

Estimate: $750+

Minimum Bid: $375

32161 #R102a, 1864, $200 Green And Red. (Used). Scarce used. Attractive manuscript cancel. Fine; 2008 PSE Certificate. (Scott $2,500).

Estimate: $1,500+

Minimum Bid: $750

32162 #R102a, 1864, $200 Green And Red. (Used). Beautiful used example with an extremely light manuscript cancel, vertical crease at the center. Very Fine; 2008 PSE Certificate. (Scott $2,500).

Estimate: $1,500+

Minimum Bid: $750

32163 #R102c, 1864, $200 Green And Red. (Used). Choice used example with bright vivid color, light manuscript cancel. Fine to Very Fine; 2008 PSE Certificate. (Scott $900).

Estimate: $700+

Minimum Bid: $350

32164 #R103a, 1871, 1c Blue & Black with Inverted Center. (No Gum). A splendid example of this desirable Invert Revenue issue. Fresh and vibrant. Very Fine and select. 2008 PSE Certificate. (Scott $1,500).

Estimate: $1,000+

Minimum Bid: $500

32165 #R109a, 1871, 10c Blue & Black with Inverted Center. (Used). A used example of this scarce Revenue Invert with herringbone cut cancel and a Straight line "Feb 20 '72" handstamped. Fine; 2008 PSE Certificate. Also, 1999 APS Certificate. (Scott $2,500).

Estimate: $1,250+

Minimum Bid: $625

32166 **#R115b, 1871, 50c Blue & Black with Inverted Center.** (Regummed). A magnificent unused example of this scarce Revenue Invert; sporting bright fresh color and detailed impressions on clean white paper, regummed. An overall Extremely Fine example destined for the finest of collections. 2008 PSE Certificate.
(Scott $2,000).

Estimate: $1,500+

Minimum Bid: $750

32167 **#R118a, 1871, $1 Blue & Black with Inverted Center.** (Used). A handsome used example of this $1 Revenue Invert, the center not only inverted, but also shifted approximately 2mm to the left. Filled in triangular punch cancel at top and a tiny corner perforation crease at bottom left, both barely visible from the back and neither affecting the overall appearance. Fine - Very Fine appearance; 2008 PF Certificate. (Scott $5,000).

Estimate: $2,500+

Minimum Bid: $1,250

32168 **#R127a, 1871, $5 Blue & Black with Inverted Center.** (Used). A handsome used example of this $5 Revenue Invert, sporting bright color and sharp impressions, with usual manuscript cancel, and a trivial pulled perf at the top which does not detract from the overall appeal. Very Fine and scarce; 2008 PF Certificate..

Estimate: $2,000+

Minimum Bid: $1,000

32169 **#R128, 1871, $10 Blue & Black.** (Used). Wonderful used strip of three, very attractive example with manuscript cancel. Extremely Fine; 2002 PSE Certificate. (Scott as singles $600).

Estimate: $500+

Minimum Bid: $250

32170 **#R129, 1871, $20 Blue & Black.** (Used). Fabulous used example, bright blue color with even ample margins for the issue. Extremely Fine; 2008 PSE Certificate. (Scott $800).

Estimate: $700+

Minimum Bid: $350

32171 **#R131, 1871, $50 Blue & Black.** (Used). Gorgeous rich color, very pretty stamp. Manuscript cancel. Very Fine to Extremely Fine; 2008 PSE Certificate. (Scott $1,000).

Estimate: $1,000+

Minimum Bid: $500

32172 **#R135b, 1871, 2c Orange & Black with Inverted Center.** (Used). An attractive used single of this third issue Revenue Invert with a manuscript "3/4/72" date cancel. Fine; 2008 PSE Certificate. (Scott $700.00).

Estimate: $500+

Minimum Bid: $250

32173 **#R135b, 1871, 2c Orange & Black, Inverted Center.** (No Gum). Spectacularly bright and vibrant, precisely centered within well balanced margins. Very Fine to Extremely Fine; 2008 PSE Certificate. (Scott $700).

Estimate: $500+

Minimum Bid: $250

32174 **#R150, 1872, $20 Org & Blk.** (Used). Manuscript cancel. Very Fine; 2008 PSE Certificate. (Scott $625).

Estimate: $700+

Minimum Bid: $350

32175 **#R150a, 1871, $20 $20 Vermilion & Black (Color Error).** (Used). Attractive example of this scarce color error. Black manuscript cancel and two tiny thin specks. Extremely Fine; 2008 PSE Certificate. (Scott $850).

Estimate: $750+

Minimum Bid: $375

32176 **#R151a, 1874, 2c Orange & Black On Green, Inverted Center.** (Partial Original Gum). Beautifully bright and clean, well centered, with a distinctive invert of the center. Original gum over most of the stamp's reverse. Fine to Very Fine and select. 2008 PSE Certificate and 1992 PF Certificate. (Scott $500).

Estimate: $500+

Minimum Bid: $250

32177 **#R151a, 1874, 2c Inverted Center.** (Used). Pleasing used example with inverted center and cut cancel. Fine; 2008 PSE Certificate. (Scott $400).

Estimate: $350+

Minimum Bid: $175

32178 **#R157, 1898, 10c Dark Green.** (Used). Bright and fresh used 'I.R.' provisional with a July 1898 manuscript cancel and a thin at the lower left. Extremely difficult stamp to obtain in any condition. Fine; 2008 PSE Certificate. (Scott $4,000).

Estimate: $2,500+

Minimum Bid: $1,250

REVENUE RARITY

32179 **#R158a, 1898, 1c Dark Yellow Green.** (Used). Extremely rare and difficult stamp to find in any condition, missing from most collections. This attractive used example with a straight line July 22 1898 cancel (with the date corrected in pen) "24, two small thins at the top, a small corner crease and a light vertical crease at the left. Fine to Very Fine; 2008 PSE Certificate. (Scott $10,000).

Estimate: $8,000+

Minimum Bid: $4,000

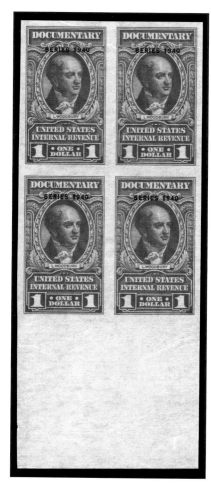

32180 **#R300A, 1940, $1 Carmine.** (No Gum As Issued). Bottom sheet margin Block of Four, diagonal natural paper wrinkle in the top pair. Very Scarce block. Extremely Fine; 2008 PSE Certificate. (Scott $550).
Estimate: $500+
Minimum Bid: $250

32181 **#R305Ab, 1940, $20 Carmine.** (No Gum As Issued). Imperforate pair. Fresh. Pair Very Fine to Extremely Fine; 2008 PSE Certificate.
Estimate: $700+
Minimum Bid: $350

32182 **#R356, 1942, 10c Carmine.** (Used). Light Blue manuscript, and red date stamp cancels. Scarce and undervalued in Scott. Fine to Very Fine PSE Certificate. (Scott $1000).
Estimate: $1,200+
Minimum Bid: $600

32183 **#R357, 1942, $60 Carmine.** (Used). Choice example. Blue manuscript cancel and red pen line cancels. Undervalued in Scott. Extremely Fine; 2008 PSE Certificate. (Scott $1850).
Estimate: $2,200+
Minimum Bid: $1,100

32184 **#R409, 1944, $500 Carmine.** (Used). A handsome used top right sheet corner single, with a manuscript cancel and an inconsequential pressed out embossed cancel at the center. Very Fine and sound example of this difficult high value. 2004 PSE Certificate. (Scott $2,600).
Estimate: $2,000+
Minimum Bid: $1,000

32185 **#R703, 1956, $2500 Carmine.** (Used). Rich color. Blue manuscript and straight-line hand-stamp cancels. Scarce. Very Fine; 2008 PSE Certificate. (Scott $800).
Estimate: $800+
Minimum Bid: $400

32186 **#R714, 1957, $10,000 Carmine.** (Used). Purple handstamp cancels. Very Fine; 2008 PSE Certificate. (Scott $500).
Estimate: $750+
Minimum Bid: $375

32187 **#R723, 1958, $10,000 Carmine.** (Used). An attention-grabbing used top right sheet corner margin single, fresh and vibrant, with handstamp and perforated initials cancels. Very Fine to Extremely Fine and choice. 2007 PF Certificate. (Scott $700).
Estimate: $1,000+
Minimum Bid: $500

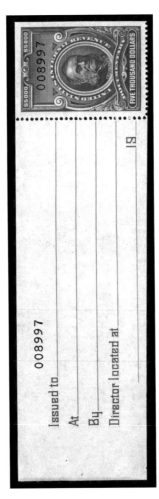

32188 **#R731, 1958, $5000 Carmine.** (Original Gum - Never Hinged). With complete receipt tab at the left, which has a fingerprint on the gum. Scarce item. Extremely Fine; 2008 PSE Certificate.
Estimate: $500+
Minimum Bid: $250

32189 **#RB6a, 1871, 6c Green And Black.** (Used). Exceptionally well-centered with Charles Osgood black handstamp on violet paper, small thin at bottom. Very attractive and scarce nonetheless. Extremely Fine; 2008 PSE Certificate.
Estimate: $500+
Minimum Bid: $250

32190 **#RB8b, 1874, 50c Green And Black.** (Used). Attractive Blue handstamp on green paper. Fine to Very Fine; 2008 PSE Certificate.
(Scott $1300).
Estimate: $1,250+
Minimum Bid: $625

32191 **#RB9a, 1873, $1 Green & Black On Violet.** (Used). A stunning used example of this difficult early Proprietary issue, with an especially light, unobtrusive purple oval handstamp cancel. A single insignificant pulled perf at the top left not noted on the certificate, otherwise free of the faults which usually plague this issue. Very Fine, choice example that will enhance the serious revenue collection. 2006 PF Certificate. (Scott $2,750).
Estimate: $2,000+
Minimum Bid: $1,000

32192 #RB10a, 1873, $5 Green And Black. (Used). Gorgeous example. Appears unused. Small faults on violet paper. Rare. Very Fine; 2008 PSE Certificate. (Scott w/Small Faults $9,000).

Estimate: $7,500+

Minimum Bid: $3,750

32194 #RD64, 1940, $100 Green. (Used). Blue Overprint, purple date, black pen line and manuscript cancels. Very Fine; 2008 PSE Certificate. (Scott $625).

Estimate: $625+

Minimum Bid: $312

32193 #RC10S, 1918, $1.00 Green. (Original Gum - Never Hinged). Unlisted mint "specimen" overprint block of four, handsome example, Fine; 2008 PF Certificate.

Estimate: $2,000+

Minimum Bid: $1,000

32195 **#RD67-85 var., 1940, 1c - $20
Bright Green, without Overprint.**
(No Gum As Issued). A most attractive and complete set of 17 mint
horizontal pairs of this scarce variety which is only listed in the catalog as a notation after the regular
issue. Remarkably bright and fresh,
with an almost proof-like quality.
Very Fine to Extremely Fine. (Scott
$1,100).

Estimate: $1,000+

Minimum Bid: $500

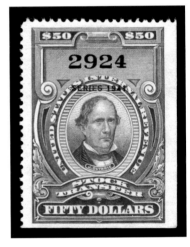

32196 **#RD112, 1941, $50 Bright Green.**
(No Gum As Issued). Bright and
Fresh. Scarce. Very Fine; 2008 PSE
Certificate. (Scott $1000).

Estimate: $1,250+

Minimum Bid: $625

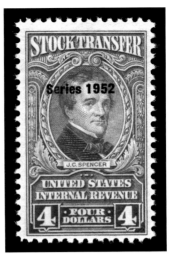

32197 **#RD370, 1952, $4 Bright Green.**
(Original Gum - Previously
Hinged). Bright color, fresh appear-
ance. Fresh gum, light hinge rem-
nant. Fine to Very Fine; 2008 PSE
Certificate.

Estimate: $1,500+

Minimum Bid: $750

32198 **#RE159A//RE184A, 1942-59, Wines
Selection.** (No Gum As Issued).
A delightful selection of thirteen
items, includes RE159A, RE165A,
RE167A & B, RE167B, RE179A,
RE180A, RE182A-E, RE183A, and
RE184A, all bright and fresh. Very
Fine to Extremely Fine. (Scott
$1,925).

Estimate: $2,500+

Minimum Bid: $1,250

32199 **#RE179, 1942, $8 Yellow Green.**
(No Gum As Issued). Scarce
as Mint. Very Fine; 2008 PSE
Certificate. (Scott $1250).

Estimate: $1,000+

Minimum Bid: $500

32200 **#RE182, 1949, $30 Yellow Green
And Black.** (No Gum As Issued).
Fabulous example, huge even
margins are beautifully centered
with radiant yellow green color.
Extremely Fine to Superb; 2008
PSE Certificate. (Scott $1,750).

Estimate: $1,750+

Minimum Bid: $875

Please visit HA.com to view other collectibles auctions.   *A 19.5% Buyer's Premium ($9 min.) Applies To All Lots*

32201 **#RE196c, 1951-54, $1.60 Yellow Green And Black.** (No Gum As Issued). Lovely example with a very fresh appearance, Very Fine; 2008 PSE Certificate.
(Scott $1,000).

Estimate: $900+

Minimum Bid: $450

32202 **#REA198, 1947, 500 Barrels, Dark Brown.** (No Gum As Issued). Fermented Malt Liquor. Pristine example with large even margins, exceptional quality. Extremely Fine; 2008 PSE Certificate. (Scott $500).

Estimate: $650+

Minimum Bid: $325

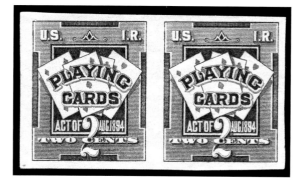

32203 **#RF2b, 1894, 2c Ultramarine.** (No Gum As Issued). Attractive example with a light natural gum bend, hinge remnant and pencil notation on the back. Very Fine; 2008 PSE Certificate. (Scott $600).

Estimate: $500+

Minimum Bid: $250

32204 **#RG58-75a, 1941, 1c - $10 Gray.** (No Gum As Issued). Horizontal imperforate pairs, without gum as issued, Very Fine to Extremely Fine.
(Scott $4,600).

Estimate: $4,000+

Minimum Bid: $2,000

32205 **#RG126, 1944, $20 Gray.** (Original Gum - Previously Hinged). Spectacular example, perfectly centered with pastel gray color on white paper, very light hinge mark at the top. Extremely Fine to Superb; 2008 PSE Certificate. (Scott $800).

Estimate: $800+

Minimum Bid: $400

32206 **#RJA48a, 1919-64, 3c Violet.** (No Gum). A magnificent unused single from the Smithsonian Revenue Deaccession auction of Feb. 12, 2005, Extremely Fine and choice; 2005 PF Certificate. (Scott $750).
> **Estimate: $1,200+**
> **Minimum Bid: $600**

32207 **#RJA99b, 1963, 20c Violet.** (Original Gum - Never Hinged). Fabulous vertical pair, dark rich violet color with a razor sharp impression. Extremely Fine to Superb; 2008 PSE Certificate. (Scott as 2 singles $1,000).
> **Estimate: $750+**
> **Minimum Bid: $375**

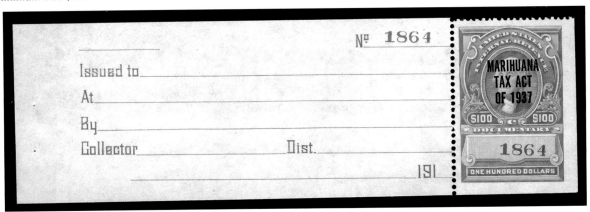

32208 **#RJM4, 1937, $100 Green.** (No Gum As Issued). Marihuana Tax Act of 1937. With complete receipt tab at left. Undervalued in Scott. Extremely Fine; 2008 PSE Certificate. (Scott $750).
> **Estimate: $1,500+**
> **Minimum Bid: $750**

32209 **#RS146c, 1862, 4c Green On Pink Paper.** (No Gum). Wonderful revenue with a tiny picked out inclusion above the "LP" in "Philadelphia" Extremely Fine; 2008 PF Certificate. (Scott $1,400).
> **Estimate: $1,200+**
> **Minimum Bid: $600**

32210 #RS199b, 1873, 2c Blue On Silk Paper. (Used). Wonderful example of the very rare blue on silk paper example, tiny pinhole outside the lettering opposite the "R" in ambrosia. Very Fine; 2008 PF Certificate. (Scott $4,250).

Estimate: $4,000+

Minimum Bid: $2,000

32211 #RS215b, 1875, 1c Lake On Silk. (No Gum). Block of eight (2x4) with a vertical crease between stamps, and a small scissor cut at right between POS. 6 & 8., great looking multiple, pencil notation on back. Extra Fine; 2008 PF Certificate. (Scott $1,280).

Estimate: $1,500+

Minimum Bid: $750

32212 #RT2d, 1878, 1c Black On Watermarked Paper. (Used). Exquisite impression and color, huge margins on three sides, Fine to Very Fine; 2008 PF Certificate. (Scott $2,750).

Estimate: $2,300+

Minimum Bid: $1,150

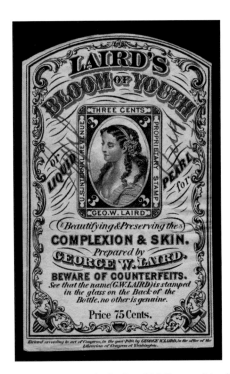

32213 **#RT15a, 1870, 3c Black On Old Paper.** (Used). Beautiful used example with a red 1871 manuscript cancel with a thin spot in the area of the word "skin", pencil notations on back. Very Fine; 2008 PF Certificate.(Scott $3,000).

Estimate: $3,000+

Minimum Bid: $1,500

32214 **#RT21c, 1872, 2c Blue On Pink Paper.** (Used). Scarce used example with several small faults, overall attractive stamp. Fine; 2008 PF Certificate.(Scott $3,750).

Estimate: $3,200+

Minimum Bid: $1,600

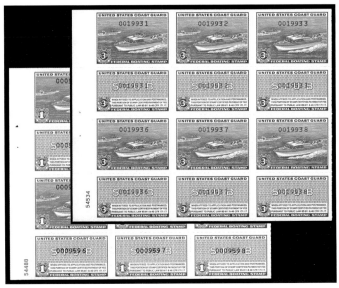

32215 **#RVB1-2, 1960, $1 & $3 Blue & Rose Red.** (Original Gum - Never Hinged). A complete run of the Boating stamps as lower left Plate No. ($1 = 54488 & $3 = 54534) blocks of six, the $3 with a gum glaze spot on the lower left stamp. Very Fine to Extremely Fine show pieces; each with 2008 PSE Certificates. (Scott as plate blocks of 4 & singles $515). (Total: 2 pages)

Estimate: $500+

Minimum Bid: $250

HUNTING PERMIT STAMPS

32216 **#RW3, 1936, $1 Brown Black.** (Original Gum - Never Hinged). Wonderful example with wide margins. Extremely Fine to Superb; 2006 PSE - Graded Certificate. (SMQ $1,100; this being one of 39 attaining this grade as of 10/08, with 19 graded higher).

Estimate: $1,000+

Minimum Bid: $500

32217 **#RW19, 1952, $2 Deep Ultramarine SUP 98 PSE.** (Original Gum - Never Hinged). Choice and Fresh. Superb PSE - Encapsulated. (SMQ $760; this being one of 7 attaining this grade as of 10/08, with none graded higher).

Estimate: $700+

Minimum Bid: $350

32218 **#RW28, 1961, $3 Multicolored GEM 100 PSE.** (Original Gum - Never Hinged). Mallard brood. Stellar quality. Gem PSE - Encapsulated. (SMQ $800; this being one of 9 attaining this grade as of 10/08, with *none* graded higher).

Estimate: $750+

Minimum Bid: $375

32219 **#RW34, 1967, $3 Multicolored SUP 98 PSE.** (Original Gum - Never Hinged). Old Squaws. Exceptional quality, wonderful eye-appeal. Superb PSE - Encapsulated.
(SMQ $540; this being one of 18 attaining this grade as of 10/08, with only 2 graded higher).

Estimate: $500+

Minimum Bid: $250

REVENUE ISSUES

32220 **#RX24, 1950, $40,000 Yellow Green And Brown.** (No Gum As Issued). Sensational example wide margins and rich color. Extremely Fine to Superb; 2008 PSE Certificate. (Scott $1,200).

Estimate: $1,200+

Minimum Bid: $600

32221 **#RX27, 1952, 3c Yellow Green And Black.** (No Gum As Issued). Dazzling example, very fresh and bright. Extremely Fine to Superb; 2008 PSE Certificate. (Scott $900).

Estimate: $900+

Minimum Bid: $450

32222 **#RX42, 1952, $1,500 Yellow Green And Black.** (No Gum As Issued). Stunning example, huge even margins with post office fresh color, wonderful stamp. Superb; 2008 PSE Certificate. (Scott $900).

Estimate: $900+

Minimum Bid: $450

32223 **#RX43, 1952, $2,000 Yellow Green And Black.** (No Gum As Issued). Fresh example on clean white paper, beauty. Extremely Fine to Superb; 2008 PSE Certificate. (Scott $700).

Estimate: $700+

Minimum Bid: $350

32224 **#RX44, 1952, $3,000 Yellow Green And Black.** (No Gum As Issued). Fabulous example, bright fresh color with wide even margins. Extremely Fine to Superb; 2008 PSE Certificate. (Scott $1200).

Estimate: $1,200+

Minimum Bid: $600

32225 **#RX45, 1952, $5,000 Yellow Green And Black.** (No Gum As Issued). Alluring example with excellent color. Extremely Fine to Superb; 2008 PSE Certificate. (Scott $600).

Estimate: $600+

Minimum Bid: $300

32226 **#RX46, 1952, $10,000 Yellow Green And Black.** (No Gum As Issued). Magnificent example, very fresh, Very Fine to Extremely Fine; 2008 PSE Certificate.
(Scott $700).

Estimate: $700+

Minimum Bid: $350

RARE FIREARMS TRANSFER TAX SHEET

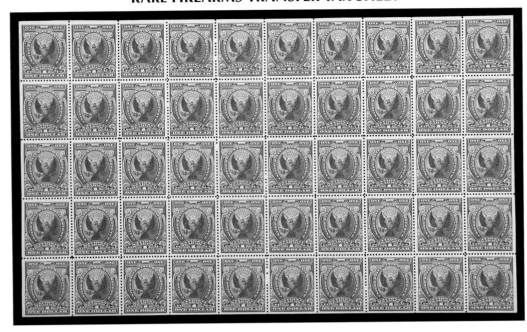

32227 **#RY3, 1938, $1 Green.** (Original Gum - Never Hinged). Rare mint revenue sheet, full sheet of fifty certificate notes "with natural gum skips, gum bends and gum wrinkles." Great looking RARE sheet. Extremely Fine to Superb; 2008 PSE Certificate. (Scott as singles $4,250).

Estimate: $3,500+

Minimum Bid: $1,750

OTHER BACK-OF-THE-BOOK ISSUES

32228 **#U464, 1920, 2c Blue.** (No Gum). Gorgeous full corner example, pristine. Extremely Fine; 2002 PF Certificate. (Scott $1,200).

Estimate: $900+

Minimum Bid: $450

32229 **#WS6, 1920, $5 Orange On Green.** (Original Gum - Previously Hinged). Rare war Savings Issue. "Several faults." Very Fine; 2008 PSE Certificate. (Scott $3,500).

Estimate: $500+

Minimum Bid: $250

32230 **#WX11, 1913, Red And Green.** (Original Gum - Previously Hinged). Bright colored example, hinge remnants. Fine to Very Fine; 2008 PF Certificate. (Scott $1,400).

Estimate: $1,100+

Minimum Bid: $550

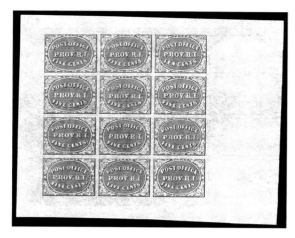

32231 **#10X2aR, 1846, 5c + 10c Gray Black, Reprint Sheet.** (Used). Complete reprint sheet of twelve (11 x 5c and 1 x 10c) with "BOGERTDURBIN" letters printed on reverse. Extremely Fine; 2008 PF Certificate. (Scott $725).

Estimate: $500+

Minimum Bid: $250

1847 MINT BLOCK OF FOUR

32232 **#1, 1847, 5c Red Brn, Bluish.** (Original Gum - Hinged). Rare world class multiple. Excellent color for a stamp minted in 1847, a detailed impression from a hand engraved plate, several vertical natural gum creases (common for this issue since the gum was brushed on by hand). A thin in the upper right stamp and a thin at the bottom center, large even margins on three sides with bottom margin just cutting into the design. Hinge remnant and pencil notations on the back, spectacular showpiece of this rare multiple. Fine to Very Fine; 2008 PSE Certificate. Scott $42,500;

Estimate: $17,500+

Minimum Bid: $8,750

32233 **#26, 1857, 3c Dull Red.** (Original Gum - Hinged). Stunning Showpiece. A lower left corner block of thirty, with double rows of horizontal perforations. Several perforation separations have been rejoined. There are several small faults including a tiny facial scuff on Position 9, facial scuffs on Position 10, an edge tear in Position 19 and staining from certain hinge remnants. Large multiples like this are extremely rare especially with the double perforations. Fabulous piece for the advanced collector. Fine. 2008 PSE Certificate.

Estimate: $3,000+

Minimum Bid: $1,500

32234 **#35, 1859, 10c Green.** (Used). A charming used block of four, deep rich color on fresh clean paper, with June 20, 1860 San Francisco, Cal. circular date stamp cancels. Fine. 2008 PSE Certificate. (Scott $650).

Estimate: $500+

Minimum Bid: $250

32235 **#36, 1857, 12c Black, Plate I.** (Used). An attention grabbing used horizontal strip of three, with Feb. 28, 1860 Mobile, Ala. double circle date stamp cancels. Fresh vibrant color on crisp clean paper, with a natural straight edge and guideline at the right, the center stamp with a very light vertical crease at the right that does not affect the appearance. Fine. 2008 PSE Certificate. (Scott as pair & single $1025).

Estimate: $750+

Minimum Bid: $375

32236 **#65, 1861, 3c Rose.** (Original Gum - Never Hinged). A mint left sheet margin block of nine, full original gum, with a insignificant tiny gum disturbance on the bottom center stamp. Fine to Very Fine. 2008 PSE Certificate. (Scott as hinged block of 4 & singles $1,400).

Estimate: $1,500+

Minimum Bid: $750

32237 **#71, 1861, 30c Orange.** (Original Gum - Hinged). A scarce mint block of four of this high value, with Post Office fresh color on clean white paper and original gum, two hinge remnants. Very Good - Fine and difficult item to find mint multiples of in any condition. 2008 PSE Certificate. (Scott $16,000).

Estimate: $8,000+

Minimum Bid: $4,000

32238 #73, 1863, 2c Black. (Original Gum - Hinged). Mint vertical block of six, the middle pair being never hinged, with a vertical crease in each vertical strip of three, the crease in the left strip not affecting the face. The top right stamp partially reperforated on the right from the top down approximately ¾ of the way down the side of that stamp. Hinge remnant on the top two stamps. Fine to Very Fine. 2008 PSE Certificate. (Scott as hinged block 4 & pair 4,800).

Estimate: $3,000+

Minimum Bid: $1,500

32239 #73, 1863, 2c Black. (Original Gum - Hinged). Horizontal block of six with small gum wrinkle at the bottom right of the top right stamp and shorter perforations in the top and bottom centered stamps. The gum has multiple hinge marks. Fine. 2008 PSE Certificate. (Scott as a block of 4 & a pair $4,800).

Estimate: $4,250+

Minimum Bid: $2,125

32240 #73, 1863, 2c Black. (Original Gum - Never Hinged). Extremely scarce never hinged block of four. Overall fine centering with ample to large margins on three sides. Very fresh appearance. Fine. 2007 PSE Certificate. (Scott as hinged $4,000)

Estimate: $3,000+

Minimum Bid: $1,500

32241 #76, 1863, 5c Brown. (Disturbed Original Gum). Rejoined block of four with disturbed part original gum, gum soaked horizontal perforations, and a vertical crease in the right stamps. Hinge remnant on position three and a pencil notation on position four. Fine to Very Fine. 2008 PSE Certificate. (Scott 8,750).

Estimate: $5,000+

Minimum Bid: $2,500

1867-68 GRILLED ISSUES

32242 **#86, 1867, 1c Blue.** (Original Gum - Never Hinged). Attention-grabbing block of four. Post Office fresh, with strong, well-defined grills. Fine. 2008 PSE Certificate. (Scott $20,000).

Estimate: $15,000+

Minimum Bid: $7,500

32243 **#99, 1867, 24c Gray Lilac.** (No Gum). Rare unused block of four with clear grills. Fresh, rich color and a natural straight edge at the left, with rejoined horizontal perforations and three creases in the top left stamp, one extending into the top right stamp. Fine and select for the specialist. 2008 PSE Certificate. (Scott as singles $14,000).

Estimate: $10,000+

Minimum Bid: $5,000

32244 **#112, 1869, 1c Buff.** (Original Gum - Previously Hinged). Bottom left sheet corner margin block of four, the top left stamp having been previously hinged, the others never hinged. A Very Good to Fine showpiece for the specialist. 2008 PSE Certificate. (Scott $850).

Estimate: $5,000+

Minimum Bid: $2,500

32245 **#113, 1869, 2c Brown.** (Original Gum - Hinged). Wonderful block of four, rich brown color with sharp impression, upper right stamp is likely to grade high. Original gum with some minor gum glazing. Fine to Very Fine. 2008 PSE Certificate. (Scott $3,750).

Estimate: $2,600+

Minimum Bid: $1,300

32246 **#114, 1869, 3c Ultramarine.** (Original Gum - Never Hinged). A top right horizontal sheet corner margin block of six with bright vibrant color on crisp white paper, overall with the grills shifted downwards so that the three bottom stamps have split grills, full original gum with small {natural} gum disturbances, short gumming on the right stamps, and a small adhesion on the gum of the top left stamp. A Fine - Very Fine show piece. 2008 PSE Certificate. (Scott as hinged block of 4 & pair $2,400).

Estimate: $5,000+

Minimum Bid: $2,500

1869 PICTORIAL - POSITION BLOCK WITH ARROW

32247 **#114, 1869, 3c Ultramarine.** (Original Gum - Never Hinged). Locomotive. Right sheet margin arrow block of four. Gum is unbelievably fresh. Scarce and desireable position piece. Fine to Very Fine. 2004 PSE Certificate. (Scott for hinged $1850).

Estimate: $3,500+

Minimum Bid: $1,750

32248 **#114 var, 1869, 3c Ultramarine.** (Original Gum - Hinged). Post Office fresh block of four, split grill variety. Original gum with several small remnants and light hinge outlines on three stamps. Fine and select for the specialist. 2008 PSE Certificate. (Scott as singles $1700).

Estimate: $1,500+

Minimum Bid: $750

1916-22 WASHINGTON-FRANKLIN ISSUE - UNWATERMARKED

32249 **#468, 1916, 6c Red Orange.** (Original Gum - Hinged). Right margin plate block of six with position 2, 3 and 6 never hinged, vivid color and impression, hinge remnant on position four, Very Fine; 2008 PSE Certificate. (Scott $1350).

Estimate: $1,100+

Minimum Bid: $550

1887-88 AMERICAN BANK NOTE CO. ISSUES

32250 **#214, 1887, 3c Vermilion.** (Original Gum - Never Hinged). Lovely lower right corner margin block of six, nice multiple example, Fine; 2008 PSE Certificate. (Scott $1380).

Estimate: $600+

Minimum Bid: $300

1890-93 SMALL BANK NOTES

32251 **#221, 1890, 3c Purple.** (Original Gum - Never Hinged). A delightful bottom margin Plate No. 21 and Imprint block of ten, plus the left corner margin vertical pair with natural straight edge at left and partial center guide arrow. Post Office fresh with pristine original gum. Fine - Very Fine; 2008 PSE Certificate. (Listed, but not valued by Scott).

Estimate: $5,000+

Minimum Bid: $2,500

32252 **#221, 1890, 3c Purple.** (Original Gum - Previously Hinged). Brightly colored block of ten with top margin part arrow, plate number and part imprint, light hinging with some minor gum disturbances and gum toning. Fine; 2008 PSE Certificate. (Scott as two blocks of four and two singles $1040).

Estimate: $500+

Minimum Bid: $250

32253 **#224, 1890, 6c Brown Red.** (Original Gum - Never Hinged). A magnificent block of four, each stamp precisely centered within well balanced margins. Bright and warm with crisp impression, pristine full original gum. Very Fine to Extremely Fine; 2008 PSE Certificate. (Scott as singles $1,000).

Estimate: $750+

Minimum Bid: $375

32254 **#227, 1890, 15c Indigo.** (Original Gum - Never Hinged). A mint block of four, gloriously rich and bold, generally well centered. Immaculate full original gum. Fine to Very Fine; 2008 PSE Certificate. (Scott as singles $3,400).

Estimate: $2,200+

Minimum Bid: $1,100

1893 COLUMBIAN EXPOSITION ISSUE

32255 **#232, 1893, 3c Green.** (Original Gum - Never Hinged). Fresh and well centered bottom margin plate number, imprint and Letter "R" block of eight. Post Office Fresh. Very Fine to Extremely Fine; 2008 PSE Certificate. (Scott $2,250).

Estimate: $2,000+

Minimum Bid: $1,000

32256 **#233, 1893, 4c Ultramarine.** (Original Gum - Never Hinged). An extraordinary, fresh, bottom margin Plate No.19, imprint and letter "D" block of eight. The shading of each stamp varying ever so slightly, creating an almost life-like motion to the Fleet scene depicted. Single insignificant short perforation at the upper right. Very Fine to Extremely Fine; 2008 PSE Certificate. (Scott $3,750).

Estimate: $3,500+

Minimum Bid: $1,750

32257 **#233, 1893, 4c Ultramarine.** (Disturbed Original Gum). A handsome mint, bottom left corner margin Plate No. 18, imprint and letter "D" block of ten. Slightly disturbed original gum, that slight disturbance being from the gum having been ever so lightly kissed by previous hinging. Paper is somewhat toned. The gum at a glance appears never hinged. Fine to Very Fine and select; 2008 PSE Certificate. (Scott $2,410).

Estimate: $1,500+

Minimum Bid: $750

1895 BUREAU ISSUES - WATERMARKED

32258 **#268, 1895, 3c Purple.** (Original Gum - Never Hinged). Attractive top plate and imprint block of six, with reduced selvage and a crease in the left corner of the salvage. Fine to Very Fine; 2008 PSE Certificate. (Scott $1300).

Estimate: $900+

Minimum Bid: $450

32259 **#277a, 1895, $2 Dark Blue.** (Original Gum - Hinged). Magnificent hinged block of four, extremely fresh block with a razor sharp impression, rare this nice. Several hinge marks. Very Fine; 2008 PSE Certificate. (Scott 5,000).

Estimate: $5,000+

Minimum Bid: $2,500

1898 TRANS-MISSISSIPPI EXPOSITION ISSUE

32260 **#287, 1898, 4c Orange.** (Original Gum - Previously Hinged). Brilliant orange color block of four with a horizontal guide line (upper right stamp previously hinged other 3 never hinged, with tiny gum disturbances). Scott $1,330; Very Fine; 2008 PSE Certificate.

Estimate: $950+

Minimum Bid: $475

32261 **#291, 1898, 50c Sage Green.** (Original Gum - Never Hinged). Rare multiple in original gum never hinged condition. Some vertical perforation separations between Position 2 and 3 , a few fingerprints on gum. Fine; 2008 PSE Certificate. (Scott as singles $13,200).

Estimate: $3,750+

Minimum Bid: $1,875

1901 PAN-AMERICAN EXPOSITION ISSUE

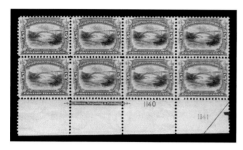

32262 **#297, 1901, 5c Ultramarine & Black.** (Original Gum - Never Hinged). Bridge at Niagara Falls. Magnificent bottom imprint and plate number block of eight, beautiful example. Very Fine; 2005 PF Certificate. (Scott as plate block of six and two singles $4,200).

Estimate: $3,600+

Minimum Bid: $1,800

32263 **#299, 1901, 10c Yellow Brown & Black.** (Original Gum - Never Hinged). Fast Ocean Navigation. A beautiful block of four, bright and vibrant, fresh as the day issued. Fine to Very Fine and choice; 2008 PSE Certificate. (Scott as singles $1,440).

Estimate: $750+

Minimum Bid: $375

1902-08 REGULAR ISSUES

32264 **#300b, 1903, 1c Blue Green.** (Original Gum - Never Hinged). Attractive and fresh Position "A" booklet pane. Fine to Very Fine; 2008 PSE Certificate. (Scott $1,150).

Estimate: $900+

Minimum Bid: $450

32265 **#300b, 1903, 1c Blue Green.** (Original Gum - Never Hinged). Beautiful and fresh Position "I" booklet pane. Fine to Very Fine; 2008 PSE Certificate. (Scott $1,150).

Estimate: $900+

Minimum Bid: $450

32266 **#301c, 1903, 2c Carmine.** (Original Gum - Never Hinged). Lovely Position "A" booklet pane. Post Office Fresh. Fine to Very Fine; 2008 PSE Certificate. (Scott $950.00).

Estimate: $700+

Minimum Bid: $350

32267 **#308, 1902, 13c Purple Black.** (Original Gum - Hinged). Top margin plate and imprint block of six with position 1,3,4,5 and 6 never hinged, position 4 with a thin, position 2 has hinge remnant. Attractive and rather scarce plate block. Fine to Very Fine; 2008 PSE Certificate. (Scott $700).

Estimate: $500+

Minimum Bid: $250

32268 **#315, 1906, 5c Blue.** (Original Gum - Previously Hinged). Wonderful right margin plate number block of six with minor natural gum wrinkling (the bottom four stamps never hinged), very light hinge on top two stamps. Very Fine; 2008 PSE Certificate. (Scott $2,750).

Estimate: $2,000+

Minimum Bid: $1,000

32270 **#324, 1904, 2c Carmine.** (Original Gum - Never Hinged). Thomas Jefferson. Handsome top margin plate number and imprint block of four, very nice color and impression, fresh original gum. Fine to Very Fine; 2008 PSE Certificate. (Scott $650).

Estimate: $300+

Minimum Bid: $150

32269 **#319n, 1903, 2c Carmine Rose.** (Original Gum - Never Hinged). Intense color, Post Office Fresh. Position G, Booklet Pane. Extremely Fine to Superb; 2008 PSE Certificate. (Scott $450.00).

Estimate: $400+

Minimum Bid: $200

32271 **#325, 1904, 3c Violet.** (Original Gum - Never Hinged). James Monroe. Deep rich violet color, very pretty top margin plate #2104 and imprint block of four. Fine; 2008 PSE Certificate. (Scott $1,100).

Estimate: $750+

Minimum Bid: $375

32272 **#326, 1904, 5c Dark Blue.** (Original Gum - Never Hinged). William McKinley. Wonderful top left corner margin plate number and imprint block of ten. Vibrant color, fresh and sharp detailed impression. Fine to Very Fine; 2008 PSE Certificate. (Scott as plate block of six and four singles $2,750).

Estimate: $2,500+

Minimum Bid: $1,250

32273 **#327, 1904, 10c Red Brown.** (Original Gum - Hinged). Map of Louisiana Purchase. Bright and fresh bottom plate# 2107 and part imprint block of four. Bottom pair never hinged, hinge remnant on position two, very light hinge mark on position one. Fine; 2008 PSE Certificate. (Scott $1325).

Estimate: $1,100+

Minimum Bid: $550

1913-15 PANAMA-PACIFIC EXPOSITION ISSUE

32274 **#400, 1913, 10c Orange Yellow.** (Original Gum - Never Hinged). Discovery of San Francisco Bay. Left margin Plate #6130 block of six, nearly blindingly bright and vibrant, immaculate original gum, the center stamps with small natural gum creases that do not affect the face. Fine to Very Fine; 2008 PSE Certificate. (Scott $3,850).

Estimate: $3,000+

Minimum Bid: $1,500

32275 #400A, 1913, 10c Orange. (Original Gum - Never Hinged). Discovery of San Francisco Bay. Exceptionally rare , top margin plate number block of six with the selvage reduced, bright orange color and sharp impression. Fine to Very Fine; 2008 PSE Certificate. (Scott $20,000).

Estimate: $12,000+

Minimum Bid: $6,000

32276 #402, 1915, 2c Carmine. (Original Gum - Hinged). Panama Canal. Top margin plate block of six (Position 1 never hinged), handsome example. Fine to Very Fine; 2008 PSE Certificate. (Scott $1950).

Estimate: $1,800+

Minimum Bid: $900

1916-22 WASHINGTON-FRANKLIN ISSUE - UNWATERMARKED

32277 #467, 1916, 5c Carmine. (Original Gum - Previously Hinged). Alluring double error in a block of twelve, both error stamps are never hinged, several stamps show lightly hinging outline and pencil notation on position two, straight edge on bottom three stamps. Fine; 2008 PSE Certificate. (Scott $2,150).

Estimate: $1,500+

Minimum Bid: $750

32278 **#467, 1916, 5c Carmine.** (Original Gum - Never Hinged). Nice mint example of the 5 cent error in a block of nine, (top center 2 cent stamp, previously hinged). Fine to Very Fine; 2008 PSE Certificate. (Scott $1,100).
Estimate: $600+
Minimum Bid: $300

1917-19 WASHINGTON-FRANKLIN ISSUE - PERF 11

32279 **#498f, 1917, 1c Green.** (Original Gum - Previously Hinged). Prepared principally for use during WWI by the U.S. Army Post Office in France, and used on soldiers' mail until General John J. Pershing's organization reached France, after which soldiers' mail was sent by free frank. A spectacular example of the Special A.E.F. booklet pane of 30, set for binding at the right, original gum, previously hinged in the first and last stamps of each row, the remaining 24 stamps being never hinged. One of the better centered examples in existence. Very Fine-Extremely Fine. 2008 PSE Certificate. (Scott $1,150).
Estimate: $1,500+
Minimum Bid: $750

RARE BOOKLET PANE

32280 **#499f, 1917, 2c Rose.** (Original Gum - Previously Hinged). Special A.E.F. booklet pane of 30, prepared during WWI for use by the U.S. Army Post Office in France and used until General John J. Pershing's organization arrived, at which time soldiers' mail was sent by free frank envelope, the pane set for binding at the right, fresh original gum showing light traces of previous hinging on the first stamp of the second row and the last stamp of the first and third rows, the rest of the stamps never hinged. A Fine to Very Fine example of this typically poorly centered pane. 2008 PSE Certificate. (Scott $28,000).

Estimate: $25,000+
Minimum Bid: $12,500

32281 **#523, 1918, $2 Orange Red And Black.** (Original Gum - Previously Hinged). Very fine centerline block of four, Beautiful block with sharp impression and fresh color. Top two stamps are lightly hinged with the bottom two stamps never hinged. Very Fine; 2008 PSE Certificate and 1983 PF Certificate. (Scott $625).

Estimate: $450+
Minimum Bid: $225

32282 **#523, 1918, $2 Orange Red And Black.** (Original Gum - Previously Hinged). Rare centerline block of four, bottom left stamp never hinged, very fresh example, very lightly hinged with no remnants, Fine to Very Fine; 2008 PSE Certificate. (Scott 2800).

Estimate: $2,400+
Minimum Bid: $1,200

1922-25 DEFINITIVES

32283 #560, 1923, 8c Olive Green. (Original Gum - Never Hinged). Beautiful left margin plate# 16452, block of six. Very Fine; 2008 PSE Certificate. (Scott $900).

Estimate: $650+

Minimum Bid: $325

32284 #567, 1923, 20c Carmine Rose. (Original Gum - Never Hinged). Attractive top margin plate number# F20038 block of six with natural gum skips on position 1 and 2, otherwise fresh original gum. Fine to Very Fine; 2008 PSE Certificate. (Scott $450).

Estimate: $350+

Minimum Bid: $175

32285 #569, 1923, 30c Olive Brown. (Original Gum - Never Hinged). Pretty bottom margin plate# 20193 block of six. (small natural gum skips on Position 5 and 6) Very Fine; 2008 PSE Certificate. (Scott $475).

Estimate: $375+

Minimum Bid: $188

32286 #570, 1922, 50c Lilac. (Disturbed Original Gum). Lovely soft pastel lilac color, wide-top top margin plate# F19143 block of six. (slight mount glaze and a few minor gum skips). Fine; 2008 PSE Certificate. (Scott $900).

Estimate: $750+

Minimum Bid: $375

32287 #571, 1923, $1 Violet Brown. (Original Gum - Never Hinged). Extremely fresh and desirable bottom margin plate# 18682 block of six, original gum, Never Hinged (few minor gum skips). Very Fine; 2008 PSE Certificate. (Scott $650).

Estimate: $450+

Minimum Bid: $225

32288 **#571, 1923, $1 Violet Brown.** (Original Gum - Never Hinged). Deep dark violet brown color, bottom margin plate# 18642 block of six. Very Fine to Extremely Fine. 2008 PSE Certificate. (Scott $650).

Estimate: $600+

Minimum Bid: $300

32289 **#572, 1923, $2 Deep Blue.** (Original Gum - Never Hinged). Stunning bottom margin plate# 14306 block of six, Fresh. Very Fine to Extremely Fine; 2008 PSE Certificate. (Scott $1200).

Estimate: $1,100+

Minimum Bid: $550

OUTSTANDING PLATE BLOCK +

32290 **#573, 1923, $5 Carmine And Blue.** (Original Gum - Never Hinged). Wide-top, Plate# F14326, F14327 and Arrow, Plate Block of 8, with four additional stamps, for a total of 12 stamps. Deep and Rich colors, very well-centered, Post Office Fresh. Extremely Fine; 2008 PF Certificate. (Scott $4,380).

Estimate: $5,000+

Minimum Bid: $2,500

End of Session Three

SESSION FOUR

Floor, Telephone, Heritage Live!™, Internet, Fax, and Mail Signature® Auction #1106
Friday, February 6, 2009, 4:00 PM CT • Dallas, Texas • Lots 32291-32666

A 19.5% Buyer's Premium ($9 minimum) Will Be Added To All Lots
You can now view full-color images and bid via the Internet at the Heritage website: HA.com/Stamps

1922-25 DEFINITIVES

32291 #573, 1922, $5 Carmine And Blue. (Original Gum - Never Hinged). Absolutely gorgeous top margin plate# F14326 and F14327 and arrow block of eight, vivid color. Choice Plate. Very Fine to Extremely Fine; 2008 PSE Certificate. (Scott $3500).
Estimate: $3,500+
Minimum Bid: $1,750

RARE USED PLATE +

32292 #573, 1922, $5 Carmine & Blue. (Used). An attention-grabbing used, top margin Plate# F14326/F14327, $5.00 and arrow block of sixteen, with small double oval cancels. Very scarce large multiple in used condition, let alone plate block of this high value issue. Fine to Very; 2008 PSE Certificate.
Estimate: $700+
Minimum Bid: $350

1924-29 COMMEMORATIVE ISSUES

32293 #634a, 1926, 2c Carmine. (Original Gum - Never Hinged). Type II. Plate# 19746. Wonderful example of this scarce lower left corner margin plate block of four, deep dark carmine color, outstanding. Very Fine; 2008 PSE Certificate. (Scott $3,000).
Estimate: $2,500+
Minimum Bid: $1,250

1930 TO DATE

32294 #716a, 1932, 2c Carmine Lake. (Original Gum - Never Hinged). Scarce Color shade, particularly in Plate Block. Plate# F20820. Very Fine; 2007 PSE Certificate. Unlisted in Scott.
Estimate: $9,000+
Minimum Bid: $4,500

32295 #832b, 1951, $1 Purple And Black. (Original Gum - Never Hinged). Large top margin block of four with natural gum skips (lower right stamp with no gum skips). Very Fine; 2008 PSE Certificate. (Scott $600).
Estimate: $500+
Minimum Bid: $250

RICHARD NIXON AUTOGRAPH ON PLATE BLOCK

32296 #992, 1950, 3c Bright Red Violet. (Original Gum - Never Hinged). Great collectors item. Mint lower left corner margin plate# 24284 block of four with typed 'The Vice Pres. of United States' across the stamps. An authentic "Richard Nixon" autograph occurs on each stamp. Extremely Fine to Superb; 2008 PSE Certificate.
Estimate: $700+
Minimum Bid: $350

SILKOTE MINT SHEET OF 100

32297 #1033a, 1954, 2c Carmine Rose on Silkote Paper. (Original Gum - Never Hinged). A complete lower left Plate# 25061 pane of 100 on experimental "Silkote" paper, a product of the S.D. Warren Co. paper manufacturer with mills at Westbrook, Maine. A total of 125 press sheets (500 panes) were quietly printed by the U.S. Bureau of Engraving and Printing in the late fall of 1954, experimentally in nature, in an attempt to overcome issues related to the extreme dampening necessary when printing on the then current sulphite paper known as "Oxford." The "Silkote" paper had a special surface that made it unnecessary for extreme dampness to be applied to the paper in the printing process. Because the "Silkote" paper did not require the extreme dampness that the "Oxford" paper did, there was less shrinkage, causing the sheets printed on this experimental paper to be somewhat mis-aligned on the perforating machines which were set to account for the shrinkage experienced with the "Oxford" paper, the net result being that the stamps from the "Silkote" sheets tended to be relatively poorly centered The pane presented here is amongst the finest of the very few sheets in existence. The majority of the individual stamps included within this particular pane tend to be amongst the finest examples we have seen of the "Silkote" issues, with high grading potentials throughout the pane. A true condition rarity for this experimental issue. 2008 PSE Certificate.

Estimate: $25,000+

Minimum Bid: $12,500

Please visit HA.com to view other collectibles auctions.   *A 19.5% Buyer's Premium ($9 min.) Applies To All Lots*

32298 **#C1, 1918, 6c Orange.** (Original Gum - Never Hinged). Lovely centerline block of four. Wonderfully centered example. Fresh. Very Fine to Extremely Fine; 2007 PF Certificate.
(Scott $540).

Estimate: $400+

Minimum Bid: $200

32299 **#C2, 1918, 16c Green.** (Original Gum - Never Hinged). Top margin Plate# 8900 and arrow block of six, fresh and vibrant. Very Fine; 2008 PSE Certificate and 2001 PF Certificate.
(Scott $1,500).

Estimate: $1,200+

Minimum Bid: $600

32300 **#C2, 1918, 16c Green.** (Original Gum - Previously Hinged). Choice mint previously hinged top margin plate# 8900 and arrow block of six (Position 1,2,4-6 never hinged), (Position 1 and 6 with small natural gum skips). Position 3 and 5 lightly hinged with no remnants. Very Fine; 2008 PSE Certificate. (Scott $1,000).

Estimate: $750+

Minimum Bid: $375

32301 **#C3, 1918, 24c Carmine Rose And Black.** (Original Gum - Never Hinged). Fresh and lively top margin plate# 8493/8492 block of twelve, with Arrow and double 'TOP' markings. Very Fine, 2008 PSE Certificate.
(Scott $2,100).

Estimate: $2,250+

Minimum Bid: $1,125

ZEP PLATE BLOCK SET - NICE TOPS

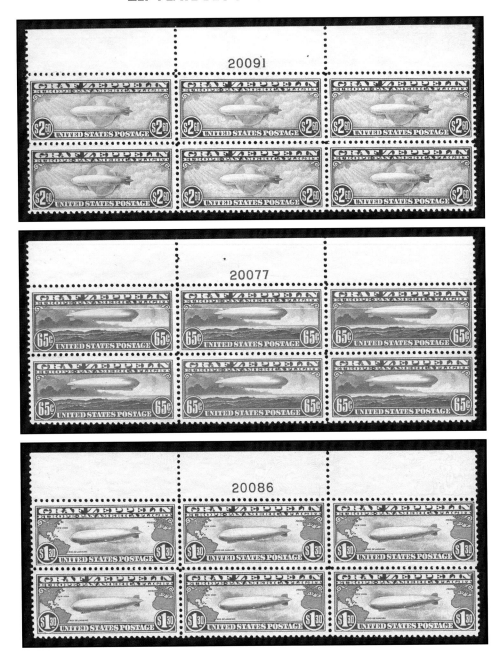

32302 **#C13-15, 1930, 65c - $2.60 COLOR.** (Original Gum - Never Hinged). Complete set of Three. Top margin Plate No. blocks (65c = P#20077, $1.30 = P# 20086, & $2,60 = P#20091), bright and fresh, immaculate full original gum with only light (and insignificant) natural gum bends that do not affect the face. Very Fine and select; each plate block with its own 2008 PSE Certificate. (Scott $33,250).

Estimate: $20,000+

Minimum Bid: $10,000

32303 **#C15, 1930, $2.60 Blue.** (Original Gum - Previously Hinged). Very desirable Graf Zeppelin block of four, vivid blue color with a superior impression, several small hinge remnants on the back. Fine to Very Fine; 2008 PSE Certificate. (Scott $3,400).

Estimate: $2,800+

Minimum Bid: $1,400

POSTAGE DUE ISSUES

32304 **#J3, 1879, 3c Pale Brown.** (Original Gum - Hinged). An attention-grabbing mint bottom margin Plate No.316 imprint and arrow strip of six, with a natural straight edge at the right (that stamp being the right sheet corner margin single), light warm pastel color and detailed impression, original gum with hinge remnants on stamps 1, 4, and 5. Stamps 2, 3, and 6 never hinged. Fine; 2008 PSE Certificate. (Scott $1,215).

Estimate: $1,000+

Minimum Bid: $500

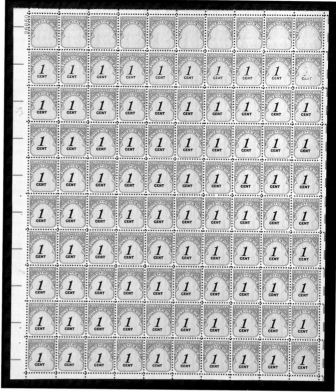

32305 **#J89a, 1959, 1c Carmine And Black.** (Original Gum - Never Hinged). Rare error, upper left corner sheet (plate number 26660), top row denomination missing. Ten Major Error stamps. Plate Block alone is an exceptional Major Error item. Extremely Fine to Superb; 2008 PSE Certificate. (Scott unpriced).

Estimate: $4,000+

Minimum Bid: $2,000

1919-22 SHANGHAI OVERPRINTS

32306 **#K8a, 1919, 16c Olive Green.** (Original Gum - Previously Hinged). Lovely bottom Plate#7742 block of 6, deep olive green color, several stamps with jumbo margins, some gum disturbances on the back. Very lightly hinged with no remnants. Original gum, Very Fine. 2008 PSE Certificate. (Scott $1,200).

Estimate: $1,500+

Minimum Bid: $750

1913 PARCEL POST ISSUES

32307 **#Q4, 1913, 4c Carmine Rose.** (Original Gum - Hinged). Top margin plate# 6392 and imprint 'FOUR' block of six with position 1,2,3 and 5 never hinged. Hinge remnants on positions 4, 6 and selvage. Lovely color, scarce Plate. Fine to Very Fine; 2008 PSE Certificate. (Scott 1000).

Estimate: $850+

Minimum Bid: $425

HUNTING PERMIT STAMPS

32308 **#RW7, 1940, $1 Sepia.** (Original Gum - Never Hinged). A beautiful and Post Office Fresh bottom right corner margin Plate# 143776 block of six, Very Fine to Extremely Fine and choice. 2008 PSE Certificate. (Scott $2,900).

Estimate: $2,000+

Minimum Bid: $1,000

32309 **#RW9, 1942, $1 Violet Brown.** (Original Gum - Never Hinged). A refreshing bottom right corner margin Plate# 149600 block of six, bright and vivid. Very Fine and choice. 2008 PSE Certificate. (Scott $2,900).

Estimate: $2,000+

Minimum Bid: $1,000

COMPLETE PANE OF 28 - RW12

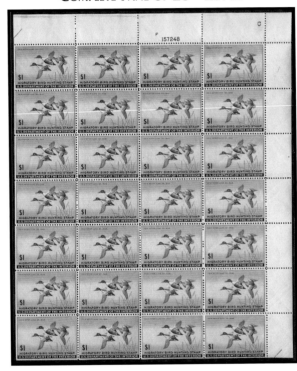

32310 **#RW12, 1945, $1 Black.** (Original Gum - Never Hinged). Complete upper right pane of 28. Very Fine; 2008 PSE Certificate. (Scott as singles $3,080).

Estimate: $2,500+

Minimum Bid: $1,250

PROOFS & ESSAYS

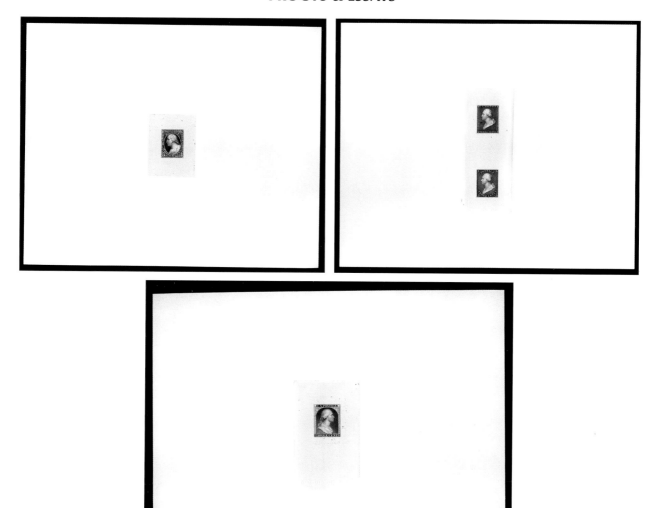

32311 **Rare 3c 1851 Essays and Essays Manuscripts.** An intriguing selection consisting of three extremely rare essay prints from original dies which had been donated to the Smithsonian. The run of prints having been limited to a "printer's proof" (which was donated to the PF) and a limited edition run where the first print went to the museum, the last to the BEP plate printer who pulled the prints from the dies, and the balance were distributed one to each of the benefactors who donated the dies to the museum. The dies correspond to Scott #11-E2 with 16 prints pulled (numbered 1-15, plus the printer's proof), and #'s11-E4 and 11-E8/11-E7, each with 10 prints pulled (numbered 1-9, plus the printer's proof). This set consists of #15 of 15 of the #11-E2 print, and number 9 of 9 of each of the other two prints, i.e.: the prints that were given to the BEP plate printer who pulled the prints for the Smithsonian, each print measuring 254 x 202-203mm, and each numbered and signed by the plate printer on the reverse. Additionally, there are two sizable manuscripts prepared as a "Study of the Three Cent Essays of 1851".
Estimate: $3,000+
Minimum Bid: $1,500

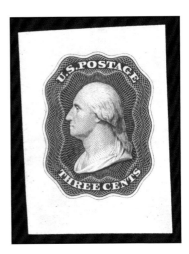

32312 **#11-E4c and 11-E12b, 1851, 3c Die Essays on India.**
Measuring 31 x 40mm and 26.5 x 36mm respectively,
both bright and fresh, the 11-E4c in scarlet and 11-E12b in
brown. Very Fine. The 11-E12b with 2006 PF Certificate.
(Scott $700).

Estimate: $600+

Minimum Bid: $350

32313 **Turner #128var, Washington Vignette Essay, Black On
Celluloid.** An exquisite Gem for the specialist, measuring
74 x 94mm. 2008 PF Certificate.

Estimate: $700+

Minimum Bid: $350

32314 **#67-E2, 1903, 5c, Die Essays Grouping.** Consists of eight
items virtually all different in color, including a mix of
67-E2a-c types. Very Fine to Extremely Fine. (Scott $970).

Estimate: $950+

Minimum Bid: $550

32315 **#67-E4f, 1903, 5c, Die II Essays on Proof Paper Printed
through a Mat.** Two different, one in yellow brown measuring 65 x 64mm, the other in black measuring 52 x
58mm. Both Extremely Fine and choice. (Scott $250).

Estimate: $300+

Minimum Bid: $200

32316 **#67-E4g, 1903, 5c Die II Essays on Colored Card.** Grouping of three including violet brown on pale green, red on light yellow, and brown on ivory, each measuring 57 x 65mm. Extremely Fine. (Scott $450).

Estimate: $600+

Minimum Bid: $375

32317 **#67-E4h, 1903, 5c Die II Essays on Green Bond.** A selection of three different including violet, black, and dull dark orange, each measuring 51 x 52mm. Extremely Fine. (Scott $375).

Estimate: $500+

Minimum Bid: $300

32318 **#67-E4k-l, 1903, 5c Die II Essays on Pelure.** Includes one each #67-E4k orange on greenish pelure measuring 45 x 55mm with 10mm of top folded back to make the essay look more squared off, and #67-E4l red brown on bluish pelure measuring 63 x 65mm. Extremely Fine. (Scott $800).

Estimate: $950+

Minimum Bid: $650

32319 **#69-E1, 1903, Vignette Die Essays Grouping.** Selection of seven essays measuring 52-74 x 51-74mm, includes five #69-E1b (blue, green, red violet, & 2x yellow brown) and two #69-E1d (dark blue on pale green & dark green on light yellow). Very Fine. (Scott $600).

Estimate: $500+

Minimum Bid: $250

32320 **#69-E1c, 1903, Vignette Die I Essays on Green Bond.**
A complete set of all three colors, each measuring 66 x
66mm, and each showing full die sinkage. Extremely Fine.
(Scott $450).

Estimate: $460+

Minimum Bid: $300

32321 **#69-E1d, 1903, Vignette Die I Essays on Colored Card.**
Selection of three including violet brown on light pink,
dark olive on buff, and dark green on light pink, each
measuring 47-49 x 47-49mm. Extremely Fine. (Scott $450).

Estimate: $500+

Minimum Bid: $300

32322 **#69-E2, 1903, 12c Die Essays Grouping.** A sizable assortment consisting of fourteen essays measuring 48-74 x
47-69mm, including nine #69-E2a with some duplication,
one #69-E2c, and four all different #69-E2e, a few overall
with trivial faults, otherwise a Very Fine selection. (Scott
$1,425).

Estimate: $900+

Minimum Bid: $450

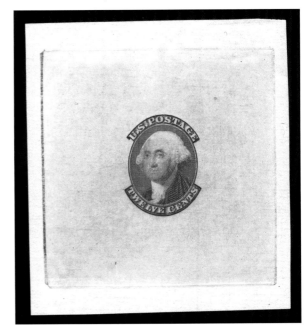

32323 **#69-E2a, 1903, Die II Essays on Proof Paper.** Seven
essays with almost all being different colors, each measuring 56-65 x 56-65mm, includes black, carmine (2), orange,
green, violet, and ultramarine. Very Fine. (Scott $525).

Estimate: $600+

Minimum Bid: $375

32324 **#69-E2e, 1903, Die I Essays on Colored Card.** Grouping of five, most measuring 46-48 x 46-49mm, one measuring 76 x 76mm and showing full die sinkage, overall includes dull red on light pink, brown on light blue, dull dark blue on ivory, violet on pale green, and dull dark blue die sunk on a tan card which is not listed in Scott. Very Fine. (Scott $750).

Estimate: $1,000+

Minimum Bid: $500

32326 **#69-E3a, 1903, 12c Die Essays on Proof Paper.** A substantial gathering consisting of twenty examples of varying colors, including some duplication. All but two showing full die sinkage, of the remaining two, one is cut to stamp size, a few trivial faults noted, one essay with a large repaired tear, otherwise a Fine to Very Fine grouping. (Scott $2,500).

Estimate: $1,500+

Minimum Bid: $750

32327 **#69-E3f, 1903, 12c Die Essays on Green Bond, Top Border Missing.** Complete set (3) of the three colors issued in, orange, green, and violet, each measuring 46-47 x 45-46mm. Very Fine. (Scott $525).

Estimate: $500+

Minimum Bid: $250

32325 **#69-E3, 12c Die Essays Selection.** Three items, two #69-E3b olive gray on old proof paper, one showing full die sinkage, and the third being #69-E3e deep blue on light pink colored card showing full die sinkage. Very Fine. (Scott $1,775).

Estimate: $1,500+

Minimum Bid: $750

32328 #70-E, 1903, 24c Die Essays Grouping. Total of seven items, all different, includes one #70-E1a, one #70-E2a with a small pulled corner at lower left, one #70-E3a, and four #70-E4f each in different colors, one with a small piece torn out at upper right and help in place by a hinge remnant. Very Fine to Extremely Fine. (Scott $720).

Estimate: $800+

Minimum Bid: $500

32329 #70-E4, 1903, 24c Die Essays Grouping. Selection of four different items, #70-E4i green on green bond, #70-E4j dark green on bond with Walls of Troy watermark, #70-E4k orange on bond with double line scallops watermark, and #70-E4l dull dark blue on pale green. Extremely Fine. (Scott $1,000).

Estimate: $1,000+

Minimum Bid: $650

32330 1861, 24c Essays Selection. Consists of two Essays, #70-E4a in lilac, on old proof paper, cut to shape, and a Brazer #70P5, Lowenberg Patent Decalcomania horizontal pair, both Essays in the pair with light vertical creases (as is often the case). Very Fine. 2005 and 2003 PF Certificates respectively.

Estimate: $500+

Minimum Bid: $250

32331 #72-E2, 1903, Die Essays Grouping. Selection of nine measuring 45-64 x 49-66mm, includes four #72-E2a (black, green, yellow brown, & lilac), three #72-E2b (yellow brown & 2x orange), and two #72-E2c (brown on ivory & violet brown on pale green). Very Fine. (Scott $1,220).

Estimate: $1,000+

Minimum Bid: $500

32332 #72-E3, 1903, Die Essays Grouping. Selection of six items measuring 45-62 x 43-61mm, includes three #72-E3a (black, dark blue, and yellow brown), one #72-E3b (violet on pale green), and two #72-E3c (black and green). Very Fine. (Scott $905).

Estimate: $650+

Minimum Bid: $325

32333 #72-E5, 1903, 90c Die Essays Grouping. Selection of six measuring 32½-64 x 37-64mm, includes four #72-E5d (black, lilac, & 2x red violet) and two #72-E5g, one of which is cut down to approximately the size of a small die proof. Very Fine. (Scott $1,200).

Estimate: $850+

Minimum Bid: $425

32334 #112-E4d/114-E4d, 1869, 1c / 3c Plate Essays on Stamp Paper, Perf 12 & Gummed, with 9x9mm Grills. (Original Gum - Previously Hinged). A small grouping of eight Essays, includes #112-E4d in chocolate, dark violet, dull red (single & pair), and orange, all original gum, previously hinged, and #114-E4d orange brown (Never Hinged), and yellow (No Gum). Fine to Very Fine. (Scott $720).

Estimate: $800+

Minimum Bid: $400

32335 #112-E4d, 1869, 1c Plate Essays on Stamp Paper, Perf 12 & Gummed, with 9x9mm Grill. Two blocks of four, one in orange, the other in yellow, both with original gum that has been previously hinged on all four essays. Fine to Very Fine. (Scott as singles $880).

Estimate: $1,000+

Minimum Bid: $500

32336 #113-E3e, 1869, 2c Plate Essays on Stamp Paper, Perf 12 & Gummed, with 9x9mm Grills. (Original Gum - Previously Hinged). Selection of eight, includes brown (2), rose, green, yellow, blue, and violet (2), all with previously hinged original gum except the green and yellow which are without gum. Fine to Very Fine. (Scott $640).

Estimate: $750+

Minimum Bid: $375

32337 **#114-E6d, 1869, 3c Plate Essays on Stamp Paper, Perf 12 & Gummed, with 9x9 Grill.** (Original Gum - Previously Hinged). Selection of five different color blocks of four, includes orange brown, black brown, green, yellow, and orange, all original gum previously hinged, except the green block which appears to be never hinged. Very Fine to Extremely Fine. (Scott $1,600).

Estimate: $1,700+

Minimum Bid: $1,150

32338 **#117-E1e, 1869, 12c Plate Essays on Stamp Paper, Perf 12 & Gummed, with 9x9mm Grill.** (Original Gum - Previously Hinged). Selection of five, red brown (3), pale rose red, and blue, all with previously hinged original gum except for the blue which is never hinged. Very Fine to Extremely Fine. (Scott $625).

Estimate: $600+

Minimum Bid: $375

32339 **#149-E5a, 1873, 7c Black, Completed Vignette Die Essay.** Die sunk on full size card. Extremely Fine. 2008 PF Certificate. (Scott $1,000).

Estimate: $1,000+

Minimum Bid: $500

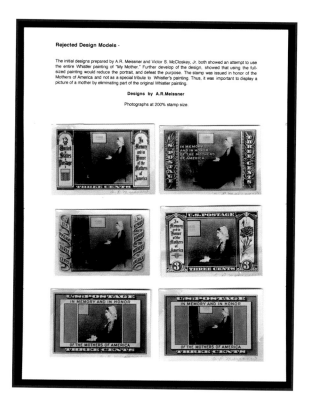

32340 **#737-Evar, 1934, 3c Black Rejected Design Models Photo Essay Collection.** Mothers of America. An impressive and quite possibly one-of-a-kind collection comprised of sixteen Rejected Design Models Photos (Photo Essays). Each measuring approximately 80-86 x 54-56mm (approximately 200% of the issued stamp size), signed by the corresponding designer, six by Alvin R. Meissner and ten by Victor S. McCluskey Jr., the entire collection meticulously presented on three exhibit-ready pages. The designs show each designer's attempt to use the entire Whistler's Mother painting, each then progressing in design by eliminating part of the original Whistler painting in consideration of the fact that the stamp was to be a tribute to Mothers of America, rather than to Whistler's painting. An Extremely Fine to Superb and most probably *unique specialist's collection*, made especially so because each model photo is individually signed by the corresponding designer.

Estimate: $500+

Minimum Bid: $250

32341 **#899E, 1940, 1c Blue Green, Large Die Essay on Wove Paper.** National Defense. Die sunk on card measuring 140 x 162mm, with fine horizontal lines in white areas of "For Defense" and without the dash (-) between "Industry" and "Agriculture", the card with inconsequential light soiling at right and small scattered toned spots on reverse. Very Fine. 2008 PF Certificate. (Scott unlisted).

Estimate: $1,000+

Minimum Bid: $500

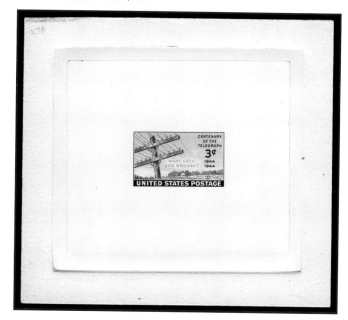

32342 **#924E, 1944, 3c Bright Red Violet, Large Die Trial Color Essay on Wove Paper.** Centenary of the Telegraph. Die Sunk on card measuring 124 x 111mm, with a few lines lacking on the pole below the upper crossbar and in the bolts of the diagonal braces, black Control (serial) No. 70145 on reverse. Very Fine. 2008 PF Certificate. (Scott unlisted).

Estimate: $1,500+

Minimum Bid: $750

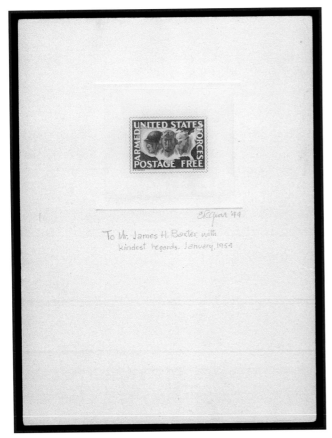

32343 1944 Armed Forces Postage Free Progressive Large Die Essays An incredible set consisting of seven essays, six being progressive to the completed seventh piece, the six progressives include the stamp frame wording on thin card, the rest of the progressives being on bond paper, with various stages of the vignette leading to a black and white essay of the proposed stamp which is signed by the designer E.R. Grove. The final essay is for the proposed stamp in full color and is die sunk on full size card measuring 151 x 202mm, signed by E.R. Grove, dated '44 *(1944)*, gifted to James H. Baxter by E.R. Grove in 1954, ten years after the design proposal. Very Fine to Extremely Fine.

Estimate: $2,500+

Minimum Bid: $1,250

32345 #40P1, 1875, 1c Bright Blue, Hybrid Large Die Proof on India. Die sunk on full size card measuring 139 x 217mm, deeply rich and clean. Extremely Fine. 2008 PF Certificate. (Scott $325).

Estimate: $400+

Minimum Bid: $200

32344 #2P1a, 1847, 10c Black. (Used). Beautiful die proof on white bond cut down. Extremely Fine. 2008 PSE Certificate. (Scott $800).

Estimate: $600+

Minimum Bid: $300

32346 **#41P1, 1875, 3c Scarlet, Hybrid Large Die Proof on India.** Die sunk on full size card measuring 139 x 217mm, luxuriously rich and vibrant, clean. Extremely Fine. 2008 PF Certificate. (Scott $325).

Estimate: $400+

Minimum Bid: $200

32347 **#42P1, 1875, 5c Orange Brown, Hybrid Large Die Proof on India.** Die sunk on full size card measuring 139 x 217mm, bright, vibrant, and clean. Extremely Fine. 2008 PF Certificate. (Scott $325).

Estimate: $400+

Minimum Bid: $200

32348 **#43P1, 1875, 10c Blue Green, Hybrid Large Die Proof on India.** Die sunk on full size card measuring 139 x 127mm, intense and clean. Extremely Fine. 2008 PF Certificate. (Scott $325).

Estimate: $400+

Minimum Bid: $200

32349 **#44P1, 1875, 12c Greenish Black, Hybrid Large Die Proof on India.** Die sunk on full size card measuring 138½ x 217mm, bright and clean. Extremely Fine. 2008 PF Certificate. (Scott $325).

Estimate: $400+

Minimum Bid: $200

32350 **#45P1, 1915, 24c Blackish Violet, Hybrid Large Die Proof on India.** Die sunk on full size measuring 139 x 217mm, intense and immaculate. Extremely Fine. 2008 PF Certificate. (Scott $325).

Estimate: $400+

Minimum Bid: $200

32352 **#47P1, 1875, 90c Deep Blue, Hybrid Large Die Proof on India.** Die sunk on full size card measuring 139 x 217mm, gorgeous and fresh. Extremely Fine. 2008 PF Certificate. (Scott $325).

Estimate: $400+

Minimum Bid: $200

32351 **#46P1, 1875, 30c Yellow Orange, Hybrid Large Die Proof on India.** Die sunk on full size card measuring 139 x 217mm, intense and warm. Extremely Fine. 2008 PF Certificate. (Scott $325).

Estimate: $400+

Minimum Bid: $200

32353 **#55-62P2 / 74P2, 1903, 1c - 90c "August" Issue Small Die Proofs.** Complete set (9) "August" issues plus 3c scarlet, each measuring 27-28 x 30-32mm, all affixed to a single original page from a Roosevelt presentation album. Extremely Fine to Superb. 2008 PF Certificate. (Scott $4,700).

Estimate: $4,000+

Minimum Bid: $2,000

32354 **#63/78P3, 1861-67, 1c - 90c, Plate Proofs on India Grouping.** Consisting of one each of #'S 63P3, 68P3, 69P3, 71P3, 72P3, 73P3, 76P3, 77P3, and 78P3, as well as #74TC3, all bright and fresh. Extremely Fine. (Scott $675).

Estimate: $700+

Minimum Bid: $400

32355 **#63/77P3, 1861-67, 1c - 90c Plate Proofs on India Grouping.** Consisting of a horizontal pair each of #'s 63P3, 68P3, 71P3, 72P3, and 77P3, each fresh and vibrant. Extremely Fine. (Scott $550).

Estimate: $600+

Minimum Bid: $325

32356 **#63/78P4, 1861-67, 1c - 90c, Plate Proofs on Card.** An attention-grabbing selection of Plate Proofs on Card consisting of #'s 63P4, 65P4, 68-69P4, 71-73P4, and 76-78P4, each proof fresh and vibrant. Very Fine to Extremely Fine and choice. (Scott $515).

Estimate: $500+

Minimum Bid: $250

32357 **1861-67, 1c - 24c Plate & Trial Color Proof Selection.** A magnificent selection consisting of #'s 69P3 (5), 74TC3 (2), 76P3 (2), and 78P3, each bright and vibrant, one of the 76P3 with a hinge remnant. An Extremely Fine and choice group. (Scott $695).

Estimate: $800+

Minimum Bid: $400

32358 **#78P3, 1862, 24c Dark Lilac, Plate Proof on India.** An attention-grabbing block of four, both intense and vibrant. Very Fine to Extremely Fine. 2008 PF Certificate. (Scott $400).

Estimate: $400+

Minimum Bid: $250

32359 **#112/22P3, 1869, 1c - 90c, Plate Proofs on India.** A charming and complete set of these regular 1869 Pictorial Plate Proofs (excluding the Re-Issue #129P3). Fine to Very Fine and undercatalogued. (Scott $855).

Estimate: $1,100+

Minimum Bid: $700

32360 **#112/21P3, 1869, 1c - 30c Plate Proofs on India Assortment.** An interesting grouping consisting of 112P3 (single & pair), 113P3 (2 singles & a Plate No.28 strip of six with imprint), 114P3 (single & pair)115P3 (single, 2 strips of four, & block of four), 116P3 block of four, 117P3 single, 119P3 (4 singles), and 121P3 (2 singles). Fine to Very Fine. (Scott $2,250).

Estimate: $2,600+

Minimum Bid: $1,500

32361 **#228P3, 1890, 30c Black Plate Proof on India.** Bottom Plate No.24 and imprint block of 12, radiantly bright and vibrant. Extremely Fine. 2008 PF Certificate. (Scott $825).

Estimate: $1,500+

Minimum Bid: $1,500

32362 **#230-45P4, 1893, 1c - $5, Plate Proofs on Card.** The complete set of sixteen, all fresh and clean. Very Fine to Extremely Fine. (Scott $1,435).

Estimate: $1,000+

Minimum Bid: $425

32363 #319P1, 1903, 2c Carmine, Large Die Proof on India.
Die sunk on full size card, with blue Bureau Control No.
105081 handstamp on reverse. Extremely Fine. 2008 PF
Certificate. (Scott $1,500).

Estimate: $1,500+

Minimum Bid: $750

**32364 #622P1a, 1926, 13c Green, Approved Large Die
Proof on Wove Paper.** Benjamin Harrison. Die sunk
on full size card, with "Approved Dec !4, 1925" and
Postmaster General's signature, blue Bureau Control No.
1363188 handstamp on reverse. Extremely Fine. 2008 PF
Certificate. (Scott unlisted).

Estimate: $850+

Minimum Bid: $425

**32365 #643P1a, 1927, 2c Carmine Rose, "Approved"
Large Die Proof on White Wove Paper.** Vermont
Sesquicentennial. Die sunk on full size card measur-
ing 146 x 202mm, with "Approved June 23, 1927" and
Postmaster General's signature, blue Bureau Control No.
69971. Extremely Fine. 2008 PF Certificate. (Scott $750).

Estimate: $800+

Minimum Bid: $400

**32366 #736P1a, 1934, 3c Carmine Rose, Large Die Proof on
White Wove Paper.** Maryland Tercentenary. Die sunk
on card measuring 152x120mm, radiantly fresh and
vibrant, with bright color, overall with trivial tiny toned
spots outside the design. Extremely Fine and undercatalogued. Alvin R. Meissner, designer; J.C. Benzing,
vignette engraver. 2008 PF Certificate. (Scott $800).

Estimate: $1,000+

Minimum Bid: $500

32367 **#736P2, 1934, 3c Carmine Rose, Small Die Proof on White Wove Paper.** Maryland Tercentenary. Measuring 30 x 26mm, brilliantly vivid and pristine. An extremely rare Gem of unrivalled quality. Victor S. McCluskey, engraver; J.C. Benzing, vignette engraver. 2008 PF Certificate. (Scott $650).

Estimate: $650+

Minimum Bid: $325

32368 **#737P1a, 1934, 3c Deep Violet, Large Die Proof on White Wove Paper.** Mothers of America. Untrimmed proof measuring 71 x 63mm. Blue Serial (Control) no. 369030 on the front. specially prepared for Hugh M. Southgate as characterized by not having been card mounted and containing the Bureau control number on the front. Extremely Fine to Superb. Victor S. McCluskey, designer; J.C. Benzing, vignette engraver. 2008 PF Certificate. ex-Southgate. (Scott $800).

Estimate: $1,000+

Minimum Bid: $500

32369 **#737P2, 1934, 3c Deep Violet, Small Die Proof on White Wove Paper.** Mothers of America. Measuring 44 x 28mm, razor sharp detail and warm pastel color on pristine paper. An exceptional Gem for the connoisseur. Victor S. McCluskey, designer; J.C. Benzing, vignette engraver. 2008 PF Certificate. (Scott $650).

Estimate: $650+

Minimum Bid: $325

32370 **#772P1a, 1935, 3c Violet, Large Die Proof on White Wove Paper.** Connecticut Tercentenary. The Charter Oak. Die sunk on card measuring 152x120mm, sumptuous warm color and a deeply etched impression producing an almost 3-dimensional look to the scene, with tiny inconsequential scattered toned spots mostly outside the design. Extremely Fine and scarce. Alvin R. Meissner, designer. 2008 PF Certificate. (Scott listed but unvalued).

Estimate: $1,500+

Minimum Bid: $750

32371 **#772P2var, 1935, 3c Violet, Small Die Proof on Thin Glazed Card.** Charter Oak. Measuring 49 x 35mm, radiantly bright and vividly detailed giving the scene depiction an almost life-like appearance, the reverse side with full original mounting adhesive not mentioned on the certificate. A rare Gem for the specialist. Victor S. McCluskey, designer; J.C. Benzing, vignette engraver. 2008 PF Certificate. (Scott unlisted).

Estimate: $1,200+

Minimum Bid: $600

32372 **#782P1var, 1936, 3c Purple, Large Die Proof on Surface Glazed Card.** Arkansas Centennial. Measuring 135x89mm showing full die sinkage, radiantly bright and vibrant, crisp and vivid, with blue Bureau handstamp "Engraver's Stock Proof / Authorized by." (initialed), and blue Control no. 468791 on reverse. Very Fine and rare, if not unique. Alvin R. Meissner, engraver; Carl T. Arlt, vignette engraver. 2008 PF Certificate. (Scott unlisted).

Estimate: $1,000+

Minimum Bid: $500

32373 **#782P2, 1936, 3c Purple, Small Die Proof on White Wove Paper.** Arkansas Centennial. Measuring 43 x 28mm, radiantly bright and vibrant, crisp impression. A pristine Gem. Alvin R. Meissner, designer; Carl T. Arlt, vignette engraver. 2008 PF Certificate. (Scott $650).

Estimate: $650+

Minimum Bid: $325

32374 **#852P2, 1939, 3c Bright Purple, Small Die Proof on White Wove Paper.** Golden Gate International Exposition. Measuring 28 x 53mm, warm and soothing, finely detailed. A pristine and undervalued Gem. 2008 PF Certificate. (Scott $600).

Estimate: $750+

Minimum Bid: $375

32375 **#854P2, 1939, 3c Bright Red Violet, Small Die Proof on White Wove Paper.** Washington Inauguration. Measuring 28 x 43mm, pristine and vivacious. An extraordinary and rare Gem for the finest collection. Alvin R. Meissner, designer; John Eissler, vignette engraver. 2008 PF Certificate. (Scott $650).

Estimate: $750+

Minimum Bid: $375

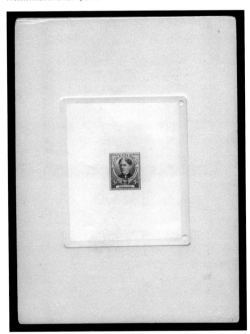

32376 **#872P1, 1940, 5c Ultramarine, Large Die Proof on India.** Frances Willard. Die sunk on full size card measuring 152 x 203mm, with blue Bureau "Engraver's Stock Proof / Authorized by." (initialed), blue Control No. 622591A, and blue "Dec 14 1939" handstamps on reverse. Extremely Fine. 2008 PF Certificate. (Scott $800).

Estimate: $800+

Minimum Bid: $400

32377 **#882P1, 1940, 5c Ultramarine, Large Die Proof on India.** Edward MacDowell. Die sunk on full size card measuring 152 x 203mm, with black Control (serial) No. 70042 on reverse, and inconsequential faint soiling at top of card. John Eissler, vignette engraver. Extremely Fine. 2008 PF Certificate. (Scott $800).

Estimate: $800+

Minimum Bid: $400

32378 **#885P1a, 1940, 2c Rose Carmine, Large Die Proof on Wove Paper.** James Whistler. Die sunk on full sized three hole punched card measuring 135 x 189mm, with black Bureau "Engraver's Stock Proof / Authorized by." (initialed) and blue Control No. 650660A handstamps on reverse, the card with light soiling and small scuff at right, and an acetate overleaf taped to reverse at right. Extremely Fine. 2008 PF Certificate. (Scott unlisted).

Estimate: $1,000+

Minimum Bid: $500

32379 #887P1, 1940, 5c Ultramarine, Large Die Proof on India.
Daniel Chester French. Die sunk on full size card measuring 152 x 203mm, with blue Bureau "Engraver's Stock Proof / Authorized by." (initialed) and blue Control No. 627028A handstamps on reverse, the card with light notation depressions at bottom that are not noted on the certificate. Very Fine to Extremely Fine. 2008 PF Certificate. (Scott $800).

Estimate: $750+

Minimum Bid: $375

32380 #888P1, 1940, 10c Dark Brown, Large Die Proof on India. Frederic Remington. Die sunk on full size card measuring 141 x 203mm, signed "Harry R. Rollins" in pencil at the bottom, with blue "Engraver's Stock Proof / Authorized by." (initialed) and blue Control No. 626309A on reverse. Extremely Fine. 2008 PF Certificate. (Scott $800).

Estimate: $800+

Minimum Bid: $400

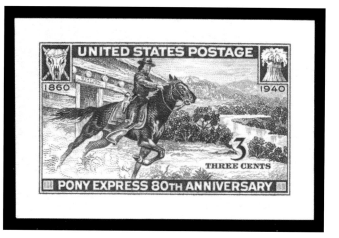

32381 #894P2, 1940, 3c Henna Brown, Small Die Proof on White Wove Paper. Pony Express. Measuring 43 x 28mm, intense and lively. A magnificent and pristine Gem exemplifying engraving mastery. William A. Roach, designer; Charles A Brooks, vignette engraver. 2008 PF Certificate. (Scott $600).

Estimate: $750+

Minimum Bid: $375

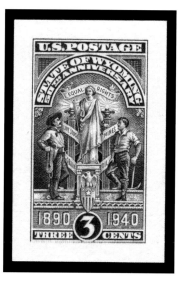

32382 #897P2, 1940, 3c Brown Violet, Small Die Proof on White Wove Paper. State of Wyoming. Measuring 28 x 43mm, both warm and effervescent, deeply etched, with a inconsequential tiny thin in the top margin which appears more like a very minor natural paper translucence, otherwise Extremely Fine. 2008 PF Certificate. (Scott $600).

Estimate: $600+

Minimum Bid: $300

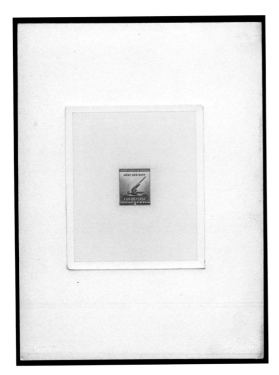

32385 **#924P1a, 1944, 3c Bright Red Violet, Large Die Proof on White Wove Paper.** Centenary of the Telegraph. Die sunk on full size card measuring 201 x 151mm, clean and vibrant, deeply etched, with red (Design Department) "Modeling" and blue Control no. 820176A handstamps on reverse. A true Gem for the specialist. Victor S. McCluskey, designer; Carl T. Arlt vignette engraver. 2008 PF Certificate. (Scott listed but unvalued).

Estimate: $1,000+

Minimum Bid: $500

32383 **#900P1a, 1940, 2c Rose Carmine, Large Die Proof on Wove Paper.** Army and Navy for Defense. Die Sunk on full size card measuring 152 x 202mm, with blue Bureau "Engraver's Stock Proof / Authorized by." (initialed) and blue Control No. 656511A handstamps on reverse, and also signed "Rollins" on reverse which is not noted on the certificate. Extremely Fine. 2008 PF Certificate. (Scott unlisted).

Estimate: $1,000+

Minimum Bid: $500

32386 **#924P2, 1944, 3c Bright Red Violet, Small Die Proof on White Wove Paper.** Centenary of the Telegraph. Measuring 43 x 28mm, sparkling bright and pristine, razor sharp etching. A masterfully produced Gem, rare and undercatalogued. Victor S. McCluskey, designer; Carl T. Arlt, vignette engraver. 2008 PF Certificate. (Scott $600).

Estimate: $750+

Minimum Bid: $375

32384 **#923P1a, 1944, 3c Violet, Large Die Proof on Wove Paper.** First Steamship to Cross the Atlantic. Die Sunk on full size three hole punched card measuring 193 x 150mm, with red Bureau "Engraver's Stock Proof / Authorized by." (initialed) and blue Control No. 819215A handstamps, the card also signed "Brooks" on reverse which is not noted on the certificate. Extremely Fine. 2008 PF Certificate. (Scott unlisted).

Estimate: $2,000+

Minimum Bid: $1,000

32387 #925P1a, 1944, 3c Deep Violet, Large Die Proof on White Wove Paper. Corregidor. Die sunk on full size card measuring 202 x 150mm, deeply etched impression, both intense and radiant at the same time, overall pristine, with red "Modeling" and blue Control no. 831498A handstamp's on reverse. A magnificent and extremely rare Gem for the specialist. William A. Roach, designer; Charles A. Brooks, vignette engraver. 2008 PF Certificate. (Scott listed but unvalued).

Estimate: $1,500+
Minimum Bid: $750

32389 #927P1a, 1945, 3c Bright Red Violet, Large Die Proof on White Wove Paper. Florida Centennial. Die sunk on full size three hole punched card measuring 202 x 150mm, luxuriously radiant and vividly detailed, with "C" security punch taped in place (as was the practice), red Bureau handstamp "Engraver's Stock Proof / Authorized by." (initialed), and blue Control no. 854730A on reverse. An exceptional Gem. William A. Roach, designer; Charles A. Brooks, vignette engraver. 2008 PF Certificate. ex-*Brooks*. (Scott listed but unvalued).

Estimate: $1,500+
Minimum Bid: $750

32388 #925P2, 1945, 3c Deep Violet, Small Die Proof on White Wove Paper. Corregidor. Measuring 43 x 28mm, both intense and radiant at the same time, with a inconsequential faint thin at top right visible only under close examination of the reverse, otherwise Extremely Fine and rare. William A. Roach, designer; Charles A Brooks, vignette engraver. 2008 PF Certificate. (Scott $600).

Estimate: $600+
Minimum Bid: $300

32390 #927P2, 1945, 3c Bright Red Violet, Small Die Proof on White Wove Paper. Florida Centennial. Measuring 43 x 28mm, gloriously rich and vibrant, deeply etched. A pristine and rare Gem for the serious collector. William A Roach, designer; Charles A Brooks, vignette engraver. 2008 PF Certificate. (Scott $600).

Estimate: $750+
Minimum Bid: $375

32391 #942P1a, 1946, 3c Deep Blue, Large Die Proof on Wove Paper. Iowa Statehood. Die sunk on full size three hole punched card measuring 191 x 193mm, with "C" security punch taped in place, as was the practice, red Bureau "Engraver's Stock Proof / Authorized by." (initialed) and blue Control No. 894878A on reverse; also with an acetate overleaf taped to the reverse. *(Note, this is correctly identified on the certificate as on wove paper, which is #942P1a and not 942P1 as noted on the certificate)* Extremely Fine. 2008 PF Certificate. (Scott unlisted).

Estimate: $1,000+

Minimum Bid: $500

32392 #946P1a, 1947, 3c Violet, Large Die Proof on Wove Paper. Joseph Pulitzer. Die sunk on full size three hole punched card measuring 203 x 152mm, with an example of the issued stamp affixed below the proof, "C" security punch taped in place, as was the practice, red Bureau "Engraver's Stock Proof / Authorized by." (initialed) and blue Control No. 917019A handstamps on the reverse, as well as lightly signed "Brooks" in pencil on the reverse which is not noted on the certificate. Extremely Fine. 2008 PF Certificate. (Scott unlisted).

Estimate: $1,500+

Minimum Bid: $750

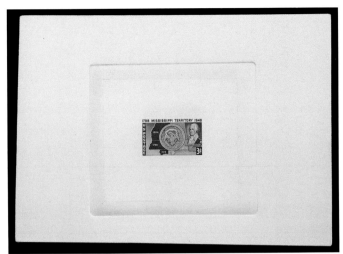

32393 #955P1a, 1948, 3c Brown Violet, Large Die Proof on Wove Paper. Mississippi Territory. Die sunk on card measuring 189 x 133-135mm (the card having been slightly reduced at the bottom by the Bureau of Printing and Engraving, with "C" security punch taped in place, violet Bureau "Engraver's Stock Proof / Authorized by." (initialed) and blue Control No. 948929A handstamps on reverse, and an acetate overleaf taped to the reverse at the bottom, the card also signed "Fenton" in pencil which is not mentioned on the certificate. Extremely Fine. 2008 PF Certificate. (Scott unlisted).

Estimate: $1,000+

Minimum Bid: $500

32394 #977P1a, 1948, 3c Rose Pink, Large Die Proof on Wove Paper. Founder of Memorial Poppy. Die sunk on full size three hole punched card measuring 202 x 151½mm, with "C" security punch taped in place, as was the practice, purple Bureau "Engraver's Stock Proof / Authorized by." (initialed) and blue Control No. 961142A handstamps, the card also signed "Brooks" in pencil which is not noted on the certificate. Extremely Fine. 2008 PF Certificate. (Scott unlisted).

Estimate: $1,500+

Minimum Bid: $750

32395 **#989P1a, 1950, 3c Bright Blue, Large Die Proof on Wove Paper.** National Capital Sesquicentennial. Die sunk on full size three hole punched card measuring 202 x 151mm, with "C" security punch taped in place, as was the practice, Purple Bureau "Engraver's Stock Proof / Authorized by." (initialed) and blue Control No. 995888A handstamp on reverse, also signed in pencil "C. Brooks" which is not noted on the certificate. Extremely Fine. 2008 PF Certificate. (Scott unlisted).

Estimate: $2,000+

Minimum Bid: $1,000

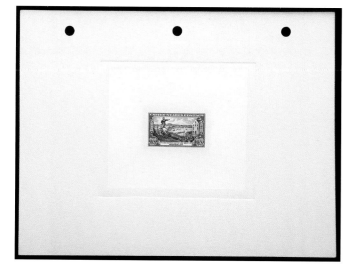

32396 **#1003P1a, 1951, 3c Violet, Large Die Proof on Wove Paper.** Washington Saves His Army at Brooklyn. Die sunk on full size three hole punched card measuring 203 x 153mm, with "C" security punch taped in place, as was the practice, purple Bureau "Engraver's Stock Proof / Authorized by." (initialed) and blue Control No. 59090B handstamps on reverse, plus signed "Brooks" in pencil on reverse which is not noted on the certificate. Extremely Fine. 2008 PF Certificate. (Scott unlisted).

Estimate: $1,500+

Minimum Bid: $750

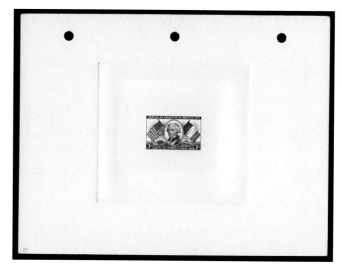

32397 **#1010P1a, 1952, 3c Bright Blue, Large Die Proof on Wove Paper.** Lafayette. Die sunk on full size three hole punched card measuring 203 x 152mm, with "C" security punch taped in place, as was the practice, with dark purple Bureau "Engraver's Stock Proof / Authorized by." (initialed) and blue Control No. 76469B, also signed in pencil "CA Brooks" on reverse, which is not noted on the certificate. Extremely Fine. 2008 PF Certificate. (Scott unlisted).

Estimate: $1,500+

Minimum Bid: $750

32398 **#1063P1a, 1954, 3c Violet Brown, Large Die Proof on Wove Paper.** Lewis & Clark. Die sunk on full size three hole punched card measuring 201 x 150mm, with purple Bureau "Engraver's Stock Proof / Authorized by." (initialed) and blue Control No. 147479B handstamps on reverse, plus signed "Brooks" in pencil on reverse which is not noted on the certificate. Extremely Fine. 2008 PF Certificate. (Scott unlisted).

Estimate: $1,000+

Minimum Bid: $500

32399 #1073P1a, 1956, 3c Bright Carmine, Large Die Proof on Wove Paper. Benjamin Franklin. Die sunk on full size three hole punched card measuring 151 x 202mm, with "C" security punch taped in place, as was the practice, violet Bureau "Engraver's Stock Proof / Authorized by." (initialed) and black Control No. 178013B handstamps on reverse, the card also signed "C. Brooks" on reverse which is not noted on the certificate. Extremely Fine. 2008 PF Certificate. (Scott unlisted).

Estimate: $1,500+
Minimum Bid: $750

32401 #2540Pa-i, 1991, $2.90 Multicolor, Progressive Plate Proofs on Gummed Stamp Paper. (Original Gum - Never Hinged). A gorgeous grouping of nine progressive plate proofs on showing all stages prior to the finished design. Very Fine to Extremely Fine. (Scott listed but unvalued).

Estimate: $1,500+
Minimum Bid: $750

32402 #2540Pj, 1991, $2.90 Multicolored, Plate Proof on Gummed Stamp Paper. (Original Gum - Never Hinged). A terrific right sheet margin horizontal pair. Very Fine to Extremely Fine. 2008 PF Certificate. (Scott listed but not valued).

Estimate: $1,500+
Minimum Bid: $750

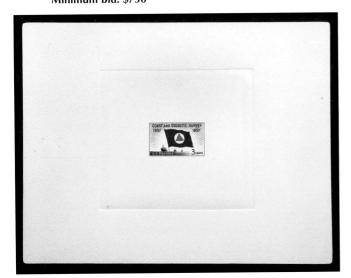

32400 #1088P1a, 1957, 3c Dark Blue, Large Die Proof on Wove Paper. Coast and Geodetic Survey. Die sunk on full size card, with "C" security punch taped in place, as was the practice, Bureau "Engraver's Stock Proof / Authorized by." (initialed) and black Control No. 198058B handstamps on reverse. Extremely Fine. 2008 PF Certificate. (Scott unlisted).

Estimate: $1,500+
Minimum Bid: $750

32403   **#2646aPb-i, 1992, 29c Multicolor, Progressive Plate Proofs on Stamp Paper, Gummed.** (Original Gum - Never Hinged). Complete set of Hummingbirds booklet pane progressive plate proofs from the files of the American Bank Note Co., consisting of eight proofs outlining the printing progression. Extremely Fine. (Scott listed but not valued).
Estimate: $3,500+
Minimum Bid: $1,750

RARE AIRMAIL SMALL DIE PROOF

32404   **#C24P2, 1939, 30c Dull Blue, Small Die Proof on White Wove Paper.** Measuring 51 x 23mm, warm yet radiant, exquisitely detailed, with *very* faint thins visible only from the reverse. Very Fine to Extremely Fine and gorgeous, this being *one of only two or three known*. Alvin R. Meissner, designer; F. Pauling, vignette engraver. 2008 PF Certificate. (Scott $2,750).
Estimate: $2,000+
Minimum Bid: $1,000

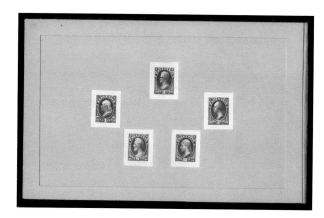

32406   **#O10-14P2, 1903, 1c - 10c Carmine, Small Die Proofs.** Complete set (5) "Executive Dept. small die proofs affixed to original page from a Roosevelt presentation album, some tiny tone spots and a tiny pencil notation. Superb. 2008 PF Certificate. (Scott as singles $500).
Estimate: $450+
Minimum Bid: $225

32405   **#O1-9P2, 1903, 1c - 90c Yellow, Small Die Proofs.** Complete set of (9) "Agriculture Dept." small die proofs affixed to original page from a Roosevelt presentation album, rare and undervalued. Superb. 2008 PF Certificate. (Scott as singles $900).
Estimate: $900+
Minimum Bid: $450

32407   **#O15-24P2, 1903, 1c - 90c Vermillion, Small Die Proofs.** Complete set (10) "Interior Dept." small die proofs affixed to original page from a Roosevelt presentation album, rare and undervalued, some scattered tiny toning spots. Superb. 2008 PF Certificate. (Scott as singles $1,000).
Estimate: $900+
Minimum Bid: $450

32408 **#O25-34P2, 1903, 1c - 90c Purple, Small Die Proofs.**
Complete set (10) "Justice Dept." small die proofs affixed
to original page from a Roosevelt presentation album, rare
and undervalued, some scattered tiny toning spots. Superb.
2008 PF Certificate. (Scott as singles $1,000).

Estimate: $1,000+

Minimum Bid: $500

32409 **#O35-45P2, 1903, 1c - 90c Ultramarine, Small Die
Proofs.** Complete set (6) "Navy Dept" small die proofs
affixed to original page from a Roosevelt presentation
album, minor scattered tone spots. Superb and undervalued. 2008 PF Certificate. (Scott as singles $1,100).

Estimate: $900+

Minimum Bid: $450

32410 **#O47-56P2, 1903, 1c - 90c Black, Small Die Proofs.**
Complete set (10) "Post Office Dept." small die proofs
affixed to original page from a Roosevelt presentation
album, some minor toning spots. Superb and undervalued.
2008 PF Certificate. (Scott as singles $1,000).

Estimate: $900+

Minimum Bid: $450

32411 **#O57-67P1, 1873, 1c - 90c Green, Large Die Proofs.**
Complete set of (11) Large Die Proofs through 90c, each
die sunk on card, each trimmed down in size to just a
touch outside the die sinkage, a few with trivial scattered
spots, otherwise Fine to Very Fine. (Scott $880).

Estimate: $500+

Minimum Bid: $250

32412 **#O57-67P2, 1903, 1c - 90c Green, Small Die Proofs.**
Complete set, (11) 1c-90c values, "State Dept." small die
proofs affixed to original page from a Roosevelt presentation album, rare and undervalued, some scattered tiny
toning spots. Superb. 2008 PF Certificate. (Scott as singles
$1,100).

Estimate: $1,100+

Minimum Bid: $550

32413 **#O68-71P2, 1903, $2 - $20 Green & Black, Small Die Proofs.** Complete set of (4) dollar values "State Dept. small die proofs affixed to original page from a Roosevelt album, some tiny toning spots. Undervalued. Superb. 2008 PF Certificate. (Scott as singles $500).

Estimate: $500+

Minimum Bid: $250

32415 **#O72-82P2, 1903, 1c - 90c Brown, Small Die Proofs.** Complete set (11) "Treasury Dept. small die proofs affixed to original page from a Roosevelt presentation album, some tiny scattered tone spots. Undervalued. Superb. 2008 PF Certificate. (Scott as singles $1,100).

Estimate: $900+

Minimum Bid: $450

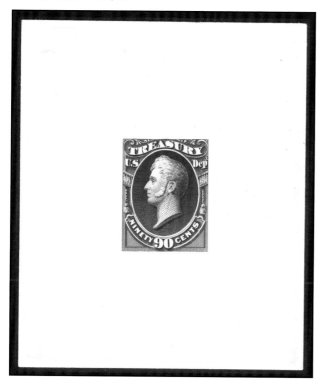

32414 **#O72//82P1, 1873, 1c - 90c Brown Large Die Proofs.** A near complete set (10) die sunk on card, missing only the 30c, each proof trimmed to just slightly larger than the die sinkage area of the card, Fine to Very Fine. (Scott $800).

Estimate: $500+

Minimum Bid: $250

32416 **#O83-93P1, 1873, 1c - 90c Rose, Large Die Proofs.** Complete set (11) proofs, each die sunk on card, each trimmed down to just outside the die sinkage, a few with scattered stains not affecting the indicia. Fine to Very Fine. (Scott $880).

Estimate: $500+

Minimum Bid: $250

32417 **#O83-93P2, 1903, 1c - 90c Rose, Small Die Proofs.**
Complete set (11) "War Dept." small die proofs affixed to
original page from a Roosevelt presentation album, rare
and undervalued, some scattered tiny toning spots. Superb.
2008 PF Certificate. (Scott as singles $1,100).

Estimate: $1,100+
Minimum Bid: $550

32420 **#R150P4, 1872, $20.00 Orange & Black, Plate Proof on
Card.** A gorgeous right margin vertical pair with imprint,
ever so slightly oxidized at top and bottom. Very Fine to
Extremely Fine. 2008 PF Certificate.

Estimate: $500+
Minimum Bid: $250

32418 **#R136P4, 1872, 4c Brown & Black Plate Proof on Card.**
A scarce bottom imprint & Plate no. 13 block of 10.
Extremely Fine. 2008 PF Certificate.

Estimate: $750+
Minimum Bid: $375

32419 **#R144P4, 1872, $1.00 Green & Black Plate Proof on
Card.** A delightful top imprint strip of five, the imprint per-
fectly centered across the three center stamps and inverted.
Very Fine. 2008 PF Certificate.

Estimate: $500+
Minimum Bid: $250

32421 **#RS153P1, 1864, 4c Black, Large Die Proof on India.** Die
sunk on full size card measuring 151 x 222mm, some tiny
toning spots, hinge remnant on the back. Superb. 2008 PF
Certificate. (Scott $450).

Estimate: $400+
Minimum Bid: $200

HUNTING PERMIT PLATE PROOFS
The following 24 lots are Newly Discovered and Unlisted
in the current Scott Catalog.

Starting with RW26P and running though RW50P, (ex RW31) Heritage is proud to present these rare and very possibly unique Federal Duck Hunting Plate Proofs.

The Scott Catalog has very similar item listings for RW 1-12P2 (Small Die proofs which catalog from $6,000 – $17,500 each). Die Proofs are taken from an actual die to a selected paper type, whereas Plate Proofs are taken from an actual printing of the stamp prior to issue. Plate Proofs may be worth more or less, as they are Imperforate specimens removed from an actual sheet and serve as a test of the accuracy of the plate.

Inasmuch as each of the Federal Duck Plate Proofs offered in this sale are a new discovery and thus far, the only examples certified by the Philatelic Foundation, we feel our $5,000 estimate per item to be rather conservative.

32422 **#RW26P, 1959, $3.00 Blue, Ocher, & Black.** (Disturbed Original Gum). Imperforate Plate Proof on Gummed Stamp paper. 2008 PF Certificate; "genuine, with disturbed OG."
Estimate: $5,000+
Minimum Bid: $2,500

32424 **#RW28P, 1961, $3.00 Multicolor.** (Disturbed Original Gum). Imperforate Plate Proof on Gummed Stamp paper. 2008 PF Certificate; "genuine, with disturbed OG.".
Estimate: $5,000+
Minimum Bid: $2,500

32423 **#RW27P, 1960, $3.00 Red Brown, Dk Blue & Bister.** (Disturbed Original Gum). Imperforate Plate Proof on Gummed Stamp paper. 2008 PF Certificate; "genuine, with disturbed OG.".
Estimate: $5,000+
Minimum Bid: $2,500

32425 **#RW29P, 1962, $3.00 Dk. Blue, Dk. Red Brn. & Black.** (Disturbed Original Gum). Imperforate Plate Proof on Gummed Stamp paper. 2008 PF Certificate; "genuine, with disturbed OG.".
Estimate: $5,000+
Minimum Bid: $2,500

32426 **#RW30P, 1963, $3.00 Multicolor.** (Disturbed Original Gum). Imperforate Plate Proof on Gummed Stamp paper. 2008 PF Certificate; "genuine, with disturbed OG.".
Estimate: $5,000+
Minimum Bid: $2,500

32427 **#RW32P, 1965, $3.00 Multicolor.** **(Slightly Disturbed Original Gum).** Imperforate Plate Proof on Gummed Stamp paper. 2008 PF Certificate; "genuine, with *slightly* disturbed OG.".
Estimate: $5,500+
Minimum Bid: $2,750

32428 **#RW33P, 1966, $3.00 Multicolor.** (Slightly Disturbed Original Gum). Imperforate Plate Proof on Gummed Stamp paper. 2008 PF Certificate; "genuine, with *slightly* disturbed OG.".
Estimate: $5,500+
Minimum Bid: $2,750

32429 **#RW34P, 1967, $3.00 Multicolor.** (Disturbed Original Gum). Imperforate Plate Proof on Gummed Stamp paper. 2008 PF Certificate; "genuine, with disturbed OG.".
Estimate: $5,000+
Minimum Bid: $2,500

32430 **#RW35P, 1968, $3.00 Multicolor.** (Disturbed Original Gum). Imperforate Plate Proof on Gummed Stamp paper. 2008 PF Certificate; "genuine, with disturbed OG and a light horizontal crease at bottom right.".
Estimate: $4,500+
Minimum Bid: $2,250

32431 **#RW36P, 1968, $3.00 Multicolor.** (Slightly Disturbed Original Gum). Imperforate Plate Proof on Gummed Stamp paper. 2008 PF Certificate; "genuine, with *slightly* disturbed OG.".
Estimate: $5,500+
Minimum Bid: $2,750

32432 **#RW37P, 1970, $3.00 Multicolor.** (Slightly Disturbed Original Gum). Imperforate Plate Proof on Gummed Stamp paper. 2008 PF Certificate; "genuine, with *slightly* disturbed OG.".

Estimate: $5,500+

Minimum Bid: $2,750

32433 **#RW38P, 1970, $3.00 Multicolor.** (Slightly Disturbed Original Gum). Imperforate Plate Proof on Gummed Stamp paper. 2008 PF Certificate; "genuine, with *slightly* disturbed OG.".

Estimate: $5,500+

Minimum Bid: $2,750

32434 **#RW39P, 1972, $5.00 Multicolor.** (Slightly Disturbed Original Gum). Imperforate Plate Proof on Gummed Stamp paper. 2008 PF Certificate; "genuine, with *slightly* disturbed OG.".

Estimate: $5,500+

Minimum Bid: $2,750

32435 **#RW40P, 1873, 1c Multicolor.** (Disturbed Original Gum). Imperforate Plate Proof on Gummed Stamp paper. 2008 PF Certificate; "genuine, with disturbed OG.".

Estimate: $5,000+

Minimum Bid: $2,500

32436 **#RW41P, 1973, $5.00 Multicolor.** (Disturbed Original Gum). Imperforate Plate Proof on Gummed Stamp paper. 2008 PF Certificate; "genuine, with disturbed OG.".

Estimate: $5,000+

Minimum Bid: $2,500

32437 **#RW42P, 1975, $5.00 Multicolor.** (Slightly Disturbed Original Gum). Imperforate Plate Proof on Gummed Stamp paper. 2008 PF Certificate; "genuine, with *slightly* disturbed OG.".

Estimate: $5,500+

Minimum Bid: $2,750

32438 **#RW43P, 1976, $5.00 Green & Black.** (Disturbed Original Gum). Imperforate Plate Proof on Gummed Stamp paper. 2008 PF Certificate; "genuine, with disturbed OG.".
Estimate: $5,000+
Minimum Bid: $2,500

32439 **#RW44P, 1977, $5.00 Multicolor.** (Slightly Disturbed Original Gum). Imperforate Plate Proof on Gummed Stamp paper. 2008 PF Certificate; "genuine, with *slightly* disturbed OG.".
Estimate: $5,500+
Minimum Bid: $2,750

32440 **#RW45P, 1978, $5.00 Multicolor.** (Slightly Disturbed Original Gum). Imperforate Plate Proof on Gummed Stamp paper. 2008 PF Certificate; "genuine, with *slightly* disturbed OG.".
Estimate: $5,500+
Minimum Bid: $2,750

32441 **#RW46P, 1979, $7.50 Multicolor.** (Slightly Disturbed Original Gum). Imperforate Plate Proof on Gummed Stamp paper. 2008 PF Certificate; "genuine, with *slightly* disturbed OG.".
Estimate: $5,500+
Minimum Bid: $2,750

32442 **#RW47P, 1980, $7.50 Multicolor.** (Slightly Disturbed Original Gum). Imperforate Plate Proof on Gummed Stamp paper. 2008 PF Certificate; "genuine, with *slightly* disturbed OG.".
Estimate: $5,500+
Minimum Bid: $2,750

32443 **#RW48P, 1980, $7.50 Multicolor.** (Disturbed Original Gum). Imperforate Plate Proof on Gummed Stamp paper. 2008 PF Certificate; "genuine, with *slightly* disturbed OG.".
Estimate: $5,500+
Minimum Bid: $2,750

32444 **#RW49P, 1982, &7.50 Multicolor.** (Slightly Disturbed Original Gum). Imperforate Plate Proof on Gummed Stamp paper. 2008 PF Certificate; "genuine, with *slightly* disturbed OG.".

Estimate: $5,500+

Minimum Bid: $2,750

32445 **#RW50P, 1983, $7.50 Multicolor.** (Slightly Disturbed Original Gum). Imperforate Plate Proof on Gummed Stamp paper. 2008 PF Certificate; "genuine, with *slightly* disturbed OG.".

Estimate: $5,500+

Minimum Bid: $2,750

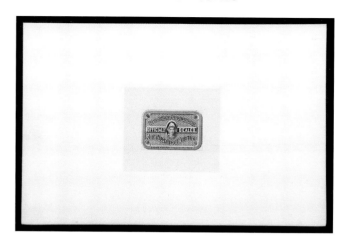

32446 **#OX2aP1, 1879 Post Office Seal, Brown, Hybrid Large Die Proof on India.** Die sunk on full size card measuring 217 x 139mm, the back of the card with a remnant at top from where an overleaf had been attached which is not mentioned on the certificate. Extremely Fine. 2008 PF Certificate. (Scott $2,500).

Estimate: $2,500+

Minimum Bid: $1,250

32447 **#9X1TC2, 1845, 5c Small Die Trial Color Proofs on Bond Selection.** Grouping of three proofs, one each in blue, green, and dark brown, measuring 43-47 x 43-47mm, each with "scar" and dot in "P" of "Post". Extremely Fine and choice. (Scott $750).

Estimate: $900+

Minimum Bid: $450

32448 **#1TC, 1847, 5c Black, Trial Color Large Die Proof on Bond.** Measuring approximately 40 x 42mm, exquisitely detailed. Very Fine. 2008 PF Certificate. (Scott $800).

Estimate: $1,500+

Minimum Bid: $750

32449 **#3-4TC, 1847, 5c & 10c, "ATLANTA" Trial Color Plate Proofs Grouping.** A nearly complete run (8) of the "ATLANTA" Trial Color Plate Proofs of the 1875 Reproductions of the 1847 Regular Issues, on thin card for the International Cotton Exhibition in Atlanta, Georgia, missing only the set in brown. Very Fine to Extremely Fine. (Scott $2,400).

Estimate: $2,750+

Minimum Bid: $1,375

32450 **#127/32TC, 1881, 10c - 90c, "ATLANTA" Trial Color Plate Proofs Group.** Selection of thirteen items, includes #127TC in brown, #128TC in brown, #129TC in brown/ blue (2), brown/black, green/blue (2), and blue/black, #130TC in green/black and black/green, #131TC in blue/ scarlet, and #132TC in scarlet/blue and blue/brown. Very Fine to Extremely Fine. (Scott $4,775).

Estimate: $6,000+

Minimum Bid: $3,000

32451 **#772TC2var, 1935, 3c Black, Trial Color Die Proof on Thin Glazed Card.** Charter Oak. Affixed to a thick card measuring 49 x 34mm, intense and bright, the card with a strip of mounting adhesive across the top on the reverse from where a protective overlay most likely had once been attached. An incomparable Gem destined for the finest collection. Victor S. McCluskey, designer; J.C. Benzing, vignette engraver. 2008 PF Certificate. (Scott unlisted).

Estimate: $1,200+

Minimum Bid: $600

32452 **#854TC1a, 1939, 3c Purple, Large Die Trial Color Proof on White Wove Paper.** George Washington Inauguration. Die Sunk on full size card measuring 152 x 203mm, intensely rich and detailed, with black Serial no. 70038 on reverse. A rare Gem for the specialist. Alvin R. Meissner, designer; John Eissler, vignette engraver. 2008 PF Certificate. (Scott unlisted).

Estimate: $1,000+

Minimum Bid: $500

32453 #876TC1, 1940, 3c Bright Red Violet, Large Die Trial Color Proof on India. Luther Burbank. Die sunk on full size card measuring 152 x 203½mm, with blue Bureau "Engraver's Stock Proof / Authorized by." (signed) and blue Control No. 627222A handstamps on reverse, as well as being signed front and back in pencil by Harry R. Rollins, which is not noted on the certificate. Extremely Fine. 2008 PF Certificate. (Scott unlisted).

Estimate: $1,500+

Minimum Bid: $750

32454 #894TC1, 1940, 3c Dark Brown, Large Die Trial Color Proof on India. Pony Express. Die sunk on full three hole punched card measuring 180 x 136mm, incredibly intense and deeply etched producing a virtually life-like scene, with blue Bureau "Engraver's Stock Proof / Authorized by." (initialed) and blue Control no. 633103A handstamps, and two small security punch holes through the design at bottom. A rare Gem for the connoisseur of premium quality rarities. William A. Roach, designer; Charles A. Brooks, vignette engraver. 2008 PF Certificate. (Scott unlisted).

Estimate: $1,000+

Minimum Bid: $500

32455 #897TC1, 1940, 3c Red Violet, Large Die Trial Color Proof on India. State of Wyoming. Die sunk on full size three hole punched card measuring 136 x 178mm, spectacularly vivid, both intense and radiant at the same time, with blue Bureau "Engraver's Stock Proof / Authorized by." (initialed) and blue Control no. 635186A handstamps on reverse, and a small security punch hole through the "3" at bottom. A rare Gem for the specialist. 2008 PF Certificate. (Scott listed but unvalued).

Estimate: $1,500+

Minimum Bid: $750

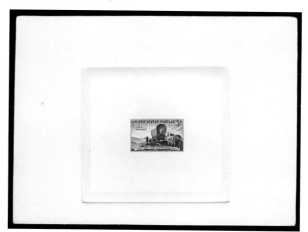

32456 #950TC1a, 1947, 3c Deep Brown, Large Die Trial Color Proof on Wove Paper. Utah Centennial. Die sunk on card measuring 191 x 136mm, with "C" security punch taped in place, as was the practice, red Bureau "Engraver's Stock Proof / Authorized by." (initialed) and blue Control No. 925800A on reverse, the number affected due to scuffing / removal of taped on overlay along the bottom. Extremely Fine. 2008 PF Certificate. (Scott unlisted).

Estimate: $1,500+

Minimum Bid: $750

ERRORS, FREAKS, & ODDITIES

32457 **#1, 1847, 5c Red Brown.** (Used). A captivating four margin single with two opened pre-print paper folds, and red grid cancel. Very Fine. 2008 PF Certificate.

Estimate: $750+

Minimum Bid: $375

AWE-INSPIRING DOUBLE IMPRESSION AND PRE-PRINTING PAPERFOLD

32458 **#114, 1869, 3c Ultramarine.** (Used). Striking and Distinct Double Impression. Unusually dark shade for issue. Also with very large diagonal Pre-Printing paperfold. Fantastic item for the 1869 Specialist. Fine. 2008 PF Certificate.

Estimate: $15,000+

Minimum Bid: $7,500

Please visit HA.com to view other collectibles auctions. *A 19.5% Buyer's Premium ($9 min.) Applies To All Lots*

32459 #279B, 1897, 2c Red. (Original Gum - Previously Hinged). A "Piece de Resistence in anyone's collection" is how this captivating block is described in a Dec. 1898 Weekly Philatelic Gazette article. A magnificent block of twenty (5x4) showing ink loss due to the presence of a thread between the printing plate and paper, or even more correct, showing that the thread was impressed into the paper under the pressure of the printing plate. Either way, an extraordinary show piece, with original gum, previously hinged, with some hinge reinforced separations to help preserve this Very Fine and *unique showpiece*. 2008 PF Certificate.

Estimate: $750+

Minimum Bid: $375

32460 #523, 1918, $2 Orange Red And Black. (Original Gum - Never Hinged). Large downward shift of the vignette. Fine to Very Fine. 2008 PSE Certificate. (Scott $1,300).

Estimate: $1,500+

Minimum Bid: $750

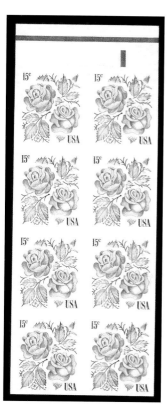

32461 #1737c, 1978, 15c Multicolored. (Disturbed Original Gum). Imperforate booklet pane of eight, original gum, while the certificate states "with the gum mostly removed from the top half of the top two stamps", examination of the pane raises the possibility that the gum may have actually been short run rather than removed, beyond that, the pane with a horizontal crease just above the top two stamps, approximately where the perforations normally would be allowing for removal from the booklet, and the as issued horizontal paper fold across the middle. Overall Very Fine to Extremely Fine for this. 2008 PSE Certificate. (Scott $2,200).

Estimate: $2,000+

Minimum Bid: $1,000

32462 **"Yellow Hat Variety", 1998, Unissued Non-Denominational "H" Rate Stamp, Multicolor.** (Original Gum - Never Hinged). A four by five block of 20, the largest known mint multiple of this unissued "Postcard Rate" stamp, originally intended to cover the 20c postcard rate in conjunction with the January 10, 1999 first class postal rate increase. Beginning with the initial discovery of ten mint examples in a kitchen drawer in a home just outside Greencastle, IN, only slightly over 100 mint examples are known, mostly discovered in Greencastle, overall with most blocks having been broken into singles, a number of which are faulty. This block is fresh and boasts even centering throughout, with rich bright colors on clean paper, and full original gum, with scattered fingerprints on the gum as is the case for most, if not all known examples, and has been previously folded along the perfs between rows two and three, with perf separations noted between positions 6 and 11, and two trivial scuffed perfs at the lower right of position 20. An Extremely Fine to Superb and extremely rare showpiece of significant importance. 2008 PSE Certificate.

Estimate: $150,000+

Minimum Bid: $75,000

PROOFS & ESSAYS

32463 **#2476P, 1991, 1c Multicolor, Die Proof on Gummed Stamp Paper.** (Original Gum - Never Hinged). Top right margin block of four. Extremely Fine. 2008 PF Certificate. (Scott $600).

Estimate: $500+

Minimum Bid: $250

32464 **#2478P, 1991, 3c Multicolor, Die Proof on Gummed Stamp Paper.** (Original Gum - Never Hinged). Top left corner margin block of four. Extremely Fine to Superb. 2008 PF Certificate. (Scott $600).

Estimate: $500+

Minimum Bid: $250

STUNNING MAJOR PRINTING ERROR

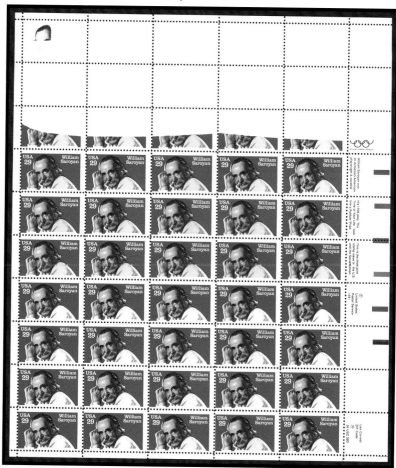

32465 **#2538, 1991, 29c Multicolored.** (Original Gum - Never Hinged). Full Pane of 50, Large Unprinted area. Top two-plus rows All Colors missing, EXCEPT Position 1 which has a partial impression of head in Black only. Positions 2-10 with all colors omitted. Positions 11-15 with all colors partially printed. A minor mis-registration of all colors (not mentioned on the Certificate) is evident on positions 11-50. Sheet contains 10 New Major Errors, and 5 fabulous freaks. A wonderfully bizarre printing error that is unlisted in Scott. 2008 PF Certificate.

Estimate: $15,000+

Minimum Bid: $7,500

32466 **#2747b, 1992, 29c Multicolor.** (Original Gum - Never Hinged). Blue Omitted. Major Error. Normal stamp inlcuded. Very Fine PF Certificate.
   Estimate: $2,500+
   Minimum Bid: $1,250

32467 **#3052Ei, 2000, 33c Multicolor.** (Original Gum - Never Hinged). Booklet pane of 20. Die-Cutting Omitted from center row. Certificate does not mention that the pane is also miscut, resulting in mis-alignment of the label. This miscutting also appears to be the cause of the Die-cut mission. Pane contains 10 error pairs. Very Fine. 2008 PF Certificate.
   Estimate: $5,000+
   Minimum Bid: $2,500

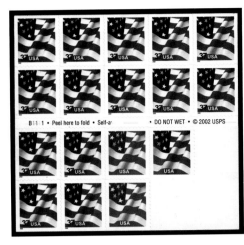

32468 **#3635a Var, 2002, 37c Multi.** (Original Gum - Never Hinged). Unlisted Major Error. Booklet Pane of 20, (3 stamps missing), Positions 13 and 18 missing Black, Positions 8, 12 14 and 17 partially missing black. Very Fine. PF Certificate.
   Estimate: $5,000+
   Minimum Bid: $2,500

32469 **#3879b, 2004, 37c, Multicolored.** (Original Gum - Never Hinged). Booklet Pane of 20, Die Cutting Omitted; Major Error. Horizontal crease between stamps at left (bar code side) and three vertical bends. *Pane contains 10 Error pairs.* Very Fine. 2008 PF Certificate.
   Estimate: $5,000+
   Minimum Bid: $2,500

32470 **#C128a, 1991, 50c Multicolored.** (Original Gum - Never Hinged). Gorgeous example of this scarce error, vertical pair imperforated horizontally, minor wrinkling in bottom margin only. Superb. 2008 PSE Certificate. (Scott $1,750).
   Estimate: $500+
   Minimum Bid: $250

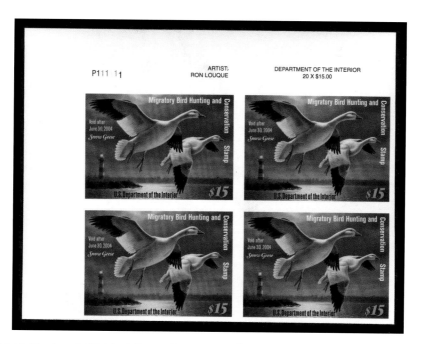

32471 **#RW70b, 2003, $15 Multicolored.** (Original Gum - Never Hinged). Rare Federal Duck Hunting permit Major Error. Imperforate upper left corner Plate Number 111111 and Imprint block of four. Extremely Fine to Superb. 2008 PSE Certificate. (Scott as pairs $15,000).
Estimate: $10,000+
Minimum Bid: $5,000

POSTAL HISTORY

1842 HAND-DELIVERED

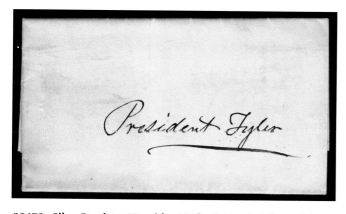

32472 **Silas Reed to "President Tyler".** Hand delivered letter addressed to president Tyler by Silas Reed dated 5 Feb 1842. Very Fine. 2008 PF Certificate.
Estimate: $300+
Minimum Bid: $150

1845-47 POSTMASTER PROVISIONALS

32473 **#9X1, 1845, 5c Black On Bluish.** (Used). Single tied by red "New York 5cts" postmark on folded letter datelined Sep 30, 1846, addressed to Washington, DC, curved "PAID" to left of the stamp, the stamp missing a small part of the top left corner; otherwise Very Fine, and fresh. 2008 PF Certificate. (Scott $650).
Estimate: $450+
Minimum Bid: $225

1847 REGULAR ISSUES

32474 **#1, 1847, 5c Brown.** (Used). Vertical pair tied by red New York square grid cancels on folded outer address sheet to Baltimore, with matching New York circular date stamp (c.d.s.). Very Fine to Extremely Fine. 2008 PSE Certificate. (Scott $1,275).

Estimate: $850+

Minimum Bid: $425

32475 **#1, 1847, 5c Red Brown.** (Used). Vertical pair, tied by red cancels on 1849 folded address sheet to Mobile, Al, with red Boston, Ma postmark at right. Fine. 2008 PF Certificate. (Scott $1,275).

Estimate: $850+

Minimum Bid: $425

32476 **#1, 1847, 5c Red Brown.** (Used). A horizontal pair tied by blue cancels on cover from Philadelphia to Wisconsin, with matching blue Philadelphia, Pa Jan 10 *(1850)* circular date stamp (c.d.s.) cancel, the right stamp with an insignificant tiny scissor cu in the bottom right margin and a vertical crease along the right frame line, the cover with a tear at the top and without the flap. Very Fine. 2008 PSE Certificate. (Scott $1,300).

Estimate: $800+

Minimum Bid: $400

32477 **#1, 1847, 5c Red Brown.** (Used). Tied by red grid cancel on August 27, 1850 folded letter from Binghamton, NY to Nanticoke Springs, NY, with red Binghamton postmark at left, the stamp being a beautiful four margin example, the cover with a lightened stain at top and lightened notations at bottom left. Very Fine. 2007 PF Certificate. (Scott $675).

Estimate: $800+

Minimum Bid: $400

32478 **#1a, 1847, 5c Dark Brown.** (Used). Two four margin singles tied by red New York square grid cancels on folded outer letter address sheet to Philadelphia, with matching red New York circular date stamp (c.d.s.), the outer address sheet missing the right side flap. Very Fine. 2008 PSE Certificate. (Scott $1,600).

Estimate: $1,000+

Minimum Bid: $500

32479 **#1a, 1847, 5c Dark Brown.** (Used). Tied by a black grid and red Boston 12 Sep *(1850)* circular date stamp (c.d.s.) cancels to New York, the stamp with inconsequential corner crease at the bottom. Very Fine. 2008 PSE Certificate. (Scott $800).

Estimate: $650+

Minimum Bid: $325

32480 **#1a, 1847, 5c Blackish Brown.** (Used). An extremely fine used single with generous margins all around, tied on folded letter by a pen cancel with a blue New York and Phil. R.R. Nov 15 *(1847)* {railroad} circular date stamp at the right, the letter with two vertical file folds. Very Fine - Extremely Fine. 2008 PSE Certificate.

Estimate: $1,000+

Minimum Bid: $500

32481 **#1a, 1847, 5c Dark Brown.** (Used). Dot in "S" variety tied by red New York grid cancel on folded letter sheet from New York to Philadelphia, with matching red New York Jul 21 *(1848)* circular date stamp (c.d.s.). Very Fine. 2008 PSE Certificate.

Estimate: $750+

Minimum Bid: $375

32482 **#1a, 1847, 5c Dark Brown.** (Used). A charming 3½ margin example, with generous margins right, left, and bottom, the top margin just clear of the frame line to generous, the stamp tied on a folded letter to New York by a blue Philadelphia, PA Oct 6 *(1849)*, "5cts." circular date stamp with a matching strike at the right, the letter with a horizontal file fold. Very Fine. 2008 PSE Certificate.

Estimate: $750+

Minimum Bid: $375

32483 **#1a, 1847, 5c Dark Brown.** (Used). Four margin single used on folded outer address sheet to Pennsylvania, the stamp with blue straight line "PAID" cancel, the cover with a matching Mar 13 Baltimore, MD postmark, heavy pre-use crease across the bottom of the stamp and the address sheet with the left flap missing and vertical file folds. Very Fine. 2008 PSE Certificate. (Scott $800).

Estimate: $500+

Minimum Bid: $250

32484 **#2, 1847, 10c Black.** (Used). Tied by red square New York grid cancel on folded letter from New York to Montreal, Canada, with matching New York Apr 24 *(1849)* circular date stamp (c.d.s.), and with red Apr 27, 1849 Montreal receiver on reverse. Very Fine. 2008 PSE Certificate. (Scott $2,100).

Estimate: $1,500+

Minimum Bid: $750

32485 **#2, 1847, 10c Black.** (Used). On a folded outer address sheet to new York tied by a red grid cancel with a matching red Saint Louis, MO. circular date stamp (c.d.s.) cancel. Very Fine. 2008PSE Certificate. (Scott $1,700).

Estimate: $1,200+

Minimum Bid: $600

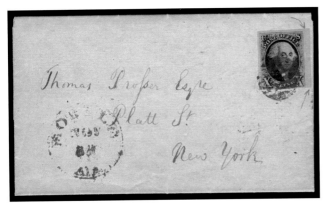

32486 #2, 1847, 10c Black. (Used). Right sheet margin single tied by red grid cancel on 1850 dated folded letter to New York, with red paint Mobile, Al postmark at the bottom left. Very Fine. 2008 PF Certificate. (Scott $1,700).

Estimate: $1,400+

Minimum Bid: $700

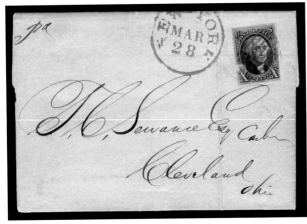

32487 #2, 1847, 10c Black. (Used). Tied by a red circular grid cancel on folded letter to Cleveland, Ohio, with matching New York Mar 28 *(1850)* circular date stamp (c.d.s.), the stamp with some white substance adhering at the lower left. Fine to Very Fine. 2008 PSE Certificate. (Scott $1,700).

Estimate: $950+

Minimum Bid: $475

32488 #2, 1847, 10c Black. (Used). Tied by a red grid cancel on cover to Pittsborough, NC with matching New York circular date stamp (c.d.s.) at the right, the stamp with an inconsequential scuff in the top left margin covered by a black ink line and the cover with trivial wear related tears at the upper left and bottom right corner. An overall Very Fine cover. 2008 PSE Certificate. (Scott $1,700).

Estimate: $850+

Minimum Bid: $425

32489 #8A & 11A, 1851, 1c Blue & 3c Brownish Carmine. (Used). Single 1c plus 3c pair and single combined usage on cover to Toronto, Canada, the stamps with black circular grid cancels, the 3c tied by red "U.S. STATES", with Roxbury, MA postmark at top, and red Stanstead and Montreal transit and black Toronto receiver on reverse, the 1c with clipped corner at top left, the 3c slightly oxidized. Very Fine. 2008 PF Certificate. (Scott $2,035).

Estimate: $1,200+

Minimum Bid: $600

32490 #13, 1855, 10c Green. (Used). A four margin single tied by Saint Louis, MO circular date stamp (c.d.s.) postmark on cover to San Francisco, the cover with an inconsequential small tear at the top. Very Fine. 2008 PSE Certificate. (Scott $1,050).

Estimate: $750+

Minimum Bid: $375

32491 **#17, 1851, 12c Black.** (Used). Tied on folded address sheet from Honolulu to Calais, ME, with red "Honolulu / U.S. Postage Paid" postmark (MH #242.03), this being *one of only 431 known strikes*, the stamp tied by bold Jul 16, 1860 San Francisco town cancel. Extremely Fine and rare. 2008 PF Certificate.

Estimate: $3,000+

Minimum Bid: $1,500

32492 **#17, 1851, 12c Black.** (Used). Vertical pair tied by black grid cancels and a red Dec 1853 Liverpool receiver on folded outer address sheet from New York to Liverpool, England, with a red New York Dec 14 credit marking. Fine to Very Fine. 2008 PSE Certificate. (Scott $850).

Estimate: $500+

Minimum Bid: $250

1857-61 FIRST ISSUES - PERFS

32493 **#19, 1857, 1c Blue.** (Used). Right sheet margin single, Position 100L4, tied by blue circular grid cancel on folded Baltimore Prices Current to Short Creek, OH, the cover signed by Ashbrook. An Extremely Fine and scarce usage. 2002 PF Certificate. *ex-Ishikawa* (Scott $13,500).

Estimate: $7,500+

Minimum Bid: $3,750

32494 #33, 1857, 10c Green. (Used). A pair and a single, each stamp with pen cancel and tied by red New York Exchange office and red boxed Aachen/Franco transit markings, on cover to Baden, with black boxed E.B. 29 Aug/Curs transit marks on reverse, the stamps with trivial stains, the left stamp with a tiny puncture at top left and small pieces replaced at upper and bottom right. Very Fine. 2008 PF Certificate.

Estimate: $750+

Minimum Bid: $375

32495 #36, 1857, 12c Black. (Used). Two singles with grid cancels on cover from Middletown, NY to Yorkshire, England, with strong sharp Middletown, NY postmark at left, red 1857 London postmark and red "3" credit markings at right, the cover with a vertical file fold at left of the stamps. Very Fine; 2008 PF Certificate. (Scott $850).

Estimate: $650+

Minimum Bid: $325

32496 #37, 1860, 24c Gray Lilac. (Used). Tied by red Philadelphia Exchange Office postmark and black grid cancel on cover to Dublin, Ireland, with manuscript "Paid" at upper left, and 1861 Dublin receiver on the reverse, the stamp with minor toned spot and slight discoloration at left, the cover with tears and edge faults and slightly reduced at left, otherwise a Very Fine and scarce usage. 2008 PF Certificate.

Estimate: $750+

Minimum Bid: $375

32497 #62B, 1861, 10c Dark Green. (Used). Used on cover from San Francisco to New York, with Dec 10, 1861 San Francisco double circular date stamp and straight line (s/l) "DUE 10" service mark alongside, the stamp with missing and frayed perforations at bottom, the cover reduced by approximately 15mm at the left. Very Fine and clean. 2008 PF Certificate. (Scott $2,000).

Estimate: $1,200+

Minimum Bid: $600

32498 #68, 1861, 10c Green. (Used). Single used on cover from Honolulu to Westfield, NY via San Francisco, with scarce red "Honolulu / U.S. Postage Paid" postmark (MH #242.03) at left, this being *one of only 431 known strikes*, and San Francisco transit at top toward the right, the cover with a toning band and insignificant tear at right. Very Fine and scarce usage. 2008 PF Certificate.

Estimate: $750+

Minimum Bid: $375

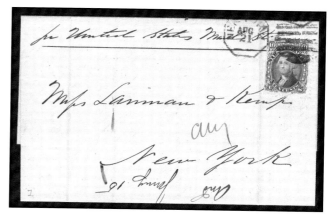

32499 **#73/73d, 1863, 2c Black.** (Used). Single with attached vertical bisect used on cover from Union, WV to Upper Belmont, NH, the stamps with cork cancels, the cover with matching Union, WV postmark, the intact stamps with trivial perforation faults. Very Fine and rare usage that includes the original correspondence. 1986 and 2008 PF Certificates. (Scott $2,070).

Estimate: $1,500+

Minimum Bid: $750

32501 **#89, 1867, 10c Green.** (Used). Tied on August 7, 1868 folded letter from St Lucia to New York, sent per the U.S. Mail Steamer, with Aug 21 *(1868)* New York receiver at top right. Very Fine. 2008 PF Certificate.

Estimate: $650+

Minimum Bid: $325

32500 **#78, 1863, 24c Lilac.** (Used). A horizontal pair tied by black cork crossroads cancels on a Barnum's City Hotel advertising cover, with a matching Baltimore, Md. circular date stamp (c.d.s.), a Jan 11, 1868 receiver on the back, the right stamp with a natural straight edge at the right, the cover with an all-over illustrated Barnum's City Hotel advertisement on the back, back flap tears and a 15mm tear at the top center. Fine to Very Fine. 2008 PSE Certificate.

Estimate: $500+

Minimum Bid: $250

32502 **#97, 1867, 12c Black.** (Used). With 3c #94, tied on a Closed Mail via England cover to Germany, the stamps tied by black New York leaf cancels and the cover with red New York Sep 30 (1868) and Verviers/Cologne transit markings - the stamps with minor perf tip toning. Very Fine. 2008 PSE Certificate.

Estimate: $500+

Minimum Bid: $250

1869 PICTORIALS

32503 **#114, 1869, 3c Ultramarine.** (Used). A single tied by a blue Stove Pipe cancel (Skinner - Eno GE-C7) on cover to Boston, Mass. with a matching blue Leominster, Ms circular date stamp (c.d.s.) at the left. Very Fine and scarce. 2008 PSE Certificate.

Estimate: $500+
Minimum Bid: $250

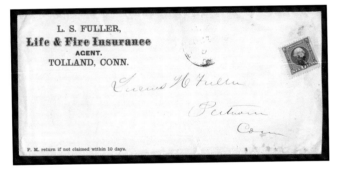

32504 **#115, 1869, 6c Ultramarine.** (Used). On L.S. Fuller Life & Fire Insurance Agent corner advertising cover (corner card cover) from Tolland to Putnam, CT, with partial Tolland, CT postmark at top center, the cover slightly reduced at right from having been opened. a Very Fine usage. 2008 PF Certificate. (Scott without premium for corner card $450).

Estimate: $500+
Minimum Bid: $250

1870-71 NATIONAL BANK NOTE CO. ISSUES - W/O GRILL

32505 **#154, 1870, 30c Black.** (Used). Used on folded letter from New York, addressed to Rieper Augener, the President of an import and export house established in Guatemala in 1860, known for advertising modest rates on German ships to England, Germany, and San Francisco, with manuscript "Sta. Rising Star / Via Panama" and blue New York Merchants 1872 circular date stamp at left. A Very Fine to Extremely Fine usage. 2008 PF Certificate.

Estimate: $1,200+
Minimum Bid: $600

1873 CONTINENTAL BANK NOTE CO. ISSUES

32506 **#161, 1873, 10c Brown.** (Used). Strip of five tied by numeral "79" cancels, along with two singles of #178, on cover from Mattapoisett, Mass. to St. Helena, with Mattapoisett Feb 19 postmark at bottom left, red New York and London transits at right, and Mar 24, 1879 St Helena receiver at center, the stamps with inconsequential perforation faults at top, and the cover with a tear at left and trivial edge faults. An overall Very Fine and attention-grabbing usage. 2008 PF Certificate.

Estimate: $750+
Minimum Bid: $375

32507 **#162, 1873, 12c Blackish Violet.** (Used). With vertical pair #156 and single #159, cork canceled on cover to Switzerland, with Dallas Texas postmark at right, red New York transit, and 1875 Basel receiver on reverse. Fine to Very Fine. 2008 PF Certificate.

Estimate: $500+

Minimum Bid: $250

32508 **#163, 1873, 15c Yellow Orange.** (Used). Used on cover from New Haven, CT to Wellington, Cape of Good Hope, with red New York and London transit markings at left, and Cape Town transit mark and Wellington receiver at right, the stamp with light horizontal crease at top, and the cover with edge tears and nicks to be expected from wear. Fine to Very Fine and scarce usage. 2008 PF Certificate.

Estimate: $1,000+

Minimum Bid: $500

1875 CONTINENTAL BANK NOTE CO. ISSUES

32509 **#178, 1875, 2c Vermilion.** (Used). Tied by magenta target cancel on U163 entire addressed to Yokohama, Japan, with Mar 11, 1879 Yokohama receiver on the reverse, the cover opened from the left side, with a slightly rounded edge at the upper left, approximately half of the reverse covered in pencil notations. an overall Very Fine and scarce usage. 2008 PF Certificate.

Estimate: $750+

Minimum Bid: $375

1890-93 SMALL BANK NOTES

32510 **#219-20, 1890, 1c & 2c Small Bank Notes.** (Used) Used on U311 entire addressed to the Chief Engineer Dutch Indies Navy in Timor, Dutch Indies, with various 1892 in route town cancels on the reverse from New York, Paris, Marseille, and Makassar, and with Sep 23, 1892 Timor receiver. Very Fine. 2008 PF Certificate.

Estimate: $500+

Minimum Bid: $250

1895 BUREAU ISSUES - WATERMARKED

32511 **#272, 1895, 8c Violet Brown.** (Used). Single tied by target cancel on Registered #U324a entire to Mexico City, with Huguenot, GA postmark to the left of the stamp, U.S. Laredo, TX registry etiquette with Mexico handstamp etiquettes below, 1899 Mexico and magenta straightline Laredo, Tex Dec 2, 1899 handstamps on reverse, the 8c stamp with faults and the cover with file folds and scattered toned spots. Very Fine. 2008 PF Certificate.

Estimate: $750+

Minimum Bid: $375

AIRMAIL ISSUES

32512 **#C3, 1918, 24c Carmine Rose & Blue.** (First Flight). A delightful First Flight usage to New York, the stamp overall fresh with well balanced margins all around is tied by an Airmail Service Philadelphia May 15, 1918 First Trip duplex cancel, with a straight line "Fee Claimed" service handstamp at the left, and a New York May 15, 1918 receiving marking on the back. Very Fine. 2008 PSE Certificate. (Scott $750).

Estimate: $750+

Minimum Bid: $375

32513 **#C4, 1923, 8c Dark Green.** (Used). Single tied on First Day cover to Detroit by Washington D.C. Aug 15, 1923 machine cancel, the cover with "The Shoreham Washington" hotel monogram on the backflap. Very Fine. 2008 PF Certificate. (Scott $400).

Estimate: $500+

Minimum Bid: $250

32514 **#C4, 1923, 8c Dark Green, First Day Cover.** The stamp tied by a Washington, DC Aug 15, 1923 slogan machine cancel. Very Fine. 2008 PSE Certificate. (Scott $400).

Estimate: $300+

Minimum Bid: $150

32515 **#C5, 1923, 16c Dark Blue, First Day Cover.** The stamp tied by a Washington, DC Aug 17, 1923 slogan machine cancel. Very Fine. 2008 PSE Certificate. (Scott $600).

Estimate: $500+

Minimum Bid: $250

32516 **#C6, 1923, 24c Carmine, First Day Cover.** The stamp tied by a Washington, DC Aug 21, 1923 duplex cancel, with violet straight line "Special Delivery" handstamp to left and a Washington DC Special Delivery duplex cancel on reverse. Very Fine. 2008 PSE Certificate. (Scott $750).

Estimate: $600+

Minimum Bid: $300

32517 **#C15, 1930, $2.60 Blue.** (Used). On a First Europe Pan America Zeppelin Flight cover, tied by a Carsick St. Sta., N.E. Apr 24, 1930 machine cancel, with the appropriate cover markings. Very Fine. 2008 PSE Certificate. (Scott $600).
Estimate: $500+
Minimum Bid: $250

LOCALS & CARRIERS

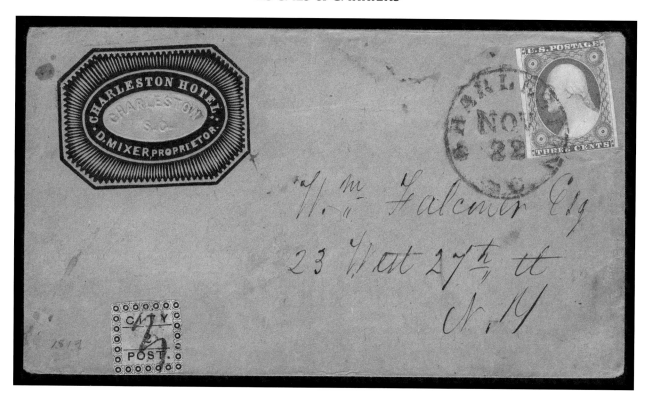

32518 **#4LB3, 1853-54, 2c Black.** (Used). On Charleston Hotel corner card cover, with 3c #11 tied by Charleston, SC town cancel, the carrier pen canceled and with an insignificant small tear at right, the 3c stamp with an inconsequential diagonal crease at top right. Very Fine. 2008 PF Certificate. (Scott $4,500).
Estimate: $5,000+
Minimum Bid: $2,500

32519 **#6LB3, 1842, 3c Black On Blue.** (Used). Single on folded letter to New York, forwarded to Rye, NY, the local with red "U.S." in octagon cancel and the cover with red Albany and New York postmarks at left. Very Fine. 2005 PF Certificate. (Scott $750).

Estimate: $600+

Minimum Bid: $300

32520 **#6LB5, 1843, 3c Black On Blue Green Glaze.** (Used). Single on folded letter addressed to New York, the stamp with red "U.S." in octagon cancel, and the cover with matching red "U.S. City Despatch Post" postmark at left. Extremely Fine. 2008 PF Certificate. (Scott $600).

Estimate: $500+

Minimum Bid: $250

32521 **#5L1, 1844, 5c Black.** (Used). Single tied by red cancel on 1844 docketed folded address sheet to New York. Very Fine. 2008 PF Certificate. (Scott $850).

Estimate: $750+

Minimum Bid: $375

32522 **#20L7, 1848, 2c Black On Green.** (Used). On cover with 5c #1, tied by red New York square grid cancel, with matching New York postmark, the local with cork cancel, and the cover with a horizontal file fold affecting the local at top. Fine to Very Fine. 2008 PF Certificate.

Estimate: $1,200+

Minimum Bid: $600

32523 **#28L5, 1855, 2c Black On Dark Blue.** (Used). Single, pen canceled, on cover addressed to Brooklyn, NY, with oval "Brooklyn City / Express Post" and straightline "PAID" handstamps at left. Very Fine to Extremely Fine. 2008 PF Certificate.

Estimate: $500+

Minimum Bid: $250

32524 **#41L1, 1860, 1c Black.** (Used). Single tied by grid of "X" in circle cancel on cover addressed to Philadelphia, the stamp with a trivial small scuff at right. Very Fine. 2008 PF Certificate. (Scott $500).

Estimate: $500+

Minimum Bid: $250

32525 **#50LU2, 1865-68 Clarke's Circular Express, Black.** (Used). Used full corner on diagonally laid paper with a strong full blue 1867 company circle cancel, the corner with some trivial toning at the top left not affecting the local. A Gem for the specialist, *the finest of three recorded examples;* 2004 PF Certificate.
(Scott $5,750).

Estimate: $5,000+

Minimum Bid: $2,500

32526 **Cummings' Express Post.** Red handstamp on a fancy "Ladies" cover addressed to New York. Very Fine to Extremely Fine. 2008 PF Certificate.

Estimate: $750+

Minimum Bid: $375

32527 **"Eagle City Post at Adams Express Wilson's Buildings"** Red handstamp on folded letter datelined Wilmington Nov 19, 1850, addressed to Philadelphia, with blue Wilmington, Del town postmark and matching numeral "5" rate handstamp. Very Fine. 2007 PF Certificate.

Estimate: $1,500+

Minimum Bid: $750

32528 **Eagle City Despatch Post** Handstamp on 1846 folded letter sent by passenger train to Philadelphia, with red "3" service handstamp, and manuscript "Passenger Train / Feb 9" at bottom, the cover with a horizontal file fold. Very Fine to Extremely Fine. ; 1993 & 2008 PF Certificates.

Estimate: $750+

Minimum Bid: $375

32529 **#72L3, 1848, 2c Black On Green Glazed.** (Used). Single tied by red New York integral rate town cancel on cover to Little Falls, NY, the local with inconsequential light creasing. Extremely Fine. 2008 PF Certificate. (Scott $650).

Estimate: $500+

Minimum Bid: $250

32530 **"Roche's City Dispatch"** Red handstamp on locally addressed stampless cover. Very Fine. 2007 PF Certificate.

Estimate: $1,000+

Minimum Bid: $500

CONFEDERATE STATES OF AMERICA

32531 **#136L9, 1849, 1c Red.** (Used). Single tied by oval "Swarts / Post Office / Chatham Square" cancel on 1853 printed publisher's notice addressed to NY, the cover with a horizontal file fold. Very Fine. 2008 PF Certificate. (Scott $400).

Estimate: $400+

Minimum Bid: $200

32532 **#U27, 1860, 3c Red On Buff.** (Used). A Very Fine entire with printed Wells Fargo & Co. "Over Our California and Coast Routes" frank addressed to Santa Cruz, NM with "Wells, Fargo & Co's / Express / from / San Mateo, Cal." label at bottom left. 2008 PF Certificate.

Estimate: $750+

Minimum Bid: $375

32534 **#6XU6, 1861, 10c Black.** (Used). Provisional entire, with original enclosure, addressed to the captain of the Fulton Dragoons, Richmond, VA, with Atlanta, GA Sept 6, 1861 postmark at upper right and Atlanta service mark at upper left. The cover with two small cover tears at top, and with backflap largely off (not mentioned on certificate); otherwise a Very Fine appearance. 2002 PF Certificate. (Scott $950.00).

Estimate: $500+

Minimum Bid: $250

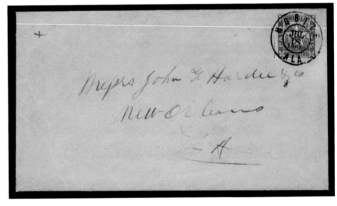

32535 **#58X2, 1861, 5c Blue.** (Used). Single tied by a strong strike of Jul 18, 1861 Mobile AL town cancel on cover to New Orleans, LA, the cover with an insignificant small closed tear at top. Extremely Fine. 2002 PF Certificate.

Estimate: $2,400+

Minimum Bid: $1,200

32533 **#143LU3, 1862, 25c Red.** (Unused). On an unused 3c pink #U34 entire, the stamped envelope with some trivial scattered light soiling. Very Fine. 2008 PF Certificate. (Scott $700).

Estimate: $500+

Minimum Bid: $250

32536 **#62X4, 1861, 5c Red Brown On Bluish.** (Used). An attractive horizontal pair of this rare Provisional issue with good to enormous margins, tied by straight line "Paid" cancels on small buff cover to Nashville TN, with New Orleans 6 Oct CDS at right (inconsequential minor tone spot on left hand stamp and cover slightly reduced at right) otherwise sound and a rare cover. Very Fine. 2008 PF Certificate. (Scott $700).

Estimate: $750+
Minimum Bid: $375

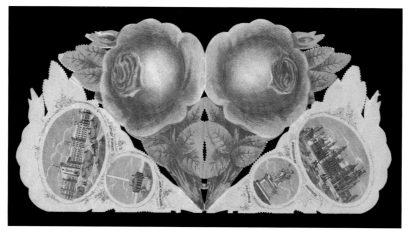

32537 **"The Rose of Washington " Grouping.** Three items including two covers and a fancy insert, the covers, both used and both with the same design, include one in all rose, and the other bi-color blue and rose, the bi-colored example with 3c #65, the insert being a fancy multicolor Rose of Washington tourism type foldout, both covers with some wear related faults and both missing the backflap. Very Fine and scarce.

Estimate: $2,000+
Minimum Bid: $1,000

32538 **#26, 1857, 3c Brownish Carmine.** (Used). Single, tied by town cancel, on reverse of Confederate 7-Star flag patriotic cover to Griffin, GA, with a blind embossed corner card for "Stovall's Excelsior Flour Mills." at the right of the address and light cover toning at top right and on the back, the backflap with a piece missing. Very Fine and rare. *ex Van Dyke MacBride*. 2002 & 2008 PF Certificates.

Estimate: $2,000+

Minimum Bid: $1,000

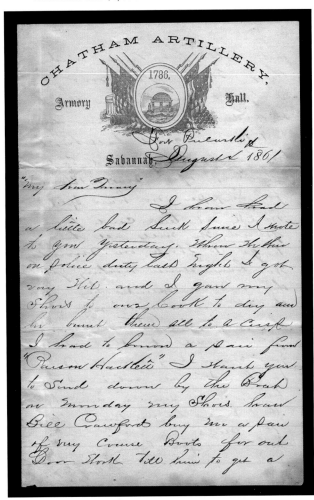

32539 **Confederate "Chatham Artillery" Letter Sheet.** Bi-colored (rose-pink & black) Armory Hall letter sheet, datelined Fort Pulaski, August 4, 1861, 4 pages of which 2 are written. Very Fine. 2008 PF Certificate and 1993 Green Certificate.

Estimate: $1,500+

Minimum Bid: $750

32540 **Unusual Stampless Confederate Illustrated 12 Star Flag Cover.** Interesting Stampless Confederate cover illustrated by 12 Star Flag, apparently sent by a Brigadier General of the Buncorbie Sharpshooters to French Broad NC: with Huntersville pmk at top left and Pd 5 at right. Very attractive and unusual. Very Fine. 2008 PF Certificate.

Estimate: $400+

Minimum Bid: $200

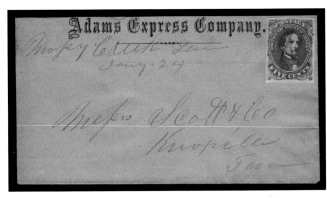

32541 **#1, 1861, 5c Green.** (Used). A fresh and attractive 5c single, pen canceled, on Buff colored Adams Express Company imprint cover addressed to Knoxville TN, with Mossy Creek manuscript at left (small repair to top of cover and slightly reduced) otherwise fine and quite scarce. Very Fine. 2008 PF Certificate.

Estimate: $750+

Minimum Bid: $375

32542 **#1, 1861, 5c Green.** (Used). An magnificent right margin single of the Jefferson Davis 5c green (stone 1) tied by circular town cancel on somewhat soiled cover with faded address (stamp with small nick at top and cover with repair and stains) nevertheless scarce usage. Fine to Very Fine. 2008 PF Certificate. (Scott $300).

Estimate: $400+

Minimum Bid: $200

32543 #2a, 1861, 10c Light Blue. (Used). An attractive small cover bearing a choice example of the 10c light blue neatly tied by Atlanta GA Town cancel addressed to Greenville TN (torn backflap) otherwise VF and scarce. Very Fine to Extremely Fine. 2008 PF Certificate.

Estimate: $500+

Minimum Bid: $250

32544 #7, 1862, 5c Blue. (Used). Horizontal pair tied on 1863 *Turned Cover* to Charleston, SC, with enclosure, the stamps tied by Laurens C.H., SC town cancel, the cover with traces of a 10c Confederate States issue (#11 or 12) inside, addressed within to Laurens C.H., SC, the cover also with an insignificant light toning band along the top edge. Very Fine. 2008 PF Certificate.

Estimate: $500+

Minimum Bid: $250

32545 #9, 1863, 10c Blue. (Used). A single 10c blue Jefferson Davis tied by black grid cancel on cover addressed to Lexington VA, (stamp with small faults and the cover is toned) otherwise quite presentable and scarce. 2008 PF Certificate. (Scott $1,650).

Estimate: $1,200+

Minimum Bid: $600

32546 #12, 1863, 10c Blue. (Used). Single tied by Richmond, VA on "Flag of Truce" cover to Richmond, VA, along with 3c #65 which is tied by Point Lookout, MD town cancel, with octagonally framed "Prisoner's Letter / Aug 12, 1864 / EXAMINED" censors handstamp at center, the 3c being oxidized and the cover remarkably sound for the period. An Extremely Fine and scarce jewel for the specialist. 2008 PF Certificate. (Scott $2,500).

Estimate: $2,000+

Minimum Bid: $1,000

32547 #13, 1863, 20c Green. (Used). A small cover to Cartersville P.O. Virginia franked by a single 20c (#13) canceled Richmond VA town cancel; (stamp has three good margins, just in at left and cover has small tear and slight stain) nevertheless overall fine and scarce usage. Fine. 2008 PF Certificate. (Scott $400).

Estimate: $750+

Minimum Bid: $375

32548 1851, 3c Washington Imperforate Issue Plate Study. An extraordinary complete plating, including both the left and right panes of Plate 2L, each pane within the study having been pain-stakenly reconstructed by a specialist using used examples, and meticulously presented on two large 278 x 354mm pages (one for each pane). Fine to Very Fine and highly specialized.

Estimate: $3,000+

Minimum Bid: $1,500

COLORFUL AND ATTRACTIVE BLACK JACK COLLECTION
1922-25 DEFINITIVES

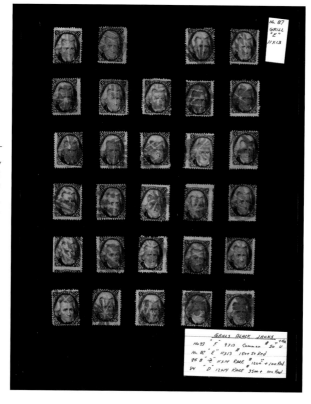

32549 Black Jacks Accumulation / Collection. An attention grabbing gathering of the ever popular "Black Jack" 3c Jackson issues of 1861-68, includes 200 stamps, mostly used, including a substantial selection with fancy cancels, many in red, plus a few in blue. Additionally there is a nice selection consisting of twenty covers, including a couple combination usages with #63. An overall Fine to Very Fine collective for the specialist.

Estimate: $4,500+

Minimum Bid: $2,250

32550#BK68, 1923, 73c White & Red, Combination Booklet. (Original Gum - Never Hinged). A complete brick of 60 booklets as issued to the Post Office, each booklet containing four panes each of #'s 552a and 554c, Fine to Very Fine. (Scott $5,100).

Estimate: $3,500+

Minimum Bid: $1,750

REVENUE ISSUES

32551 Match & Medicine Collection. An absolutely wonderful collection mounted on pages and housed in three separate volumes. Although some faults are to be expected, the overall condition is much better than typical for the issues; add to that a number of higher value items, and the result is a collection well worth checking out. Very Fine to Extremely Fine. (Scott $5,700+).

Estimate: $3,500+

Minimum Bid: $1,750

REMARKABLE COLLECTION OF RAILROAD CANCELLATIONS

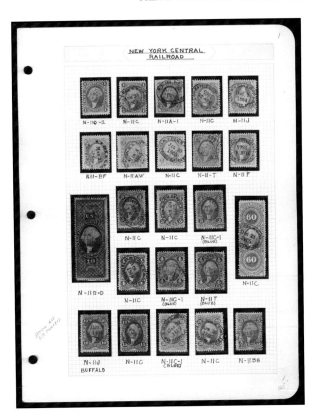

32552 1857-70, Collection of Revenue issues in 3 Ring Binder. (Used). An impressive collection of over 800 Revenue stamps neatly mounted on quadrille pages and housed in a 3 ring binder, containing a fascinating array of scarce and highly desirable Railroad cancellations and in particular several of the rarer Machine made type. The collection includes a number of colored cancellations, and there are also a number of multiples present including blocks pairs and strips. The Railroads are too numerous to mention in detail but each stamp appears to have been selected with an eye not only for scarcity but also for quality, all of which goes to make this one of the most fascinating and desirable collections we have the pleasure to offer. Very Fine to Extremely Fine.

Estimate: $3,000+

Minimum Bid: $1,500

HUNTING PERMIT STAMPS

32553 #RW1-RW65, (Original Gum - Never Hinged). Fantastic Hunting Permit Stamp (Duck) collection, housed on White Ace album pages, consisting of Scott #'s RW1-65. All stamps appear mint with never hinged original gum. An exceptionally clean grouping from a true collector, a few stamps with inconsequential natural gum bends or skips, as is typically the case; otherwise, a Very Fine collection well suited for the enthusiast. (Scott $6,975).

Estimate: $5,500+

Minimum Bid: $2,750

POSSESSIONS & ADMINISTRATIONS
CANAL ZONE

32554 **#15, 1905, 8c on 50c Bister Brown.** (Disturbed Original Gum). A striking mint example of this scarce overprinted issue, with "PANAMA" 13mm long, exceptionally well centered, original gum {disturbed} from interleaving, with nibbled perfs and a tiny margin tear at left. Very Fine to Extremely Fine. *One of only 435 issued.* 2007 APS Certificate. (Scott $2,600).

Estimate: $1,000+

Minimum Bid: $500

32555 **#59, 1920, 1b Dark Violet & Black.** (Used). Tied by town cancel on registered cover from Balboa Heights, CZ to Saginaw, MI, violet handstamped registration etiquette at left, with 1921 Balboa Heights, Cristobal, and New Orleans registry handstamps on the reverse. Very Fine. 2008 PF Certificate. (Scott $1,000).

Estimate: $800+

Minimum Bid: $400

GUAM

32556 **#7, 1899, 8c Violet Brown.** (Original Gum - Previously Hinged). Spectacular violet brown color and impression, barely hinged, bottom imprint and Plate No.929 block of six. Fine to Very Fine; 2008 PF Certificate. (Scott $1,700).

Estimate: $1,500+

Minimum Bid: $750

HAWAII

32557 **#13, 1859, 2c Light Blue On Bluish White Paper.** (Used). Very rare used example. Plate 3-B, Type IX, Position 9, with a red circular Hawaii handstamp cancel and a sealed paper break at right. Very-Fine. 2008 PF Certificate. (Scott $5,000).

Estimate: $2,500+

Minimum Bid: $1,250

32558 **#29, 1869, 2c Red.** (Original Gum - Previously Hinged). Horizontal block of fifteen, fresh and vibrant, original gum, positions 3, 6-10, and 12-14 being never hinged, the balance with light evidence of previous hinging. Extremely Fine. 2008 PF Certificate. (Scott as blocks of 4 & singles $765).

Estimate: $750+

Minimum Bid: $375

New Double Overprint "Type" Discovery

32559 **#62 var, 1893, 12c Black, Double Overprint Type III.** (Used). An exceptional used example of a double overprint type previously unlisted by Scott for this issue, previously known to exist with types I and II double overprints, this incredible example is the first documented by the Philatelic Foundation with the double overprint type III where the second overprint is of light or weak strength, the stamp with trivial tiny corner creases at the bottom left. A Very Fine and most likely *unique* stamp for the specialist. 2008 PF Certificate. (Scott unlisted).

Estimate: $2,500+
Minimum Bid: $1,250

32560 **#R12, 1901, $50.00 Slate Blue & Carmine.** (Original Gum - Never Hinged). A delicate though complete mint sheet of this high value Revenue issue. Bold rich colors and detailed impression make for an eye-catching presentation, the sheet with full original gum, some stamps with small insignificant thin spots and the top selvage mostly separated from having been stuck to black mounting paper. Very Fine. 2008 PF Certificate. (Scott as singles $9,100).

Estimate: $7,500+
Minimum Bid: $3,750

32561 **#R12, 1901, $50.00 Slate Blue & Carmine.** (Original Gum - Never Hinged). Bottom left corner margin block of six with imprint in both selvages, fresh and vibrant, with unblemished full original gum. Fine to Very Fine. 2008 PF Certificate. (Scott $780).

Estimate: $1,000+
Minimum Bid: $500

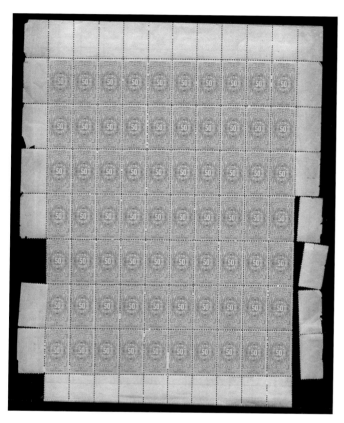

32562 #R13, 1913, 50c Yellow Orange. (Original Gum - Never Hinged). A fragile, yet complete mint sheet of 70. Bright and vivid, centering varying throughout, with a few VF-XF examples noted, and with full original gum. The entire sheet is lightly toned (from the adhesive used at the time), several stamps with small toned spots visible primarily from the reverse, and selvage tabs missing or separated at left and right. An overall Fine to Very Fine and rare sheet. 2008 PF Certificate. (Scott as singles $2,520).

Estimate: $1,500+

Minimum Bid: $750

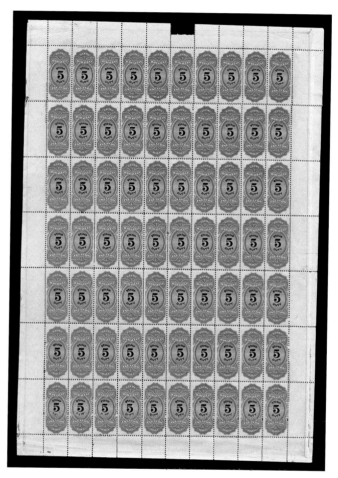

32563 #R15, 1910, $5.00 Vermilion & Violet Blue. (Original Gum - Never Hinged). An attention-grabbing complete mint sheet of 70. Bright and vibrant with full original gum; a few stamps with tiny toned spots and a few with tiny black adherences on the back. Small portion of selvage missing at top center. Extremely Fine and rare sheet. 2008 PF Certificate. (Scott as singles $7,000).

Estimate: $6,000+

Minimum Bid: $3,000

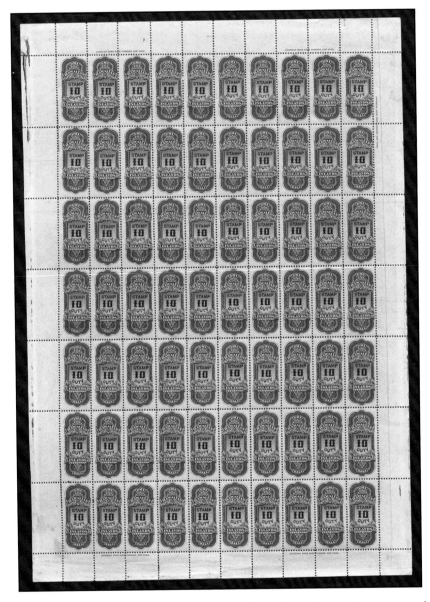

32564 #R16, 1910, $10.00 Reddish Brown & Green. (Original Gum - Never Hinged). A captivating complete mint sheet of this high value Revenue stamp. Remarkably rich and vibrant, with a few singles noted that would be of premium centering for the issue, and fresh full original gum with a few stamps with insignificant tiny toned spots. A Very Fine and rare sheet for the connoisseur of Hawaiian philately. 2008 PF Certificate. (Scott as singles $7,000).

Estimate: $10,000+

Minimum Bid: $5,000

Please visit HA.com to view other collectibles auctions.

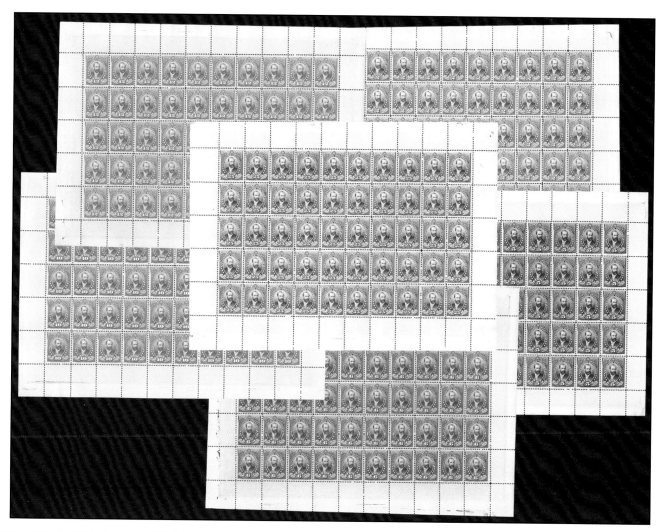

32565 #O1-6, 1896, 2c - 25c Officials. (Original Gum - Never Hinged). The Hawaii Officials issues complete as six mint Never Hinged sheets (six sheets in total), each sheet being bright and fresh, with immaculate full original gum. A Very Fine and rare set for the aficionado' of Hawaiian philately. (Scott as singles $33,250).

Estimate: $25,000+

Minimum Bid: $12,500

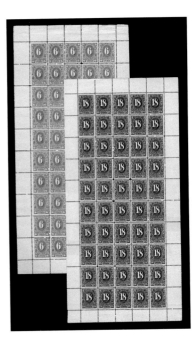

32568 **#78S, 1894, 12c Blue, Specimen.** (Original Gum - Never Hinged). Horizontal block of eight, each stamp overprinted "SPECIMEN" in red, bright and vibrant, with the plate positions penciled on the reverse. Very Fine to Extremely Fine. 2008 PF Certificate.

Estimate: $1,500+

Minimum Bid: $750

32566 **1894, 6c & 18c Kahului Railroad Parcel Stamps.** (No Gum). A complete unused pane of 50 each of the 6c red and 18c black issues, the 18c sheet with some scotch taped separations between the 6th, 7th, and 8th horizontal rows preserving the overall eye-appeal. A Fine to Very Fine pair of sheets for the specialist. Both sheets with 2008 PF Certificates. (Scott unlisted).

Estimate: $500+

Minimum Bid: $250

32569 **#80S, 1899, 1c Dark Green Specimen.** (Original Gum - Never Hinged). Vertical gutter block of four, each stamp overprinted "SPECIMEN" and with security punch hole. Very Fine. 2008 PF Certificate.

Estimate: $750+

Minimum Bid: $375

32567 **#74S, 1894, 1c Yellow, Specimen.** (Original Gum - Never Hinged). Bottom sheet margin horizontal block of eight with imprint, each stamp overprinted "SPECIMEN" in red and with security punch hole at bottom right, with plate positions penciled on the reverse. Fine to Very Fine. 2008 PF Certificate.

Estimate: $750+

Minimum Bid: $375

32570 **1860 Honolulu, Hawaii Stampless Cover.** Addressed to San Francisco, Cal., sent per the Steamer "Tornado", with red Honolulu/Hawaiian Islands postmark (MH #243.03), fancy "Ship/6" handstamp, and 1860 San Francisco receiver, the cover slightly reduced at left. Very Fine. 2008 PF Certificate.

Estimate: $1,200+

Minimum Bid: $600

32571 **#65, 1893, 2c Vermilion, "Provisional Govt. 1893" Overprint.** (Used). Horizontal pair tied on locally carried cover by Honolulu first class mail duplex cancel (Type 231.72), the cover with a horizontal opening tear at top. Very Fine. 2008 PF Certificate. (Scott $525).

Estimate: $500+

Minimum Bid: $250

PHILIPPINES

32572 **#229, 1904, 4c Brown, XF 90 PF.** (Original Gum - Never Hinged). Magnificent, with rich color and fresh gum. Extremely Fine. 2008 PF Graded Certificate. (Scott as Very Fine $175).

Estimate: $500+

Minimum Bid: $250

32573 **#232, 1903, 8c Violet Black, XF 90 PF.** (Original Gum - Never Hinged). Amazingly fresh and attractive with vibrant color, a sharp impression, and Post Office fresh gum. Extremely Fine. 2008 PF Graded Certificate. (Scott for Very Fine $125).

Estimate: $500+

Minimum Bid: $250

32574 **#234VAR, 1903, 13c Purple Black.** (No Gum). Exciting unused horizontal pair of this rare red "O.B." overprint variety. Unlisted by Scott. Very Fine. 2008 PF Certificate.

Estimate: $600+

Minimum Bid: $300

32575 **#236, 1894, 10c Vermilion.** (No Gum). Handsome and rare unused pair with red "O.B." overprint, both stamps with faint creases. Very Fine. 2008 PF Certificate.

Estimate: $500+

Minimum Bid: $250

32576 **#J7, 1901, 50c Deep Claret.** (Original Gum - Previously Hinged). Scarce Philippines mint bottom right sheet corner margin block of four. Only 2,140 stamps issued. Rich and bold with some perforation separations on the right top margin and reinforced perforations throughout the block. Fine to Very Fine. 2008 PF Certificate. (Scott as singles $1,000).

Estimate: $500+

Minimum Bid: $250

CANADA & PROVINCES - NEWFOUNDLAND

32577 **Unitrade #2 (Scott #2), 1857, 2p Scarlet Vermilion.** (No Gum). A very presentable unused example of this rare 2 pence from the Heraldic Flowers issue, with fresh color and narrow margins: two being clear margins and two just in at top and bottom: otherwise a sound stamp of fine appearance. Fine. Signed A Brun on reverse. 2002 Sismondo Certificate & 1959 RPS Certificate. (Unitrade CAN $10,000/Scott $17,500).

Estimate: $3,000+

Minimum Bid: $1,500

32578 **Unitrade #4 (Scott #4), 1857, 4p Scarlet Vermilion.** (Used). A used example of this scarce 4 pence Heraldic Flowers issue, canceled by bars with narrow margins just barely clear on all 4 sides (minute corner crease) otherwise fault free and very collectible. Reverse bears *Thier's* expert mark. Fine. 2002 Sismondo Certificate. (Unitrade CAN$3,000 / Scott $3,750).

Estimate: $1,500+

Minimum Bid: $750

32579 **Unitrade #7 (Scott #7), 1857, 6½p Scarlet Vermilion.** (No Gum). A fresh unused example (without gum) of this scarce 6½ pence Heraldic Flowers issue with fresh Scarlet Vermillion color and 2 close, 1 enormous margin the fourth margin just cutting in at base: otherwise fault free a very collectible example of this difficult stamp. Fine; 2002 Sismondo Certificate. (Unitrade CAN$3,000 / Scott $4,500).

Estimate: $800+

Minimum Bid: $400

CANADA

A CHOICE EXAMPLE OF THE RARE "BLACK BROWN" SHADE OF THE 10C

32580 **Unitrade #16 (Scott #16), 1859, 10c Black Brown.** (Used). A choice used example of this rare "Black Brown" Prince Albert issue with deep rich color, neat unobtrusive cancel and VF centering for the issue: an exceptional example accompanied by a clear 2008 Greene Foundation Certificate. (Unitrade CAN $8,000).

Estimate: $4,000+

Minimum Bid: $2,000

32581 **Unitrade #28i (Scott #28var), 1868, 12½c Milky Blue, VF-XF 85 PF.** (Original Gum - Previously Hinged). An impressive mint example of this scarce "Large Queen" with rich color and hinged OG (hinge remnant). Unpunched perf at bottom. An exceptional stamp. Very Fine - Extremely Fine. 2007 PF Graded Certificate. (Unitrade CAN$3,000).

Estimate: $1,800+

Minimum Bid: $900

32582 **Unitrade #30b (Scott #30b), 1868, 15c Blue Gray.** (Original Gum - Previously Hinged). An impressive mint top sheet margin strip of four, with full imprint, of the 15c "Large Queen" in the scarce blue gray shade, having fresh color and hinged or lightly hinged OG. Very scarce and Unpriced as such. Very Fine to Extremely Fine. 2008 PF Certificate. (Unitrade as singles CAN$1,200).

Estimate: $800+

Minimum Bid: $400

32583 **Unitrade #36iii (Scott #36var), 1870, 2c Deep Green On Yellowish Paper.** (Used). A superb Imperforate Pair of this "Small Queen" (Ottawa) issue neatly tied on piece of 2c surcharged postal stationery with large margins all round, fresh color and neat Jan 25 circular date stamps. A very scarce usage listed but unpriced in Unitrade and unlisted in Scott. Extremely Fine to Superb. 2005 Greene Foundation Certificate.

Estimate: $600+

Minimum Bid: $300

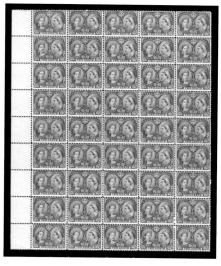

32584 Unitrade #43 (Scott #43), 1888, 6c Red Brown XF 90 XQ PF. (Original Gum - Previously Hinged). A choice mint bottom sheet margin example, with rich color and full very lightly hinged OG - an exceptional example Graded as XF 90 XQ ("Exceptional Quality"). 2008 PF Graded Certificate. (Unitrade for Very Fine CAN$250).

Estimate: $500+

Minimum Bid: $250

32585 Unitrade #51 (Scott #51), 1897, 1c Orange. (Original Gum - Never Hinged). A superb mint 5x10 block of 50 with left sheet margin, having fresh color and full clean never hinged OG, except for positions 46 & 47 which are previously hinged, (7 stamps at upper left have a natural gum crease) otherwise a very spectacular and scarce multiple. Fine to Very Fine. 2008 PF Certificate. (Unitrade as singles CAN$4,380).

Estimate: $3,000+

Minimum Bid: $1,500

32586 #52, 1897, 2c Green. (Original Gum - Never Hinged). A superb mint 5x9 block of 45 with left sheet margin, having fresh color and full clean never hinged OG, except for position 45 which is previously hinged, (position 18 with a tiny thin spot) otherwise a very spectacular and scarce multiple. Very Fine to Extremely Fine. 2008 PF Certificate. (Unitrade as singles CAN$4,655).

Estimate: $2,500+

Minimum Bid: $1,250

UNLISTED VARIETY

32587 Unitrade #56 var (Scott #56 var), 1897, 8c Dark Violet. (Original Gum - Never Hinged). A superb mint corner marginal example showing the variety "extended frameline" (unlisted in both Unitrade and Scott) with rich color, enormous well balanced margins and full clean OG. Exceptional and rare thus. Extremely Fine to Superb. 2008 PF Certificate and 1979 Greene Foundation Certificate.

Estimate: $4,500+

Minimum Bid: $2,250

32588 Unitrade #63 (Scott #63), 1897, $3 Yellow Bister. (Original Gum - Never Hinged). A superb mint example of the $3 Jubilee with fresh color & full never hinged original gum, an exceptional example. Extremely Fine. 2007 Greene Foundation Certificate. (Unitrade CAN$6,000).

Estimate: $3,500+

Minimum Bid: $1,750

32589 Unitrade #65 (Scott #65), 1897, $5 Olive Green. (Original Gum - Never Hinged). A very fresh and attractive mint example of the $5 Jubilee with rich color and full never hinged OG quite exceptional and very scarce thus. Very Fine. 2007 Greene Foundation Certificate. (Unitrade CAN$6,000).

Estimate: $3,500+

Minimum Bid: $1,750

32590 Unitrade #71 (Scott #71), 1897, 6c Brown. (Original Gum - Never Hinged). A superb mint example of this 6c Maple Leaf issue beautifully centered within very large to jumbo margins, with deep rich color and full never hinged Original Gum.
Extremely Fine to Superb. 2006 Greene Foundation Certificate. (Unitrade CAN$525).

Estimate: $300+

Minimum Bid: $150

32591 Unitrade #72 (Scott #72), 1897, 8c Orange. (Original Gum - Never Hinged). A magnificent mint example of this scarce 8c maple leaf issue with vibrant color, very well centered between four particularly large margins. Very Fine to Extremely Fine. 2008 PF Certificate. (Unitrade $1,050).

Estimate: $600+

Minimum Bid: $300

32592 Unitrade #77d (Scott #77d), 1899, 2c Carmine. (No Gum As Issued). A spectacular block of four of the imperforate 2c "numeral" issue in the rare Die II with bright colors and large margins all round (without gum as issued). Very Fine to Extremely Fine. 2008 PF Certificate. (Unitrade as pairs CAN$5,000).

Estimate: $2,000+

Minimum Bid: $1,000

32593 Unitrade #80a (Scott #80a), 1898, 6c Brown. (Original Gum - Previously Hinged). A very fresh and attractive mint imperforate pair of the 6c QV numeral issue with rich color, enormous balanced margins and hinged OG (right hand stamp with natural internal crease), an excellent example of this rare stamp of which only 200 were printed. Very Fine Very Fine to Extremely Fine. 2008 PF Certificate. (Unitrade CAN$1,500).

Estimate: $900+

Minimum Bid: $450

32594 Unitrade #83ii (Scott #83var), 1898, 10c Brown Violet. (No Gum As Issued). A magnificent mint imperforate pair of this scarce 10c numeral issue (without gum as issued) with deep rich color, enormous margins including right sheet margin printed on clean never hinged paper. An exceptional pair. Extremely Fine to Superb. 2008 PF Certificate. (Unitrade CAN$1,250).

Estimate: $1,000+

Minimum Bid: $500

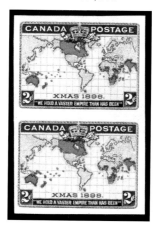

32595 Unitrade #85a (Scott #85a), 1898, 2c Black, Lavender & Carmine. (No Gum As Issued). A choice unused pair of this scarce Imperial Penny Postage issue imperforate vertically with fresh colors, enormous margins printed on clean, fresh paper (without gum as issued) Only 200 stamps issued. Very Fine to Extremely Fine. 2008 PF Certificate. (Unitrade CAN$700).

Estimate: $400+

Minimum Bid: $200

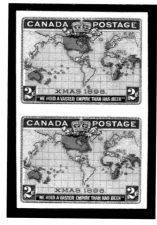

32596 Unitrade #86bii (Scott #86b var), 1898, 2c Black, Deep Blue & Carmine. (No Gum As Issued). A magnificent mint imperforate vertical pair of this popular Imperial Penny Postage issue (without gum - as issued) in the deeper blue shade, with rich colors, very large margins all round and clean, fresh paper. Very Fine to Extremely Fine. 2008 PF Certificate. (Unitrade CAN$700).

Estimate: $475+

Minimum Bid: $238

32597 Unitrade #89-91 (Scott #89-91), 1903, 1c - 5c. (Original Gum - Never Hinged). A choice mint selection of 3 of these scarce ED VII issues, comprising the 1c -5c with fresh colors and full never hinged OG. Extremely Fine. (Unitrade CAN$1,230).

Estimate: $500+

Minimum Bid: $250

32598 Unitrade #104-22 (Scott #104-22), 1911-25, 1c - $1. (Original Gum - Never Hinged). Complete set (20) of George V "Admiral" issue in blocks of four, including #'s 112a and 117ii, bright and fresh, the 10c plum block with trivial tiny scattered printing ink smears that are not immediately apparent when looking at the block. Fine to Very Fine. (Unitrade as singles CAN$20,820).

Estimate: $10,000+

Minimum Bid: $5,000

32599 Unitrade #125-30 (Scott #125-30), 1912-24, 1c - 3c. (Original Gum - Never Hinged). A superb mint complete set of 6 of the GV Admiral coil pairs perforated 8 vertically with rich colors, fresh. Very Fine to Extremely Fine. (Unitrade CAN$1,455).

Estimate: $500+

Minimum Bid: $250

32600 Unitrade #136-38 (Scott #136-38), 1924, 1c-3c. (Original Gum - Never Hinged). A superb mint set (3) of these scarce GV Admiral imperforate issues in spectacular blocks of 4 with fresh colors Fresh. Extremely Fine. (Unitrade as pairs CAN$1,000).

Estimate: $500+

Minimum Bid: $250

32601 **Unitrade #217-27 (Scott #217-27), 1935, 1c - $1.** (Original Gum - Never Hinged). Complete set (11) of the George V Pictorial issue in mint blocks of four, fresh and vibrant. Very Fine. (Unitrade as singles CAN$1,282).

Estimate: $500+

Minimum Bid: $250

OFFICIAL ISSUES

32602 **Unitrade #O1-10 (Scott #O1-10), 1949-50, 1c - $1.** (Original Gum - Never Hinged). War and Peace complete set (9), in mint blocks of four, all especially well centered within large well balanced margins, bright and fresh. Extremely Fine. (Catalog #05 does not exist). (Unitrade as singles CAN$1,408).

Estimate: $750+

Minimum Bid: $375

AIRMAIL ISSUES

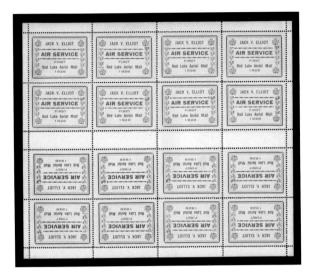

32603 **Unitrade #CL7c (Scott #CL7), 1926, 25c Red On Yellow.** (Original Gum - Never Hinged). An impressive complete tete-beche gutter sheet of 16 of the 25c Jack Elliot Private Airline etiquette with fresh colors and full clean never hinged OG: spectacular and very scarce thus. Extremely Fine to Superb; 2008 PF Certificate. (Unitrade CAN$3,000).

Estimate: $3,500+

Minimum Bid: $1,750

32604 **Unitrade #CL12e (Scott #CL12b), 1926, 25c Ultramarine.** (Original Gum - Never Hinged). A superb mint example of this scarce Fairchild Private Airmail carrier in a full sheet of 10 with 5 tete beche pairs, having rich color and full clean never hinged OG. Very scarce and desirable. Very Fine to Extremely Fine. 2008 PF Certificate. (Unitrade CAN$3,375).

Estimate: $2,000+

Minimum Bid: $1,000

PROOFS & ESSAYS

SCARCE PRIVATE AIR COMPANY PROOF SETS WITH VARIETIES

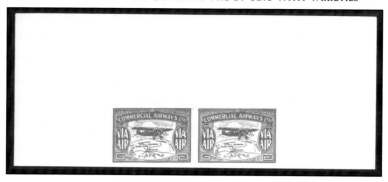

32605 Unitrade #CL47i, 47iv (Scott unlisted), 1929, Commercial Airways Ltd. (No Gum As Issued). A very fresh and attractive complete set of 8 pairs of these scarce Northern Alberta & Northwest Territories Private Air company proofs printed on card without gum as issued. Each pair showing the variety "broken "C" in the adjacent pair: All with bright colors and enormous margins. Very Scarce and Unusual. Extremely Fine to Superb. (Unitrade CAN$4,200).

Estimate: $3,000+

Minimum Bid: $1,500

SCARCE SET OF PRIVATE AIR COMPANY PROOF PAIRS

32606 Unitrade #CL47iii (Scott unlisted), 1929, Commercial Airways Ltd. (No Gum As Issued). A fresh and attractive complete set of 6, very scarce Alberta & Northwest Territories private Air Company "Air Fee" proofs pairs printed on card, without gum as issued. Fresh colors, and enormous margins. Interesting and unusual. Extremely Fine. (Unitrade CAN$3,000).

Estimate: $2,400+

Minimum Bid: $1,200

32607 Unitrade #50-65P (Scott #50-65P), 1897, 1c - $5 Plate Proofs. A complete set (16) Jubilee Plate Proofs as vertical pairs. Fresh and clean, with large margins all around. Very Fine to Extremely Fine. (Unitrade CAN$12,020).

Estimate: $6,000+

Minimum Bid: $3,000

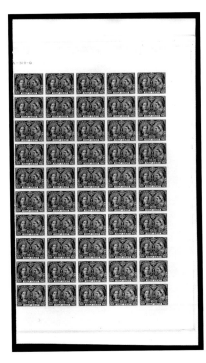

32608 **Unitrade #50P (Scott #50P3), 1897, ½c Black, Plate Proof.** A magnificent plate proof of the ½c Jubilee in a half sheet of 50, mounted on card with rich color and enormous margins - spectacular and a very scarce multiple. Extremely Fine. 2008 PF Certificate. (Unitrade as singles CAN$3,750).

Estimate: $2,200+

Minimum Bid: $1,100

32610 **Unitrade #52P (Scott #52P3), 1897, 2c Green, Plate Proof.** A magnificent plate proof of the 2c Jubilee in a half sheet of 50, mounted on card with rich color and enormous margins, spectacular and a very scarce multiple. Extremely Fine. 2008 PF Certificate. (Unitrade as singles CAN$2,500).

Estimate: $1,300+

Minimum Bid: $650

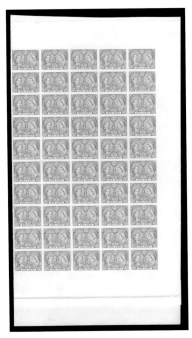

32609 **Unitrade #51P (Scott #51P3), 1897, 1c Orange, Plate Proof.** A magnificent plate proof of the 1c Jubilee in a half sheet of 50, mounted on card with rich color and enormous margins - spectacular and a very scarce multiple. Extremely Fine. 2008 PF Certificate. (Unitrade as singles CAN$2,500).

Estimate: $1,300+

Minimum Bid: $650

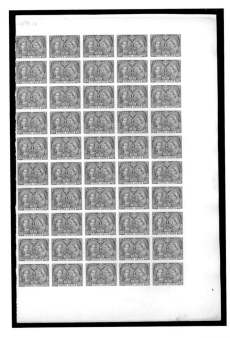

32611 **Unitrade #53P (Scott #53P4), 1897, 3c Bright Rose, Plate Proof** A magnificent plate proof of the 3c Jubilee in a half sheet of 50, mounted on card with rich color and enormous margins (positions 1, 6 & 11 with slight edge faults at left) - nevertheless a spectacular and scarce multiple. Extremely Fine. 2008 PF Certificate. (Unitrade as singles CAN$2,000).

Estimate: $1,200+

Minimum Bid: $600

32612 Unitrade #54P (Scott #54P), 1897, 5c Deep Blue, Plate Proof. A magnificent plate proof of the 5c Jubilee in a half sheet of 50, mounted on card with rich color and enormous margins (positions 41 & 46 with edge faults) - nevertheless spectacular and a very scarce multiple. Very Fine to Extremely Fine. 2008 PF Certificate. (Unitrade as singles CAN$3,750).

Estimate: $1,800+

Minimum Bid: $900

32613 Unitrade #62P (Scott #62P3), 1897, $2.00 Dark Purple, Plate Proof. A superb Plate Proof of the $2 Jubilee issue, in a magnificent block of 10, mounted on card with rich color and excellent margins including left and right sheet margins. An exceptional and rare multiple. Extremely Fine to Superb; 2008 PF Certificate. (Unitrade as singles CAN$7,000).

Estimate: $4,500+

Minimum Bid: $2,250

32614 Unitrade #63P (Scott #63P3), 1897, $3.00 Yellow Bister, Plate Proof A superb Plate Proof of the $3 Jubilee issue, in a magnificent block of 10, mounted on card with rich color and excellent margins including left and right sheet margins. An exceptional and rare multiple. Extremely Fine to Superb. 2008 PF Certificate. (Unitrade as singles CAN$7,000).

Estimate: $4,500+

Minimum Bid: $2,250

32615 Unitrade #64P (Scott #64P3), 1897, $4.00 Purple, Plate Proof. A superb Plate Proof of the $4 Jubilee issue, in a magnificent block of 10, mounted on card with rich color and excellent margins including left and right sheet margins. An exceptional and rare multiple. Very Fine to Extremely Fine. 2008 PF Certificate. (Unitrade as singles CAN$7,000).

Estimate: $4,500+

Minimum Bid: $2,250

A Rare Plate Proof of the $5 Jubilee in a Margin Block of 10

32616 Unitrade #65P (Scott #65P3), 1897, $5.00 Olive Green, Plate Proof. A choice Plate Proof of the $5 Jubilee issue in an impressive right and left margin block of 10 (5x2), printed on India, card mounted: without gum as issued. A rare multiple. Superb. 2008 PF Certificate. (Unitrade as singles CAN$7,000).

Estimate: $4,500+

Minimum Bid: $2,250

32617 Unitrade #66-73P (Scott #66-73P), 1897, ½c - 10c, Plate Proofs. A complete set of these scarce QV maple leaf issues in Plate Proofs mounted on card, each in magnificent block of four, with large margins and rich colors. A very scarce set. Extremely Fine to Superb. (Unitrade as singles CAN$8,000).

Estimate: $6,000+

Minimum Bid: $3,000

32618 Unitrade #74-84P (Scott #74-84P), 1898, ½c - 20c, Plate Proofs. A very fresh complete set of 10 of QV Numeral issue, each in a magnificent Plate Proof blocks of 4, all with bright colors and enormous margins. Extremely Fine. (Unitrade as singles CAN$16,000).

Estimate: $9,000+

Minimum Bid: $4,500

32619 Unitrade #217-27P (Scott #217-27P), 1935, 1c - $1 Plate Proofs. A superb set of plate proofs on card of this scarce GV pictorial issue featuring the Champlain monument, each in a magnificent cross gutter block of 4, with fresh colors, enormous margins all round and a spectacular "Post Office Fresh" group. Extremely Fine to Superb. (Unitrade as regular pairs CAN$7,000).

Estimate: $4,500+

Minimum Bid: $2,250

CANADA - POSTAL HISTORY AIRMAIL ISSUES

UNUSUAL & RARE AERO CLUB OF CANADA SPECIAL STAMP ON ILLUSTRATED FLIGHT COVER

32620 #CLP1, 1918, 25c Black & Red. (Used). A charming and unusual Pictorial cover whose reverse shows views of Ottawa and is additionally franked with a sound example of the rare "Aero Club of Canada First Flight" special stamp. Appropriately canceled with the violet Toronto Flight cachet. The front bears a (slightly faulty) single War Tax stamp, (Sc Mr4). The cover is toned (with small faults): nevertheless a rare unusual Canadian Postal History item (only 167 of the Aero Club stamps extant). Fine to Very Fine. 2008 PF Certificate.

Estimate: $3,000+

Minimum Bid: $1,500

32621 #CLP1, 1918, 25c Black & Red. (Used). A very scarce Aero Flight of Canada, 1st flight cover sent to Toronto with blue green " By Aeroplane Aug 27, 1918 Ottawa Canada" cachet at top center, a single 2c (MR4) tax stamp at right and blue receiving stamp at left: the reverse bears a faulty (25c) Semi Official Stamp tied by purple flight cachet and Exhibition and appropriate arrival stamps. A colorful and very scarce Semi Official Flight cover. Fine to Very Fine; 2008 PF Certificate.

Estimate: $2,000+

Minimum Bid: $1,000

RARE AERO CLUB OF CANADA SEMI-OFFICIAL STAMP ON 1ST FLIGHT COVER

32622 #CLP2, 1918, 25c Black & Red. (Used). The rare Aero Club of Canada 25c Semi Official stamp (with numerals of value) tied to 1st Flight cover addressed to Ottawa with Toronto 1918 Duplex cancel, reverse shows violet Ottawa "Dead Letter Office" and "Returned for Additional Postage" handstamps, requiring the additional 2c Tax stamp (MR4) which was later affixed to the front (The semi Official stamp is creased and the cover has faults) nevertheless a very desirable Airmail & Postal History item. Very Fine. 2008 PF Certificate.

Estimate: $4,000+

Minimum Bid: $2,000

RARE MOOSE JAW FLYING CLUB STAMP ON COVER

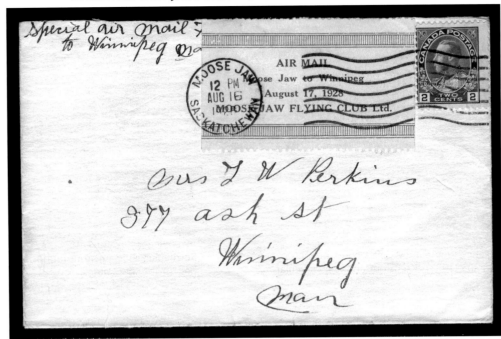

32623 **#CLP7, 1927, $1.00 Red.** (Used). A superb example of the rare "Moose Jaw Fling Club "special flight" stamp together with single 2c green (#207), both neatly tied on small clean cover by neat Moose Jaw Sask Aug 16 cancel, and addressed to Winnipeg Man, with appropriate Aug 17, 1928 receiving mark on reverse. Very rare and possibly unique. Very Fine to Extremely Fine. 2008 PF Certificate.

Estimate: $4,500+

Minimum Bid: $2,250

EXTREMELY RARE NORTHERN AIR SERVICE FIRST FLIGHT

32624 **Unitrade #CL5, 1925, Northern Air Service.** A very fresh and attractive small 1st flight cover, being *one of only eight* carried on the Northern Air Service experimental flight to Haileybury Ont, Rouyn Lake Ont, with appropriate "First Experimental Flight from Rouyn lake to Haileybury", violet handstamp and further franked with the 1c & 2c regular issues (Sc105,107), both canceled with May 18th 1925 CDS: accompanied by a sworn affidavit certifying that this is one of the eight covers that were carried on this flight. A very scarce 1st flight cover. (Noted but un-priced in Unitrade or Scott). Extremely Fine. 2008 PF Certificate.

Estimate: $3,250+

Minimum Bid: $1,625

32625 **Unitrade #CL5, 107VAR, 1922-25, Northern Air Service.** An attractive "First Flight" franked by a single 2c and a diagonally bisected 2c (Scott 107 var) both neatly tied to cover by Rouyn Lake; June 27 1925 cancels, addressed to Richmond Hill ONT; the reverse bears a Northern Air Service etiquette (CL5) canceled by Haileybury ONT Pmk and First Flight cachet and is further signed by Pilot: BW Broach. Very scarce and unusual. Very Fine. 2008 PF Certificate.

Estimate: $1,800+

Minimum Bid: $900

SCARCE FAIRCHILD PRIVATE AIRMAIL TETE-BECHE PAIR ON COVER.

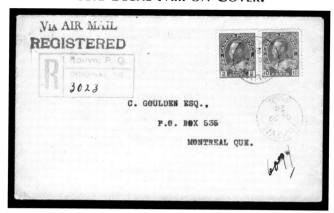

32626 Unitrade #CL11a, 1926, 25c Deep Blue. (Used). A superb First Flight / Registered Airmail cover bearing 2c & 10c regular issue (107,118) on front and a spectacular tete - beche pair of the 25c blue Fairchild Private Airline stamp on the reverse. Canceled by Rouyn PQ Oct 22 / 26 CDS and with violet First flight Cachet signed by Pilot. Spectacular & Scarce. Extremely Fine. 2008 PF Certificate.

Estimate: $1,200+

Minimum Bid: $600

RARE PATRICIA AIRWAYS IMPERF - BETWEEN AIRMAIL PAIR ON COVER

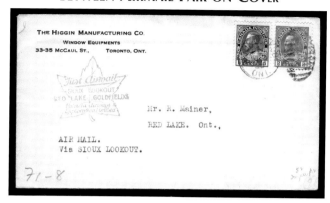

32627 Unitrade #CL13a, 1913, 25c Yellow Green. (Used). A magnificent private Airmail cover bearing a single 2c & 5c regular issue on front and a rare Imperf - between pair of the 25c Patricia Airways Private Airmail stamps on reverse, both canceled by Red Lake ONT Jul 7 / 1926 CDS. Blue leaf shaped commemorative cancel on front and reverse, Spectacular & rare since only 4 such covers are believed to be extant. Extremely Fine; 2008 PF Certificate.

Estimate: $3,500+

Minimum Bid: $1,750

GREAT BRITAN

REGULAR ISSUES

A MAGIFICENT EXAMPLE OF THE 1D BLACK & WORLD'S 1ST STAMP

32628 Stanley Gibbons #1 (Scott #1), 1840, May, 1p Black, XF-S 95 PF. (Used). A superb used example of the famous 1d black from plate 2 (lettered MK) in the scarcer intense black shade with four enormous margins. Neat Red Maltese Cross cancellation. Extremely Fine to Superb. 2007 PF Graded Certificate. (Stanley Gibbons £425).

Estimate: $950+

Minimum Bid: $475

A MAGNIFICENT MINT PAIR
FAMOUS 2D BLUE

32629 Stanley Gibbons #5 (Scott #2), 1840, 2p Blue. (Original Gum - Hinged). A magnificent mint pair of the famous 2d Blue; the world's second stamp. This scarce pair sports four large well-balanced margins and fabulously deep rich color, with full fresh original gum showing only very light traces of a prior hinging using the large side of the hinge, a few trivial small natural gum skips not mentioned on the certificates, and an inconsequential small natural inclusion above the letter "L" of the left stamp. An overall exceptional example, rare in all respects. Extremely Fine to Superb. 2008 Brandon Certificate and 2008 PF Certificate. (Stanley Gibbons as singles £54,000 / Scott $65,000).

Estimate: $35,000+
Minimum Bid: $17,500

32630 Stanley Gibbons #ES11d (Scott #4), 1841, 2p Blue. (No Gum). A very attractive unused example, Plate 3, (without gum) of this scarce second 2d issue with white lines added (lettered PB) with rich color and four enormous margins (small scissor cut in upper margin clear of design) otherwise quite superb & fault free. 2008 Brandon Certificate and 2008 PF Certificate. (Stanley Gibbons £4,250).

Estimate: $1,000+
Minimum Bid: $500

32631 Stanley Gibbons #4 (Scott #2), 1840, 2p Deep Blue. (Partial Original Gum). A fresh mint example of this rare stamp (lettered BJ) in die 1 with deep rich color, four clear to good margins, and what the certificates note as "small part original gum", that small part being approximately a 50/50 scattered mix of original gum and prior hinging marks. Fault free & Fine to Very Fine; 2008 Brandon Certificate, as well as 2008 Sismondo and 2002 Philatelic Expertising:GB Certificates. (Stanley Gibbons £35,000 / Scott $17,500).

Estimate: $7,500+
Minimum Bid: $3,750

32632 Stanley Gibbons #ES14 (Scott #4), 1849, 2p Blue. (Original Gum - Hinged). A fresh mint example of this very scarce 2d imperforate issue Lettered QF (Plate 4 with white lines) with good color and original gum that shows light traces of prior hinging at the top, including some trivial small bits of hinge remnant. Fine to Very Fine. 2008 Brandon Certificate and 2008 PF Certificate. (Stanley Gibbons £4,250).

Estimate: $1,000+
Minimum Bid: $500

GREAT BRITAIN 1858 1D RED COMPLETE
PLATE #'s 71- 225

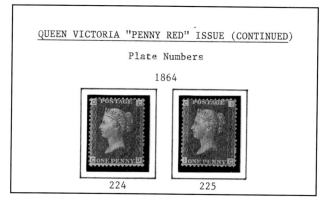

32633 Stanley Gibbons #43-44 (Scott #33), 1858, 1d red. (Original Gum - Hinged). A remarkable entirely mint collection of all the 153 stamps that comprise the complete issue of 1d red plate numbers from #71 - # 225 (ex #77) all very fresh and fine with hinged or often lightly hinged OG - a very scarce and VF group for the advanced collector. Very Fine to Extremely Fine. 2008 Brandon Certificate. (Stanley Gibbons £12,343).

Estimate: $8,500+
Minimum Bid: $4,250

An exceptional complete plating of the 2d blue P.14 issue

32634 Stanley Gibbons #45-47 (Scott #29-30), 1858, 2d Blue. (Original Gum - Hinged). A mint complete plating of the 1858 2d blue issue, P. 14 with white lines added comprising 7 stamps (plates 7-15), generally with fresh colors, and lightly hinged or hinged OG. (Couple of small hinge remnants and natural gum creases) otherwise overall fresh and fine and a rare grouping. Fine to Very Fine. (Stanley Gibbons £5,970).

Estimate: $1,800+

Minimum Bid: $900

A complete plating of 15 stamps including the Rare Plate 9

32635 Stanley Gibbons #48 (Scott #58), 1870, 1/2p Rose. (Original Gum - Hinged). A very fresh complete plating of 15 stamps of this scarce issue all generally with good color and full clean hinged or lightly hinged OG some natural gum creases common to the issue otherwise Very Fine. 2008 Brandon Certificate for the plate 9. (Stanley Gibbons £8,000).

Estimate: $3,500+

Minimum Bid: $1,750

32636 Stanley Gibbons #118 (Scott #55), 1867, 2sh Blue. (Partial Original Gum). A fresh mint example of this scarce stamp (Plate 1) with rich color and part OG (small hinge remnant and small surface scuff on Queens neck) Very Fine; 2008 Brandon Certificate. (Stanley Gibbons £2,800).

Estimate: $700+

Minimum Bid: $350

32637 Stanley Gibbons #187-96 (Scott #98-107), 1883, 1/2p - 1sh. (Original Gum - Hinged). An exceptionally bright and fresh set of 10 of these scarce issues each with good color and previously hinged or lightly hinged OG. Very Fine. (Stanley Gibbons £4,020).

Estimate: $1,700+

Minimum Bid: $850

32638 Stanley Gibbons #180 (Scott #108), 1884, 5sh Carmine Rose. (Original Gum - Hinged). A very fresh and attractive mint example of this scarce stamp with rich color and original gum with three remnants from a large hinge and some small inconsequential adherences most likely from an album page. Also noted is a trivial tiny gum crease in lower margin, primarily visible under close examination of the reverse. An overall Very Fine to Extremely Fine and desirable example. 2008 Brandon Certificate and 2008 PF Certificate. (Stanley Gibbons £950).

Estimate: $450+

Minimum Bid: $225

32639 Stanley Gibbons #183 (Scott #109), 1884, 10sh Ultramarine. (Original Gum - Hinged). A very fresh and attractive mint example of this scarce stamp with bright color and original gum with scattered remnants from two larger hinges and a couple inconsequential small adherences that appear to be from having been slightly stuck down on an album page at some point. Also noted is a minor natural gum crease that does not detract from the overall appearance. Very Fine to Extremely Fine and choice. 2008 Brandon Certificate and 2008 PF Certificate. (Stanley Gibbons £2,000).

Estimate: $1,000+

Minimum Bid: $500

32640 Stanley Gibbons #404 (Scott #176a), 1913, £1 Dull Blue Green. (Used). A sound used example of the very scarce 1 Pound Seahorse in the scarcer dull blue green shade with good color and neat unobtrusive CDS. Fault free & Fine; 2008 Brandon Certificate. (Stanley Gibbons £1,500).

Estimate: $750+

Minimum Bid: $375

A RARE & UNUSUAL MULREADY WITH
ILLUSTRATED ADDRESS

32641 1840, 1p Black, Mulready Stereo A236 Form 6. (Used). An interesting and usage of the 1d Mulready letter sheet with illustrated address in the form of a label and two 1d coins addressed to Gloster (misspelt) with Ipswich & Gloucester receiving marks. Some reinforcement along folds and a little soiled nevertheless very scarce & unusual. Very Fine to Extremely Fine. 2008 PF Certificate.

Estimate: $3,000+

Minimum Bid: $1,500

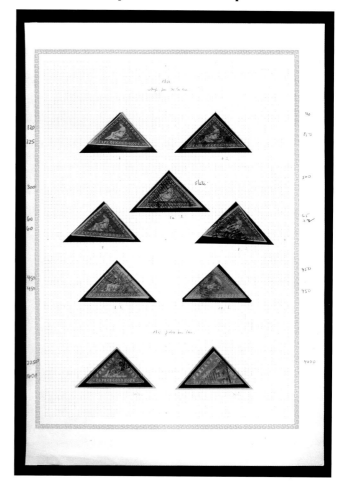

32642 1853-64, Cape of Good Hope Triangles Advanced Collection. A fairly advanced and quite specialized essentially used collection of these scarce and popular "Cape Triangles" all neatly mounted on 6 Quadrille pages. The collection includes singles, pairs, blocks, shades and some varieties. Of particular a note are a number of three margined examples of the 1d from the 1853 issues on blue paper, notably a superb pair (SG 3b) with watermark sideways (2008 Brandon cert), a fine block of 4 of the 4d blue on deeply blued paper (SG2) couple of small faults (2008 Brandon cert) and a fine showing of the succeeding issues including examples of the 1d, 4d (including a steel blue (2008 Brandon cert) the 6d & 1s with shades from all the printers. Last but not least, are examples of the 1d & 2d "Woodblocks", both of fine appearance: the 1d with small faults and the 2d rebacked (both with 2008 Brandon certs). A total of 47 items (not counting two reference items) with several scarce and even rare stamps and very high catalog value. Some faults as to be expected but overall a fine collection for which closer inspection by a specialist could prove rewarding. Fine to Very Fine. (Stanley Gibbons £10,000 +).

Estimate: $4,500+

Minimum Bid: $2,250

THE RARE COGH 1D ERROR OF COLOR

32643 Stanley Gibbons #13c (Scott #7d), 1861, 1p 1P Pale Blue (Error). (Used). A used example of the rare Cape Triangle, 1d error of color: printed in pale blue instead of Vermillion. The stamp has a tiny sealed tear on first "O" of Good and two somewhat close margins, the third being cut into at base: nevertheless a very collectible example of this world class rarity of which only a few exist. Fine. 2008 Brandon Certificate, also 2008 Sismondo and 1952 BPA Certificates. (Stanley Gibbons £28,000).

> **Estimate: $8,000+**
> **Minimum Bid: $4,000**

THE RARE COGH 4D ERROR OF COLOR

32644 Stanley Gibbons #14e (Scott #9f), 1861, 4p 4P Vermilion (Error). (Used). A very presentable used example of this rare Cape Triangle being the 4d error of color printed in Vermillion instead of Blue. The stamp has good color and close margins (and as with most of the few that exist has small faults, such as small tears and pressed out creases), nevertheless of very fine appearance and a better than average example of this world class rarity. Fine to Very Fine. 2008 Brandon Certificate and 2007 Sismondo Certificate. (Stanley Gibbons £40,000).

> **Estimate: $10,000+**
> **Minimum Bid: $5,000**

BRITISH GUIANA
AN ATTRACTIVE EXAMPLE OF THE 4C MAGENTA FROM THIS LEGENDARY ISSUE

32645 Stanley Gibbons #24 (Scott #14), 1856, 4c Magenta. (Used). An attractive used example of this legendary British Guiana 4c "Ship" issue bearing manuscript initials E.D.W (E.D. Wright, Postmaster) with all printed letters complete within clear margins, cut octagonally as usual and canceled by neat Berbice AU 1856 CDS (2 1/2 mm sealed tear at upper left, some thins on the reverse and a few surface abrasions) all common to this difficult and delicate issue: nevertheless very fine appearance and a quite desirable example of this popular rarity. Fine. 2008 Sismondo Certificate and 1972 PF certificate. (Stanley Gibbons £8,500 / Scott $16,000).

Estimate: $3,500+

Minimum Bid: $1,750

MAURITIUS
A SUPERB EXAMPLE OF THE LEGENDARY 1D MAURITIUS EARLIEST IMPRESSION

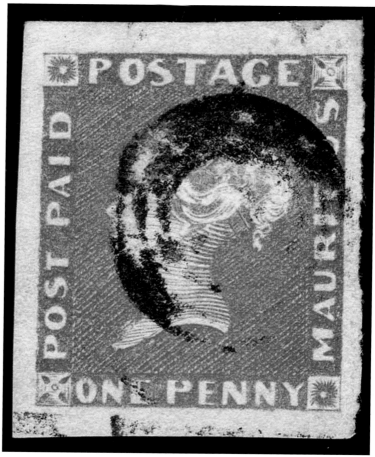

32646 Stanley Gibbons #3 (Scott #3), 1848, 1p Orange. (Used). A superb used example of this early Mauritius 1d in the Orange Vermillion shade, being the earliest impression (plate 2) with vibrant rich color, four enormous margins and 3 ring numeral "1"cancellation: a truly magnificent and fault free example of this legendary rarity. Superb. 2008 Brandon Certificate, also 2008 Sismondo and 1981 RPS Certificates. (Stanley Gibbons £14,000 / Scott $17,500).

Estimate: $8,000+

Minimum Bid: $4,000

QUEENSLAND

An exceptional example of this rare #1

32647 **Stanley Gibbons #1 (Scott #1), 1860, 1p Deep Rose.**
(Used). A remarkable used example of this rare stamp with portion of the adjoining stamp, plus a further portion (separated) thereby showing complete QL postmark. Fault free. Extremely Fine to Superb. 2008 Brandon Certificate, also with clear 2008 Sismondo certificate and 1963 Bolaffi Certificate indicating it very possibly to be one of the finest extant. (Stanley Gibbons £800).

Estimate: $1,200+
Minimum Bid: $600

TASMANIA

32648 **Stanley Gibbons #15, 17 (Scott #5, 6), 1855 (2), 2p & 4p Green & Deep Blue.** (Used). An attractive small cover franked by the 1855 2d green & 4d blue both tied by Oval Grid cancels to folded letter addressed to Philadelphia. Red 1857 Launceston Pmk at right, Red London transit Pmk at center and Philadelphia Pmk at right (2d stamp is cut in at bottom), nevertheless overall VF appearance and a scarce usage. Fine. 2008 PF Certificate. (Stanley Gibbons £1610+).

Estimate: $500+
Minimum Bid: $250

WORLDWIDE
AUSTRIA

SEMI-POSTAL ISSUES

32649 **#B111, 1933, 50g + 50g.** (Original Gum - Previously Hinged). A choice mint example of this scarce and popular "Wipa" Souvenir sheet of 4 with fresh colors and full original gum showing only the barest trace of previous hinging, with the stamps within the sheet being never hinged. Extremely Fine. 2008 PF Certificate. (Scott $2,500).

Estimate: $1,250+
Minimum Bid: $625

32650 **#B185-88, 1946, 1s+1s - 5s+5s Renner Souvenir Sheets.** (Original Gum - Previously Hinged). A choice mint complete set of 4 of these scarce and popular Renner Souvenir sheets (each of eight stamps) with fresh colors and full original gum, very lightly to extremely lightly kissed by previous hinging. Extremely Fine. 2008 PF Certificate for each sheet. (Scott as NH $2,000).(Total: 4 pages)

Estimate: $900+
Minimum Bid: $450

NEWSPAPER ISSUES

32651 **#PR4, 1858, 4kr Brown.** (Used). An attractive used example of this very scarce Newspaper stamp with good color, neat Double Eagle cancel and close (but clear) to enormous margins. Fine. 2008 PF Certificate. (Scott $1,100).

Estimate: $500+

Minimum Bid: $250

32652 **#PR3, 1858, 4kr Red.** (Used). A very presentable example of this rare newspaper issue with bright color,bold face free Verona cancel and three large margins: fourth cut into at left (small tone spot at bottom left) nevertheless a very collectible example. Fine. 2008 PF Certificate. (Scott $2,400).

Estimate: $500+

Minimum Bid: $250

CHINA

PROOFS & ESSAYS

32653 **#605TCE1, 1945, Trial Color Essay, Black.** (No Gum). A choice Trial Color Essay on India , die sunk on card for the Chang Kai -Chek commemorative issue of 1945 design (A70) printed by American Banknote Co with pencil notation "F 11811" on reverse. Attractive and scarce. Extremely Fine. 2008 PF Certificate.

Estimate: $1,000+

Minimum Bid: $500

CUBA

REGULAR ISSUES

SCARCE EARLY STAMPLESS COVER TO THE US

32654 **1850 Havana to New York.** An attractive small stampless cover addressed to New York with red S/L Habana hand stamp, 1850 postmarks and 12 1/2 in a circle New York handstamp. Unusual and scarce. Extremely Fine. 2008 PF Certificate.

Estimate: $300+

Minimum Bid: $150

FINLAND

32655 **#16, 1875, 32p Lake.** (Original Gum - Previously Hinged). A well centered mint single with post office fresh color and detailed impression on crisp clean paper, original gum, previously hinged with a hinge remnant and light penciling on the gum which is not mentioned on the certificate. Very Fine. 2008 PF Certificate. (Scott $2,400).

Estimate: $1,200+

Minimum Bid: $600

FRANCE

32656 **#6c, 1849, 25c Light Blue on Bluish, Tete-Beche Pair.** (Used). An attention-grabbing used tete-beche pair on piece with lozenge of dots cancel. Very Good to Fine. 2008 PF Certificate. (Scott $13,500).

Estimate: $3,000+

Minimum Bid: $1,500

32657 **#7f, 1849, 40c Orange On Yellowish, Type II.** (Used). A scarce used pair of the type II issue, with bright fresh color and lozenge of dots cancel, the pair with faint thinning at the top not affecting the overall appearance or desirability, and with light pencil notations on the back not mentioned on the certificate. Overall Fine appearance. 2008 PF Certificate. (Scott $52,500).

Estimate: $5,000+

Minimum Bid: $2,500

GERMANY

SEMI-POSTAL ISSUES

ITALIAN STATES - SARDINIA

32660 **#2, 1851, 20 c Blue.** (Partial Original Gum). A fresh mint example of this scarce stamp with good color, four good margins for the issue, and part original gum with album page adhesions, and a couple small hinge remnants that are not noted on the certificate. An overall sound stamp with a Very Fine appearance for this scarce issue. Signed Calves and Diena, and with a 2008 Sismondo Certificate. (Scott $8,250).

Estimate: $1,200+

Minimum Bid: $600

A RARE SARDINIAN INVERT

32658 **#B33, 1930, 8pf-50pf Multicolor.** (Used). An attractive used example of this very scarce "IPOSTA" souvenir sheet with good colors and neat Berlin 15.9.30 cancel at left together with appropriate exhibition cancellations both on the stamps and below (inconsequential very faint toning) nevertheless very collectible. Very Fine. 2008 PF Certificate. (Scott $1,250).

Estimate: $450+

Minimum Bid: $225

32661 **#10f, 1863, 5c Green.** (Used). An attractive used example of this rare 5c showing the variety: "inverted embossed head", with fresh color, neat Trevi CDS and clear to good margins. Fine to Very Fine Sismondo Certificate also E. Diena Certificate. (Scott $3,250).

Estimate: $1,000+

Minimum Bid: $500

32659 **#B68, 1935, 3pf-25pf Sheet Of 4.** (Used). A choice used example of this scarce "OSTROPA" Souvenir sheet with rich colors, neat exhibition cancels and full OG: a scarce sheet without the usual faults. Very Fine to Extremely Fine. 2008 PF Certificate. (Scott $700).

Estimate: $550+

Minimum Bid: $275

ITALY - SOCIAL REPUBLIC

AIRMAIL ISSUES

RARE BALBO TRANSATLANTIC TRYPTICH ISSUE IN TWO COMPLETE SHEETS OF 20

32662 **#C48-49, 1933, 5l+19.75 & 5.25+44.75 Red, Blue & Green.** (Original Gum - Never Hinged). A spectacular set of these 2 scarce Balbo Transatlantic Flight triptychs issues presented in two complete sheets of 20 stamps each (40 stamps in all) with bright colors and full never hinged OG - (couple of insignificant tone spots as often and pen mark in lower selvedge) nevertheless quite superb and much better than usual. (Scott as singles $11,500).

Estimate: $10,000+
Minimum Bid: $5,000

JAPAN

REGULAR ISSUES

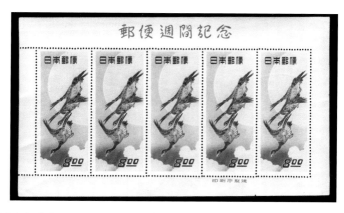

32663 **#479a, 1949, 8y Purple.** (Original Gum - Never Hinged). Fresh and Attractive example of this scarce miniature sheet. Tiny margin nicks at the bottom, Minor natural gum creases not mentioned on certificate, both common to the issue. Very Fine. 2008 PF Certificate. (Scott $600).

Estimate: $300+
Minimum Bid: $150

MADEIRA

A SCARCE MADEIRA COMBINATION COVER TO THE US

32664 **#5 & 14, 1868, 100r & 120r.** (Used). An attractive small cover bearing the 100r lilac imperforate & the 120r blue perforate issues neatly tied by grid cancels to small cover addressed sent from Madeira to Philadelphia, with 1869 Funchal postmark at left and red London and New York transit marks at lower right (120r with inconsequential tone spot in top margin - mentioned only for accuracy, and backflap fault affecting back stamp) nevertheless attractive and very scarce. Very Fine. 2008 PF Certificate.

Estimate: $2,000+

Minimum Bid: $1,000

MONACO

Monaco 1956 Pigeons & Helicopter
unissued (J39, 48 var)

32665 **Dally #491A-B, 1956, 30 Fr / 1Fr unissued tete - beche pair Multicolored.** (Original Gum - Never Hinged). A superb mint vertical tete - beche pair of these extremely rare un- issued stamps, featuring Helicopters & Pigeons, with fresh colors and full never hingedOG. Offered with R. Calves Certificate for the block of 4from which this pair was taken. Listed in the French Catalog Dally (#491A-B). Extremely Fine to Superb. 2008 R. Calves Certificate. (Dally Euro10,500)**.**

Estimate: $5,500+

Minimum Bid: $2,750

POLAND

SEMI-POSTAL ISSUES

32666 **1946 Polish Education Work Issue.** (Original Gum - Never Hinged). Includes #'s B49, B49A-B, and B49Bc. A very fresh and attractive complete set of these scarce "Educational" issues in special mini - sheets of 12, offered together with the corresponding Souvenir sheet of 3, all with bright colors and full clean never hinged OG (tiny inconsequential natural inclusion in the margin of the B49B sheet) nevertheless a VF and scarce group. Very Fine to Extremely Fine. (Scott $1,745).

Estimate: $800+

Minimum Bid: $400

End of Session Four

SESSION FIVE - Non Floor

Floor, Telephone, Heritage Live!™, Internet, Fax, and Mail Signature® Auction #1106
Saturday, February 7, 2009, 12:00 PM CT • Dallas, Texas • Lots 32667-33210

A 19.5% Buyer's Premium ($9 minimum) Will Be Added To All Lots
You can now view full-color images and bid via the Internet at the Heritage website: HA.com/Stamps

1847 REGULAR ISSUES

32667 #1, 1847, 5c Red Brown, F 70 PSE. (Used). Four margined used single, blue circular grid cancel, Fine. PSE - Encapsulated. (SMQ $355; this being one of 22 attaining this grade as of 10/08, with 214 graded higher).

Estimate: $300+

Minimum Bid: $150

32668 #1, 1847, 5c Red Brown. (Used). An incredibly handsome used single, precisely centered within four wonderfully generous margins, with a red grid cancel, and expertly sealed 2mm tear at the bottom left, below the "I" of "FIVE." Very Fine appearance; 2008 PSE Certificate. (Scott $600).

Estimate: $300+

Minimum Bid: $150

32669 #1, 1847, 5c Red Brown, G 30 PSE. (Used). Used single with red "PAID / 5" cancel, Good; PSE - Encapsulated. (SMQ $200; this being one of 44 attaining this grade as of 10/08, with 301 graded higher).

Estimate: $250+

Minimum Bid: $125

32670 #1, 1847, 5c Red Brown F 70 PSE. (Used). Red Grid cancel, a tad heavy. Four margin copy, with obvious point deduction for cancel. Fine PSE - Encapsulated. (SMQ $355; this being one of 22 attaining this grade as of 10/08, with 214 graded higher).

Estimate: $250+

Minimum Bid: $125

32671 #1, 1847, 5c Red Brown F 70 PSE. (Used). Fine PSE - Encapsulated. (SMQ $355; this being one of 22 attaining this grade as of 10/08, with 214 graded higher).

Estimate: $250+

Minimum Bid: $125

32672 #1b, 1847, 5c Orange Brown, VG 50 PSE. (Used). A charming 3½ margin used single, margins varying from just in the frame line at the upper left to monstrous at the right, red circular grid cancels. Very Good; PSE - Encapsulated. (SMQ $375; this being one of 3 attaining this grade as of 10/08, with 26 graded higher).

Estimate: $250+

Minimum Bid: $125

1875 REPRINT OF 1857-61 ISSUE

32673 #3, 1875 Reprint, 5c Red Brown. (No Gum As Issued). Handsome example, with tiny closed pinhole at the upper right which is barely detectable in watermark fluid. Very Fine; 2008 PSE Certificate. (Scott $800).

Estimate: $800+

Minimum Bid: $400

1851-57 FIRST ISSUES - IMPERF

32674 #7, 1851, 1c Blue VF-XF 85 PSE. (Used). Extremely light black cancel on four margin example with pretty blue color. Very Fine to Extremely Fine; 2008 PSE - Graded Certificate. (SMQ $265; this being one of 13 attaining this grade as of 10/08, with 58 graded higher).

Estimate: $220+

Minimum Bid: $110

32675 #9, 1851, 1c Blue XF 90 PSE. (Used). Almost a jumbo, very fresh example, Position 61R1L, black circular date stamp (c.d.s.) cancel, Extremely Fine; 2005 PSE - Graded Certificate, 2004 PF Certificate. (SMQ $310; this being one of 48 attaining this grade as of 10/08, with 74 graded higher).

Estimate: $300+

Minimum Bid: $150

32676 #9, 1851, 1c Blue XF 90 PSE. (Used). Bright and fresh, with a black circular date stamp (c.d.s.), Extremely Fine; 2008 PSE - Graded Certificate. (SMQ $310; this being one of 48 attaining this grade as of 10/08, with 74 graded higher).

Estimate: $250+

Minimum Bid: $125

32677 #9, 1851, 1c Blue VF-XF 85 PSE. (Used). Bright and vibrant, nice unobtrusive light cancel. Very Fine to Extremely Fine and choice. 2008 PSE - Graded Certificate. (SMQ $200; this being one of 27 attaining this grade as of 10/08, with 129 graded higher).

Estimate: $150+

Minimum Bid: $1

32678 #9, 1851, 1c Blue. (Used). Horizontal strip of three, with strong Jul 6, Berkley Springs, West Virginia circular date stamp cancel on the middle stamp. Fine to Very Fine and choice; 2008 PSE Certificate. (Scott $450).

Estimate: $400+

Minimum Bid: $200

32679 #11, 1851, 3c Dull Red. (Disturbed Original Gum). A classic beauty, refreshingly vibrant, with slightly disturbed original gum. Very Fine to Extremely Fine; 2006 PF Certificate. (Scott $325).

Estimate: $250+

Minimum Bid: $125

32680 #13, 1851, 10c Green VF 80 PSE. (Used). Red and black cancels, with a very shallow thin spot, Very Fine PSE - Encapsulated. (SMQ $890; this being one of 4 attaining this grade as of 10/08, with 35 graded higher).

Estimate: $450+

Minimum Bid: $225

32681 #14, 1851, 10c Green XF 90 PSE. (Used). Luscious dark green example with large to jumbo margins, sharp black grid cancel. Extremely Fine PSE - Encapsulated. (SMQ $415; this being one of 26, attaining this grade as of 10/08, with 55 graded higher) .

Estimate: $400+

Minimum Bid: $200

32682 #14, 1851-57, 10c Green. (Used). Gorgeous used example tied on piece by black circular grid cancel. Very Fine to Extremely Fine; 2008 PSE Certificate. (Scott $200).

Estimate: $200+

Minimum Bid: $100

32683 #14, 1855, 10c Green. (Used). Position 55R1, with large Boston PAID grid cancel. Very Fine to Extremely Fine; 2003 PSE Certificate. (Scott $200).

Estimate: $200+

Minimum Bid: $100

32684 #15, 1855, 10c Green. (Used). A Fine to Very Fine used single with black New Orleans, La circular date stamp (c.d.s.) cancel. 2005 PSE Certificate. (Scott $200).

Estimate: $400+

Minimum Bid: $200

32685 #17, 1851, 12c Black VF 80 PSE. (Used). Pretty copy. Very light cancel, four margin copy. Very Fine PSE - Encapsulated. (SMQ $335; this being one of 18 attaining this grade as of 10/08, with 74 graded higher).

Estimate: $300+

Minimum Bid: $150

1857-61 FIRST ISSUES - PERFS

32686 #20, 1857, 1c Blue F 70 PSE. (Original Gum - Hinged). Plate 12. Pencil mark on gum. Fine PSE - Encapsulated. (SMQ $650; this being one of 1 attaining this grade as of 10/08, with only 6 graded higher).

Estimate: $400+

Minimum Bid: $200

32687 #21, 1857, 1c Blue. (Used). Fresh used example, Position 99R2 with a black circular date stamp (c.d.s.) cancel, short perforation at the right and a light horizontal crease. Very Good to Fine; 2008 PSE Certificate, 1971 PF Certificate. (Scott $2,750).

Estimate: $1,100+

Minimum Bid: $550

32688 #37, 1857, 24c Gray Lilac, VF 80 PSE. (Used). Well centered, with black circular grid cancel. Very Fine PSE - Encapsulated. (SMQ $410; this being one of 10 attaining this grade as of 10/08, with 22 graded higher).

Estimate: $350+

Minimum Bid: $175

32689 #37, 1857, 24c Gray Lilac. (Used). A charming used single, with red circular grid cancels and a red "PD" in circle marking. Very Fine; 2008 PSE Certificate. (Scott $440).

Estimate: $240+

Minimum Bid: $120

32690 #37, 1857, 24c Gray Lilac. (Used). A handsome used single with black straight line "PAID" cancel, short perf at bottom left, trivial light crease top left corner and bottom left corner perf, and an inconsequential repunched perf hole top right corner, an overall Very Fine appearance. 2008 PSE Certificate. (Scott $425).

Estimate: $240+

Minimum Bid: $120

32691 #28, 1857-61, 5c Red Brown F 70 PSE. (Used). Rich color, light town cancel, sound. Fine PSE - Encapsulated. (SMQ $700; this being one of 2 attaining this grade as of 10/08, with 15 graded higher).

Estimate: $500+

Minimum Bid: $250

32692 #28b, 1857, 5c Bright Red Brown G 30 PSE. (Partial Original Gum). Rich color and strong detailed impression. Nice example with part OG. Good PSE - Encapsulated. (this being one of 1 attaining this grade as of 10/08, with only 9 graded higher).

Estimate: $750+

Minimum Bid: $375

32693 #33, 1857, 10c Green VF 80 PSE. (Used). With San Francisco, Cal. circular date stamp (c.d.s.) cancel, Very Fine; 2007 PSE - Graded Certificate. (SMQ $310; this being one of 8 attaining this grade as of 10/08, with 28 graded higher).

Estimate: $300+

Minimum Bid: $150

32694 #39, 1857-61, 90c Blue F 70 PSE. (No Gum). Scarce in any grade, beautiful color, nice addition for a collector, Fine PSE - Encapsulated. (SMQ $610; this being one of 2, attaining this grade as of 10/08, with only 4 graded higher).

Estimate: $500+

Minimum Bid: $250

1861-66 SECOND ISSUES

32695 #64, 1861, 3c Pink. (Used). Terrific example of a true pink color, well centered with balanced margins, used with pen cancel. Very Fine to Extremely Fine; 2008 PSE Certificate. (Scott $1,000).

Estimate: $500+

Minimum Bid: $250

32696 #65, 1861, 3c Rose VF 80 PSE. (Original Gum - Never Hinged). Post Office fresh, with full original, Never Hinged gum. Very Fine; 2008 PSE - Graded Certificate. (SMQ $385; this being one of 5 attaining this grade as of 10/08, with 13 graded higher).

Estimate: $350+

Minimum Bid: $175

32697 #69, 1861, 12c Black. (Used). Light unobtrusive cancel, Very Fine; 2008 PSE Certificate. (Scott $120).

Estimate: $90+

Minimum Bid: $1

32698 #70, 1861-62, 24c Red Lilac, VG 50 PSE. (No Gum). Bright and appealing example, very minor perforation faults, Very Good PSE - Encapsulated. Minor perf faults (SMQ $380; this being one of 2 attaining this grade as of 10/08, with none graded higher).

Estimate: $350+

Minimum Bid: $175

32699 #76, 1863, 5c Brown, XF 90 PSE. (Used). Extremely Fine; 2007 PSE - Graded Certificate. (SMQ $450; this being one of 18 attaining this grade as of 10/08, with 10 graded higher).

Estimate: $400+

Minimum Bid: $200

32700 #78, 1861, 24c Lilac. (Used). Bright Color, with a light cancel. Fine to Very Fine; 2008 PSE Certificate. (Scott $250).

Estimate: $200+

Minimum Bid: $100

1867-68 GRILLED ISSUES

32701 #83, 1867, 3c Rose. (Used). Alluring example with large margins on three sides, used with a black crossroads cancel and short perforations at the top and bottom. Fine to Very Fine; 2008 PSE Certificate. (Scott $1,100).

Estimate: $450+

Minimum Bid: $225

32702 #85E, 1867, 12c Black. (Used). An attention-grabbing used example of this "Z" grilled issue, sporting a strong grill, faintly canceled giving an unused appearance, with a tiny corner crease at the bottom left and a tiny perforation tear at the upper right, both trivial and unobtrusive to the overall eye appeal. Fine to Very Fine appearance. 2008 PF Certificate. (Scott $2,500).

Estimate: $1,500+

Minimum Bid: $750

32703 #100, 1867, 30c Orange, G-VG 40 PSE. (No Gum). A beautiful unused single, well centered within the usual tight margins, clear grill, trivial scuffed perf at top, Good to Very Good; PSE - Encapsulated. (this being the only example attaining this grade as of 10/08, with only 2 graded higher).

Estimate: $700+

Minimum Bid: $350

32704 #101, 1867, 90c Blue VG, 50 PSE. (Used). A handsome used single, clear grill, non-obtrusive cancel, trivial tiny scuff and pulled perf. Very Good; PSE - Encapsulated. (SMQ $570; this being one of 3 attaining this grade as of 10/08, with only 8 graded higher).

Estimate: $400+

Minimum Bid: $200

1869 PICTORIALS

32705 #115, 1869, 6c Ultramarine F 70 PSE. (Partial Original Gum). Fine PSE - Encapsulated. (SMQ $590; this being one of 2 attaining this grade as of 10/08, with 10 graded higher).

Estimate: $450+

Minimum Bid: $225

32706 #116, 1869, 10c Yellow XF 90 PSE. (Used). Lovely used example with good color and margins. Extremely Fine; 2008 PSE - Graded Certificate, 2007 PF Certificate. (SMQ $395; this being one of 30 attaining this grade as of 10/08, with 17 graded higher).

Estimate: $350+

Minimum Bid: $175

32707 #116, 1869, 10c Yellow. (Used). Wonderful used example, large margins with a fabulous black Hiogo, Japan cancel, a short perforation at the top left and a tiny pencil mark on the back. Very Fine to Extremely Fine; 2008 PSE Certificate. (Scott $150).

Estimate: $400+

Minimum Bid: $200

32708 #117, 1869, 12c Green, VF 80 PSE. (Used). With complimentary red cancel, and light pencil notations on the reverse not noted on the capsule insert. Very Fine; PSE - Encapsulated. (SMQ $160; this being one of 12 attaining this grade as of 10/08, with 72 graded higher).

Estimate: $150+

Minimum Bid: $1

32709 #118, 1869, 15c Brown & Blue, VG 50 PSE. (No Gum). Fresh and bright unused single, detailed impression on clean paper, grill shifted slightly from the center. Very Good; PSE - Encapsulated. (SMQ $990; this being one of 2 attaining this grade as of 10/08, with only 4 graded higher).

Estimate: $700+

Minimum Bid: $350

32710 #118, 1869, 15c Brown & Blue G 30 PSE. (Original Gum - Previously Hinged). Handsome overall example, very attractive for the grade, slight toning and crease on back, light pencil notation. Good PSE - Encapsulated. (SMQ $2,000; this being the only example attaining this grade as of 10/08, with only 3 graded higher).

Estimate: $1,500+

Minimum Bid: $750

32711 #118a, 1869, 15c Brown & Blue FR-G 20 PSE. (Partial Original Gum). Nice example with an almost invisible tear, Fair - Good PSE - Encapsulated.
1 mm tear at top (SMQ unpriced).

Estimate: $200+

Minimum Bid: $100

32712 #119, 1869, 15c Brown & Blue, VF 80 PSE. (Used). With unobtrusive cancel, Very Fine; PSE - Encapsulated. (SMQ $280; this being one of 13 attaining this grade as of 10/08, with 33 graded higher).

Estimate: $200+

Minimum Bid: $100

32713 #119, 1869, 15c Brown And Blue. (Used). Simply gorgeous appearing example, used with extremely light red and black cancels, red cancel cuts the paper at the bottom center. Extremely Fine; 2008 PSE Certificate. (Scott $275).

Estimate: $400+

Minimum Bid: $200

32714 #119, 1869, 15c Brown & Blue. (Used). Very well centered used single, with a black circle of wedges cancel and a shorter perf at the right, Very Fine; 2008 PSE Certificate. (Scott $275).

Estimate: $200+

Minimum Bid: $100

32715 #120, 1869, 24c Green & Violet, VG 50 PSE. (No Gum). Bright and fresh unused single, with detailed impression on crisp paper, clear grill, Very Good; PSE - Encapsulated. (SMQ $1,050; this being one of 2 attaining this grade as of 10/08, with 11 graded higher).

Estimate: $700+

Minimum Bid: $350

32716 #122, 1869, 90c Carmine & Black, G 30 PSE. (No Gum). Bright and vibrant unused single. Good; PSE - Encapsulated. (SMQ $1,100; this being one of 2 attaining this grade as of 10/08, with only 8 graded higher).

Estimate: $850+

Minimum Bid: $425

1870-71 NATIONAL BANK NOTE CO. ISSUES - W/O GRILL

32717 #151, 1870-71, 12c Dull Violet F 70 PSE. (Regummed). True dull violet color. Fine PSE - Encapsulated. (SMQ $500; this being one of 4 attaining this grade as of 10/08, with only 6 graded higher).

Estimate: $250+

Minimum Bid: $125

32718 #151, 1870, 12c Dull Violet. (No Gum). Fresh and bright, unused. Fine; 2008 PSE Certificate. (Scott $1,200).

Estimate: $400+

Minimum Bid: $200

32719 #153, 1870-71, 24c Purple F-VF 75 PSE. (No Gum). Lovely pastel color, fresh. Fine - Very Fine. PSE - Encapsulated. (this being one of 2 attaining this grade as of 10/08, with only 1 graded higher).

Estimate: $400+

Minimum Bid: $200

32720 #153, 1870-71, 24c Purple F 70 PSE. (Disturbed Original Gum). Scarce stamp, toned with weak strike, disturbed original gum. Fine PSE - Encapsulated. (SMQ $1,200; this being one of 3 attaining this grade as of 10/08, with only 4 graded higher).

Estimate: $600+

Minimum Bid: $300

1873 CONTINENTAL BANK NOTE CO. ISSUES

32721 #166, 1873, 90c Rose Carmine VF-XF 85 PSE. (Used). Bright and lively used example, better than usual color on white paper, black cancel. Very Fine - Extremely Fine. PSE - Encapsulated. (SMQ $435; this being one of 9 attaining this grade as of 10/08, with 12 graded higher).

Estimate: $350+

Minimum Bid: $175

1879 AMERICAN BANK NOTE CO. ISSUES

32722 #183, 1879, 2c Vermillion. (Original Gum - Previously Hinged). Attractive example with even margins and lively color, original gum, light hinging. Extremely Fine. (SMQ $320; this being one of 4 attaining this grade as of 10/08, with only 2 graded higher).

Estimate: $300+

Minimum Bid: $150

32723 #185, 1879, 5c Blue VF 80 PSE. (Disturbed Original Gum). Very Fine PSE - Encapsulated. (this being the only one attaining this grade as of 10/08, with none graded higher).

Estimate: $300+

Minimum Bid: $150

32724 #188, 1879, 10c Brown. (Original Gum - Previously Hinged). A mint single, original gum, very light hinge mark, with creases that appear more like light natural gum bends, and a tiny margin thin that does not detract from the overall appearance, light hinge mark and several gum skips across the back. Fine. 2006 APS Certificate. (Scott $2,500) .

Estimate: $1,000+

Minimum Bid: $500

32725 #189, 1879, 15c Red Orange VF 80 PSE. (Original Gum - Previously Hinged). Very fine example with attractive color, pleasing. Very Fine. PSE - Encapsulated. (SMQ $350; this being one of 6 attaining this grade as of 10/08, with 28 graded higher).

Estimate: $250+

Minimum Bid: $125

1882 AMERICAN BANK NOTE CO. ISSUE

32726 #205, 1882, 5c Gray Brown XF-S 95 PSE. (Used). One of the finest used examples, very light black cancel, pretty stamp. Extremely Fine to Superb; 2008 PSE - Graded Certificate. (SMQ $305; this being one of 3 attaining this grade as of 10/08, with only 2 graded higher).

Estimate: $300+

Minimum Bid: $150

1881-82 DESIGNS OF 1873 RE-ENGRAVED

32727 #208a, 1881-82, 6c Deep Brown Red F 70 PSE. (Original Gum - Never Hinged). Very close right margin, beautiful example otherwise. Fine PSE - Encapsulated. (SMQ $730; this being one of 2 attaining this grade as of 10/08, with only 4 graded higher).

Estimate: $500+

Minimum Bid: $250

32728 #209, 1881-82, 10c Brown. (Original Gum - Previously Hinged). Horizontal pair with huge top margin, lightly hinged. Fine to Very Fine; 2008 PSE Certificate. (Scott $425).

Estimate: $350+

Minimum Bid: $175

1887-88 AMERICAN BANK NOTE CO. ISSUES

32729 #213, 1887, 2c Green XF-S 95 PSE. (Used). Undervalued in SMQ. Gorgeous with mild face-free cancel. Extremely Fine to Superb; 2008 PSE - Graded Certificate. (SMQ $150; this being one of 3 attaining this grade as of 10/08, with only 5 graded higher).

Estimate: $200+

Minimum Bid: $100

32730 #214, 1887, 3c Vermillion VF 80 PSE. (Original Gum - Never Hinged). Appealing example with blazing and rich vermilion color. Post Office Fresh gum. Very Fine; 2008 PSE - Graded Certificate. (SMQ $220; this being one of 12 attaining this grade as of 10/08, with 49 graded higher).

Estimate: $200+

Minimum Bid: $100

32731 #214, 1887, 3c Vermillion XF 90 PSE. (Used). Unobtrusive New York town cancel. Extremely Fine; 2008 PSE - Graded Certificate. (SMQ $185; this being one of 8 attaining this grade as of 10/08, with only 4 graded higher).

Estimate: $200+

Minimum Bid: $100

32732 #217, 1888, 30c Orange Brown XF 90 PSE. (Used). Lovely example with a black Philadelphia, PA. double oval cancel. Extremely Fine; 2008 PSE - Graded Certificate. (SMQ $320; this being one of 6 attaining this grade as of 10/08, with only 4 graded higher).

Estimate: $250+

Minimum Bid: $125

32733 #219, 1890, 1c Dull Blue SUP 98 PSE. (Original Gum - Never Hinged). Superb; 2007 PSE - Graded Certificate. (SMQ $360; this being one of 3 attaining this grade as of 10/08, with only 1 graded higher).

Estimate: $350+

Minimum Bid: $175

32734 #219D, 1890-93, 2c Lake F 70 PSE. (Original Gum - Never Hinged). Wonderful lake example, nice overall appearance, tiny scattered gum disturbance spots. Fine. PSE - Encapsulated. (SMQ $305; this being one of 4 attaining this grade as of 10/08, with 25 graded higher).

Estimate: $200+

Minimum Bid: $100

32735 #219D, 1890, 2c Lake XF-S 95 PSE. (Used). Alluring example of the lake color, extremely well centered with a black cancel, pencil notations on back. Extremely Fine - Superb. PSE - Graded Certificate. (SMQ $230; this being one of 2 attaining this grade as of 10/08, with only 5 graded higher).

Estimate: $300+

Minimum Bid: $150

32736 #220, 1890, 2c Carmine XF-S 95J PSE. (Used). Enormous jumbo, intense color with black machine cancel. Extremely Fine to Superb. 2008 PSE - Graded Certificate. (this being one of 6 attaining this grade as of 10/08, with only 2 graded higher).

Estimate: $200+

Minimum Bid: $100

32737 #220, 1890, 2c Carmine, XF-S 95J PSE. (Used). Huge used example in jumbo with deep rich color, light black cancel. Extremely Fine to Superb. PSE - Encapsulated. (this being one of 6 attaining this grade as of 10/08, with only 2 graded higher).

Estimate: $300+

Minimum Bid: $150

32738 #223, 1890-93, 5c Chocolate VF 80 PSE. (Original Gum - Never Hinged). Choice example, warm chocolate color with fresh mint appearance. Very Fine. PSE - Encapsulated. (SMQ $300; this being one of 4 attaining this grade as of 10/08, with 24 graded higher).

Estimate: $250+

Minimum Bid: $125

32739 #224, 1890-93, 6c Brown Red VF 80 PSE. (Original Gum - Never Hinged). Fresh. Very Fine. PSE - Encapsulated. (SMQ $265; this being one of 4 attaining this grade as of 10/08, with 46 graded higher).

Estimate: $200+

Minimum Bid: $100

32740 #228, 1890-93, 30c Black, F 70 PSE. (Original Gum - Hinged). Looks nicer than the grade, close in on the left with nice even margins on the other three sides, color and impression are very good. Fine. PSE - Encapsulated. (SMQ $225; this being one of 6 attaining this grade as of 10/08, with 18 graded higher).

Estimate: $150+

Minimum Bid: $1

32741 #229, 1890-93, 90c Orange, F-VF 75 PSE. (Disturbed Original Gum). Pretty example with good color, disturbed gum seems to be multiple hinge remnants. Fine to Very Fine. PSE - Encapsulated. (this being one of 3 attaining this grade as of 10/08, with only 3 graded higher).

Estimate: $200+

Minimum Bid: $100

1893 COLUMBIAN EXPOSITION ISSUE

32742 #234, 1893, 5c Chocolate XF-S 95J PSE. (Used). A splendid example of premium quality, vividly fresh, an Extremely Fine to Superb Jumbo margin example. 2008 PSE - Graded Certificate.
(this being one of 4 attaining this grade as of 10/08, with only 2 graded higher).

Estimate: $400+

Minimum Bid: $200

32743 #236, 1893, 8c Magenta XF 90J PSE. (Original Gum - Previously Hinged). Monster jumbo, Fabulous eye-appeal, perfect centering for the shape, stunning color and impression, barely hinged, should bring multiples of catalogue. Extremely Fine. PSE - Encapsulated. (this being one of 6 attaining this grade as of 10/08, with 12 graded higher).

Estimate: $250+

Minimum Bid: $125

32744 #240, 1893, 50c Slate Blue VF 80 PSE. (Disturbed Original Gum). Very Fine. 2007 PSE - Graded Certificate. (SMQ $600; this being one of 6 attaining this grade as of 10/08, with 13 graded higher).

Estimate: $500+

Minimum Bid: $250

32745 #240, 1893, 50c Slate Blue F 70 PSE. (Original Gum - Never Hinged). Recall Of Columbus. Fine. 2007 PSE - Graded Certificate. (SMQ $680; this being one of 2 attaining this grade as of 10/08, with 32 graded higher).

Estimate: $450+

Minimum Bid: $225

32746 #240, 1893, 50c Slate Blue VG 50 PSE. (Original Gum - Previously Hinged). Wonderful slate blue example. Lightly hinged and creased. Very Good. PSE - Encapsulated. (SMQ $180; this being one of 8 attaining this grade as of 10/08, with 98 graded higher).

Estimate: $200+

Minimum Bid: $100

32747 #241, 1893, $1 Salmon F 70 PSE. (Used). Nice collectable example with light double oval cancel in black. Fine. PSE - Encapsulated. (SMQ $360; this being one of 5 attaining this grade as of 10/08, with 32 graded higher).

Estimate: $300+

Minimum Bid: $150

32748 #242, 1893, $2 Brown Red, F-VF 75 PSE. (Used). Attractive example with very light black corner cancel. Fine to Very Fine. PSE - Encapsulated. (this being one of 7 attaining this grade as of 10/08, with 27 graded higher).

Estimate: $400+

Minimum Bid: $200

32749 #242, 1893, $2 Brown Red, G-VG 40 PSE. (No Gum). Columbus in Chains. Unused single, warm pastel color on white paper. Good to Very Good; PSE - Encapsulated.
(this being one of 4 attaining this grade as of 10/08, with 31 graded higher).

Estimate: $300+

Minimum Bid: $150

32750 #243, 1893, $3 Yellow Green F-VF 75 PSE. (Regummed). Desirable example, professionally regummed. Fine to Very Fine. PSE - Encapsulated. (this being one of 2 attaining this grade as of 10/08, with 13 graded higher).

Estimate: $400+

Minimum Bid: $200

32751 #243, 1893, $3 Yellow Green, F-VF 75 PSE. (Used). Strong impression and color example, very light black cancel. Fine to Very Fine. PSE - Encapsulated. (this being the only example attaining this grade as of 10/08, with 19 graded higher).

Estimate: $700+

Minimum Bid: $350

32752 #243, 1893, $3 Yellow Green, F 70 PSE. (Original Gum - Previously Hinged). Columbus Describing Third Voyage. Lovely mint example, sharp impression with striking color, original gum, hinge remnant. Fine. 2007 PSE - Graded Certificate. (SMQ $1,100; this being one of 8 attaining this grade as of 10/08, with 28 graded higher).

Estimate: $900+

Minimum Bid: $450

32753 #244, 1893, $4 Crimson Lake, VG 50 PSE. (No Gum). Isabella and Columbus. Unused single, luxuriously radiant and fresh. Very Good; PSE - Encapsulated. (SMQ $690; this being one of 7 attaining this grade as of 10/08, with 27 graded higher).

Estimate: $600+

Minimum Bid: $300

32754 #245, 1893, $5 Black, VG-F 60 PSE. (No Gum). Unused single, intense color and detailed impression on crisp fresh paper. Shorter perfs at top. Very Good to Fine; PSE - Encapsulated.
(this being one of 3 attaining this grade as of 10/08, with 31 graded higher).

Estimate: $500+

Minimum Bid: $250

32755 #245, 1893, $5 Black, VG 50 PSE. (Original Gum - Hinged). Columbus. Previously hinged with a natural horizontal gum wrinkle. Very Good. 2002 PSE - Graded Certificate. (SMQ $1,150; this being one of 4 attaining this grade as of 10/08, with 64 graded higher).

Estimate: $700+

Minimum Bid: $350

1894 BUREAU ISSUES - UNWATERMARKED

32756 #261A, 1894, $1 Black F-VF 75 PSE. (Used). Sharp jet black example with crisp white paper, black duplex cancel. Fine to Very Fine. PSE - Encapsulated. (this being the only example attaining this grade as of 10/08, with only 7 graded higher).

Estimate: $400+

Minimum Bid: $200

32757 #262, 1894, $2 Bright Blue F 70 PSE. (Original Gum - Previously Hinged). Jumbo margins on bottom and right, overall very collectable mint example. Fine. PSE - Encapsulated. (SMQ $1,600; this being one of 3 attaining this grade as of 10/08, with 10 graded higher).

Estimate: $1,200+

Minimum Bid: $600

1895 BUREAU ISSUES - WATERMARKED

32758 #268, 1895, 3c Purple VF-XF 85 PSE. (Original Gum - Never Hinged). Extremely nice for the grade, well centered bottom plate number single. Very Fine to Extremely Fine. PSE - Encapsulated. (SMQ $230; this being one of 14 attaining this grade as of 10/08, with 15 graded higher).

Estimate: $200+

Minimum Bid: $100

32759 #271, 1895, 6c Dull Brown. (Original Gum - Previously Hinged). Lovely bottom margin imprint and plate number strip of three, lightly hinged. Fine; 2008 PSE Certificate. (Scott $390).

Estimate: $250+

Minimum Bid: $125

32760 #274, 1895, 15c Dark Blue, F 70J PSE. (Original Gum - Never Hinged). Jumbo with the darkest of blue color. Fine. PSE - Encapsulated. (this being one of 2 attaining this grade as of 10/08, with 23 graded higher).

Estimate: $200+

Minimum Bid: $100

32761 #277, 1895, $2 Bright Blue, F 70 PSE. (Original Gum - Previously Hinged). Handsome for the grade. Fine. PSE - Encapsulated. (SMQ $570; this being one of 2 attaining this grade as of 10/08, with 34 graded higher).

Estimate: $400+

Minimum Bid: $200

1898 TRANS-MISSISSIPPI EXPOSITION ISSUE

32762 #292, 1898, $1 Black, VF 80 PSE. (No Gum). Cattle in the Storm. A gorgeous unused single, intensely rich, with full bodied detail on bright white paper. Very Fine; PSE - Encapsulated. (SMQ $570; this being one of 5 attaining this grade as of 10/08, with only 3 graded higher).

Estimate: $500+

Minimum Bid: $250

32763 #293, 1898, $2 Orange Brown, F 70 PSE. (No Gum). Mississippi River Bridge. A fresh unused single. Fine; PSE - Encapsulated. (SMQ $710; this being one of 6 attaining this grade as of 10/08, with only 7 graded higher).

Estimate: $650+

Minimum Bid: $325

1901 PAN-AMERICAN EXPOSITION ISSUE

32764 #294, 1901, 1c Green And Black XF-S 95 PSE. (Original Gum - Never Hinged). Attention-getting example, sharp impression with lovely color. Extremely Fine to Superb. 2008 PSE - Graded Certificate. (SMQ $445; this being one of 26 attaining this grade as of 10/08, with 15 graded higher).

Estimate: $400+

Minimum Bid: $200

32765 #295, 1901, 2c Carmine & Black, XF-S 95 PSE. (Original Gum - Never Hinged). Extra larger margins and bold color, outstanding example. Extremely Fine to Superb. PSE - Encapsulated. (SMQ $380; this being one of 84 attaining this grade as of 10/08, with 37 graded higher).

Estimate: $300+

Minimum Bid: $150

1902-08 REGULAR ISSUES

32766 #304, 1902-03, 5c Blue. (Original Gum - Never Hinged). Wonderful example, bright blue color on white paper. Fine to Very Fine; 2008 PSE Certificate. (Scott $300).

Estimate: $250+

Minimum Bid: $125

32767 #311, 1902-03, $1 Black VF 80 PSE. (Original Gum - Hinged). Very Fine. PSE - Encapsulated. (SMQ $670; this being one of 7 attaining this grade as of 10/08, with 42 graded higher).

Estimate: $500+

Minimum Bid: $250

32768 #312, 1902-03, $2 Dark Blue, F 70 PSE. (Original Gum - Hinged). Close margin on the right prevents a higher grade, superb color and strike. Fine. PSE - Encapsulated. (SMQ $520; this being one of 8 attaining this grade as of 10/08, with 47 graded higher).

Estimate: $400+

Minimum Bid: $200

32769 #313, 1902-03, $5 Dark Green VG 50 PSE. (Original Gum - Hinged). Deep and sharp impression, with short perf at the right. Very Good and desirable. PSE - Encapsulated. (SMQ $740; this being one of 6 attaining this grade as of 10/08, with 66 graded higher).

Estimate: $600+

Minimum Bid: $300

32770 #313, 1902-03, $5 Dark Green, F 70 PSE. (Used). Well centered stamp with good color, graded 70 due to slightly heavy black cancel. Fine. PSE - Encapsulated. (SMQ $375; this being one of 7 attaining this grade as of 10/08, with 16 graded higher).

Estimate: $250+

Minimum Bid: $125

32771 #314, 1906, 1c Blue Green GEM 100J PSE. (Original Gum - Never Hinged). Portion of 8 adjoining stamps. Gem. 2007 PSE - Graded Certificate. (this being one of 9 attaining this grade as of 10/08, with *none* graded higher).

Estimate: $300+

Minimum Bid: $150

32772 #314, 1906, 1c Blue Green, GEM 100 PSE. (Original Gum - Never Hinged). Absolutely perfect, large side margin. Gem. PSE - Encapsulated. (this being one of 7 attaining this grade as of 10/08, with only 9 graded higher).

Estimate: $200+

Minimum Bid: $100

32773 #319, 1903, 2c Carmine XF-S 95J PSE. (Used). A magnificent used condition rarity, precisely centered within huge well balanced margins. Extremely Fine to Superb; PSE - Encapsulated. (this being one of 6 attaining this grade as of 10/08, with only 2 graded higher).

Estimate: $500+

Minimum Bid: $250

32774 #319, 1903, 2c Carmine. (Used). Huge margins, very well centered, black machine cancel. Superb. (SMQ $365; this being one of 1 attaining this grade as of 10/08, with only 1 graded higher).

Estimate: $300+

Minimum Bid: $150

1904 LOUISIANA PURCHASE EXPOSITION ISSUE

32775 #326, 1904, Apr. 30, 5c Dark Blue VF-XF 85 PSE. (Original Gum - Never Hinged). Rich dark blue color with a razor sharp impression. Very Fine to Extremely Fine; 2008 PSE - Graded Certificate. (SMQ $415; this being one of 20 attaining this grade as of 10/08, with 46 graded higher).

Estimate: $350+

Minimum Bid: $175

1908-09 WASHINGTON FRANKLIN ISSUE - DBL. LINE WMK.

32776 #332, 1908, 2c Carmine VF-XF 85J PSE. (Original Gum - Never Hinged). Huge jumbo on experimental paper. Very Fine to Extremely Fine; 2008 PSE - Graded Certificate.

Estimate: $200+

Minimum Bid: $100

32777 #346, 1909, 4c Orange Brown, GEM 100 PSE. (Original Gum - Never Hinged). A magnificent bottom sheet margin single, with partial inscription and portions of the adjoining stamps showing left right top and both top corners. Gem; 2008 PSE - Graded Certificate. (this being one of 4 attaining this grade as of 10/08, with none graded higher).

Estimate: $400+

Minimum Bid: $200

32778 #346, 1908-09, 4c Orange Brown SUP 98J PSE. (Original Gum - Never Hinged). Huge right side margin single with partial inscription and 5 point star Superb; 2006 PSE - Graded Certificate. (this being one of 2 attaining this grade as of 10/08, with only 4 graded higher).

Estimate: $300+

Minimum Bid: $150

32779 #348, 1908, 1c Green XF 90 PSE. (Original Gum - Never Hinged). Coil Pair. Pretty example, strong 90. Extremely Fine. 2006 PSE - Graded Certificate. (SMQ $335; this being one of 6 attaining this grade as of 10/08, with 16 graded higher).

Estimate: $300+

Minimum Bid: $150

32780 #348, 1908, 1c Green VF 80 PSE. (Original Gum - Never Hinged). Coil guide line pair, with immaculate full original gum. Very Fine; 2007 PSE - Graded Certificate. (SMQ $600; this being one of 4 attaining this grade as of 10/08, with 29 graded higher).

Estimate: $500+

Minimum Bid: $250

32781 #350, 1908, 4c Orange Brown. (Regummed). Attractive coil guide line pair, excellent color, regummed, (1988 PF certification as original gum). Fine to Very Fine; 2008 PSE Certificate. (Scott $1,250).

Estimate: $800+

Minimum Bid: $400

32782 #350, 1908-10, 4c Orange Brown, F-VF 75 PSE. (Original Gum - Never Hinged). Coil single. Great impression with rich color. Fine to Very Fine. PSE - Encapsulated. (this being the only example attaining this grade as of 10/08, with 13 graded higher).

Estimate: $200+

Minimum Bid: $100

1909 BLUISH PAPERS

32783 #366, 1909, 15c Pale Ultramarine F 70 PSE. (Original Gum - Previously Hinged). Prior hinge mark, no remnant. Fine. PSE - Encapsulated. (SMQ $720; this being one of 4 attaining this grade as of 10/08, with 11 graded higher).

Estimate: $500+

Minimum Bid: $250

1909 COMMEMORATIVES

32784 #367, 1909, 2c Carmine SUP 98 PSE. (Original Gum - Never Hinged). Post Office Fresh. Superb; 2008 PSE - Graded Certificate. (SMQ $460; this being one of 9 attaining this grade as of 10/08, with only 2 graded higher).

Estimate: $400+

Minimum Bid: $200

32785 #367, 1909, 2c Carmine SUP 98 PSE. (Original Gum - Never Hinged). Superb PSE - Encapsulated. (SMQ $460; this being one of 9 attaining this grade as of 10/08, with only 2 graded higher).

Estimate: $400+

Minimum Bid: $200

32786 #369, 1909, 2c Carmine, VF 80 PSE. (Original Gum - Previously Hinged). A handsome mint example of this Bluish paper issue, bright and vibrant, original gum, with small disturbance across the middle from previous hinging. Very Fine; PSE - Encapsulated. v(SMQ $175; this being one of 11 attaining this grade as of 10/08, with 22 graded higher).

Estimate: $150+

Minimum Bid: $1

1910-11 WASHINGTON-FRANKLIN ISSUE - SGL. LINE WMK.

32787 #379, 1911, 6c Red Orange XF-S 95J PSE. (Original Gum - Hinged). A gorgeous mint single. Original gum, previously hinged including an insignificant tiny hinge remnant. Extremely Fine to Superb; PSE - Encapsulated. (this being one of 2 attaining this grade as of 10/08, with only 2 graded higher).

Estimate: $200+

Minimum Bid: $100

32788 #393, 1910, 2c Carmine, VF 80 PSE. (Original Gum - Hinged). Coil guide line pair, original gum, with two very small pieces of hinge remnant. Very Fine; 2004 PSE - Graded Certificate. (SMQ $300; this being one of 1 attaining this grade as of 10/08, with only 5 graded higher).

Estimate: $250+

Minimum Bid: $125

32789 #395, 1910, 4c Brown. (Original Gum - Never Hinged). Coil guide line pair, with pristine full original gum, Fine; 2006 APS Certificate. (Scott $1,100).

Estimate: $600+

Minimum Bid: $300

32790 #396, 1913, 5c Blue XF-S 95 PSE. (Original Gum - Previously Hinged). Coil Pair. Fresh. Light hinge mark on left stamp only, right stamp never hinged. Extremely Fine to Superb PSE - Encapsulated. (SMQ $340; this being one of 1 attaining this grade as of 10/08, with only 4 graded higher).

Estimate: $300+

Minimum Bid: $150

32791 #396, 1910, 5c Blue, XF 90 PSE. (Original Gum - Never Hinged). Coil single, Extremely Fine; 2008 PSE - Graded Certificate. (SMQ $330; this being one of 17 attaining this grade as of 10/08, with 17 graded higher).

Estimate: $300+

Minimum Bid: $150

1913-15 PANAMA-PACIFIC EXPOSITION ISSUE

32792 #397, 1913, 1c Green XF-S 95J PSE. (Original Gum - Never Hinged). Extremely Fine to Superb; 2007 PSE - Graded Certificate. (this being one of 14 attaining this grade as of 10/08, with 32 graded higher).

Estimate: $350+

Minimum Bid: $175

32793 #397, 1913, 1c Green XF-S 95 PSE. (Original Gum - Never Hinged). Extremely Fine to Superb. 2006 PSE - Graded Certificate. (SMQ $370; this being one of 66 attaining this grade as of 10/08, with 46 graded higher).

Estimate: $300+

Minimum Bid: $150

32794 #397, 1913, 1c Green, XF-S 95 PSE. (Original Gum - Never Hinged). A pristine mint single with a wonderfully crisp and clear impression. Extremely Fine to Superb. PSE - Encapsulated. (SMQ $370; this being one of 66 attaining this grade as of 10/08, with 46 graded higher).

Estimate: $300+

Minimum Bid: $150

32795 #397, 1913, 1c Green, XF-S 95 PSE. (Original Gum - Never Hinged). Striking example, large margins, sharp looking. Extremely Fine to Superb. PSE - Encapsulated. (SMQ $370; this being one of 66 attaining this grade as of 10/08, with 46 graded higher).

Estimate: $300+

Minimum Bid: $150

32796 #397, 1913, 1c Green XF-S 95 PSE. (Original Gum - Never Hinged). Gorgeous and fresh, Extremely Fine to Superb; PSE - Encapsulated. (SMQ $370; this being one of 66 attaining this grade as of 10/08, with 46 graded higher).

Estimate: $300+

Minimum Bid: $150

32797 #398, 1913, 2c Carmine XF-S 95J PSE. (Original Gum - Never Hinged). Spectacular jumbo, as fresh as the day it was printed. Extremely Fine to Superb. 2006 PSE - Graded Certificate. (this being one of 7 attaining this grade as of 10/08, with 21 graded higher).

Estimate: $350+

Minimum Bid: $175

32798 #398, 1913, 2c Carmine XF-S 95 PSE. (Original Gum - Never Hinged). Bright, fresh, and beautiful. Extremely Fine to Superb. PSE - Encapsulated. (SMQ $380; this being one of 52 attaining this grade as of 10/08, with 28 graded higher).

Estimate: $400+

Minimum Bid: $200

32799 #400, 1913, 10c Never Hinged, XF-S 95 PSE. (Original Gum - Hinged). Precisely centered, original gum that has been previously hinged towards the center. Extremely Fine to Superb PSE - Encapsulated. (SMQ $405; this being one of 12 attaining this grade as of 10/08, with only 6 graded higher).

Estimate: $350+

Minimum Bid: $175

32800 #400, 1913, 10c Orange Yellow XF 90J PSE. (Original Gum - Previously Hinged). Discovery of San Francisco Bay. Light hinge mark only. Large margins. Extremely Fine. PSE - Encapsulated. (this being one of 2 attaining this grade as of 10/08, with 18 graded higher).

Estimate: $300+

Minimum Bid: $150

32801 #400A, 1913, 10c Orange XF 90J PSE. (Original Gum - Previously Hinged). Discovery of San Francisco Bay. Small portion of prior hinge remnant. Large margins. Extremely Fine PSE - Encapsulated. (this being one of 6 attaining this grade as of 10/08, with 28 graded higher).

Estimate: $300+

Minimum Bid: $150

32802 #400A, 1913, 10c Orange, VF-XF 85 PSE. (Original Gum - Hinged). Beautifully bright and vibrant, original gum, couple of hinge marks. Very Fine to Extremely Fine; PSE - Encapsulated. (SMQ $255; this being one of 13 attaining this grade as of 10/08, with 53 graded higher).

Estimate: $200+

Minimum Bid: $100

32803 #400A, 1913, 10c Orange F 70 PSE. (Original Gum - Never Hinged). Top margin example with very fine impression. Fine PSE - Graded Certificate. (SMQ $200; this being one of 6 attaining this grade as of 10/08, with 124 graded higher).

Estimate: $150+

Minimum Bid: $1

1912-14 WASHINGTON - FRANKLIN ISSUE

32804 #406, 1912, 2c Carmine XF-S 95 PSE. (Original Gum - Never Hinged). Post Office Fresh. Extremely Fine to Superb; 2008 PSE - Graded Certificate. (SMQ $245; this being one of 15 attaining this grade as of 10/08, with 11 graded higher).

Estimate: $200+

Minimum Bid: $100

32805 #410, 1912, 1c Green XF-S 95 PSE. (Original Gum - Never Hinged). Awesome line pair, very well centered, nice original look. Extremely Fine to Superb. PSE - Encapsulated. (SMQ $290; this being one of 2 attaining this grade as of 10/08, with only 9 graded higher).

Estimate: $300+

Minimum Bid: $150

32806 #412, 1912, 1c Green, XF-S 95 PSE. (Original Gum - Never Hinged). Deep color, perfect margins. Extremely Fine to Superb. PSE - Encapsulated. (SMQ $255; this being one of 4 attaining this grade as of 10/08, with only 4 graded higher).

Estimate: $250+

Minimum Bid: $125

32807 #415, 1912, 9c Salmon Red XF 90 PSE. (Original Gum - Never Hinged). Post office fresh in all respects. Extremely Fine and most desirable. 2008 PSE - Graded Certificate. (SMQ $425; this being one of 15 attaining this grade as of 10/08, with 13 graded higher).

Estimate: $400+

Minimum Bid: $200

1913-15 WASHINGTON-FRANKLIN ISSUE - SGL. LINE WMK.

32808 #437, 1914, 15c Gray, GEM 100 PSE. (No Gum). A magnificent stamp for the collector more interested in the face than the gum, perfectly centered, with full even perforations all around, warm pastel color on clean paper, unused (no gum), Gem; PSE - Encapsulated. (this being the only example attaining this grade as of 10/08, with none graded higher).

Estimate: $500+

Minimum Bid: $250

32809 #440, 1914-15, 50c Violet, F 70 PSE. (Original Gum - Hinged). Gorgeous pastel color, detailed impression, original gum with a small hinge remnant just above the center, Fine; PSE - Encapsulated. (SMQ $280; this being one of 5 attaining this grade as of 10/08, with 35 graded higher).

Estimate: $240+

Minimum Bid: $120

32810 #443, 1914, 1c Green XF-S 95 PSE. (Original Gum - Never Hinged). Deep green color, mint large margins. Extremely Fine to Superb PSE - Encapsulated. (SMQ $305; this being one of 6, attaining this grade as of 10/08, with only 1 graded higher) .

Estimate: $300+

Minimum Bid: $150

32811 #443, 1914, 1c Green, XF 90 PSE. (Original Gum - Previously Hinged). A magnificent mint coil guide line pair, each stamp spectacularly centered, luxuriously vibrant and finely detailed, original gum, light traces of previous hinging on left stamp only, the right stamp never hinged, Extremely Fine; PSE - Encapsulated. (SMQ $240; this being the only example attaining this grade as of 10/08, with only 1 graded higher).

Estimate: $200+

Minimum Bid: $100

32812 #443, 1914, 1c Green. (Original Gum - Never Hinged). Coil guide line pair. Very Fine; 2004 PF Certificate. (Scott $325).

Estimate: $300+

Minimum Bid: $150

32813 #444, 1914, 2c Carmine. (Original Gum - Previously Hinged). A mint coil guide line pair. Fine; 2005 PSE Certificate. (Scott $325).

Estimate: $200+

Minimum Bid: $100

32814 #445, 1914, 3c Violet. (Original Gum - Previously Hinged). A mint "paste-up" pair, original gum, with previous hinging at top of left stamp only, the right stamp being never hinged. Fine; 2006 APS Certificate. (Scott as a normal pair $575).

Estimate: $300+

Minimum Bid: $150

1913-15 WASHINGTON-FRANKLIN ISSUE - SGL. LINE WMK.

32815 #445, 1914, 3c Violet, VF 80 PSE. (Original Gum - Previously Hinged). Fresh and bright, original gum, light previous hinging at upper left. Very Fine; PSE - Encapsulated. (SMQ $225; this being one of 3 attaining this grade as of 10/08, with only 8 graded higher).

Estimate: $200+

Minimum Bid: $100

32816 #447, 1914, 5c Blue, VF-XF 85 PSE. (Original Gum - Previously Hinged). Post Office fresh, Very Fine to Extremely Fine; PSE - Encapsulated. (SMQ $300; this being one of 5 attaining this grade as of 10/08, with only 8 graded higher).

Estimate: $300+

Minimum Bid: $150

32817 #454, 1915, 2c Red. (Original Gum - Previously Hinged). A mint coil joint line pair. Previous hinging at top center of the pair. Very Fine; 2005 PSE Certificate. (Scott $425).

Estimate: $250+

Minimum Bid: $125

32818 #456, 1916, 3c Red Violet VF 80 PSE. (Original Gum - Previously Hinged). Handsome and fresh coil pair, light pastel color, uniformly well centered, original gum, very light traces of previous hinging at the top center of the pair. Very Fine; PSE - Encapsulated. (SMQ $570; this being one of 5 attaining this grade as of 10/08, with only 8 graded higher).

Estimate: $400+

Minimum Bid: $200

32819 #457, 1915, 4c Brown, XF 90 PSE. (Original Gum - Never Hinged). Bright and vibrant with a deeply etched impression on crisp paper. Extremely Fine and desirable; PSE - Encapsulated. (SMQ $240; this being one of 10 attaining this grade as of 10/08, with only 8 graded higher).

Estimate: $200+

Minimum Bid: $100

32820 #459, 1914, June 30, 2c F-VF 75 PSE. (Original Gum - Previously Hinged). Handsome and fresh horizontal pair, full original gum, with the barest kiss of previous hinging. Fine to Very Fine; PSE - Encapsulated.
(this being the only example attaining this grade as of 10/08, with only 5 graded higher).

Estimate: $300+

Minimum Bid: $150

32821 #459, 1914, 2c Carmine, VF 80 PSE. (Original Gum - Never Hinged). Post Office fresh, with owner's handstamp on reverse. Very Fine. PSE - Encapsulated. (SMQ $290; this being one of 4 attaining this grade as of 10/08, with 57 graded higher).

Estimate: $240+

Minimum Bid: $120

1916-22 WASHINGTON-FRANKLIN ISSUE - UNWATERMARKED

32822 #475, 1916, 15c Gray, VF-XF 85 PSE. (Original Gum - Hinged). Fresh, original gum, with a hinge remnant at top. Very Fine to Extremely Fine. PSE - Encapsulated. (SMQ $245; this being one of 7 attaining this grade as of 10/08, with 22 graded higher).

Estimate: $200+

Minimum Bid: $100

32823 #476, 1916, 20c Ultramarine, VF-XF 85 PSE. (Original Gum - Previously Hinged). Luxuriously fresh and vibrant, original gum showing only light traces of previous hinging. Catalog number in pencil on back. Very Fine to Extremely Fine; PSE - Encapsulated. (SMQ $315; this being one of 11 attaining this grade as of 10/08, with 12 graded higher).

Estimate: $260+

Minimum Bid: $130

32824 #477, 1917, 50c Light Violet, F 70 PSE. (Original Gum - Hinged). Mint single, original gum, previously hinged, with the catalog number lightly penciled on the gum. Fine PSE - Encapsulated. (SMQ $520; this being one of 4 attaining this grade as of 10/08, with 33 graded higher).

Estimate: $400+

Minimum Bid: $200

32825 #480, 1917, $5 Light Green, VF 80 PSE. (Original Gum - Previously Hinged). Mint single, original gum that shows only light traces of previous hinging. Very Fine; 2007 PSE - Graded Certificate. (SMQ $190; this being one of 11 attaining this grade as of 10/08, with 60 graded higher).

Estimate: $250+

Minimum Bid: $125

32826 #486, 1916, 1c Green, SUP 98 PSE. (Original Gum - Never Hinged). Simply superb. PSE - Encapsulated. (SMQ $185; this being one of 7 attaining this grade as of 10/08, with only 6 graded higher).

Estimate: $200+

Minimum Bid: $100

32827 #489, 1916, 3c Violet, XF-S 95 PSE. (Original Gum - Never Hinged). Pretty mint single. Extremely Fine to Superb. PSE - Encapsulated. (SMQ $185; this being one of 18 attaining this grade as of 10/08, with 12 graded higher).

Estimate: $185+

Minimum Bid: $1

32828 #492, 1916, 2c Carmine, XF-S 95 PSE. (Original Gum - Never Hinged). Outstanding example of the coil pair. Extremely Fine to Superb. PSE - Encapsulated. (SMQ $220; this being one of 5 attaining this grade as of 10/08, with only 3 graded higher).

Estimate: $200+

Minimum Bid: $100

32829 #495, 1916, 4c Orange Brown XF-S 95 PSE. (Original Gum - Never Hinged). Coil pair. Extremely Fine to Superb. PSE - Encapsulated. (SMQ $215; this being one of 7 attaining this grade as of 10/08, with only 9 graded higher).

Estimate: $200+

Minimum Bid: $100

32830 #495, 1916, 4c Orange Brown XF-S 95 PSE. (Original Gum - Never Hinged). Strong 95. Extremely Fine to Superb. PSE - Encapsulated. (SMQ $215; this being one of 7 attaining this grade as of 10/08, with only 9 graded higher).

Estimate: $200+

Minimum Bid: $100

32831 #498, 1917, 1c Green, SUP 98 PSE. (Original Gum - Never Hinged). Superb. PSE - Encapsulated. (SMQ $280; this being one of 16 attaining this grade as of 10/08, with 10 graded higher).

Estimate: $280+

Minimum Bid: $140

1917-19 WASHINGTON-FRANKLIN ISSUE - PERF 11

32832 #499, 1917, 2c Rose SUP 98 PSE. (Original Gum - Never Hinged). Superb PSE - Encapsulated. (SMQ $300; this being one of 10 attaining this grade as of 10/08, with only 2 graded higher).

Estimate: $300+

Minimum Bid: $150

32833 #501, 1917, 3c Light Violet XF-S 95 PSE. (Original Gum - Never Hinged). Extremely Fine to Superb; 2008 PSE - Graded Certificate. (SMQ $305; this being one of 24 attaining this grade as of 10/08, with only 10 graded higher).

Estimate: $250+

Minimum Bid: $125

32834 #506, 1917, 6c Red Orange XF-S 95 PSE. (Original Gum - Never Hinged). Choice. Extremely Fine to Superb. PSE - Encapsulated. (SMQ $295; this being one of 46 attaining this grade as of 10/08, with 15 graded higher).

Estimate: $300+

Minimum Bid: $150

32835 #509, 1917, 9c Salmon Red, XF-S 95 PSE. (Original Gum - Never Hinged). Extremely Fine to Superb. PSE - Encapsulated. (SMQ $355; this being one of 32 attaining this grade as of 10/08, with 15 graded higher).

Estimate: $350+

Minimum Bid: $175

32836 #511, 1917, 11c Light Green, XF-S 95 PSE. (Original Gum - Never Hinged). Vivacious deep dark bluish-green (slab notes light green). Extremely Fine to Superb. PSE - Encapsulated. (SMQ $225; this being one of 47 attaining this grade as of 10/08, with 19 graded higher).

Estimate: $225+

Minimum Bid: $112

32837 #512, 1917, 12c Claret Brown XF-S 95 PSE. (Original Gum - Never Hinged). Strong for grade. Extremely Fine to Superb. PSE - Encapsulated. (SMQ $250; this being one of 23 attaining this grade as of 10/08, with 15 graded higher).

Estimate: $250+

Minimum Bid: $125

32838 #512, 1917, 12c Claret Brown XF-S 95 PSE. (Original Gum - Never Hinged). Fresh and gorgeous. Extremely Fine to Superb. 2008 PSE - Graded Certificate. (SMQ $250; this being one of 23 attaining this grade as of 10/08, with 15 graded higher).

Estimate: $200+

Minimum Bid: $100

32839 #513, 1917, 13c Apple Green XF-S 95 PSE. (Original Gum - Never Hinged). Extremely Fine to Superb; 2007 PSE - Graded Certificate. (SMQ $305; this being one of 29 attaining this grade as of 10/08, with 22 graded higher).

Estimate: $250+

Minimum Bid: $125

32840 #513, 1919, 13c Apple Green, XF-S 95 PSE. (Original Gum - Never Hinged). Extremely Fine to Superb; 2008 PSE - Graded Certificate. (SMQ $305; this being one of 29 attaining this grade as of 10/08, with 22 graded higher).

Estimate: $250+

Minimum Bid: $125

1918-20 WASHINGTON-FRANKLIN ISSUE - OFFSET ISSUES

32841 #534, 1918, 2c Carmine, GEM 100 PSE. (Original Gum - Never Hinged). A monstrous Gem showing traces of the frame lines from the adjoining stamps left, right, and bottom. 2007 PSE - Graded Certificate. (this being one of 7 attaining this grade as of 10/08, with only 3 graded higher).

Estimate: $350+

Minimum Bid: $175

32842 #534, 1918, 2c Carmine GEM 100 PSE. (Original Gum - Never Hinged). Absolute perfection, maximum size margins. Gem; 2008 PSE - Graded Certificate. (this being one of 7 attaining this grade as of 10/08, with only 3 graded higher).

Estimate: $200+

Minimum Bid: $100

1919-20 ISSUES

32843 #537, 1919, 3c Violet XF-S 95J PSE. (Original Gum - Never Hinged). Victory of the Allies in World War I. Extremely Fine to Superb Jumbo; 2004 PSE - Graded Certificate. (this being one of 24 attaining this grade as of 10/08, with 24 graded higher).

Estimate: $350+

Minimum Bid: $175

32844 #537, 1919, 3c Violet XF-S 95 PSE. (Original Gum - Never Hinged). Extremely Fine to Superb; PSE - Encapsulated. (SMQ $190; this being one of 40 attaining this grade as of 10/08, with 48 graded higher).

Estimate: $175+

Minimum Bid: $1

32845 #543, 1921, 1c Green SUP 98 PSE. (Original Gum - Never Hinged). Superb; 2007 PSE - Graded Certificate. (SMQ $240; this being one of 15 attaining this grade as of 10/08, with none graded higher).

Estimate: $200+

Minimum Bid: $100

32846 #547, 1920, $2 Carmine And Black VF 80 PSE. (Original Gum - Never Hinged). Lovely example with fabulous color. Very Fine; 2007 PSE - Graded Certificate, 1998 PF Certificate. (SMQ $325; this being one of 19 attaining this grade as of 10/08, with 105 graded higher).

Estimate: $275+

Minimum Bid: $138

32847 #547, 1920, $2 Carmine & Black F-VF 75 PSE. (Original Gum - Never Hinged). Post Office Fresh. Fine to Very Fine PSE - Encapsulated. (this being one of 6 attaining this grade as of 10/08, with 124 graded higher).

Estimate: $220+

Minimum Bid: $110

1920 PILGRIM TERCENTENARY ISSUE

32848 #548, 1920, 1c Green XF-S 95; PSE. (Original Gum - Never Hinged). The Mayflower. Extremely Fine to Superb; 2005 PSE - Graded Certificate. (SMQ $210; this being one of 20 attaining this grade as of 10/08, with 23 graded higher).

Estimate: $200+

Minimum Bid: $100

32849 #550, 1920, 5c Deep Blue, XF 90 PSE. (Original Gum - Never Hinged). Signing of the Compact. Extremely Fine. 2008 PSE - Graded Certificate. (SMQ $260; this being one of 32 attaining this grade as of 10/08, with 52 graded higher).

Estimate: $250+

Minimum Bid: $125

1922-25 DEFINITIVES

32850 #551-73, 1922, ½c - $5. (Original Gum - Never Hinged). Complete set (23) of 1922 flat plate Definitive's, fresh and vibrant. Fine to Very Fine. (Scott $1,222). (Total: 1 pages)

Estimate: $500+

Minimum Bid: $250

32851 #551, 1925, 1/2c Olive Brown, SUP 98J PSE. (Original Gum - Never Hinged). Superb. PSE - Encapsulated. (this being one of 17 attaining this grade as of 10/08, with only 6 graded higher).

Estimate: $200+

Minimum Bid: $100

32852 #551, 1922, 1/2c Olive Brown, SUP 98 PSE. (Original Gum - Never Hinged). Superb. PSE - Encapsulated. (SMQ $225; this being one of 32 attaining this grade as of 10/08, with 23 graded higher).

Estimate: $200+

Minimum Bid: $100

32853 #551, 1922, 1/2c Olive Brown SUP 98 PSE. (Original Gum - Never Hinged). Superb; 2008 PSE - Graded Certificate. (SMQ $225; this being one of 32 attaining this grade as of 10/08, with 23 graded higher).

Estimate: $200+

Minimum Bid: $100

32854 #552, 1922, 1c Never Hinged SUP 98; PSE. (Original Gum - Never Hinged). Superb PSE - Encapsulated. (SMQ $310; this being one of 16 attaining this grade as of 10/08, with only 3 graded higher).

Estimate: $300+

Minimum Bid: $150

32855 #552, 1922, 1c Deep Green, SUP 98 PSE. (Original Gum - Never Hinged). Superb. PSE - Encapsulated. (SMQ $310 ; this being one of 16 attaining this grade as of 10/08, with only 3 graded higher).

Estimate: $300+

Minimum Bid: $150

32856 #553, 1922, 11/2c Yellow Brown SUP 98 PSE. (Original Gum - Never Hinged). Plate No.16869. Superb. PSE - Encapsulated. (SMQ $365; this being one of 17 attaining this grade as of 10/08, with only 9 graded higher).

Estimate: $400+

Minimum Bid: $200

32857 #554, 1922, 2c Carmine, SUP 98; PSE. (Original Gum - Never Hinged). Superb. PSE - Encapsulated. (SMQ $320; this being one of 10 attaining this grade as of 10/08, with 10 graded higher).

Estimate: $300+

Minimum Bid: $150

32858 #555, 1922, 3c Violet XF-S 95J PSE. (Original Gum - Never Hinged). Extremely Fine to Superb. 2008 PSE - Graded Certificate. (this being one of 7 attaining this grade as of 10/08, with 14 graded higher).

Estimate: $400+

Minimum Bid: $200

32859 #555, 1922, 3c Red Violet XF-S 95 PSE. (Original Gum - Never Hinged). Extremely Fine to Superb; 2007 PSE - Graded Certificate. (SMQ $325; this being one of 45 attaining this grade as of 10/08, with 21 graded higher).

Estimate: $250+

Minimum Bid: $125

32860 #556, 1922, 4c Yellow Brown XF-S 95 PSE. (Original Gum - Never Hinged). Extremely Fine to Superb; 2007 PSE - Graded Certificate. (SMQ $410; this being one of 31 attaining this grade as of 10/08, with 11 graded higher).

Estimate: $300+

Minimum Bid: $150

32861 #558, 1922, 6c Red Orange, XF 90 PSE. (Original Gum - Never Hinged). Extremely Fine. 2006 PSE - Graded Certificate. (SMQ $200; this being one of 33 attaining this grade as of 10/08, with 48 graded higher).

Estimate: $200+

Minimum Bid: $100

32862 #564, 1922, 12c Brown Violet, SUP 98 PSE. (Original Gum - Never Hinged). Superb. PSE - Encapsulated. (SMQ $435; this being one of 25 attaining this grade as of 10/08, with only 8 graded higher).

Estimate: $450+

Minimum Bid: $225

32863 #564, 1922, 12c Brown Violet SUP 98; PSE. (Original Gum - Never Hinged). A luxurious mint example, impeccably centered, fresh and vibrant. Superb. PSE - Encapsulated. (SMQ $435; this being one of 25 attaining this grade as of 10/08, with only 8 graded higher).

Estimate: $400+

Minimum Bid: $200

32864 #566, 1922, 15c Never Hinged XF-S 95 PSE. (Original Gum - Never Hinged). Extremely Fine to Superb. 2006 PSE - Graded Certificate. (SMQ $345; this being one of 40 attaining this grade as of 10/08, with 41 graded higher).

Estimate: $300+

Minimum Bid: $150

32865 #566, 1922, 15c Gray XF-S 95 PSE. (Original Gum - Never Hinged). Extremely Fine to Superb. 2007 PSE - Graded Certificate. (SMQ $345; this being one of 40 attaining this grade as of 10/08, with 41 graded higher).

Estimate: $300+

Minimum Bid: $150

32866 #567, 1922, 20c Carmine Rose, XF-S 95J PSE. (Original Gum - Never Hinged). Extremely Fine to Superb. 2004 PSE - Graded Certificate. (this being one of 7 attaining this grade as of 10/08, with 23 graded higher).

Estimate: $350+

Minimum Bid: $175

32867 #568, 1922, 25c Yellow Green, XF-S 95 PSE. (Original Gum - Never Hinged). Extremely Fine to Superb. PSE - Encapsulated. (SMQ $330; this being one of 46, attaining this grade as of 10/08, with 26 graded higher).

Estimate: $330+

Minimum Bid: $165

32868 #569, 1922, 30c Olive Brown, XF-S 95J PSE. (Original Gum - Never Hinged). Magnificent jumbo with deep color. Extremely Fine to Superb. 2005 PSE - Graded Certificate. (this being one of 14 attaining this grade as of 10/08, 17 graded higher).

Estimate: $450+

Minimum Bid: $225

32869 #569, 1922, 30c Never Hinged XF-S 95 PSE. (Original Gum - Never Hinged). Extremely Fine to Superb; 2008 PSE - Graded Certificate. (SMQ $470; this being one of 25 attaining this grade as of 10/08, with 31 graded higher).

Estimate: $375+

Minimum Bid: $188

32870 #570, 1922, 50c Lilac XF 90J PSE. (Original Gum - Never Hinged). Extremely Fine; 2007 PSE - Graded Certificate. (this being one of 10 attaining this grade as of 10/08, with 56 graded higher).

Estimate: $200+

Minimum Bid: $100

32871 #571, 1922, $1 Violet Black, XF-S 95J PSE. (Original Gum - Never Hinged). Extremely Fine to Superb. 2008 PSE - Graded Certificate. (this being one of 2 attaining this grade as of 10/08, with 19 graded higher).

Estimate: $400+

Minimum Bid: $200

32872 #571, 1922, $1 Never Hinged XF-S 95 PSE. (Original Gum - Never Hinged). Extremely Fine to Superb; 2008 PSE - Graded Certificate. (SMQ $600; this being one of 56 attaining this grade as of 10/08, with 21 graded higher).

Estimate: $500+

Minimum Bid: $250

32873 #571, 1922, $1 Violet Black, XF-S 95 PSE. (Original Gum - Never Hinged). Extremely Fine to Superb; 2008 PSE - Graded Certificate. (SMQ $600; this being one of 56 attaining this grade as of 10/08, with 21 graded higher).

Estimate: $400+

Minimum Bid: $200

32874 #573, 1922-25, $5 Carmine & Blue VF 80 PSE. (Original Gum - Never Hinged). Very Fine PSE - Encapsulated. (SMQ $200; this being one of 35 attaining this grade as of 10/08, with 245 graded higher).

Estimate: $150+

Minimum Bid: $1

32875 #585, 1923, 4c Yellow Brown XF-S 95 PSE. (Original Gum - Never Hinged). Extremely Fine to Superb; 2007 PSE - Graded Certificate. (SMQ $500; this being one of 18 attaining this grade as of 10/08, with 13 graded higher).

Estimate: $400+

Minimum Bid: $200

32876 #588, 1923, 7c Black XF-S 95 PSE. (Original Gum - Never Hinged). Post Office Fresh. Extremely Fine to Superb; 2005 PSE - Graded Certificate. (SMQ $400; this being one of 23 attaining this grade as of 10/08, with only 9 graded higher).

Estimate: $350+

Minimum Bid: $175

1924-29 COMMEMORATIVE ISSUES

32877 #615, 1924, 2c Carmine Rose XF-S 95 PSE. (Original Gum - Never Hinged). Extremely Fine to Superb. PSE - Graded Certificate. (SMQ $190; this being one of 32 attaining this grade as of 10/08, with 16 graded higher).

Estimate: $150+

Minimum Bid: $1

32878 #617, 1925, 1c Deep Green, SUP 98 PSE. (Original Gum - Never Hinged). Superb PSE - Encapsulated. (SMQ $260; this being one of 36 attaining this grade as of 10/08, with 12 graded higher).

Estimate: $250+

Minimum Bid: $125

32879 #617, 1925, 1c Deep Green SUP 98 PSE. (Original Gum - Never Hinged). Superb; 2007 PSE - Graded Certificate. (SMQ $260; this being one of 36 attaining this grade as of 10/08, with 12 graded higher).

Estimate: $200+

Minimum Bid: $100

32880 #617, 1925, 1c Deep Green SUP 98 PSE. (Original Gum - Never Hinged). Vividly bright, with a virtually life-like quality. Superb; 2008 PSE - Graded Certificate. (SMQ $260; this being one of 36 attaining this grade as of 10/08, with 12 graded higher).

Estimate: $200+

Minimum Bid: $100

32881 #618, 1925, 2c Carmine Rose, SUP 98 PSE. (Original Gum - Never Hinged). Superb PSE - Encapsulated. (SMQ $295; this being one of 38 attaining this grade as of 10/08, with only 8 graded higher).

Estimate: $300+

Minimum Bid: $150

32882 #618, 1925, 2c Carmine Rose, SUP 98 PSE. (Original Gum - Never Hinged). Superb PSE - Encapsulated. (SMQ $295; this being one of 38 attaining this grade as of 10/08, with only 8 graded higher).

Estimate: $300+

Minimum Bid: $150

32883 #619, 1925, 5c Dark Blue XF-S 95J PSE. (Original Gum - Never Hinged). Lexington-Concord. Extremely Fine to Superb Jumbo; 2005 PSE - Graded Certificate. (this being one of 13 attaining this grade as of 10/08, with 35 graded higher).

Estimate: $350+

Minimum Bid: $175

32884 #619, 1925, 5c Dark Blue XF-S 95 PSE. (Original Gum - Never Hinged). Extremely Fine to Superb; 2006 PSE - Graded Certificate. (SMQ $220; this being one of 106 attaining this grade as of 10/08, with 48 graded higher).

Estimate: $175+

Minimum Bid: $1

32885 #620, 1925, 2c Carmine & Black SUP 98 PSE. (Original Gum - Never Hinged). Superb; 2008 PSE - Graded Certificate. (SMQ $280; this being one of 20 attaining this grade as of 10/08, with only 7 graded higher).

Estimate: $250+

Minimum Bid: $125

32886 #620, 1925, 2c Carmine & Black SUP 98 PSE. (Original Gum - Never Hinged). Norse-American. Superb; 2008 PSE - Graded Certificate. (SMQ $280; this being one of 20 attaining this grade as of 10/08, with only 7 graded higher).

Estimate: $250+

Minimum Bid: $125

32887 #621, 1925, 5c Dark Blue & Black, XF-S 95 PSE. (Original Gum - Never Hinged). Extremely Fine to Superb. PSE - Encapsulated. (SMQ $185; this being one of 62 attaining this grade as of 10/08, with 36 graded higher).

Estimate: $200+

Minimum Bid: $100

32888 #628, 1926, 5c Gray Lilac SUP 98 PSE. (Original Gum - Never Hinged). Superb; 2008 PSE - Graded Certificate. (SMQ $385; this being one of 28 attaining this grade as of 10/08, with only 6 graded higher).

Estimate: $300+

Minimum Bid: $150

32889 #629, 1926, 2c Carmine Rose, SUP 98 PSE. (Original Gum - Never Hinged). Superb. PSE - Encapsulated. (SMQ $255; this being one of 20 attaining this grade as of 10/08, with only 7 graded higher).

Estimate: $250+

Minimum Bid: $125

32890 #634A, 1928, 2c Carmine F-VF 75 PSE. (Original Gum - Never Hinged). Type II. Fine to Very Fine PSE - Encapsulated. (this being one of 10 attaining this grade as of 10/08, with 49 graded higher).

Estimate: $400+

Minimum Bid: $200

32891 #636, 1926, 4c Yellow Brown SUP 98 PSE. (Original Gum - Never Hinged). Superb PSE - Encapsulated. (SMQ $440; this being one of 11, attaining this grade as of 10/08, with only 3 graded higher) .

Estimate: $440+

Minimum Bid: $220

32892 #636, 1926, 4c Yellow Brown SUP 98 PSE. (Original Gum - Never Hinged). Superb; 2007 PSE - Graded Certificate. (SMQ $440; this being one of 11 attaining this grade as of 10/08, with only 3 graded higher).

Estimate: $350+

Minimum Bid: $175

32893 #639, 1926, 7c Black SUP 98 PSE. (Original Gum - Never Hinged). Superb PSE - Encapsulated. (SMQ $440; this being one of 16, attaining this grade as of 10/08, with 13 graded higher) .

Estimate: $440+

Minimum Bid: $220

32894 #639, 1926, 7c Black SUP 98 PSE. (Original Gum - Never Hinged). Just about the finest color and impression possible, amazing. Superb; 2008 PSE - Graded Certificate. (SMQ $440; this being one of 16 attaining this grade as of 10/08, with 13 graded higher).

Estimate: $400+

Minimum Bid: $200

32895 #641, 1926, 9c Rose SUP 98 PSE. (Original Gum - Never Hinged). Superb; 2007 PSE - Graded Certificate. (SMQ $440; this being one of 10 attaining this grade as of 10/08, with only 3 graded higher).

Estimate: $400+

Minimum Bid: $200

32896 #644, 1927, 2c Carmine Rose SUP 98 PSE. (Original Gum - Never Hinged). Superb PSE - Encapsulated. (SMQ $295; this being one of 20, attaining this grade as of 10/08, with only 9 graded higher) .

Estimate: $300+

Minimum Bid: $150

32897 #645, 1928, 2c Carmine Rose GEM 100 PSE. (Original Gum - Never Hinged). Gem; 2008 PSE - Graded Certificate. (this being one of 5 attaining this grade as of 10/08, with *none* graded higher).

Estimate: $400+

Minimum Bid: $200

32898 #645, 1928, 2c Carmine Rose SUP 98 PSE. (Original Gum - Never Hinged). Superb PSE - Encapsulated. (SMQ $230; this being one of 13, attaining this grade as of 10/08, with only 6 graded higher) .

Estimate: $200+

Minimum Bid: $100

32899 #646, 1928, 2c Carmine SUP 98 PSE. (Original Gum - Never Hinged). Superb PSE - Encapsulated. (SMQ $315; this being one of 19, attaining this grade as of 10/08, with only 10 graded higher) .

Estimate: $300+

Minimum Bid: $150

32900 #654, 1929, 2c Carmine Rose SUP 98J PSE. (Original Gum - Never Hinged). Superb; 2008 PSE - Graded Certificate. (this being one of 5 attaining this grade as of 10/08, with only 1 graded higher).

Estimate: $250+

Minimum Bid: $125

32901 #655, 1929, 2c Carmine Rose SUP 98 PSE. (Original Gum - Never Hinged). Superb; 2007 PSE - Graded Certificate. (SMQ $330; this being one of 20 attaining this grade as of 10/08, with only 1 graded higher).

Estimate: $250+

Minimum Bid: $125

32902 #656, 1929, 2c Carmine Rose SUP 98 PSE. (Original Gum - Never Hinged). Superb PSE - Encapsulated. (SMQ $420; this being one of 6, attaining this grade as of 10/08, with only 1 graded higher) .

Estimate: $420+

Minimum Bid: $210

32903 #657, 1929, 2c Carmine Rose SUP 98 PSE. (Original Gum - Never Hinged). Superb PSE - Encapsulated. (SMQ $190; this being one of 23, attaining this grade as of 10/08, with only 4 graded higher) .

Estimate: $190+

Minimum Bid: $1

32904 #657, 1929, 2c Carmine Rose, SUP 98 PSE. (Original Gum - Never Hinged). Superb; 2007 PSE - Graded Certificate. (SMQ $190; this being one of 23 attaining this grade as of 10/08, with only 4 graded higher).

Estimate: $150+

Minimum Bid: $1

32905 #657, 1929, 2c Carmine Rose SUP 98 PSE. (Original Gum - Never Hinged). Superb PSE - Graded Certificate. (SMQ $190; this being one of 23 attaining this grade as of 10/08, with only 4 graded higher).

Estimate: $150+

Minimum Bid: $1

1929 KANSAS / NEBRASKA OVERPRINTS

32906 #658, 1929, 1c Green XF-S 95J PSE. (Original Gum - Never Hinged). Extremely Fine to Superb; 2005 PSE - Graded Certificate. (this being one of 3 attaining this grade as of 10/08, with only 8 graded higher).

Estimate: $225+

Minimum Bid: $112

32907 #661, 1929, 3c Violet XF-S 95 PSE. (Original Gum - Never Hinged). Extremely Fine to Superb; 2008 PSE - Graded Certificate. (SMQ $450; this being one of 24 attaining this grade as of 10/08, with only 9 graded higher).

Estimate: $400+

Minimum Bid: $200

32908 #667, 1929, 9c Light Rose XF-S 95 PSE. (Original Gum - Never Hinged). Nebraska Overprint. Extremely Fine to Superb; 2008 PSE - Graded Certificate. (SMQ $340; this being one of 15 attaining this grade as of 10/08, with 13 graded higher).

Estimate: $300+

Minimum Bid: $150

32909 #671, 1929, 2c Carmine SUP 98 PSE. (Original Gum - Never Hinged). Superb; 2008 PSE - Graded Certificate. (SMQ $480; this being one of 6 attaining this grade as of 10/08, with only 3 graded higher).

Estimate: $500+

Minimum Bid: $250

32910 #674, 1929, 5c Deep Blue XF-S 95 PSE. (Original Gum - Never Hinged). Extremely Fine to Superb; 2008 PSE - Graded Certificate. (SMQ $400; this being one of 19 attaining this grade as of 10/08, with only 4 graded higher).

Estimate: $350+

Minimum Bid: $175

32911 #679, 1929, 10c Orange Yellow VF-XF 85 PSE. (Original Gum - Never Hinged). Nebraska Overprint. Very Fine to Extremely Fine; 2007 PSE - Graded Certificate. (SMQ $315; this being one of 19 attaining this grade as of 10/08, with 78 graded higher).

Estimate: $250+

Minimum Bid: $125

1930 TO DATE

32912 #682, 1930, 2c Carmine Rose SUP 98 PSE. (Original Gum - Never Hinged). Superb PSE - Graded Certificate. (SMQ $190; this being one of 12 attaining this grade as of 10/08, with only 2 graded higher).

Estimate: $150+

Minimum Bid: $1

32913 #683, 1930, 2c Carmine Rose SUP 98 PSE. (Original Gum - Never Hinged). Superb PSE - Encapsulated. (SMQ $210; this being one of 9, attaining this grade as of 10/08, with only 4 graded higher) .

Estimate: $200+

Minimum Bid: $100

32914 #684, 1930, 1½c Brown, SUP 98 PSE. (Original Gum - Never Hinged). Superb; 2008 PSE - Graded Certificate. (SMQ $275; this being one of 19 attaining this grade as of 10/08, with only 4 graded higher).

Estimate: $250+

Minimum Bid: $125

32915 #688, 1930, 2c Never Hinged SUP 98 PSE. (Original Gum - Never Hinged). Superb; 2008 PSE - Graded Certificate. (SMQ $220; this being one of 8 attaining this grade as of 10/08, with only 3 graded higher).

Estimate: $160+

Minimum Bid: $1

32916 #689, 1930, 2c Carmine Rose SUP 98 PSE. (Original Gum - Never Hinged). Superb PSE - Encapsulated. (SMQ $185; this being one of 16, attaining this grade as of 10/08, with only 7 graded higher) .

Estimate: $200+

Minimum Bid: $100

32917 #690, 1931, 2c Carmine Rose SUP 98 PSE. (Original Gum - Never Hinged). Superb PSE - Encapsulated. (SMQ $170; this being one of 12, attaining this grade as of 10/08, with only 9 graded higher) .

Estimate: $200+

Minimum Bid: $100

32918 #700, 1931, 30c Brown XF-S 95 PSE. (Original Gum - Never Hinged). Extremely Fine to Superb; 2008 PSE - Graded Certificate. (SMQ $195; this being one of 28 attaining this grade as of 10/08, with 15 graded higher).

Estimate: $200+

Minimum Bid: $100

32919 #702, 1931, 2c Black And Red SUP 98 PSE. (Original Gum - Never Hinged). Superb PSE - Encapsulated. (SMQ $170; this being one of 25, attaining this grade as of 10/08, with only 3 graded higher) .

Estimate: $200+

Minimum Bid: $100

32920 #725, 1932, 3c Violet SUP 98J PSE. (Original Gum - Never Hinged). Enormous margin jumbo with bold impression and color. Fresh. Superb; 2007 PSE - Graded Certificate. (SMQ $220; this being one of 13 attaining this grade as of 10/08, with only 4 graded higher).

Estimate: $250+

Minimum Bid: $125

32921 #728, 1933, 1c Yellow Green GEM 100 PSE. (Original Gum - Never Hinged). Registry quality, finest to date. Gem; 2008 PSE - Graded Certificate. (SMQ $380; this being one of 1 attaining this grade as of 10/08, with none graded higher).

Estimate: $400+

Minimum Bid: $200

32922 #721, 1932, 3c Never Hinged GEM 100 PSE. (Original Gum - Never Hinged). Coil Single. Gem; 2008 PSE - Graded Certificate. (this being one of 2 attaining this grade as of 10/08, with *none* graded higher).

Estimate: $250+

Minimum Bid: $125

32923 #774, 1935, 3c Purple GEM 100 PSE. (Original Gum - Never Hinged). Gem PSE - Encapsulated. (SMQ $300; this being one of 3 attaining this grade as of 10/08, with only 1 graded higher).

Estimate: $275+

Minimum Bid: $138

32924 #789, 1936, 5c Ultra, GEM 100 PSE. (Original Gum - Never Hinged). Gem PSE - Encapsulated. (SMQ $400; this being one of 1 attaining this grade as of 10/08, with only 1 graded higher).

Estimate: $350+

Minimum Bid: $175

32925 #792, 1936, 3c Purple GEM 100 PSE. (Original Gum - Never Hinged). Gem PSE - Encapsulated. (SMQ $350; this being one of 3, attaining this grade as of 10/08, with only 0 graded higher) .

Estimate: $350+

Minimum Bid: $175

32926 #794, 1936, 5c Ultra, GEM 100 PSE. (Original Gum - Never Hinged). Gem PSE - Encapsulated. (SMQ $400; this being one of 3 attaining this grade as of 10/08, with only 0 graded higher).

Estimate: $350+

Minimum Bid: $175

32927 #809, 1938, 41/2c Dark Gray GEM 100 PSE. (Original Gum - Never Hinged). Gem PSE - Encapsulated. (SMQ $305; this being one of 39 attaining this grade as of 10/08, with *none* graded higher).

Estimate: $200+

Minimum Bid: $100

32928 #839, 1939, 1c Green SUP 98 PSE. (Original Gum - Never Hinged). Coil Line Pair. Superb; PSE Graded Certificate. (SMQ $390; this being one of 13 attaining this grade as of 10/08, with only 1 graded higher).

Estimate: $350+

Minimum Bid: $175

32929 #860, 1940, 2c Rose Carmine GEM 100 PSE. (Original Gum - Never Hinged). Gem PSE - Encapsulated. (SMQ $330; this being one of 6 attaining this grade as of 10/08, with none graded higher).

Estimate: $300+

Minimum Bid: $150

32930 #861, 1940, 3c Bright Red Violet GEM 100 PSE. (Original Gum - Never Hinged). Gem PSE - Encapsulated. (SMQ $310; this being one of 11 attaining this grade as of 10/08, with none graded higher).

Estimate: $280+

Minimum Bid: $140

32931 #863, 1940, 10c Dark Brown GEM 100 PSE. (Original Gum - Never Hinged). Gem; PSE - Encapsulated. (SMQ $320; this being one of 8 attaining this grade as of 10/08, with none graded higher).

Estimate: $300+

Minimum Bid: $150

32932 #864, 1940, 1c Bright Blue Green, GEM 100 PSE. (Original Gum - Never Hinged). Gem PSE - Encapsulated. (SMQ $300; this being one of 13 attaining this grade as of 10/08, with none graded higher).

Estimate: $250+

Minimum Bid: $125

32935 #869, 1940, 1c Bright Blue Green GEM 100 PSE. (Original Gum - Never Hinged). Gem PSE - Encapsulated. (SMQ $300; this being one of 15 attaining this grade as of 10/08, with none graded higher).

Estimate: $250+

Minimum Bid: $125

32938 #876, 1940, 3c Bright Red Violet GEM 100 PSE. (Original Gum - Never Hinged). Gem PSE - Encapsulated. (SMQ $330; this being one of 6 attaining this grade as of 10/08, with none graded higher).

Estimate: $300+

Minimum Bid: $150

32941 #884, 1940, 1c Bright Blue Green GEM 100 PSE. (Original Gum - Never Hinged). Gem PSE - Encapsulated. (SMQ $310; this being one of 11 attaining this grade as of 10/08, with none graded higher).

Estimate: $280+

Minimum Bid: $140

32944 #890, 1940, 2c Rose Carmine GEM 100 PSE. (Original Gum - Never Hinged). Gem; PSE - Encapsulated. (SMQ $320; this being one of 9 attaining this grade as of 10/08, with none graded higher).

Estimate: $275+

Minimum Bid: $138

32933 #866, 1940, 3c Bright Red Violet GEM 100 PSE. (Original Gum - Never Hinged). Gem example; PSE - Encapsulated. (SMQ $310; this being one of 11 attaining this grade as of 10/08, with none graded higher).

Estimate: $250+

Minimum Bid: $125

32936 #870, 1940, 2c Rose Carmine GEM 100 PSE. (Original Gum - Never Hinged). Gem; PSE - Encapsulated. (SMQ $330; this being one of 7 attaining this grade as of 10/08, with none graded higher).

Estimate: $275+

Minimum Bid: $138

32939 #877, 1940, 5c Ultramarine GEM 100 PSE. (Original Gum - Never Hinged). Dr. Walter Reed. Gem PSE - Encapsulated. (SMQ $280; this being one of 20 attaining this grade as of 10/08, with None graded higher).

Estimate: $250+

Minimum Bid: $125

32942 #887, 1940, 5c Ultramarine GEM 100 PSE. (Original Gum - Never Hinged). Gem; PSE - Encapsulated. (SMQ $320; this being one of 8 attaining this grade as of 10/08, with none graded higher).

Estimate: $300+

Minimum Bid: $150

32945 #891, 1940, 3c Bright Red Violet GEM 100 PSE. (Original Gum - Never Hinged). Gem; PSE - Encapsulated. (SMQ $280; this being one of 23 attaining this grade as of 10/08, with only 1 graded higher).

Estimate: $225+

Minimum Bid: $112

32934 #868, 1940, 10c Dark Brown GEM 100 PSE. (Original Gum - Never Hinged). Gem; PSE - Encapsulated. (SMQ $300; this being one of 15 attaining this grade as of 10/08, with none graded higher).

Estimate: $250+

Minimum Bid: $125

32937 #872, 1940, 5c Ultramarine GEM 100 PSE. (Original Gum - Never Hinged). Gem; PSE - Encapsulated. (SMQ $320; this being one of 8 attaining this grade as of 10/08, with none graded higher).

Estimate: $300+

Minimum Bid: $150

32940 #877, 1940, 5c Ultramarine GEM 100 PSE. (Original Gum - Never Hinged). Gem, PSE - Encapsulated. (SMQ $280; this being one of 20 attaining this grade as of 10/08, with none graded higher).

Estimate: $225+

Minimum Bid: $112

32943 #888, 1940, 10c Dark Brown GEM 100 PSE. (Original Gum - Never Hinged). Gem; PSE - Encapsulated. (SMQ $310; this being one of 12 attaining this grade as of 10/08, with none graded higher).

Estimate: $250+

Minimum Bid: $125

32946 #891, 1940, 3c Bright Red Violet GEM 100 PSE. (Original Gum - Never Hinged). Gem; PSE - Encapsulated. (SMQ $280; this being one of 23 attaining this grade as of 10/08, with only 1 graded higher).

Estimate: $225+

Minimum Bid: $112

32947 #892, 1940, 5c Ultramarine GEM 100 PSE. (Original Gum - Never Hinged). Gem; PSE - Encapsulated. (SMQ $320; this being one of 8 attaining this grade as of 10/08, with none graded higher).

Estimate: $300+

Minimum Bid: $150

32948 #909, 1943, 5c Multicolored GEM 100 PSE. (Original Gum - Never Hinged). Gem; PSE - Encapsulated. (SMQ $160; this being one of 91 attaining this grade as of 10/08, with none graded higher).

Estimate: $100+

Minimum Bid: $1

32949 #909c, 1943, 5c Multicolor SUP 98 PSE. (Original Gum - Never Hinged). Reverse printing of black. Superb; 2008 PSE - Graded Certificate. (this being one of 5 attaining this grade as of 10/08, with only 2 graded higher).

Estimate: $200+

Minimum Bid: $100

32950 #910a, 1943, 5c, Blue Violet, Blue, Bright Red and Black.(Original Gum - Never Hinged). Double Impression of "Czechoslovakia." Very Fine; 2008 APS Certificate. .

Estimate: $500+

Minimum Bid: $250

32951 #910, 1943, 5c Multicolored GEM 100 PSE. (Original Gum - Never Hinged). Gem; PSE - Encapsulated. (SMQ $180; this being one of 59 attaining this grade as of 10/08, with none graded higher).

Estimate: $125+

Minimum Bid: $1

32952 #911, 1943, 5c Multicolored GEM 100 PSE. (Original Gum - Never Hinged). Gem; PSE - Encapsulated. (SMQ $180; this being one of 62 attaining this grade as of 10/08, with none graded higher).

Estimate: $125+

Minimum Bid: $1

32953 #912, 1943, 5c Multicolored GEM 100 PSE. (Original Gum - Never Hinged). Gem; PSE - Encapsulated. (SMQ $160; this being one of 76 attaining this grade as of 10/08, with none graded higher).

Estimate: $100+

Minimum Bid: $1

32954 #913, 1943, 5c Multicolored GEM 100 PSE. (Original Gum - Never Hinged). Gem; PSE - Encapsulated. (SMQ $180; this being one of 63 attaining this grade as of 10/08, with none graded higher).

Estimate: $125+

Minimum Bid: $1

32955 #915, 1943, 5c Multicolored GEM 100 PSE. (Original Gum - Never Hinged). Gem; PSE - Encapsulated. (SMQ $135; this being one of 156 attaining this grade as of 10/08, with none graded higher).

Estimate: $100+

Minimum Bid: $1

32956 #916, 1943, 5c Multicolored GEM 100 PSE. (Original Gum - Never Hinged). Gem; PSE - Encapsulated. (SMQ $215; this being one of 27 attaining this grade as of 10/08, with none graded higher).

Estimate: $150+

Minimum Bid: $1

32957 #917, 1943, 5c Multicolored GEM 100 PSE. (Original Gum - Never Hinged). Gem; PSE - Encapsulated. (SMQ $180; this being one of 49 attaining this grade as of 10/08, with none graded higher).

Estimate: $125+

Minimum Bid: $1

32958 #918, 1943, 5c Multicolor GEM 100 PSE. (Original Gum - Never Hinged). Gem; PSE - Encapsulated. (SMQ $180; this being one of 51 attaining this grade as of 10/08, with none graded higher).

Estimate: $125+

Minimum Bid: $1

32959 #920, 1943, 5c Multicolored GEM 100 PSE. (Original Gum - Never Hinged). Gem; PSE - Encapsulated. (SMQ $215; this being one of 26 attaining this grade as of 10/08, with none graded higher).

Estimate: $150+

Minimum Bid: $1

32960 #921, 1943, 5c Multicolored GEM 100 PSE. (Original Gum - Never Hinged). Gem; PSE - Encapsulated. (SMQ $215; this being one of 38 attaining this grade as of 10/08, with none graded higher).

Estimate: $150+

Minimum Bid: $1

32961 #946, 1947, 3c Purple GEM 100 PSE. (Original Gum - Never Hinged). Gem; 2008 PSE - Graded Certificate. (this being one of 3 attaining this grade as of 10/08, with none graded higher).

Estimate: $200+

Minimum Bid: $100

32962 #991, 1950, 3c Light Violet GEM 100 PSE. (Original Gum - Never Hinged). Gem; 2008 PSE - Graded Certificate. (this being one of 10 attaining this grade as of 10/08, with none graded higher).

Estimate: $200+

Minimum Bid: $100

32963 #1003, 2008, 3c Violet GEM 100 PSE. (Original Gum - Never Hinged). Gem; 2008 PSE - Graded Certificate. (this being one of 5 attaining this grade as of 10/08, with none graded higher).

Estimate: $200+

Minimum Bid: $100

32964 #1025, 1953, 3c Violet GEM 100 PSE. (Original Gum - Never Hinged). Gem; 2008 PSE - Graded Certificate. (this being one of 5 attaining this grade as of 10/08, with none graded higher).

Estimate: $200+

Minimum Bid: $100

32965 #1052, 1958, $1 Bright Purple GEM 100 PSE. (Original Gum - Never Hinged). Gem PSE - Encapsulated (SMQ $380; this being one of 4 attaining this grade as of 10/08, with none graded higher).

Estimate: $350+

Minimum Bid: $175

32966 #1053, YEAR, $5 COLOR SUP 98 PSE. (Original Gum - Never Hinged). Superb PSE - Encapsulated. (SMQ $180; this being one of 41 attaining this grade as of 10/08, with only 9 graded higher).

Estimate: $180+

Minimum Bid: $1

32967 #1129, 1959, 8c Rose Lake GEM 100 PSE. (Original Gum - Never Hinged). Gem; 2008 PSE - Graded Certificate. (this being one of 1 attaining this grade as of 10/08, with none graded higher).

Estimate: $200+

Minimum Bid: $100

AIRMAIL ISSUES

32968 #C1-6, 1918-23, 6c - 24c. (Original Gum - Never Hinged). Complete set (6) of the first airmails, bright and fresh. Fine to Very Fine. (Scott $800). (Total: 6 pages)

Estimate: $400+

Minimum Bid: $200

32969 #C1, 1918, 6c Orange XF 90 PSE. (Original Gum - Never Hinged). Extremely Fine; 2007 PSE - Graded Certificate. (SMQ $250; this being one of 59 attaining this grade as of 10/08, with only 52 graded higher).

Estimate: $200+

Minimum Bid: $100

32970 #C2, 1918, 16c Green XF 90 PSE. (Original Gum - Never Hinged). Strong 90. Extremely Fine; 2007 PSE - Graded Certificate. (SMQ $250; this being one of 63 attaining this grade as of 10/08, with 66 graded higher).

Estimate: $250+

Minimum Bid: $125

32971 #C2, 1918, 16c Green XF 90 PSE. (Original Gum - Never Hinged). Extremely Fine; 2006 PSE - Graded Certificate. (SMQ $250; this being one of 63 attaining this grade as of 10/08, with only 66 graded higher).

Estimate: $200+

Minimum Bid: $100

32972 #C3, 1918, 24c Carmine Rose & Blue XF 90 PSE. (Original Gum - Never Hinged). Vivid color. Extremely Fine; 2008 PSE - Graded Certificate. (SMQ $250; this being one of 62 attaining this grade as of 10/08, with 101 graded higher).

Estimate: $250+

Minimum Bid: $125

32973 #C3, 1918, 24c Carmine Rose And Blue XF 90 PSE. (Original Gum - Never Hinged). Extremely Fine; 2008 PSE - Graded Certificate. (SMQ $250; this being one of 62 attaining this grade as of 10/08, with 101 graded higher).

Estimate: $200+

Minimum Bid: $100

32974 #C4, 1923, 8c Dark Green XF-S 95 PSE. (Original Gum - Never Hinged). Bottom plate number single; Plate# 14824. Extremely Fine to Superb; 2008 PSE - Graded Certificate. (SMQ $215; this being one of 63 attaining this grade as of 10/08, with 30 graded higher).

Estimate: $200+

Minimum Bid: $100

32975 #C4, 1923, 8c Dark Green XF-S 95 PSE. (Original Gum - Never Hinged). Fresh. Extremely Fine to Superb; 2008 PSE - Graded Certificate. (SMQ $215; this being one of 63 attaining this grade as of 10/08, with only 30 graded higher).

Estimate: $200+

Minimum Bid: $100

32976 #C9, 1927, 20c Yellow Green SUP 98 PSE. (Original Gum - Never Hinged). Superb; PSE - Encapsulated. (SMQ $265; this being one of 29 attaining this grade as of 10/08, with 13 graded higher).

Estimate: $200+

Minimum Bid: $100

32977 #BKC1, 1928, 61c Blue. (Original Gum - Never Hinged). Four complete booklets of the Lindbergh "Spirit of St. Louis" issue. Very Fine. (Scott $1,100). (Total: 4 pages)

Estimate: $500+

Minimum Bid: $250

32978 #C12, 1930, 5c Never Hinged SUP 98 PSE. (Original Gum - Never Hinged). Near jumbo, deep color, original gum, Never Hinged, Superb PSE - Encapsulated. (SMQ $390; this being one of 11 attaining this grade as of 10/08, with only 9 graded higher).

Estimate: $350+

Minimum Bid: $175

32979 #C13-15, 1930, 65c - $2.60 **Graf Zeppelins.** (Original Gum - Never Hinged). A complete mint set, full original gum. Fine to Very Fine, the 65c and $1.30 each with 2008 PSE Certificate, and the $2.60 with 2007 PSE Certificate. (Scott $2,600).

Estimate: $1,500+

Minimum Bid: $750

32980 #C13, 1930, 65c Green XF 90 PSE. (Original Gum - Never Hinged). Extremely Fine PSE - Encapsulated. (SMQ $610; this being one of 133, attaining this grade as of 10/08, with 133 graded higher) .

Estimate: $450+

Minimum Bid: $225

32981 #C13, 1930, 65c Green VF-XF 85 PSE. (Original Gum - Previously Hinged). Previously hinged. Very Fine to Extremely Fine PSE - Encapsulated. (SMQ $240; this being one of 17, attaining this grade as of 10/08, with only 64 graded higher) .

Estimate: $200+

Minimum Bid: $100

32982 #C13, 1930, 65c Green VF-XF 85 PSE. (Original Gum - Never Hinged). A mint right sheet margin, Plate No. 20077, tiny natural paper inclusion at the center, Very Fine - Extremely Fine 2008 PSE - Graded Certificate. (SMQ $470; this being one of 145, attaining this grade as of 10/08, with 279 graded higher) .

Estimate: $400+

Minimum Bid: $200

32983 #C13, 1930, 65c Green VF-XF 85 PSE. (Original Gum - Never Hinged). Very Fine to Extremely Fine; 2007 PSE - Graded Certificate. (SMQ $470; this being one of 145 attaining this grade as of 10/08, with 279 graded higher).

Estimate: $400+

Minimum Bid: $200

32984 #C13, 1930, 65c Green F-VF 75 PSE. (Original Gum - Never Hinged). Post Office Fresh. Fine to Very Fine PSE - Encapsulated.
(this being one of 26 attaining this grade as of 10/08, with 574 graded higher).

Estimate: $300+

Minimum Bid: $150

32985 #C13, 1930, 65c Green. (Original Gum - Never Hinged). Post office fresh mint single. Very Fine; 2008 PSE Certificate. (Scott $425) .

Estimate: $350+

Minimum Bid: $175

32986 #C13, 1930, 65c Green. (Original Gum - Never Hinged). Post Office fresh, with two small natural gum skips not mentioned on the certificate. Fine; 2008 PSE Certificate. (Scott $425).

Estimate: $300+

Minimum Bid: $150

32987 #C13, 1930, 65c Green VF-XF 85 PSE. (Used). Natural paper bends. Very Fine to Extremely Fine PSE - Encapsulated. (SMQ $215; this being one of 9 attaining this grade as of 10/08, with 23 graded higher).

Estimate: $170+

Minimum Bid: $1

32988 #C14, 1930, $1.30 Never Hinged XF-S 95 PSE. (Original Gum - Previously Hinged). Fresh gum with very light hinge mark only. Extremely Fine to Superb; 2007 PSE - Graded Certificate. (SMQ $650; this being one of 22 attaining this grade as of 10/08, with only 6 graded higher).

Estimate: $500+

Minimum Bid: $250

32989 #C14, 1930, $1.30 Brown. (Original Gum - Never Hinged). Fresh, original gum without the usual gum bends. Fine to Very Fine; 2008 PSE Certificate. (Scott $900).

Estimate: $475+

Minimum Bid: $238

32990 #C14, 1930, $1.30 Brown F-VF 75 PSE. (Used). Crease at the bottom right. Fine to Very Fine PSE - Encapsulated. (this being one of 4 attaining this grade as of 10/08, with only 52 graded higher).

Estimate: $250+

Minimum Bid: $125

32991 #C18, 1933, 50c Green XF-S 95J PSE. (Original Gum - Never Hinged). Extremely Fine to Superb PSE - Encapsulated. (this being one of 23 attaining this grade as of 10/08, with 28 graded higher).

Estimate: $300+

Minimum Bid: $150

32992 #C18, 1933, 50c Green XF-S 95 PSE. (Original Gum - Never Hinged). Baby Zeppelin. Extremely Fine to Superb; 2006 PSE - Graded Certificate. (SMQ $200; this being one of 96 attaining this grade as of 10/08, with 51 graded higher).

Estimate: $200+

Minimum Bid: $100

32993 #C25, 1941, 6c Carmine SUP 98 PSE. (Original Gum - Never Hinged). Superb PSE - Encapsulated. (SMQ $220; this being one of 26 attaining this grade as of 10/08, with none graded higher).

Estimate: $200+

Minimum Bid: $100

32994 #C34, 1947, 10c Black GEM 100 PSE. (Original Gum - Never Hinged). Gem PSE - Encapsulated. (SMQ 300; this being one of 2 attaining this grade as of 10/08, with only 0 graded higher).

Estimate: $300+

Minimum Bid: $150

SPECIAL DELIVERY ISSUES

32995 #E1, 1885, 10c Blue F 70 PSE. (Original Gum - Never Hinged). Messenger Running. Natural gum bend. Fine PSE - Encapsulated. (SMQ $440; this being one of 3 attaining this grade as of 10/08, with 20 graded higher).

Estimate: $300+

Minimum Bid: $150

32996 #E3, 1893, 10c Orange, F 70 PSE. (Original Gum - Never Hinged). Messenger Running. Fine PSE - Encapsulated. (SMQ $220; this being one of 7 attaining this grade as of 10/08, with 27 graded higher).

Estimate: $200+

Minimum Bid: $100

32997 #E4, 1894, 10c Blue, F 70 PSE. (Original Gum - Previously Hinged). Messenger Running, original 'crackly' gum, previously hinged. Fine; PSE - Encapsulated. (SMQ $400; this being one of 4 attaining this grade as of 10/08, with 23 graded higher).

Estimate: $260+

Minimum Bid: $130

32998 #E4, 1894, 10c Dark Blue F 70 PSE. (Original Gum - Hinged). Messenger Running. Portion of selvage remains as hinge remnant. Fine PSE - Encapsulated. (SMQ $400; this being one of 4 attaining this grade as of 10/08, with 23 graded higher).

Estimate: $300+

Minimum Bid: $150

32999 #E5, 1895, 10c Blue F-VF 75 PSE. (Original Gum - Never Hinged). Messenger Running. Fine to Very Fine PSE - Encapsulated. (this being one of 2 attaining this grade as of 10/08, with 21 graded higher).

Estimate: $250+

Minimum Bid: $125

33000 #E7, 1908, 10c Green XF 90 PSE. (Original Gum - Never Hinged). Extremely Fine; 2007 PSE - Graded Certificate. (SMQ $350; this being one of 28, attaining this grade as of 10/08, with 30 graded higher) .

Estimate: $300+

Minimum Bid: $150

33001 #E11, 1917, 10c Ultramarine XF-S 95 PSE. (Original Gum - Never Hinged). Extremely Fine to Superb PSE - Encapsulated. (SMQ $290; this being one of 28, attaining this grade as of 10/08, with 22 graded higher) .

Estimate: $300+

Minimum Bid: $150

33002 #E13, 1922, 15c Never Hinged XF-S 95 PSE. (Original Gum - Never Hinged). Extremely Fine to Superb PSE - Encapsulated. (SMQ $295; this being one of 24, attaining this grade as of 10/08, with 14 graded higher) .

Estimate: $300+

Minimum Bid: $150

33003 #E13, 1922, 15c Deep Orange XF-S 95 PSE. (Original Gum - Never Hinged). Messenger on Motorcycle. Extremely Fine to Superb; 2005 PSE - Graded Certificate. (SMQ $295; this being one of 24 attaining this grade as of 10/08, with 14 graded higher).

Estimate: $250+

Minimum Bid: $125

33004 #E14, 1922, 20c Never Hinged SUP 98 PSE. (Original Gum - Never Hinged). Superb PSE - Encapsulated. (SMQ $220; this being one of 12 attaining this grade as of 10/08, with only 9 graded higher).

Estimate: $200+

Minimum Bid: $100

POSTAGE DUE ISSUES

33005 #J6, 1879, 30c Brown, F-VF 75 PSE. (Original Gum - Hinged). Warm and fresh, original gum, with hinge remnant at top, and a trivial natural gum crease. Fine to Very Fine; PSE - Encapsulated. (this being one of 3 attaining this grade as of 10/08, with only 3 graded higher).

Estimate: $200+

Minimum Bid: $100

33006 #J18, 1884, 5c Pale Red Brown, VF 80 PSE. (Partial Original Gum). Handsome and fresh, partial original gum, the top third of the stamp without gum and with a paper hinge remnant, horizontal crease along the bottom visible primarily from the reverse. Very Fine; PSE - Encapsulated. (SMQ $600; this being the only example attaining this grade as of 10/08, with only 6 graded higher).

Estimate: $500+

Minimum Bid: $250

33007 #J27, 1891, 30c Bright Claret, F 70 PSE. (Original Gum - Hinged). Bright and fresh. Previously hinged at top. Fine; PSE - Encapsulated. (SMQ $325; this being one of 2 attaining this grade as of 10/08, with only 6 graded higher).

Estimate: $300+

Minimum Bid: $150

33008 #J28, 1891, 50c Bright Claret. (Original Gum - Previously Hinged). Deep bright color and impression, previously hinged. Fine to Very Fine; 2008 PSE Certificate. (Scott $700).

Estimate: $400+

Minimum Bid: $200

33009 #J29, 1894, 1c Vermilion, F 70 PSE. (Original Gum - Previously Hinged). Fine; PSE - Encapsulated. (SMQ $1,300; this being one of 2 attaining this grade as of 10/08, with only 1 graded higher).

Estimate: $600+

Minimum Bid: $300

33010 #J30, 1894, 2c Vermillion FR-G 20 PSE. (Original Gum - Never Hinged). Nice mint example with a natural straight edge at the right and a natural gum wrinkle at the bottom. Fair to Good; 2008 PSE - Graded Certificate. (SMQ $2,100; this being one of 1 attaining this grade as of 10/08, with only 6 graded higher).

Estimate: $500+

Minimum Bid: $250

33011 #J36, 1894, 30c Never Hinged. (Original Gum - Previously Hinged). Terrific deep claret color, three huge margins and very close at the top, rough perforations at the bottom. Fine; 2008 PSE Certificate. (Scott $600).

Estimate: $400+
Minimum Bid: $200

33012 #J43, 1895, 30c Deep Claret, F-VF 75 PSE. (Original Gum - Hinged). Bright and vibrant, original gum with a small hinge remnant at top. Fine to Very Fine; PSE - Encapsulated. (this being one of 2 attaining this grade as of 10/08, with only 6 graded higher).

Estimate: $500+
Minimum Bid: $250

33013 #J44, 1895, 50c Deep Claret, VF 80 PSE. (Original Gum - Previously Hinged). Post Office fresh, full original gum only extremely lightly kissed by prior hinge. Very Fine; PSE - Encapsulated. (SMQ $430; this being one of 2 attaining this grade as of 10/08, with only 9 graded higher).

Estimate: $400+
Minimum Bid: $200

33014 #J50, 1915, 50c Deep Claret. (No Gum). Minor creases. Very Fine; 2008 PSE Certificate. (Scott $1,150).

Estimate: $400+
Minimum Bid: $200

33015 #J58, 1914, 50c Carmine Lake. (Used). Fresh used example with a removed horizontal crayon line cancel at the base of the numeral 50. Fine; 2008 PSE Certificate. (Scott $1,500).

Estimate: $500+
Minimum Bid: $250

33016 #J69, 1930, 1/2c Carmine SUP 98 PSE. (Original Gum - Never Hinged). Superb PSE - Encapsulated. (SMQ $330; this being one of 2 attaining this grade as of 10/08, with only 1 graded higher).

Estimate: $300+
Minimum Bid: $150

33017 #J89, 1959, DENOMINATION Carmine Rose And Black SUP 98 PSE. (Original Gum - Never Hinged). Superb PSE - Graded Certificate. (SMQ unpriced; this being one of 2 attaining this grade as of 10/08, with none graded higher).

Estimate: $200+
Minimum Bid: $100

1913 PARCEL POST ISSUES

33018 #JQ1, 1913, 1c Dark Green XF-S 95J PSE. (Original Gum - Never Hinged). Extremely Fine to Superb; 2007 PSE - Graded Certificate. (this being one of 2 attaining this grade as of 10/08, with only 3 graded higher).

Estimate: $250+
Minimum Bid: $125

33019 #JQ2, 1913, 2c Dark Green XF-S 95 PSE. (Original Gum - Previously Hinged). Extremely Fine to Superb; 2006 PSE - Graded Certificate. (SMQ $230; this being one of 3 attaining this grade as of 10/08, with only 1 graded higher).

Estimate: $200+
Minimum Bid: $100

1919-22 SHANGHAI OVERPRINTS

33020 #K1-18, 1919-22, 2c on 1c - $2 on $1. (Original Gum - Previously Hinged). Shanghai overprints complete (18), bright and fresh, all with previously hinged original gum except for #'s K10 (20c on 10c), K14 (60c on 30c), and K18 (4c on 2c) which are never hinged. Fine to Very Fine. (Scott $2,640).

Estimate: $1,200+
Minimum Bid: $600

OFFICIAL ISSUES

33021 #O2, 1873, 2c Yellow. (Original Gum - Previously Hinged). Owner's stamp on the reverse. Very Fine. 2005 PF Certificate. (Scott $240).

Estimate: $220+
Minimum Bid: $110

33022 #O12, 1873, 3c Carmine F-VF 75 PSE. (Original Gum - Hinged). The highest Graded copy to date. No remnant, but obvious prior hinge removal. Fine to Very Fine PSE - Encapsulated.
(this being one of 1 attaining this grade as of 10/08, with none graded higher).

Estimate: $500+
Minimum Bid: $250

33023 #O19, 1873, 10c Vermilion XF 90 PSE. (Original Gum - Never Hinged). Extremely Fine PSE - Encapsulated. (this being the only example attaining this grade as of 10/08, with only 2 graded higher) .

Estimate: $400+
Minimum Bid: $200

33024 #O25, 1873, 1c Purple VF-XF 85 PSE. (Original Gum - Hinged). Very Fine to Extremely Fine; 2008 PSE - Graded Certificate. (SMQ $420; this being one of 3 attaining this grade as of 10/08, with only 2 graded higher).

Estimate: $350+
Minimum Bid: $175

33025 #O34, 1873, 90c No Gum F 70 PSE. (Disturbed Original Gum). Fine PSE - Encapsulated. (SMQ $800; this being one of 1 attaining this grade as of 10/08, with *none* graded higher).

Estimate: $500+
Minimum Bid: $250

33026 #O67, 1873, 90c No Gum VF 80J PSE. (No Gum). Enormous margins. Very Fine PSE - Graded Certificate. (this being one of 1 attaining this grade as of 10/08, with only 2 graded higher).

Estimate: $300+

Minimum Bid: $150

33027 #O68, 1873, $2 Green And Black VG-F 60 PSE. (Disturbed Original Gum). Two shorter perfs, pencil mark on back. Very Good to Fine PSE - Encapsulated. (this being one of 1 attaining this grade as of 10/08, with only none graded higher).

Estimate: $500+

Minimum Bid: $250

33028 #O94, 1879, 1c Yellow, FR-G 20 PSE. (No Gum As Issued). Mint single, no gum as issued, with a vertical purple ink line. Fair to Good. PSE - Encapsulated. (this being the only example attaining this grade as of 10/08, with only 2 graded higher).

Estimate: $500+

Minimum Bid: $250

NEWSPAPER ISSUES

33029 #PR74, 1879, $9 Orange. (No Gum). Very fresh with excellent color. Very Fine. (SMQ $240; this being one of 2 attaining this grade as of 10/08, with only 2 graded higher).

Estimate: $200+

Minimum Bid: $100

REVENUE ISSUES

33030 #R83a, 1863, $2 Red. (Used). Manuscript cancel, small thin at the top and a small corner crease at the bottom left. Very Fine. 2005 PSE Certificate. (Scott $750) .

Estimate: $400+

Minimum Bid: $200

33031 #R95a, 1862, $10 Green. (Used). Handsome example, manuscript cancel and paper wrinkle at the bottom right. Fine; 2008 PSE Certificate. (Scott $650).

Estimate: $200+

Minimum Bid: $100

33032 #R98a, 1862, $20 Orange. (Used). Handsome used example with black hand stamp cancel. Very Fine to Extremely Fine. 2008 PSE Certificate. (Scott $150).

Estimate: $350+

Minimum Bid: $175

1913 PARCEL POST ISSUES

33033 #Q2, 1913, 2c Carmine XF-S 95J PSE. (Original Gum - Never Hinged). City Carrier. Very large margin, fresh example. Extremely Fine to Superb; 2005 PSE - Graded Certificate. (this being one of 5 attaining this grade as of 10/08, with 14 graded higher).

Estimate: $550+

Minimum Bid: $275

33034 #Q2, 1913, 2c Never Hinged XF-S 95 PSE. (Original Gum - Never Hinged). Extremely Fine to Superb PSE - Encapsulated. (SMQ $325; this being one of 27 attaining this grade as of 10/08, with 19 graded higher).

Estimate: $300+

Minimum Bid: $150

33035 #Q8, 1913, 20c Carmine Rose F-VF 75 PSE. (Original Gum - Never Hinged). Airplane Carrying Mail. Light gum creases. Fine to Very Fine PSE - Encapsulated. (this being one of 4 attaining this grade as of 10/08, with 52 graded higher).

Estimate: $200+

Minimum Bid: $100

33036 #Q9, 1913, 25c Carmine Rose XF 90 PSE. (Original Gum - Never Hinged). Manufacturing. Extremely Fine. PSE - Encapsulated. (SMQ $485; this being one of 16 attaining this grade as of 10/08, with 13 graded higher).

Estimate: $400+

Minimum Bid: $200

SPECIAL DELIVERY ISSUES

33037 #QE1, 1925, 10c Yellow Green SUP 98 PSE. (Original Gum - Never Hinged). Superb. PSE - Encapsulated. (SMQ $155; this being one of 5 attaining this grade as of 10/08, with only 2 graded higher).

Estimate: $200+

Minimum Bid: $100

33038 #QE4, 1925, 25c Deep Green SUP 98 PSE. (Original Gum - Never Hinged). Superb. 2008 PSE - Graded Certificate. (SMQ $440; this being one of 26 attaining this grade as of 10/08, with only 2 graded higher).

Estimate: $350+

Minimum Bid: $175

33039 #QE4, 1925, 25c Yellow Green XF-S 95 PSE. (Original Gum - Never Hinged). Extremely Fine to Superb PSE - Encapsulated. (SMQ $200; this being one of 41, attaining this grade as of 10/08, with only 33 graded higher) .

Estimate: $200+

Minimum Bid: $100

33040 #QE4, 1925, 25c Yellow Green XF-S 95 PSE. (Original Gum - Never Hinged). Extremely Fine to Superb; 2007 PSE - Graded Certificate. (SMQ $200; this being one of 41 attaining this grade as of 10/08, with 33 graded higher).

Estimate: $150+

Minimum Bid: $1

33041 #QE4a, 1925, 25c Deep Green SUP 98 PSE. (Original Gum - Never Hinged). Superb. PSE - Encapsulated. (SMQ $385; this being one of 10 attaining this grade as of 10/08, with only 1 graded higher).

Estimate: $400+

Minimum Bid: $200

33042 #QE4a, 1925, 25c Yellow Green SUP 98 PSE. (Original Gum - Never Hinged). Superb; 2008 PSE - Graded Certificate. (SMQ $385; this being one of 10 attaining this grade as of 10/08, with only 1 graded higher).

Estimate: $300+

Minimum Bid: $150

REVENUE ISSUES

33043 #R36a, 1862, 10c Inland Exchange, Blue. (Used). A handsome used single, deep rich color on fresh paper with manuscript cancel, Very Fine; 2008 **PSE Certificate.** (Scott $350) .

Estimate: $250+

Minimum Bid: $125

33044 #R74c, 1862, $1 Passage Ticket, Red. (Used). Manuscript cancel. Fine - Very Fine. 2008 PSE Certificate. (Scott $275.00)

Estimate: $200+

Minimum Bid: $100

33045 #R84a, 1863, $2.50 Purple. (Used). Extremely rare used example with manuscript cancel, horizontal crease and filled thin. Fine; 2002 PSE Certificate (Scott $7,000).

Estimate: $2,250+

Minimum Bid: $1,125

33046 #R87a, 1863, $3.50 Blue. (Used). Brilliant bright blue color on white paper, used example with a manuscript cancel, some small thin spots and horizontal diagonal creases. Very Fine. 2008 PF Certificate. (Scott $7,000).

Estimate: $3,500+

Minimum Bid: $1,750

33047 #R102c, 1862, $200 Green & Red. (Used). A used single with the usual manuscript cancel, bright fresh colors and detailed impressions, a pulled perf at the bottom left, otherwise sound. Fine. 2008 PSE Certificate. (Scott $900.00).

Estimate: $500+

Minimum Bid: $250

33048 #R102c, 1862, $200 Green And Red. (Used). Pretty used example with blue hand stamp cancel and a vertical crease at the center ending in a 4 mm tear at the bottom. Fine. 2008 PSE Certificate. (Scott $900).

Estimate: $300+

Minimum Bid: $150

33049 #R115b, 1871, 50c Blue & Black with Inverted Center. (Used). A used single with herringbone cut cancel and a repair at the lower right edge *(associated with the herringbone cut cancel)* not affecting the overall appearance, Fine to Very Fine. 2008 PSE Certificate. (Scott $2,000).

Estimate: $1,000+

Minimum Bid: $500

33050 #R653, 1953, $10000 Carmine. (Used). Magnificent example with black handstamp, cut cancel and staple holes, Extremely Fine to Superb; 2008 PSE Certificate. (Scott $1750).

Estimate: $1,000+

Minimum Bid: $500

HUNTING PERMIT STAMPS

33051 #RW7, 1940, $1 Sepia XF 90 PSE. (Original Gum - Never Hinged). Charming example of this sepia colored waterfowl issue. Extremely Fine. 2005 PSE - Graded Certificate. (SMQ $380; this being one of 31 attaining this grade as of 10/08, with 27 graded higher).

Estimate: $300+

Minimum Bid: $150

33052 #RW7, 1940, $1 Sepia XF 90 PSE. (Original Gum - Never Hinged). Noticeable natural gum bend visible on face, not mentioned on certificate. Extremely Fine. 2006 PSE - Graded Certificate. (SMQ $380; this being one of 31 attaining this grade as of 10/08, with 27 graded higher).

Estimate: $250+

Minimum Bid: $125

33053 #RW18, 1934, $1 Blue XF-S 95 PSE. (Original Gum - Never Hinged). Fresh, couple natural gum wrinkles. Extremely Fine to Superb; 2006 PSE - Graded Certificate. (SMQ $215; this being one of 39 attaining this grade as of 10/08, with 19 graded higher).

Estimate: $200+

Minimum Bid: $100

33054 #RW22, 1955, $2 Dark Blue SUP 98 PSE. (Original Gum - Never Hinged). Magnificent example. Very nice margins. Superb PSE - Encapsulated. (SMQ $390; this being one of 24 attaining this grade as of 10/08, with only 2 graded higher).

Estimate: $350+

Minimum Bid: $175

33055 #RW24, 1957, $2 Emerald, SUP 98 PSE. (Original Gum - Never Hinged). Superb PSE - Encapsulated. (SMQ $420; this being one of 22 attaining this grade as of 10/08, with only 1 graded higher).

Estimate: $380+

Minimum Bid: $190

33056 #RW25, 1958, $2 Black SUP 98 PSE. (Original Gum - Never Hinged). Superb PSE - Encapsulated. (SMQ $475; this being one of 11 attaining this grade as of 10/08, with only 2 graded higher).

Estimate: $425+

Minimum Bid: $212

33057 #RW25, 1958, $2 Black, XF-S 95 PSE. (Original Gum - Never Hinged). Bottom margin Plate No.166755 single. Extremely Fine to Superb. 2008 PSE - Graded Certificate. (SMQ $205; this being one of 41 attaining this grade as of 10/08, with 14 graded higher).

Estimate: $200+

Minimum Bid: $100

33058 #RW26, 1959, $3 Multicolored SUP 98 PSE. (Original Gum - Never Hinged). Superb PSE - Encapsulated. (SMQ $390; this being one of 27 attaining this grade as of 10/08, with only 4 graded higher).

Estimate: $325+

Minimum Bid: $162

33059 #RW27, 1960, $3 Multicolored XF-S 95 PSE. (Original Gum - Never Hinged). Extremely Fine to Superb. 2006 PSE - Graded Certificate. (SMQ $180; this being one of 79 attaining this grade as of 10/08, with 46 graded higher).

Estimate: $150+

Minimum Bid: $1

33060 #RW29, 1962, $3 Multicolored, SUP 98 PSE. (Original Gum - Never Hinged). Superb. PSE - Encapsulated (SMQ $390; this being one of 35 attaining this grade as of 10/08, with none graded higher).

Estimate: $350+

Minimum Bid: $175

33061 #RW30, 1963, $3 Multicolored SUP 98 PSE. (Original Gum - Never Hinged). Superb. PSE - Encapsulated. (SMQ $390; this being one of 25 attaining this grade as of 10/08, with only 4 graded higher).

Estimate: $350+

Minimum Bid: $175

33062 #RW31, 1964, $3 Multicolored SUP 98 PSE. (Original Gum - Never Hinged). Superb. PSE - Encapsulated. (SMQ $435; this being one of 17 attaining this grade as of 10/08, with none graded higher).

Estimate: $400+

Minimum Bid: $200

33063 #RW32, 1965, $3 Multicolored SUP 98 PSE. (Original Gum - Never Hinged). Superb PSE - Encapsulated. (SMQ $390; this being one of 29 attaining this grade as of 10/08, with none graded higher).

Estimate: $350+

Minimum Bid: $175

33064 #RW33, 1966, $3 Multicolored SUP 98 PSE. (Original Gum - Never Hinged). Superb. PSE - Encapsulated. (SMQ $390; this being one of 25 attaining this grade as of 10/08, with only 6 graded higher).

Estimate: $350+

Minimum Bid: $175

33065 #RW38, 1971, $3 Multicolored GEM 100 PSE. (Original Gum - Never Hinged). Gem. PSE - Encapsulated. (SMQ $400; this being one of 17 attaining this grade as of 10/08, with none graded higher).

Estimate: $380+

Minimum Bid: $190

33066 #RW39, 1972, $5 Multicolored SUP 98 PSE. (Original Gum - Never Hinged). Superb. PSE - Encapsulated. (SMQ $340; this being one of 20 attaining this grade as of 10/08, with only 6 graded higher).

Estimate: $300+

Minimum Bid: $150

33067 #RW40, 1973, $5 Multicolored GEM 100 PSE. (Original Gum - Never Hinged). Gem. PSE - Encapsulated. (SMQ $290; this being one of 18 attaining this grade as of 10/08, with none graded higher).

Estimate: $250+

Minimum Bid: $125

33068 #RW47, 1980, $7.50 Multicolored GEM 100 PSE. (Original Gum - Never Hinged). Gem. PSE - Encapsulated. (SMQ $320; this being one of 8 attaining this grade as of 10/08, with none graded higher).

Estimate: $300+

Minimum Bid: $150

33069 #RW50, 1983, $7.50 Multicolored GEM 100 PSE. (Original Gum - Never Hinged). Gem. PSE - Encapsulated. (SMQ $320; this being one of 9 attaining this grade as of 10/08, with none graded higher).

Estimate: $300+

Minimum Bid: $150

33070 #RW54, 1987, $10 Multicolored GEM 100 PSE. (Original Gum - Never Hinged). Gem. PSE - Encapsulated. (SMQ $220; this being one of 38 attaining this grade as of 10/08, with none graded higher).

Estimate: $200+

Minimum Bid: $100

33071 #RW60, 1993, $15 Multicolored, GEM 100 PSE. (Original Gum - Never Hinged). Gem PSE - Encapsulated. (SMQ $240; this being one of 34 attaining this grade as of 10/08, with none graded higher).

Estimate: $200+

Minimum Bid: $100

33072 #RW61, 1994, $15 Multicolored, GEM 100 PSE. (Original Gum - Never Hinged). Gem. PSE - Encapsulated. (SMQ $220; this being one of 48 attaining this grade as of 10/08, with none graded higher).

Estimate: $200+

Minimum Bid: $100

33073 #RW68, 2001, $15 Multicolored GEM 100 PSE. (Original Gum - Never Hinged). Gem. PSE - Encapsulated. (SMQ $240; this being one of 26 attaining this grade as of 10/08, with none graded higher).

Estimate: $200+

Minimum Bid: $100

33074 #RW69, 2002, $15 Multicolored, GEM 100 PSE. (Original Gum - Never Hinged). Gem. PSE - Encapsulated. (SMQ $290; this being one of 20 attaining this grade as of 10/08, with none graded higher).

Estimate: $300+

Minimum Bid: $150

33075 #RW70, 2003, $15 Multicolored GEM 100 PSE. (Original Gum - Never Hinged). Gem. PSE - Encapsulated. (SMQ $290; this being one of 16 attaining this grade as of 10/08, with none graded higher).

Estimate: $300+

Minimum Bid: $150

33076 #RW71, 2004, $15 Multicolored, GEM 100 PSE. (Original Gum - Never Hinged). Gem. PSE - Encapsulated. (SMQ $180; this being one of 66 attaining this grade as of 10/08, with none graded higher).

Estimate: $200+

Minimum Bid: $100

33077 #RW72, 2005, $15 Multicolored, GEM 100 PSE. (Original Gum - Never Hinged). Gem. PSE - Encapsulated. (SMQ $240; this being one of 30 attaining this grade as of 10/08, with none graded higher).

Estimate: $250+

Minimum Bid: $125

33078 #RW74b, 2007, $15 Multicolored XF-S 95 PSE. (Original Gum - Never Hinged). Extremely Fine to Superb. PSE - Encapsulated. (this being one of 153 attaining this grade as of 10/08, with 104 graded higher).

Estimate: $150+

Minimum Bid: $1

LOCALS & CARRIERS

33079 #20LUX3, 1876, 2c Black. (Used). An Extremely Fine used example, with a inconsequential horizontal crease near the bottom, otherwise free of the myriads of wear related faults usually associated with the Boyd's Bank Notices. 2008 PF Certificate. (Scott $250).

Estimate: $300+

Minimum Bid: $150

33080 #26L2, 1851, 1c Black. (Original Gum - Previously Hinged). Delightful example. Very Fine; 2003 PF Certificate. (Scott $250).

Estimate: $200+

Minimum Bid: $100

OTHER BACK-OF-THE-BOOK ISSUES

33081 #UX1, 1873, 1c Brown On Buff. (Unused). An unused example of this first Postal Card, with scattered lightened manuscript markings and trivial extraneous blue markings in area around the indicia which are barely visible even under magnification (towards the upper right corner), Fine to Very Fine; 2008 PF Certificate. (Scott $375).

Estimate: $200+

Minimum Bid: $100

33082 #WS5, 1919, $5 Carmine. (Used). On a War Savings Certificate. Fine to Very Fine; 2008 PSE Certificate. (Scott $350).

Estimate: $300+

Minimum Bid: $150

33083 #WX11, 1913, Red & Green. (Original Gum - Never Hinged). Reperforated at the left. Very Fine to Extremely Fine. 2008 PF Certificate. (Scott $1,400).

Estimate: $700+

Minimum Bid: $350

33084 #PC6-9, 1862, 5c - 50c Postage Currency Grouping. Four items, each handsome, each with use-related minor faults; primarily scattered creasing. An overall Fine to Very Fine selection. (Scott $600). (Total: 4 pages)

Estimate: $240+

Minimum Bid: $120

CONFEDERATE STATES OF AMERICA

33085 #8, 1863, 2c Brown Red. (Original Gum - Never Hinged). Scarce stamp in original gum never hinged condition, large balanced margins. Extremely Fine. 2008 PF Certificate. (Scott as hinged $70).

Estimate: $200+

Minimum Bid: $100

1893 COLUMBIAN EXPOSITION ISSUE

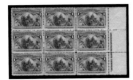

33086 #230, 1893, 1c Deep Blue. (Original Gum - Previously Hinged). Block of nine, with a horizontal crease in the bottom three, top six are never hinged. Fine to Very Fine. 2008 PSE Certificate. (Scott as singles $420).

Estimate: $500+

Minimum Bid: $250

33087 #230, 1893, 1c Deep Blue. (No Gum). It is a genuine unused, no gum, top margin Plate No. 55, Imprint and Letter K block of eight, with an 18mm horizontal tear in the selvage at the upper right, fresh color, clean back. Gem 2008 PSE Certificate. (Scott as hinged $750).

Estimate: $200+

Minimum Bid: $100

33088 #234, 1893, 5c Chocolate. (Original Gum - Hinged). Columbus Soliciting Aid of Isabella. Top margin Plate No.7, imprint and letter "B" block of eight (positions 1, 4, and 5-8 being Never Hinged), with a vertical crease through the selvage and positions 4 and 8, separated horizontal perforations at the middle and rejoined perforations and a sealed tear at the top center. Fine to Very Fine. 2008 PSE Certificate. (Scott $2,750).

Estimate: $950+

Minimum Bid: $475

1901 PAN-AMERICAN EXPOSITION ISSUE

33089 #299, 1901, 10c Yellow Brown & Black. (Original Gum - Never Hinged). Bottom margin Plate No. 1151 and Imprint block of six, with rejoined vertical perforations at the right, nicely etched impression, Fine to Very Fine. 2008 PSE Certificate. (Scott $6,750) .

Estimate: $4,500+

Minimum Bid: $2,250

1904 LOUISIANA PURCHASE EXPOSITION ISSUE

33090 #324, 1904, Apr. 30, 2c Carmine. (Original Gum - Never Hinged). Appealing top margin plate and imprint block of four. Very Fine to Extremely Fine; 2008 PSE Certificate. (Scott $350).

Estimate: $350+

Minimum Bid: $175

33091 #325, 1904, Apr. 30, 3c Violet. (Original Gum - Never Hinged). Desirable block of four with deep color. Fine; 2008 PSE Certificate. (Scott as singles $880).

Estimate: $400+

Minimum Bid: $200

1908-09 WASHINGTON FRANKLIN ISSUE - DBL. LINE WMK.

33092 #337, 1908, 8c Olive Green. (Original Gum - Previously Hinged). Top margin plate and imprint block of six, reduced selvage, positions 1,2,3 and 6 never hinged. Fine to Very Fine; 2008 PSE Certificate. (Scott $525).

Estimate: $350+

Minimum Bid: $175

1918-20 WASHINGTON-FRANKLIN ISSUE - OFFSET ISSUES

33093 #536, 1919, Aug. 15, 1c Gray Green. (Original Gum - Never Hinged). Pretty left margin plate number block of six, Fine; 2008 PSE Certificate. (Scott $375).

Estimate: $200+

Minimum Bid: $100

1922-25 DEFINITIVES

33094 #571, 1922-25, $1 Violet Black. (Original Gum - Previously Hinged). Well centered top margin arrow and plate number block of ten, light hinging on four stamps top row, balance never hinged. Very Fine to Extremely Fine. 2008 PSE Certificate. (Scott as P/B 6 & 4 singles $520).

Estimate: $450+

Minimum Bid: $225

1924-29 COMMEMORATIVE ISSUES

33095 #620, 1925, 2c Carmine & Black. (Original Gum - Previously Hinged). Nice top margin arrow, 2c and plate number block of eight, lightly hinged in selvage only. Fine to Very Fine; 2008 PSE Certificate. (Scott $200).

Estimate: $200+

Minimum Bid: $100

33096 #621, 1925, 5c Dark Blue And Black. (Original Gum - Previously Hinged). Handsome example, never hinged (previously hinged in selvage only) top margin arrow and plate number block of eight. Fine to Very Fine; 2008 PSE Certificate. (Scott $500).

Estimate: $400+

Minimum Bid: $200

33097 #630, 1926, 2c Carmine Rose. (Original Gum - Previously Hinged). Two White Plains sheets of 25, one being the lower right position, the other being the upper left, both with original gum, previously hinged in the selvage only. Fine to Very Fine. The lower right position sheet with 2008 PSE Certificate. (Scott $750). (Total: 2 pages)

Estimate: $450+
Minimum Bid: $225

1930 TO DATE

33098 #834, 1938, $5 Carmine And Black. (Original Gum - Never Hinged). Pretty left arrow margin block of four (minor mount glaze in the selvage only). Very Fine. 2008 PSE Certificate. (Scott $375).

Estimate: $300+
Minimum Bid: $150

AIRMAIL ISSUES

33099 #C3, 1918, 24c Carmine Rose & Blue. (Original Gum - Previously Hinged). A bottom left sheet corner margin block of four with siderographer's initials, bright fresh colors and detailed impressions on crisp white paper, the vignette shifted slightly to the left and downward making the plane appear to be approaching for a landing, previously hinged original gum, with 3mm short gumming across the bottom pair and hinged reinforcing of the bottom selvage. Fine. 2008 PSE Certificate. (Scott $280).

Estimate: $200+
Minimum Bid: $100

33100 #C6, 1923, 24c Carmine. (Original Gum - Previously Hinged). Mint block of four, bright and fresh, original gum, the bottom pair being never hinged, the top pair showing very light evidence of previous hinging towards the bottom of each stamp. Very Fine to Extremely Fine. 2008 PSE Certificate. (Scott as singles $470).

Estimate: $750+
Minimum Bid: $375

POSTAGE DUE ISSUES

33101 #J22, 1891, 1c Bright Claret. (Original Gum - Never Hinged). Top margin block of four. Very Good to Fine; 2008 PSE Certificate. (Scott $380).

Estimate: $250+
Minimum Bid: $125

REVENUE ISSUES

33102 #R103, 1871, 1c Blue & Black. (Disturbed Original Gum). Lovely mint block of four with disturbed original gum. Very Fine to Extremely Fine. 2008 PSE Certificate. (Scott $400).

Estimate: $350+
Minimum Bid: $175

33103 #R110, 1871, 15c Blue & Black. (Original Gum - Hinged). Terrific mint block of four, fresh, moderately hinged on several stamps. Very Fine. 2008 PSE Certificate. (Scott $225).

Estimate: $200+
Minimum Bid: $100

HUNTING PERMIT STAMPS

33104 #RW15, 1948, $1 Bright Blue. (Original Gum - Never Hinged). Top right corner margin Plate no. 160099 block of six, with an insignificant natural gum wrinkle in the bottom right stamp. Fresh. Very Fine; 2008 PSE Certificate. (Scott $425).

Estimate: $375+
Minimum Bid: $188

PROOFS & ESSAYS

33105 #70Evar, 1861, 24c Francis Patent Essay on Blue Green Wove Paper. A stunning horizontal pair, original gum, with a hinge remnant, the left essay with a light vertical crease at left which is not visible from the face and appears more to be a natural gum bend. 2003 and 2008 PF Certificates.

Estimate: $200+
Minimum Bid: $100

33106 #70E4h, 1903, 24c Dark Blue Large Die Essay on Bond. Measuring 64 x 66mm. Gorgeous. 2003 and 2008 PF Certificates.

Estimate: $200+
Minimum Bid: $100

33107 #70-E4K, 1903, 24c Light Blue. (Used). Fantastic example, die proof on bond, double line of scallops watermark. Superb; 2006 PF Certificate. (Scott $300).

Estimate: $300+
Minimum Bid: $150

33108 #72-E1, 1903, 90c Vignette Die Essays. Selection of three, includes #72-E1a Die on proof paper in green showing full die sinkage, and two #72E1c Die on dull light blue green bond, one in dusky blue, and the other in red violet, Very Fine to Extremely Fine. (Scott $430).

Estimate: $400+
Minimum Bid: $200

33109 #RO68E, 1864, 1c Black, Large Die Essay on India. Die sunk on card measuring 150 x 107½mm, showing full die sinkage, intensely rich and vibrant. Very Fine to Extremely Fine. 2008 PF Certificate.

Estimate: $350+
Minimum Bid: $175

33110 #RO68E, 1864, 1c Black. Gorgeous match and medicine die essay on India paper, deep jet black color. Very Fine; 2008 PF Certificate.

Estimate: $300+
Minimum Bid: $150

33111 #63/78P4, 1861-67, 1c - 90c, Plate Proofs on Card. A gorgeous selection of Plate Proofs consisting of numbers 63P4, 65P4, 71P4, 72P4, 73P4, 76P4, 77P4, and 78P4. Fresh as the day printed. Very Fine to Extremely Fine and undercatalogued. (Scott $455).

Estimate: $400+

Minimum Bid: $200

33112 #78P3, 1862, 24c Lilac Plate Proof on India. A spectacular left margin single, fresh and bright, Extremely Fine to Superb and undercatalogued; 2008 PF Certificate. (Scott $80).

Estimate: $200+

Minimum Bid: $100

33113 #299P1, 1901, 10c Yellow Brown & Black, Large Die Proof on India. Die sunk on a non-contemporary card backing measuring 83 x 72mm, the proof itself being especially bright and vibrant, Extremely Fine; Raymond Ostrander Smith, designer; 2008 PF Certificate. (Scott $575).

Estimate: $300+

Minimum Bid: $150

33114 #J5-7P3, 1879, 10c - 50c Brown, Plate Proofs on India. Sequential top margin Plate No. (331, 332, & 333 respectively) blocks of twelve with imprint, each block with vertical creases, the 10c and 30c being through the second vertical pair, and lighter creases on the 50c through the first and last vertical pairs; otherwise a Very Fine to Extremely Fine appearance for these scarce positions. (Scott $2,025).

Estimate: $1,200+

Minimum Bid: $600

33115 #O57-71P4, 1873, 1c - $20 Green, Plate Proofs on Card. Complete set of 15, fresh and clean. Very Fine. (Scott $228).

Estimate: $100+

Minimum Bid: $1

33116 #RO47P1, 1880, 1c Black. Large die proof on India, die sunk on card, 152 x 226mm, some very tiny toning spots. Superb; 2008 PF Certificate. (Scott $225).

Estimate: $200+

Minimum Bid: $100

33117 #RS60P1, 1880, 1c Black. Full die sunk black large die proof on India measuring 64 x 103mm, stain spot at top. Very Fine; 2008 PF Certificate. (Scott $175).

Estimate: $200+

Minimum Bid: $100

33118 #RS65P1, 1869, 4c Black. Full die sunk black large die proof on India measuring 94 x 55mm, pencil notation on front. Very Fine; 2008 PF Certificate. (Scott $175).

Estimate: $200+

Minimum Bid: $100

33119 #9X1TC2, 1845, 5c Trial Color Proofs on India Paper. (No Gum As Issued). A selection of six different shades including dull dark violet, brown violet, dark green, orange yellow, brown, and scarlet; the dark green, brown, and scarlet examples being sound; the dull dark violet with a facial scrape, the brown violet with a trivial at the top right, and the scarlet with thins, none of which detract from the overall appearance; Very Good - Fine. (Scott $1700)

Estimate: $1,250+

Minimum Bid: $625

33120 #39TC5, 1861, 90c Trial Color Plate Proof on Wove Paper. Mounted on non-contemporary bond paper, the proof in dark violet brown, with a small tear at top through the "T" of "Postage", and a repair at lower right, both inconsequential to the overall Very Fine appearance of this scarce proof; 2008 PF Certificate. (Scott $625).

Estimate: $350+

Minimum Bid: $175

33121 #RS33TC1, 1863, 1c Green. Full die sunk Turner die 1 green trial color die proof on India measuring 50 x 75mm, small thin spot at bottom left. Very Fine; 2008 PF Certificate. (Scott $225).

Estimate: $200+

Minimum Bid: $100

33122 #RS33TC1, 1863, 1c Green. Full die sunk Turner die 111 green trial color die proof on India, horizontally broken die measuring 65 x 83mm, thin above design. Very Fine; 2008 PF Certificate. (Scott $225).

Estimate: $200+

Minimum Bid: $100

33123 #RS50TC1, 1877, 1c Black. Full die sunk black trial color die proof on India measuring 50 x 64mm, small thin spot at top. Very Fine; 2008 PF Certificate. (Scott $300).

Estimate: $250+

Minimum Bid: $125

33124 #RS86TC1, 1869, 1c Black, Large Die Trial Color Die Proof on India. Die sunk on card measuring 150 x 112mm showing full die sinkage. Very Fine to Extremely Fine; 2008 PSE Certificate. (Scott $225).

Estimate: $200+

Minimum Bid: $100

33125 #RS196TC1, 1876, 1c Green, Large Die Trial Color Proof on India. Die sunk on card measuring 111 x 151mm, deep rich pastel color and detailed impression, clean. Very Fine to Extremely Fine; 2008 PF Certificate. (Scott $225).

Estimate: $200+

Minimum Bid: $100

33126 #RS221TC1, 1863, 4c Blue. Full die sunk blue trial die proof on India measuring 85 x 64mm, several small thins. Very Fine; 2008 PF Certificate. (Scott $225).

Estimate: $200+

Minimum Bid: $100

33127 #RS261TC1, 1877, 4c Blue. Full die sunk blue trial color die proof on India measuring 72 x 57mm, thin spot at bottom right, tiny pencil notation on the front. Very Fine; 2008 PF Certificate (Scott $500).

Estimate: $400+

Minimum Bid: $200

OTHER BACK-OF-THE-BOOK ISSUES

33128 1812, "Albert Gallatin" Free Frank as Secretary of Treasury. On stampless folded letter to Gloucester, Mass., datelined May 20, 1812, with a brown Wash. City May 21 circular date stamp (c.d.s.) cancel at upper left corner, the letter front with a sealed tear at top center that does not affect the signature. Fine to Very Fine; 2008 PSE Certificate.

Estimate: $250+

Minimum Bid: $125

1847 REGULAR ISSUES

33129 #1, 1847, 5c Brown. (Used). Tied on folded outer address sheet by a pen cancel and a blue Middlebury, Ct. town receiving mark, with a blue Oxford, Mass. circular date stamp (c.d.s.) postmarking and matching blue "5" rate mark, the stamp with light stains, a clipped corner at the bottom left and a 5mm vertical tear at the bottom left. Fine; 2008 PSE Certificate. (Scott $675).

Estimate: $250+

Minimum Bid: $125

1851-57 FIRST ISSUES - IMPERF

33130 #9, 1852, 1c Blue. (Used). Three singles tied by Washington, DC Nov 15, 1856 circular date stamp (c.d.s.) cancels on fully intact cover to Staunton, VA, the right stamp with trivial corner creases at the top right, the cover itself with lightly penciled description attributed to Chase, but not mentioned on the certificate. Very Fine; 2008 PSE Certificate. (Scott $410).

Estimate: $240+

Minimum Bid: $120

33131 #10A, 1851, 3c Orange Brown. (Used). Position 86R2E, tied by blue circular grid cancel on 1851 folded letter to Concord, New Hampshire, with a matching Lowell, MS Oct 22, 3c PAID postmark, the letter with a vertical file fold and some toning spots. Very Fine; 2008 PSE Certificate. (Scott $210).

Estimate: $200+

Minimum Bid: $100

33132 #10A, 1851, 3c Orange Brown. (Used). Single on cover to Attleboro, MA, with Pawtucket, RI postmark at top left, the stamp with red circular grid cancel, also with a trivial small corner crease at bottom left. Very Fine; 2008 PF Certificate. (Scott $210).

Estimate: $200+

Minimum Bid: $100

33133 #14, 1855, 10c Green. (Used). A handsome four margin single tied by blue Baltimore, MD circular date stamp (c.d.s.) on cover to San Francisco. Very Fine; 2008 PSE Certificate. (Scott $260).

Estimate: $200+

Minimum Bid: $100

33134 #15, 1855, 10c Green. (Used). Tied by blue Johnstown, Wis. circular date stamp (c.d.s.) on cover to Yankee Jims, Cal., the cover reduced by about 28mm at the left and with a stain at the lower left. Very Fine; 2008 PSE Certificate. (Scott $260).

Estimate: $150+

Minimum Bid: $1

1857-61 FIRST ISSUES - PERFS

33135 #26, 1857, 3c Dull Red. (Used). Used on cover from University of Virginia, VA to Clayton, Alabama, where a second stamp was applied and the cover was readdressed to Lynchburg, Virginia, the stamps with small faults and the cover with opening tears at top, Fine to Very Fine; 2008 PF Certificate and the cover signed Ashbrook.

Estimate: $200+

Minimum Bid: $100

33136 #36b, 1860, 12c Black. (Used). Two singles on a cover to Dumfries, Scotland, the stamps which have been lifted and replaced are canceled with black grids and tied by a red Philadelphia Dec 24, 1860 transit marking, both stamps with heavy horizontal creases and small tears, the cover with Jan 1861 receivers on the back and pinholes. Fine to Very Fine; 2008 PSE Certificate.

Estimate: $300+

Minimum Bid: $150

1861-66 SECOND ISSUES

33137 #64, 1861, 3c Pink. (Used). Single tied by blue Baltimore, MD postmark on 1861 dated folded letter to Philadelphia, with a double oval merchant handstamp at lower left. The stamp has a small nick at left and a small nick and tear at the top left, the cover with a minor scotch tape repaired tear at top; otherwise, a Fine to Very Fine usage; 2008 PF Certificate. (Scott $1,100).

Estimate: $450+

Minimum Bid: $225

33138 #73, 1863, 2c Black. (Used). A horizontal pair, along with a horizontal pair #68, tied by black circular waffle grid cork cancels and a red New York City cancel on an 1865 cover to Yorkshire, England, with red London transit at lower left, and a Crowe receiver on the reverse, the cover missing the backflap. Fine to Very Fine; 2008 PSE Certificate.

Estimate: $350+

Minimum Bid: $175

33139 #78b, 1862, 24c Gray. (Used). A single tied by Buffalo, NY postmark on cover to Knaresboro, England, with London transit, 1866 Knaresboro receiver on the reverse, the stamp with an insignificant small corner crease at the top right. Fine to Very Fine usage; 2008 PF Certificate. (Scott $325).

Estimate: $250+

Minimum Bid: $125

1869 PICTORIALS

33140 #112-13, 1869, 1c - 2c Pictorials. (Used). Single of each tied by target cancels on cover from Augusta to Alma, Wisconsin. Very Fine; 2008 PF Certificate. (Scott $400).

Estimate: $300+

Minimum Bid: $150

33141 #113, 1869, 2c Brown. (Used). A horizontal strip of three tied on cover to Leeds, England, the stamps with black cork cancels and tied by a black Feb. 9, 1870 London transit mark, the cover reduced by 2mm at the top, and has a red New Haven, CT double circle postmark, red New York and London transits, and a black Leeds receiver on the back. Very Fine; 2008 PSE Certificate.

Estimate: $300+

Minimum Bid: $150

33142 #119, 1869, 15c Brown & Blue. (Used). Usage on a folded cover front to Austria, the stamp tied black circle of wedges cork cancel, a red New York Jan 26 (1870) 'PAID ALL' marking and a red French transit marking. Very Fine; 2008 PSE Certificate. (Scott $275).

Estimate: $200+

Minimum Bid: $100

1893 COLUMBIAN EXPOSITION ISSUE

33143 #230//240, 1893, 1c - 50c COLOR. (Used). Partial set (10), missing only the 8c and the dollar values, tied on a Philatelic cover to Kansas City, MO by Ft. Wayne, Ind Dec 4, 1894 machine cancels. The 1c tied by the 2c stamp and the handstamp cancel across both stamps, contrary to the certificate's assertion that the 1c is not tied. The 1c, 5c, 6c, 10c, 15c, and 30c stamps with faults and the cover with a opening related tear at top left, otherwise a Fine to Very Fine and scarce combination cover; 2008 PSE Certificate. (Scott $851).

Estimate: $350+

Minimum Bid: $175

AIRMAIL ISSUES

33144 Zeppelins Plus Flight Group (Used). A group of four covers, three being Round the World Zeppelin flights, one with #C4-6 complete as blocks of four plus 13c, 50c & $1 Definitive issues, one round trip via Tokio, Japan with two #C4 blocks of four and a pair of #C6, the reverse side with U.S. Air Mail Routes map and 1c Definitive, the third with 5c, 50c, $1, & $2 Definitive's, each cover with the appropriate flight markings, with the fourth being a #C10a usage (without selvage) on a Midwestern Philatelic Exhibition commemorative cover, a Fine to Very Fine grouping for the specialist. (Total: 4 pages)

Estimate: $400+

Minimum Bid: $200

33145 #C14, 1930, $1.30 Brown. (Used). Used on a U219 Zeppelin flown entire, the stamp tied by a Whittier, Cal Apr 23, 1930 circular date stamp (c.d.s.) and by the Zeppelin flight marking, the stamp with a small scuff in the upper left margin, and the cover with Friedrichshafen and New York markings on the back. Very Fine; 2008 PSE Certificate.

Estimate: $350+

Minimum Bid: $175

33146 #C14, 1930, $1.30 Brown. (Used). 1930 machine cancel, on cacheted Graf Zeppelin flight cover addressed to Waterbury CT, Friedrichshafen & green 1930 New York special Graf Zeppelin postmark on reverse. Very Fine; 2008 PF Certificate. (Scott $400).

Estimate: $300+

Minimum Bid: $150

33147 #C15, 1930, $2.60 Blue. (Used). Tied on Zeppelin flown #U422a, along with #C11, addressed to San Francisco, the Zeppelin stamp tied by New York duplex cancel, with Graf Zeppelin flight cachets, and green New York special Graf Zeppelin postmark on reverse; the stamp with a small tear at top through "F" in "Graf". A Very Fine appearance and usage; 2008 PF Certificate.

Estimate: $450+

Minimum Bid: $225

33148 #C15, 1930, $2.60 Blue. (Used). On a First Europe Pan America Zeppelin Flight cover, tied by a Washington, D.C. Apr 24, 1930 machine cancel, with the appropriate cover markings - the cover opened at the top and reduced 5mm at the right. Fine to Very Fine; 2008 PSE Certificate. (Scott $600).

Estimate: $400+

Minimum Bid: $200

LOCALS & CARRIERS

33149 #3LB1, 1849, 1c Blue. (Used). On 1850 docketed folded letter to Surry, Me, the local tied by red Boston integral rate town cancel, the cover with a vertical file fold through the top of the stamp and a repaired nick at the bottom. Fine to Very Fine; 2008 PF Certificate. (Scott $275).

Estimate: $200+

Minimum Bid: $100

33150 #7LB11, 1850, 1c Black On Black Glazed. (Used). Uncancelled single on 1852 dated folded letter to Providence, RI along with 3c #11A which is tied by blue Philadelphia town cancel. Very Fine; 2008 PF Certificate.

Estimate: $200+

Minimum Bid: $100

33151 "Adams & Co. / Express / San Jose" Blue oval handstamp on 1859 docketed folded letter sheet to San Francisco, with blue "PAID" in circle at top left. Very Fine to Extremely Fine; 2008 PF Certificate.

Estimate: $250+

Minimum Bid: $125

33152 #15L14, 1861, 1c Blue & Pink. (Used). Used on cover with 3c #11 to Lancaster, PA, the local acid tied, the 3c tied by Philadelphia, PA May 20 circular date stamp (c.d.s.), the cover with a Blood's Despatch May 20, 1857 circular date stamp (c.d.s.) at top center, and with a horizontal fold that does not affect either stamp. Fine to Very Fine; 2008 PSE Certificate. (Scott $375).

Estimate: $250+

Minimum Bid: $125

33153 #20LU14, 1867, 2c Red On Cream. (Used). Locally addressed entire, the stamp design tied by "Blood's Dispatch / 41 Fulton St." cancel, the cover with a trivial small tear at right. Fine to Very Fine; 2008 PF Certificate. (Scott $300).

Estimate: $200+

Minimum Bid: $100

33154 #36L1a, 1849, G. Carter's Despatch, 2c Black on Ribbed Paper. On 1849 dated folded letter to Danville, PA, with blue Philadelphia postmark, the local pen canceled and with a tint tear at right. Fine to Very Fine; 2003 PF Certificate. (Scott $300).

Estimate: $200+

Minimum Bid: $100

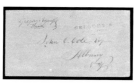

33155 "Gregory's Express Office / San Francisco" Blue triple straight line handstamp, with the "X" in "Express" directly below the first "R" in "Gregory's" on cover to Albany, NY with manuscript "Gregory's Express / Paid" at left. Very Fine; 2008 PF Certificate.

Estimate: $350+

Minimum Bid: $175

33156 "Kinsley & Co's Express" Fancy "Forwarded By." company handstamp on Boston 1850 datelined folded letter to Philadelphia. Very Fine to Extremely Fine; 2008 PF Certificate.

Estimate: $350+

Minimum Bid: $175

33157 "Pacific Express" Frank. On 3c #U10 entire addressed to Red Bluffs, CA, with red "Pacific Express Co. / Shasta" cancel, the cover with light edge wear and soiling. Fine to Very Fine; 2008 PF Certificate.

Estimate: $250+

Minimum Bid: $125

33158 #136L10, 1849, 1c Pink. (Used). Single tied on locally addressed cover by oval "Swart's Post Office / Chatham Square" cancel, with framed "Paid / Swarts" handstamp at left. Very Fine; 2008 PF Certificate. (Scott $250).

Estimate: $250+

Minimum Bid: $125

33159 #145L1, 1853, 2c Gold. (Used). Westtown local Type II uncancelled on cover to Winchester, Virginia, with #26 tied by Street Road, PA town cancel, both the stamps and cover sound, Very Fine; 2008 PF Certificate. (Scott $200).

Estimate: $250+

Minimum Bid: $125

33160 #145L1, 1853, 2c Gold. (Used). Westtown local Type III, uncancelled on cover to Pennsylvania, with 3c #26 tied by Westchester, Pa circular date stamp (c.d.s.) town cancel, the 3c stamp with trivial small faults, the cover with minor back flap faults from opening, Very Fine; 2008 PF Certificate.

Estimate: $200+

Minimum Bid: $100

33161 #145L1, 1853, 2c Gold. (Used). Westtown local Type II on cover front, uncancelled, with 3c #26A, to Yardville, NJ, the 3c tied by Westtown, PA circular date stamp (c.d.s.) cancel and with a small nick at the top left, Very Fine; 2008 PF Certificate. (Scott $200).

Estimate: $200+

Minimum Bid: $100

33162 #145L2, 1853, 2c Gold. (Used). Westtown local Type VII, uncancelled on reverse of cover from Street Road, PA to Colora, MD, along with #158 with target cancel, Very Fine and clean; 2008 PF Certificate.

Estimate: $400+

Minimum Bid: $200

33163 #U9, 1853, 3c Red. (Used). Clean and Very attractive entire, with printed Wells Fargo frank addressed to San Francisco, with oval "Wells Fargo & Co / Express / Chinese Camp" cancel. Extremely Fine; 2008 PF Certificate.

Estimate: $250+

Minimum Bid: $125

CONFEDERATE STATES OF AMERICA

33164 #26, 1857, 3c Dull Red. (Used). A single used on bi-color "Forever Float, Our Banner Bright." Union Patriotic cover to Palmyra, ME, from Madison, Wis., with Madison, Wis. postmark at the center, the stamp oxidized, and the cover with a small inconsequential mended nick at the right. Very Fine; 2008 PF Certificate.

Estimate: $250+

Minimum Bid: $125

33165 #1, 1861, 5c Green. (Used). A horizontal pair on cover from New Orleans to Virginia, the cover reduced at top. Very Fine; 2008 PF Certificate. (Scott $475).

Estimate: $300+

Minimum Bid: $150

33166 #2a, 1862, 10c Light Blue. (Used). A single used on cover to Augusta, GA, with Richmond, VA postmark, the stamp with trivial diagonal crease at top. Very Fine; 2008 PF Certificate. (Scott $325).

Estimate: $250+

Minimum Bid: $125

33167 #11a, 1863, 10c Milky Blue. (Used). Single tied on "Turned" cover addressed to Cool Well P.O., VA, the stamp tied by Richmond town cancel. Fine to Very Fine; 2008 PF Certificate.

Estimate: $375+

Minimum Bid: $188

33168 #11, 1863, 10c Blue. (Used). Single tied on "Turned" cover addressed to Galveston P.O., Texas, the stamp tied by Harrisburgh, Tex town cancel, the "other" usage carried "out of the mail", the cover with light water-staining at right. Fine to Very Fine; 2008 PF Certificate.

Estimate: $350+

Minimum Bid: $175

COLLECTIONS / BALANCES

33169 1857-1944, Extensive & Valuable mint Collection. (Original Gum - Hinged). A fairly substantial collection of essentially mint United States stamps housed in a beautiful old Scott National Album replete with several hundred issues from most issues and periods far too numerous to describe in detail: however we noted (mint unless otherwise indicated) a VF 5c (10 X 1) reprint, followed by a good selection of the 1857 1c, 3c P. 15 issues with pairs, 1861 issues P.12 with a number of 1c & 3c, a good selection of the succeeding "Banknotes", mainly lower values but several VF or better examples, Columbians to 8c with shades, a good selection of the 1895 Bureau issues to 10c with several shades, Trans Mississippi 1c-4c including MNH blocks of the 1c & 2c, a good showing of the 1902 issues to 13c with several additional shades also pairs, coil pairs and imperforate varieties , Louisiana Purchase incomplete but including a block of the 1c, (two MLH & 2 MNH), and the Pilgrim issues to 2c including blocks. There follows a fairly extensive showing of the most of the Franklin - Washington issues to the $1, including blocks, pairs, coil pairs (some questionable) strips and varieties, Panama Pacific P.12 to 5c, & P. 10 to 2c with plate number singles, 1922 Regular issues P.11 complete to $2 Capitol Hill, Kansas Nebraska complete, plus a block of the Kansas 6c MNH and fairly complete thereafter including Parks, Prexies to $5 etc to 1946. Finally an interesting selection of BOB issues, with sparse airmails, but fairly extensive Special Delivery issues, Postage Dues, Parcel post, both Coast Guards, a selection of Officials, Guam 1c - 50c & 10c Special Deliver, some Canal Zone, Motor Vehicle appears complete, Newspapers PR 114-125, Potato Tax R1-13, Silver Tax 108-120 all mint, $5 War savings, mint small grease spot and much more, including in addition a brimming Scott National album with 1000's of less expensive issues. All in all a very interesting group with specialist material & high catalog value. Fine to Very Fine.

Estimate: $3,500+

Minimum Bid: $1,750

33170 #551//568, 1922-25, ½c - 25c, Plate Blocks. (Original Gum). Selection consisting of seventeen mint plate blocks of six including #'s 551-59 and 561-68, all are never hinged except for the 1c, 3c, and 15c which had been previously lightly hinged, the 20c with scattered small natural gum skips. An overall Fine to Very Fine grouping. (Scott $4,327).

Estimate: $2,500+

Minimum Bid: $1,250

33171 1847-1947, Specialized Cancellation Collection. (Used). A old Scott National Album filled with over 1,000 used United States stamps covering most periods and clearly focused cancellations, shades and types or varieties, with particular interest in colored and fancy cancels. We noted a good showing of the 1847 1c & 3c, the 1857 perf. 15 with examples of the 1c, 3c & 10c, the 1861 "Banknotes" are also well represented with numerous examples of most values and especially the 24c of which there are 10, the 1869 Pictorials are quite well represented with several examples of the 3c & 10c with a variety of shades and cancellations and notably a magnificent pair of the 3c with a bright blue cork cancel. The 1870 - 1887 Banknote issues are also well represented as are most of the succeeding issues including Columbians to the 30c, Trans Mississippi to the 10c, the latter VF unused , Pan Pac and most of the succeeding issues often complete with some $1& $2 values present. There are numerous Franklin - Washington's with a number of coils and coil pairs (some questionable), several strips, blocks, multiples and varieties and thereafter fairly complete to Kansas Nebraska - generally used with a few mint or unused examples here and there. The collection includes an interesting BOB selection with a fairly complete Airmails including a mint "Baby Zepp" (but no C13-15), fairly complete showings of Special Delivery, Parcel Post, Special Handling, Postage Dues (including a superb #J60, VFU), several officials including some complete sets, several Locals (including a "Blood" on cover), a fine used example of the 10c Hamburg American Packet Co. issue), some Match & Medicine and several Revenues, and much more. Some faults and a few questionable items but overall condition is fine, and an unusual & interesting lot well worth closer inspection. Fine to Very Fine.

Estimate: $2,000+

Minimum Bid: $1,000

33172 Mint U.S. Collection, 1893-1949. Nice mint accumulation in green album, lots of airmails, Columbians, definitive's and too many other stamps to list. Condition is mixed with hinged and never hinged, overall sound examples but some faults are to be expected. Very good dealer or intermediate collectors group. Fine to Very Fine. (Approximate Scott Value $3,000).

Estimate: $900+

Minimum Bid: $450

33173 1870-1910, Collection of Fancy cancels.(Used). A fascinating collection of several 100 "Fancy Cancels" mounted on 20 stock pages and a few album pages all contained in a 3 ring binder: includes 7 covers and numerous stamps on piece: An interesting and unusual group. Fine to Very Fine.

Estimate: $750+

Minimum Bid: $375

33174 1851-1981 United States Collection. (Mint &Used). A good starter collection contained in a beautiful old Scott National album: fairly sparse for the early years with only a smattering of issues present, generally used, a small selection of Banknotes, used and various other issues generally partially complete or used thereafter, including Columbians unused to the 10c (without gum), Trans Mississippi unused to 8c (couple with OG) various Franklin- Washington mint and used, including 1917 Flat Plate complete to the $1 mint OG, 1926 Rotary complete to 50c mint OG, Nebraska complete mint OG, thereafter fairly complete to 1980, also some airmails and a small amount of BOB: some faults here and there but generally fine and a good basis for expansion. Fine to Very Fine.

Estimate: $600+

Minimum Bid: $300

33175 #230//236, 1893, 1c - 8c Columbians, VF 80 PSE. (Original Gum - Never Hinged). Nice group of PSE certified stamps in original gum, Never Hinged, 80 or better, includes #'s 230 graded 80J (2006), 232 graded 83 (2001), 233 graded 80 (2005), and 236 graded 80 (2005). Very Fine PSE - Graded Certificate. (SMQ $640);

Estimate: $400+

Minimum Bid: $200

33176 Group of four 1902-08 Regular Issues. (Original Gum - Never Hinged). Perfectly matched group of the 1902-08 Regular Issue series, Scott numbers 302, 303, 307 and 308, all PSE graded 80, terrific lot, Very Fine PSE - Graded Certificate. (SMQ $575).

Estimate: $350+

Minimum Bid: $175

33177 Mixed group with PSE Certification (Original Gum - Never Hinged). Small group of PSE certified as 80 original gum, Never Hinged, Scott numbers 286,402 and 572, very nice lot. Very Fine. PSE - Graded Certificate. (SMQ $475).

Estimate: $250+

Minimum Bid: $125

33178 Group of Three Kansas/Nebraska Overprints (Original Gum - Never Hinged). Wonderful lot of three, includes #'s 665-66, and 677. All graded 80. Very Fine. PSE - Graded Certificate. (SMQ $315).

Estimate: $150+

Minimum Bid: $1

33179 #38, 1955, 3c + 4c + 8c Multicolored Souvenir Sheet. (Original Gum - Never Hinged). Thirteen post office fresh souvenir sheets. Very Fine to Extremely Fine. (Scott $1,560).

Estimate: $1,000+

Minimum Bid: $500

CANADIAN PROVINCES NOVA SCOTIA
REGULAR ISSUES

33180 Unitrade #1 (Scott #1), 1851, 1p Red Brown ('53). (Used). An attractive used example of this scarce #1 with good color, unobtrusive cancellations and close, but clear to enormous margins all round. Fault free. Fine to Very Fine. 2008 PF Certificate. (Unitrade CAN$400).

Estimate: $200+

Minimum Bid: $100

33181 #2b, 1857, 3p Pale Blue. (Used). An attractive small cover franked by a pair of the 3d blue Heraldic Flowers issue tied to cover by grid cancels with red " Paid 10" in circle Handstamp at left and 1859 Amherst transit PMK on reverse (left stamp is defective at lower left and the right has a few small tears at bottom right) nevertheless a scarce usage. Fair to Good; 2008 PF Certificate. (Scott $565).

Estimate: $200+

Minimum Bid: $100

GREAT BRITAN

33182 Stanley Gibbons #8 (Scott #3), 1841, 1p Red Brown On Bluish. (Original Gum - Previously Hinged). A superb mint example (lettered MK) with rich color on bluish paper with 4 good to enormous margins, very lightly hinged. Extremely Fine PF Certificate. (Stanley Gibbons £500).

Estimate: $280+

Minimum Bid: $140

33183 Stanley Gibbons #8 (Scott #3), 1841, 1d Red Brown On Bluish. (Original Gum - Previously Hinged). A fresh mint example (lettered JH) with rich color on bluish paper, close (but clear) to excellent margins all round and hinged OG (small hinge remnant) Fine to Very Fine; 2008 PF Certificate. (Stanley Gibbons £500).

Estimate: $200+

Minimum Bid: $100

33184 Stanley Gibbons #8 (Scott #3), 1841, 1d Red Brown On Bluish. (Original Gum - Previously Hinged). A fresh mint example (lettered RC) with rich color on bluish paper, clear to good margins all round and lightly hinged OG (natural gum crease) otherwise Fine to Very Fine; 2008 PF Certificate. (Stanley Gibbons £500).

Estimate: $120+

Minimum Bid: $1

33185 Stanley Gibbons #8 a (Scott #3), 1841, 1 d Red Brown On Very Blue Paper. (Original Gum - Previously Hinged). A very fresh mint example (lettered BF) with rich red brown color on very blue paper; with four good to enormous margins, small hinge remnant and light vertical crease at left and diagonal crease at top right. Very Fine to Extremely Fine; 2008 PF Certificate. (Stanley Gibbons £600).

Estimate: $160+

Minimum Bid: $1

33186 #U3, 1840, 1p Black. (Used). An attractive used example of the Mulready letter sheet addressed to London with red Maltese Cross cancel and Canterbury July 10 1840 CDS on reverse and red London receiving mark: filing folds and edge nicks not mentioned on certificate, nevertheless a better than average example 2008 PF Certificate. (Scott $425).

Estimate: $200+

Minimum Bid: $100

BRITISH COMMONWEALTH
GUERNSEY

33187 #N1, N2, 1941, 1/2p, 1p Light Green, Red. (Used). Oversized registered cover addressed to Vale, Guernsey bearing seven 1/2 d stamps and eight 1d stamps canceled by Guernsey Channel islands 6 Dec 1941 CDS with Express Delivery etiquette.(Usual blue registry crayon affecting a couple of stamps) a colorful and scarce WWII German Occupation cover. Very Fine; 2008 PF Certificate.

Estimate: $150+

Minimum Bid: $1

PAPUA NEW GUINEA

33188 #57, 1911, 2sh6p Rose. (Used). An attractive small clean registered cover addressed to New York, City franked by a single example of the 2s 6p rose Lakatoi issue which is tied by Samarai CDS: with Red Samarai registry etiquette at bottom right and Melbourne, San Francisco & New York transit and receiving markings on reverse. Scarce usage. Very Fine; 2008 PF Certificate. (Stanley Gibbons £300 +).

Estimate: $300+

Minimum Bid: $150

TONGA
A SCARCE CENTENARY OF EMANCIPATION FDC

33189 #CO1- 6: 2d - 1 pound set on cover (Used). A colorful "Centenary of Emancipation" First Day cover bearing the complete set of the scarce Air Post Officials overprinted "Official Airmail - 1862 - Tau'ataina - Emancipation - 1962" in Red all neatly tied by neat Nukualofa 7 Feb 1962 cancels: a very scarce usage on an O.H.M.S. cover addressed to the deputy Premier , HRH Tuipehahake. Very Fine; 2008 PF Certificate.
.

Estimate: $200+

Minimum Bid: $100

WORLDWIDE
CAPE VERDE

33190 #7a, 1877, 100r Lilac. (Used). An interesting small clean cover bearing the 100r lilac (Scott 7a) tied by neat blue San Vincente cancel and addressed to Auburndale MA, sent via London & New York with appropriate transit and receiving marks on reverse (cover open at top and left and partially at right). Very scarce usage. Very Fine; 2008 PF Certificate.

Estimate: $250+

Minimum Bid: $125

AUSTRIA

33191 #B110, 1933, 50g + 50g Deep Ultramarine. (Used). Tied on piece by exhibition cancel. Very Fine; 2008 PF Certificate. (Scott $150.00).

Estimate: $100+

Minimum Bid: $1

GERMANY

33192 #B91-92, 1936, (Original Gum - Hinged). Two fresh sets of these attractive Souvenir sheets issued for the 1936 Berlin Olympics one signed and dated 10-9-36 by Jesse Owens, winner of four Gold medals at the 1936 Olympics, the other signed by Glenn Morris winner of the John Sullivan Decathlon Memorial Award - dated Jan 13 1937: each written up and neatly mounted on an album page: Spectacular and a rare and unusual piece of Postal History. .

Estimate: $400+

Minimum Bid: $200

ITALIAN STATES - SARDINIA

33193 #2, 1851, 20 c Blue. (No Gum). A very fresh unused (without gum) example of this scarce stamp with good color and clear to good margins all round. Fault free & Fine to Very Fine; 2008 Sismondo Certificate &1995 APS Certificate (Scott $2,000).

Estimate: $240+

Minimum Bid: $120

33194 #9, 1854, 40 c Brick Red. (Used). An attractive used example of this scarce stamp with rich color, good embossing, neat Genva 15 GEN CDS, and three good margins (fourth is just cutting frame line at top left) otherwise fault free and of fine appearance. Signed Diena & Calves Fine to Very Fine; 2008 Sismondo Certificate & 1995 APS Certificate (Scott $3,250).

Estimate: $280+

Minimum Bid: $140

JAPAN

33195 National Park Souvenir Sheets (Original Gum - Never Hinged). A selection of three mint souvenir sheets including Scott #'s 288a with original folder, and 318a and 323a in their original combined folder. All three sheets are post office fresh, with unblemished full original gum, Never Hinged. A Very Fine grouping. (Scott without folders $410).

Estimate: $300+

Minimum Bid: $150

33196 #422a, 1948, 5y Brown. (Original Gum - Never Hinged). A very fresh never hinged example of this scarce souvenir sheet of 5 known as "Beauty Looking Back" 2008 PF Certificate. (Scott $475).

Estimate: $250+

Minimum Bid: $125

NEW HEBRIDES (FRENCH)

33197 #3, 5, 1908 (2), 25c, 1fr Blue On Greenish, Blue On Yel. Green. (Used). An interesting registered cover mailed from Vila, French New Hebrides to New York via Sydney NSW & London. Franked by 1908 25c & 1fr overprinted issues (usual blue registry marks and missing corner to cover) otherwise unusual and scarce usage. Very Fine; 2008 PF Certificate.

Estimate: $150+

Minimum Bid: $1

SWITZERLAND

33198 #30, 1855, 1fr Lavender. (Used). A used upper marginal example of this scarce early Swiss 1fr Sitting Helvetia issue with good color (black silk thread) and neat diamond grill cancel (lower margin cut into and some light toning) otherwise sound & scarce. Very Good to Fine; 2008 PF Certificate. (Scott $950).

Estimate: $200+

Minimum Bid: $100

33199 #31, 1855, 1fr Lavender. (Used). A used example of the 1 fr. lavender "Sitting Helvetia" (yellow silk thread) with neat blue grid cancel, good color and close to clear margins: overall sound & Fine; 2008 PF Certificate. (Scott $925.00).

Estimate: $200+

Minimum Bid: $100

COLLECTIONS / BALANCES

33200 1840-1970 Collection of Austria. (Mint & Used). An interesting accumulation of Austria , including some Lombardy & Venetia, housed in 8 albums & Binders containing 1,000's of mint & used stamps and a few covers. Strength in 19th century material with a number of scarce stamps present but also several better semi postal's and a fairly substantial amount of unusual "back of the book material" and interest in cancellations and varieties. Some duplication (since there are in reality at least 2 collections present) and we noted a few faults here and there but generally VF with substantial value. Viewing recommended. Fine.

Estimate: $4,000+

Minimum Bid: $2,000

33201 1947-65, Collection of "Black Proofs". (No Gum As Issued). A very interesting collection of these scarce "Schwarzdrucke" (black proofs) housed in a special album containing some 100 of these imperforate proofs all neatly mounted on specially printed pages (written in German) giving the history and philatelic background of each issue. Overall VF and scarce and an important reference work for the specialist. Very fine.

Estimate: $500+

Minimum Bid: $250

33202 1843-1975, Collection of Switzerland. (Used). A fairly substantial collection of mainly used stamps mounted on quadrille pages all housed in a 3 ring binder containing a good selection of early issues including 2L3 (appears to be genuine but not counted) followed by a handful of the early Federal issues (some faults but generally in better than average condition) and a good showing of both the imperforate and perforate sitting Helvetia's, several VF amongst which we noted some interesting cancels. There is also a good selection of the succeeding standing Helvetia's with perforation varieties, some better back of the book and not forgetting a complete PAX set. An interesting valuable collection worth closer inspection.

Estimate: $1,500+

Minimum Bid: $750

33203 1840 - 2000 World Wide Collection. (mint & used) A massive "One mans" collection comprised of thousands of mint & used stamps contained in some 45 well filled albums and stock books (most of the albums being Scott Internationals). While the collection includes a number of 19th century issues mostly in average to poor condition there is strength is in later 20th century issues - nothing rare but a number of better regular and semi postal's from European countries such as Scandinavia, Belgium, Germany & Area , France & Colonies, Monaco, Liechtenstein, Switzerland, some Portugal & Spain, Italy, Baltic States etc. there is a smattering of Asia including little Japan & China and a small amount of GB & Colonies- but strength is in Western Europe (no U.S.). Also noted are two older sets of Scott catalog and some other reference items. Some faults as to be expected in a collection so large but overall condition is VF with very high Catalog value. Inspection recommended. Fine to Very Fine.(Total: 9 pages)

Estimate: $15,000+

Minimum Bid: $7,500

33204 1850 - 1975, Worldwide balance collections. (Mint & Used). A vast accumulation of "Worldwide Collection Balances" comprised of some 50 Albums and Binders containing a vast array of mint and used stamps plus some covers: while some of the albums are only sparsely filled there are several well filled better collections, including British Empire, Spain and some specialized groupings. There are also a couple of beautiful old "Turn of the Century" French albums "Albums de Timbres Postes" with better world wide classic material including some British Empire, France , Spain, Germany & Italian States etc. Overall an interesting and valuable lot well worth closer inspection. Fine to Very Fine.

Estimate: $5,000+

Minimum Bid: $2,500

33205 1840-1950, Worldwide Collection. (Mint & Used). A fairly large holding comprised of 16 albums (including a lovely old Schaubeck), plus several binders and folders all containing a wide array of mint & used stamps of the world plus a few covers, all housed in a large carton: countries include Switzerland with some better classics and semi postal's, good airmails and several better souvenir sheets including a Naba (appears MNH), also Germany & States, Italian States, France with better mint semi postal's, and some BE & Asia with general worldwide in the Schaubeck. Some faults here and there as to be expected but overall fine and a very useful lot with some substantial value. Fine to Very Fine.

Estimate: $3,000+

Minimum Bid: $1,500

33206 1840-1950, Large Accumulation of Worldwide Stamps & Covers.(Mint & Used). An accumulation of several 1,000 mint and used stamps plus several covers housed in 4 cardboard file box and two cover binders all contained in a box: mostly comprised of stamps of lower value but we noted a number of better items in the $50 - $100 + range andseveral scarce covers including two 1 penny blacks on cover and some German Zeppelin flights. An interesting lot well worth closer inspection. Fine to Very Fine.

Estimate: $3,000+

Minimum Bid: $1,500

33207 Miscellaneous Collection / Balances. Large collection of post cards, covers, stampless envelopes, etc. Well over 1,000 pieces. Great dealer lot. Fine to Very Fine.

Estimate: $1,000+

Minimum Bid: $500

33208 COLLECTION LOT / BALANCES Large US and Foreign Collection. Mint and used with mixed condition. Some nice Japan and China from a quick examination. Take a look, it is worth examining. Fine to Very Fine.

Estimate: $750+

Minimum Bid: $375

33209 1850 - 1950, Worldwide Collections & Balances. (Used). An accumulation of mint & used stamps of the world contained 10 Albums and Binders which include some lovely "old- time" albums including an "Imperial" album (sparsely filled, all housed in a large carton: a vast number of countries are represented mainly with lower value material but it includes items of a value of up about $50, most of Europe is represented including GB & colonies, and we noticed some China & Japan , Russia & Poland and a little BNA & South America , some faults here and there as to be expected but overall fine and a very useful little lot. Fine to Very Fine. Fine to Very Fine.

Estimate: $750+

Minimum Bid: $375

33210 1870-1960, China Collection. (Mint & Used). A fairly substantial collection of mint & used stamps and a few covers mounted on some 20 large stock pages - back and front - all contained in a binder, and including issues from Imperial china, PRC & ROC: generally lower value singles and sets and souvenir sheets but interest in cancellations and includes some US, German Offices. Some faults but an interesting lot. Fine to Very Fine.

Estimate: $450+

Minimum Bid: $225

End of Auction

398   Please visit HA.com to view other collectibles auctions.   *A 19.5% Buyer's Premium ($9 min.) Applies To All Lots*

Heritage Auction Galleries Staff

Steve Ivy - Co-Chairman and CEO

Steve Ivy began collecting and studying rare coins in his youth, and as a teenager in 1963 began advertising coins for sale in national publications. Seven years later, at the age of twenty, he opened Steve Ivy Rare Coins in downtown Dallas, and in 1976, Steve Ivy Numismatic Auctions was incorporated. Steve managed the business as well as serving as chief numismatist, buying and selling hundreds of millions of dollars of coins during the 1970s and early 1980s. In early 1983, James Halperin became a full partner, and the name of the corporation was changed to Heritage Rare Coin Galleries. Steve's primary responsibilities now include management of the marketing and selling efforts of the company, the formation of corporate policy for long-term growth, and corporate relations with financial institutions. He remains intimately involved in numismatics, attending all major national shows. Steve engages in daily discourse with industry leaders on all aspects of the rare coin/currency business, and his views on grading, market trends and hobby developments are respected throughout the industry. He serves on the Board of Directors of the Professional Numismatists Guild (and was immediate past president), is the current Chairman of The Industry Council for Tangible Assets, and is a member of most leading numismatic organizations. Steve's keen appreciation of history is reflected in his active participation in other organizations, including past or present board positions on the Texas Historical Foundation and the Dallas Historical Society (where he also served as Exhibits Chairman). Steve is an avid collector of Texas books, manuscripts, and national currency, and he owns one of the largest and finest collections in private hands. He is also a past Board Chair of Dallas Challenge, and is currently the Finance Chair of the Phoenix House of Texas.

James Halperin - Co-Chairman

Jim Halperin and the traders under his supervision have transacted billions of dollars in rare coin business, and have outsold all other numismatic firms every year for over two decades. Born in Boston in 1952, Jim attended Middlesex School in Concord from 1966 to 1970. At the age of 15, he formed a part-time rare coin business after discovering that he had a knack (along with a nearly photographic memory) for coins. Jim scored a perfect 800 on his math SATs and received early acceptance to Harvard College, but after attending three semesters, he took a permanent leave of absence to pursue his full-time numismatic career. In 1975, Jim personally supervised the protocols for the first mainframe computer system in the numismatic business, which would catapult New England Rare Coin Galleries to the top of the industry in less than four years. In 1983, Jim merged with his friend and former archrival Steve Ivy, whom Jim had long admired. Their partnership has become the world's largest and most successful numismatic company, as well as the third-largest auctioneer in America. Jim remains arguably the best "eye" in the coin business today (he won the professional division of the PCGS World Series of Grading). In the mid-1980s, he authored "How to Grade U.S. Coins" (now posted on the web at www.CoinGrading.com), a highly-acclaimed text upon which the NGC and PCGS grading standards would ultimately be based. Jim is a bit of a Renaissance man, as a well-known futurist, an active collector of EC comics and early 20th-century American art (visit www.jhalpe.com), venture capital investor, philanthropist (he endows a multimillion-dollar health education foundation), and part-time novelist. His first fictional novel, "The Truth Machine," was published in 1996 and became an international science fiction bestseller, and was optioned for movie development by Warner Brothers. Jim's second novel, "The First Immortal," was published in early 1998 and immediately optioned as a Hallmark Hall of Fame television miniseries. Jim is married to Gayle Ziaks, and they have two sons, David and Michael. In 1996, with funding from Jim and Gayle's foundation, Gayle founded Dallas' Dance for the Planet, which has grown to become the largest free dance festival in the world.

Greg Rohan - President

At the age of eight, Greg Rohan started collecting coins as well as buying them for resale to his schoolmates. By 1971, at the age of ten, he was already buying and selling coins from a dealer's table at trade shows in his hometown of Seattle. His business grew rapidly, and by 1985 he had offices in both Seattle and Minneapolis. He joined Heritage in 1987 as Executive Vice-President and Manager of the firm's rare coin business. Today, as an owner and as President of Heritage, his responsibilities include overseeing the firm's private client group and working with top collectors in every field in which Heritage is active. Greg has been involved with many of the rarest items and most important collections handled by the firm, including the purchase and/or sale of the Ed Trompeter Collection (the world's largest numismatic purchase according to the Guinness Book of World Records), the legendary 1894 San Francisco Dime, the 1838 New Orleans Half Dollar, and the 1804 Silver Dollar. During his career, Greg has handled more than $1 billion of rare coins, collectibles and art, and provided expert consultation concerning the authenticity and grade condition of coins for the Professional Coin Grading Service (PCGS). He has provided expert testimony for the United States Attorneys in San Francisco, Dallas, and Philadelphia, and for the Federal Trade Commission (FTC). He has worked with collectors, consignors, and their advisors regarding significant collections of books, manuscripts, comics, currency, jewelry, vintage movie posters, sports and entertainment memorabilia, decorative arts, and fine art. Additionally, Greg is a Sage Society member of the American Numismatic Society, and a member/life member of the PNG, ANA, and most other leading numismatic organizations. Greg is also Chapter Chairman for North Texas of the Young Presidents' Organization (YPO), and is an active supporter of the arts. Greg co-authored "The Collectors Estate Handbook," winner of the NLG's Robert Friedberg Award for numismatic book of the year. Mr. Rohan currently serves on the seven-person Advisory Board to the Federal Reserve Bank of Dallas, in his second appointed term. He and his wife, Lysa, are avid collectors of rare wine, Native American artifacts, and American art.

Paul Minshull - Chief Operating Officer

As Chief Operating Officer, Paul Minshull's managerial responsibilities include integrating sales, personnel, inventory, security and MIS for Heritage. His major accomplishments include overseeing the hardware migration from mainframe to PC, the software migration of all inventory and sales systems, and implementation of a major Internet presence. Heritage's successful employee-suggestion program has generated 200 or more ideas each month since 1995, and has helped increase employee productivity, expand business, and improve employee retention. Paul oversees the company's highly-regarded IT department, and has been the driving force behind Heritage's web development, now a significant portion of Heritage's future plans. As the only numismatic auction house that combines traditional floor bidding with active Internet bidding, the totally interactive system has catapulted Heritage to the top rare coin website (according to Forbes Magazine's "Best of the Web"). Paul was born in Michigan and came to Heritage in 1984 after 12 years as the General Manager of a plastics manufacturing company in Ann Arbor. Since 1987, he has been a general partner in Heritage Capital Properties, Sales Manager, Vice President of Operations, and Chief Operating Officer for all Heritage companies and affiliates since 1996. Paul maintains an active interest in sports and physical fitness, and he and his wife have three children.

Todd Imhof - Vice President

Todd Imhof did not start collecting coins in his teens, unlike most professional numismatists. Shortly after graduating college, Todd declined an offer from a prestigious Wall Street bank to join a former high school classmate in his small rare coin firm in the Seattle area. In the mid-1980s, the rare coin industry was rapidly changing, with the advent of third-party grading and growing computer technologies; as a newcomer, Todd more easily embraced these new dynamics. He soon discovered a personal passion for rare coins, and for working with high-level collectors; in 1991, he co-founded Pinnacle Rarities, a firm specialized in servicing the savviest and most prominent collectors in numismatics. At 25, he was accepted into the PNG, and currently serves on its Consumer Protection Committee and its Legislation/Taxation Issues Committee. In 1992, he was invited to join the Board of Directors for the Industry Council for Tangible Assets, later serving as its Chairman (2002-2005).

Todd enjoys a reputation that is envied by the entire numismatic community, and his relationship with Heritage's most prominent clients, who seek his expertise and integrity, has only strengthened over the years. Clients and colleagues are impressed by his ability to navigate complex deals with unsurpassed professionalism. By understanding what each collector is trying to accomplish, Todd has the uncanny ability to identify the perfect coins at the right prices. In the famous Phillip Morse Auction, he became the only person in history to purchase two separate $1mm+ coins during a single auction session! Todd is an avid competitive sailor, and collector of fine wines and Olympic medals. He and his wife have two sons and a daughter.

Leo Frese - Vice President

Leo has been involved in numismatics for nearly 40 years, a professional numismatist since 1971, and has been with Heritage for over 20 years. He literally worked his way up the Heritage "ladder" through dedication, hard work, and a belief that the client is the most important asset Heritage has. He worked with Bob Merrill for nearly 15 years and now is the Director of Consignments. Leo has been actively involved in assisting clients sell nearly $500,000,000 in numismatic material. Leo was recently accepted as a member of PNG, is a life member of the ANA, and holds membership in FUN, CSNS, and other numismatic organizations. He believes education is the foremost building block in numismatics. Leo encourages all collectors to broaden their horizons, be actively involved in the hobby, and donate freely to YN organizations. Leo's interests include collecting Minnesota pottery and elegant Depression glass. Although travel is an important element of his job, he relishes time with his wife Wendy, children Alicen and Adam, and son-in-law Jeff.

Jim Stoutjesdyk - Vice President

Jim Stoutjesdyk was named Vice President of Heritage Rare Coin Galleries in 2004. A Michigan native, Jim became involved in numismatics at a young age and was named the ANA's Outstanding Young Numismatist of the Year in 1987. A University of Michigan graduate, he was first employed by Superior Galleries, eventually becoming their Director of Collector Sales. Since joining Heritage in 1993, Jim has assumed many responsibilities including Gallery Manager for the retail showroom, retail clientele development, editor of Heritage's Insider magazine from 1998 to 2000, and wholesale trading at coin shows across the nation. Jim's duties now include buying and selling, pricing all new purchases, assisting with auction estimates and reserves, and overseeing the daily operations of the rare coin department. Jim met his wife Amy at Heritage; they married in 1998 and have a son Blake and a daughter Emily. While away from Heritage Jim enjoys spending time with his family and traveling to new places. Jim serves on the Board of Directors of Families for Effective Autism Treatment and has raised tens of thousands of dollars to provide education, advocacy, and support to families in the North Texas area who are affected by autism.

Norma L. Gonzalez - VP of Auction Operations

Born in Dallas, Texas, Norma joined the U.S. Navy in August of 1993. During her five-year enlistment, she received her Bachelor's Degree in Resource Management and traveled to Japan, Singapore, Thailand and lived in Cuba for three years. After her enlistment, she moved back to Dallas where her family resides. Norma joined Heritage in 1998; always ready for a challenge, she spent her days at Heritage and her nights obtaining an M. B. A. She was promoted to Vice President in 2003. She currently manages the operations departments, including Coins, Currency, World & Ancient Coins, Sportscards & Memorabilia, Comics, Movie Posters, Pop Culture and Political Memorabilia. Norma enjoys running, biking and spending time with her family. In February 2004 she ran a 26.2-mile marathon in Austin, Texas and later, in March she accomplished a 100-mile bike ride in California.

Debbie Rexing - VP - Marketing

Debbie's marketing credentials include degrees in Business Administration in Marketing and Human Resource Management from The Ohio State University, as well as sales experience for General Foods. After joining Heritage in 2001, Debbie rapidly became an integral part of the marketing teams involved with Heritage's most exciting and successful specialties, including U.S. Coins, World Coins, Currency, Music & Entertainment, Vintage Movie Posters, Americana, and U.S. Tangibles Inc. Her varied responsibilities included cross-functional coordination of photography, auction logistics, and marketing. Debbie has been active in coin auctions, staffing the podium, executing client bids, and in lot viewing. Her wide experience in many aspects of the business has provided her with a broad perspective of Heritage's activities. She and her husband Rick have three children – Trent, Abbey, and Claire – and her hobbies include interior design, entertaining and exercise, the beach and water activities, and watching Ohio State football.

Kelley Norwine - VP - Media and Client Relations

Born and raised in South Carolina, Kelley pursued a double major at Southern Wesleyan University, earning a BA in Music Education and a BS in Business Management. A contestant in the Miss South Carolina pageant, Kelley was later Regional Manager & Director of Training at Bank of Travelers Rest in South Carolina. Relocating to Los Angeles, Kelley became the Regional Manager and Client Services Director for NAS-McCann World Group, an international Advertising & Communications Agency where she was responsible for running one of the largest offices in the country. During her years with NAS Kelley was the recipient of numerous awards including Regional Manager of the Quarter and the NAS Courage and Dedication award. After relocating to Dallas, Kelley took a job as Director of Client Services for TMP/Monster Worldwide and joined Heritage in 2005 as Director of Client Development. She was named VP of Marketing for Heritage in 2007. A cancer survivor, Kelley is an often-requested motivational speaker for the American Cancer Society. In her spare time, she writes music, sings, and plays the piano.

Patricia Castillo - Director of Auctions & Client Service

Patricia Castillo lived all over the country before settling down in Ferris, Texas, near Dallas. She began her career working in Customer Service, and in 2001 joined the Heritage family assisting in Client Services and live auctions. Patricia's knowledge grew with the company, and her hard work led to her promotion to Director of Auctions and Client Services. Patricia is directly involved in the training and management of the Client Services team. A cancer survivor, Patricia enjoys spending time with her two beautiful little girls, attending softball games, and spending time with family and friends.

Andrea Voss - Live-Auction & Event Coordinator

Andrea Voss is a true Texas native – born and educated in the Dallas area, with a degree in Journalism from the University of North Texas in Denton. Andrea joined the Heritage family in 2004, and after assisting Client Services with e-mail inquiries, she earned the opportunity to become the Auction Supervisor. Her responsibilities have grown with her experiences, and she is now the Live-Auction & Event Coordinator. Clients may see her in the back of the live auction room supervising, or in the front using her Auctioneer license. In her off hours, Andrea enjoys time on her patio with her dog and cat, and still dreams of one day being a writer.

Devin Jackson - Auction Client Services/Live Auction Supervisor

Devin Jackson joined Heritage in 2005 as a member of the Client Services Group. Devin is a native Texan, growing up in a small suburb south of Dallas. Devin later attended the University of North Texas and graduated with a Bachelor's Degree in Kinesiology. A life long sports fanatic, Devin briefly coached high school football, basketball, and track in his home town of Ferris, TX after graduating from college. Devin later joined the staff of Heritage Auction Galleries, assisting with Live Auctions and Client Services. Devin has collected sports cards and memorabilia since he was a young boy and he continues to collect memorabilia from his favorite professional sports teams, including the San Francisco 49ers.

Marti Korver - Manager - Credit/Collections

Marti has been working in numismatics for more than three decades. She was recruited out of the banking profession by Jim Ruddy, and she worked with Paul Rynearson, Karl Stephens, and Judy Cahn on ancients and world coins at Bowers & Ruddy Galleries, in Hollywood, CA. She migrated into the coin auction business, running the bid books for such memorable sales as the Garrett Collection and representing bidders as agent at B&R auctions for 10 years. She also worked as a research assistant for Q. David Bowers for several years. Memorable events included such clients (and friends) as Richard Lobel, John Ford, Harry Bass, and John J. Pittman. She is married to noted professional numismatist and writer, Robert Korver, (who is sometimes seen auctioneering at coin shows) and they migrated to Heritage in Dallas in 1996. She has an RN daughter (who worked her way through college showing lots for Heritage) and a son (who is currently a college student and sometimes a Heritage employee) and a type set of dogs (one black and one white). She currently collects kitschy English teapots and compliments.

Becky Dirting - Managing Director, Collectibles Division

Becky joined Heritage in 2005 and was named Managing Director of the Collectibles Departments in 2007, providing direct oversight for such auction specialties as Historical Books & Manuscripts, Americana & Political, Civil War, Western, Americana Indian Art, Texana, Comics & Comic Art, Music & Entertainment, Vintage Movie Posters, Sports Collectibles, Illustration Art, and Natural History. Becky's career path included PwC Consulting in Learning and Knowledge Management, and she remains focused on staff development, training, operations and process development, knowledge management, budget management, and contract negotiation. She enjoys spending time with her wonderful husband, sons, extended family, friends and beloved pets, and is a talented chef.

Julie Gonzalez - Director of Auction Operations

After working part-time for Heritage for many years, Julie Gonzalez was so excited about the growth opportunities that she joined us on a full-time basis! As the Operations Manager for Americana, she led her team through several successful auctions, and was then promoted to lead the operations staff and consignment coordinators for a third of Heritage's specialty auctions. Her work ethic, determination and tenacity are supporting Heritage's growth. Away from work, you might spot Julie outside enjoying time with her family and friends, or running.

Rare Stamp Department Specialists

Steven Crippe - Director, Philatelic Sales
Before joining Heritage in 2008, Steve Crippe made his name in Philatelics as the founder and President of GradedStamps.com. He is known for his broad general knowledge of the field, and is recognized as one of the leading experts in the Error sub-specialty of stamps. He retired from the newspaper business in 1999 to launch a full-time, rare stamp business, soon thereafter he developed a custom-software web site dedicated to the sale of rare stamps. He was the first national-level stamp dealer to embrace PSE's third-party grading, which quickly became the norm in the stamp trade. He is a current member of the American Stamp Dealers Association, American Philatelic Society, United States Stamp Society, Error, Freaks and Oddities Collectors Club and the Florida Stamp Dealers Association.

Brian Degen - Director, Philatelic Operations & Cataloger
Brian Degen's interest in Philately also started in his childhood, collecting alongside his father. He began working for dealers, and over time, his collecting focused on classic U.S. and Israeli issues. His reputation as a hobbyist led to establishing his own philatelic firm, and he then joined a major international auction house, specializing in U.S. Postal history, British North America, Germany, U.S. classics, banknotes, Confederates, locals, airmails, and other back-of-the-book areas. Prior to his philatelic career, Brian worked in the health insurance and financial management sectors, and in Information Technology. Brian's interests also include martial arts, photography, and science fiction.

Mike Japp - Senior Philatelic Consultant
A successful advertising professional, Mike Japp left the ad world behind in the early 1990s to join Sotheby's as a Philatelic consultant. After four years there, he joined the New York office of Phillips DePury, Luxemburg, as head of the Rare Stamps department. He re-joined Sotheby's in 2000, helping to produce several important auctions. Since leaving Sotheby's, Mike founded Angle American Appraisal Service, Inc., specializing in rare stamps. He joined Heritage as a Senior Consultant in 2008, and still continues to consult with many major auction houses and high net worth clients. He is a member of the American Philatelic Society and the American Stamp Dealers Association.

Rick Passo - Consignment Director
Rick Passo joined Heritage in 2008 and brings his well-regarded expertise as a noted stamp generalist with a specialty in classical U.S. stamps. He earned his Jurist Doctorate at the University of Tulsa, using his knowledge of stamps and collecting to pay for his education. He is known for having an eye for rare quality and brings more than 20 years of experience to his position as consignment director at Heritage.

Jose Berumen - Operations Manager
Jose Berumen was born and raised in the Dallas area and in 2004 he started his career with Heritage Auction Galleries, working part-time in the Rare Coin department while attending school at night. After a year and a half of hard work and dedication he was promoted to Currency Operations Manager. While in this position Jose has streamlined processes and increased the productivity amongst his team. Jose travels to most of the Numismatic Auctions as a member of the traveling auction staff and is a high valued team member. When not traveling to a show or meeting a deadline in Dallas, Jose enjoys going to the gym, running at the lake and spending time with his family. He also enjoys watching football, basketball, and playoff hockey. Jose has a daughter named Amber

Cataloged by: Steven Crippe, Brian Degen, Rick Passo, Mike Japp, George Chua

Edited by: Steven Crippe, Brian Degen

Operations Support by: Jose Berumen, Sally Martinez, Alma Villa & Doris Villareal

Catalog and Internet Imaging by: Jose Berumen, Sally Martinez, Heather Wise, Stephanie Krause, Travis Awalt, Colleen McInenery, Brenna Wilson, Tony Webb, Kristin Bazan, Dennis Nowicki, Lori McKay, Maribel Cazares

Production and Design by: Tim Hose, Matt Pegues, Mary Hermann, Mark Masat, Debbie Rexing

Terms and Conditions of Auction

Auctioneer and Auction:

1. This Auction is presented by Heritage Auction Galleries, a d/b/a/ of Heritage Auctions, Inc., or its affiliates Heritage Numismatic Auctions, Inc., or Heritage Vintage Sports Auctions, Inc., or Currency Auctions of America, Inc., as identified with the applicable licensing information on the title page of the catalog or on the HA.com Internet site (the "Auctioneer"). The Auction is conducted under these Terms and Conditions of Auction and applicable state and local law. Announcements and corrections from the podium and those made through the Terms and Conditions of Auctions appearing on the Internet at HA.com supersede those in the printed catalog.

Buyer's Premium:

2. On bids placed through Auctioneer, a Buyer's Premium of fifteen percent (15%) will be added to the successful hammer price bid on lots in Coin and Currency auctions, or nineteen and one-half percent (19.5%) on lots in all other auctions. There is a minimum Buyer's Premium of $9.00 per lot. In Gallery Auctions (sealed bid auctions of mostly bulk numismatic material), the Buyer's Premium is 19.5%.

Auction Venues:

3. The following Auctions are conducted solely on the Internet: Heritage Weekly Internet Auctions (Coin, Currency, Comics, and Vintage Movie Poster); Heritage Monthly Internet Auctions (Sports, and Stamps). Signature® Auctions and Grand Format Auctions accept bids from the Internet, telephone, fax, or mail first, followed by a floor bidding session; Heritage Live and real-time telephone bidding are available to registered clients during these auctions.

Bidders:

4. Any person participating or registering for the Auction agrees to be bound by and accepts these Terms and Conditions of Auction ("Bidder(s)").
5. All Bidders must meet Auctioneer's qualifications to bid. Any Bidder who is not a client in good standing of the Auctioneer may be disqualified at Auctioneer's sole option and will not be awarded lots. Such determination may be made by Auctioneer in its sole and unlimited discretion, at any time prior to, during, or even after the close of the Auction. Auctioneer reserves the right to exclude any person from the auction.
6. If an entity places a bid, then the person executing the bid on behalf of the entity agrees to personally guarantee payment for any successful bid.

Credit:

7. Bidders who have not established credit with the Auctioneer must either furnish satisfactory credit information (including two collectibles-related business references) well in advance of the Auction or supply valid credit card information. Bids placed through our Interactive Internet program will only be accepted from pre-registered Bidders; Bidders who are not members of HA.com or affiliates should pre-register at least 48 hours before the start of the first session (exclusive of holidays or weekends) to allow adequate time to contact references. Credit may be granted at the discretion of Auctioneer. Additionally Bidders who have not previously established credit or who wish to bid in excess of their established credit history may be required to provide their social security number or the last four digits thereof to us so a credit check may be performed prior to Auctioneer's acceptance of a bid.

Bidding Options:

8. Bids in Signature® Auctions or Grand Format Auctions may be placed as set forth in the printed catalog section entitled "Choose your bidding method." For auctions held solely on the Internet, see the alternatives on HA.com. Review at HA.com/common/howtobid.php.
9. Presentment of Bids: Non-Internet bids (including but not limited to podium, fax, phone and mail bids) are treated similar to floor bids in that they must be on-increment or at a half increment (called a cut bid). Any podium, fax, phone, or mail bids that do not conform to a full or half increment will be rounded up or down to the nearest full or half increment and this revised amount will be considered your high bid.
10. Auctioneer's Execution of Certain Bids. Auctioneer cannot be responsible for your errors in bidding, so carefully check that every bid is entered correctly. When identical mail or FAX bids are submitted, preference is given to the first received. To ensure the greatest accuracy, your written bids should be entered on the standard printed bid sheet and be received at Auctioneer's place of business at least two business days before the Auction start. Auctioneer is not responsible for executing mail bids or FAX bids received on or after the day the first lot is sold, nor Internet bids submitted after the published closing time; nor is Auctioneer responsible for proper execution of bids submitted by telephone, mail, FAX, e-mail, Internet, or in person once the Auction begins. Internet bids may not be withdrawn until your written request is received and acknowledged by Auctioneer (FAX: 214-4438425); such requests must state the reason, and may constitute grounds for withdrawal of bidding privileges. Lots won by mail Bidders will not be delivered at the Auction unless prearranged.
11. Caveat as to Bid Increments. Bid increments (over the current bid level) determine the lowest amount you may bid on a particular lot. Bids greater than one increment over the current bid can be any whole dollar amount. It is possible under several circumstances for winning bids to be between increments, sometimes only $1 above the previous increment. Please see: "How can I lose by less than an increment?" on our website. Bids will be accepted in whole dollar amounts only. No "buy" or "unlimited" bids will be accepted.

The following chart governs current bidding increments.

Current Bid	Bid Increment
<$10	$1
$10 - $29	$2
$30 - $49	$3
$50 - $99	$5
$100 - $199	$10
$200 - $299	$20
$300 - $499	$25
$500 - $999	$50
$1,000 - $1,999	$100
$2,000 - $2,999	$200
$3,000 - $4,999	$250
$5,000 - $9,999	$500
$10,000 - $19,999	$1,000

Current Bid	Bid Increment
$20,000 - $29,999	$2,000
$30,000 - $49,999	$2,500
$50,000 - $99,999	$5,000
$100,000 - $199,999	$10,000
$200,000 - $299,999	$20,000
$300,000 - $499,999	$25,000
$500,000 - $999,999	$50,000
$1,000,000 - $1,999,999	$100,000
$2,000,000 - $2,999,999	$200,000
$3,000,000 - $4,999,999	$250,000
$5,000,000 - $9,999,999	$500,000
>$10,000,000	$1,000,000

12. If Auctioneer calls for a full increment, a bidder may request Auctioneer to accept a bid at half of the increment ("Cut Bid") only once per lot. After offering a Cut Bid, bidders may continue to participate only at full increments. Off-increment bids may be accepted by the Auctioneer at Signature® Auctions and Grand Format Auctions. If the Auctioneer solicits bids other than the expected increment, these bids will not be considered Cut Bids.

Conducting the Auction:

13. Notice of the consignor's liberty to place bids on his lots in the Auction is hereby made in accordance with Article 2 of the Texas Business and Commercial Code. A "Minimum Bid" is an amount below which the lot will not sell. THE CONSIGNOR OF PROPERTY MAY PLACE WRITTEN "Minimum Bids" ON HIS LOTS IN ADVANCE OF THE AUCTION; ON SUCH LOTS, IF THE HAMMER PRICE DOES NOT MEET THE "Minimum Bid", THE CONSIGNOR MAY PAY A REDUCED COMMISSION ON THOSE LOTS. "Minimum Bids" are generally posted online several days prior to the Auction closing. For any successful bid placed by a consignor on his Property on the Auction floor, or by any means during the live session, or after the "Minimum Bid" for an Auction have been posted, we will require the consignor to pay full Buyer's Premium and Seller's Commissions on such lot.
14. The highest qualified Bidder recognized by the Auctioneer shall be the buyer. In the event of any dispute between any Bidders at an Auction, Auctioneer may at his sole discretion reoffer the lot. Auctioneer's decision and declaration of the winning Bidder shall be final and binding upon all Bidders. Bids properly offered, whether by floor Bidder or other means of bidding, may on occasion be missed or go unrecognized; in such cases, the Auctioneer may declare the recognized bid accepted as the winning bid, regardless of whether a competing bid may have been higher.
15. Auctioneer reserves the right to refuse to honor any bid or to limit the amount of any bid, in its sole discretion. A bid is considered not made in "Good Faith" when made by an insolvent or irresponsible person, a person under the age of eighteen, or is not supported by satisfactory credit, collectibles references, or otherwise. Regardless of the disclosure of his identity, any bid by a consignor or his agent on a lot consigned by him is deemed to be made in "Good Faith." Any person apparently appearing on the OFAC list is not eligible to bid.
16. Nominal Bids. The Auctioneer in its sole discretion may reject nominal bids, small opening bids, or very nominal advances. If a lot bearing estimates fails to open for 40–60% of the low estimate, the Auctioneer may pass the item or may place a protective bid on behalf of the consignor.
17. Lots bearing bidding estimates shall open at Auctioneer's discretion (approximately 50% of the low estimate). In the event that no bid meets or exceeds that opening amount, the lot shall pass as unsold.
18. All items are to be purchased per lot as numerically indicated and no lots will be broken. Auctioneer reserves the right to withdraw, prior to the close, any lots from the Auction.
19. Auctioneer reserves the right to rescind the sale in the event of nonpayment, breach of a warranty, disputed ownership, auctioneer's clerical error or omission in exercising bids and reserves, or for any other reason and in Auctioneer's sole discretion. In cases of nonpayment, Auctioneer's election to void a sale does not relieve the Bidder from their obligation to pay Auctioneer its fees (seller's and buyer's premium) and any other damages or expenses pertaining to the lot.
20. Auctioneer occasionally experiences Internet and/or Server service outages, and Auctioneer periodically schedules system downtime for maintenance and other purposes, during which Bidders cannot participate or place bids. If such outages occur, we may at our discretion extend bidding for the Auction. Bidders unable to place their Bids through the Internet are directed to contact Client Services at 1-800-872-6467.
21. The Auctioneer or its affiliates may consign items to be sold in the Auction, and may bid on those lots or any other lots. Auctioneer or affiliates expressly reserve the right to modify any such bids at any time prior to the hammer based upon data made known to the Auctioneer or its affiliates. The Auctioneer may extend advances, guarantees, or loans to certain consignors, and may extend financing or other credits at varying rates to certain Bidders in the auction.
22. The Auctioneer has the right to sell certain unsold items after the close of the Auction. Such lots shall be considered sold during the Auction and all these Terms and Conditions shall apply to such sales including but not limited to the Buyer's Premium, return rights, and disclaimers.

Payment:

23. All sales are strictly for cash in United States dollars (including U.S. currency, bank wire, cashier checks, travelers checks, eChecks, and bank money orders, all subject to reporting requirements). All are subject to clearing and funds being received In Auctioneer's account before delivery of the purchases. Auctioneer reserves the right to determine if a check constitutes "good funds" when drawn on a U.S. bank for ten days, and thirty days when drawn on an international bank. Credit Card (Visa or Master Card only) and PayPal payments may be accepted up to $10,000 from non-dealers at the sole discretion of the Auctioneer, subject to the following limitations: a) sales are only to the cardholder, b) purchases are shipped to the cardholder's registered and verified address, c) Auctioneer may pre-approve the cardholder's credit line, d) a credit card transaction may not be used in conjunction with any other financing or extended terms offered by the Auctioneer, and must transact immediately upon invoice presentation, e) rights of return are governed by these Terms and Conditions, which supersede those conditions promulgated by the card issuer, f) floor Bidders must present their card.
24. Payment is due upon closing of the Auction session, or upon presentment of an invoice. Auctioneer reserves the right to void an invoice if payment in full is not received within 7 days after the close of the Auction. In cases of nonpayment, Auctioneer's election to void a sale does not relieve the Bidder from their obligation to pay Auctioneer its fees (seller's and buyer's premium) on the lot and any other damages pertaining to the lot.
25. Lots delivered in the States of Texas, California, or other states where the Auction may be held, are subject to all applicable state and local taxes, unless appropriate permits are on file with Auctioneer. Bidder agrees to pay Auctioneer the actual amount of tax due in the event that sales tax is not properly collected due to: 1) an expired, inaccurate, inappropriate tax certificate or declaration, 2) an incorrect interpretation of the applicable statute, 3) or any other reason. The appropriate form or certificate must be on file at and verified by Auctioneer five days prior to Auction or tax must be paid; only if such form or certificate is received by Auctioneer within 4 days after the Auction can a refund of tax paid be made. Lots from different Auctions may not be aggregated for sales tax purposes.
26. In the event that a Bidder's payment is dishonored upon presentment(s), Bidder shall pay the maximum statutory processing fee set by applicable state law. If you attempt to pay via eCheck and your financial institution denies this transfer from your bank account, or the payment cannot be completed using the selected funding source, you agree to complete payment using your credit card on file.
27. If any Auction invoice submitted by Auctioneer is not paid in full when due, the unpaid balance will bear interest at the highest rate permitted by law from the date of invoice until paid. If the Auctioneer refers any invoice to an attorney for collection, the buyer agrees to pay attorney's fees, court costs, and other collection costs incurred by Auctioneer. If Auctioneer assigns collection to its in-house legal staff, such attorney's time expended on the matter shall be compensated at a rate comparable to the hourly rate of independent attorneys.

28. In the event a successful Bidder fails to pay any amounts due, Auctioneer reserves the right to sell the lot(s) securing the invoice to any underbidders in the Auction that the lot(s) appeared, or at subsequent private or public sale, or relist the lot(s) in a future auction conducted by Auctioneer. A defaulting Bidder agrees to pay for the reasonable costs of resale (including a 10% seller's commission, if consigned to an auction conducted by Auctioneer). The defaulting Bidder is liable to pay any difference between his total original invoice for the lot(s), plus any applicable interest, and the net proceeds for the lot(s) if sold at private sale or the subsequent hammer price of the lot(s) less the 10% seller's commissions, if sold at an Auctioneer's auction
29. Auctioneer reserves the right to require payment in full in good funds before delivery of the merchandise.
30. Auctioneer shall have a lien against the merchandise purchased by the buyer to secure payment of the Auction invoice. Auctioneer is further granted a lien and the right to retain possession of any other property of the buyer then held by the Auctioneer or its affiliates to secure payment of any Auction invoice or any other amounts due the Auctioneer or affiliates from the buyer. With respect to these lien rights, Auctioneer shall have all the rights of a secured creditor under Article 9 of the Texas Uniform Commercial Code, including but not limited to the right of sale. In addition, with respect to payment of the Auction invoice(s), the buyer waives any and all rights of offset he might otherwise have against the Auctioneer and the consignor of the merchandise included on the invoice. If a Bidder owes Auctioneer or its affiliates on any account, Auctioneer and its affiliates shall have the right to offset such unpaid account by any credit balance due Bidder, and it may secure by possessory lien any unpaid amount by any of the Bidder's property in their possession.
31. Title shall not pass to the successful Bidder until all invoices are paid in full. It is the responsibility of the buyer to provide adequate insurance coverage for the items once they have been delivered to a common carrier or third-party shipper.

Delivery; Shipping; and Handling Charges:

32. Buyer is liable for shipping and handling. Please refer to Auctioneer's website www.HA.com/common/shipping.php for the latest charges or call Auctioneer. Auctioneer is unable to combine purchases from other auctions or affiliates into one package for shipping purposes. Lots won will be shipped in a commercially reasonable time after payment in good funds for the merchandise and the shipping fees is received or credit extended, except when third-party shipment occurs.
33. Successful international Bidders shall provide written shipping instructions, including specified customs declarations, to the Auctioneer for any lots to be delivered outside of the United States. NOTE: Declaration value shall be the item'(s) hammer price together with its buyer's premium and Auctioneer shall use the correct harmonized code for the lot. Domestic Buyers on lots designated for third-party shipment must designate the common carrier, accept risk of loss, and prepay shipping costs.
34. All shipping charges will be borne by the successful Bidder. Any risk of loss during shipment will be borne by the buyer following Auctioneer's delivery to the designated common carrier or third-party shipper, regardless of domestic or foreign shipment.
35. Due to the nature of some items sold, it shall be the responsibility for the successful bidder to arrange pick-up and shipping through third-parties; as to such items Auctioneer shall have no liability. Failure to pick-up or arrange shipping in a timely fashion (within ten days) shall subject Lots to storage and moving charges, including a $100 administration fee plus $10 daily storage for larger items and $5.00 daily for smaller items (storage fee per item) after 35 days. In the event the Lot is not removed within ninety days, the Lot may be offered for sale to recover any past due storage or moving fees, including a 10% Seller's Commission.
36. The laws of various countries regulate the import or export of certain plant and animal properties, including (but not limited to) items made of (or including) ivory, whalebone, turtleshell, coral, crocodile, or other wildlife. Transport of such lots may require special licenses for export, import, or both. Bidder is responsible for: 1) obtaining all information on such restricted items for both export and import; 2) obtaining all such licenses and/or permits. Delay or failure to obtain any such license or permit does not relieve the buyer of timely compliance with standard payment terms. For further information, please contact Bill Taylor at 800-872-6467 ext. 1280.
37. Any request for shipping verification for undelivered packages must be made within 30 days of shipment by Auctioneer.

Cataloging, Warranties and Disclaimers:

38. NO WARRANTY, WHETHER EXPRESSED OR IMPLIED, IS MADE WITH RESPECT TO ANY DESCRIPTION CONTAINED IN THIS AUCTION OR ANY SECOND OPINE. Any description of the items or second opine contained in this Auction is for the sole purpose of identifying the items for those Bidders who do not have the opportunity to view the lots prior to bidding, and no description of items has been made part of the basis of the bargain or has created any express warranty that the goods would conform to any description made by Auctioneer. Color variations can be expected in any electronic or printed imaging, and are not grounds for the return of any lot.
39. Auctioneer is selling only such right or title to the items being sold as Auctioneer may have by virtue of consignment agreements on the date of auction and disclaims any warranty of title to the Property. Auctioneer disclaims any warranty of merchantability or fitness for any particular purposes. All images, descriptions, sales data, and archival records are the exclusive property of Auctioneer, and may be used by Auctioneer for advertising, promotion, archival records, and any other uses deemed appropriate.
40. Translations of foreign language documents may be provided as a convenience to interested parties. Auctioneer makes no representation as to the accuracy of those translations and will not be held responsible for errors in bidding arising from inaccuracies in translation.
41. Auctioneer disclaims all liability for damages, consequential or otherwise, arising out of or in connection with the sale of any Property by Auctioneer to Bidder. No third party may rely on any benefit of these Terms and Conditions and any rights, if any, established hereunder are personal to the Bidder and may not be assigned. Any statement made by the Auctioneer is an opinion and does not constitute a warranty or representation. No employee of Auctioneer may alter these Terms and Conditions, and, unless signed by a principal of Auctioneer, any such alteration is null and void.
42. Auctioneer shall not be liable for breakage of glass or damage to frames (patent or latent); such defects, in any event, shall not be a basis for any claim for return or reduction in purchase price.

Release:

43. In consideration of participation in the Auction and the placing of a bid, Bidder expressly releases Auctioneer, its officers, directors and employees, its affiliates, and its outside experts that provide second opines, from any and all claims, cause of action, chose of action, whether at law or equity or any arbitration or mediation rights existing under the rules of any professional society or affiliation based upon the assigned description, or a derivative theory, breach of warranty express or implied, representation or other matter set forth within these Terms and Conditions of Auction or otherwise. In the event of a claim, Bidder agrees that such rights and privileges conferred therein are strictly construed as specifically declared herein; e.g., authenticity, typographical error, etc. and are the exclusive remedy. Bidder, by non-compliance to these express terms of a granted remedy, shall waive any claim against Auctioneer.
44. Notice: Some Property sold by Auctioneer are inherently dangerous e.g. firearms, cannons, and small items that may be swallowed or ingested or may have latent defects all of which may cause harm to a person. Purchaser accepts all risk of loss or damage from its purchase of these items and Auctioneer disclaims any liability whether under contract or tort for damages and losses, direct or inconsequential, and expressly disclaims any warranty as to safety or usage of any lot sold.

Dispute Resolution and Arbitration Provision:

45. By placing a bid or otherwise participating in the auction, Bidder accepts these Terms and Conditions of Auction, and specifically agrees to the alternative dispute resolution provided herein. Arbitration replaces the right to go to court, including the right to a jury trial.
46. Auctioneer in no event shall be responsible for consequential damages, incidental damages, compensatory damages, or any other damages arising or claimed to be arising from the auction of any lot. In the event that Auctioneer cannot deliver the lot or subsequently it is established that the lot lacks title, or other transfer or condition issue is claimed, In such cases the sole remedy shall be limited to rescission of sale and refund of the amount paid by Bidder; in no case shall Auctioneer's maximum liability exceed the high bid on that lot, which bid shall be deemed for all purposes the value of the lot. After one year has elapsed, Auctioneer's maximum liability shall be limited to any commissions and fees Auctioneer earned on that lot.
47. In the event of an attribution error, Auctioneer may at its sole discretion, correct the error on the Internet, or, if discovered at a later date, to refund the buyer's purchase price without further obligation.
48. Arbitration Clause: All controversies or claims under this Agreement or arising from or pertaining to: this Agreement or related documents, or to the Properties consigned hereunder, or the enforcement or interpretation hereof of this or any related agreements, or damage to Properties, payment, or any other matter, or because of an alleged breach, default or misrepresentation under the provisions hereof or otherwise, that cannot be settled amicably within one (1) month from the date of notification of either party to the other of such dispute or question, which notice shall specify the details of such dispute or question, shall be settled by final and binding arbitration by one arbitrator appointed by the American Arbitration Association ("AAA"). The arbitration shall be conducted in Dallas, Dallas County, Texas in accordance with the then existing Commercial Arbitration Rules of the AAA. The arbitration shall be brought within two (2) years of the alleged breach, default or misrepresentation or the claim is waived. The prevailing party (a party that is awarded substantial and material relief on its claim or defense) may be awarded its reasonable attorney's fees and costs. Judgment upon the award rendered by the arbitrator may be entered in any court having jurisdiction thereof; provided, however, that the law applicable to any controversy shall be the law of the State of Texas, regardless of its or any other jurisdiction's choice of law principles and under the provisions of the Federal Arbitration Act.
49. No claims of any kind can be considered after the settlements have been made with the consignors. Any dispute after the settlement date is strictly between the Bidder and consignor without involvement or responsibility of the Auctioneer.
50. In consideration of their participation in or application for the Auction, a person or entity (whether the successful Bidder, a Bidder, a purchaser and/or other Auction participant or registrant) agrees that all disputes in any way relating to, arising under, connected with, or incidental to these Terms and Conditions and purchases, or default in payment thereof, shall be arbitrated pursuant to the arbitration provision. In the event that any matter including actions to compel arbitration, construe the agreement, actions in aid or arbitration or otherwise needs to be litigated, such litigation shall be exclusively in the Courts of the State of Texas, in Dallas County, Texas, and if necessary the corresponding appellate courts. For such actions, the successful Bidder, purchaser, or Auction participant also expressly submits himself to the personal jurisdiction of the State of Texas.
51. These Terms & Conditions provide specific remedies for occurrences in the auction and delivery process. Where such remedies are afforded, they shall be interpreted strictly. Bidder agrees that any claim shall utilize such remedies; Bidder making a claim in excess of those remedies provided in these Terms and Conditions agrees that in no case whatsoever shall Auctioneer's maximum liability exceed the high bid on that lot, which bid shall be deemed for all purposes the value of the lot.

Miscellaneous:

52. Agreements between Bidders and consignors to effectuate a non-sale of an item at Auction, inhibit bidding on a consigned item to enter into a private sale agreement for said item, or to utilize the Auctioneer's Auction to obtain sales for non-selling consigned items subsequent to the Auction, are strictly prohibited. If a subsequent sale of a previously consigned item occurs in violation of this provision, Auctioneer reserves the right to charge Bidder the applicable Buyer's Premium and consignor a Seller's Commission as determined for each auction venue and by the terms of the seller's agreement.
53. Acceptance of these Terms and Conditions qualifies Bidder as a client who has consented to be contacted by Heritage in the future. In conformity with "do-not-call" regulations promulgated by the Federal or State regulatory agencies, participation by the Bidder is affirmative consent to being contacted at the phone number shown in his application and this consent shall remain in effect until it is revoked in writing. Heritage may from time to time contact Bidder concerning sale, purchase, and auction opportunities available through Heritage and its affiliates and subsidiaries.
54. Rules of Construction: Auctioneer presents properties in a number of collectible fields, and as such, specific venues have promulgated supplemental Terms and Conditions. Nothing herein shall be construed to waive the general Terms and Conditions of Auction by these additional rules and shall be construed to give force and effect to the rules in their entirety.

State Notices:

Notice as to an Auction in California. Auctioneer has in compliance with Title 2.95 of the California Civil Code as amended October 11, 1993 Sec. 1812.600, posted with the California Secretary of State its bonds for it and its employees, and the auction is being conducted in compliance with Sec. 2338 of the Commercial Code and Sec. 535 of the Penal Code.

Notice as to an Auction in New York City. These Terms and Conditions are designed to conform to the applicable sections of the New York City Department of Consumer Affairs Rules and Regulations as Amended. This is a Public Auction Sale conducted by Auctioneer. The New York City licensed Auctioneers are Kathleen Guzman, No.0762165, and Samuel W. Foose, No.0952360, who will conduct the Auction on behalf of Heritage Auctions, Inc. ("Auctioneer"). All lots are subject to: the consignor's right to bid thereon in accord with these Terms and Conditions of Auction, consignor's option to receive advances on their consignments, and Auctioneer, in its sole discretion, may offer limited extended financing to registered bidders, in accord with Auctioneer's internal credit standards. A registered bidder may inquire whether a lot is subject to an advance or reserve. Auctioneer has made advances to various consignors in this sale.

Notice as to an Auction in Texas. In compliance with TDLR rule 67.100(c)(1), notice is hereby provided that this auction is covered by a Recovery Fund administered by the Texas Department of Licensing and Regulation, P.O. Box 12157, Austin, Texas 78711 (512) 463-6599. Any complaints may be directed to the same address.

Rev. 11_18_08

Additional Terms & Conditions:
STAMPS & PHILATELIC ITEMS

STAMPS & PHILATELIC ITEMS TERM A: Signature® Auctions are not on approval. No certified material may be returned because of possible differences of opinion with respect to the grade offered by any third-party organization, dealer, or service. No guarantee of grade is offered for ungraded Property sold and subsequently submitted to a third-party grading service. There are absolutely no exceptions to this policy. Under extremely limited circumstances, (e.g. gross cataloging error) a purchaser, who did not bid from the floor, may request Auctioneer to evaluate voiding a sale: such request must be made in writing detailing the alleged gross error; submission of the lot to the Auctioneer must be pre-approved by the Auctioneer; and bidder must notify Brian Degen (1-800-872-6467 Ext. 1767) in writing of such request within three (3) days of the non-floor bidder's receipt of the lot. Any lot that is to be evaluated must be in our offices within 30 days after Auction. Grading does not qualify for this evaluation process nor do such complaints constitute a basis to challenge the authenticity of a lot. Lots returned must be housed intact in their original holder. No lots purchased by floor Bidders may be returned (including those acting through agents). Late remittance for purchases may be considered just cause to revoke all return privileges.

STAMPS & PHILATELIC ITEMS TERM B: Auctions conducted solely on the Internet THREE (3) DAY RETURN POLICY: Certified Stamps, and Certified and Uncertified Philatelic Items paid for within seven days of the weekly or monthly Internet Auction closing are sold with a three (3) day return privilege. You may return lots under the following conditions: Within three days of receipt of the lot, you must first notify Auctioneer by contacting Client Service by phone (1-800-872-6467) or e-mail (Bid@HA.com), and immediately ship the lot(s) fully insured to the attention of Returns, Heritage, 3500 Maple Avenue, 17th Floor, Dallas TX 75219-3941. Lots must be housed intact in their original holder and condition. You are responsible for the insured, safe delivery of any lots. A non-negotiable return fee of 5% of the purchase price ($10 per lot minimum) will be deducted from the refund for each returned lot or billed directly. Postage and handling fees are not refunded. After the three-day period (from receipt), no items may be returned for any reason. Late remittance for purchases revokes these Return privileges.

STAMPS & PHILATELIC ITEMS TERM C: Multiple stamp / item lots, including sets, collections, large lots, and small group lots, whether certified or not, are not sold on approval, and are sold "As Is" Without Warranty. There are absolutely no exceptions to this policy.

STAMPS & PHILATELIC ITEMS TERM D: Stamps and Philatelic Items sold referencing a third-party certification or grading service are sold "As Is" Without Warranty. Bidder shall solely rely upon warranties of the authentication provider issuing the Certificate or opinion. Grading, condition or other attributes of any lot may have a material effect on its value, and the opinion of others, including third-party grading services such as PSE, PF, and APEX may differ with that of Auctioneer. Auctioneer shall not be bound by any prior or subsequent opinion, determination, or certification by any grading service. Bidder specifically waives any claim to right of return of any item because of the opinion, determination, or certification, or lack thereof, by any grading service. Certain warranties may be available from the grading services and the Bidder is referred to them for further details: Professional Stamp Experts (PSE), P.O. Box 6170, Newport Beach, CA 92658; Philatelic Foundation (PF), 70 West 40th St., 15th Floor, New York, NY 10018; American Philatelic Expertising Service (APEX), 100 Match Factory Place, Bellefonte, PA 16823; or, for other services, as otherwise noted on the Certificate. Third party graded stamps are not returnable for any reason whatsoever. Auctioneer shall not be liable for any patent or latent defect or controversy pertaining to or arising from any encapsulated collectible. In any such instance, purchaser's remedy, if any, shall be solely against the service certifying the collectible.

STAMPS & PHILATELIC ITEMS TERM E: In the event Auctioneer cannot deliver the lot or subsequently it is established that the lot lacks title, or other transfer or condition issue is claimed, Auctioneer's liability shall be limited to rescission of sale and refund of purchase price; in no case shall Auctioneer's maximum liability exceed the high bid on that lot, which bid shall be deemed for all purposes the value of the lot. After one year has elapsed from the close of the Auction, Auctioneer's maximum liability shall be limited to any commissions and fees Auctioneer earned on that lot.

STAMPS & PHILATELIC ITEMS TERM F: Grading is a matter of opinion, an art and not a science, and therefore the opinion rendered by the Auctioneer or any third party grading service may not agree with the opinion of others (including trained experts), and the same expert may not grade the same item with the same grade at two different times. Although consensus grading is employed by most grading services, it should be noted as aforesaid that grading is not an exact science. In fact, it is entirely possible that if a lot is broken out of a plastic holder and resubmitted to another grading service or even to the same service, the lot could come back with a different grade assigned.

STAMPS & PHILATELIC ITEMS TERM G: Auctioneer does not warrant provenance of a stamp or philatelic item; it is the responsibility of the Bidder to arrive at their own conclusion prior to bidding.

STAMPS & PHILATELIC ITEMS TERM H: Due to changing grading standards over time, differing interpretations, and to possible mishandling of items by subsequent owners, Auctioneer reserves the right to grade items differently than shown on certificates from any grading service that accompany the items. Auctioneer also reserves the right to grade items differently than the grades shown in the prior catalog should such items be reconsigned to any future auction.

STAMPS & PHILATELIC ITEMS TERM I: Certification does not guarantee protection against the normal risks associated with potentially volatile markets. The degree of liquidity for certified and graded stamps and collectibles will vary according to general market conditions and the particular lot involved. For some lots there may be no active market at all at certain points in time.

STAMPS & PHILATELIC ITEMS TERM J: Storage of purchased stamps and philatelic items: Purchasers are advised that certain types of plastic may react with a stamp's ink(s), gum and/or paper or transfer plasticizer to stamps and may cause damage. Caution should be used to avoid storage in materials that are not inert.

WIRING INSTRUCTIONS:
Bank Information: JP Morgan Chase Bank, N.A., 270 Park Avenue, New York, NY 10017
Account Name: HERITAGE NUMISMATIC AUCTIONS MASTER ACCOUNT
ABA Number: 021000021
Account Number: 1884827674
Swift Code: CHASUS33

Rev. 10_13_08

Your five most effective bidding techniques:

1 Interactive Internet™ Proxy Bidding
(leave your maximum Bid at HA.com before the auction starts)

Heritage's exclusive Interactive Internet™ system is fun and easy! Before you start, you must register online at HA.com and obtain your Username and Password.

1. Login to the HA.com website, using your Username and Password.

2. Chose the specialty you're interested in at the top of the homepage (i.e. coins, currency, comics, movie posters, fine art, etc.).

3. Search or browse for the lots that interest you. Every auction has search features and a 'drop-down' menu list.

4. Select a lot by clicking on the link or the photo icon. Read the description, and view the full-color photography. Note that clicking on the image will enlarge the photo with amazing detail.

5. View the current opening bid. Below the lot description, note the historic pricing information to help you establish price levels. Clicking on a link will take you directly to our Permanent Auction Archives for more information and images.

6. If the current price is within your range, Bid! At the top of the lot page is a box containing the Current Bid and an entry box for your "Secret Maximum Bid" – the maximum amount you are willing to pay for the item before the Buyer's Premium is added. Click the button marked "Place Bid" (if you are not logged in, a login box will open first so you can enter your username (or e-mail address) and password.

7. After you are satisfied that all the information is correct, confirm your "Secret Maximum Bid" by clicking on the "Confirm Absentee Bid" button. You will receive immediate notification letting you know if you are now the top bidder, or if another bidder had previously bid higher than your amount. If you bid your maximum amount and someone has already bid higher, you will immediately know so you can concentrate on other lots.

8. Before the auction, if another bidder surpasses your "Secret Maximum Bid", you will be notified automatically by e-mail containing a link to review the lot and possibly bid higher.

9. Interactive Internet™ bidding closes at 10 P.M. Central Time the night before the session is offered in a floor event. Interactive Internet™ bidding closes two hours before live sessions where there is no floor bidding.

10. The Interactive Internet™ system generally opens the lot at the next increment above the second highest bid. As the high bidder, your "Secret Maximum Bid" will compete for you during the floor auction. Of course, it is possible in a Signature® or Grand Format live auction that you may be outbid on the floor or by a Heritage Live bidder after Internet bidding closes. Bid early, as the earliest bird wins in the event of a tie bid. For more information about bidding and bid increments, please see the section labeled "Bidding Increments" elsewhere in this catalog.

11. After the auction, you will be notified of your success. It's that easy!

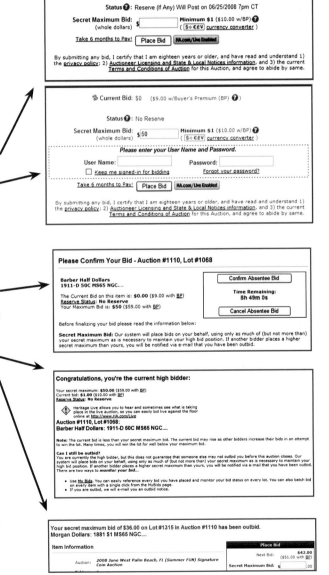

2 HERITAGE Live!™ Bidding
(participate in the Live auction via the Internet)

1. Look on each auction's homepage to verify whether that auction is "HA.com/Live Enabled." All Signature® and Grand Format auctions use the HERITAGE Live!™ system, and many feature live audio and/or video. Determine your lots of interest and maximum bids.

2. Note on the auction's homepage the session dates and times (and especially time zones!) so you can plan your participation. You actually have two methods of using HERITAGE Live!™: a) you can leave a proxy bid through this system, much like the Interactive Internet™ (we recommend you do this before the session starts), or b) you can sit in front of your computer much as the audience is sitting in the auction room during the actual auction.

3. Login at HA.com/Live.

4. Until you become experienced (and this happens quickly!) you will want to login well before your lot comes up so you can watch the activity on other lots. It is as intuitive as participating in a live auction.

5. When your lot hits the auction block, you can continue to bid live against the floor and other live bidders by simply clicking the "Bid" button; the amount you are bidding is clearly displayed on the console.

3 Mail Bidding
(deposit your maximum Bid with the U.S.P.S. well before the auction starts)

Mail bidding at auction is fun and easy, but by eliminating the interactivity of our online systems, some of your bids may be outbid before you lick the stamp, and you will have no idea of your overall chances until the auction is over!

1. Look through the printed catalog, and determine your lots of interest.

2. Research their market value by checking price lists and other price guidelines.

3. Fill out your bid sheet, entering your maximum bid on each lot. Bid using whole dollar amounts only. Verify your bids, because you are responsible for any errors you make! Please consult the Bidding Increments chart in the Terms & Conditions.

4. Please fill out your bid sheet completely! We also need: a) Your name and complete address for mailing invoices and lots; b) Your telephone number if any problems or changes arise; c) Your references; if you have not established credit with Heritage, you must send a 25% deposit, or list dealers with whom you have credit established; d) Total your bid sheet; add up all bids and list that total in the box; e) Sign your bid sheet, thereby agreeing to abide by the Terms & Conditions of Auction printed in the catalog.

5. Mail early, because preference is given to the first bid received in case of a tie.

6. When bidding by mail, you frequently purchase items at less than your maximum bid. Bidding generally opens at the next published increment above the second highest mail or Internet bid previously received; if additional floor, phone, or HERITAGE Live!™ bids are made, we act as your agent, bidding in increments over any additional bid until you win the lot or are outbid. For example, if you submitted a bid of $750, and the second highest bid was $375, bidding would start at $400; if no other bids were placed, you would purchase the lot for $400.

7. You can also Fax your Bid Sheet if time is short. Use our exclusive Fax Hotline: 214-443-8425.

4 Telephone Bidding (when you are traveling, or do not have access to HERITAGE Live!™)

1. To participate in an auction by telephone, you must make preliminary arrangements with Client Services (Toll Free 866-835-3243) at least three days before the auction.

2. We strongly recommend that you place preliminary bids by mail or Internet if you intend to participate by telephone. On many occasions, this dual approach has reduced disappointments due to telephone (cell) problems, unexpected travel, late night sessions, and time zone differences. Keep a list of your preliminary bids, and we will help you avoid bidding against yourself.

5 Attend in Person (whenever possible)

Auctions are fun, and we encourage you to attend as many as possible – although our HERITAGE Live!™ system brings all of the action right to your computer screen. Auction dates and session times are printed on the title page of each catalog, and appear on the homepage of each auction at HA.com. Join us if you can!

Take 4 Months to Pay...

Heritage will Finance Your Purchase

We're collectors too, and we understand that on occasion there is more to buy than there is cash. Consider Heritage's Extended Payment Plan [EPP] for your purchases totaling $2,500 or more.

Extended Payment Plan [EPP] Conditions

- Minimum invoice total is $2,500.
- Minimum Down Payment is 25% of the total invoice.
- A signed and returned EPP Agreement is required.
- The EPP is subject to a 3% *fully refundable* Set-up Fee (based on the total invoice amount) payable as part of the first monthly payment.
- The 3% Set-up Fee is refundable provided all monthly payments are made by eCheck, bank draft, personal check drawn on good funds, or cash; and if all such payments are made according to the EPP schedule.
- Monthly payments can be automatically processed with an eCheck, Visa, or MasterCard.
- You may take up to four equal monthly payments to pay the balance.
- Interest is calculated at only 1% per month on the unpaid balance.
- Your EPP must be kept current or additional interest may apply.
- There is no penalty for paying off early.
- Shipment will be made when final payment is received.
- All traditional auction and sales policies still apply.

There is no return privilege once you have confirmed your sale, and penalties can be incurred on cancelled invoices. To avoid additional fees, you must make your down payment within 14 days of the auction. All material purchased under the EPP will be physically secured by Heritage until paid in full.

To exercise the EPP option, please notify **Eric Thomas** at **214.409.1241** or email at **EricT@HA.com** upon receipt of your invoice.

We appreciate your business and wish you good luck with your bidding.